www.wadsworth.com

wadsworth.com is the World Wide Web site for
Wadsworth and is your direct source to dozens
of online resources.

At *wadsworth.com* you can find out about
supplements, demonstration software, and
student resources. You can also send e-mail to
many of our authors and preview new publications
and exciting new technologies.

wadsworth.com
Changing the way the world learns®

Music in Western Civilization

Volume C:
Romanticism to the Present

Craig Wright
Yale University

Bryan Simms
University of Southern California

Australia • Brazil • Canada • Mexico • Singapore • Spain • United Kingdom • United States

THOMSON

✳

SCHIRMER

Music in Western Civilization
Volume C: Romanticism to the Present
Craig Wright, Bryan Simms

Publisher: Clark Baxter
Senior Development Editor: Sue Gleason
Senior Assistant Editor: Julie Yardley
Editorial Assistant: Emily Perkins
Executive Technology Project Manager: Matt Dorsey
Executive Marketing Manager: Diane Wenckebach
Marketing Assistant: Rachel Bairstow
Marketing Communications Manager: Patrick Rooney
Project Manager, Editorial Production: Trudy Brown
Creative Director: Rob Hugel
Executive Art Director: Maria Epes

Print Buyer: Karen Hunt
Permissions Editor: Sarah Harkrader
Production Service: Johnstone Associates
Text and Cover Designer: Diane Beasley
Photo Researcher: Roberta Broyer
Copy Editor: Judith Johnstone
Autographer: Ernie Mansfield
Cover Image: Carlo Saraceni (1585–1620), *Saint Cecilia*. Galleria Nazionale d'Arte Antica, Rome, Italy. Scala/Art Resource, NY.
Compositor: Thompson Type
Text and Cover Printer: Quebecor World/Dubuque

Printed in the United States of America
1 2 3 4 5 6 7 09 08 07 06 05

ISBN 0-495-00869-9

Thomson Higher Education
10 Davis Drive
Belmont, CA 94002-3098
USA

For more information about our products, contact us at:
Thomson Learning Academic Resource Center
1-800-423-0563
For permission to use material from this text or product, submit a request online at
http://www.thomsonrights.com.
Any additional questions about permissions can be submitted by e-mail to **thomsonrights@thomson.com.**

BRIEF CONTENTS

Part

VIII

CONTEMPORARY MUSIC

DETAILED CONTENTS

Part

VII   THE EARLY TWENTIETH CENTURY

Musical Interlude 7
Music After 1900   592

Part
VIII

CONTEMPORARY MUSIC

Musical Interlude 8
After World War II   720

PREFACE

The decision to write a new history of Western music must appear to others, as it occasionally still does to its authors, as an act of madness. Of course, we have taken up this challenge in order to create a book that will best serve our students and our own goals as teachers. But it seems appropriate at the outset to inform prospective readers—and even to remind ourselves—what these goals are and what specific things we think make this text better than other histories of Western music.

❀ THE "PLACE" OF MUSIC

Music is the expressive voice of a culture, and often that voice is clearest in one particular city, country, or region. For this reason, we have centered our discussion of music in the places where it took deepest root. For example, we link much of the presentation of medieval music to the city of Paris; Handel to London; Beethoven to Vienna; Richard Strauss to Berlin; jazz to Harlem. We have not attempted daring or esoteric connections. But by placing music in a culturally resonant setting, we can help our students to see and hear how the sociopolitical life of certain places not only gave rise to musical genres and styles but also broadened and shaped all of Western civilization. To accomplish our overarching goal, we made certain pedagogical decisions based on our many years of teaching music history.

❀ CONTENT AND ORGANIZATION

The most visible difference in the organization of this book is its arrangement of topics into 83 brief chronological chapters. The book includes everything we thought most important to cover, and its many brief chapters promote three main goals. First, the arrangement of chapters makes it easier for instructors to present the material to students in any order that best suits their courses. For example, we are accustomed to teaching the instrumental music of Bach before his vocal music. But instructors more comfortable leading with vocal music can easily do so by assigning Chapter 40 before Chapter 39. Second, as instructors all know, students do not invariably bring to their studies an unquenchable desire to read the assigned text material. We have found that assigning a smaller passage for every class session yields better results than long chapters. Third, short chapters allow time for supplementary or source readings, and thus promote a better-rounded treatment of the subject at hand.

To provide variety for the student while studying the basic materials and musical selections, we engage special topics in **Boxes.** These are always germane to the subject under discussion, and they give the student a momentary diversion on some relevant issue in the history of music. For example, students enjoy the quirky observations on sixteenth-century social dancing made by aging priest Thoinot Arbeau, so we have highlighted his *Orchésographie* in Chapter 22. Similarly, students are generally astonished to find that people were paid to attend opera performances in the nineteenth century and to applaud on cue, so a box in Chapter 62 explains the existence of the *claque*. Nine longer **Musical Interludes** appear between various chapters. These discussions—music printing in the Renaissance, the critical concept of romanticism, and the birth of rock, among others—deal with larger issues that characterize an entire musical and cultural age, and their greater length and placement between chapters reflect their added importance.

A comprehensive **Timeline** of composers interwoven with the important political, social, and artistic events of that era opens each of eight parts of the book. We intend each timeline to provide a visual synopsis of a major historical period and a cultural context for the many musical events that we will discuss in the chapters that follow.

At the root of any study of music history, of course, lies the music itself, and our 267 CD tracks represent the major genres, composers, and works in the history of Western music. The discussion in each chapter moves quickly from a geographical and cultural context to a close study of these works, which are placed in students' hands in the form of excellent recordings and scores. A **Listening Cue** in the text alerts the reader whenever the time is right to leave the text, pick up headphones and the Anthology, and grapple with the primary materials of music.

In our selection of music, we have emphasized the **coverage of women composers** by including works by Hildegard of Bingen, Beatriz de Dia, Barbara Strozzi, Elizabeth Jacquet de La Guerre, Clara Schumann, Alma Mahler, Lili Boulanger, Bessie Smith, Ruth Crawford Seeger, and Joan Tower. We are mindful that many important composers—male as well as female—have of necessity been omitted from our discussion to produce a text of reasonable size. We invite comments about our choices and have appended our e-mail addresses to the end of this preface for this and any other issues readers may wish to discuss with us. In rare instances, where we were unable to include a piece on the CD set, the Listening Cue directs the reader to the book's website or to the Internet.

MATERIAL TAILORED TO YOUR COURSE

Most schools offer music history for music majors in a sequence covering one, two, or three semesters. A few lucky colleagues have four or more semesters to cover this subject. We both teach at schools that devote three semesters to the history survey, and we are well aware of the problems that arise in adapting any one text to sequences of different durations. But the emerging web economy has taught us and our students that we must provide greater choices.

Accordingly, we offer the book, the Anthology, and the thirteen CDs that accompany the text in combinations that match a typical two- or three-semester course—march time or waltz time, as it were. The book is also available, of course, as a single-volume text, in hardcover for durability over the course of a year or more. Students rightly complain if they must buy a book and then are assigned only part of it. Our flexible configuration of print and audio material allows instructors to require students to buy only as much material as they will actually use. The ISBN and order information for these several print and audio options appear on the back cover of the text.

For teaching formats that we have not anticipated but may best fit your unique course syllabus, please write your local Thomson-Schirmer sales representative to craft a print medium customized to your course. For help contacting this person, use the Rep Locator on the Schirmer home page: www.Wadsworth.com/music.

 ANCILLARIES

Several remarkable ancillaries accompany the text.

Anthology

Timothy Roden of Ohio Wesleyan University has joined us to create a splendid anthology of Scores. It contains all of the central works discussed in the text with the exception of a few jazz and modern pieces that lack scores. Tim has added informative introductory notes to each selection and supplied new translations for all works with texts in foreign languages. As mentioned earlier, the complete Anthology is available in two or three volumes.

Audio CDs and Web

Virtually every piece that we discuss in the text appears on one of thirteen audio CDs; recordings of a few works can be located on the book's website (www.Wadsworth.com/music). The recordings are of the highest quality; for example, much of the recorded medieval music comes from the prestigious Harmonia Mundi label. Recordings of hitherto unrecorded pieces have been specially commissioned from professional groups and performers, including The Washington Cornett and Sackbut Ensemble.

Workbook

Timothy Roden has also written a unique student workbook of analytical exercises and probing questions that will help students examine each piece of music in the Anthology and prepare for exams and quizzes. Nothing like it exists now, and by engaging the student, these exercises bring the music to life. The Workbook also includes an essay by Sterling Murray, "Writing a Research Paper on a Musical Subject," as well as a bibliography for students designed to help in the process of writing papers. The bibliography can also be found on the website (www.Wadsworth.com/music).

Instructor's Resource CD-ROM

An all-inclusive CD ROM contains ExamView computerized testing, as well as an electronic version of the Instructor's Manual/Test Bank. Also found here are PowerPoint presentations that include outlines for lectures, additional illustrations, musical examples in the text, audio clips, and other materials for use in the classroom.

ACKNOWLEDGMENTS AND THANKS

A project this comprehensive and complex is naturally the work of many hands. We are grateful to colleagues who gave generously of their time, ideas, and good will to make this undertaking a success. Some read and critiqued large portions of the text, others answered specific questions, and still others graciously provided materials. We are sincerely grateful to all of the following for their help.

Jonathan Bellman, *University of Northern Colorado*

Jane Bernstein, *Tufts University*

Francisco Lorenzo Candelaria, *University of Texas, Austin*

Tim Carter, *University of North Carolina, Chapel Hill*

Cynthia J. Cyrus, *Blair School of Music, Vanderbilt University*

Jeffrey Dean, *The New Grove Dictionary of Music and Musicians*

Charles Dill, *University of Wisconsin, Madison*

Christine Smith Dorey, *Case Western Reserve University*

Lawrence Earp, *University of Wisconsin, Madison*

Robert Eisenstein, *University of Massachusetts and Mount Holyoke College*

Robert Galloway, *Houghton College*

David Grayson, *University of Minnesota*

James Grymes, *University of North Carolina, Charlotte*

Barbara Haggh-Huglo, *University of Maryland*

James Hepokoski, *Yale University*

Michael Holmes, *University of Maryland*

Derek Katz, *University of California, Santa Barbara*

Terry Klefstad, *Southwestern University*

Walter Kreyszig, *University of Saskatchewan*

James Ladewig, *University of Rhode Island*

Paul Laird, *University of Kansas*

Bruce Langford, *Citrus College*

Charles S. Larkowski, *Wright State University*

Lowell Lindgren, *Massachusetts Institute of Technology*

Dorothea Link, *University of Georgia*

Daniel Lipori, *Central Washington University*

Ralph Lorenz, *Kent State University*

Patrick Macey, *Eastman School of Music*

Thomas J. Mathiesen, *Indiana University*

Charles Edward McGuire, *Oberlin College Conservatory of Music*

Bryce Mecham, *Brigham Young University*

Donald C. Meyer, *Lake Forest College*

Sharon Mirchandani, *Westminster Choir College of Rider University*

Sterling Murray, *West Chester University*

Giulio Ongaro, *University of Southern California*

Leon Plantinga, *Yale University*

Keith Polk, *University of New Hampshire*

Hilary Poriss, *University of Cincinnati*

John Rice, *Rochester, Minnesota*

Anne Robertson, *University of Chicago*

Ellen Rosand, *Yale University*

David Rothenberg, *Colby College*

Ed Rutschman, *Western Washington University*

Christopher J. Smith, *Texas Tech University School of Music*

Tony C. Smith, *Northwestern State University of Louisiana*

Kerala Snyder, *Eastman School of Music*

Pamela Starr, *University of Nebraska*

Marica Tacconi, *Pennsylvania State University*

JoAnn Taricani, *University of Washington*

Susan Thompson, *Yale University*

Jess B. Tyre, *State University of New York at Potsdam*

Zachariah Victor, *Yale University*

Scott Warfield, *University of Central Florida*

Mary A. Wischusen, *Wayne State University*

Gretchen Wheelock, *Eastman School of Music*

Several colleagues who specifically asked to remain anonymous

Closer to home, we wish to thank our respective wives, Sherry Dominick and Charlotte E. Erwin, for reading and evaluating the text, for giving advice on many fronts, and, most of all, for their support and patience. Having ready access to the music libraries at Yale and the University of Southern California has been a special boon, and we are grateful to Kendall Crilly, Richard Boursy, Suzanne Lovejoy, and Eva Heater for help in acquiring materials, and to Karl Schrom and Richard Warren for advice with regard to recordings. Also offering invaluable assistance during the creation of new recordings were Richard Lalli and Paul Berry. At the end of the project we could not have done without the indefatigable labors of graduate students Pietro Moretti and Nathan Link in researching, editing, proofreading, and preparing materials for the instructor's CD; in the course of this project the students became the mentors.

Finally, the authors wish to thank the staff of Thomson-Schirmer that has helped to produce this volume. First of all, the guiding light, from beginning to end, was our publisher and friend, Clark Baxter; in many ways, this book is his. Joining Clark in this enterprise were a number of exceptionally talented people including Trudy Brown, who coordinated with great finesse the production of every part of this massive undertaking. Judy Johnstone merged, with her accustomed skill and forbearance, countless print and electronic chapters, images, and autography into a book that Diane Beasley's design has made exceptionally attractive. Sharon Poore and Sue Gleason helped us develop the manuscript itself. Julie Yardley worked closely with us and with Tim Roden on the ancillaries, especially on the Anthology. Emily Perkins, Clark's remarkable assistant, kept an ocean of paper and electronic material moving in the right direction, and on schedule. Matt Dorsey oversaw the development of the book's website and the Instructor's Resource CD-ROM. Finally, a word of thanks to Diane Wenckebach, who brought boundless energy and commitment to the marketing of this text, and who, with Patrick Rooney, prepared its promotional material.

Craig Wright
(craig.wright@yale.edu)

Bryan Simms
(simms@usc.edu)

Music in Western Civilization

THE ROMANTIC PERIOD

The nineteenth century—beginning with the age of Beethoven and Schubert and continuing to the time of Richard Strauss and Gustav Mahler—is commonly called the "Romantic period" in the history of music. The distinctness of this era comes both from a common spirit in music composed during this century and from great social and political upheavals that drew lines through the historical continuum. One such point of demarcation came in 1814, the year in which Napoleon's subjugation of Europe ended. After this time, art was increasingly shaped by the initiatives toward democratic government, the decline in aristocratic privilege, industrialization,

1750	1800	1850

CLASSICAL PERIOD (1750–1820) **ROMANTIC PERIOD**

Ludwig van Beethoven (1770–1827)

1848–1849 Uprisings throughout Europe

Louis Philippe (1773–1850), French monarch (r. 1830–1848)

Carl Maria von Weber (1786–1826)

Modest Mussorgsky

1789–1799 French Revolution

Peter Ilyich

Giacomo Meyerbeer (1791–1864)

Gioachino Rossini (1792–1868)

Franz Schubert (1797–1828)

Arthur Sullivan

Hector Berlioz (1803–1869)

1804–1814 Napoleonic Wars

Felix Mendelssohn (1809–1847)

Frédéric Chopin (1810–1849)

Robert Schumann (1810–1856)

Franz Liszt (1811–1886)

Richard Wagner (1813–1883)

Giuseppe Verdi (1813–1901)

◆ **1814 Fall of Napoleon**

Clara Schumann (1819–1896)

Anton Bruckner (1824–1896)

Johann Strauss, Jr. (1825–1899)

Jacques-Louis David, Napoleon on Horseback at the St. Bernard Pass

Corbis

Johannes Brahms (1833–1897)

Corbis

burgeoning national identity, and other products of Napoleon's legacy. The year 1914, in which World War I began, is another line drawn deeply in the sands of history. After the horrific destruction of this "Great War," people throughout the world felt the need to end the forms of artistic expression that had their origins a hundred years before. Between these two cataclysmic events lies the Romantic period, and its musical features will be the subject of the chapters that follow.

Part VI

1850   1900   1950

(1820–1914)

◆ c1900 *Belle Époque*

Edward Elgar (1857–1934)

(1839–1881)

1914–1918 World War I

Tchaikovsky (1840–1893)

Ralph Vaughan Williams (1872–1958)

Alma Mahler (1879–1964)

(1842–1900)

Lili Boulanger (1893–1918)

Gabriel Fauré (1845–1924)

Giacomo Puccini (1858–1924)

Gustav Mahler (1860–1911)

Claude Debussy (1862–1918)

Arturo Toscanini (1867–1957)

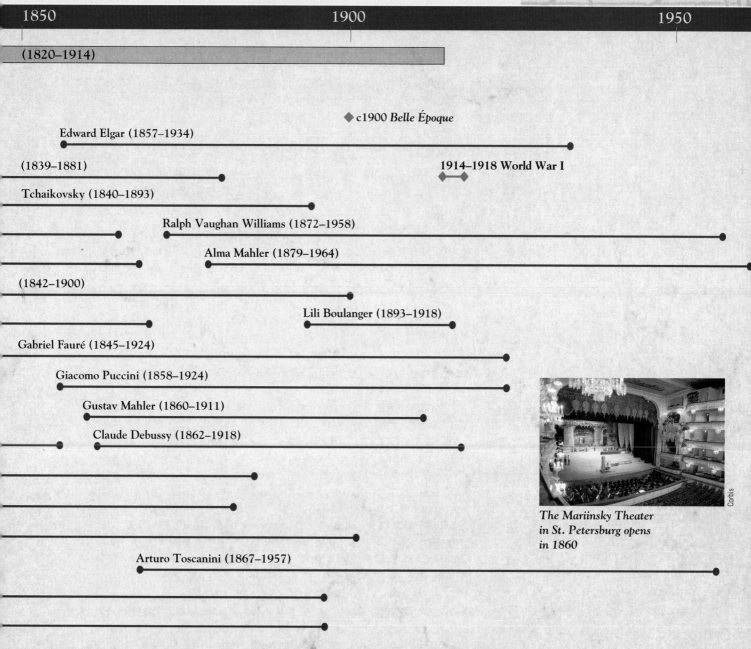

The Mariinsky Theater in St. Petersburg opens in 1860

Corbis

Musical Interlude

6

Romanticism

The Romantic period in the history of music designates both a chronological era—corresponding roughly to the nineteenth century—and also a spirit that characterizes music created in that century. People use the terms "romantic" and "romanticism" to designate this distinctive style, although these words are not precise in their meaning. They suffer from the pitfalls of all generalizations about musical style—suggesting similarity where none may exist, and rarely being susceptible to a concrete definition. But, despite these dangers, the idea that much of the music of the nineteenth century is romantic has long persisted, and it fulfills a need for a concept that separates the type of music composed in this century from that before or later.

Early in the nineteenth century, critics began to describe contemporary music as romantic, bringing this and related words over from studies of literature. A "romance" at this time was a work of fiction set in a remote time and place, shrouded in mystery, and often turning more on characters' emotions than on their powers of reason. The writer and musician E.T.A. Hoffmann found these qualities in Beethoven's Symphony No. 5. In an 1813 review of the work, Hoffmann pointed to "that infinite longing which is the essence of romanticism." He continues:

> Beethoven's instrumental music opens up to us also the realm of the monstrous and the immeasurable. Burning flashes of light shoot through the deep night of this realm, and we become aware of giant shadows that surge back and forth, driving us into narrower and narrower confines until they destroy us.[1]

Although Hoffmann does not limit the romantic spirit in music to any one century, he highlights a common feature of music in the 1800s—its tendency toward a vivid expression of feelings and passionate states of mind. As we will see in the chapters ahead, romantic music often embodies complex ideas and strong emotions. Music of this type is no longer only for pleasure, no longer simply an elevated pastime. In the eighteenth century these were widely accepted as the real purpose of music. Mozart said as much in a letter to his father in 1781: "Music, in the most terrible situations, must never offend the ear, but must instead please the hearer, or in other words must never cease to be *music*."[2] Not so with romantic music!

The emotions that characterize romanticism are no mere abstractions, but more often those experienced by the individual composer. A personal voice is heard nowhere so clearly as in music of the Romantic period. In many of his greatest works, Beethoven leads us into his own emotional world, and this element of self-exploration remains in music of Berlioz, Brahms, Mahler, and Strauss later in the century.

The nineteenth century was indeed the era of the individual. The French Revolution, which marked the beginning of this period, was carried forward by the idea of the individual's rights, expressed in the motto *liberté, égalité, fraternité*—"liberty, equality, brotherhood." This was the age when absolute monarchies were overturned throughout western Europe, feudalism was all but ended, and wealth and power passed once and for all from the aristocracy to the middle classes. It was a time when the hero was celebrated and the accomplishments of the individual, whether a military genius such as Napoleon or a virtuoso performer such as Nicolò Paganini or Franz Liszt, commanded the admiration of people from all walks of life.

The emphasis on individualized expression in music produced many innovations in musical style. The melodies and themes in romantic music often reveal asymmetrical shapes that better convey a temperamental content than the balanced and periodic melodies of the Classical period. Harmony becomes more suggestive, especially through an increased use of dissonant chords and modulations to remote keys. Composers of the Romantic era were inclined to greater diversity in the choice of keynotes, indicating that certain keys are inherently more evocative of certain emotional states than other keys. Pieces in the minor mode became much more prevalent as composers delved more deeply into the realm of the subjective. Musicians looked for novel ways of unifying long musical compositions, striving for the same degree of continuity and oneness as in a play by William Shakespeare, whose dramas were appreciated in the nineteenth century as never before. Above all, the music of the nineteenth century wears its heart on its sleeve. It dispenses with classical restraint in favor of overt display, exaggeration, and impetuosity of feeling.

Chapter
52

Franz Schubert

Beethoven's funeral in Vienna on 29 March 1827, attended by thousands, began with a great procession that transported Beethoven's casket from his last residence to the nearby Holy Trinity Church. Vienna's leading musicians walked alongside, some carrying candles, others flowers. Beethoven's friends and students—including Carl Czerny and Ignaz Schuppanzigh—were among the candle bearers. Also marching beside the coffin was Franz Schubert (1797–1828), a younger Viennese musician whose reputation was on the rise. Beethoven had heard of Schubert mainly from reports by mutual acquaintances. Beethoven's assistant, Anton Schindler, had brought him some of Schubert's songs and recalled Beethoven's reaction to them: "Truly there is a divine spark in this Schubert."

❀ SCHUBERT'S LIFE

Although Schindler is notorious for his unreliable testimony concerning Beethoven, this recollection is at least accurate—there was unquestionably a divine spark in Schubert. Unlike many of the city's other leading composers, he was a native Viennese, born in a northern suburb only a few blocks from Beethoven's last residence. Beethoven's apartment had eight rooms while Schubert's birthplace had one room, which he shared with his parents and three brothers. His father, an amateur musician, ran an elementary school and provided his son with his first musical and general education.

At the age of eleven Schubert was admitted by audition to the choir of the Court Chapel. Since women were not allowed to sing in this ensemble, boys were needed to sing the alto and soprano parts. (Recall that Haydn, at the age of eight, was enrolled similarly in the choir of the Cathedral of St. Stephen, across town from the

Court Chapel.) The boy choristers were very well treated. They resided free of charge at the City Seminary and were enrolled in a nearby gymnasium, a school with a strong academic program that would prepare them later to enroll in a university.

Schubert had many musical opportunities in addition to choral singing. He played violin in his school's orchestra and studied composition privately with Antonio Salieri. In 1812, after his voice changed, he could no longer sing in the choir. But, unlike Haydn, who was summarily turned out of his choir school to earn his living as best he could, Schubert was allowed to complete his course of study at the gymnasium. Instead of continuing, however, he resigned and in 1813 enrolled in a training school to qualify as an elementary teacher. In the following year he joined the faculty at his father's school. All the while he composed—songs, choral music, chamber music, symphonic works—in astonishing abundance. In 1815 alone he composed some one hundred forty songs; another hundred followed in 1816. Schubert was also absorbed in literature and art, interests developed through regular meetings with a circle of close friends. They created an intellectual atmosphere and social network on which Schubert relied for the remainder of his life.

By 1818, encouraged by his friends, Schubert had quit the career of schoolteacher to become an independent professional musician, and from 1821 he began to have his compositions published. His friend Anselm Hüttenbrenner described his working habits:

> Schubert . . . used to sit down at his writing desk every morning at 6 o'clock and compose straight through until 1 o'clock in the afternoon. . . . Schubert never composed in the afternoon; after the midday meal he went to a coffee house, drank a small portion of black coffee, smoked for an hour or two and read the newspapers at the same time.— In the evening he went to one or other of the theatres.[1]

But there were factors that darkened Schubert's prospects as a professional musician. He was shy, more inclined to make music in intimate surroundings among sympathetic acquaintances than in the harsh public spotlight. Also, he was not a great performer compared to a Beethoven or Mozart in their youth. Schubert was a competent pianist and singer—he often accompanied himself in singing his own songs—but his performing was not at a level that would open doors for him in an era when composition and performance were still closely intertwined.

Nevertheless, Schubert was soon positioned to break into the leading ranks of Viennese composers. By about 1823 he had become reasonably well known as a writer of songs, piano pieces, and church music. He had scored several modest successes as an opera composer, and he was receiving an income from commissions, publications, and public performances. His music was also heard in private gatherings, especially at musical parties called **Schubertiads** that were assembled by his friends, where he could try out new works. The parties typically ended with dining, dancing, and socializing.

Schubert's career and the spread of his reputation were held back, however, by increasingly self-destructive habits, which ultimately brought about his death at the age of only thirty-one. He contracted syphilis in 1822 or 1823, and its effect on his health was only worsened by alcohol and probably narcotics. He fell increasingly into fits of depression, at times showing no interest in his own well-being, at other times acting normally. During his final years he sometimes retreated into isolation to struggle with his demons.

Around 1825 his prospects seemed to brighten as his health improved and his life became better regulated. He was inspired by the beauty of nature during a long stay in the Austrian alps on the Traun Lake near Salzburg, where he composed one of

Schubert's Appearance

Anselm Hüttenbrenner (1794–1868) was an Austrian composer who was an acquaintance of both Schubert and Beethoven. This is an excerpt from a memoir concerning Schubert written in 1854.

. . . . Schubert's outward appearance was anything but striking or prepossessing. He was short of stature, with a full, round face and was rather stout. His forehead was very beautifully domed. Because of his short sight he always wore spectacles, which he did not take off even during sleep. Dress was a thing in which he took no interest whatever: consequently he disliked going into smart society, for which he had to take more trouble with his clothes. As a result many a party anxiously awaited his appearance and would have been only too glad to overlook any negligence in his dress; sometimes, however, he simply could not bring himself to change his everyday coat for a black frock coat; he disliked bowing and scraping, and listening to flattering talk about himself he found downright nauseating. . . .

When the merry musical brotherhood, of whom there were often ten, met together intimately anywhere, each had his own nickname. Our Schubert was called *Schwammerl* [little mushroom]. What a pity that such musical truffles are so rare.— We were young, gay people and, in our dear capital, enjoyed ourselves as much as possible and used to go along arm-in-arm. . . .[2]

FIGURE 52-1
Franz Eybl's 1827 portrait of Schubert shows the composer without his ever-present spectacles.

his very greatest works, the Symphony No. 9 in C Major. His music was being performed in concerts of Vienna's important Gesellschaft der Musikfreunde (Society of the Friends of Music), of which Schubert himself had been elected a member, and publishers were by then competing for his songs and piano pieces.

In March 1828 Schubert finally decided to put himself in the public eye by organizing a concert devoted entirely to his own music—the kind of event, called an "academy," that had so greatly benefited Mozart and Beethoven. The concert was given in the hall of the Gesellschaft, and the program mixed chamber music, songs, and choral works. The concert was a great success and brought the composer a tidy profit, and it was followed by a burst of creativity. Songs including the beautiful "Der Hirt auf dem Felsen" ("The Shepherd on the Rock"), three of his greatest piano sonatas, and the String Quintet in C Major were all composed in little more than two months in the late summer of 1828. But disease then quickly overtook him, and he died on November 19 of that year.

SCHUBERT'S MUSIC: WORKS FOR VOICES

Despite his short life and the battles that he waged with himself, Schubert composed an astoundingly large and diverse body of music. He worked in all of the standard genres of his time with the exception of the concerto, which he never attempted. The sheer quantity of his music makes an accounting of it complex, all the more so because he often left compositions incomplete. Many works—including some of his very greatest ones—were not published during his lifetime. Given these uncertainties, identifying Schubert's music is often done by "D." numbers—similar to Mozart's "K." numbers—which are the numbers assigned to them chronologically in a catalog assembled in 1951 by Otto Erich Deutsch.

Schubert was best known in his own day, as in ours, as a composer of songs (or **Lieder,** the German word for songs), of which there are over six hundred. Most of these are short, independent pieces, but there are also **song cycles,** which are groups of songs that belong together in poetry and music. His two authentic cycles are *Die schöne Müllerin* (*The Lovely Maid of the Mill,* 1823) and *Winterreise* (*Winter's Journey,* 1827). After Schubert's death a publisher created a cycle of fourteen independent songs, called *Schwanengesang* (*Swan Song,* 1828).

Like Mozart and Haydn before him, Schubert composed many works for the Catholic services of worship. These include six Masses and numerous shorter, motet-like pieces for chorus alone or with organ or orchestra accompanying. He wrote about one hundred fifty compositions for chorus, including cantatas and some one hundred pieces for male chorus. He aspired to make a name for himself as an opera composer, but had limited success, in part because of the poor librettos he selected. His incidental music for the play *Rosamunde* (1823) contains some of his most delightful music.

✿ CHAMBER, PIANO, AND ORCHESTRAL COMPOSITIONS

Schubert's chamber music continues the genres developed by Haydn, Mozart, and Beethoven. Schubert composed string quartets, trios, an octet, and two quintets. One of these last—the Quintet for piano, violin, viola, cello, and bass in A major—is fondly called the "Trout" Quintet because Schubert brings the melody from his song "Die Forelle" ("The Trout," Ex. 52-1) into its fourth movement.

EXAMPLE 52-1

In a bright little brook the happy trout darts like an arrow.

Schubert's piano music is among the greatest and most original of its type. He wrote fifteen piano sonatas (some probably incomplete) and a larger number of short **character pieces**—brief compositions that quickly establish a definite mood or atmosphere. These include six *Moments musicaux* (*Musical Moments*) and eight *Impromptus* (*Extemporizations*). There are also many dance pieces for piano—mainly Ecossaises (Scottish Dances), waltzes, waltz-like Ländler (country dances), and "Deutsche" (German dances). Most of these were written by the composer to accompany social dancing, especially at his Schubertiads.

Also like Mozart and Beethoven, Schubert composed several fantasies for piano, works having a nonstandard form and often an improvisatory character. The most imposing and virtuosic of these is the Fantasy in C Major (1822), nicknamed the

"Wanderer" Fantasy because in one section Schubert quotes a melody from his song "The Wanderer." The form of the piano work—which was apparently original with Schubert and very influential upon later composers—continues the tendency already seen in Beethoven's "Eroica" Symphony (see Chapter 50) to achieve continuity rather than compartmentalization throughout a large, multimovement instrumental composition. The "Wanderer" Fantasy has four movements (*allegro/adagio/presto/allegro*) like one of the large piano sonatas of Beethoven. But these are all run together without pause, and each movement has a principal theme that shares motives with the first theme of the first movement. The openings of these themes are shown in Example 52-2.

EXAMPLE 52-2

This large-scale thematic integration also affects the use of formal archetypes. Each movement has its own recognizable form, but the entire four-movement work is built on a single sonata-form plan. The first movement outlines a sonata design of its own, which breaks off within the development section. The development is then continued in the *adagio* and *presto* movements. The fugal finale returns plainly to the theme of the first movement, thus marking the beginning of a large-scale recapitulation.

None of Schubert's symphonies was published in his lifetime, which seems ironic, since these are among the great works of their type. Schubert completed seven symphonies and left several others incomplete or in sketches. The most famous of the latter group is the Symphony in B Minor (1822), nicknamed the "Unfinished" since Schubert left it—for reasons unknown—as a torso, containing only two movements and sketches for a third.

In 1826 Schubert submitted his last symphony, Symphony No. 9 in C Major (1825–1826), to the orchestra of the Gesellschaft der Musikfreunde, which rehearsed it but found it too difficult for a public performance. The work had its premiere only in 1839, under the leadership of Felix Mendelssohn in Leipzig.

This "Great" C-Major Symphony mixes traditional symphonic features with others that look toward the future. It has a standard four-movement form, but, as in Beethoven's "Eroica" Symphony and Symphony No. 9, these are greatly elongated. Schubert uses the standard late eighteenth-century orchestra, expanded only by three trombones, but he gives far more melodic material to the woodwinds and brass than even Beethoven did. The work has many formal novelties. The first movement, for example, begins with a slow passage that is more of an exposition than an introduction since its themes are fully formed and return explicitly later in the movement. The first of these themes, shown in Example 52-3, returns climactically at the end of the first movement.

EXAMPLE 52-3

SCHUBERT'S SONGS

Schubert was the first major composer to put songs front-and-center in his compositional oeuvre. The genre itself had been long cultivated, its history reaching back even to the Middle Ages, where it is found in the settings of love poetry by the French troubadours and trouvères (see Chapter 6). Songs of the modern type— short compositions for solo voice accompanied by piano—were written by Haydn, Mozart, and Beethoven, but these composers considered such works to be sidelights to their larger musical undertakings, such as operas, symphonies, or concertos. Composers of more modest reputation from the same time, such as Johann Friedrich Reichardt (1752–1814), wrote songs in a simplified style for use in the home. An example is Reichardt's 1794 setting of Goethe's poem "Erlkönig" ("Erlking"). The poem has eight stanzas, and Reichardt's music for each is virtually the same, creating a simple **strophic form**. The setting of the first stanza is shown in Example 52-4, in which Reichardt's music, simplified almost to the point of becoming formulaic, can be observed.

EXAMPLE 52-4

Performing Schubert's Songs

There is no reason that we should today perform Schubert's songs precisely as he did himself, even if we could know how he performed them. Still, the modern performer wisely seeks out Schubert's ideas as a guide to the proper realization of these subtly complex works.

To learn about Schubert's own performance practices, we begin with the study of **Johann Michael Vogl** (1768–1840), a singer who was the most important interpreter of Schubert's songs during the composer's lifetime. Schubert met Vogl in 1817, when Vogl was a celebrated Viennese operatic singer. In 1814 Vogl had performed the role of Pizarro in Beethoven's *Fidelio* in Vienna, and toward the end of his career he was one of the first singers to specialize in song recitals. Everyone loved to hear Vogl sing Schubert's songs, although his occasional affectations—"a tonelessly spoken word, a sudden outburst, a falsetto note," to quote one contemporary—were tolerated but not approved by the composer.

Vogl observed many of the practices still used by the modern Lieder singer, including free transpositions of songs. But Schubert would have disagreed with modern singing that becomes too dramatic. He was adamant that a strict tempo must be kept and that vocal mannerisms had to be eliminated. "Schubert always indicated exactly where he wanted or permitted a *ritardando*, an *accelerando* or any kind of freer delivery," wrote his friend Leopold von Sonnleithner. "But where he did not indicate this, he would not tolerate the slightest arbitrariness or the least deviation in tempo."

Unaffected and melodious singing was what Schubert apparently wanted, not melodramatic effects. Sonnleithner continued: "He never allowed violent expression in performance. The Lieder singer, as a rule, only relates experiences and feelings of others; he does not himself impersonate the characters whose feelings he describes. Poet, composer and singer must conceive the song *lyrically*, not *dramatically*."

🌿 FIGURE 52-2
Moritz von Schwind, "Schubert Evening at the Home of Joseph von Spaun," 1868. Johann Michael Vogl—the first important interpreter of Schubert's songs—is accompanied by the composer at a Schubertiad.

Bridgeman Art Library

Longer and more complex songs were also written in the late eighteenth century. Those by Johann Zumsteeg (1760–1802), the opera conductor in the city of Stuttgart, were much admired by Schubert. At the time, these were usually called "ballads," "arias," or "cantatas," reserving the term *Gesang* or *Lied* for shorter strophic songs like Reichardt's "Erlkönig." The musical forms encountered in these longer songs were often like scenes from an opera, sometimes mixing tuneful passages with recitatives, and not following any simple repetitive or symmetrical musical plan. This type of song is said to be **through composed.**

Schubert wrote songs of both simple and complex types, and in both he brought to the genre a musical richness and intensity of expression that far surpass the works of a Reichardt or Zumsteeg. A celebrated example of his longer songs is "Erlkönig" (1815), in which he used the same poem as had Reichardt. The poet is **Johann Wolfgang von Goethe** (1749–1832)—the most celebrated German writer of his time—whose poetry stimulated the rise in importance of song writing among composers throughout the German-speaking world. The writings of Goethe (pronounced, approximately, GRR-tuh)—novels, plays (such as *Faust*), opera texts, and poetry—are filled with strophic verse that invites musical treatment. Goethe's poetry was mined repeatedly by the great song composers throughout the nineteenth century.

The text of "Erlkönig" is what at the time was called a **ballad,** which is a poem in stanzas that tells a story and rises quickly to a dramatic climax. Goethe wrote the poem in 1782 for a play with music called *Die Fischerin* (*The Fisher Girl*), in which it was set to music by a Weimar singer and actress named Corona Schröter. It tells an eerie tale, drawn from Danish folklore, of a father riding toward home carrying his sick child. The child sees the sinister erlking, who tries to lure him away and finally takes him by force. When the father arrives at his destination, he finds the child dead in his arms. We can easily understand why Schubert, Reichardt, and numerous other song composers were attracted to the poem. It is strongly musical, with its own strict rhythm and hard consonant sounds that evoke the horse's headlong gallop. It is also tensely dramatic—the erlking speaks seductively to the child who cries out in terror, only to be reassured by the father. The minuscule drama is framed by the impassive words of a narrator.

Schubert composed "Erlkönig" when he was only eighteen years old, but he could find no publisher for it until 1821, shortly after it was performed at a public benefit concert at Vienna's Kärntnertor Theater. It was his first important publication, and marked the beginning of his rise to wider recognition in Vienna's musical circles. While Reichardt had used music only as a neutral backdrop to the poem, Schubert puts the music and words on an equal footing. The form of the song is complex. It is essentially through composed, since each stanza has different music. At the same time, a motive suggesting the child's fear (Ex. 52-5) is repeated in stanzas 4, 6, and 7, each time a half tone higher, which brings into the song an element of strophic form.

EXAMPLE 52-5

The music is grippingly dramatic. Schubert treats the four characters—narrator, father, son, and erlking—in clearly distinguishable ways. The father sings soothingly in the low register, the son higher in a shrill and repetitive fashion, and the erlking's music is sickly sweet. Schubert brings forward an enriched harmonic palette reminiscent of Beethoven to underscore the emotional state of the child, as in the chain of diminished chords that accompanies its cries. The tonal framework for the song is G minor, although the key becomes unstable, almost disorienting, in the dialogues between the father and son. In the erlking's three stanzas the key is absolutely clear and stable—the erlking knows what he wants.

The role of the piano is far from the simple accompaniment of Reichardt's setting, functioning in Schubert's song as an independent expressive tool. The impetuous triplet figure in the right hand conveys the headlong dash of the horse and rider, which continues throughout the song except in the stanzas where the erlking sings. There it evaporates into a simple lilting accompaniment, and at the very end it comes to a standstill, as the horse reaches its destination.

Schubert saves his most dramatic touch for this last poetic line, which occurs in the last three measures of the song. The horse's hooves fall silent in measure 146, but we know that the song is not finished because the cadential motion is incomplete, having paused on a Neapolitan sixth chord. Now the narrative voice changes to recitative to complete the grim tale—"in his arms the child was dead." The piano then quickly finishes the progression, as though snapping the storybook shut.

LISTENING CUE

FRANZ SCHUBERT
"Erlkönig" (1815)

CD 9/1
Anthology, No. 144

A second example of a song of the longer type is "Ganymed" ("Ganymede," 1817). Like "Erlkönig" it is based on a poem by Goethe, but the two poems are very different in form and emotional content. This poem deals with the Greek legend of Ganymede, a handsome Trojan youth. The god Zeus was so captivated by his beauty that he transformed himself into an eagle, swooped down, and carried the boy off to become a god. The legend has been interpreted as showing a homoerotic practice among the Greek gods, but Goethe's poetic treatment is more spiritualized than worldly. The speaker—who represents Ganymede—is enraptured by the beauty of nature. He embraces it with a sensual passion and finally imagines that he soars upward—just as Ganymede did as he was transformed by Zeus into a god—to become absorbed within nature. In Goethe's pantheistic vision, nature becomes god, the "all-loving father" of the last line.

This symbolic poem must have posed a great challenge to Schubert in the creation of a satisfying song. First of all, its meaning is complex, and it is written in an ecstatic and exalted language that Goethe often used in the 1770s, under the influence of the *Sturm und Drang* style evident in German literature of that period (see Chapter 45). Its poetic structure is entirely irregular and prose-like; it has no consistent stanzas, line lengths, or rhyme. How could Schubert make such a poem into a song?

He does so by approaching the text as though it were a fragment of an opera libretto. The song that results is like a detached operatic passage that moves through contrasting sections, changes from tuneful to recitational melody, and avoids symmetric repetitions or even a concentric tonal plan. The word **scena**, or "scene," is sometimes used to describe a song of this operatic type. Schubert divides Goethe's poem into three groups of lines: in the first the speaker praises the splendor of nature, in the second he feels the morning breeze and hears the song of the nightingale, in the third he soars upward to embrace the god of nature. The three groups are set musically to three distinct musical sections, rather like an aria in an opera of the time. Recall the plan underlying Leonore's aria "Abscheulicher!" from Beethoven's

Fidelio (Chapter 50). It begins in the key of G minor and moves through several contrasting sections, alternating recitative and slow melody. Finally it settles into the key of E major for a fast and conclusive final section in which phrases are repeated for emphasis.

Although Schubert does not exactly follow this order of events, his plan for the song is still related to it. The first group of lines (mm. 1–45) is set to a slow, lyrical melody that begins in the key of A♭ major (Ex. 52-6). The melody for the second group (mm. 46–74) is more recitational and the key is unstable. Finally, the song settles into a stable F major for the third and final group (mm. 75 to end), in which the singer ecstatically repeats musical phrases to extol his union with nature. For Schubert to end his piece in a different key from its beginning is very unusual in the genre of the song, although typical of the progressive key plans in contemporaneous opera arias. In both, the openness of the key plan has a dramatic purpose, showing vividly that the narrating character has been transformed from the beginning to end.

EXAMPLE 52-6

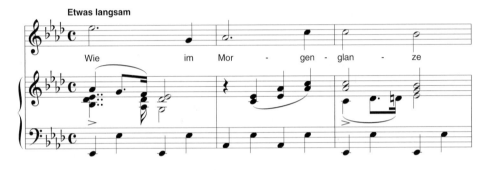

LISTENING CUE

FRANZ SCHUBERT
"Ganymed" (1817)

CD 9/2
Anthology, No. 145

The operatic trappings of "Ganymed" and the condensed drama of "Erlkönig" are generally absent in Schubert's many short songs. These tend to be strophic in structure, often folk-like in their naive sentiments, and reasonably simple and artless. Some of Schubert's short songs take on a heightened degree of artistry within their simple framework. One such is "Nähe des Geliebten" ("Nearness of the Beloved"), which Schubert composed in 1815, again on a poem by Goethe.

The narrator of the poem thinks longingly of a distant beloved, whose image is evoked by the elements of nature. In the narrator's imagination, the beloved seems to come closer and closer as we move through the poem's four stanzas. At first he is only thought of, then seen and heard, and finally he is there. But it is all imagined, and at the end the despondent lover can only cry out "O, would that you were here!" Schubert responds to Goethe's folk-like sentiments and strict poetic regularity by writing a song that is strophic in form. Following a short piano introduction, each of the poem's four stanzas is set to exactly the same music. But just as Goethe brings depth of emotion and artistic subtlety to the poem, Schubert writes a strophic song that is anything but formulaic. The piece begins with a two-measure piano introduction in a mood of scarcely containable excitement, as though representing the mind of the narrator searching feverishly for memories of the beloved (Ex. 52-7). The music begins with throbbing repeated chords, far distant from the tonic harmony, and its top line rises chromatically in increasing anticipation. Finally, the ascending line strikes upon the tonic note, G♭, which seems to force the voice to sing out, "Ich denke dein," "I think of you." Only then does self-control return, as the music moves quickly to a cadence in the home key.

EXAMPLE 52-7

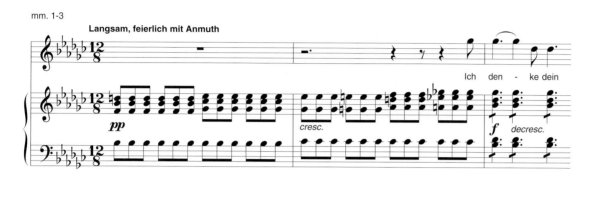

LISTENING CUE

FRANZ SCHUBERT

"Nähe des Geliebten" (1815)

CD 9/3

Anthology, No. 146

 ## SUMMARY

The music of the Viennese composer Franz Schubert (1797–1828) contains most of the genres cultivated by his great forebears, including Beethoven and Mozart, although Schubert placed more emphasis on smaller and more intimate types of music—the character piece for piano and the song. Schubert made the song into a major musical genre. His memorable lyricism and ingenious ways of depicting poetry musically have been models for song composition to the present day. Schubert's songs include short, strophic pieces (as in "Nähe des Geliebten") and longer through-composed types (such as "Erlkönig"). Some of the more complex songs (such as "Ganymed") imitate passages from opera. Schubert's symphonies, piano sonatas, and chamber works continue and expand the forms inherited from earlier Viennese composers.

 ## KEY TERMS

Schubertiad	strophic form	Johann Wolfgang von Goethe
Lied (pl., Lieder)	Johann Michael Vogl	ballad
song cycle	through-composed form	scena (type of song)
character piece		

Chapter 53

Music in Paris Under Louis Philippe: Berlioz and Chopin

After the fall of Napoleon in 1814, the Bourbons were restored as the legitimate kings of France, although their powers were then restrained by a constitution that promoted a limited sharing of power with the middle classes. But the Parisian people still remembered the suffering of the Revolution and its aftermath—endured in part for the sake of personal liberty and greater social equality—and they looked with alarm on the actions of their kings, which seemed to be moving France back to the days when monarchs wielded absolute power. King Charles X, who rose to the French throne in 1824, had attempted to restrict the press, limit the right to vote, and return financial privileges to the aristocracy and Church. In July 1830 measures such as these triggered an insurrection among Parisians from all walks of life (Fig. 53-1), and within three days the king was forced to abdicate and flee to England. In his place, **Louis Philippe** (1773–1850), formerly Duke of Orléans, was declared the new monarch and dubbed the "citizen king."

Eugène Delacroix's painting, seen in Figure 53-1, is far from a realistic recording of any single event in the **July Revolution.** It is instead a passionate and larger-than-life allegory concerning the advance of liberty, which is personified by the partially nude female figure at the top center. She strides—armed, fearless, and unstoppable—over barricades and a tangle of bodies, carrying the three-color flag of the French Revolution and leading a motley band of warriors drawn from all stations of Parisian society. To her left is youth, to her right a businessman with top hat (possibly a self-portrait of the artist), and further to the right, a man in worker's clothing carrying a saber. In its emotionality, energy, and dark tone, the painting's style befits its revolutionary subject, and during the reign of King Louis Philippe (1830–1848) these same qualities would increasingly appear in French music.

At this time, Paris displaced Vienna as the center of European musical culture. The profession of music in Paris was entirely different from that of Vienna, reflecting the different social structures of the two cities. In Beethoven's day, the aristocracy in Vienna was still able to provide a haven for musicians; recall the lifetime annuity that Beethoven received in 1809 from a group of music-loving noblemen. An opportunity like this scarcely existed for Parisian musicians. After the Revolution, the wealth of the French aristocracy was largely confiscated, and under Louis Philippe its prerogatives shifted almost completely to the middle classes. Louis Philippe himself had a great interest in the arts, and he often gave sums of money and commissions to deserving artists. But there was no longer a patronage system in existence after the Revolution that could support French musicians. They made their livelihood instead from their

❧ FIGURE 53-1

Liberty Leading the People by Eugène Delacroix (1798–1863) depicts the July Revolution of 1830 in Paris, when the French people deposed their monarch, King Charles X. Delacroix witnessed the event and was reportedly filled with pride to see the tricolor waving above Notre Dame. The cathedral is seen rising above the smoke on the right side of this famous painting.

Bridgeman Art Library

interaction with a large and faceless audience, which they reached by teaching, organizing concerts, publishing music, and composing operas.

In Vienna, the large churches hired musicians, presented new music, and allowed common people to hear music performed. But this opportunity too was unavailable to the French musician because, following the Revolution, churches had little in the way of music beyond simple chanting. Musical life in Paris was concentrated instead in the opera house and concert hall. Opera was by far the leading genre, and it was fostered by three principal opera companies: the Opéra, the Théâtre-Italien, and the Opéra-Comique. The "Opéra" (actually, the Académie Royale de Musique) presented operas strictly in the French language, and a rule barred works with spoken dialogue. The Opéra theater, which could seat nearly two thousand, was located on the Rue le Peletier, not far from the future site of the great Palais Garnier, which became its home in 1875 and still stands in the center of Paris.

❖ MUSICAL CULTURE IN PARIS

Just when Louis Philippe came to power in 1830, a new operatic style, called **grand opera,** appeared in the repertory of the Opéra. The name came from the grandiose lengths, lavish use of chorus and ballet, and spectacular scenic effects in such works. The Berlin-born **Giacomo Meyerbeer** (1791–1864) was the most successful composer in this style. Meyerbeer first came to European attention as a piano virtuoso, and in the 1820s, while living in Italy, he made a name for himself as a composer of opera.

Meyerbeer's *Robert le diable* (*Robert the Devil*), given triumphantly at the Paris Opéra in 1831, firmly established the identity of the new genre. Meyerbeer followed up on its success with two additional grand operas, *Les Huguenots* (*The Huguenots*, 1836) and *L'africaine* (*The African Girl*, 1865). In these works, Meyerbeer used librettos written for him by **Eugène Scribe** (1791–1861), who was one of the most popular French playwrights of his time. For his grand operas, Scribe adopted historical or legendary subjects, into which he wrote complicated plots full of conflict, action, and surprising turns of events.

The grand operas of Meyerbeer and Scribe astonished contemporary audiences by their realistic and spectacular staging. This was what amazed Frédéric Chopin when he saw Meyerbeer's *Robert le diable* shortly after it opened in Paris in 1831. He wrote about it enthusiastically to a friend in Poland:

> If ever magnificence was seen in a theatre I doubt whether it reached the level of splendour shown in *Robert le diable*, the very latest five-act opera of Meyerbeer... Devils (the huge chorus) sing through megaphones and spirits in groups of fifty or sixty rise from their graves.... Toward the end, you see the inside of a church and the whole church itself as at Christmas or Easter, all lit up, with monks and congregation seated, with censers and what's more with a grand organ, whose sound, when heard on the stage, enchants and amazes and practically drowns the whole orchestra. No one will ever stage anything like it![1]

Musically, Meyerbeer's grand operas were as up-to-date as their staging. Although ostensibly still "number" operas—divided into a succession of arias, ensembles, and choruses connected by recitatives—the numbers are effectively absorbed into long, action-filled scenes. Each of these contains a fluid alternation of different types of singing, among which choral passages are especially frequent. Meyerbeer further ties his operas together by bringing back prominent melodies to underscore a recurring dramatic idea. Near the beginning of *Robert le diable*, for example, the minstrel

Raimbaut sings a "ballad" that reveals that Robert, the leading character, was born of the devil (Ex. 53-1). In later references to this, as far removed as in the final act, the ballad melody returns.

EXAMPLE 53-1

Once there ruled in Normandy a noble and brave prince. His daughter, the pretty Bertha, rejected all suitors…

Despite his amazement at the scenic wonders of grand opera, Chopin preferred the singing at the Théâtre-Italien. Here, Italian operas, including works by Gioachino Rossini, Vincenzo Bellini, and Gaetano Donizetti, were heard in their original language. The Opéra-Comique put on a mixed repertory of French-language operas whose only distinguishing feature was the inclusion of spoken dialogue.

In addition to opera, Parisians could also hear orchestral music excellently played. The principal orchestra in Paris in 1830 was sponsored by the Société des Concerts du Conservatoire (Society of Conservatory Concerts), led by the violinist-conductor François Habeneck. The precision of this orchestra—comprising mainly students and alumni of the Paris Conservatory—was praised by almost everyone who heard it. Habeneck's programming emphasized the orchestral music of Beethoven, which was virtually unknown in Paris before the Société was founded in 1828.

Pianists also flocked to Paris, where there was a culture for pianism fostered by the piano manufacturers Pleyel and Erard. Erard's instruments had gained a technical advantage over the competition by the invention of a **double escapement action** by which a hammer, after striking a string, falls back first to an intermediary position, from which it can then quickly re-strike the string. This innovation allowed for the rapid repetition of a note, an effect quickly embraced by Paris's crowd of competing virtuoso-composers. Members of the piano fraternity supported themselves by giving public and private concerts, teaching, and publishing piano music.

The competition among them increased in 1824 when the 12-year-old Franz Liszt, born in Hungary, gave his first Paris concert. Typically, Liszt played a concerto

and a set of variations, but then he got down to the more serious business of improvising. He took up the theme of the aria "Non più andrai" from Mozart's *Marriage of
Figaro* (Ex. 53-2), on which he then extemporized to the amazement of everyone. "I
am convinced that the soul and spirit of Mozart have passed into the body of young
Liszt," concluded one critic. Around 1840, Liszt introduced a new type of public
concert, the **recital,** in which a pianist played alone (also see Chapter 57).

EXAMPLE 53-2

HECTOR BERLIOZ

Perhaps the most distinctive voice in the musical culture in Paris of the 1830s and
1840s was that of Hector Berlioz (pronounced BEAR-lee-ohs, 1803–1869). He was
born in a village in southeastern France, near Grenoble, to the family of a physi-
cian. Largely self-taught in music, he learned to play flute and guitar and to compose. In 1821 he moved to Paris, which became his permanent residence, to study
medicine. But he lost interest in this field after witnessing his first autopsy. "When
I entered that fearful human charnel-house," he wrote, "littered with fragments of
limbs, and saw the ghastly faces and cloven heads, the bloody cesspool in which we
stood, with its reeking atmosphere, the swarms of sparrows fighting for scraps, and
the rats in the corners gnawing bleeding vertebrae, such a feeling of horror pos-
sessed me that I leapt out of the window, and fled home as though Death and all his
hideous crew were at my heels."[2]

Understandably, he dropped medicine and looked toward music as his desired
profession. He studied with Jean François Lesueur (1760–1837), one of the city's
leading teachers of composition, and in 1830 he won France's most coveted award
for a young composer—the **Prix de Rome** (Rome Prize). Awarded by the Institut de
France until 1968, the Prix de Rome conferred a four-year living stipend and two
years' residency at the Villa Medici in Rome. Among later winners of the prize were
Claude Debussy, Georges Bizet, and Lili Boulanger.

Berlioz returned to Paris from Rome in 1832 and his reputation as a composer
continued to grow. He supplemented his income by writing musical criticism, at
which he was gifted. His musical activities were concentrated upon the organization of concerts—several per year—which showcased his music. When interest in
them flagged among Parisian audiences, Berlioz looked abroad for support. In the
1840s and 1850s he toured repeatedly throughout Europe, giving orchestral concerts of his own music, and his works found approval especially among musicians
and audiences in Germany. He also earned a reputation as a leading conductor.
Near the end of his life, his health and spirits declined. One of his last occupations
was the completion of his *Memoirs,* in which he recounts his life and times in a
uniquely lively and personalized narrative.

Berlioz's Music

Typical of the French composer of his period, Berlioz aspired to make his reputation
in the field of opera. But his three main works of this type—*Benvenuto Cellini*
(1837), *Les Troyens* (*The Trojans,* 1858), and *Béatrice et Bénédict* (1862)—had little

Berlioz as Conductor

By Berlioz's time, the art of conducting had come a long way. In the seventeenth century, in France, conductors often marked time by pounding the floor with a cane or staff, a practice that could have fatal consequences. Recall from Chapter 35 that the great opera composer Jean-Baptiste Lully (1632–1687), while leading a chorus and orchestra in his *Te Deum*, accidentally struck his toe with his staff and two months later died from the gangrenous wound. In the eighteenth century, multiple conductors were common. The orchestra was normally led by its concertmaster, and a keyboardist—whether having an obbligato part or not—was often on hand to join in with the setting of tempos. This was the way that Haydn's symphonies were performed in London in the 1790s; Haydn conducted at the piano and Johann Peter Salomon also conducted from his concertmaster's chair.

Berlioz was one of the first orchestral conductors to modernize these practices. In his treatise "On Conducting" (1855), he insists that conductors use a full score—not just the first violin part, as was done by François Habeneck and others. He recommends the use of a baton, twenty inches long, and insists that he be watched and followed constantly by his players. His recommendations for the orchestra's seating arrangement seem odd to us now. Berlioz placed the cellos and basses on risers behind the woodwinds and horns, who were themselves seated behind the violins and violas. The brass and percussion were in the back.

Despite these oddities, Berlioz's judgments on the virtues and failings of the conductor are as valid today as in 1850:

> The conductor must *see* and *hear*, he must be resourceful and energetic, he must know the nature and the range of the instruments and be able to read a score. . . . He must have other, almost indefinable gifts, without which the invisible contact between him and the performers cannot be established. Lacking these, he cannot transmit his feelings to the players and has no dominating power or guiding influence. He is no longer a director and leader, but simply a time-beater, provided he is able to beat and divide time regularly.[3]

success with Parisian audiences. Berlioz found more support for his orchestral music and concert works for voices. He wrote four symphonies, each unusual in medium, form, and poetic content. The earliest is *Symphonie fantastique* (1830), which will be discussed presently. Next came *Harold in Italy* (1834), in which Berlioz experiments with joining a programmatic symphony to a concertante treatment of viola. The title refers to the last part of Lord Byron's poem *Childe Harold's Pilgrimage* (1812–1818). Berlioz's third symphony is *Romeo and Juliet* (1839), which depicts scenes from Shakespeare's tragedy and brings in chorus and solo voices. The last symphony, *Grande symphonie funèbre et triomphale* (*Grand Funereal and Triumphal Symphony*, 1840), also uses voices. Berlioz wrote shorter works that he called overtures—including *Waverly*, *King Lear*, *The Roman Carnival*, and *The Corsair*—which he intended for concert purposes rather than as preludes to any longer composition. Pieces of this type are now called **concert overtures,** and they are forerunners of the "symphonic poem" (see Chapter 57).

Berlioz's large choral works include *La damnation de Faust* (*The Damnation of Faust*, 1846), a Requiem Mass (1837), and *L'enfance du Christ* (*The Childhood of Christ*, 1854). The first is a cantata-like composition for solo voices, chorus, and orchestra, using texts from Goethe's drama *Faust*. Berlioz wrote his own text for *L'enfance du Christ*, which tells dramatically of the flight of the Holy Family from the vengeful King Herod. In addition to his large choral works, Berlioz also wrote songs, of which the collection *Les nuits d'été* (*Summer Nights*, 1841) was orchestrated for use in his tours.

Symphonie fantastique

An emerging orchestral culture in Paris in the late 1820s and the impact of Beethoven's symphonies—performed at the Société des Concerts—inspired the youthful Berlioz to turn toward symphonic composition. But, even in his first symphony, which he called *Symphonie fantastique* (literally, *"Fantastic" Symphony*, 1830), he was plainly unwilling to continue with the type of symphony cultivated by the Viennese masters. Instead, he reinterpreted the genre as a fully programmatic type of music, in which dramatic ideas could be made as concrete and coherent as in an opera.

Berlioz's point of departure for this new conception was the tendency in Beethoven, found especially in the "Eroica" Symphony (discussed in Chapter 50) and Symphony No. 6 ("Pastoral"), to imbue an instrumental composition with extramusical meaning. Recall that Beethoven intended his "Eroica" Symphony to "celebrate the memory of a great man," which he did by bringing in musical symbols and allusions to the idea of heroism. Berlioz, whose musical imagination could never be contained by an abstract language of tones, went further, and fully transformed the genre into a musical "novel," to use his own analogy. The term **programmatic symphony** is used today to designate a multi-movement symphonic work of this type.

Another tendency hinted at in Beethoven and brought front and center by Berlioz in his *Symphonie fantastique* is music as autobiography. Certainly, Beethoven's personal voice is heard in many works. The lament for the fallen hero of the Funeral March of the "Eroica" Symphony, for example, is, at least in part, Beethoven's own lament. But typical of composers of an earlier time, this personal voice is muted, spoken in a universalized rather than idiosyncratic tone. The subject of Berlioz's *Symphonie fantastique* is no such timeless vision, but Berlioz himself.

The story that the symphony conveys was written by the composer and originally given the title *Épisode de la vie d'un artiste: Symphonie fantastique en cinq parties* (*Episode in the Life of an Artist: Fantastic Symphony in Five Parts*). It recounts Berlioz's own passionate infatuation for an Irish actress, Harriet Smithson (1800–1854), whom he saw in Shakespearean roles in Paris from 1827 to 1829. Although they never met until after the Symphony was completed, and despite rumors concerning her morality, Berlioz had declared himself hopelessly in love with her. To his friend Ferdinand Hiller he wrote: "Today it is a year since I saw HER for the last time—oh! unhappy woman! how I loved you—trembling I write, HOW I LOVE YOU! If there is another world, shall we find each other again?"[4]

At the first performance of the Symphony in December, 1830, Berlioz distributed the story to the audience. There were five movements (or "parts"), each with a title, and a brief elaboration (here paraphrased):

1. Reveries – Passions. A young musician sees a woman who embodies his ideals, and he falls desperately in love. The mere thought of her brings to his mind an obsessive melody. In the first movement his state of mind progresses from a melancholy reverie to fitful passions.

2. A Ball. Even at a ball the obsessive thought of the beloved and its melody return.

3. Scene in the Country. In the country, the artist's mind is calmed by shepherds piping a folk melody. Suddenly a dark thought comes to him—perhaps the beloved is not as perfect as he has imagined.

4. March to the Scaffold. In despair he takes opium and has a hellish nightmare. He imagines that he has killed his beloved and his punishment is death. A grim march accompanies him to the guillotine, and he thinks one last time of her before the blade falls.

5. Dream of a Witches' Sabbath. He awakens in hell, surrounded by witches. Their number is joined by the beloved, who has come to taunt him in a devilish orgy. Funeral bells and the funeral chant "Dies irae" ("Day of Wrath") are heard, and the witches then dance gleefully around him.

At the 1830 concert, Berlioz informed his audience that the music would not entirely depict this extended narrative, only fill in its gaps by conveying certain emotional states experienced by the artist protagonist. Berlioz used the analogy of an opera with spoken dialogue. The printed program was like the dialogue—realistic and narrational—while the orchestral music was like an operatic number that is static and emotive.

Still, there is much realism and storytelling in Berlioz's music. His main device for making the symphony capable of narration is the recurrent symbolic theme. The obsessive idea of the beloved is symbolized by a melody that is similarly obsessive, since it returns in every movement and changes to mirror the changes in her image in the artist's febrile imagination. Berlioz referred to this recurrent melody as an **idée fixe,** or "obsession."

When it is first heard in the first movement (Ex. 53-3), it embodies her initial qualities, "passionate but at the same time noble and shy." At the end of the second movement's ball, it appears with a waltz rhythm; in the third movement it is passed among woodwinds indecisively. In the grim fourth movement, the *idée fixe* melody returns almost as first heard, only to be chopped off—along with the artist's head—after a few measures. In the finale it is made grotesque and played by the shrill clarinet in E♭, just as the beloved has revealed herself as a vengeful witch. The beginnings of these appearances of the central melody are summarized in Example 53-3.

EXAMPLE 53-3

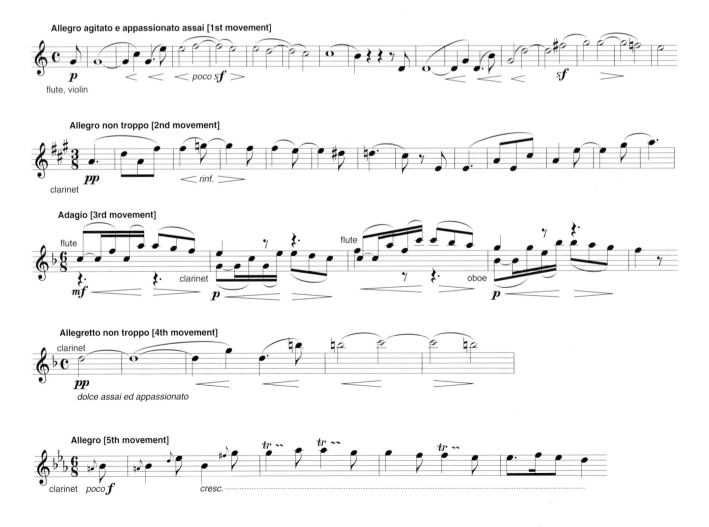

The explicit recurrence of a theme in several movements of a multi-movement composition—called **cyclicism**—has both a formal and a rhetorical function. It serves to unify Berlioz's long and structurally diverse work, and the transformed re-appearances of the theme reinforce its programmatic meaning. Like other aspects of Berlioz's symphony, the cyclic use of themes was forecast in Beethoven's instrumental music (see Chapters 50 and 51), there taking the form of subtle motivic inter-relationships among themes in different movements. Berlioz makes explicit what was only hinted at by Beethoven, all in the service of a more concrete expression of ideas.

Many of the additional ways by which Berlioz makes his symphony operatic are encountered in the fourth movement, "March to the Scaffold" (Berlioz's complete programmatic explanation for the movement is given in the Anthology). The formal plan for the march is irregular, although it has features suggesting sonata form. After a short introduction, a main theme begins in G minor; a second theme begins in the relative major, B♭, and the exposition is then repeated (Ex. 53-4). The analogy with sonata form breaks down at this point, although a varied recapitulation of the main theme in G minor occurs at measure 114. The music then becomes almost cinematic, building in intensity as we see the prisoner approach the guillotine. His last thought of the beloved turns briefly to the major mode, then the blade falls and his head bounces down the stairs of the scaffold (Ex. 53-5). A drum roll and G-major chords announce that justice has been served.

EXAMPLE 53-4

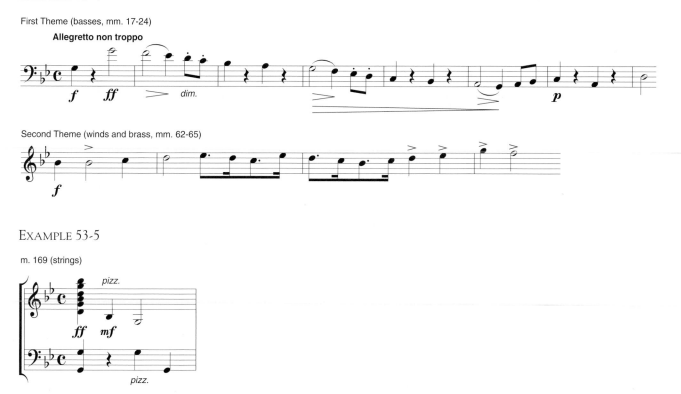

First Theme (basses, mm. 17-24)

Allegretto non troppo

Second Theme (winds and brass, mm. 62-65)

EXAMPLE 53-5

m. 169 (strings)

Berlioz's orchestra resembles the colorful ensembles of French grand opera far more than the symphony orchestra of Beethoven. Instruments not used in Beethoven's symphonies are brought in—English horn, small clarinets, cornets, and **ophicleides** (keyed brass instruments that are now normally replaced by tubas)—and the entire orchestra is swollen to about ninety players. The composer constantly searches for new combinations of instruments, often played in unusual ways, to create a sound that will make special dramatic effects, as in the bouncing-head music of Example 53-5.

LISTENING CUE

HECTOR BERLIOZ   CD 9/4
Symphonie fantastique (1830)   Anthology, No. 147
Fourth movement, "March to the Scaffold"

Later Developments

The course of Berlioz's life after the premiere of *Symphonie fantastique* in December 1830 would seem far-fetched even as a soap opera. Just as quickly as he had fallen in love with Harriet Smithson, Berlioz transferred his affections to a teenaged pianist, Marie Moke, to whom he became engaged in 1830, before leaving for his sojourn in Rome. There, he received news that his fiancée had married another man. In a rage he left Rome for Paris, intending to murder Mlle. Moke, her husband, and her conniving mother. About halfway to Paris, and after a half-hearted attempt at suicide, he calmed down and returned to Rome. He set about writing a sequel to *Symphonie fantastique* that was at first called *The Return to Life*, later retitled *Lélio*, which calls for solo voices, chorus, and orchestra. Between movements, a narrator impersonates the artist of the symphony, who has awakened from his bad dream and decides to live henceforth for art and music.

Berlioz returned to Paris in the winter of 1832 and organized a concert at which *Symphonie fantastique* (revised during his stay in Italy) was performed together with *The Return to Life*. Harriet Smithson, who had also returned to Paris, was brought to this performance, and she recognized herself as Berlioz's muse. Finally, she met the composer, and Berlioz impetuously declared his love for her, marrying her in the following year. But the soap opera has an unhappy ending, as Berlioz and Smithson quickly drifted apart, their marriage desperately unhappy for both. Following Smithson's death in 1854, Berlioz married a singer, Marie Recio, with whom he had long toured.

"Absence" from *Les nuits d'été*

One of the pieces sung by Marie Recio in her tours with Berlioz was the song "Absence," which shows an understated side of the composer's genius. The song had been composed around 1840 for voice and piano, one of a group of six songs based on poetry by Théophile Gautier (1811–1872) that was published under the title *Les nuits d'été* (*Summer Nights*). They are best known in a later version with orchestral accompaniment. The six pieces form a **song collection** rather than a cycle, since they share no striking musical or poetic ideas, and Berlioz did not insist that they be performed as a group.

The genre of the song was of less interest to French composers of the 1830s and 1840s than it was to the Germans following Schubert. The most popular type of song in France was the **romance,** which was a simple strophic piece with little musical sophistication. Later in the nineteenth century, French composers began to write songs of more complex form and greater artistry that were often called

mélodies (an example from the works of Claude Debussy will be discussed in Chapter 63). Berlioz's songs from *Les nuits d'été* are forerunners of this later type.

In "Absence," Berlioz uses only three stanzas of a longer poem by Gautier that speaks of the pain of separation between lovers. The first stanza opens with the plea, "Come back, come back, my beloved," and Berlioz reinforces this appeal by repeating the first stanza after the second and again after the third. The music follows a similar plan, taking on the rondo shape **A B A B' A.** In addition to the great melodic beauty and poignant atmosphere created by Berlioz's music, the harmonic language is ingenious in its embodiment of the feelings expressed in the poem. As shown in Example 53-6, the voice begins with an upward leap of a fourth, C♯ to F♯, which is stated twice over, on the words "Come back, come back. . . ." The second time, the motive is expanded by the insertion of the leading tone E♯, which meets the bass in a stark tritone—suggesting the bitter feelings of separation—then resolves upward to the tonic note F♯. The melody of section B becomes recitational and harmonically aimless, as the speaker thinks of the distance between herself and her lover.

EXAMPLE 53-6

Come back, come back, my beloved!

LISTENING CUE

HECTOR BERLIOZ
"Absence" from *Les nuits d'été* (1840)

CD 9/5
Anthology, No. 148

❀ FRÉDÉRIC CHOPIN

The wind has blown me here, where one breathes freely; but perhaps for that very reason—because it's so easy—one falls to sighing still more. Paris is whatever you care to make of it. You can enjoy yourself, get bored, laugh, cry, do anything you like, and no one takes any notice because thousands here are doing exactly the same. Everyone goes his own way. Well, I really don't know whether any place contains more pianists than Paris, or whether you can find anywhere more asses and virtuosos.[5]

This was Frédéric Chopin's reaction to the city of Paris, written shortly after his arrival in the fall of 1831 on a leg of a European concert tour. "I may stay longer than I intended," he confessed in another letter, and in fact Paris remained his permanent home.

Chopin (1810–1849) was born in Poland, near Warsaw, and grew up there in the family of a French-born schoolteacher. He was a child prodigy as both pianist and composer, and he attended the conservatory in Warsaw, where his teacher, Józef Elsner, had no trouble describing him on the final report card—"a musical genius," Elsner wrote. Piano concerts in the larger European capitals followed. In these performances Chopin, typical of the virtuoso performer of the day, played much of his own music, especially concertos and other brilliant pieces including rondos and variations. Chopin was especially gifted in the art of improvisation, whose freedom and spontaneity is felt in his compositions. His first public concert in Paris came in February 1832, and its program consisted again of mixed fare—chamber pieces, a piano concerto with orchestra, and vocal music.

Chopin soon tired of the public spotlight and made a comfortable living by teaching, playing privately, and selling piano pieces to publishers. In 1838 he began a nine-year affair with the novelist Aurore Dudevant (1804–1876), who was called by her pen name, **George Sand.** Known to her contemporaries for eccentric dress, leftist politics, and tumultuous love affairs, Sand is now held as one of the most important French writers of her day and a founder of the feminist outlook in literature. She was uniquely positioned to observe Chopin's creative process, its mixture of inspiration and labor:

> His creation was spontaneous, miraculous. He found without search or foresight. It came out of the keyboard, sudden, complete, sublime, or it sang in his head as he sauntered, and he hastened back to cast it on the instrument and hear it aloud. But then began the most crushing labor I have ever witnessed. It was a train of efforts, waverings, frustrated stabs at recapturing certain details of the theme that he had heard; what he had conceived as a unity he now overanalyzed in his desire to get it down, and his chagrin at not being able to rediscover it whole and clear plunged him into a sort of despair. He withdrew into his room for days, weeping, pacing up and down, breaking his pens, playing a measure a hundred times over, changing it each time, then writing it out and erasing it as many times, and beginning all over again on the morrow with painstaking and desperate perseverance.[6]

The couple spent the winter of 1838 on the island of Majorca, where Chopin completed his Preludes for piano, Opus 28, but where his health began a relentless decline due to the effects of tuberculosis. Summers were spent in seclusion at Sand's estate, called Nohant, located in central France. These visits brought the composer in touch with writers and artists from Sand's circle, including the painter Eugène Delacroix, with whom Chopin formed a close friendship. The painter described life at Nohant during a visit in the summer of 1842:

> This is a delightful place and my hosts do everything in their power to make life agreeable. When we are not together for dinner, lunch, billiards or walks, one can read in one's room or sprawl on one's sofa. Every now and then there blows in through your window, opening on to the garden, a breath of the music of Chopin, who is at work in his room, and it mingles with the song of the nightingales and the scent of the roses. You see that so far I am not much to be pitied.[7]

In 1847 Chopin and Sand parted company, and the composer's health continued to decline. He visited London and Scotland to give concerts, but his disease had sapped his energy and spirits. To his childhood friend Julius Fontana he could only compare his condition to that of a worn-out piano:

> The sound board is perfect, only the strings have snapped and a few pegs have jumped out. But the only real trouble is this: we are the creation of some famous maker, in his way a kind of Stradivari, who is no longer there to mend us. In clumsy hands we can-

Chopin and the Musical Hoax

In 1945 the world of Chopin scholarship was churned by the appearance of texts purporting to be copied from letters written by Chopin to Countess Delphine Potocka, a wealthy Polish émigrée living in Paris, whose company Chopin is known to have kept. The language is highly erotic. Chopin repeatedly describes his creative instinct as closely related to sex, which he describes using frank and often vulgar language. This is entirely different from the tactful and reserved tone that Chopin's other correspondence reveals. "My romance with Sandowa [Sand] has taught me quite a lot," he says to the Countess. "You'll see how you will become my pupil and I'll teach you some love tricks which are absolutely new and frightfully *piquant*." Later he adds, "With us creators the process is like child bearing is with you—one woman has a terrible time while another spits out a baby like a plum stone."

Many accepted the Potocka letters as genuine, even though they were only known in copies made by a certain Mme. Czernicka, a more-than-slightly psychotic Chopin groupie who committed suicide in 1949, on the centennial of the composer's own death. Ultimately, the many contradictions contained in these texts proved that they were entirely fraudulent.

not give forth new sounds and we stifle within ourselves those things which no one will ever draw from us, and all for lack of a repairer. I can scarcely breathe—I am just about ready to give up the ghost.[8]

Chopin returned to Paris in the winter of 1848 and died there in October 1849, at the age of thirty-nine.

Chopin's Music

All of Chopin's music involves the piano, and most of it consists of character pieces. Recall from Chapter 52 that these are works of brief or moderate length that establish a particular mood or style. Some of the pieces imitate dances, including waltzes, polonaises, and mazurkas. Chopin concentrated especially on the **mazurka,** composing some sixty such works that reflect his lifelong interest in Polish culture. The mazurka is an old Polish country dance in triple time, with accents often on beats two or three of a measure. Chopin's interpretation of the dance produced pieces of endless variety and imagination.

The compositions called ballades and scherzos are longer, and Chopin also composed three piano sonatas. His **nocturnes,** of which there are twenty-one, have a special character that will be described shortly, and he wrote numerous **études** (studies) that stem from his piano teaching but achieve at the same time a great artistry.

Chopin composed relatively little other music. There are two youthful piano concertos that he composed for his early public performances, a late cello sonata (1846), and some Polish language songs.

Nocturne in D♭ Major

The nocturne was a type of piano character piece made popular in the early nineteenth century by John Field (1782–1837), an Irish player and composer whom Chopin especially admired. In Field's hands the nocturne took on a distinct style—delicate and dreamy in its evocations of the night—which was very different from the brilliant and bombastic variations and rondos that were the stock-in-trade of a touring virtuoso. Field's nocturne style involved a simple, singing melody in the right hand, accompanied by broken chords in the left, the harmonies blended by a liberal use of the sustaining pedal.

Chopin's Nocturne in D♭ Major, Op. 27, No. 2 (1835), conforms in general to this character, although Chopin goes far beyond Field in the originality that he brings to the genre. Our attention is first captured by the beautiful sound that Chopin coaxes from the instrument, as he explores the changing sonorities inherent in the piano's different registers and gauges just the right spacing of chordal tones.

The sound is always rhythmically alive and filled with light and air. Chopin's way of playing his own music involved an almost constant rubato. "Chopin *could* not play in strict time," Berlioz remarked about his friend. We also marvel at the beauty and glittering ornament of the melodies, which may have been suggested to the composer by the operatic singing that he heard at the Théâtre-Italien.

The work uses no standard form, but an improvisatory alternation of two melodic ideas (Ex. 53-7). One appears at the outset and returns twice later in the piece, in rondo fashion. The other, more unstable harmonically and built on sequence, alternates with the first. A coda rounds the piece off from measure 62.

EXAMPLE 53-7

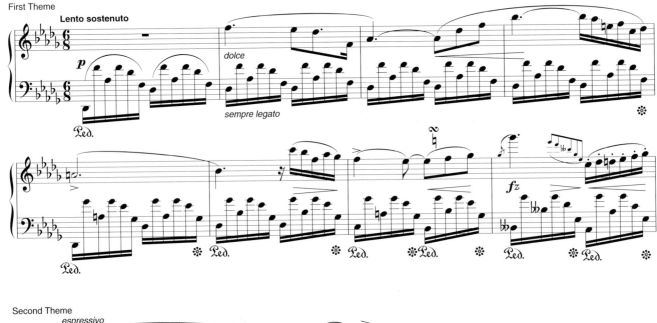

Chopin's originality is expressed especially in his harmonic and tonal language. The key of the work, D♭ major, is at the far flat side of the tonal spectrum, which in music of the nineteenth century often suggests a relaxed and lyrical spirit. Compare it to the yearning and tension implicit in the key of F♯ major, on the far sharp side, in Berlioz's song "Absence." Chopin's entire nocturne remains reasonably close to the home key, although the composer finds imaginative ways of connecting primary chords in that key. Consider, for example, the chords between the tonic harmony in measure 4 and the dominant-seventh chord at the end of measure 8 (see Ex. 53-7). It is futile to try to explain the chords between these two points by roman numerals. Instead, the harmonic coherence of this linking passage is created by a downward stepwise motion in the bass voice, D♭–C–B♭–B♭♭–A♭. The voices above the bass move smoothly by stepwise or common-tone connections.

LISTENING CUE

FRÉDÉRIC CHOPIN
Nocturne in D♭ Major, Op. 27, No. 2 (1835)

CD 9/6
Anthology, No. 149

SUMMARY

Paris in the 1830s and 1840s, during the reign of the monarch Louis Philippe, became the musical capital of Europe. Operas flourished there, and a new type, "grand opera," was characterized by grandiose lengths, lavish use of chorus and ballet, and spectacular scenic effects. The leading composer of grand opera was Giacomo Meyerbeer. Paris was also home to pianists, who arrived from all of Europe. Orchestras were on the rise, stimulated by performances of the symphonies and concertos of Beethoven.

Hector Berlioz and Polish-born Frédéric Chopin were among the leading composers in Paris during this period. Berlioz aspired to success as a composer of opera, but he was better known for his orchestral and choral music. His *Symphonie fantastique* (1830) is an overtly programmatic work, dealing with a narrative that was provoked by Berlioz's own infatuation with an Irish actress. The work explores new ways in which symphonic music can be made concretely dramatic, such as the recurrent appearance of a melody (an *idée fixe*, as the composer called it) that symbolizes an element in the story.

Chopin's compositions were largely for his own instrument, the piano. In addition to a few large works—three piano sonatas and two piano concertos—Chopin wrote character pieces, which were works of brief or moderate length that establish a particular mood. Over twenty of these are called "nocturnes," which are lyrical works that use a distinctive texture made from a singing melody in the right hand and an arpeggiated accompaniment in the left.

KEY TERMS

Louis Philippe	recital	song collection
July Revolution	Prix de Rome	romance (type of song)
grand opera	concert overture	*mélodie*
Giacomo Meyerbeer	programmatic symphony	George Sand
Eugène Scribe	*idée fixe*	mazurka
double escapement	cyclicism	nocturne
action	ophicleide	étude

Chapter 54

Leipzig and the Gewandhaus: Felix Mendelssohn and the Schumanns

In his tour of Germany in 1843, Hector Berlioz was invited by his old acquaintance Felix Mendelssohn to visit Leipzig—a city in the east-central part of what is now Germany (Map 54-1)—to have his music played by the local orchestra. Berlioz readily accepted the invitation, but during his visit he was surprised by several things. The orchestra seemed limited in its instrumental resources compared to the French orchestras. Berlioz could find no English horn, harp, or ophicleide to cover these parts in the performance of his *Symphonie fantastique*. Even more perplexing to Berlioz was the taste for older music that he found in Leipzig. In this city, new compositions had to share the stage with works from the past, even those going back a hundred years to the time of Bach and Handel. Mendelssohn, Berlioz concluded, was "a little too fond of the dead."

✺ MUSIC IN SAXONY

Unknown to Berlioz in 1843, the mixed taste that prevailed in Leipzig was a harbinger of the present day, in which classical music draws its sustenance from both the past and present. The city's conservatism stemmed in part from the greatness of its musical heritage. After all, this was the city where Johann Sebastian Bach had worked for twenty-seven years (see Chapter 40). Just as Bach in his own music looked both to the past and the present, Leipzig's later musicians found ways of stitching together old and new, often so seamlessly as to defy any distinction between them. In the nineteenth century, Leipzig was home to Robert and Clara Schumann, and, in the twentieth century, to Max Reger (1873–1916), all of whom shared Mendelssohn's multi-stylistic outlook on music.

✺ MAP 54-1

Europe after the Congress of Vienna.

When Berlioz visited in 1843, Leipzig was a city of some 45,000 people located in the Kingdom of Saxony. This was one of thirty-nine sovereign states that were allied into the so-called German Confederation, which was formed to replace the Holy Roman Empire that Napoleon had eliminated. The president of this alliance was the emperor of Austria, although its most powerful state was the Kingdom of Prussia to the north. Saxony's wealth came mainly from its textile industry, and its high reputation derived from the intellectual and artistic achievements of its people. Robert Schumann commented that the aristocracy of Leipzig was not its wealthy and privileged citizens but its "150 bookstores, 50 printing establishments, and 30 newspapers."

A university was founded there in 1409, and in the eighteenth century this was one of the first institutions where the discipline of *Musikwissenschaft*—"musical science," or roughly what we now call musicology—was taught. One of the first professor-musicologists in

Leipzig was Lorenz Christoph Mizler (1711–1778), who had been a student of Bach at the Saint Thomas School. He had an essentially new idea for teaching music in a university—as a discipline that would "bring science to music and to explore and bring order to its history," as he said. Music theory, in addition to music history, was a part of the new study of musical science, and at the end of the nineteenth century one of the world's leading theorists, **Hugo Riemann** (1849–1919), was on the Leipzig faculty. Riemann developed a simple way of discussing **functional harmony.** Any chord, he said, represents one of only three harmonic functions within a key—that of its tonic, dominant, or subdominant. His theory is the origin of our present-day outlook on harmonic progressions as motions toward tonics and dominants by way of chords functioning as dominant preparations.

Leipzig in the nineteenth and early twentieth centuries was also the world's leading center for music publishing. It was home to the great firms of C. F. Peters and Breitkopf & Härtel. The latter company was the first publisher of important works by Beethoven, Berlioz, Chopin, and Schubert. Beginning in the mid nineteenth century, it pioneered a new type of musical edition, one containing the **complete works** of a great composer of the past. Such editions were primarily intended for study and reference rather than performance, and Leipzig's own J. S. Bach was the first composer whom Breitkopf honored in this way.

Leipzig had an opera house, but its main claim to fame in music of the nineteenth century was its orchestra. This was called the **Gewandhaus Orchestra,** named after the hall in which it performed (Fig. 54-1). The orchestra's small auditorium occupied an upper floor of a building used earlier to display cloth, or *Gewand* in German, from the city's fabric industry. In Mendelssohn's day the women in the audience sat separate from the men—people went to a concert to hear music, not to flirt.

🌿 FIGURE 54-1

Felix Mendelssohn was a skillful painter in addition to being a gifted musician, and here he depicts Leipzig's Gewandhaus in watercolor. The city's orchestra performed in a hall on the second floor.

🌿 FIGURE 54-2

Wilhelm von Schadow's portrait of Felix Mendelssohn, 1834, when the composer was in his mid-twenties.

❋ FELIX MENDELSSOHN: LIFE AND MUSIC

The rise of the Gewandhaus Orchestra to international fame began in 1835, when a gifted musician from Düsseldorf, Felix Mendelssohn (1809–1847; Fig. 54-2), was appointed music director. Mendelssohn grew up in Berlin in the family of an affluent, cultured banker. He received his education at the hands of distinguished private tutors and through carefully organized travel. Mendelssohn and his siblings—including his musically talented sister Fanny (1805–1847)—converted in 1816 from Judaism to Christianity, whereupon they added the name **Bartholdy** to their family name. This was done at a time when many European Jews sought a greater degree of professional and social assimilation by embracing Christianity; later composers to follow the same path include Gustav Mahler and Arnold Schoenberg. Mendelssohn's education continued at the University of Berlin, where he attended lectures on aesthetics given by the great philosopher Georg Friedrich Hegel.

Mendelssohn's principal tutor in music was Carl Friedrich Zelter (1758–1832). He was well known in Berlin as a composer and as the conductor of the city's main choral society, the Singakademie (Singing Academy). This

was one of the few organizations during the early nineteenth century that performed choral music by Johann Sebastian Bach, who at this time was remembered primarily as a composer of keyboard music. In 1829 Mendelssohn, with Zelter's support, conducted the Singakademie in a performance of Bach's mammoth *St. Matthew Passion,* a work that one hundred years after its first performance was still unpublished and largely unknown. Mendelssohn's concert was a huge success, and a revelation to German audiences. It provoked the so-called **Bach Revival,** in which Bach's music in its entirety was at last performed, published, and studied.

The later years of Mendelssohn's short life were taken up by the dual careers of composer and conductor. His main position was in Leipzig as *Kapellmeister* (conductor) of the Gewandhaus Orchestra (1835–1847), and from 1840 he divided his time in Leipzig with an appointment as music director in the city of Berlin. He traveled repeatedly to music festivals throughout Germany and made ten highly successful visits to England, where his music was keenly appreciated.

During his twelve years as conductor of the Gewandhaus Orchestra, Mendelssohn selected music for performance in a way that was unusual for its time but similar to the approach of an orchestra in the present day. His programs mixed styles and historical periods of origin, without the uniform emphasis on recently composed works, which was more typical of concert planning at the time. Mendelssohn searched for seemingly timeless works from the past—Handel's *Messiah,* Bach's keyboard concertos, symphonies by Haydn, Mozart, and Beethoven—and mixed these in with new orchestral compositions, such as those of a Berlioz or Robert Schumann. One of his greatest discoveries, made during his search through the orchestra literature of the past, was Schubert's Symphony No. 9 in C Major (see Chapter 52). It had never been performed in public, or published, when its manuscript was sent to Mendelssohn by his friend and fellow Leipziger Robert Schumann. Mendelssohn recognized its greatness and in 1839 conducted its first performance.

Mendelssohn's philosophy of programming took a first step toward the establishment of the **canon,** the term used nowadays for the generally accepted body of musical works, composed almost entirely in the eighteenth and nineteenth centuries, that has come to dominate our serious musical culture.

Piano Trio in D Minor

Mendelssohn's mixed approach to programming is reflected in the style of his own music, which uses elements from the past that he cautiously extends by new thinking. He was one of the great composers of orchestral music of his time, but his works for this medium avoid the experimental aspects of a composer such as Berlioz in favor of a continuation of the classical lines established by Haydn, Mozart, and Beethoven. Mendelssohn composed five mature symphonies, in addition to thirteen symphonies for string orchestra that were written during his student period. He also wrote concertos—two for piano and one for violin—and, like Berlioz, he composed concert overtures (including the ever-popular *Fingal's Cave*). His chamber music includes six string quartets, two piano trios, and several sonatas. An excellent pianist, Mendelssohn composed primarily character pieces for this instrument. He wrote two large oratorios, *St. Paul* (1836) and *Elijah* (1846), in addition to many other works for chorus. Although Mendelssohn wrote no major operas, he often composed incidental music to spoken plays, including music to Shakespeare's *A Midsummer Night's Dream.* This has become Mendelssohn's most often performed work.

Getting into the Canon

Musicians can agree on one thing at least: the world of classical music today is dominated by the works of a relatively small number of composers. Their compositions have taken on such prestige and authority as to be tantamount to a canon, a term also used for the books that make up the Bible and are accepted by the faithful as the word of God.

The musicians whose compositions make up this canon, or "standard repertory," of classical music come from a relatively similar background. All are men, all are Europeans, and virtually all lived in the eighteenth and nineteenth centuries. To many in the present day, this sounds more than a bit objectionable—smacking of elitism, sexism, and similar small-minded thinking. Why is it that Robert Schumann and Felix Mendelssohn are in, while Clara Schumann and Fanny Mendelssohn—female composers of note—are out?

Even today, musicians do not agree on this question. Some believe that the canon is like an exclusive club that needs to be opened to women, minorities, and non-Europeans. Composers in the canon are there arbitrarily, it is said, in part because writers of textbooks return to them in edition after edition.

Other musicians respond that those in the canon are there because they wrote better music. People want to hear Felix Mendelssohn, not Fanny Mendelssohn, they say. But if this is so, what makes Felix's music better than his sister Fanny's? Again, no agreement. Some hold that a close study of musical works can show the superiority of one piece over another. This was an idea that motivated the Austrian theorist Heinrich Schenker (1868–1935), who looked intensely at the harmonic and contrapuntal technique of composers and found about ten European male composers whose music, he concluded, was inherently superior.

His conclusions do not satisfy everyone. Why should an ingenuity of musical structure make a piece good or enduring? Isn't simplicity a good thing? The French composer Maurice Ravel threw up his hands over the whole issue: "I consider it impossible to explain or judge a work of musical art," he declared. For a musician like Ravel, the only objective criterion for judging music is viability. Works in the canon are those that for long periods of time—for whatever reason—have lived; they have been performed, studied, and recorded, and have stimulated people's imagination.

The Trio in D Minor, Op. 49, illustrates the composer's marriage of old and new. Trios for piano, violin, and cello (called simply "piano trios") were an important type of music for the Viennese composers. Beethoven's piano trios, for example, are second in number only to his string quartets among the chamber genres. Mendelssohn's D-Minor Trio, written in 1839, has a classical exterior—four movements in the sequence *allegro/andante/scherzo/allegro*, each using a traditional form. The whole work is concise—about a half-hour in length—and its overall tonal plan is similar to that of a trio composed fifty years earlier.

Comparison of the first movement of Mendelssohn's trio with a movement from Berlioz's *Symphonie fantastique* (see Chapter 53) reveals the varying ways that Beethoven influenced the generation of composers that followed him. Berlioz picks up ideas subtly present in Beethoven—programmaticism, cyclicism, formal liberty—and carries them to such lengths as to create a whole new conception of the symphony. Mendelssohn, on the contrary, takes Beethoven's ideals of musical form and expression only a small and measured step forward.

One feature of Mendelssohn's movement that plainly derives from Beethoven is the presence throughout of a clash between two opposing ideas—one of them stable though passionately lyric, the other agitated and eruptive. This battle of opposites is often seen in Beethoven's first movements, as in his famous Piano Sonata in D Minor, Op. 31, No. 2 (nicknamed "The Tempest"). Beethoven's work opens with a dreamy arpeggio on an A-major triad, followed immediately by an impulsive, downward-moving line in the tonic D minor (Ex. 54-1). These starkly contrasted moods compete for the remainder of the movement.

EXAMPLE 54-1

In Mendelssohn's trio movement, also in the key of D minor, the conflict is embodied in two main themes, one in the cello at the beginning and the second following immediately in the piano (Ex. 54-2). The cello's theme is richly melodious, the piano's unstable, agitated, fragmented. These opposites are later represented in the movement by sudden juxtapositions of minor and major, triple versus duple divisions of the beat, and piano set against the strings. Also like Beethoven is the creation of an uninterrupted continuity throughout the entire sonata-form movement. Mendelssohn moves toward this sense of connectedness by omitting the familiar double bar with repeat signs at the end of the exposition, something occasionally done by Beethoven in his first movements. Both composers promote musical unity, despite the contrasts on the musical surface, by subtly carrying over motives from one theme to another.

We will find an example in Mendelssohn's movement by comparing the two principal subsidiary (or "second") themes that arise toward the end of the exposition (Ex. 54-3). Outwardly, these embody the same contrasts seen at the beginning. The first one is lyrical, proceeds in quarter-note values, and is played by the cello; the other erupts into agitated triplets, is not very melodious, and is given to the piano. But beneath these contrasts there is a sameness created by an ascending triadic motive, E - A - C♯ - E, shown by the bracket in the example.

EXAMPLE 54-2

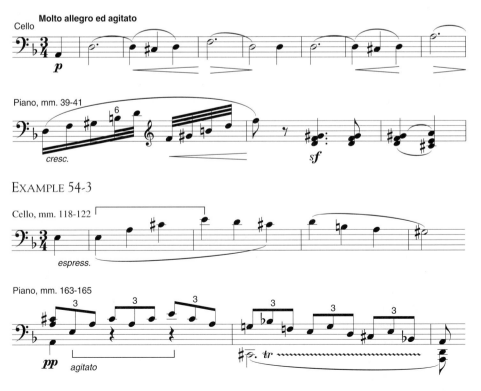

EXAMPLE 54-3

In other ways, Mendelssohn apparently wished to move the music beyond the classical style of Beethoven and bring it closer, however cautiously, to the spirit of his own day. The piano part has some of the flashy virtuosity typical of the age of Chopin and Liszt. The timbre of the music is dark and the first main theme is richly songful, even operatic, in character. Mendelssohn's method of development is entirely different from Beethoven's; he tends to keep his melodies intact, only to lead them through a quickly changing tonal environment. Look at the passage in the development section from measures 250 to 284. Here the first subsidiary theme returns repeatedly, almost intact, although it quickly traverses the keys of Bb major, G minor, and finally D minor.

The Trio in D Minor thus reveals Mendelssohn's conservative interpretation of the romantic spirit: its first movement maintains Beethoven's approach to sonata form, underscoring Beethoven's ways of promoting motivic and tonal unity beneath an apparent diversity on the surface of the music. At the same time its concentration on a warm and affective melody allies it with contemporary musical trends.

LISTENING CUE

FELIX MENDELSSOHN
Piano Trio in D Minor, Op. 49 (1839)
First movement, *Molto allegro ed agitato*

CD 9/7
Anthology, No. 150

ROBERT SCHUMANN

Mendelssohn's stylistic conservatism was fully supported by his fellow Leipzig musician Robert Schumann (1810–1856). "He is the Mozart of the nineteenth century," wrote Schumann approvingly about Mendelssohn, "the most brilliant musician, the one who sees most clearly through the contradictions of this period and for the first time reconciles them."[1]

Schumann was born in the Saxon town of Zwickau, about forty miles south of Leipzig. As a child his imagination was fired equally by music and literature, and he aspired to be a concert pianist. In 1828 he enrolled at the University of Leipzig in law, although Schumann had no interest in this area, cut classes regularly, and concentrated instead on piano and composition. He studied piano with a well-known teacher in Leipzig, Friedrich Wieck, although his prospects as a player were set back by an injury to his hand. He admired the virtuosity of Wieck's prize student and daughter, Clara, whom Schumann would marry in 1840.

Like Berlioz before him, Schumann combined his talents for literature and music by writing musical criticism. In 1833 he collaborated on the founding of the **Neue [Leipziger] Zeitschrift für Musik** (*New Journal for Music*), which he edited and wrote almost single-handedly until 1844. This journal is still in existence. Music criticism at this time was different from its modern counterpart. Instead of passing judgments on performances like the reviewer of today, Schumann wrote primarily about newly published music, and his opinions were insightful. He immediately recognized the greatness of Chopin: "Hats off, gentlemen, a genius!" he declared in 1831 after examining the score of Chopin's early Variations, Op. 2. After studying a piano reduction of *Symphonie fantastique* he declared Berlioz's art to be a "flaming sword," although he found many eccentricities and was bothered by the explicit program that Berlioz used in the work. In 1853 he recognized the youthful Johannes Brahms as "a young creature over whose cradle graces and heroes stood guard."

After his marriage to Clara Wieck, Schumann often traveled with his wife on her concert tours. The pair moved in 1844 from Leipzig to the nearby city of Dresden—the capital of Saxony—and in 1850 again to Düsseldorf, where Schumann was appointed conductor of the local orchestra and chorus. Schumann waged a lifelong struggle with mental illness—its origins are uncertain—and in Düsseldorf his illness took a dire turn. He suffered several nervous breakdowns and tried studying counterpoint to focus his thoughts. Gradually his mind filled with voices and visions. "He heard entire pieces from beginning to end, as if played by a full orchestra," wrote Clara, "and the sound would remain on the final chord until Robert directed his thoughts to another composition." His psychosis only worsened, and in 1854 he attempted to drown himself in the Rhine River. He was then committed to a mental institution, where he died in 1856.

Schumann's Music

In the 1830s Schumann began his compositional career by writing almost exclusively for piano, something typical of the aspiring piano virtuoso. In addition to sonatas conceived on a large scale, he created miniature character pieces that were often gathered into cycles. *Papillons* (*Butterflies*, 1831), *Carnaval* (*Carnival*, 1835), and *Kinderscenen* (*Scenes from Childhood*, 1838) are some of the best known. These miniature works are fully imbued with the romantic spirit that originated with Schubert. As in Schubert's piano waltzes, impromptus, and "musical moments," Schumann's pieces bring the most intense expressivity and innovative musical materials into miniature dimensions. As with Berlioz's *Symphonie fantastique*, they are personalized and autobiographical, but, unlike Berlioz, this personal element is spoken under the breath, not intended for everyone to hear.

Examples of Schumann's sometimes cryptic allusions to his own world are found in **Carnaval,** a collection of more than twenty small pieces, each bearing a title of a person or event at an imaginary masked ball during carnival season. Musicians including Chopin and Nicolò Paganini—the great violin virtuoso—are at the dance, represented by pieces that bear their names and imitate their styles of composition. We meet Schumann himself in the pieces titled "Florestan" and "Eusebius," which were the names that he gave to the impetuous and the dreamy sides of his personality, respectively. Clara is there in a piece titled "Chiarina," which Schumann marks *passionato*. But his affections were apparently still divided among several women. The alto part of its opening phrase contains a descending line A♭-G-F-E♭-D, which—according to one hypothesis—Schumann used in later music as his private motto for Clara (Ex. 54-4). But the opening three notes in the soprano line, A♭-C-B♮, refer to one of her rivals. In German solfège, these note names are spelled As-C-H, and Asch was the hometown of Ernestine von Fricken, another of Wieck's female students.

EXAMPLE 54-4

mm. 1-5

In 1840, just before his marriage to Clara in September, Schumann turned his attention from piano music to songs, and in that year alone he poured out some one hundred seventy works of this type, including his great cycles *Dichterliebe* (*Poet's Love*), *Frauenliebe und -leben* (*Women's Love and Life*), and *Myrthen* (*Myrtles*). As with the piano miniatures, his model for song-writing was Schubert, whose deeply expressive approach to the genre of song Schumann adopts and extends.

After their marriage, Clara urged her husband to take up the larger musical forms, and he responded by hurriedly composing the first two of his four symphonies. He later wrote concertos for piano and for cello, three string quartets, and important chamber works with piano—a Quintet, Op. 44, Quartet, Op. 47, and three piano trios. In these later works Schumann partly turns away from the exuberant, affective style of the early piano pieces and songs in order to recapture a more classical form and measured expression. Schumann wrote one opera, *Genoveva* (1849).

Symphony No. 1 in B♭ Major ("Spring")

Schumann's four symphonies have a complex history. The first of them, in B♭ major, was written in a burst of creativity spanning only four days in January 1841. Later in that year he composed another symphony, in D minor, although it was not fully orchestrated until 1851, whereupon it was called Symphony No. 4. In the intervening years he wrote two additional symphonies, one in C major (called Symphony No. 2) and another in E♭ major (Symphony No. 3, nicknamed the "Rhenish" Symphony after the Rhine River). These four are among the greatest works in the entire symphonic literature.

Schumann began his Symphony No. 1 as a subtly programmatic work, much as Beethoven had done in his "Eroica" and "Pastoral" symphonies. His subject would be springtime, and he at first referred to a poem by a Leipzig writer named Adolf Böttger (1815–1870), although the verse has little apparent relevance to the finished work. He gave each of the movements a descriptive subtitle: Spring's Beginning, Evening, Happy Games, Spring Bursting Out. But Schumann was never in favor of the overt programmaticism used by Berlioz, which for Schumann could only limit the freedom of a listener's imagination. "What remains as really important," he wrote, "is whether the music, without text and explanation, has intrinsic value, and especially whether it is imbued with spirit."[2] When his symphony was published later in 1841, Schumann removed all of the verbal references to spring, although the work is still commonly known as the "Spring" Symphony.

There is much about it that is springlike. In the first movement, a triangle is brought in, giving the work a festive sound. The flute twitters like a bird, and the music—as often with Schumann—has the freshness of a spring day. The work has the overall shape of a symphony by Beethoven or Schubert. There are the customary four movements (fast with slow introduction/slow/scherzo/fast) and the whole symphony is moderate in length, about thirty-five minutes. The orchestra is virtually identical to the one used in Schubert's Symphony No. 9 in C Major, which had been played repeatedly by the Gewandhaus Orchestra beginning in 1839, and was certainly in Schumann's ear as he wrote his B♭ symphony.

The audience at the Gewandhaus for the premiere of Schumann's "Spring" Symphony, which Mendelssohn conducted in March 1841, must have noted from the very outset the similarities with Schubert's Ninth. The two works begin similarly, with slow introductions launched by brass motives that underlie later themes (Schumann's opening motive is shown in Ex. 54-5; see Schubert's in Chapter 52). In both works, the motive returns climactically later in the movement, at the beginning of the recapitulation in Schumann, in the coda in Schubert. Both first movements take liberties with the customary sequence of events in sonata form.

EXAMPLE 54-5

Horns, trumpets

Schumann looks to Beethoven's gestures of continuity and large-scale unity in the symphony as a fertile area for development. The slow movement and the scherzo of Symphony No. 1 are played without pause, and they are further linked by a hymn-like figure in the trombones at the end of the slow movement that is immediately transformed into the main scherzo theme (Ex. 54-6a). A theme subtly shared between the outer movements is shown in Example 54-6b.

EXAMPLE 54-6

Schumann's slow movement is unusual in its tempo and lyric character. Symphonic slow movements before this time were normally marked *andante*, but Schumann's is slower—a broad *larghetto*—and its main melody (Ex. 54-7) is unusually intense, reminiscent of an operatic melody, or one by Chopin. A model for this type of slow movement may have been the slow movement, marked *adagio*, of Beethoven's "Pastoral" Symphony, which has a similar character. Beethoven's *Adagio* also shares with Schumann's *Larghetto* a busy accompaniment in the strings, one that always poses a problem in balance.

Example 54-7

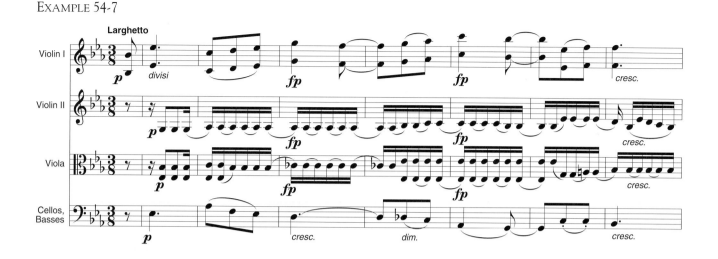

LISTENING CUE

ROBERT SCHUMANN
Symphony No. 1, "Spring" (1841)
Second movement, *Larghetto*

CD 9/8
Anthology, No. 151

CLARA SCHUMANN

Clara Schumann (1819–1896) was one of the great piano virtuosos of the nineteenth century (Fig. 54-3). Growing up in Leipzig, where she was relentlessly pushed to succeed by her father, she proved herself an extraordinary child prodigy. She played at the Gewandhaus at the age of only nine and in 1831, at the age of eleven, she began to tour throughout Europe. She continued to concertize virtually to the end of her long life, even through numerous pregnancies during her sixteen years of marriage (the Schumanns had eight children).

A special chapter in her life following Robert Schumann's untimely death concerns her friendship with the composer Johannes Brahms. He introduced himself to the Schumanns in 1853 and was warmly embraced by them both. After Schumann's death, Brahms and Clara Schumann continued a platonic, artistic relationship that endured for the remainder of Clara's life. In 1896, as Clara's health began to fail, Brahms composed *Four Serious Songs*, Op. 121, a collection that was his memorial to her and to their 43-year friendship. He sent a copy of the songs to Clara's daughter with a poignant explanation of their content:

> Deep in the heart of man something often whispers and stirs, quite unconsciously perhaps, which in time may ring out in the form of poetry or music. . . . I beg you to regard these [songs] as a true memorial to your beloved mother.[3]

FIGURE 54-3
Eduard Kaiser's lithograph of Robert and Clara Schumann, 1847. The Schumanns lived in Dresden when this was made.

CORBIS

The programs that Clara Schumann played spanned a general change in the idea of the piano concert—from a gala event with many players and differing genres, to the recital, in which the pianist plays alone or nearly so. In the earlier type, Clara Schumann played improvisations, her own compositions, flashy studies, variations on opera melodies, and concertos. Later she changed to a more modern soloistic repertory that mixed sonatas by Domenico Scarlatti and Beethoven, fugues by Bach, works by her husband (always), and other modern pieces (especially those by Brahms). These were chosen for their artistry rather than showmanship, for which she had only disdain. She toured far and wide, from Russia to England (where she visited nineteen times), although never to America. She ended her days as a professor of piano playing at the Conservatory in Frankfurt. There are no recordings of her playing.

Clara Schumann also composed, primarily because this was part of the art of the virtuoso in her day. Most of her music—a piano concerto, character works for this instrument, variations, and songs—were pieces intended for her concerts. Her songs show an introspective side of her musical personality, one that was plainly stimulated by the songs of her husband. She wrote "Liebst du um Schönheit" ("If You Love Beauty") in 1841, and it was published in a collection of songs to texts by Friedrich Rückert, some composed by her husband during his great song year of 1840, some by her.

The poetry of Friedrich Rückert (1788–1866) was set to music by many of the greatest nineteenth-century Lieder composers—Schubert, Gustav Mahler, and Robert and Clara Schumann are only a few. In Chapter 60 we will return to Rückert's poem "Um Mitternacht," where it is found in a song by Gustav Mahler. The poem "Liebst du um Schönheit" is frank in its emotionality. Love me only for the sake of love, says the narrator, not for beauty, youth, or wealth, for which you can do better elsewhere. These same direct sentiments are captured in the music, which is unsophisticated and repetitive, although affective in its melodic warmth.

LISTENING CUE

CLARA SCHUMANN
"Liebst du um Schönheit" (1841)

CD 9/9
Anthology, No. 152

SUMMARY

Music in the city of Leipzig in the early nineteenth century had a conservative tone, mixing elements of eighteenth-century music with modern ideas. The city was a center of orchestral music, thanks to its excellent Gewandhaus Orchestra, which was conducted by Felix Mendelssohn from 1835 to 1847. Mendelssohn composed music in a mixed style, close to the models provided by Mozart and Beethoven, but cautiously expanded by more modern notions. His Trio in D Minor, Op. 49, shows this combination of old and new.

Robert Schumann lived in Leipzig from 1831 to 1844, during which he composed piano music, songs, and, beginning in 1841, orchestral music. His symphonies show the same mixture of stylistic elements as in Mendelssohn. His Symphony No. 1 in

B♭ Major ("Spring") uses a form inherited from Beethoven and Schubert, although the four movements are linked together by shared themes and other gestures toward continuity. The slow movement, *Larghetto,* is especially songful.

Clara Wieck Schumann, who married Robert Schumann in 1840, was one of the great piano virtuosos of the nineteenth century. Like most professional pianists, she also composed, and her song "Liebst du um Schönheit" achieves an affecting beauty despite its artlessness and simplicity of form.

KEY TERMS

Hugo Riemann
functional harmony
complete works (type of
   musical edition)

Gewandhaus Orchestra
Bartholdy
Bach Revival
canon

Neue Zeitschrift für Musik
Carnaval

German Opera of the Nineteenth Century: Weber and Wagner

Opera in the early nineteenth century retained its unique importance within the world of music. Like other musical genres, it was partly a diversion, but it also had the special capacity to deal with the real social and historical issues of its time. Mozart's *Marriage of Figaro* attracted attention in part because it questioned the right of the aristocracy to privilege. Beethoven's *Fidelio* touched on the legitimate limits of the power of the state over the individual. Giuseppe Verdi's *Nabucco* alluded to the plight of a people having no homeland, a condition felt by many of Verdi's Italian countrymen when the opera was first heard in 1842.

Opera in the nineteenth century was not only relevant but highly popular. In virtually all of the major European capitals of this time, the genre flourished as never before. New and larger opera houses were being built with updated staging and lighting equipment. Opera singers had become international celebrities, and new ideas about operatic composition flowed, at first from France and Italy, and later from Germany. Fame and fortune awaited the successful opera composer to a degree unknown by composers in any other medium.

But, with a few exceptions such as Mozart and Beethoven, German musicians had been underachievers in the genre. Schubert, Mendelssohn, and Schumann composed operas, but they were never very successful. Recall from Chapter 48 that German opera in the eighteenth century existed primarily in a form called **Singspiel** (literally, "play with singing"). In *Singspiel,* simple musical numbers were inserted into a lighthearted or folkish spoken play. Works of this type continued to be composed after 1800, but in musical terms they seemed unsophisticated and old-fashioned. To most audiences, even in German lands, *Singspiel* paled in comparison to the intensely human comedies found in Gioachino Rossini's Italian operas, or the spectacular French operas by Giacomo Meyerbeer, or the studies in heroism found in the French operas of Gaspare Spontini.

Singspiel was far more modest. Its performers were typically members of a traveling company who performed spoken plays one day and opera the next. The art of purely operatic singing was scarcely known among them. In the eighteenth century, King Frederick the Great had said unkindly that a horse could sing opera better than a German. If so, little had changed by the early nineteenth century. "Where in all our German fatherland are there training schools for higher vocal culture?" asked Richard Wagner in 1834. "The higher vocal art, solo singing, is in manifest decline, and many a mile might we journey before we could assemble a couple of dozen good singers really worthy of the name."[1]

✱ CARL MARIA VON WEBER

German opera took on new vitality and identity in the works of Carl Maria von Weber (pronounced VAY-ber, 1786–1826). He was born in Eutin, a small town in the far north of Germany, and his life was unsettled by almost constant travel and by a career divided among composing, conducting, performing (he excelled at both guitar and piano), writing musical criticism, and managing theaters. In 1817 he was appointed director of an opera troupe in the city of Dresden, the capital of Saxony, where he staged *Singspiele* and French operas in German translation. An Italian opera company was also in residence in the city, and a heated rivalry soon developed between the two. Weber was determined to bring the level of German opera above the Italian, which, except for its excellent singing, he found thin in artistic content. He poked fun at the make-up of a typical Italian work as something where "oboes double the flutes, clarinets double the oboes, flutes double the violins, bassoons double the bass. Second violins double the firsts, viola doubles the bass. Voice ad libitum. Violins double the voice."[2]

In Dresden, Weber composed his greatest opera, *Der Freischütz* (freely, *The Bewitched Marksman*, 1821). It has much in common with Beethoven's *Fidelio* (see Chapter 50). The characters are strictly types, not drawn to the measure of real individuals, and the musical form is an old-fashioned succession of traditional operatic numbers interspersed into a spoken play. In light of these features, both *Der Freischütz* and *Fidelio* are related to *Singspiel,* and both works also incorporate styles from French and Italian operas of their time.

Der Freischütz also has features that look to the future of opera. The libretto, written by **Friedrich Kind** (an amateur writer who lived in Dresden), avoids the more typical themes of contemporary operas of the day—the comic farce or the tragedy stemming from heightened, conflicting human emotions. Instead, Kind adapted a ghost story, making it into a morality play in which good is pitted against the forces of evil. Mysterious events take place and there is an aura of the supernatural, just as in a popular type of literature of the time called the "romance." Because of this similarity, Weber designated his opera, not as old-fashioned *Singspiel,* but by the more up-to-date term, **romantic opera.**

In addition to characters representing everyman (Max), the pure woman (Agathe), religion (the Holy Man), the good ruler (Prince Ottokar), and the fallen individual (Caspar), there is also a strong presence of common people—plain folk—who live in harmony with nature. In their rousing choruses Weber quotes several folk songs, as he wished to give his opera a nationalistic flavor at a time when Germans were discovering patriotism after their long subjugation by the French under Napoleon.

Synopsis of *Der Freischütz*

The hunter Max is dejected over his poor shooting, and he knows that he must do better in tomorrow's shooting match in order to win the hand of his beloved Agathe, daughter of the chief forester. A fellow hunter, Caspar, tells Max that he can supply enchanted, or "free," bullets, that will go wherever the shooter wishes. These can be had if Max meets him that night in the haunted Wolf's Glen. Despite Agathe's premonitions, Max agrees, and the two hunters cast seven magic bullets. But, unknown to Max, the spirit of the devil, Samiel, is lurking near, and he will control the seventh bullet himself.

At the next day's shooting contest, Max is unbeatable. For his seventh and final shot, Prince Ottokar picks an easy target—a dove sitting on a nearby branch. Just as he aims, Agathe darts from behind the tree. "Don't shoot, Max, I am the dove!" But the shot rings out and Agathe falls to the ground. To everyone's relief, she has only fainted and the bullet has instead killed Caspar, who had earlier sold his soul to Samiel. After confessing his crimes and receiving support from a Holy Man, Max is given a year's probation, after which he can marry Agathe. All praise the goodness of God.

Weber's most original accomplishment in *Der Freischütz* is to unify the diverse elements that make up an opera on the basis of its drama. He achieves this especially in the work's orchestral music, which closely follows and underscores the drama. No longer is the orchestra simply an accompaniment to singing, as often in Italian opera. Weber instead elevates its role by a network of musical symbols—specifically, by identifying orchestral motives, tonalities, and specific instruments with certain characters or situations. The idea of using musical elements as explicit dramatic symbols was not entirely new with Weber, but in the context of German opera he brought the notion to a higher and more systematic level than had been done before, and his achievements were carefully studied by later opera composers, including Hector Berlioz and Richard Wagner.

The keys of C major and D major, for example, are used in *Der Freischütz* whenever the good characters—especially Agathe and choruses representing the people—sing. The villainous Caspar sings primarily in B minor and D minor, and the devil, Samiel, doesn't sing at all; instead, he speaks over an unstable diminished chord played by the orchestra. Max, the hero and hunter, is accompanied most often by the French horns; the pure Agathe by the pure sound of the clarinet; Samiel by the devilish timpani.

The most striking, and always the most popular, part of *Der Freischütz* is the finale to Act 2, also called the **Wolf's Glen Scene.** Recall from Chapter 48 that an operatic finale is a longish number occurring at the end of an act. It is made from several contrasting but connected musical sections in differing vocal styles, although ensemble singing usually dominates. Several of the leading singer-actors appear in a finale to bring the plot either to a crisis point or to some resolution. Weber, like Beethoven at the climactic beginning of Act 2 of *Fidelio*, underscores the dramatic tension of his finale by using **melodrama,** in addition to normal singing. In melodrama—which was favored among French composers of the day—the voices speak in alternation with or accompanied by orchestral music.

In the finale of Act 2, Max has foolishly agreed to meet Caspar in the haunted Wolf's Glen to cast magic bullets. Caspar arrives first, greeted by a chorus of invisible spirits in the key of F♯ minor, and he calls on Samiel to appear. We know Samiel arrives when we hear the orchestra play the motive by which he is always accompanied (Ex. 55-1). His motive is no arbitrary symbol. It is made from a sustained diminished-seventh chord, always with the notes A-C-E♭-G♭ regardless of the tonal context, and it is always played quietly with the timpani muttering on offbeats. It has the same shadowy, slippery quality as the diabolical creature that it represents. The key then shifts to C minor, and Caspar asks Samiel for an extension to his time on earth in return for Caspar's bringing him the soul of Max. Samiel seems to agree to this arrangement, and Caspar builds a fire in a forge to cast the magic bullets. The hunting horns announce Max's arrival as the key turns to E♭ major—the key of the hero ever since Beethoven's Symphony No. 3.

EXAMPLE 55-1

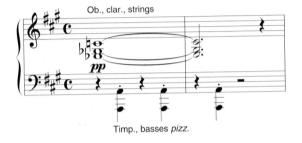

The casting of the seven bullets forms the climactic last section of the finale (Anthology, No. 153). The orchestral music begins in A minor and depicts the furnace's crackling fire. Caspar shouts out the number of each new bullet as it is tossed from its mold, and after each one there is an eerie vision, as though nature protests what is happening. A wild boar crashes through the bushes, the Wild Huntsman (a character from folklore) rides through the air, and finally a great thunderstorm rises. Audiences of the 1820s were fascinated by the dramatic realism of Weber's staging, especially by a wooden owl whose eyes glowed and wings flapped. Like the orchestral music, the scenery was no longer a neutral backdrop but instead an active expressive tool. When the seventh bullet is cast, both Caspar and Max are thrown to the ground, and as the key returns to F♯ minor Samiel reaches out for Max's hand.

In addition to creating a network of musical and visual symbols in this scene, Weber looks for subtle ways of instilling continuity in the music, which is necessary if it is to be as dramatic as the words. He finds in the work's tonal plan a dimension for promoting musical integration. This is unified and concentric, as in a symphony or concerto of the day, but unusual in an opera. The entire opera returns at its end to a home key, here C major, in which it began. The Wolf's Glen Scene—like an inner movement from a symphony—begins and ends in a contrasting key, F♯ minor.

Integration of key and harmony is also felt on the smaller scale, always with reference to the work's drama. In the Wolf's Glen Scene, for example, the succession of principal tonic notes which span the entire passage— F♯, C, E♭, A, then back to F♯ at the end—make up on the large scale the same diminished-seventh chord that represents Samiel in his small motive. By this integration of timespans, Weber shows us that Samiel controls the scene from beginning to end, ruthlessly wielding his power over such frail human beings as Caspar and Max.

LISTENING CUE

CARL MARIA VON WEBER
Der Freischütz (1821)
Act 2, Wolf's Glen Scene, concluding section

CD 9/10
Anthology, No. 153

RICHARD WAGNER

Weber's creation of an opera unified in music and drama was developed later in the nineteenth century by Richard Wagner (pronounced VAHG-ner, 1813–1883; Fig. 55-1). Wagner was born in Leipzig and grew up there and in nearby Dresden. Like his fellow Saxon, Robert Schumann, he was strongly attracted to literature and later wrote voluminously on music. Wagner was largely self-taught as a composer, and at the age of nineteen he had a symphony performed by the Gewandhaus Orchestra. On the same program Clara Wieck, thirteen years old, also played, and she teased her friend Robert Schumann about Wagner's progress: "Listen, Mr. Wagner has got ahead of you. His symphony was performed, and it's said to be almost exactly like Beethoven's Symphony [No. 7] in A Major."[3]

In 1839 Wagner moved to Paris to try to advance his career as a composer of opera in the world's operatic capital. He began to write musical criticism to earn money, but he had no success in finding a stage for his early operas. His breakthrough came in 1842, when his opera *Rienzi*—a work in the style of French grand opera although having a German text—was accepted for production in Dresden. Its success led to Wagner's appointment there as *Kapellmeister*, in a position earlier held by Carl Maria von Weber. His next two operas—*Der fliegende Holländer* (*The Flying Dutchman*, 1841) and *Tannhäuser* (1845)—also had their premieres in Dresden, and his *Lohengrin* (1848) was readied for the 1849 season.

But, in the spring of 1849, Wagner's burgeoning career was derailed by his participation in an uprising in Dresden directed against the rule of Friedrich Augustus II, the king of Saxony and also Wagner's employer. The insurgency was quickly put down, but some two hundred people were killed and a warrant was issued for Wagner's arrest. Using a faked passport, he escaped a possible death sentence by fleeing to Zurich in neutral Switzerland. With an arrest warrant looming permanently over him, Wagner was effectively banished from visiting countries in the German Confederation, and, as a specialist in German opera, his prospects as a composer were in tatters. In 1860 the king of Saxony granted Wagner a limited amnesty, and only then could he return to German lands without fear of arrest.

In Switzerland, Wagner's interests first turned toward literary matters. He wrote aesthetic treatises on the state of opera and its relation to contemporary and future society, and he continued to hatch ideas for new works. Following the breakup of his marriage in 1859, Wagner left Switzerland and began an unsettled period of travel, hounded by increasing debt and frustrated musical ambitions.

In 1864 Wagner was living in a Stuttgart hotel and literally down to his last dollar. He was found there by a secretary to Ludwig II—eighteen years old and newly enthroned as the king of Bavaria—who invited Wagner to meet him in the Bavarian capital of Munich. Needless to say, Wagner accepted the invitation. Although not especially musical, King Ludwig was a passionate admirer of Wagner's writings and music, and he immediately paid off Wagner's debts, gave him a salary and a place to live, and underwrote the expenses for the premier performances of the operas *Tristan und Isolde* (1859) and *Die Meistersinger von Nürnberg* (*The Master Singers of Nuremberg*, 1867).

The large expenses arising from having Wagner as a guest soon made it necessary for the king to ask Wagner to leave Munich, and the composer then returned to Switzerland and lived near Lucerne. In 1870 he married Cosima Liszt, daughter of Franz Liszt and formerly the wife of Liszt's student Hans von Bülow. In Lucerne, Wagner pushed ahead on a longstanding project of epic proportions—*Der Ring des Nibelungen* (*The Ring of the Nibelung*)—a cycle of four related operas.

Bridgeman Art Library

FIGURE 55-1

Portrait of Richard Wagner by Franz von Lenbach. Lenbach, a personal friend of Wagner and his wife, painted many of the leading personalities of his day.

For their staging he felt that he needed a special theater where the operas could be performed in a festival-like atmosphere. With King Ludwig's financial help, Wagner purchased property in the Bavarian village of **Bayreuth** and began to raise money to build a theater specifically for the performance of his own works (Fig. 55-2). He also built a permanent residence in Bayreuth, moving there in 1872 to oversee the first complete performances of the *Ring* operas. These took place in the summer of 1876. Wagner then turned his attention to his last opera, *Parsifal* (1882), a work that he thought should only be performed in the Bayreuth theater. In February 1883, while visiting Venice, the composer suffered a fatal heart attack, and he is buried on the grounds of his villa in Bayreuth.

Vanni/Art Resource

🌿 FIGURE 55-2
The Bayreuth Festival Theater is located on a hill on the outskirts of the town of Bayreuth. The auditorium seats about 1,500.

🌸 WAGNER'S MUSIC AND THEORIES OF OPERA

Wagner was a specialist in operatic composition, a genre that best combined his literary and musical talents. Not counting a few youthful experiments, he wrote a total of eleven operas, although he did not consider the first of these, *Rienzi*, to be a mature work. There are also a few songs, piano pieces, choral music, and orchestral works such as the delightful *Siegfried Idyll* for chamber orchestra (1870).

All of Wagner's operas use texts that he wrote himself. He developed an idea for a new composition by his literary readings and by calling on his own experiences and ideas. He worked these stimuli into a prose outline and from there into a poetic libretto which was usually published immediately. Composition then followed, and Wagner sometimes returned to a completed work to make substantial revisions.

The first three of the ten principal operas—*The Flying Dutchman*, *Tannhäuser*, and *Lohengrin*—form a related group, not too distant in style from Weber's *Der Freischütz*. Wagner based their texts on old German legends, and the stories bring in magical and supernatural elements in the same way as *Der Freischütz*. Wagner called each of these a "romantic" opera, using Weber's term. Like *Der Freischütz*, *The Flying Dutchman* is clearly divided into operatic numbers, although Wagner dispenses with the old-fashioned spoken dialogue of Weber's time. In *Tannhäuser* and *Lohengrin*, the division into numbers is less apparent because they are absorbed into larger divisions, or scenes, in which there is a fluid alternation among soloistic, ensemble, and choral singing. The scenes are all connected without pause, so that there is no encouragement for the audience to break the concentration by applause.

After *Lohengrin*, Wagner went into his Swiss exile and wrote a series of books and articles on the state of opera and its future prospects, and his theories guided him in his later musical works. Wagner believed that opera in his day was out of balance, since the musical element had taken on too much importance and the dramatic part had, he thought, become trivial. He wanted to redress this imbalance by elevating the drama of opera to a more sophisticated level and creating an integrated equilibrium among text, music, and staging. Opera, he said, should become a **Gesamtkunstwerk (total work of art),** not just an occasion for singing. Thinking as always in utopian terms, Wagner proposed that this integrated and dramatic artwork would become the ideal of **music of the future.**

The best subjects for the artwork of the future, Wagner speculated, were drawn from myths, since these were products of a collective imagination and inherently understandable by everyone. Myths, he said, deal with the essential problems facing humanity—the nature of love, the concept of property, the idea of God—and big ideas such as these could become the stuff of opera. But, for this to happen, the artificialities of the genre as it then existed would have to be reformed. The stop-and-go of number opera had to be eliminated in favor of a continuous and uninterrupted form. Melody would have to avoid regular and symmetric phrases and instead continually reshape motives and ride upon an enriched, expressive harmony. The virtuoso singing of opera would be reined in and made to share the burden of expression with the orchestra. The orchestra would not be the "huge guitar" of Italian opera—a mere accompaniment—but a continuation of Weber's idea of the opera orchestra as an independent expressive voice that abstractly communicates the drama through a network of musical symbols.

A model for the operatic artwork of the future, said Wagner, could be found in ancient Greek tragedy. These plays were given in festival-like productions involving an entire community, and they were performed with the combination of poetry, dance, choral chanting, and expressive acting that suggests a total work of art. Using symbolic motives, the orchestra of future opera could be like a Greek chorus, an independent voice that continuously comments on and judges the actions presented on stage. Ultimately, Wagner's ideal for the future of the genre seemed so different from his contemporary opera that he proposed a new name for it, not opera but **music drama** (Wagner eventually found this term also to be misleading).

❋ DAS RHEINGOLD

Many of Wagner's theories on music of the future were realized in the four operas—*Das Rheingold* (*The Rhine Gold*, 1854), *Die Walküre* (*The Valkyrie*, 1856), *Siegfried* (1869), and *Götterdämmerung* (*Twilight of the Gods*, 1874)—that make up the cycle *The Ring of the Nibelung*. Wagner based his sprawling tale on characters and events drawn from Old Norse and medieval German mythology. He even imitated the literary style of his ancient sources by replacing normal rhyme with alliteration (as in "Peter Piper picked a peck of pickled peppers"). He also imitated the old figure of speech called "kenning," by which an object is named by its observed characteristics (for example, a battle becomes a "storm of swords"). As in the old sagas, certain objects—a ring, a sword, a spear—take on a broad symbolic meaning. This affected style makes the *Ring* texts difficult to read now, although they still have a literary value in themselves, and readers will find many similarities with J. R. R. Tolkien's *Lord of the Rings*.

The doings of the old gods and the deeds of medieval heroes in the *Ring* operas are only the outer shell of an underlying statement about the prospects of modern people in a society that Wagner believed to be devoid of compassion and gripped by material values. In general terms, at least, Wagner makes the symbolism of the story plain. The gold and its ring stand for wealth, which, as Alberich says, confers great power but brings with it anxiety and animosity, diminishing the capacity for love. Wealth rightly belongs only to nature, represented by the Rhine River. The magical golden tarnhelm suggests that a person in possession of wealth becomes deceptive and hypocritical, not what he seems. Wotan's dilemma arises because he, like other beings, craves material possessions, such as Valhalla. This weakness prevents him from leading the universe to a peaceful and ethical state where love can exist.

The answer to Wotan's dilemma comes only after four days of opera, during which the gods gradually stand aside and allow humanity to act freely and to discover on its own a capacity for love. The message of the *Ring* operas is both complex and

Synopsis of *The Rhine Gold*

The opera is in four scenes. In the Rhine River, mermaids, or "Rhine Maidens," frolic playfully around a horde of gold, whose beauty delights them. Alberich, one of the dwarfish Nibelungs who live in the earth, swims up and learns from the ladies that a ring made from the gold will allow its wearer to rule the world. But this person would have to renounce love, something that for them is unthinkable. To their horror, Alberich steals the gold. "I renounce love and curse it," he yells as he swims away.

The scene shifts to the mountains, where the chief god, Wotan, lives with his wife, Fricka. He proudly gazes over to his new castle, called Valhalla, which has just been built for him by giants, although Fricka is alarmed to learn that her sister Freia has been promised to the giants in payment. Wotan has no intention of giving Freia to such beasts; he is counting on his ability as a wheeler-dealer to get better terms. His shifty advisor Loge suggests paying off the giants by stealing Alberich's gold. Although Wotan is pledged to maintain ethics in the universe, he sees no alternative.

Loge and Wotan descend into the earth, where they find that Alberich has used the golden ring to enslave his fellow Nibelungs. From the treasure Alberich's brother Mime has made him a "tarnhelm," a magical mask by which he can change identity. It is clear that Alberich plans nothing less

than bringing down the gods and dominating the world. To show what the tarnhelm can do, Alberich uses it to turn himself into a toad, and Wotan cleverly traps him with his foot.

Back in the mountains, Wotan demands the entire treasure for Alberich's release. He agrees, but repeats the curse of the ring; it will confer power but its owner will suffer fear and ultimately death. The owner of the ring will actually be its slave. When the giants demand the ring in addition to the rest of the treasure, Wotan refuses. Just then Erda, the mother goddess of the earth, rises up to warn Wotan that all things will perish. Give up the ring, she demands, and Wotan sullenly obeys. As they pack up their treasure, the giants argue over it and one slays the other. The ring has claimed its first victim.

Although relieved to have ransomed Freia, Wotan has a dilemma on his hands. How can he create an orderly universe in which love can flourish when he himself has had continually to break his own moral laws? He picks up a sword left over from the Nibelung's horde, and a great idea comes to him: he will turn over ethical authority to mortals acting of their own free will. In high spirits he leads the gods over a rainbow bridge toward **Valhalla.**

---

disarmingly simple: there are two great forces in the universe, Wagner says, the power of love and the power of wealth. The power of love is shown to be the higher.

To create a musical context appropriate to this titanic message, Wagner resorted to a much expanded medium and time frame. Lasting about three hours, *The Rhine Gold* is the shortest of the four operas (it is a prelude of sorts and there is no intermission); the other three last between four and five hours each. The voice parts—especially the leading male roles, given generally to the tenor voice—demand such strength and endurance that they are mastered by relatively few singers.

True to his theories, Wagner in *The Rhine Gold* dispenses with divisions into operatic numbers and creates instead a relatively continuous musical texture. Even during the changes of scenery, the music keeps going in the form of descriptive orchestral interludes. Except for the ensemble singing by the Rhine Maidens, all of the singing in the opera is soloistic—there are no choruses or other ensembles—nor is there any rigid distinction in the solo singing between recitative and aria. The voices sing in a midway style, the text always clearly audible, with the melody sometimes becoming recitational and at other times lyrical.

One of the great joys of listening to Wagner's operas is their orchestral music. No composer has ever made an orchestra sound better or more expressive than Wagner. The orchestra of the *Ring* operas is enlarged and enriched by new instruments. Wagner writes for eight French horns, and he calls for the other brass and woodwinds in fours. There are six harps and a large percussion section (sixteen anvils are needed in the interlude before Scene 3), and the composer specifies that sixty-four string players should cover the customary five lines. New instruments appear in the brass.

For example, Wagner calls for four mid-range brass instruments now called **Wagner tubas.** These are played by hornists, and together they produce an unusually mellow and dignified tone, creating the precise atmosphere that Wagner wanted us to experience when we first see Valhalla at the beginning of Scene 2.

Wagner greatly expands upon Weber's idea of giving symbolic motives to the orchestra, which allows it to comment upon and narrate elements of the drama directly. These figures are now called **leitmotives** (leading, or associative, motives) although Wagner himself did not use this term. The motives usually appear in the orchestra, sometimes migrating into the voice parts for emphasis. Some of them appear concretely and unchangingly, functioning as a musical label for a person or thing. An example is the motive that identifies the sword found by Wotan as he enters Valhalla at the end of the opera (Ex. 55-2). It is always played by the brass, usually in C major, and it surges upward energetically and climactically—all suggesting the thing that it represents.

EXAMPLE 55-2

Other motives are more flexible in their use and shadowy in their symbolism, making any labeling of them arbitrary or misleading. An example of this more subtle level of symbolism is seen by comparing the motives for the ring and for Valhalla, which are shown in Example 55-3 in their first occurrences in the opera. They are very similar, suggesting that Wagner found some underlying relation between the ring and the castle. In the final scene of *The Rhine Gold,* the so-called Entrance of the Gods into Valhalla, Wagner alternates between them to make a subtle dramatic point. As the gods gaze at the new castle, the Valhalla motive is stated repeatedly. But when Wotan comments that the castle was built from toil and care, from which it will now be a shelter, the Valhalla figure is made to resemble the motive of the ring, which is a symbol suggesting care and anxiety.

EXAMPLE 55-3

In many of Wagner's operas, the final sections of acts and scenes create a memorable climax, and this is certainly the case in the music of *The Rhine Gold* that Wagner composes for the gods as they enter their new home. The scene is unified by a central key, D♭ major, which is generally used by Wagner whenever the drama focuses on Valhalla. The passage begins with an introductory orchestral portrait of a thunderstorm, in B♭ major. Donner and Froh, the gods of thunder and rain, send out a great lightning bolt that clears away the clouds and reveals the magnificent castle in the

Wagner and Anti-Semitism

Wagner's writings contain outright and repeated hostility toward Jews, and this outlook casts a dark shadow over his undeniable greatness as an artist and musician. His first overtly anti-Semitic essay was titled "Judaism in Music," published under a pseudonym in the *Neue Zeitschrift für Musik* in 1850. Here Wagner reinforces many of the invidious stereotypes used against Jews at the time, and his anti-Semitic diatribes only increased in his later writings.

Wagner's unapologetic racism considerably advanced the acceptability in Germany of anti-Semitic thinking, which later contributed to the rise of the Nazis and, ultimately, to the unspeakable tragedy of the Holocaust. Fortunately, none of Wagner's music is overtly polluted by his racist attitudes. But his writings have made it difficult for many in the present day to listen to this music with the whole-hearted sympathy that Wagner himself asked of his audiences. Even today, Wagner's music is virtually never performed in the state of Israel.

There can be no excuse for the anti-Semitic element in Wagner's writings. Still, the modern listener must evaluate Wagner's personal failings in light of a broader range of personal and artistic factors. These include the high-minded content of his operas in general and the likelihood that Wagner would have opposed the violence inflicted upon the Jews during the Nazi period. In *Das Rheingold*, when Wotan is negotiating with the giants, his thuggish lieutenant, Donner, threatens to slay them with his hammer. Wotan—who speaks for Wagner himself—stops Donner cold. "Nothing through force!" he commands.

distance. A spectacular rainbow bridges the valley, and the gods prepare to walk triumphantly over it. But, as usual, something spoils Wotan's pleasure. The Rhine Maidens are heard from the river valley lamenting the loss of their beautiful gold. "Tell those insufferable creatures to be quiet!" he snaps to Loge. But they continue. Only in the river, the depths of nature, is there truth, they say; what is above is false and weak.

These dramatic events are shadowed by vividly descriptive orchestral music and its leitmotives. In addition to the motives already illustrated that represent the sword, the ring, and Valhalla, there are four other important motives that appear in the passage, and these are shown in Example 55-4 in their initial forms.

EXAMPLE 55-4

Rhine gold! Rhine gold! Radiant joy…

LISTENING CUE

RICHARD WAGNER
Das Rheingold (1854)
Entrance of the Gods into Valhalla

CD 9/11
Anthology, No. 154

SUMMARY

In the early nineteenth century, operas in the German language at first lagged behind the sophistication and popularity of such works coming from Italy and France. But in the hands of the composers Carl Maria von Weber and Richard Wagner, German opera became the source of new ideas. In *Der Freischütz,* Weber expands upon the old form of *Singspiel* to create an opera in which the dramatic element takes on a new emphasis. Weber was especially resourceful in making the orchestra not simply an accompaniment but, through its use of a network of musical symbols, directly expressive.

Wagner continued Weber's initiatives and strove toward a conception of opera as a dramatic genre in which text, music, and staging are balanced and integrated. Wagner elevated the literary element of opera and changed its traditional musical form by removing musical numbers in favor of a homogeneity of vocal styles and an uninterrupted continuity. A distinctive feature of his operas is the use of leitmotives in the orchestral music. These are short musical figures that symbolize elements in the drama.

His most imposing realization of his theories about opera is found in *Der Ring des Nibelungen* (*The Ring of the Nibelung*), which is a gigantic cycle of four related operas that uses ideas drawn from ancient German mythology to critique the society in which the composer lived. Since 1876 Wagner's operas have been performed in a special festival theater that he personally had constructed in the Bavarian town of Bayreuth.

KEY TERMS

Singspiel
Friedrich Kind
romantic opera
Wolf's Glen Scene
melodrama (in opera)

Bayreuth
total work of art
    (*Gesamtkunstwerk*)
music of the future
music drama

Valhalla
Wagner tuba
leitmotive

Chapter

Opera in Italy: Rossini and Verdi

56

Italian opera in the nineteenth century was more closely linked to operatic traditions than was its German counterpart, and it was more in line with the spirit of its own time than with any utopian "music of the future." During the nineteenth century, the leading Italian composers guardedly expanded upon traditional operatic

✿ FIGURE 56-1

One of the most popular and influential composers of the nineteenth century, Gioachino Rossini was also an accomplished chef and famous for his wit.

form based on the familiar musical numbers of aria, duet, ensemble, and chorus, all inherited from the eighteenth century. Italian librettos adhered to familiar subjects—especially the tragedy brought on by irreconcilable human desires. Singers continued to rule the genre, just as they had in the eighteenth century. The intention of the Italian opera composer was, as always, to please the audience, and the leading figures were extraordinarily successful in doing this.

The most successful of the early nineteenth-century Italian composers of opera was Gioachino Rossini (1792–1868; Fig. 56-1), whose works were performed and acclaimed all over the world. In 1823 the French novelist Stendhal extravagantly declared Rossini to be a second Napoleon:

> Napoleon is dead; but a new conqueror has already shown himself to the world; and from Moscow to Naples, from London to Vienna, from Paris to Calcutta, his name is constantly on every tongue. The fame of this hero knows no bounds save those of civilization itself.[1]

Later in the century, the operas of Giuseppe Verdi (1813–1901) provoked similar raves. Following the premiere of Verdi's *Otello* in Milan in 1887, the composer's carriage was mobbed by the ecstatic audience, the horses unleashed, and the wagon then partly carried, partly pulled by the composer's admirers to his hotel. Verdi's wife insisted that this enthusiasm came ultimately from an appreciation of the music: "This passionate demonstration comes from a high esteem, an affection that is heavy with understanding," she wrote.

✿ GIOACHINO ROSSINI

Rossini brought the various strands of Italian opera of the early nineteenth century into a classic form that was maintained, at least in general outline, for nearly a hundred years in the hands of his successors Vincenzo Bellini (1801–1835), Gaetano Donizetti (1797–1848), Giuseppe Verdi, and Giacomo Puccini (1858–1924). Rossini was born in Pesaro, on the Adriatic coast, to a family of musicians, and he grew up in Bologna in north central Italy. Here he attended the local conservatory, the Liceo Musicale, and began to compose. His career as a major opera composer was launched when he was only eighteen years old, and over the next ten years he composed no fewer than thirty operas. During this time he traveled almost constantly between cities where his works were staged, especially the Italian opera capitals of Venice, Rome, Milan, and Naples.

His works were soon taken up by opera companies outside of Italy, and his presence was in demand all over Europe. In 1822 he visited Vienna for a festival of his operas and found himself a celebrity there. During his stay in Vienna he met Beethoven. In 1823 Rossini settled in Paris and became director of the Théâtre-Italien (see Chapter 53), and here he wrote operas in French for the Paris Opéra. After *Guillaume Tell* (*William Tell*, 1829), he went into a forty-year retirement, wrote no further operas, and lived alternately in Italy and France.

Rossini specialized in operatic composition. He wrote thirty-nine operas in all, some of which are French revisions of earlier works in Italian. Additionally, he composed music for the church, including several Masses and a *Stabat mater* (1832). Toward the end of his life he wrote a large number of small, lighthearted pieces—mainly songs and piano music—which he called *Péchés de vieillesse* (*Sins of Old Age*).

The Barber of Seville

Early in his meteoric career, Rossini concentrated on comic opera, later on serious opera, although the musical styles and forms in either type had by the nineteenth century become largely interchangeable. The typical early Rossini opera begins with an overture, although this is sometimes omitted in his later works. As in opera of the preceding century, acts are divided into a succession of musical numbers—arias, duets, other ensembles, and choruses. In the early operas, the numbers are connected by **simple recitative** (accompanied by a keyboard instrument, or sometimes by the cello or bass), although Rossini subsequently dropped this old-fashioned element. He retained passages of recitative accompanied by the orchestra, and these usually function as introductions or transitions within a number.

The elimination of simple recitative made it necessary for the narrative aspect of his operas to be absorbed into the regular musical numbers, and this caused Rossini to make these numbers longer and mixed in style. Such complex numbers were already found in earlier Italian opera in the finales of acts, which typically consist of several sections in different tempos, and mix together ensemble, choral, and soloistic singing.

Il barbiere di Siviglia (*The Barber of Seville*, 1816) is by far Rossini's most famous opera. The steps through which it came into existence provide a vivid example of the way the Italian opera business worked at this time. Rossini signed a contract for a new opera with the **impresario** (manager) of a theater in Rome (he agreed on a fee that was less than half that of the company's leading singer). He had only a few weeks to compose the new work (which was plenty of time for Rossini), he had to use whatever libretto the impresario provided, and he agreed to conduct the initial performances from the keyboard.

The impresario hired a local amateur writer, Cesare Sterbini, to come up with a comic libretto. Sterbini then dashed one off by revising two well-known sources—Beaumarchais's French play *Le barbier de Séville* (*The Barber of Seville*, 1775) and the libretto of an Italian comic opera by Giovanni Paisiello (1782) that was itself based on Beaumarchais's famous comedy. Rossini needed only about three weeks to compose the music, in part because the forms making up an opera at the time were well established and because he had no hesitation about borrowing musical passages from earlier works that would be unknown to his audience. In other operas, Rossini occasionally farmed out the composing of some of the music to an assistant (much as film composers do today). Many of the characters of *The Barber of Seville* will be familiar from Mozart's *Marriage of Figaro* (see Chapter 48), because both operas are based on related comedies by Beaumarchais, *Marriage* being a sequel to *Barber*.

Although the first performance of *The Barber of Seville* was greeted by an uproar provoked by various staging mishaps, the work became an instant success, its fame soon spreading over the whole world. The *Barber*'s popularity has never waned. Hans von Bülow, long an associate of Richard Wagner, found its greatness in its whole-hearted acceptance of its own genre, needing none of the reform that Wagner found necessary:

> In this work there is an eternal youthfulness that mocks the ravages of time. It is a bouquet of flowers that never fade and keep their full fragrance, a champagne euphoria

Synopsis of *The Barber of Seville*

The young Count Almaviva, disguised as a poor student, tries to attract the attention of the lovely Rosina, who lives in Seville with her guardian, Dr. Bartolo. The count turns for advice to his former servant, Figaro, now a barber, who hatches a series of schemes to get Almaviva into Bartolo's house and in touch with Rosina. Bartolo has plans to marry Rosina himself, and he is ready to use any and all means to defeat Almaviva. After a series of ludicrous escapades, misunderstandings, and changes of disguise, the Count reveals his true identity to Rosina and proposes marriage. Seeing that he is defeated, Bartolo blesses their union. (The opera is in two acts, although in some editions and performances the first act is divided in two.)

with no morning after. In brief, this *Barber* remains a truly classic opera, since this term describes "whatever pleases everywhere and for all times."[2]

The music for *The Barber of Seville* exemplifies Rossini's early style, which is fairly close to that found in such eighteenth-century models as Mozart's *Marriage of Figaro*. The work is strictly a number opera because it consists musically of self-contained pieces (arias, ensembles, and choruses). These are separated by simple recitative, in which the story is pushed forward. Applause could be expected at the end of each number, bringing the opera to a complete halt, and a number would be repeated immediately if the audience demanded it.

The first number of Act 1 following the overture is an example of a special type of operatic piece called an *introduzione*, or **introduction.** These were regularly found in comic operas of the late eighteenth and early nineteenth centuries (Mozart's *Don Giovanni* and *Magic Flute*, for example, begin with introductions). The introduction balances the finale, the last number of an act, since both are relatively long and multi-sectional, made from a succession of contrasting passages that mix choral, ensemble and solo singing.

The introduction in *Barber* has a symmetric and entirely self-contained **ABA'** form. Brief transitions between the sections are accomplished by recitative accompanied by the orchestra. The first section is devoted mainly to the singing of a chorus of musicians whom Fiorello (a servant of the Count) has quietly positioned in front of Bartolo's house to accompany the Count in singing a serenade below Rosina's window. The second section is aria-like, a love song "Ecco ridente in cielo" ("Look, Smiling in Heaven") that is filled with an overblown sentimentality. The third section begins with a reprise of the melodies of the first section, but this is soon interrupted when the musicians are paid and create a comic hubbub—just what the love-struck Count was hoping to avoid.

Our attention in the introduction is drawn mainly to the second of its three sections, which contains the Count's aria-like serenade. This has a two-part form already encountered in the aria "Abscheulicher!" from Beethoven's *Fidelio* (see Chapter 50), although here the form is shorter and simpler. Rossini calls it a **cavatina,** which is his term for an entrance aria. (Recall that Beethoven had used this term, although in an entirely different way, for the slow movement of his String Quartet in B♭ Major, Op. 130.)

The first of the two parts of the aria covers two stanzas of text. The music is slow in tempo, intensely lyrical, and strophic in form—all typical features of the begin-

---

The Audience Greets the Barber

The opening night of *The Barber of Seville* in Rome's Teatro Argentina was a fiasco. Rossini's biographer, Alexis-Jacob Azevedo, reports:

... The crowning disaster occurred when, during the wonderful finale [of Act 1], a cat appeared on stage and ran among the singers. The excellent Figaro, Zamboni, shooed it off to one side but it returned from the other and leapt up onto the leg of Bartolo-Botticelli. The hapless pupil of the doctor and respectable Marceline [Berta], fearing a scratch, nimbly avoided the prodigious leaps of the crazed animal, which paid attention only to the sword of the police guard. The charitable audience called to it, imitated its meowing, and with yells and gestures egged it on in its improvised role. An athletic young fellow seated in the middle of the parterre—he wasn't part of the claque, that's for sure—found the finale too serious, climbed up on his seat and called out in a loud voice, 'It's a funeral . . . .'" [3]

---

ning of the traditional two-part aria. The second part is fast and full of vocal fireworks, the sort of passage that was called a cabaletta at the time. It covers two additional poetic stanzas, of which the second is extended by repetitions within the text. Here the tenor shows how many notes he can sing (he probably would have extemporaneously added to the already considerable number of ornaments written out by the composer).

The third section begins as a simple reprise of the opening part, but, when the musicians erupt in excitement, the tempo shifts to *allegro vivace* for a climactic final passage called a **stretta**. Rossini sharpens the sense of climax at this point by bringing in one of his trademarks: the so-called **Rossini crescendo**. This is made from a series of crescendos that coincide with repetitions of ever-shorter phrases, a steady thickening of orchestration, and an ever-quicker harmonic motion.

LISTENING CUE

GIOACHINO ROSSINI
The Barber of Seville (1816)
Act 1, No. 1 (*Introduzione*)

CD 9/12–13
Anthology, No. 155

GIUSEPPE VERDI

In a letter of 1898, Giuseppe Verdi reflected on the importance to him of the works of Rossini: "I cannot help believing that *The Barber of Seville*, for abundance of ideas, for comic verve, and for truth of declamation, is the most beautiful comic opera in existence." In Verdi's operas the spirit of Rossini is very much alive as Verdi continues to expand the basic forms inherited from Rossini and makes Rossini's marriage of music and drama ever more intimate. At the same time, Verdi modernized Italian opera, making it into a more realistic dramatic entity and bringing to it the advances in orchestration and harmony that characterize the later nineteenth century.

Verdi was born in a small village, Roncole, in north Italy. Roncole is about fifteen miles from the city of Parma, which was the seat of government of a small duchy that from 1814 was ruled by a relative of the Austrian Hapsburg emperors. Much of Italy during Verdi's life was either directly ruled by or closely allied to Austria, a situation that offended the composer's patriotic sensibilities and formed a subject touched on explosively in his early operas. As a child he showed a prodigious gift for music, and in 1832 he moved to Milan to further his musical education, but at the age of eighteen he was found too old to be accepted at the Conservatory in Milan, so he studied privately instead.

In 1839 Verdi's first opera, *Oberto*, was performed in Milan at the **Teatro alla Scala,** and its impresario, Bartolomeo Merelli, then commissioned additional works. One of these was *Nabucco*, based on the biblical story of King Nebuchadnezzar, which scored a huge success at La Scala in 1842 and launched Verdi's international operatic career. Like Rossini before him, Verdi capitalized on his fame by quickly composing new operas and traveling constantly among theaters to oversee new productions. He lived abroad for long periods, especially in Paris, and then from 1857 settled on a farm near the town in which he was born. From about 1874, after completing a Requiem Mass in honor of the Italian patriot and novelist Alessandro Manzoni (1785–1873), Verdi composed less, although in his final years he returned to the stage with two operas based on Shakespearean subjects, *Otello* (1887) and *Falstaff* (1893).

One of Verdi's last concerns was the founding in the city of Milan of the Casa di Riposo per Musicisti—a retirement home for musicians that still exists. Following his death in 1901, the composer donated his considerable wealth to support this home, and it is where he and his wife, Giuseppina Strepponi, are buried.

❋ VERDI AND THE *RISORGIMENTO*

Verdi composed twenty-eight operas and relatively little else, although his great Requiem is frequently heard. His early operas became symbols of the **Risorgimento** (resurgence), which was the movement toward Italian political and social unification that began after Napoleon's defeat in 1814 and culminated in 1870, when virtually all of Italy was at last brought into a single nation under the leadership of King Victor Emmanuel II. Although Verdi's energies were almost totally claimed by his musical career, he was plainly sympathetic to the objectives of the *Risorgimento*. In his operas, his countrymen found many supportive allusions to their hopes of ridding Italy of Austrian domination. Often the leading characters in his operas choose duty, even death, over personal happiness. Frequently, two nations are at war, one of which is easily identified with the Austrians, the other with the Italians. For example, in the story of the opera *I lombardi alla prima crociata* (*The Lombards at the First Crusade*, 1843), Italians from the region of Lombardy (an ancient kingdom surrounding the city of Milan) battle the Saracens in the crusades. Those in Verdi's audience immediately saw the parallel with Italy and Austria in their own day, and they responded enthusiastically to the leading character's call for war to liberate a Holy Land.

In 1859 Verdi was all the more closely identified with the cause of Italian unification when warfare between the Kingdom of Sardinia (which encompassed not only the island of Sardinia but also much of northern Italy) erupted with Austria. Many in the *Risorgimento* thought that an alliance with Sardinia and its king, Victor Emmanuel II, was the best way of achieving unification for all of Italy. Their patriotic cry was "Viva VERDI!" which evoked both the name of their compatriot composer

Synopsis of *Otello*

The action takes place on the island of Cyprus, an outpost of the Republic of Venice. The fearless soldier Othello ("Otello" is the Italian equivalent) has battled the Turks and, as the opera begins, his ship returns to port in a fearsome storm. The storm abates, the ship arrives, and Othello announces that victory has been won. All are elated except for the soldier Iago, who hates Othello and schemes to bring him down. Iago leads a drinking song, which produces a drunken brawl that Othello quells, after which he sings a love duet with his wife, Desdemona (in Italian, pronounced des-DAY-mona). Iago sings a "credo" in which he asserts that we are the fools of fate, and all is false and meaningless. Slyly, Iago plants seeds of doubt in Othello's mind, hinting that Desdemona is having an affair with Cassio, Othello's lieutenant. He offers a contrived proof by planting in Cassio's pocket Desdemona's handkerchief, which is seen by the jealous Othello.

Preparing for bed, Desdemona senses that she will be murdered by Othello. She sings the "Willow Song" of a lovelorn girl who sadly faced the grave, then a prayer-like "Ave Maria." Othello silently enters her bedchamber, kisses her, then strangles her despite her avowals of fidelity to him. Her maid calls for help, and Iago's lies are explained to him. Othello stabs himself and dies after one final kiss for his dead wife.

and an acronym for their king, **V**ittorio **E**manuele **R**e d'**It**alia (Victor Emmanuel, King of Italy).

Otello

By the time Italian unification was finally completed in 1870, Verdi (Fig. 56-2) had become cynical about politics, and he turned in his later operas to purely musical and dramatic matters. He closely oversaw the creation of his librettos, favoring tragic subjects drawn from classic literature. In *Otello* Verdi and his librettist, Arrigo Boito (1842–1918), turned to Shakespeare's tragedy *Othello*. As usual in the creation of an opera libretto, the literary model was preserved only in its characters and external action. Little of Shakespeare's memorable poetry or subtlety of characterization is kept, as Boito flattens the roles into types, changes the narrative to allow for traditional operatic numbers, and simplifies the action.

Vestiges of number opera from the days of Rossini are still visible in *Otello*. The first act, for example, consists of four numbers: a chorus depicting the storm in which Othello's boat is caught, a second chorus during which the townsfolk celebrate by a bonfire, a drinking duet for Iago and Cassio (a cliché of Italian opera called a **brindisi**), and a love duet for Othello and Desdemona.

But, unlike an opera by Rossini, these are not free-standing divisions, since they are connected without pause by interludes that push the story forward. The interludes are themselves complex, consisting of a quick alternation of solo singing, ensemble, chorus, and recitation. The numbers themselves are equally complex, not the simple duets and choruses of earlier years but more fluid and dramatic passages that mix together bits of soloistic singing into an ensemble or choral context. It is characteristic of Verdi's later works that he diminishes the importance of the large aria as the principal means of expression, replacing it with duets and choruses. The dramatic role of the orchestra is also much increased by its capacity vividly to depict images and emotions.

❋ FIGURE 56-2

In 1877, when this portrait was made, Giuseppe Verdi had entered retirement to rest on the laurels of his Requiem Mass and the worldwide success of *Aida*, his last opera. But his creative spark was soon to be fanned by the prospect of composing a new opera based on Shakespeare's *Otello*.

The opera's climactic fourth act also has four main musical numbers, and in this instance they agree with the division of the act into four **scenes** (a scene is a passage calling a particular selection of characters to the stage). After introductory measures in the orchestra, the first scene is devoted to an aria-like song for Desdemona, the famous "Willow Song," which is cast in a strophic form with recitational introduction and coda. The second scene follows without pause and contains Desdemona's "Ave Maria," a prayer to the Virgin in simple ternary form. Like the brindisi of Act 1, the prayer scene, or **preghiera,** was a common feature of Verdian opera.

The murder scene follows, and musically it has no precedent in traditional Italian opera because it does not rely primarily on singing to convey its dramatic message. Instead, it is the orchestra—its motivic symbolism, harmonic language, and tonal plan—that takes over the burden of affective communication. The voices are confined to a more rudimentary declamation of their lines.

The scene opens with a gripping orchestral portrait of Othello's inner conflict, incoherence, and confusion. Two fragmentary melodic ideas alternate—one in the basses and the other in the celli (marked A and B in Ex. 56-1)—and these represent Othello's love for Desdemona versus his murderous jealousy. The tonal plan in this virtual tone poem provides no coherence because the keys constantly change and conflict.

EXAMPLE 56-1

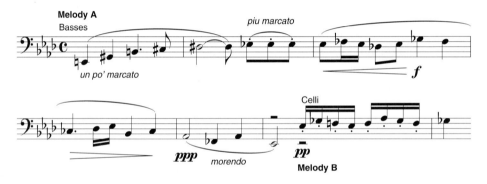

Finally, Othello arrives at the bedside of the sleeping Desdemona, draws back the curtains, and kisses her. At this moment the theme that accompanied their kiss in the love duet of Act 1 returns in the same taut key of E major (Ex. 56-2). Othello's accusations and Desdemona's denials follow, in a tortured crescendo in which the jealousy motive in the orchestra takes complete control.

EXAMPLE 56-2

LISTENING CUE

GIUSEPPE VERDI
Otello (1887)
Act 4, scene 3

CD 10/1
Anthology, No. 156

The fourth scene of Act 4 is like the familiar operatic finale. The singing is mainly devoted to an ensemble of all the remaining characters, and the music moves through several contrasting sections. Here the drama is brought to a denouement.

 VERDI AND WAGNER

Many of the new ideas that Verdi introduced to Italian opera in *Otello* are similar to those encountered in the operas of Richard Wagner (see Chapter 55). The murder scene is especially like a scene from Wagner, in which a climactic dramatic action is presented by declamation intensified by orchestration, harmony, motivic symbolism, and key scheme. The continuity in *Otello*—promoted by connecting the sections and by the symbolic motive of the kiss that returns outside of the boundaries of a single number—has an obvious resonance in Wagner's theory of operatic structure. The enriched harmonies of the kiss motive may sound more like those of Wagner than Verdi.

But Verdi was indignant over the idea that he had copied from Wagner. To his publisher, Ricordi, he dismissed the allegation that "... after all I was an imitator of Wagner!!! What a fine result after twenty-five years, to end up as an *Imitator*!!!"[4] Although Verdi rarely had anything good to say about Germans, he recognized Wagner's importance. Upon learning of Wagner's death in 1883, he again wrote to Ricordi: "A great individualist has disappeared! A name that leaves a very powerful mark on the history of Art!!! Addio, addio."[5]

It is unlikely that Verdi was directly influenced by Wagner. Instead, both Wagner and Verdi were influenced by a common spirit in music of their time, which encouraged formal continuity, plausible drama, and harmonic intricacy. It is not surprising that their music should have evolved to produce similarities.

SUMMARY

Italian opera of the nineteenth century was closely linked to operatic traditions. The leading composers, including Gioachino Rossini and Giuseppe Verdi, expanded in an orderly way upon traditional operatic form based on a division into familiar musical numbers. Rossini's *The Barber of Seville* (1816) is a comic opera that is especially close to the form of eighteenth-century works. Its libretto is based upon a comic farce by Beaumarchais, and Rossini's music is made from a succession of arias, duets, ensembles, and choruses linked together by simple recitative.

As a "modern" composer of the late nineteenth century, Verdi enriched Rossini's forms. In his opera *Otello*—based on Shakespeare's tragedy—music is used to create a plausible drama. The "kiss motive" heard in the first act recurs in the fourth act, to link the music organically to the drama, and the old operatic numbers, though still in evidence, are made more complex and linked together continuously.

KEY TERMS

simple recitative	cavatina (in Rossini's operas)	*Risorgimento*
impresario	stretta	brindisi
introduction (as an operatic number)	Rossini crescendo	scene
	Teatro alla Scala	preghiera

Chapter

Nationalism and Virtuosity: Franz Liszt

By the middle of the nineteenth century, a new consciousness of national identity began to appear in many parts of the world. The birth of **nationalism**—the love for and allegiance to one's region of birth and its people, culture, and language—occurred in Europe in the aftermath of Napoleonic imperialism. Previously, the concept of nationhood was limited or dim, and personal allegiances were more typically directed to a sovereign ruler rather than to a native land. But this circumstance began to change as Napoleon's conquests in the early nineteenth century placed many distant parts of Europe under French domination. After Napoleon's overthrow in 1814, nationalism became a powerful political factor in the reorganization of European culture.

It was expressed principally in two related movements: one toward political unification of people having a common language, and the other toward independence from foreign rule. The strivings toward unification were felt most strongly on the Italian peninsula and in German lands, and these areas achieved political unification in 1861 and 1871, respectively. Foreign rule of whole nations remained widespread in Europe even by the mid-nineteenth century. Poles and Finns were still governed by Russians, Italians by Austrians, and Rumanians by Hungarians.

The frictions created by these political alignments were especially heated in the Austrian Empire. At the time of the Congress of Vienna (1814–1815), the sprawling lands of the Hapsburg rulers—which formed Austria in the broad sense—came to include most of Italy and Eastern Europe, in addition to the ancestral Hapsburg lands in modern-day Austria. The Hapsburgs themselves were Germans by language, but their kingdom contained many nationalities vying for independence. The most powerful of these were the Hungarians, who in 1867 were granted a privileged status by the formation of the so-called **Austro-Hungarian Monarchy.**

As the century progressed, growing nationalistic sentiments made an important mark on music. We have seen in Chapter 56 how the texts of Verdi's early operas were influenced by the desire, shared by the composer's Italian countrymen, to escape from the rule of Austria and to establish an independent homeland. Other composers used their music to celebrate their nation and its history. This was done on a broad scale by the Czech composer **Bedřich Smetana** (1824–1884) in his cycle of six orchestral works called *Má vlast* (*My Fatherland*, 1874–1879).

Many composers looked into the soul of their own people by collecting and arranging the folk songs of their native lands. These materials, which seemed to embody the spirit of a nation, were often brought into original compositions. In Chapter 59 we will encounter a group of Russian musicians of the late nineteenth century, called the *kuchka* (handful) or "The Five," who demonstrated a special affinity for folk song. One of them, Nicolai Rimsky-Korsakov (1844–1908), arranged and published one hundred forty Russian folk songs, which contained for him "pictures of the ancient pagan period and spirit" of his land. The symphonies and operas of the Czech composer Antonín Dvořák (1841–1904) often evoke the folk songs and dances of his native land. Even the most cosmopolitan of nineteenth-century composers sometimes wrote nationalistic music. One of them is Franz Liszt (1811–1886), probably the greatest pianist of the century and a musician at home virtually anywhere in the world.

LISZT'S LIFE AND WORKS

Liszt was born in the village of Raiding, some fifty miles south of Vienna. This town lies just inside the Hungarian regions of the Hapsburg Empire. Although Liszt's family spoke German, many of his ancestors were Hungarians, and Liszt gradually came to think of Hungary as his true homeland. "I remain from my birth to the grave Magyar in heart and mind," he wrote in 1873.[1]

His father was a good amateur cellist and an employee of the Esterházy family—Haydn's patrons of old. When the young Liszt's prodigious talent as a pianist was revealed, the elder Liszt gave up his position to promote his son's musical development and career. The first step was education. In 1821 the Liszt family moved to Vienna, where Franz became a student of Carl Czerny in piano and Antonio Salieri in composition. Czerny took the 11-year-old wunderkind to play for his own teacher, Beethoven, and Liszt later recalled the occasion:

> Beethoven asked me whether I could play a Bach fugue. I chose the C-minor fugue from the Well-Tempered Clavier. "And could you also transpose the fugue at once into another key?" Beethoven asked me. Fortunately I was able to do so. After my closing chord I glanced up. The great master's darkly glowing gaze lay piercingly upon me. Yet suddenly a gentle smile passed over his gloomy features, and Beethoven came quite close to me, stooped down, put his hand on my head, and stroked my hair several times. "A devil of a fellow," he whispered. . . ."[2]

Next came European tours, during which the child prodigy traveled as far as Paris and London, amazing all who heard him. Liszt and his father settled in Paris in 1823, and his tours continued to take him far and wide. He composed primarily for his own instrument, and in Paris he became a close acquaintance of both Berlioz and Chopin (see Chapter 53).

His personal life proved controversial even in a period when artists often felt unconstrained by accepted principles of morality. In 1834 he began an affair with the French writer Marie d'Agoult (1805–1876; see Box), who left her husband and child to live and travel with Liszt (Fig. 57-1). Although they never married, they had three children, including Cosima Liszt (1837–1930), later the wife of Richard Wagner. Liszt and Marie drifted apart in the 1840s, whereupon Liszt took up with a wealthy Russian-Polish Princess, Carolyne von Sayn-Wittgenstein (1819–1887). She would be his principal companion for the remainder of his life, although the two never married.

During the period from 1839 to 1847, Liszt undertook virtually nonstop touring and performing, which brought him to the four corners of Europe and to a level of fame and adulation never before achieved by a musician. He was swarmed by his admirers in a way now known only to rock stars. Heinrich Heine described his emotional effect on his audiences as **Lisztomania.** Although travel at this time was still done largely by horse-drawn carriage, Liszt performed in more than one hundred seventy cities in this eight-year span.

He retired from his grueling tours in 1848 and settled into a position as conductor of the court orchestra in Weimar. This

FIGURE 57-1
Ary Scheffer, "Liszt in Geneva," 1835. "He was tall and extremely thin. His face was pale and his large sea-green eyes shone like a wave when the sunlight catches it" (Marie d'Agoult describes her first glimpse of Liszt).

LISZT.

Marie d'Agoult

At a musical gathering in Paris in 1833, Countess Marie d'Agoult caught her first glimpse of Franz Liszt. "A wonderful apparition appeared before my eyes," she recalled in her *Memoirs* about the 21-year-old pianist. "I can find no other word to describe the sensation aroused in me by the most extraordinary person I had ever seen. He was tall and extremely thin. His face was pale and his large sea-green eyes shone like a wave when the sunlight catches it." That night, so the Countess recalled, her sleep was disrupted by bizarre dreams.

Her attraction to Liszt was plain enough, but Marie at the time was married and the mother of two small children. She aspired to be a writer, not just a wealthy pa-troness of the arts, so in 1835 she abandoned her family for a daring artistic alliance with Franz Liszt. The pair lived alternately in Paris, Switzerland, and Italy, and three children were born to them.

Liszt's concertizing made any semblance of family life impossible. Marie returned in 1840 to Paris with the children, and her relationship with Liszt gradually deteri-orated. In 1844 the two finally broke up, and Marie worked out her bitter-ness at Liszt in a novel called *Né-lida*, which became a bestseller in France. The heroine, Nélida, is plainly a self-portrait. She falls in love with an artist, Guermann Regnier (Liszt in disguise). Guer-mann treats her shabbily, dreams only of cheap success, and finally abandons her. With this, his cre-ativity vanishes.

Bridgeman Art Library

❋ FIGURE 57-2
Henri Lehmann, portrait of Marie d'Agoult, 1839.

town in eastern Germany was the seat of government of a small duchy called Saxe-Weimar, and it was earlier home to the great writers Goethe and Friedrich von Schiller (1759–1805), and earlier still to J.S. Bach. Here, Liszt led the orchestra in concerts and operatic performances, and his interests as a composer came to include orchestral music. In his programming he was a stalwart supporter of modern compo-sitions, and he conducted new works by Hector Berlioz and Richard Wagner that at the time were still baffling to many audiences.

In 1861 Liszt resigned from his position in Weimar and moved to Rome, where he found solitude in the company of priests and monks. In 1865 he took the lower orders of the Catholic priesthood, which allowed him to use the title "abbé" but did not seriously interfere with his lifestyle. From 1869 until his death he alternated residences among Rome, Weimar, and Budapest, giving master classes, composing, and occasionally playing the piano in public. He died in 1886 in Bayreuth, where he had gone to hear Wagner's operas and visit with his daughter Cosima. Liszt is buried in Bayreuth.

Liszt composed an astonishingly large amount of music, more than seven hun-dred compositions in all. More than a hundred pieces are for solo piano, and Liszt also made important contributions to the orchestral, choral, and song literature.

His solo piano music includes a Sonata in B Minor (1853) and character pieces of all types, some gathered into collections with titles such as *Années de pèlerinage* (*Years of Pilgrimage*), *Harmonies poétiques et religieuses* (*Poetic and Religious Harmonies*), and *Légendes* (*Legends*). His études for piano reach to new levels of technical difficulty, and many of his piano works incorporate national or folk-like themes. These include *Hungarian Rhapsodies*, to be discussed momentarily, which are artistic arrangements of Hungarian and Gypsy music.

The arrangement was one of Liszt's most distinctive specialties. From existing songs, symphonies, and operas, he made some two hundred such transcriptions and paraphrases for piano, creating concert pieces out of a hitherto functional type of music. Toward the end of his life he wrote a series of small piano works whose spareness and unusual harmonic materials are unlike anything in music before their time.

His orchestral music includes thirteen **symphonic poems** (discussed below), two programmatic symphonies (*A Faust Symphony*, 1854–1857, and *A Symphony on Dante's "Divine Comedy,"* 1856), and two piano concertos. He found time also to write a large number of songs and works for chorus that include Masses and the oratorios *The Legend of St. Elizabeth* (1862) and *Christus* (1867). Liszt almost entirely avoided chamber music and opera.

❋ LISZT AND THE PIANO

Partly for practical reasons, during his tours from 1839 to 1847 Liszt dispensed with the traditional format of the piano concert, which earlier had required hiring an orchestra and bringing in singers to perform operatic excerpts. Instead, he played either entirely alone or with only a few other performers, creating a new type of concert called the **recital.**

His repertory was broad and highly original. He continued to present the staples of earlier piano concerts, including showy character pieces of his own composition, fantasies and variations upon popular operatic tunes, and improvisations. To these he added his massively virtuosic transcriptions of music originating in other media—the symphonies of Beethoven, for example—and he began to present classics from the past, including Beethoven piano sonatas, fugues by J.S. Bach, and sonatas by Domenico Scarlatti.

Liszt usually played from memory, something still unusual at the time, and he often alternated among several different pianos placed on the stage. His appearance—tall, thin, with shoulder-length black hair, often bedecked with medals and wearing a ceremonial sword—was straight from Hollywood. Between numbers he typically walked into the audience to chat with his fans.

Hungarian Rhapsody No. 15 ("Rákóczy March")

Liszt's music for piano adheres to no uniform style. Some works are lengthy, others relatively short. Some are original compositions, and many others are artistic transcriptions and arrangements of music by other composers. Some are relatively easy to play while others approach the very limits of human dexterity. Some are bombastic and grandiloquent, others understated.

His *Hungarian Rhapsodies* for piano illustrate the virtuosic side of Liszt's musical imagination as well as the element of nationalism that he brought periodically into his works. In 1839 he returned to Hungary to give concerts following an absence of sixteen years, and there he found himself a national hero. His consciousness of

At a Liszt Recital

The Russian journalist Vladimir Stasov heard Liszt play in St. Petersburg in 1842 and reported:

> Just at that moment Liszt, noting the time, walked down from the gallery, elbowed his way through the crowd and moved quickly toward the stage. But instead of using the steps he leaped onto the platform. He tore off his white kid gloves and tossed them on the floor, under the piano. Then after bowing low in all directions to a tumult of applause such as had probably not been heard in Petersburg since 1703 [the year the city was founded], he seated himself at the piano. Instantly the hall became deadly silent. Without any preliminaries Liszt began playing the opening cello phrase of the *William Tell* Overture [by Rossini]. As soon as he finished the overture and while the hall was still rocking with applause, he moved swiftly to a second piano facing the opposite direction. . . . On this occasion Liszt also played the Andante from *Lucia* [*di Lammermoor*, by Gaetano Donizetti], his fantasy on Mozart's *Don Giovanni*, piano transcriptions of Schubert's [songs] "Ständchen" and "Erlkönig," Beethoven's [song] "Adelaide" and in conclusion his own [*Grand*] *Galop chromatique*.
>
> We had never in our lives heard anything like this. We had never been in the presence of such a brilliant, passionate, demonic temperament, at one moment rushing like a whirlwind, at another pouring forth cascades of tender beauty and grace.[3]

Liszt elevated the piano to a new status. In his playing, and in his compositions for the instrument, he showed the piano's capacity to rival the newly expanded orchestra. He demonstrated that pianists could rise above previous limitations of technique and make the instrument create unsuspected new sounds and expressive effects. "My piano is to me what his vessel is to the sailor, his horse to the Arab," Liszt wrote:

> Nay even more, till now it has been myself, my speech, my life. It is the repository of all that stirred my nature in the passionate days of my youth. I confided to it all my desires, my dreams, my joys, and my sorrows. Its strings vibrated to my emotions, and its keys obeyed my every caprice.[4]

❀ FIGURE 57-3
An 1845 caricature of Liszt in typical recital mode.

Bridgeman Art Library

himself as a Hungarian was awakened, and he began to collect Hungarian melodies and make brilliant arrangements of them for use in his concerts.

Liszt came to view these pieces as tantamount to a Hungarian national epic, told in music rather than in words. Just as the *Iliad* and *Odyssey*—the epic stories of ancient Greece and its people—were recited in public by professional orators called rhapsodes, Liszt saw himself as the rhapsode of his Hungarian musical epic. He wrote:

> By the word **"Rhapsody"** the intention has been to designate the fantastically *epic* element which we deem this music to contain. Each one of these productions has always seemed to us to form part of a poetic cycle, remarkable by the unity of its inspiration, eminently national. The conditions of this unity are fulfilled by the music belonging exclusively to the one people whose soul and intimate sentiments it accurately depicts; sentiments moreover which are nowhere else so well expressed and which are cast into a form proper to this one nation; having been invented and practiced exclusively by them.[5]

Between 1851 and 1853 he selected fifteen of his Hungarian arrangements—most of which were revisions of pieces from the 1840s—and published them as a loose cycle of *Hungarian Rhapsodies*. Later in his career he added several more works with this title.

But what is the "Hungarian" music that forms the basis of Liszt's rhapsodies? The composer pondered this question at length. The Magyars—those who spoke Hungarian as their native language—formed only one of many ethnic groups living side by side in the lands thought of as Hungary. The Magyars were primarily farmers who, according to Liszt, showed no particular genius for music.

Living in their midst were Gypsies, nomadic people who were often professional musicians of great skill. Liszt considered them and their music to be just as Hungarian as that of the Magyars. Gypsy bands—typically featuring a solo violin and a dulcimer called the **cimbalom**—were popular throughout Hungary, where they played dance music and flashy improvisations on folk or traditional melodies. Their music, which Liszt had heard even as a child, had many other distinctive features. It was often based on a **Gypsy scale,** which is a minor scale with raised fourth and seventh degrees. These alterations produce two augmented seconds in the scale, as seen in this example on the keynote D: D E F G♯ A B♭ C♯ D. Gypsy music typically had a flexibility of rhythm and meter, and in spirit it could be subdued, or rise to the level of "a furious orgy of wild beasts," as Liszt described it.

In his *Hungarian Rhapsody* No. 15 (published in 1853), we see Liszt mingle together aspects of Gypsy and Magyar music. The piece is an arrangement of the "Rákóczy March," which in Liszt's day had become a patriotic favorite among Hungarians, played by military bands and Gypsy ensembles alike. Liszt described the march to Marie d'Agoult as "a kind of aristocratic Hungarian *Marseillaise*" (the *Marseillaise* is the national anthem of France). The composer of the march has never been conclusively identified, but he was probably a minor Hungarian composer active around the year 1800. The march was named in honor of Francis II Rákóczy (1676–1735), who led Hungarian armies in an uprising against their Hapsburg overlords that in 1707 created a short-lived independent republic.

The "Rákóczy March" is typical of the band march around 1800. It has a duple meter and opens with several themes that are repeated in symmetrical fashion. These lead to a contrasting section, called the **trio,** then to a reprise of the opening music. Its main themes are shown in Example 57-1.

EXAMPLE 57-1

First theme

Tempo di Marcia animato

First trio theme

Un poco meno allegro

Liszt interprets this familiar framework as though the march were played by a Gyspy band (which it frequently was). An introduction lays out a Gypsy scale with its distinctive augmented seconds. Later in the work, in a cadenza that Liszt situates at the end of the trio, the sound of the cimbalom is imitated by glissandos in the pianist's right hand. The flashy ornamentation for which Gypsy musicians were famous is reinterpreted by Liszt as pianistic virtuosity—including a blur of octaves in both hands, gymnastic leaps over the entire keyboard, and free dissonances.

LISTENING CUE

FRANZ LISZT   CD 10/2
Hungarian Rhapsody No. 15 ("Rákóczy March") (1853)   Anthology, No. 157

❋ LISZT, WAGNER, AND THE NEW GERMAN SCHOOL

The nationalism apparent in his *Hungarian Rhapsodies* represents only one element of Liszt's remarkable musical career and historical importance. He also played a major role in establishing a modernist faction in the European musical culture of his time, one that was clearly distinct from the conservative approach to nineteenth-century music practiced by Mendelssohn and the Schumanns. Although honoring the classical past in music, Liszt believed that the more important role of leading composers was to prepare for the future. In a letter of 1874 he emphasized this aspiration: "My sole ambition as a musician," he wrote, "has been and shall be to hurl my lance into the infinite expanse of the future."[6]

In his commitment to the future, Liszt found a kindred spirit in Richard Wagner. They met in Paris in 1840, and Liszt came to admire Wagner's early operas. He performed *Tannhäuser* in Weimar in 1849. Later in that year he was helpful in arranging for Wagner's escape from German lands following the Dresden uprisings (see Chapter 55), and he then boldly conducted the premiere of Wagner's *Lohengrin* in 1850, during its composer's forced exile in Switzerland.

While Wagner was banished from German lands, Liszt took over the leadership of the modernist faction in European music, and Weimar became home to critics, composers, and performers of like mind. They proudly used Wagner's term "music of the future" as their slogan and, later, the **New German School** as their name. Their numbers steadily grew and came to include such talented musicians as Hans von Bülow (1830–1894), Carl Tausig (1841–1871), Peter Cornelius (1824–1874), and the American Edward MacDowell (1860–1908).

Their arch rivals were located nearby in Leipzig, later in Vienna. At first there were friendly relations between the two camps, but a split opened up on the question of how the great music of the past should be played. Under Mendelssohn, there was a careful adherence to the letter of the score of a work by Bach, Mozart, or Beethoven. But when Liszt played the classics, there was no such reverence. He freely interpreted, rearranged, and altered the works of the old masters. Mendelssohn remarked on this after hearing Liszt play in Leipzig in 1842: "Here he added six bars, there omitted seven; here he played the wrong chords, and later introduced other similar corruptions, and there in the most gentle passages made a dreadful *fortissimo*, and, in my view, it was all sorry nonsense."[7] Liszt's guideline for performing, on the other hand, was "the letter kills the spirit, a thing to which I will never subscribe."

Younger musicians were also beginning to choose sides. The youthful Johannes Brahms introduced himself to Liszt in 1853 and promptly dozed off while Liszt was playing his own Piano Sonata. In 1860 Brahms and three other musicians were emboldened to publish a manifesto directly attacking the music of "the leaders [Liszt and Wagner] and pupils of the so-called New German School . . . as contrary to the innermost spirit of music."[8]

Liszt's relations with his allies were sometimes as choppy as with his enemies. His life as a pious abbé in Italy was disrupted by the knowledge that his daughter Cosima—since 1857 the wife of his student Hans von Bülow—was engaged in a scandalous affair with his friend Wagner, who was the father of two of Cosima's children (conceived while Wagner and the Bülows lived in a bizarre *ménage à trois*). In the fall of 1867, Liszt traveled to Switzerland to confront Wagner and express his outrage and disapproval. After Father made his obligatory protest, the tensions apparently eased and the two got down to the more serious business of making music. Liszt sightread the orchestra part of *Die Meistersinger* at the keyboard while Wagner sang the vocal roles.

MUSIC FOR ORCHESTRA: THE SYMPHONIC POEM

Liszt's intention to hurl his lance into the future was realized especially in his orchestral music. When he ended his career as a touring piano virtuoso in 1848 and took up the baton as orchestral conductor in Weimar, he turned his composer's attention toward the orchestra. It was a difficult transition, especially since he had little experience in scoring his ideas for orchestra. At first he relied on assistance from other Weimar musicians—August Conradi (1821–1873) and Joseph Joachim Raff (1822–1882)—to orchestrate his music, but later he felt confident to take over this aspect of his craft.

As an orchestral composer, Liszt concentrated first on the one-movement programmatic orchestral piece, a genre that by mid-century had been well established in the concert overtures of Beethoven, Berlioz, and Mendelssohn. Liszt called his works of this type not overtures but "symphonic poems," to emphasize their affinity with the art of poetry.

The programmatic element in them is very different from the one used by Hector Berlioz in a work such as his *Symphonie fantastique*. For Berlioz, the program suggests, step by step, what might occur musically in the course of the piece. For Liszt, on the other hand, the program usually indicates only a certain mood or feeling that can be formulated in words and which runs parallel to the spirit of the music. The program in Liszt's symphonic poems provides at most a means for the listener to interpret correctly the atmosphere or emotional content of a work.

In addition to their programmaticism, Liszt's symphonic poems are highly original in form. The composer often uses a standard design, such as sonata form, but he typically changes the order of events and tonalities in a free way that is better geared to capture the spirit or character that he had in mind. He also tends to draw the work's themes out of a common melodic prototype, heard at the outset, although changing its character at each reappearance. This technique of thematic unity, called **transformation of themes,** had been prefigured by Berlioz in *Symphonie fantastique* (see Chapter 53) and by Schubert in his "Wanderer" Fantasy (see Chapter 52). Liszt was very familiar with both of these works because he had transcribed Berlioz's symphony for piano and arranged Schubert's fantasy for piano and orchestra.

An example of Liszt's approach to the transformation of themes is found in his symphonic poem *Les préludes* (*The Preludes*, 1854), a work that is freely based on a poem of the same name by Alphonse de Lamartine (1790–1869). The melodic prototype for all of the work's main themes is given out in the strings in the opening measures (Ex. 57-2a). Note especially the distinctive head motive (C-B-E) of this theme and also its pentatonic content of pitches. Except for the lower neighbor tone B, all other notes in the theme are drawn from the pentatonic scale G-A-C-(D)-E. These basic materials are then transformed to create the other main themes of the movement.

EXAMPLE 57-2

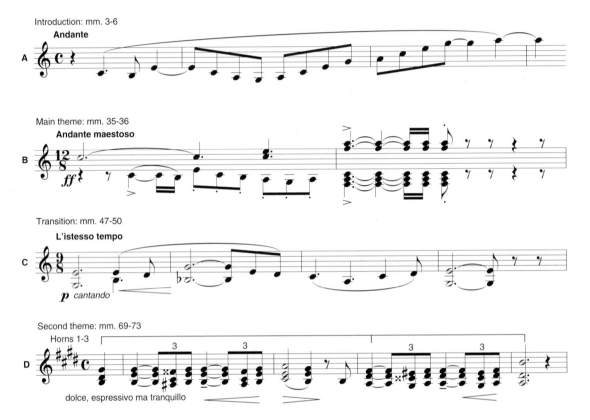

The first transformation occurs in the first theme of the sonata form proper (Ex. 57-2b). Its materials plainly come from the introductory prototype, although its character is made majestic rather than lyric. The transition to the second thematic area begins with a seemingly new theme (Ex. 57-2c), but this too derives from the prototype. Its character takes yet another turn, as it is played *cantando* in the lower strings. Finally, the principal second theme arrives in the horns (Ex. 57-2d). Here the degree of transformation is more extensive, although the head motive of the prototype is apparent in the framing tones G♯-F♯-B, which are marked by a bracket in the example.

 SUMMARY

Musical nationalism was an important factor in nineteenth-century music. This phenomenon is seen in music that celebrates a composer's homeland or embodies elements of its musical folklore or culture. Examples are found in the *Hungarian Rhapsodies* for piano by Franz Liszt (1811–1886). In these works, Liszt transcribes

Hungarian and Gypsy melodies and evokes the playing of Gypsy bands, which the composer had heard in his childhood in Hungary and during his concert tours there in the 1840s.

Liszt's early career was centered on piano playing—he was one of the greatest virtuosos of the instrument—and composing for this instrument. In the late 1840s and 1850s he turned his attention to composing for orchestra, specializing in programmatic music, both multi-movement programmatic symphonies and shorter, one-movement "symphonic poems." The programmatic element in these works is often unrelated to the formal plan of a composition and intended instead to aid the listener in locating a mood or spirit in which the work is best heard. The forms encountered in Liszt's compositions are usually freely—not strictly—derived from classical archetypes. Liszt also practiced an economy of themes (often termed "transformation of themes") by which an initial melodic prototype is apparent in the subsequent melodies in a work, only transformed in character and in details. A similar technique had been used earlier in music by Hector Berlioz and Franz Schubert.

KEY TERMS

nationalism	symphonic poem	trio (of a march)
Austro-Hungarian	recital	New German School
Monarchy	rhapsody	transformation of themes
Bedřich Smetana	cimbalom	
Lisztomania	Gypsy scale	

Chapter

58

Vienna in the Late Nineteenth Century: Brahms and Bruckner

In 1862 Johannes Brahms (1833–1897) arrived in Vienna for what he expected would be a short stay. By then he was well known as a composer, conductor, and pianist, and he was anticipating an appointment to a good position, probably as conductor of the orchestra in his home town of Hamburg. Although this was not granted to him, he increasingly found Vienna to be a congenial home, and by the later 1860s decided to make it his permanent place of residence.

 ## VIENNA IN THE 1860s

The Vienna that he encountered in 1862 was a far cry from the one in which Beethoven and Schubert had lived thirty-five years before. Under the rule of the Austrian emperor, Franz Joseph, Vienna became a huge and sprawling metropolis whose population had doubled since the 1820s. When Franz Joseph came to power after the uprisings of 1848, the old central city remained much as it had been for centuries, still surrounded by battlements that were themselves circled by a broad esplanade (Fig. 58-1). Beyond this open space, a newer city had grown up as a hodge-podge of suburban villages.

In 1857 the emperor turned the circular open space over to the city government to begin a massive urban renewal, and over the next thirty years the Vienna of the present day was created. On the western flank of the circular band, the city planners built imposing governmental and educational structures—a parliament, city hall, and university—each in a distinctive historical style of architecture. The eastern side was devoted to large commercial and residential buildings, and the southern portion to structures for the arts, including the Kunsthistorisches Museum (Museum for Historical Art), Opera, and a home for the Vienna Philharmonic Orchestra and the city's music conservatory. The complex reconstruction of this part of Vienna was tied together by a broad, tree-lined avenue called the Ringstrasse (Ring Street), which today lends the Austrian capital much of its distinctive charm and grandeur.

FIGURE 58-1
Jakob Alt, "View of Vienna's Karlskirche," 1820. The old city of Vienna was ringed by an open area (called a "glacis") used partly as a park, partly by the military.

The development of the Ringstrasse symbolized the return of Vienna to its old vigor as a musical center. In 1869 a new theater for the Vienna Opera was completed; it was a splendidly ornate, neo-Renaissance structure that seated more than 2,000. Although destroyed during World War II, this imposing theater was rebuilt keeping its old appearance, and it remains today one of the world's great opera houses. In 1870 Vienna's Gesellschaft der Musikfreunde (Society of the Friends of Music)—a name usually shortened to **"Musikverein"** (Music Society)—built a new home near the Opera. The building contains a splendid auditorium (the "Golden Hall") that is still one of Europe's acoustically most perfect concert sites (Fig. 58-2). It is home to the Vienna Philharmonic Orchestra, which began to present regular concerts in 1860, drawing its personnel from the orchestra of the Opera.

In addition to its reputation for higher musical arts, Vienna was also known throughout the nineteenth century for popular music, especially music for the dance. Social dancing had long been a craze among the Viennese, and in the nineteenth century the dance of choice for people from all walks of life was the **waltz.** Dance halls had cropped up across the city, and for a small entrance fee the Viennese could waltz the night away to the accompaniment of a piano or small orchestra (Fig. 58-3).

Waltzing and its music had a questionable reputation early in the century. When Chopin visited Vienna in 1830 he reported to his parents: "Best known among the many Viennese entertainments are those evenings in the beer-halls where Strauss or Lanner . . . play waltzes during supper," he wrote. "The audience is so delighted that they can scarcely contain themselves. It just shows you how corrupted the taste of the Viennese public is."[1]

But by the 1860s the waltz had moved out of Vienna's beer gardens and into its palaces, and it came to embody a sophisticated happi-

FIGURE 58-2
Built in 1870, the "Golden Hall" of the Musikverein is the home of the Vienna Philharmonic Orchestra. Its best-known concert is the one that takes place yearly on New Year's Day.

ness that characterizes Vienna and its people. The leading composer of waltzes was **Johann Strauss, Jr.** (1825–1899)— known as the "Waltz King"—whose dance orchestras played all over the city. When he conducted them, he stood with his violin amid the orchestra and led his musicians in a famously energetic and precise manner. His waltzes—*The Blue Danube, Tales from the Vienna Woods, The Emperor's Waltz,* and a hundred others—continue to delight the whole world.

Bridgeman Art Library

✻ BRAHMS'S LIFE AND WORKS

Brahms was born to the family of a musician in the city of Hamburg in north central Germany, which then as now is Germany's busiest seaport. He quickly advanced as a pianist and composer, and in 1853 set off on a tour as accompanist to the Hungarian violinist Eduard Reményi. He brought with him his own early compositions, including two piano sonatas, songs, and chamber works, and these attracted the attention of the influential musicians whom he met.

✻ FIGURE 58-3

The waltz, danced here at a court ball, captured the sophisticated pleasure that was prized by the Viennese.

Most important was his encounter in Düsseldorf with Robert and Clara Schumann, who immediately recognized his genius. Robert Schumann was moved to write his final review, titled "New Paths," for the *Neue Zeitschrift für Musik* to call attention to the still unknown Brahms (excerpted in Box). In 1854 Schumann was institutionalized, and Brahms returned to Düsseldorf to assist Clara Schumann and her seven children. The romantic attachment that arose between her and Brahms was touched on in Chapter 54.

Brahms at first aimed for a career that combined conducting and composing, along the lines already laid out by Schumann and Mendelssohn. After moving to Vienna in 1862 he held a position as conductor of a chorus, and following upon the example of Mendelssohn he performed early music (especially the choral works of J.S. Bach) together with modern compositions. From 1872 to 1875 he was the artistic director of the concerts of the Musikverein in Vienna, but after this time he concentrated more fully on composing.

A new chapter in his creative life was opened in 1876 with the premiere of his Symphony No. 1, on which he had worked sporadically for more than twenty years. It was followed quickly by three additional symphonies, which helped to solidify his position as one of the very greatest composers of his or any other time. Following his death from cancer in April 1897, tributes poured in from around the world. In a gesture that may never again be accorded to a classical musician, the flags on the great ships in the port of Hamburg, Brahms's home town, were flown in his honor at half mast.

The body of music composed by Brahms is very different in its finite quantity and orderly status from that of a Schubert or Liszt. Those musicians left behind a far larger amount of music, many pieces incomplete, others existing in multiple versions, and many probably not intended for publication at all. But Brahms destroyed all such imperfect works, self-consciously leaving behind only complete compositions in a definitive form, all of which satisfied him artistically.

Brahms's orchestral music consists of four symphonies (1876–1885), several concert overtures, the popular *Variations on a Theme by Joseph Haydn,* and one concerto for violin, two for piano, and a double concerto for violin and cello. He wrote a

New Paths by Robert Schumann

Following a concert tour in the fall of 1853, Johannes Brahms traveled to Düsseldorf to meet Robert and Clara Schumann, and a deep mutual admiration arose immediately among them. Robert Schumann— earlier one of Germany's leading music critics—took up the pen one final time to call attention to the youthful Brahms. Here are excerpts from his article, titled *Neue Bahnen* (*New Paths*):

. . . I have thought that in the course of events there would and must someday suddenly appear one who would be called to utter the highest expression of the time in an ideal manner, someone who presents us with mastery not through a gradual development but like Minerva springing fully armed from the head of Kronion. And he has arrived, a young blood, at whose cradle graces and heroes stood guard. His name is *Johannes Brahms*, from Hamburg, working there in quiet obscurity but under an excellent and enthusiastic teacher (Eduard Marxsen), trained in the strictest rules of art and recommended to me not long ago by an honored and renowned master. He came just as he was billed, even in appearance. He is a natural. Sitting at the piano he began to reveal wondrous lands. We were drawn ever more into his magical circle. He played ingeniously, coaxing from the piano an orchestra of multicolored and joyous voices—his sonatas were more disguised symphonies. Then there were songs whose poetry one could understand without knowing the words, while a deep lyric melody penetrated everything. Then single piano pieces, some having a demonic character with the most clever form. Then sonatas for violin and piano, next quartets for string instruments. And each so different from the others that they all seemed to flow from some different source. And then he seemed to bring them like a gathering storm together into a waterfall, over whose tumbling waves a peaceful rainbow stretched and at whose edge butterflies flitted about to the song of nightingales. . . .[2]

large amount of chamber music, including instrumental sonatas, string quartets, sextets, and works combining piano and strings. For piano there are three early sonatas and many character pieces, in addition to chorale preludes for organ. His vocal works include songs, choruses and pieces for vocal ensemble. Among the latter are two collections of waltzes, called *Liebeslieder* (*Love Songs*) that have a distinctively Viennese flavor.

After the death of Mendelssohn and Schumann, Brahms took over the leadership of the conservative branch of European musical culture. His traditionalism is seen in his concentration on "absolute" musical genres—those having no explicit programmatic content—as in his chamber works and his symphonies of a classical type. His allegiance to classical forms—sonata form, variations, rondo, and simple ternary—was stronger than in a musician such as Liszt. Brahms did not write opera, thus avoiding comparisons with Wagner.

At the same time, strongly romantic and progressive elements are apparent in virtually all of his music. These include an intensely lyrical impulse, a darkly enriched tone, advanced harmonic and tonal thinking, and a passionately affective content. His forms—on the surface seemingly familiar from the Classical period—are highly intricate beneath and continue the movement toward unity that allies him, albeit in a different way, with the most progressive musicians of the nineteenth century.

Symphony No. 3

During the period 1876–1885 when Brahms completed his four symphonies, orchestral culture was flourishing throughout Europe. Orchestras were on the rise everywhere, as in Vienna, where the Vienna Philharmonic Orchestra had begun its permanent subscription concerts in 1860 and moved into its splendid home in the Musikverein in 1870.

At this time, three types of music were being written specifically for orchestra: symphonies, one-movement programmatic pieces (called overtures or symphonic poems), and concertos. Symphonies came in several types that reflect the split existing at this time between conservative and progressive composers. The symphony preserving the classical form of four movements without program was still the leading genre, with important examples appearing in the 1870s from Anton Bruckner, the Czech composer Antonín Dvořák, and a whole school of Russian symphonists headed by Peter Ilych Tchaikovsky and his teacher, Anton Rubinstein (1829–1894).

An alternative to the classical-type symphony was the programmatic symphony, an example of which has been seen in Berlioz's *Symphonie fantastique*. In addition to the overt presence of a program, this type of symphony is more variable in its form than its classical cousin. It often has more than four movements and these can extend to unusual lengths. Typically, the orchestra is enlarged beyond the classical makeup.

Brahms's approach to the genre of the symphony allied him—at least outwardly—with the traditionalists, and specifically with the genre as it existed in the hands of Beethoven during his middle period (see Chapter 50). All of Brahms's symphonies have four movements with a customary sequence of tempos (fast/slow/lilting/fast), and they are all moderate in length (none as long as Beethoven's "Eroica" Symphony). All use traditional forms—all of the first movements are in sonata form, for example—and all call for an orchestra of moderate size. None of the four is programmatic.

Brahms's Symphony No. 3 in F Major, Op. 90 (1883), illustrates his moderate extension of Beethoven's symphonic style. The first movement is the longest of the work's four, as in the classical model. Other conservative features are plain to see. The movement uses an uncomplicated version of sonata form, including a repeat of the exposition and a long coda, as in most of the symphonic first movements of Beethoven. The orchestra is moderate in size, calling for even fewer instruments than Beethoven did sixty years earlier in his Ninth Symphony.

Progressive features are equally evident. Brahms's tonal plan is far from the classical norm. The home key is F major, but the second theme appears in the mediant key, A major, and this subsidiary material returns in the recapitulation in D major and minor, the submediant key. The metric structure of the movement is unstable, as it contains many hemiola figures and otherwise almost constantly shifts its metric patterns in defiance of the bar line. Here, as in much of his music, Brahms almost completely avoids the regular four- and eight-measure phrases of the classicists.

The work is also tightly unified by recurrences of a small motive that precedes the main theme (Ex. 58-1). The top line of the motive, played by Flute I, contains the ascending melodic figure F - A♭ - F, which Brahms's biographer Max Kalbeck interpreted as a recurrent personal motto in Brahms's music representing the words **F**rei **a**ber **f**roh, "free but happy." Brahms himself was entirely silent about any such idea.

EXAMPLE 58-1

Brass, woodwinds

In various shapes, the motive reappears throughout the movement. It is embedded in different themes and turns up frequently in the bass line and in fleeting figures in inner voices. Its multiple appearances at the beginning of the main theme—to cite only one of many such examples of its use—are marked by brackets in Example 58-2. The listener is reminded of a similar phenomenon in works by Beethoven, notably the famous short-short-short-long motto that opens Beethoven's Symphony No. 5. Brahms goes beyond Beethoven's Fifth by explicitly bringing back the central motive in its original form at the end of the fourth movement of the Third Symphony. In this way he brings the symphony closer to the unified, cyclic forms of a composer such as Liszt.

EXAMPLE 58-2

LISTENING CUE

JOHANNES BRAHMS
Symphony No. 3 (1883)
First movement, *Allegro con brio*

CD 10/3
Anthology, No. 158

BRAHMS'S VOCAL MUSIC

Among Brahms's many outstanding works for chorus, his *Ein deutsches Requiem* (*A German Requiem*, 1868) is perhaps the greatest. The piece was begun as early as 1857 and achieved its completed form—with seven movements that call for mixed chorus, orchestra, and solo voices—in 1868. It is not an example of the traditional genre of the requiem (or Requiem Mass) as encountered in Chapter 48 in connection with Mozart's Requiem. That was a composition geared for use in the official Catholic funeral service, but Brahms, like several earlier composers, uses the term "Requiem" to designate a work that more freely addresses the idea of death. His *German Requiem* is more appropriate to the concert hall than to a service of worship.

Brahms selected his texts from the German Bible, choosing passages that speak of comfort for the bereaved, the impermanence of life, and the joyful prospect of the afterlife. The whole composition has a symmetrical form that begins and ends in F major and reaches its crowning center in the fourth movement, "Wie lieblich sind Deine Wohnungen" ("How Lovely Are Thy Dwelling Places"). The music here is blissfully melodious.

Brahms composed nearly two hundred songs for voice and piano, and in these works he brought the genre established by Schubert to new heights of warmth and expressivity. Toward the end of the nineteenth century composers wrote two types of songs: one aspired to be a literary event, the other a musical event. We will encounter literary songs in pieces by Gustav Mahler and Claude Debussy (see Chapters 60 and 63). Brahms's tastes leaned strongly toward the latter type. In his songs a certain simplicity and conservatism reigns. Their affective content resides mainly in a lyric melody in the voice, and the piano is relegated largely to an accompanimental role. The form of Brahms's songs is most often strophic or varied strophic, and these works often have an artlessly folkish flavor. The composer once declared that the folk song was his "ideal" in all song writing.

We see a folk-like simplicity at work in his song "Feldeinsamkeit" ("Alone in the Country"), Op. 86, No. 2 (c1879). This is a setting of an unpretentious poem in two stanzas by Hermann Allmers (1821–1902), a minor German poet. Lying in the grass, the narrator gazes peacefully at the clouds and feels dead to the world. Brahms's setting keeps Allmers's artless tone. The song has a simple varied strophic form, and the piano is confined to the role of accompaniment, with no elaborate prelude or postlude.

Despite these gestures toward a superficial simplicity, the song uses an advanced harmonic language that is filled with chromatic motions. The music also persistently mirrors the text. We experience the narrator's passive gazing into the sky in the long pedal point on the tone F at the beginning. When the narrator finds himself surrounded by crickets, we hear their chirping in a pungent ninth chord, and when the blue sky that he sees above him opens up before our eyes, the tonic minor triad is suddenly transformed into a major triad (Ex. 58-3).

EXAMPLE 58-3

...while crickets around me chirp ceaselessly, with the blue of heaven...

In Chapter 75 we will study another setting of Allmers' poem "Feldeinsamkeit" by the American composer Charles Ives.

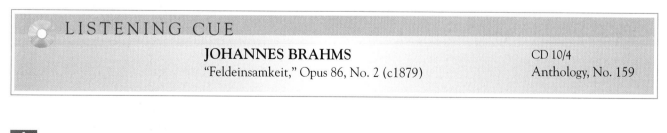

LISTENING CUE

JOHANNES BRAHMS
"Feldeinsamkeit," Opus 86, No. 2 (c1879)

CD 10/4
Anthology, No. 159

ANTON BRUCKNER

The great and immediate success of Brahms's symphonies with audiences all over the world long eluded those of his Viennese contemporary Anton Bruckner (1824–1896). Bruckner was born in a village near the city of Linz, which lies midway between Salzburg and Vienna. Until the age of forty-four, he led the life of a provincial church musician and school teacher. He was an excellent organist, especially known for his improvisations, and in his early years he composed almost exclusively choral music for use in the Catholic liturgy.

In 1868 Bruckner moved to Vienna, where he worked primarily as a music professor, first at the Vienna Conservatory and later also at the University of Vienna. His many students include Gustav Mahler, Arnold Schoenberg, and the theorist Heinrich Schenker. As a composer in Vienna, Bruckner turned decisively to the symphony, ultimately composing nine mature symphonies, of which the ninth was left incomplete when he died in 1896.

These compositions pledge conflicting allegiances in the war of the conservatives versus the futurists. In some ways they exhibit Classical features. None of them is overtly programmatic, all have four movements in a customary succession of tempos and movement types, and, except for the final symphonies, they all use an orchestra of moderate size.

But virtually everything else about them suggests the thinking of a composer from the New German School. They are epic in length, about twice as long as Brahms's symphonies. Most are cyclic, as themes from the first movements are brought back in the finales (although we have seen Brahms hint at this in his Third Symphony). The forms encountered in their individual movements—especially the sonata forms in the first and last movements—are extensively reinterpreted relative to the classical norm, just as Berlioz did in the first movement of his *Symphonie fantastique* or Liszt in his *Les préludes*. Given the unprecedented way that Bruckner organizes and expresses musical ideas, it is not at all surprising that many audiences of his time found his symphonies incoherent rather than original.

In one of the great ironies of music history, Bruckner allowed himself to be persuaded by his friends and students to make radical cuts and other revisions in all of his symphonies, hoping to make them more acceptable to audiences of his day.

Bruckner's symphonies all have trademark features. Their first movements usually open with a gesture reminiscent of the opening of Beethoven's Ninth Symphony. Over mysterious chords in the strings, a melody is gradually pulled up from fragments of open fourths and fifths. A theme then forces its way out at the end of a long and repetitive crescendo. The music that follows is unapologetically full of clichés—rhythms constantly alternating groupings of twos and threes, ostinatos carried out through long crescendos, extended motionless harmonies over pedal points, moments of utter bombast placed beside those of serenity. Bruckner's liberated outlook on musical form and expression found its only approval in the progressive faction of European musicians led by Wagner and Liszt.

Bruckner made several trips to visit Wagner, whom he worshiped in a child-like way. Bruckner traveled to Bayreuth for the premiere of *Parsifal* in 1882, and Wagner greeted him and asked how he liked the new work. "While still holding his hand," Bruckner later recalled, "I knelt down, pressed his precious hand to my lips, and kissed it, saying, 'O master, I worship you!!!' The Master responded, 'Calm down, Bruckner, good night!!!' These were the Master's last words to me. On the following day he sat behind me at the *Parsifal* performance and scolded me for applauding too loudly."[3]

Bruckner's Motets: *Christus factus est*

Bruckner concentrated on only two types of music—symphonies and choral compositions for the Catholic liturgy. His mature works of the latter type consist of three Masses (1864–1868), a *Te Deum* (a Latin text praising God that can be performed at virtually any celebration), a setting of Psalm 150 ("Hallelujah! Praise the Lord in His Holy Place"), and a number of mostly unaccompanied Latin motets.

Christus factus est (1884) is a handsome example of the last of these. Recall from Chapter 21 that a motet, during its heyday in the late Renaissance period, was a setting for unaccompanied chorus of a sacred Latin text. Depending on the words used, such pieces might have been performed within the Catholic liturgy or used outside of the church for private devotion or reflection. Following the Renaissance, major composers continued to write motet-like compositions, but there was increasingly less homogeneity in their styles or purposes. Mozart, for example, often wrote motets—such as his exquisite *Ave verum corpus* (Hail, True Body, 1791). His works of this type are usually for the medium of chorus and orchestra and they were intended for church performance. Among the early nineteenth-century composers, Schubert, Mendelssohn, Berlioz, and Liszt wrote motet-like works, again in a mixed style that preserved some antique features (such as an imitative texture) combined with more modern forms of expression.

Bruckner's *Christus factus est* is appropriate to the Catholic Mass on Maundy Thursday, the Thursday before Easter, when the Church celebrates the founding of the eucharist (a symbolic recreation of the Last Supper). The words are taken from the Gradual for that feast, and in a celebration of Mass in Bruckner's time, the chorus might well have substituted this motet for the more normal chanting of this text:

Christus factus est pro nobis obediens	Christ was for us obedient
usque ad mortem, mortem autem crucis.	unto death, unto death on the cross.
[verse] Propter quod et Deus exaltavit illum,	Therefore God exalted him,
et dedit illi nomen,	and gave him a name
quod est super omne nomen.	that is above every other name.

In Bruckner's day, there was a movement afoot in the Catholic Church in German lands, called **Cecilianism,** that urged a greater uniformity in church music based on the seemingly pure style of religious works from the time of Palestrina (see Chapter 25). To musicians of the nineteenth century, this suggested a serene and uniform mood in which the chorus sang unaccompanied in simplified rhythms with a light counterpoint, sometimes using the church modes and quoting from Gregorian chant. Although Bruckner found Cecilian church music to be unimaginative, the goals of this movement are partly evident in his motet *Christus factus est.*

Echoes of Renaissance polyphony are plain to hear. Bruckner's motet is unaccompanied, simple in rhythm, and it alternates homophonic passages with others using a light imitation. The harmonies consist largely of root-position triads. The words are always clearly audible, and these govern the form of the piece and also trigger word paintings. From measure 7, on the word "obediens" (obedient), the altos and basses obediently follow one another downward through a chain of suspensions. On the word "mortem" (death) the music sinks low and arrives in measure 15 on a dissonant chord with notes separated by whole tones. The voices then repeatedly soar into their highest register on the words "quod est super omne nomen" ("that is above every other name"). All of these features are derived from the motet style of composers of the sixteenth century.

But the tonal language of the work comes straight from Wagner. The voice leading is densely chromatic, dissonances are freely admitted, and the triadic cadence points in the interior of the work have little relevance to the framing tonality of

D minor and major. As in his symphonies, Bruckner in *Christus factus est* pours new wine into old bottles.

 LISTENING CUE

ANTON BRUCKNER
Christus factus est (1884)

CD 10/5
Anthology, No. 160

 SUMMARY

Vienna in the 1860s regained its preeminence in the world of music. New structures—including a new Opera house and a new concert hall called the "Musikverein" ("Music Society")—were built in that decade, and Vienna continued to be a center for sophisticated popular music, as in the waltzes of Johann Strauss, Jr.

Johannes Brahms emerged in this decade as Vienna's leading composer of serious music. In the public's mind, he was allied with musical conservatives, although his symphonies and choral music (such as his *A German Requiem* of 1868) defy any real distinctions between old and new. In his music there is an intense melodiousness, an advanced harmonic language, irregular phrases—all cast into traditional forms. Many of Brahms's two hundred songs have a folk-like spirit, although their chromatic harmonies link the composer with his most progressive contemporaries.

As a proponent of Wagner and the New German School, Anton Bruckner, a resident of Vienna from 1868 until his death in 1896, was on the other side of the critic's fence. Despite their seemingly classical exterior, his symphonies reveal a profound originality in form and substance. Before (and occasionally after) arriving in Vienna, Bruckner composed mainly choral music for the Catholic liturgy. His motet *Christus factus est* uses a chromatic harmony reminiscent of Wagner's music, although this is placed in a form drawn from motets at the time of Palestrina.

KEY TERMS

"Musikverein"
waltz

Johann Strauss, Jr.
Cecilianism

 *Chapter* **59**

Music and Ballet in Nineteenth-Century Russia: Mussorgsky and Tchaikovsky

A native culture for artistic music was slow to develop in Russia. During the reign of Tsar Peter the Great (1682–1725), the artistic life of Russia was placed in the hands of foreigners who came to the capital city of St. Petersburg to design its architectural monuments, occupy court positions in the arts and letters, and make music. During the rule of Catherine the Great (1762–1796) Italian opera flourished in the Russian court. The Queen brought in a succession of leading Italian opera composers—Baldassare Galuppi, Tommaso Traetta, Giovanni Paisiello, and Giuseppe Sarti among others—to compose and to oversee new works, and Italian opera found a devoted following among Russia's aristocracy.

The first significant and original Russian-born composer was **Mikhail Glinka** (1804–1857). He spent his adult life mainly in St. Petersburg, with long sojourns in Paris, Berlin, Milan, and other European cities. He was largely self-taught as a musician and worked as a governmental employee while approaching music as an amateur. Most of his compositions—which include the operas *A Life for the Tsar* and *Ruslan and Lyudmila*, symphonic works, and songs—speak with a Russian accent through the use of national themes and folk-song quotations or imitations. Glinka's basic language, all the same, is that of German and Italian music.

ST. PETERSBURG IN THE LATE NINETEENTH CENTURY

During the reign of Tsar Alexander II (1855–1881) the culture for classical music in St. Petersburg was greatly modernized, and opportunities for native composers brightened. In 1860 the **Mariinsky Theater** (called the Kirov Theater during the Soviet period) was opened and placed at the disposal of a state-supported Russian opera troupe (see Part VI timeline). A rival Italian company gradually lost out in popularity as the native-born Russian musicians revealed a great genius for music. The Mariinsky Theater soon became the focal point for music throughout the city, where a taste for opera and ballet was solidly entrenched. In 1862 a conservatory was established that provided for the training of native performers and composers, the latter including Peter Ilyich Tchaikovsky, Sergei Prokofiev, and Dmitri Shostakovich. Although opera and ballet were supreme, orchestral music began to flourish with the founding of the Russian Musical Society (1859), Russian Symphonic Concerts (1885), and the establishment of a permanent Court Orchestra (1882).

THE *KUCHKA*

As musical culture in St. Petersburg by the 1860s began to produce outstanding native composers, conflict with the older domination by foreigners and by Western musical models became unavoidable. Some of the leaders of musical life at that time, such as the virtuoso pianist Anton Rubinstein (1829–1894), thought that Russian music would best develop by continuing to imitate traditional European values, including accepted styles of composition, strict conservatory training, and a cosmopolitan outlook that could blend with the familiar musical tastes of the Germans, French, and Italians. To these westward-looking Russians, the styles of Schumann, Wagner, Verdi, and Brahms were perfectly acceptable.

Rubinstein's pro-Western philosophy was opposed by a circle of influential St. Petersburg musicians and music critics who gathered around the brilliant pianist and composer **Mily Balakirev** (pronounced Ba-LA-kir-ef, 1837–1910). He distrusted the regimented and doctrinaire teaching of traditional musical conservatories, which he believed restrained new ideas and inhibited creative freedom. He was also a Slavic nationalist who was annoyed by the dominance of European music in Russian concert halls and opera houses. In its place he wanted to hear a distinctively

Russian voice in new music, such as Glinka had achieved by the use of folk songs and stories, and he also encouraged the development of new musical materials that broke with European traditions. Balakirev supported the appearance of oriental themes in music—as in his virtuosic *Islamey* for piano. Such compositions, he thought, celebrated the extension of the Russian empire into Asia.

Younger St. Petersburg musicians were drawn to Balakirev's powerful personality and great musicianship. "His influence over those around him," wrote his student Nicolai Rimsky-Korsakov, "was boundless, and resembled some magnetic or mesmeric force."[1] Following an orchestral concert that Balakirev conducted in St. Petersburg in 1867 featuring his own works and those of others in his circle, the writer Vladimir Stasov pointed approvingly to Balakirev's nationalistic outlook: "How much poetry, feeling, talent, and ability there is," Stasov wrote, "in the small but already mighty handful (*moguchaya kuchka*) of Russian musicians."[2] The epithet **kuchka,** "handful," caught on as a name for Balakirev's circle, whose other principal members were the composers Rimsky-Korsakov, César Cui (1835–1918), Alexander Borodin (1833–1887), and Modest Mussorgsky (1839–1881). (The group is also sometimes called **The Five.**) In 1867 all were still musical amateurs lacking in any systematic musical education, something that Balakirev thought unnecessary. Their background made them all the more sympathetic to rough-and-ready experimentation into new musical resources. All wanted a distinctive Russian profile in their music.

✜ MODEST MUSSORGSKY

Mussorgsky's career characterizes the interests of the group, although his development of a nationalistic, realistic, and non-Westernized musical language went further than his *kuchka* comrades toward a distinctively original and influential style. He was largely self-taught as a composer, receiving guidance from several friends, especially from the magnetic Balakirev. Although passionate about composing, he made his living as an army officer and later as a government worker, and he enjoyed little recognition as an artist during his own lifetime. A self-destructive and manic personality, Mussorgsky died from alcohol poisoning at the age of only forty-two. Even his friends from the *kuchka* could not always take him seriously, given his personal habits and his disdain for conventional modes of composition.

Mussorgky's greatest work is the opera **Boris Godunov,** based on a play by Alexander Pushkin that deals with the life of an early Russian tsar. Mussorgsky completed it in 1869, although he could not arrange for a performance. He revised it in 1872, whereupon it was performed at the Mariinsky Theater. His other principal works are the tone poem *Night on Bald Mountain,* the cycle of piano pieces *Pictures at an Exhibition* (best known in Maurice Ravel's orchestration of 1922), and three song cycles (*The Nursery, Sunless,* and *Songs and Dances of Death*).

The song "Within Four Walls" that opens the cycle *Sunless* (1874) shows Mussorgsky's realism and a novel approach to the genre itself. The poem, written by Arseny Golenishchev-Kutuzov (an amateur poet whom the composer had befriended), consists of a series of melancholy exclamations, made by an individual trapped by life and sustained only by a glimmer of hope for future happiness. Although poetically unsophisticated, the words express a non-sentimental and realistic outlook on life that surely rang true with the composer during his depressive moods.

A gritty realism was at the very root of Russian art of the 1870s (also see Chapter 65), and it was a guiding principle in Mussorgsky's choice of song poetry. The composer explained his attachment to realistic images to the painter Ilya Repin: "It is the people I want to depict: when I sleep I see them, when I eat I think of them, when I drink—I can visualize them, integral, big, unpainted, and without any tinsel. And what an *awful* (in the true sense of the word) richness there is in the people's speech for a musical figure."[3] Repin's own realistic style as a painter is evident in his searing portrait of the composer (Fig. 59-1), made only days before Mussorgsky's untimely death. It shows the subject "without any tinsel," in the final stages of his battle with alcohol and depression.

To match the realistic text, Mussorgsky created music that is stripped bare of artifice. The song has virtually no tune, only an artful imitation of the text as it would be spoken. "My music must be an artistic reproduction of human speech in all its finest shades, that is, *the sounds of human speech*, as the external manifestations of thought and feeling," he wrote in 1868. "That is the ideal toward which I strive."[4]

The piano accompaniment in the song adds bare and loosely connected chords that hover statically around a D-major triad (the opening line is shown in Ex. 59-1). There are no distractions coming from normal harmonic progressions or traditional voice leading. Mussorgsky's partial removal of functional harmonic progressions in songs such as "Within Four Walls" would later prove to be a powerful influence on the music of Claude Debussy (see Chapter 63).

EXAMPLE 59-1

✻ FIGURE 59-1
Ilya Repin painted this portrait of his friend Mussorgsky only days before Mussorgsky's death from the effects of alcoholism.

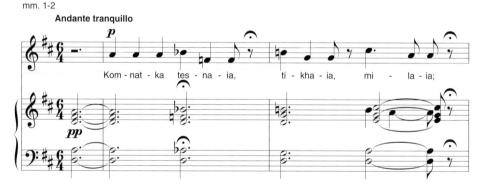

mm. 1-2

Andante tranquillo

Kom - nat - ka tes - na - ia, ti - kha - ia, mi - la - ia;

My room is small, quiet, pleasant; ...

🔘 LISTENING CUE

MODEST MUSSORGSKY
Sunless, "Within Four Walls" (1874)

CD 10/6
Anthology, No. 161

✿ PETER ILYICH TCHAIKOVSKY

Balakirev and his *kuchka* were well-known to Peter Ilyich Tchaikovsky (1840–1893), Russia's greatest composer of the nineteenth century. Tchaikovsky met Balakirev in Moscow in 1867, and Balakirev shortly afterward conducted his music in St. Petersburg.

Tchaikovsky's works from this time had much that appealed to Balakirev, including their quotations of folk songs and other nationalistic gestures. Balakirev freely offered the young composer advice about composing, and he guided Tchaikovsky through the creation of one of his first great works, the concert overture *Romeo and Juliet*. But Tchaikovsky was wary of Balakirev's overbearing personality and the anti-Western element in his aesthetic program. Living in Moscow rather than the *kuchka* stronghold of St. Petersburg, Tchaikovsky always kept a cautious distance from Balakirev's circle.

Born in a mining village near the Ural Mountains, Tchaikovsky as a child moved with his family to St. Petersburg, and in 1865 he was one of the earliest graduates from the city's new conservatory, where he studied composition with Anton Rubinstein. His career path was very different from those of the *kuchka*, since he was determined to be a professional musician, not an amateur. Immediately after leaving the St. Petersburg Conservatory, he was appointed to the faculty of Moscow's new conservatory, where he taught until 1878. His life was otherwise unsettled, as he traveled almost constantly between European cities and various locations in Russia. A remarkable chapter in his life concerns his relationship with a wealthy admirer of his music, Countess Nadezhda von Meck, with whom he exchanged an extensive and highly personal correspondence but whom he never met. For a period, Mme. Meck supported the composer financially.

Tchaikovsky was a master of all of the musical genres of his day. He wrote operas (including *Eugene Onegin* and *The Queen of Spades*), six symphonies, symphonic poems, piano character pieces, songs, three string quartets, and concertos. He was also the first leading composer of the late nineteenth century to write music for ballet, in his *Swan Lake* (1876), *The Sleeping Beauty* (1889), and *The Nutcracker* (1892).

✿ BALLET

A **ballet**—in the modern sense—is a theatrical presentation in which a story or idea is communicated by music, mime, and dancing. The genre has a long history, although it emerged as an independent art form only in the late eighteenth century. Nowhere was it more popular than in Paris, where dancing had long been a principal courtly entertainment (see Chapter 35). Parisian audiences of the 1820s were enchanted by the dancing of **Marie Taglioni** (1804–1884), who was the first ballerina to specialize in dancing *en pointe*, on the toes, which is done with the aid of special shoes (Fig. 59-2). Her graceful and fluent movements fit in well with romantic ballet **scenarios,** or stories, that typically featured supernatural creatures, evoked the passions of unrequited love, and created the atmosphere of fairy tale.

Although a ballet in the nineteenth century was a collaborative creation, the **choreographer** (often called the "ballet master") was the leading figure. He often wrote or adapted the scenario, devised a structure for the work as a whole, commissioned the writing of music, and created the dance steps used in each section.

The layout of a typical ballet in the nineteenth century had much in common with traditional opera. A ballet, like an opera, normally begins with an overture. The story—which in opera is largely told in recitative—is conveyed in ballet by passages in **mime,** where the leading dancers communicate by way of standardized hand movements, poses, and facial expressions. These are interspersed with danced numbers. Some involve the entire company (the *corps de ballet*), rather like a chorus in an opera. Other numbers are ensembles—passages for a few leading dancers such as in a *pas de deux* (for two dancers, normally a man and woman). Still other dances, called **variations,** are for a single performer, comparable to an operatic aria. Ballets often

Marie Taglioni

Marie Taglioni created the art of the modern ballerina. Strictly trained by her father, the choreographer Filippo Taglioni, Marie developed a style of dancing and a stage persona that by the 1830s brought her to the top of her profession and created a model for dancing that still exists today.

She perfected the idea of vertical line for the ballerina—an elegant extension of the body and an elevation that seemed to free her from all gravitational limits. She also emphasized dancing on the points of the toes, which creates the illusion of elongation and detachment from the stage. Although she did not invent this practice, she brought it to the prominence it still enjoys in theatrical dance. Her costumes were also revolutionary. She rejected realistic dress in favor of a bell-shaped skirt made from white tulle, worn with bare arms and shoulders. Her motions were praised for their fluidity and lightness. In all, Marie Taglioni represented the essence of what we now call "classical ballet."

Her greatest role was in the ballet *La sylphide*, whose choreography was created by her father for the Paris Opéra in 1832. Here she impersonated a sylph, one of a band of imaginary winged creatures who frolic in the woods. She falls in love with a mortal, who pursues her through the forest and finally embraces her. With this her wings fall to earth and she dies.

After her initial triumph in Paris, Taglioni traveled throughout Europe to delight ballet audiences everywhere. From 1837 she was in residence at the Mariinsky Theater in St. Petersburg, where she developed a cult-like following. Her departure was the occasion of a bizarre event among her Russian fans. As a memento, she had left behind a pair of ballet slippers, which her following seized upon and had cooked into an edible form. They then devoured the shoes as a culinary delicacy.

Bridgeman Art Library

❧ FIGURE 59-2
Marie Taglioni created the modern art of the ballerina, especially in her refinement of techniques for dancing *en pointe*.

---

contain interludes called **divertissements** ("entertainments"), which are episodes with dancing and spectacle that have little connection to the surrounding story.

In the traditional nineteenth-century ballet, music has a secondary role. Although occasionally written by accomplished composers such as the Frenchmen Adolphe Adam (1803–1856, composer of the ballet *Giselle*) and Léo Delibes (1836–1891, composer of *Coppélia* and *Sylvia*), the music was more typically written by an obscure composer on the staff of a theater. In writing the music, the composer took strict orders from the choreographer and aspired only to produce a tuneful score that would serve as a backdrop to the dancing. No originality or self-expression was expected.

❀ BALLET IN RUSSIA: *THE NUTCRACKER*

Early in the nineteenth century, visiting French dancers and choreographers firmly established the French style of ballet in St. Petersburg, where an enthusiasm for the genre was as great as in Paris. Toward the end of the century, the leading figure in

Scenario of *The Nutcracker*

Preparations for Christmas are in full swing at the Silberhaus home, where the tree is being trimmed and presents assembled for the children. A family friend, the mysterious Drosselmayer, arrives, bringing life-sized dolls as presents for his godchildren, Clara and Fritz Silberhaus. Father insists that these be safely stored, whereupon Drosselmayer produces another toy, a small nutcracker in the shape of a toy soldier, which Fritz immediately breaks. Clara sadly wraps up the injured toy and places it in her doll bed, whereupon the party ends and the children are sent to bed.

Late at night Clara steals back into the room to check on the nutcracker, and she is astonished to see the tree growing large and all the toys coming alive. Mice do battle with the toy soldiers, and the Mouse King gains the upper hand over the Nutcracker, who has now come alive to lead his army against the mice. He is saved by Clara, who throws her slipper at the Mouse King. Magically, the Nutcracker turns into a charming Prince, who escorts Clara toward the tree, whereupon they disappear into its branches and fly through a snowstorm.

In the second act the Prince brings Clara to his home, where they meet the kindly Sugar Plum Fairy. A divertissement is ordered for Clara's entertainment, at the end of which the Sugar Plum Fairy dances a *pas de deux* with her consort.

Russian ballet was the French émigré **Marius Petipa** (1818–1910), who came to St. Petersburg in 1847 as a dancer and soon rose to the position of the principal choreographer at the Imperial Ballet of the Mariinsky Theater. He collaborated with Tchaikovsky on two ballet scores—*The Sleeping Beauty* and *The Nutcracker*—which remain masterpieces of their type and are among Tchaikovsky's most beloved works.

The Nutcracker was intended for the Christmas season, and it is geared to the enjoyment of children and adults alike. Since its premiere at the Mariinsky Theater in the week before Christmas 1892, it has been given at Christmas by ballet companies around the world, and it is now by far the most often performed work of its genre. Its scenario is loosely based on a children's story, "Nutcracker and Mouse King" (1819), by E.T.A. Hoffmann, although the narrative was extensively rewritten by Petipa to create a ballet scenario.

The story itself begins with a clear narrative, but by the end of Act 1 it dissolves into pure fantasy. The entire second act is devoted to a divertissement, and we never learn more about the mysterious Drosselmayer, the Mouse King, or other characters from the opening. Ballet—far more than opera—can accommodate such inconsistencies, and these have not prevented *The Nutcracker* from achieving its enduring popularity. Another unusual aspect of the work is that the leading roles, Clara and the Nutcracker Prince, were intended to be enacted by children (actually, younger students from the ballet school of the Mariinsky Theater). Their dancing is simple, and the more virtuosic choreography is given to the subsidiary roles of the Sugar Plum Fairy, her consort, and the figures who perform variations in the divertissement of Act 2.

Tchaikovsky wrote the music for the work based on an outline given him by Petipa. In this document the ballet master sketched out the story, which he divided preliminarily into forty-six sections. Typical of the choreographer in his relation with a composer, Petipa instructed Tchaikovsky concerning the length and character of each dance and Tchaikovsky closely adhered to this outline. For example, in a section toward the end of Act 1, just after Clara dispatches the Mouse King with her slipper, Petipa gave these instructions:

> The Nutcracker turns into an enchanting prince. One or two chords. He runs to aid Clara, who regains consciousness. Here begins emotional music, which changes into a

poetic *andante,* and ends in a grandiose fashion. 64 bars. The decor changes. A fir forest in winter. Gnomes with torches are standing around the Christmas tree to pay homage to the Prince, Clara, and the dolls, who are placed around the tree. A grouping. All this takes place within the *andante* of 64 bars.[5]

The music that Tchaikovsky wrote for this passage (Act 1, no. 8) is almost exactly what Petipa ordered. It opens with two measures stating a C major chord and then progresses through a succession of phrases that are *andante* in tempo and, as Petipa instructed, highly poetic and emotional in character. A lesser composer for ballet would probably have followed Petipa's instructions even more explicitly by writing a succession of eight eight-measure phrases, for a total of sixty-four bars. But Tchaikovsky avoids such a purely formulaic plan by introducing asymmetrical extensions to some of the phrases, while still writing music that is generally regular in structure.

Here, as elsewhere in Tchaikovsky's oeuvre, the composer promotes ease of understanding by a high degree of repetitiveness of melodic material. The whole number uses a simple repetitive form (**A B A'** coda), and each of the three main parts begins with a phrase that is then immediately repeated, in the manner of a melodic period. (For some listeners, past and present, the amount of simple repetition is a weakness in Tchaikovsky's music.) The composer achieves the emotionalism that Petipa wanted in a way also commonly seen in his other works: as the music approaches the reprise, the orchestration is thickened, the tempo dramatically broadens, and, with the crash of cymbals at the point of reprise, the melody is thrust grandiosely into the upper register. The music contains no harmonic surprises and remains unambiguously in C major.

In *The Nutcracker,* as in his other ballet scores, Tchaikovsky did not attempt to duplicate the close expressive connection between music and dramatic ideas and characters that was found in opera of the same period. There is instead a far looser and more general resemblance between the music and the drama, conveyed by tempo, meter, length, and spirit ("emotional," "poetic," "grandiose"—the sentiments that were specified by Petipa). There remains enough freedom so that virtually any section of the ballet can subsequently be re-choreographed. In modern productions of Act 1, no. 8, for example, the change to a snowy winter scene envisioned by Petipa is often replaced by a *pas de deux* for the adults now commonly cast in the roles of Clara and the Prince, with a suggestion of romantic interest between the two. There is no incongruity between the music and this revised choreography.

LISTENING CUE

PETER ILYICH TCHAIKOVSKY
The Nutcracker (1892)
Act 1, scene 8

CD 10/7
Anthology, No. 162

Tchaikovsky strengthened the connection between music and character in one area not addressed by Petipa—in the work's orchestration. In *The Nutcracker,* as in his symphonies, Tchaikovsky shows a profound understanding of the orchestra and a resourcefulness in finding new color combinations that evoke images and ideas. When the mysterious Drosselmayer appears in Act 1, no. 4, for example, his music is given to the low strings, trombones, and the horns playing *bouché* (with the tone tightly stopped by a mute or by the hand in the bell). The sound is just right for the character's unnerving eccentricity. Tchaikovsky uses the ethereal sound of the **celesta** to accompany the Sugar Plum Fairy in her variation in the *pas de deux* near the end of the ballet. This bell-like instrument controlled by a keyboard had been invented by Auguste Mustel only shortly before, and it was heard by the composer on a trip to Paris in 1890. Immediately Tchaikovsky asked his Moscow publisher, Peter Jurgenson, to purchase the instrument. "In the meantime I would prefer it to be shown to nobody," he warned, "or I am afraid that [Nicolai] Rimsky-Korsakov and [Alexander] Glazunov will get wind of it and use its unusual effects sooner than me."[6]

Immediately upon completing the score to *The Nutcracker*, Tchaikovsky arranged excerpts into an orchestral **suite,** for use as a concert work. There are also suites of excerpts from the ballets *The Sleeping Beauty* and *Swan Lake*, but these were created by musicians after the composer's death in 1893.

SUMMARY

Russian musical culture until the mid nineteenth century was dominated by foreigners. Native-born Russians began to assert their genius and originality for music in the later part of the century. In the capital city, St. Petersburg, a group of composers know as the *kuchka* (handful), or "The Five," was led by Mily Balakirev. They favored a nationalistic profile in their works (often achieved by quoting Slavic folk songs in original compositions) and a freedom from traditional European styles and musical materials. These qualities are seen especially in the works of one of their number, Modest Mussorgsky, whose opera *Boris Godunov* and songs project a realistic image of Russian life. In Mussorgsky's song "Within Four Walls" from the cycle *Sunless,* this realism is captured by a simple declamatory melody and by chords whose progressions are remote from the central key.

Peter Ilyich Tchaikovsky was sympathetic to the nationalistic aspirations of the *kuchka* group, although he was more strongly connected to developments in the European music of his day. Tchaikovsky was the first major composer of the nineteenth century to write important works for ballet. His final ballet score, *The Nutcracker,* is based on a fanciful Christmas story. His music is memorably tuneful, repetitive, and skilled in orchestration, although he avoids the innovative harmonic experiments of many of his contemporaries.

KEY TERMS

Mikhail Glinka	ballet	divertissement
Mariinsky Theater	Marie Taglioni	Marius Petipa
Mily Balakirev	scenario	celesta
kuchka ("handful")	choreographer	suite
The Five	mime	
Boris Godunov	variations (ballet)	

Chapter 60

Vienna at the Turn of the Twentieth Century: Gustav and Alma Mahler

In the fall of 1875, Gustav Mahler—then fifteen years old—arrived in Vienna to enroll in the Conservatory of the Musikverein (see Chapter 58) and to begin training for the career of a virtuoso pianist. Home to Johannes Brahms and to the waltzes of Johann Strauss, Jr., Vienna by this time had fully regained the greatness of musical culture that it enjoyed during the time of Haydn, Mozart, and Beethoven.

The two main focal points for serious music—the Opera and the Musikverein—were flourishing in 1875 as never before. The repertory of the Opera was filled with important new works coming from all over Europe. In 1875 alone, Verdi traveled to Vienna to conduct his *Aida* and Requiem, Wagner arrived to oversee productions of *Lohengrin* and *Die Meistersinger,* and Georges Bizet's *Carmen* received its Viennese premiere. The Vienna Philharmonic Orchestra continued to play in the magnificent "Golden Hall" of the Musikverein, which opened five years before Mahler's arrival. The membership of the Philharmonic was, and continues to be, drawn from the orchestra of the Opera, although the Vienna Philharmonic Orchestra itself is self-governing. Even the conductor is elected by its members, which ensures a uniquely reciprocal relation between them and their leaders, who have included Hans Richter, Wilhelm Furtwängler, Karl Böhm, Herbert von Karajan, and Leonard Bernstein, in addition to Mahler himself. The repertory of the Philharmonic at this time had a distinctly conservative flavor, although new music was not neglected. Between 1873 and 1881 the Philharmonic gave the premier performances of Bruckner's Symphonies No. 2, 3, and 4, and Brahms was a regular visitor to its concerts, as piano soloist, conductor, and composer of new works.

Mahler's arrival in Vienna in 1875 was itself a testament to the continuing changes in Austrian society. Mahler was born to a Jewish family living in a small village, Kalist, northwest of Vienna, and in an earlier time his legal right to relocate within the Austrian Empire—not to mention his professional opportunities—would have been strictly limited. Beginning with the uprisings of 1848, and finally in 1867, Jews in the empire were accorded full civil liberties, which allowed them to move freely and to enter any profession. These liberal measures resulted in a great migration of Jews from the eastern regions of the empire into the capital city of Vienna, where they were quickly assimilated into a cosmopolitan German-speaking society and became leaders in the arts and sciences.

MAHLER'S LIFE

When Mahler concluded his training at the conservatory, he enrolled at the University of Vienna and attended lectures on a variety of topics. These included harmony, which was taught by Anton Bruckner, with whom he formed a friendly relationship. He soon faced a dilemma shared with other aspiring composers of his day: how to make a living. The solution available to many a composer born near the end of the nineteenth century was to perform as a touring virtuoso, but Mahler had given up on this idea. Others such as Bruckner made teaching their livelihood, but Mahler had no affinity for this profession. His plan, which Richard Strauss was

❧ FIGURE 60-1

Mahler in 1902, when this photograph was made, had reached the pinnacle of his fame as conductor at the Vienna Court Opera.

choosing at the same time, was to make his living as a conductor (primarily of opera) and to compose when time permitted, mainly in the summer months. In 1880 he acquired his first conducting position, initiating a career that would lead him ultimately to the very pinnacle of success: his appointment in October 1897 by the emperor himself, as director of the Opera in Vienna (Fig. 60-1). In 1907 Mahler resigned this position to conduct at the Metropolitan Opera in New York, and he ended his career as conductor of the New York Philharmonic Orchestra. Unlike his friend Strauss, however, Mahler never lived to see his music accepted by the public to an extent that allowed him to reduce his grueling schedule of conducting. By his own rueful estimation, he remained a lifelong "summer composer."

❀ MAHLER'S SONGS

Mahler specialized in two of the main musical genres of his day: the song and symphony. At the end of the nineteenth century, the song continued to attract composers of every nationality, much as it had since the time of Schubert and Schumann. Recall from Chapter 58 that songs at this time were sometimes folk-like and relatively simple in musical style, at other times more sophisticated in musical resources and literary in tone.

Although Mahler wrote songs of both types, he increasingly emphasized the literary song. In his works of this type, the poetry attracts our attention nearly as much as the music. The texts are often sophisticated and subtle, written by leading literary figures. The burden of expression is shared between the voice and the accompaniment—piano or orchestra—and principal themes are located mainly in the latter. The harmonic and tonal language is expressive in its own right and highly enriched in sonority, and the form of such songs is usually through composed. Composers like Mahler often linked together several such songs into integrated cycles.

Mahler composed songs throughout his career, often as a way to exteriorize some deeply emotional event in his own life. He wrote the poetry himself for his first important cycle, the *Lieder eines fahrenden Gesellen* (*Songs of a Wayfarer*) of 1884–1885, which speaks about an unhappy love affair. Here, as often in his later songs, Mahler uses an orchestral accompaniment, although all of his songs also exist in authentic versions with piano alone. He believed that poetry of deep emotion could only be interpreted musically through an orchestral medium. "A large-scale composition that plumbs the depths of the subject unconditionally demands the orchestra," he told his friend Natalie Bauer-Lechner.[1] The large medium of the orchestra helped the composer to plumb those depths.

For the songs he composed just after the *Lieder eines fahrenden Gesellen*, Mahler selected song poetry from **Des knaben Wunderhorn** (*The Youth's Magic Horn*), a collection of some seven hundred German folk poems edited by Achim von Arnim and Clemens Brentano that was published in three volumes from 1805 to 1808. This folk poetry, which was freely modified by the editors, had already proved influential upon German romantic literature, but Mahler was the first major composer to explore it extensively as song text. The verses paint a variety of mundane scenes. Conversations between lovers, the dreary life of soldiering, humorous tales, the joys of nature, and stories involving the supernatural are characteristic.

By the turn of the century, Mahler's enthusiasm for the *Wunderhorn* poems waned, and he turned for song texts to the poetry of Friedrich Rückert, whom we have already encountered in Clara Schumann's song "Liebst du um Schönheit" (Chapter 54). In its highly intellectualized and introspective character, Rückert's verse is entirely different from the artless folk style. For his cycle *Kindertotenlieder* (*Songs on the Death of Children*, 1904), Mahler chose five wrenchingly emotional poems written by Rückert in 1834 following the death of his two children. In 1901 and 1902 Mahler composed five additional Rückert songs, including "Liebst du um Schönheit" ("If You Love Beauty"), the one set to music sixty years earlier by Clara Schumann.

Another of Mahler's Rückert songs is "Um Mitternacht" (1901). In this poem, the narrator awakens in the dead of night with a troubled mind. He looks for comfort alternately in the stars and in himself, but he finds none. He thinks next of his fellow man, but there he sees only suffering. Finally, having no other conceivable recourse, he turns to God, in whom he recognizes the guardian of all life.

Mahler's treatment of this sophisticated poem is typical of the literary song of the turn of the century. The accompaniment is provided by an orchestra, and the composer selects only those instruments—brass, woodwinds, piano, harp, and percussion—that seem to fit with the sentiments of the poem. Among the woodwinds he includes a prominent part for **oboe d'amore**—a sometimes ungainly alto oboe that Strauss used in his *Symphonia domestica* at about the same time. (The oboe d'amore is replaced by oboe in some editions.) Throughout his songs and symphonies, Mahler constantly experimented with such new combinations of sound: "Here is the future of all orchestral technique," he told his friend Josef Foerster.

Typical of the literary song, the form of "Um Mitternacht" avoids all simple repetitive patterns and remains close to the model of through composition. Musical materials from the opening stanza recur in each of the later ones, but always in a flexible and developmental manner that allows for the introduction of new ideas. Mahler's principle of form was embodied in the perpetual development of material, never in its simple repetition. He explained this to Bauer-Lechner:

> I have come to recognize a perpetual evolution of content in song, in other words, through-composition as the true principle of music. In my writing, from the very first, you won't find any more repetition from strophe to strophe; for music is governed by the law of eternal evolution, eternal development—just as the world, even in one and the same spot, is always changing, eternally fresh and new.[2]

The through-composed form allows the composer to follow closely upon the ideas of the poem. At the opening, for example, the key and mode are not firmly established, which suggests the narrator's ambivalent frame of mind, and the recurrent descending bass line in the accompaniment suggests his depression (Ex. 60-1). The harmonies of the song deserve careful study, both for their syntactic and expressive meaning. Prior to the fifth stanza, for example, Mahler totally avoids the dominant harmony in the key, again suggesting the narrator's uncertainty. But when his thoughts turn to God, the mode shifts to major and the harmonic progressions become absolutely clear and normative in the principal tonality. (Mahler himself was apparently undecided about the key of "Um Mitternacht." He sketched the song in the key of B♭ and had it published in 1905 in separate editions, one in the key of A, another in the key of B.)

EXAMPLE 60-1

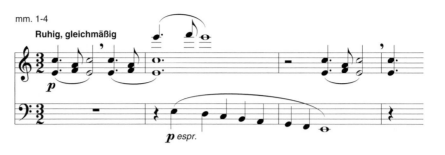

mm. 1-4
Ruhig, gleichmäßig

LISTENING CUE

GUSTAV MAHLER
"Um Mitternacht" (1901)

CD 10/8
Anthology, No. 163

MAHLER'S SYMPHONIES

When Mahler completed his Symphony No. 1 in 1888, the genre of the symphony had risen to a position of supreme importance throughout the world of serious music. Surprisingly, its dominance had not been foreseen even by the leading composers of the earlier Romantic period. In his theory concerning "music of the future," formulated at mid-century, Richard Wagner said that the symphony had exhausted itself with Beethoven's Ninth Symphony, and that the future of music would tend toward an integrated musical drama distantly akin to opera. Plainly, Wagner was incorrect in this prediction. By the end of the century the symphony—not opera—was the supreme challenge for a composer. Virtually all of the principal figures of this time wrote symphonies, many of whom (including Brahms, Bruckner, Jean Sibelius, and Mahler himself) neglected opera entirely.

The writing of a new symphony in the 1880s confronted the composer with a number of critical choices. One was the makeup of the orchestra. The symphonists of conservative sentiment, including Brahms, wrote symphonies at this time for an orchestra of moderate size, whose constitution was similar to that of Beethoven's symphonies except for the inclusion of tuba, which was needed to give a bass voice to the brass choir. Symphonic composers of more modernist inclination—Mahler and Richard Strauss are examples—tended to follow Wagner in his expansion and diversification of the orchestra. Beethoven's idea of adding chorus and solo voices to the symphonic medium had waned among composers late in the century, but it was revived by Mahler, who included voices in his Symphonies No. 2, 3, 4, and 8.

Another question concerned the overall form of the symphony, and in this area there was little agreement among even the most successful composers. The conservatives preserved the classical four-movement sequence, consisting of a fast opening movement in sonata form, interior movements that were slow or dance-like, and a fast finale that tended to take on ever more weight. A more experimental solution, associated with Liszt and the New German School and reaching back to the time of Schubert's "Wanderer" Fantasy (see Chapter 52), was to write long and integrated one-movement works. Orchestral works of this type might have been considered tone poems or symphonies per se, and they typically had contrasting sections unified by the reappearance of common themes. Strauss's *Symphonia domestica* (1903) is an example. It has four main sections (a connected sequence fast/scherzo/slow/ fast) that suggest a four-movement symphony. A third formal alternative, the one favored by Mahler, was to avoid all accepted plans and to rethink the overall form of the symphony freely and anew for each work.

The most vexing question of all for the aspiring symphonist of the 1880s concerned the content of a new work. Would the composer follow Brahms by avoiding any overt statement of non-musical content? Or would he take a midway position, as did Beethoven in the "Pastoral" Symphony or Schumann in his Symphony No. 1 ("Spring") by suggesting extra-musical ideas through movement titles and a freedom of form? Or would he follow the Berlioz of *Symphonie fantastique* and write an unabashedly programmatic symphony, in which the musical materials were placed directly in the service of a detailed narrative?

In his symphonies, Mahler was always ambiguous about this question. His writings make it clear that he was thoroughly skeptical about attaching programmatic meaning to orchestral music. To Alma Schindler in 1901 he described a program as something "that leads directly to misunderstanding, to a flattening and coarsening, and in the long run to such distortion that the work, and still more its creator, is utterly unrecognizable."[3] He was even more detailed in a letter of 1896 to the Berlin music critic Max Marschalk:

> I know that, so far as I myself am concerned, as long as I can express an experience in words I should never try to put it into music. The need to express myself musically— in symphonic terms—begins only on the plan of *obscure* feelings, at the gate that opens into the "other world," the world in which things no longer fall apart in time and space. — Just as I find it banal to compose programme-music, I regard it as unsatisfactory and unfruitful to try to make programme notes for a piece of music. This remains so despite the fact that the *reason* why a composition comes into being at all is bound to be something the composer has experienced, something real, which might after all be considered sufficiently concrete to be expressed in words.[4]

Despite these reservations, Mahler was aware that programmaticism in symphonic music helped to promote its understanding and acceptance, especially for new works that were unfamiliar in style. This had been proved by the great success of Richard Strauss's symphonic poems, works that were concrete in their programmatic content. Perhaps feeling a rivalry with Strauss, Mahler first presented his Symphonies Nos. 1–4 (composed 1888–1900) as overtly programmatic compositions that deal with the life, aspirations, and fate of a hero who is unnamed, although certainly the composer himself. Mahler's way of making his music relate to this program would have been familiar to audiences at the end of the century, since it included such familiar strategies as quoting from his own earlier music, associating themes with specific elements of the program, creating unusual forms that suggest a narrative, and fashioning irregular tonal plans whose meaning seemed to reside in an extra-musical dimension.

But in 1897, when Mahler began to publish his early symphonies, the programmatic element was strictly suppressed, and, in his symphonies beginning with No. 5, all programmatic allusions were banished. His Symphonies Nos. 5–7 (1902–1905) also eliminate the voices that were present in Nos. 2–4, although the Eighth Symphony (1906, called "Symphony of a Thousand" for its gigantic medium) brings the chorus back to sing texts from Goethe's *Faust* and the Pentecost hymn "Veni creator spiritus" ("Come, Creative Spirit"). Mahler's next major work, *Das Lied von der Erde* (*The Song of the Earth*, 1908–1909), combines the genres of symphony and song. The Ninth Symphony (1909) is remarkable for its abstraction and stylistic advancement, and his Symphony No. 10 was left incomplete upon his death in 1911, although the work is now performed using any of several reconstructions.

Mahler's Symphony No. 5

Mahler's Fifth Symphony (1902) initiated a new phase in the composer's creative life, although it has much about it that still hints at the openly programmatic works of the past. As in his earlier symphonies, he quotes in the first and fifth movements from his own earlier songs (from "Nun will die Sonn' so hell aufgeh'n" ["Now the Sun Will Brightly Rise"] from *Kindertotenlieder* and "Lob des hohen Verstandes" ["In Praise of Lofty Intellect"], a *Wunderhorn* song). The first movement is a grim funeral march, like the first movement of the Second Symphony, and, like the Fourth Symphony, the whole work has a non-concentric tonal plan, here beginning in C♯ minor and ending in D major. Also like Symphony No. 4, the five movements are linked into an integrated cycle by varied recurrence of themes.

A new and more classical direction is also plain to see. The orchestra is moderate in size, and, after the opening funeral march (which Mahler compared to a prelude), the normal sequence of four symphonic movements (fast/scherzo/slow/fast) is apparent. The work is also far shorter than the sprawling Symphonies Nos. 1–3. There is a new spirit present that is less self-conscious and introspective in expression and more given to a delight in pure and virtuosic music making.

The slow fourth movement, titled *Adagietto*, has a lost-to-the-world character that reappears throughout Mahler's oeuvre—notably in the finales of the Third and Ninth Symphonies and also in the orchestral song "Ich bin der Welt abhanden gekommen" ("I've Lost Track of the World"), which Mahler composed concurrently with the Fifth Symphony. Like the interior movements of most of his symphonies, the *Adagietto* has the character of an interlude, little resembling the outer movements in materials or mood. In its reduced orchestration for harp and strings it appears as a relaxed moment before the symphony's main musical issues are taken up again in the finale.

Our attention in the *Adagietto* is drawn most to the melody, which is passed between the violins and cellos. Its phrases are drawn out so leisurely as to make any regular beat or meter seem unapparent and any firm sense of cadence elusive. The principal melody, in a simple **ABA** form, has a teasing relationship to the underlying harmonies. On the downbeat of virtually every measure, the last melodic tone from the preceding measure is suspended over the bar, as though the melody is in no hurry to move on. This lazy hanging back is also evident in the free treatment of non-harmonic tones. At the end of the first phrase, for example, the music in measure 9 settles on the dominant chord (C major) in the key of F, but the third (E) of this chord is displaced by the tone F, suspended over from the preceding measure, and the expected resolution to the chordal tone E is reached only after the next melodic phrase has begun (Ex. 60-2).

EXAMPLE 60-2

mm. 8-11 (strings only)

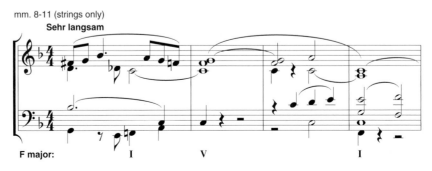

Choosing a Tempo

Mahler marked the tempo of his *Adagietto* movement in the Fifth Symphony simply *Sehr langsam*—"very slow." He left behind nothing more specific, no metronome marking or recordings to help future musicians find the proper tempo. The time signature is a plain $\frac{4}{4}$, so this is not much help, other than to suggest the quarter-note as the unit corresponding to the beat.

It is known that Mahler himself conducted with generally quick tempos. In a letter to Albert Neisser in 1906, he states that the entire Fifth Symphony lasts about 45 minutes. This means that Mahler's tempos in the work were astonishingly fast (virtually no modern recordings of the symphony have a duration of less than an hour). The conductor Bruno Walter (1876–1962)—an associate conductor with Mahler in Vienna and present in Cologne for the premier performance of the Fifth Symphony in 1904 under Mahler's own leadership—later recorded the *Adagietto* with a quick tempo. Under his baton, the movement lasted about 7 minutes, 30 seconds.

The tempos have slowed since Walter's time. Leonard Bernstein's recording of 1964 stretched to 11 minutes,

Herbert von Karajan's of 1973 to 12 minutes, and Bernard Haitink in a 1988 recording weighed in at just under 14 minutes, almost twice as long as in Walter's interpretation.

Can any of these tempos be judged absolutely right or wrong? The question itself is ambiguous. Many conductors believe that a tempo even far slower than Mahler's own can be musical, or "right," if other factors support it, especially the rare ability of an orchestra to play convincingly at a slow tempo. But Mahler himself was no relativist when it came to choosing tempos. In his writings he had no hesitation to speak of certain tempos as absolutely right or wrong.

Mahler's thinking on the subject of tempo reflects the ideas of Richard Wagner, especially those recorded in Wagner's landmark discussion in the essay "On Conducting" (1869). In an *Adagio* movement, Wagner writes, the conductor must set the tempo as slow as possible provided that its melodies can still be effectively sung. It is the singer's ability to regulate the breath, to create phrases, and to shape the line that governs tempo—even when the singer is absent!

No one movement—not even one so memorable as the *Adagietto* from the Fifth Symphony—can illustrate the inexhaustible inspiration and diversity of Mahler's symphonies. In his hands the genre became a truly total work of art, able to record nature in all its variety as well as the passions of the human soul in all their depth and subtlety. In a conversation in 1907 with the Finnish symphonic composer Jean Sibelius, Mahler summarized his viewpoint concerning the symphony. "The symphony must be like the world," Mahler insisted. "It must embrace everything."[5]

LISTENING CUE

GUSTAV MAHLER
Symphony No. 5 (1902)
Fourth movement, *Adagietto*

CD 10/9
Anthology, No. 164

ALMA MAHLER: MUSICIAN AND MUSE

In the spring of 1902, Vienna was transfixed by news of the wedding engagement of Gustav Mahler—one of the city's most eligible bachelors—and the beautiful Alma Schindler (1879–1964; Fig. 60-2), daughter of a prominent family of Viennese artists. No one expected it to be a typical marriage. Mahler was known as impatient and domineering, Alma as creative, headstrong, and—nearly twenty years younger than her fiancé—evidently irresistible to men.

Schindler was also a talented musician. She was a good pianist, and when she met Mahler in 1901 she was a student in composition of **Alexander Zemlinsky**

FIGURE 60-2
Alma Schindler, before her marriages to three world-famous men: Gustav Mahler, Walter Gropius, and Franz Werfel.

(1871–1942). She composed primarily piano pieces and songs—a hundred of them, as she later claimed. After Mahler died in 1911, Alma married the architect Walter Gropius and, following their divorce, the novelist Franz Werfel. Most of her musical compositions were lost when she fled from Hitler on an odyssey that ultimately brought her in 1940 to the United States. She lived first in California, later in New York City, until her death in 1964.

Mahler made it a condition of their marriage that she give up composing. "The role of 'composer,' the 'worker's' role falls to me," he insisted, "yours is that of the loving companion and understanding partner."[6] Alma reluctantly complied, although in 1910 Mahler relented in his opposition to her creative work. He then encouraged Alma to return to her earlier compositions and to prepare some of the songs for publication, after both he and Alma had revised them. A total of fourteen of her songs were published between 1910 and 1924.

The song "Die stille Stadt" ("The Quiet City") was placed first in the 1910 publication, suggesting that it was a favorite of both Mahlers. The song reveals melodic and expressive warmth and a daring harmonic originality. The date of composition is unknown, but it was probably in 1900 or 1901, during Alma's period of study with Zemlinsky. The poet of "Die stille Stadt," Richard Dehmel (1863–1920), was admired by Zemlinsky, as he was by many other progressive German musicians of the day. The poem is romantic stuff. A narrator describes a town swallowed by a darkness and fog so dense as to strike fear in the hearts of its visitors. The anxiety is dispelled by the simple sound of a child singing, which is like a ray of light that cannot be dimmed.

The harmonic language of the song brings to it an element of strangeness that matches the disoriented feelings of the narrator as fog descends on the city. Tonic and dominant chords in the keys of D major and minor (the parallel modes are used interchangeably) appear at structural junctures in the song, like the tops of spires and bridges peeping up through the fog in Dehmel's poem. But, between these guideposts, the harmonic motions seem to get lost, arriving on chords that are distant from the harmonic road map, only then suddenly to regain a tonal point of orientation.

Such harmonic detours arise at the very opening of the song (Ex. 60-3). The short piano introduction begins on a tonic triad but by the second beat it has slipped into the fog of a diminished chord. Another try leads only to a greater disorientation, represented on beat four by an augmented-sixth chord (D♭-F-A♭-B♮) with no clear function in the home key. The tonic then suddenly reappears on the downbeat of measure 2, and, however briefly, we know where we are.

EXAMPLE 60-3

mm. 1-2

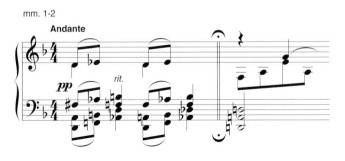

> ## LISTENING CUE
> ### ALMA MAHLER
> "Die stille Stadt" (c1901)
>
> CD 10/10
> Anthology, No. 165

SUMMARY

New music flourished in Vienna at the time Mahler lived there (1875–1880 as a student, and 1897–1907 as conductor and director of the Opera). His career was divided between conducting and composing, and in the latter capacity he wrote primarily songs and symphonies. For his early songs he drew upon folk poetry from the anthology *Des knaben Wunderhorn*, and later from the works of Friedrich Rückert. The song "Um Mitternacht" is an example of a song with literary emphasis: the music closely interprets the text, the song is accompanied by an orchestra of unusual makeup, and it is through composed and continually developmental.

Mahler wrote ten symphonies (the last one left incomplete) and a "song symphony" called *Das Lied von der Erde*. The first four were presented as autobiographical programmatic works, although these were later published as absolute music with the programmatic apparatus removed. His later symphonies are even more in the absolute vein. Symphony No. 5 is the first of the later group, and, although it shares much in style with the earlier symphonies, its relative brevity, moderate-sized orchestra, and musical virtuosity suggest a new phase in the composer's work. Its fourth movement, *Adagietto*, is celebrated for its melodiousness and spirit of detachment.

Mahler's wife, Alma, was a skillful composer in the late Romantic style of the turn of the twentieth century. She composed mainly songs, of which fourteen were published during her lifetime. Her "Die stille Stadt" is remarkable for its advanced harmonic thinking and intense expressivity.

KEY TERMS

Des knaben Wunderhorn   oboe d'amore   Alexander Zemlinsky

Chapter

England at the End of the Romantic Period: Elgar and Vaughan Williams

61

The great wealth and political might of England in the late nineteenth century supported a thriving musical culture. By 1901 the population of greater London had risen to an astounding 6.6 million residents, and these numbers, together with an affluence generated by industrialization and empire, created in the capital city a uniquely large demand for music. Music also flourished in smaller English cities, where orchestras, choir festivals, and amateur music making had grown in popularity throughout the nineteenth century.

Oddly, this demand for music was satisfied—as it had been for almost two hundred years—primarily by imported music and foreign composers. For reasons that are not at all clear, England after the time of Purcell did not, until the twentieth century, produce native composers who were widely recognized beyond their own land. In the eighteenth century, the leading "English" figures were German immigrants, including George Frideric Handel and John Christian Bach, and other foreigners such as the Rome-born pianist Muzio Clementi (1752–1832) were also leaders in English music.

European composers flocked to London throughout the nineteenth century to organize special concerts and to write works on commission. Carl Maria von Weber composed and conducted his last opera, *Oberon*, for Covent Garden, and Mendelssohn wrote his late oratorio *Elijah* for the Birmingham Festival in 1846. Clara Schumann performed in England no less than nineteen times. The elderly Franz Liszt came to London in 1886 for what proved a triumphant performance of his oratorio *The Legend of St. Elizabeth* at the Crystal Palace. During this stay he was invited to Windsor Castle to meet Queen Victoria, who was herself highly musical. "We asked him to play," she wrote in her diary, "which he did, several of his own compositions. He played beautifully."[1]

Although London held out the promise of financial gain for visiting composers, the complex entrepreneurship that existed in the city could easily cast visiting artists into financial disaster. This was the outcome of Richard Wagner's visit to London in 1877. Hoping to reduce the debt incurred in the first Bayreuth festival and aware of his great popularity in London, he arranged for a series of concerts at the huge Royal Albert Hall. Apparently unknown to Wagner, many of the seats were permanently leased to patrons who could attend any event without additional cost. Wagner's visit was an artistic success but a financial debacle.

The most successful of the native English composers of the late nineteenth century was **Arthur Sullivan** (1842–1900). Following training at the conservatory in Leipzig, he attracted attention in London for his serious choral and orchestral music. But he made his most lasting mark in the genre of **operetta,** a type of light opera that was well established in Paris and Vienna by mid-century. In 1871 he began to collaborate on comic works with the London writer **William Gilbert,** and in 1875 the team of Gilbert and Sullivan scored their first major success with the operetta *Trial by Jury*. Their collaboration endured until 1896, resulting in fourteen works including *H. M. S. Pinafore*, *The Pirates of Penzance*, *The Mikado*, and *The Yeomen of the Guard*.

❋ THE ENGLISH CHOIR FESTIVALS

Although known for his light music, Arthur Sullivan spent much of his career as a conductor and composer for **choir festivals.** Summer festivals that featured choral singing took place in Germany and elsewhere during the nineteenth century, but they had a special importance for English musical life. Often lasting for several days at a time, they brought together amateur choruses and church choirs from an entire region to perform choral classics and new works. Their popularity was advanced by the enduring demand throughout England to hear the choral music of Handel and by a longstanding tradition of amateur choral singing. By the end of the nineteenth century, the festivals had taken on their own character, with huge numbers of performers, long programs that mixed choral and symphonic music, and a gala atmosphere in which entire communities were brought together.

The most famous of these events in London was the **Handel Festival,** which took place every third year beginning in 1857. Similar occasions outside of London also had a great appeal. The Three Choirs Festival figures prominently in the careers of several leading English musicians, especially Edward Elgar. In its early history in the eighteenth century, it brought together the cathedral choirs from Gloucester, Worcester, and Hereford, rotating its location yearly among these three cities. By the mid nineteenth century, the Three Choirs Festival extended for six consecutive days, with participation by amateur choruses throughout the region accompanied by a professional festival orchestra.

The festivals also had importance for English society. The singers, from all walks of life, encountered music not as onlookers but participants in an activity whose importance reinforced a sense of national unity. A reporter at the Leeds Festival of 1898 commented on its galvanizing atmosphere:

> It was here that the crowds—for there was a crowd outside all three main entrances— gaped most, and stared and jostled and pushed in their energetic attempts to see the Festival from without. And in sooth it was a brave sight to see the gaily dressed ladies tripping from the steps of the broughams and up over the red-carpeted steps, with the gentlemen behind shouting directions to the Jehus and giving a final pat for the satisfactory adjustment of their white tie. . . . Hither and thither hurried people—greybeards, youths, elderly ladies, maidens—with 'scores' rolled under their arms.[2]

❀ EDWARD ELGAR

The choir festivals provoked a broad involvement of the English people in amateur music-making, and they finally contributed to the emergence of one of the great composers of the late Romantic period, Edward Elgar (1857–1934; Fig. 61-1). His early career is typical of such lesser nineteenth-century English musicians as Hubert Parry, Charles Stanford, and Alexander Mackenzie. He grew up in the town of Worcester and frequently attended concerts in London, which by train was four hours distant. His father ran a music shop, and he learned to play violin and keyboard instruments, although his knowledge of composition was entirely self-taught. Until well into his forties he made his living as a freelance violinist, church organist, and music teacher. His compositions did not attract attention far beyond his home town.

His musical career was then rooted in a regional culture whose main institutions were choir festivals, glee club performances, and amateur orchestras. His imagination as a creative musician ultimately could not be contained within this provincial milieu, and he looked beyond it for a musical language that could express more universal matters.

Elgar found in German music a model for his fully romantic spirit. Like many English musicians of the late nineteenth century, Elgar became a staunch Germanist. The cultural interchange between England and German lands had been strong

❀ FIGURE 61-1
Edward Elgar was the outstanding English composer of the late Romantic period.

since 1714, when the Elector of Hanover rose to the English throne as George I. Queen Victoria's mother was German-born, as was her husband, Prince Albert. Elgar was especially attracted to the new works of Brahms and Wagner, as well as to those of younger German progressivists such as Richard Strauss. In Brahms, Elgar noted the absence of a regionalism that was so pronounced in his own musical environment. Brahms's Symphony No. 3, he wrote, was "free from any provincialism or expression of national dialect (the charming characteristic of lesser men: Gade, Dvořák, Grieg)." Brahms, continued Elgar, "writes for the whole world and for all time—a giant—lofty and unapproachable." Wagner was equally esteemed. On his score of *Tristan und Isolde*, Elgar wrote: "The best and the whole of the best of this world and the next."

In the 1890s Elgar and his wife (who shared his admiration for German culture) traveled repeatedly to Munich and Bayreuth to hear Wagner. On one such pilgrimage they were joined by a family friend, Rosa Burley, who recalled the occasion in her memoirs:

> The *Ring* impressed me chiefly by its interminable length, and I was quite unable to understand the Genius's [Elgar's] enthusiasm. But *Tristan* was a shattering experience—Mrs. Elgar, always deeply affected by romantic music, was the most touched . . . but on all of us the heavily erotic melodies worked such a spell as to make sleep impossible for the whole night.[3]

Elgar primarily wrote for chorus and orchestra and for orchestra alone—the two types of music that could be most readily marketed to festivals in the England of his day. In the late 1890s, his music begin to attract attention in London, and finally in 1899 his Variations on an Original Theme (*Enigma*) brought him international celebrity. The work was followed by the oratorio *The Dream of Gerontius* (1900), and by a series of short orchestral compositions including the overtures *Cockaigne* (1901) and *In the South* (1904), and by five orchestral marches titled **Pomp and Circumstance** (see Box). In 1904 he was knighted by King Edward VII, making him "Sir Edward Elgar." The main successes of his later years were works for orchestra: two symphonies (1908 and 1911), and concertos for violin (1910) and cello (1919).

Variations on an Original Theme ("Enigma")

Sets of variations are not especially prominent in the nineteenth-century orchestral literature, although Brahms's *Variations on a Theme by Joseph Haydn* (1873) may have been a model for Elgar when he wrote his "Enigma" Variations, Op. 36, in 1898–1899. Both works proceed through a number of variations having strongly contrasting character and end in a climactic finale. Unlike Brahms's Variations, the "Enigma" Variations is an intensely programmatic composition in the late nineteenth-century German progressive manner. Like Mahler's early symphonies, it concerns the composer's own life in its outward and inward dimensions, although both Elgar and Mahler kept exact details of such programmatic meaning strictly out of sight.

The existence of Elgar's personalized program is hinted at in familiar ways—titles of movements, quotations from pre-existing music (from Mendelssohn's overture *Meeresstille und glückliche Fahrt* [*Calm Seas and Prosperous Journey*] in Variation 13), and the use of a melody in Variation 1 that was sung and played in the Elgar household.

But for public consumption, Elgar gave away only superficial ideas: "This work, commenced in a spirit of humour & continued in deep seriousness, contains

Pomp and Circumstance

There are some few compositions in the history of music that immediately please everyone and continue to do so indefinitely, seemingly impervious to passing time and changing taste. One such is the "Hallelujah" chorus from Handel's *Messiah*. Even though we have all heard it countless times, the "Hallelujah" chorus still brings us to our feet. We stand not just because of a tradition of doing so, but because this music is filled with so much electricity that we cannot stay in our seats. Audiences have always felt its power. After the first performance in Dublin, Ireland, in 1742, a reviewer wrote that *Messiah* "was allowed by the greatest Judges to be the finest composition of Musick that ever was heard."

Edward Elgar's *Pomp and Circumstance* contains another such timeless moment in music. In 1901 Elgar wrote two

short marches for orchestra, which he called *Pomp and Circumstance*, drawing the title from a line in Shakespeare's *Othello*. His jealousy aroused by Iago, Othello exclaims, "Farewell the tranquil mind! Farewell . . . pride, pomp, and circumstance of glorious war!"

Elgar knew all along that the melody in the trio of the first of the two marches was something special (its beginning is shown below). He had written about it to his publisher, "Gosh! Man I've got a tune in my head!" The early audiences of the march shared Elgar's enthusiasm. When March No. 1 was first performed at a Promenade concert in London in 1901, the conductor, Henry Wood, had to play it three times before the audience would let the concert continue.

It has never lost its inspiring power. Nowadays the *Pomp and Circumstance* March No. 1 and its famous trio are played at every American high school graduation, regally accompanying the entrance of the proud graduates and always bringing tears of joy to the eyes of their parents.

There is no possibility of explaining the longevity or the uniquely inspiring effect of this work on purely technical grounds. The melody seems simple and unremarkable as it

marches down the scale from G to A, accompanied by the simplest of chords. Its appeal may well be in its perfect balance of materials, which seem to achieve just the right mixture of things that are original with others that can be readily anticipated. There is neither too much complication nor simplicity, and a perfect marriage is formed in it between the expected and the unexpected.

sketches of the composer's friends. It may be understood that these personages comment or reflect on the original theme & each one attempts a solution of the Enigma, for so the theme is called."[4]

What is this "enigma" contained in the theme (its beginning is shown in Ex. 61-1)? On this question Elgar was more than a little evasive:

The Enigma I will not explain—its "dark saying" must be left unguessed, and I warn you that the apparent connexion between the Variations and the Theme is often of the slightest texture; further, through and over the whole set another and larger theme "goes", but is not played. . . . So the principal Theme never appears, even as in some late dramas—e.g., Maeterlinck's "L'Intruse" and "Les sept Princesses"—the chief character [Death] is never on the stage.[5]

EXAMPLE 61-1

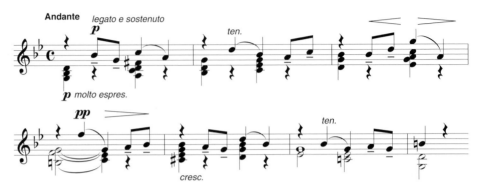

The work consists of a theme in G minor and major followed by fourteen variations, of which the last is marked "Finale." Each of the variations is headed by initials of (or other references to) the name of an acquaintance of the composer, the music being "what I think they w[oul]d have written, if they were asses enough to compose," as he told his publisher. The first variation, for example, refers to Elgar's wife, Alice, and the last one to Elgar himself.

The true nature of the central enigma and the identity of the unplayed "principal theme" have been infinitely debated, with no unanimous agreement about what Elgar might have meant. Some have held that the missing theme is a melody ("Auld Lang Syne" has been suggested) that could form a counterpoint with the actual theme, although many other solutions have also been proposed, involving music that ranges from Mozart's "Prague" Symphony to the **B-A-C-H motive** (B♭-A-C-B♮, the musical letters of Bach's name). Others believe that Elgar referred not to a musical theme but to a musical problem posed by the theme, which the variations then gradually resolve.

In purely musical terms, there is much about the theme that is complex and possibly enigmatic. Although it has a simple ternary form, it opens with phrases that are divided into breathless one-measure units (see Ex. 61-1). Its many leaps suggest that at least two melodic strands exist in it simultaneously, their notes touched alternately to form what is called a **compound melody.** The leaps of a descending-seventh in measures 3 and 4 are especially distinctive.

The centerpiece and longest section of the work is the ninth variation, which is often performed as a separate composition. It is subtitled "**Nimrod**," the name of the "mighty hunter" from the Book of Genesis. This is a reference to Elgar's friend and editor, August Johannes Jaeger (the German word *Jaeger* means "hunter"— Elgar was fond of puns). Elgar paints a highly sympathetic portrait of Jaeger in this variation. The rich sound of the orchestra comes from Elgar's skillful adaptation of the German style of orchestration, which aimed at a blended sound. When the full orchestra plays, the important primary and subsidiary lines are doubled, so as to mix elements from several of the orchestra's main choirs—strings, woodwinds, and brass. No one sonority is made to stand out, as it does in contemporaneous French and Russian orchestral works from the same period.

The Nimrod variation preserves the ternary form of the theme and clearly paraphrases its opening melodic shapes, including the distinctive downward leaps. But much is changed. The disjointed phrases of the theme are made continuous, and the minor mode that hung clouds over the theme has changed to major and revealed a blissfully blue sky. In these ways it may be that Nimrod has begun to solve Elgar's enigma.

LISTENING CUE

EDWARD ELGAR

"Enigma" Variations (1899)
Theme and ninth variation ("Nimrod")

CD 10/11–12
Anthology, No. 166

ENGLISH MUSIC AFTER ELGAR: RALPH VAUGHAN WILLIAMS

Following the turn of the twentieth century, Edward Elgar's unabashedly romantic music—bursting with emotion and plainly using the nineteenth-century language of Wagner—seemed to many audiences to be out of touch with broader developments in music of the day. It was not a musical style that could be unquestioningly accepted by younger English composers. Ralph Vaughan Williams (1872–1958; Fig. 61-2) continued some of the romantic traits of Elgar's music, especially its expressive melodiousness and emphasis on traditional orchestral and choral forms and genres. But, at the same time, Vaughan Williams looked for alternatives that could stamp his music as English rather than German, and a product of the twentieth century rather than the nineteenth.

Vaughan Williams grew up in London and received his musical education at the Royal College of Music and Cambridge University. His attention as a church organist and choir master was drawn to the hymnody of the Anglican Church, and in 1906 he helped to edit a new collection called the **English Hymnal**. Here he included some of his own hymns ("Hail Thee, Festival Day!," "Down Ampney," and "Sine Nomine"—Ex. 61-2—are especially well known). He also created hymns by joining folk songs to hymn texts and by reviving the music of numerous Renaissance musicians.

FIGURE 61-2
Vaughan Williams brought new ideas to the romantic style of Elgar.

EXAMPLE 61-2

As a composer, Vaughan Williams concentrated on symphonies—he wrote nine of these—and works for chorus. He also composed shorter orchestral pieces, such as the *Fantasia on a Theme by Thomas Tallis* (1910). It is based on a hymn that he included in the *English Hymnal,* "When Rising from the Bed of Death," the music from the English composer Thomas Tallis (1505–1585). Vaughan Williams had found Tallis's hymn in a collection of sixteenth-century psalm tunes, where it appears in Phrygian mode with a simple four-part harmonization (see Chapter 26). Its first phrase is shown in Example 61-3, as Vaughan Williams presents Tallis's piece in the *English Hymnal* with the melody in the soprano voice.

EXAMPLE 61-3

Vaughan Williams's interest in English folk song and early English polyphony suggests a new way of thinking about music that differs from the romantic outlook of Elgar and the great nineteenth-century German musicians like Brahms and Wagner. For these composers, music was a universal and timeless language, but Vaughan Williams's works suggest that it can just as well be rooted in a particular place. In his lecture-essay "Should Music Be National?" (1932), Vaughan Williams rejects the notion of music of the future and the cult of the genius, both central to Elgar's aesthetic. He would never have praised Brahms, as did Elgar, for being "for the whole world and for all time." Music, wrote Vaughan Williams, was primarily for the present time and for the composer's region, and only in this context could it project a healthy nationalism. The larger-than-life works of Wagner held little appeal to him.

SUMMARY

Music in England in the late nineteenth century was supplied largely by foreign composers, although the popular choir festivals created a demand for new music, and the operettas of Gilbert and Sullivan were universally admired. Edward Elgar adopted the musical language of German romantic composers, especially Wagner, although he used it in a highly original way in his orchestral and choral works. His first international success was with his so-called "Enigma" Variations for orchestra, in which one striking variation is subtitled "Nimrod," named after the hunter in Genesis. The revival in English music begun by Elgar was continued by his younger contemporaries, including Ralph Vaughan Williams. In his use and imitation of English folk song and Renaissance melodies, Vaughan Williams partly turned away from Elgar's Germanic romanticism and developed a harmonic language based on the old church modes.

KEY TERMS

Arthur Sullivan	Handel Festival	"Nimrod"
operetta	*Pomp and Circumstance*	*English Hymnal*
William Gilbert	B-A-C-H motive	
choir festival	compound melody	

Opera in Milan after Verdi: Puccini, Toscanini, and *Verismo*

When Verdi's *Otello* received its triumphant premiere at the Teatro alla Scala in Milan in 1887, the city's musical and operatic culture was well on its way to becoming fully modernized and cosmopolitan. How different this was from the situation at La Scala when Verdi's first opera, *Oberto*, was heard there in 1839. The enterprise of opera at La Scala was then almost entirely in the hands of its impresario, Bartolomeo Merelli, and the works in any one season rotated among recent compositions that Merelli commissioned or rented. A successful opera was repeated until the audience for it dwindled, whereupon the composer or his publisher tried to market it to other cities. A notable success by a well-known figure such as a Vincenzo Bellini or Gaetano Donizetti could be revived for as many years as there was a demand for it, but it was thought inevitable that even the most admired opera would fade into oblivion after a few years.

THE OPERA BUSINESS

The economic viability of opera early in the nineteenth century depended on the creation of new works, and the **impresario** was their catalyst. He offered contracts to promising composers, placed them in touch with librettists whom he also hired, and worked closely with a publisher to promote the sale or rental of works to other houses, for which he normally received a commission. The operas performed at La Scala in the 1830s were almost entirely by living Italian composers, as older works seemed woefully outdated and compositions by foreigners were looked on with a good deal of skepticism.

By 1887 the opera business in Italy had changed. The role of the impresario had been taken over by publishing houses, which coordinated the creation and marketing of new works. Verdi's publisher was the powerful Milan firm of **Ricordi,** whose representatives worked directly with the composer—as they did later with Giacomo Puccini—to promote the creation of new works. Verdi's *Otello* (see Chapter 56) came into being largely through Ricordi's urging, and such a major operatic success was no longer merely a local phenomenon but a worldwide event.

The practice of operatic performance by 1887 was also on its way to modern standards. The challenging orchestra part of *Otello*, for example, was played by La Scala's large and excellent orchestra, led by the well-known conductor Franco Faccio. This was a far cry from the first performance of *Oberto*, which had been directed—as was the custom in the 1830s—only by the orchestra's first violinist, with the composer at his side.

The deportment of the opera audience had also changed. In the 1830s the atmosphere at an opera was almost like a sports event in the present day: people cheered, booed, and hurled sarcastic remarks. The booing could bring a performance to an early end if the crowd didn't like what it heard. The audience especially guarded its right to demand an immediate repetition of an enjoyable part of an opera, even though this practice was certain to obscure the coherence of the work as a whole. The performance of encores was finally ended at La Scala only in the 1906–1907 season, when it was officially banned by the management.

The Claque

One of the oddities of nineteenth-century operatic culture was the claque. This was a group of professional applauders (*claquer* is the French word for clapping). They were hired, usually by the opera management, to attend opera performances and to applaud on cue. The effect of their work was just like having canned laughter in a TV comedy.

The claque was most valuable at the premiere of a new opera. In a large theater at such an event, the claque could number more than one hundred clappers, all well-rehearsed and coordinated. Their work was highly prized by composers and performers since they could create enthusiasm, underscore a high point in an unknown work, and guide those in the audience as to when applause was needed and when not.

The institution of the claque reached its heights at the Paris Opéra in the 1830s. Its leader was known simply as Auguste, and his power to make a success or failure out of a new opera was legendary. He had no hesitation to tell a composer what needed to be changed, and he was not inclined to waste his efforts on a work he didn't like. Hector Berlioz recalled Auguste's response to a minor composer who had asked for his support: "I can't do it, sir. It would compromise me in the eyes of the public, of the artists, and of my colleagues. I have my reputation to maintain; . . I cannot allow myself to be hissed."

✹ INNOVATIONS AT LA SCALA

The modernization of operatic culture at La Scala in the 1880s was most evident in the expansion of its repertory to include works by leading foreign composers (always given in Italian translation) and a new readiness to restage classic works from the past. The number of operas and performances in a season was much reduced in comparison to 1839. In that year's playbill, seventeen operas were given no fewer than 221 performances. In 1887, only five operas were in the repertory, and these received a total of sixty-two presentations. Classics of the past were now amply represented: Donizetti—by far the most popular opera composer at La Scala in 1839—was still in the repertory in 1887 with his *Lucrezia Borgia*, which was composed over a half-century earlier. The Milanese audiences long had a taste for French opera (Jules Massenet and Charles Gounod were especially well-liked), and in the 1880s Wagner's works were poised to take the city by storm. In 1889 *Lohengrin* (by "Riccardo Wagner") had seventeen performances, and in the 1890s his works had become staples of the city's operatic diet. Many of Milan's leading younger composers—including Giacomo Puccini and Pietro Mascagni—declared themselves to be Wagnerians.

✹ ARTURO TOSCANINI

The internationalization of La Scala was advanced by the appointment in 1898 of **Arturo Toscanini** (1867–1957) as artistic director and principal conductor. Toscanini began his career as a cellist. He had played in the La Scala orchestra at the premiere of *Otello* in 1887, and even then he was considered one of Italy's rising young conductors. He had many of the same qualities that made Gustav Mahler a controversial success in Vienna: excellent musicianship, high standards, and the willpower to impose a unified artistic conception on a large and often contentious group of musicians.

At La Scala, Toscanini insisted on the highest level of technical excellence from the orchestra and singers, and he also demanded respect from the audience, not just for the singing but for the work as a whole. His career led him increasingly away from Milan to other cities of the world, although he periodically returned to La Scala for important events. One of the most poignant of these followed the death in 1924 of his friend Puccini. At the funeral in Milan's great Duomo (cathedral), Toscanini conducted Puccini's music with La Scala's orchestra. Two years later he led the premier performance of Puccini's last opera, *Turandot*, whose ending the composer did not live to complete. Instead of using Franco Alfano's reconstruction of Puccini's sketches for these concluding minutes, Toscanini ended it with the last measures that Puccini himself had composed—Liù's funeral music—whereupon he turned to the audience to state movingly that the composer had died at that point.

What primarily separated Toscanini from other Italian conductors of the day was his breadth of repertory. He was equally at home with the symphonic literature as with opera, and he was also open to complex modern music. In addition to his great understanding of the works of Verdi and Puccini, Toscanini also specialized in the operas of Wagner. He inaugurated his tenure as music director in Turin in 1895 by conducting Wagner's *Götterdämmerung* and at La Scala with *Die Meistersinger*. In 1930 he was the first non-German to conduct at Bayreuth.

He crossed paths with Gustav Mahler only briefly, in New York in 1909 and 1910, when both were on the staff of the Metropolitan Opera, both competing for the Wagnerian repertory. Just as in Milan and Turin, he wished first to conduct Wagner at the Met, but to his credit he stepped aside when Mahler protested that this would conflict with his own native specialty.

PUCCINI AT LA SCALA

Like Verdi before him, Giacomo Puccini (1858–1924) was closely associated with the city of Milan and its Teatro alla Scala (Fig. 62-1). He attended the Conservatory in Milan from 1880 to 1883, during which time he composed his earliest opera, *Le villi*. His first real success came in 1893 with *Manon Lescaut*, in which he took up a literary source already used by Jules Massenet in the 1884 French opera *Manon*. More operatic successes followed: *La Bohème* (1896), *Tosca* (1900), *Madama Butterfly* (1904), *La fanciulla del West* (1910, based on the American play *Girl of the Golden West*) and *Turandot* (1924). Like Wagner and Verdi before him, Puccini specialized strictly in operatic composition. After his student days, he wrote no large-scale works of any other type. He explained in a letter to his librettist Giuseppe Adami: "The Almighty touched me with his little finger and said, 'Write for the theater— only for the theater!' And I have obeyed the supreme command."

Madama Butterfly received a stormy premiere at La Scala in February 1904, after which it underwent a series of extensive revisions. It is based on the play *Madame Butterfly* by the American writer David Belasco and on a short story of the same title by John Luther

🌿 FIGURE 62-1

Puccini and Arturo Toscanini in Paris, where they planned the Metropolitan Opera premiere of *La fanciulla del West*.

Photo courtesy of *Opera News*

Synopsis of *Madama Butterfly*

On a hill overlooking Nagasaki harbor, the marriage broker, Goro, shows a house to the American naval officer Benjamin Franklin Pinkerton. He is to be married to the Japanese girl Cho-Cho-San (called "Butterfly"). In Pinkerton's aria "Dovunque al mondo," he explains that he travels the world sampling the best of local delights, leaving them all quickly behind. The American consul, Sharpless, disapproves of this philosophy. Butterfly arrives with her large family, and just as the marriage ceremony is concluded her uncle, the Bonze, bursts in to chastise Butterfly for marrying outside of her culture and religion. Left alone, Pinkerton and Butterfly profess their love.

When Act 2 opens, three years have passed with no word from Pinkerton, who has left Butterfly and her servant, Suzuki, behind. Butterfly is confident that he will return as he promised, when the robins return to their nests. Sharp-less and Goro arrive to try to arrange another marriage for Butterfly, to a Japanese-American businessman named Yamadori, but she will hear none of it. Butterfly shows Sharpless the son born after Pinkerton's departure. At last, Pinkerton's ship is seen entering the harbor, and Butterfly elatedly dresses in her wedding gown to greet Pinkerton upon his return.

Act 3 begins at dawn. Pinkerton has still not arrived and Butterfly has fallen asleep. Sharpless, Pinkerton, and his American wife, Kate, quietly enter. Filled with shame and sorrow, Pinkerton leaves Sharpless and Kate to try to convince Butterfly to allow the child to be brought up in America. She agrees, provided that Pinkerton makes the request in person. Behind a screen she stabs herself to death as Pinkerton rushes in. "Butterfly! Butterfly!" he cries.

Long, which was also Belasco's source. As usual in a new opera by Puccini, the libretto was created by multiple hands, including Puccini's own and those of his publisher, Giulio Ricordi. An outline was first made by Luigi Illica, and the poetic text itself was written by Giuseppe Giacosa, both writers working for Ricordi.

The literary sources provided only a shell of what eventually became the musical text (see Box). The librettists freely added episodes and characters, and they had no hesitation to change the entire tone of the work. The first act of the libretto, for example, was created almost entirely by Illica and Giacosa. It has no counterpart in Belasco's play (although some of its episodes are outlined in Long's story). The character of Butterfly is flattened into a one-dimensional type that is far removed from Belasco's character. In the play she is a primitive and almost clownish figure; in the opera, a sensitive victim of exploitation who, typical of Puccini's heroines, sacrifices everything for love.

Puccini's music contains a mixture of styles: the Verdian reliance on emotional expression through vocal melody is still the central element, although the voices also sing for long stretches in a more conversational mode. Puccini—always interested in the new harmonic resources of his day—gives the score pungency by whole-tone and pentatonic passages, the latter reinforcing the Japanese setting. (Puccini also quotes several authentic Japanese folk songs.)

The structure of the opera represents an updating that shows the composer's effort to make opera plausible as drama as well as music. To do this he merges traditional principles of Italian opera with the newer thinking of modern French and German composers. The acts contain numerous operatic numbers—arias, duets, ensembles, and choruses—each of which has a reasonably closed or symmetrical form. These numbers are floated into a more continuous music sung by ensembles with changing numbers of characters. Here the singing is declamatory, and these ensembles fulfill a narrative function provided in earlier opera by recitative.

Puccini's new structural synthesis is apparent at the beginning of Act 1. The work begins without an overture in a narrative ensemble in which the number of characters steadily increases. It begins with Goro and Pinkerton, who are soon joined by Butterfly's servants including Suzuki, then by Sharpless. At each arrival of a new character and at each change of topic, a new section of music begins, usually with a new tempo, key, and melody. The singing has the character of a melodious declamation, musically midway between aria and recitative.

Puccini is plainly interested in promoting continuity throughout these conversational ensembles by bringing back themes and motives at points far distant from one another. For example, the opera opens with the theme shown in Example 62-1, which is first presented in the orchestra as the subject of a four-part fugue. The figure returns frequently throughout the first act, serving to bind the music together.

EXAMPLE 62-1

Puccini also uses a more subtle principle of motivic recurrence that links together several themes on the basis of a common melodic profile. Three of the most important themes heard near the beginning of the opera (Ex. 62-2) are associated in this way. Their affinity comes from their sharing an ascending major triad (bracketed in the example). The second one quotes the opening of the American national anthem, which frames Pinkerton's aria "Dovunque al mondo" (discussed below). The other melodies are sung by Pinkerton and Sharpless, the two principal American characters, Puccini's apparent objective being to give these related figures related melodic material. But the composer does not go so far as to make themes into Wagnerian leitmotives; he does not use them so pervasively or with such clear symbolism as does Wagner.

EXAMPLE 62-2

The opening narrative ensemble is interrupted by the first traditional operatic number, Pinkerton's aria "Dovunque al mondo" ("Wherever in the World"). Typical of the traditional Italian opera, the text is reflective rather than narrative. Here Pinkerton declares his philosophy of life—to travel the world seeking pleasure with no concern about its consequences.

The aria has a symmetrical form: it is framed by the quotations of the American national anthem and it has two stanzas which begin with essentially the same music. Puccini also looks for ways to bring dramatic action even into a self-contained aria. Within the number, Pinkerton continues his conversation with Sharpless. Both of Pinkerton's stanzas lead into recitational music in which Sharpless interrupts to disapprove of Pinkerton's philosophy of life. They cannot resolve their argument, and the music finally breaks off in the middle of a harmonic progression, far from having reached its completion in the home key of G♭ major. Pinkerton then finds an idea on which they can agree: "America forever!" he sings in English. With this the music returns to the tonic chord, Sharpless concurs by singing the same line, and the aria ends.

LISTENING CUE

GIACOMO PUCCINI	CD 10/13
Madama Butterfly (1904)	Anthology, No. 167
Aria "Dovunque al mondo"	

❀ VERISMO OPERA

In the 1890s Milan was also prominent in the origin of a new type of Italian opera, called **verismo** (realism). Such operas are short and musically condensed, usually spanning only a single act, and they are typically set among people from the lower social classes who are driven by uncontrollable passions to acts of violence. Musically, the *verismo* opera has a small cast that is dominated by a soprano and tenor. The action moves quickly to its climax, dispensing with all character portraits and subsidiary plots. The traditional operatic numbers are still present, but they are so abbreviated as to appear blended together into a continuous action.

Verismo opera was a response by Italian composers to an ever-growing competition from abroad. Wagner's operas had begun to attract attention in Italy, and French operas were increasingly popular. Georges Bizet's immensely influential French opera *Carmen* (1875) offered the Italians a model for the new direction that led to *verismo*. In Bizet's fast-moving work, the character Don José is driven by love and jealousy to murder his beloved Carmen after seeing her with the dashing bullfighter, Escamillo.

The first *verismo* opera was *Cavalleria rusticana* (*Rustic Chivalry*, 1890) by **Pietro Mascagni** (1863–1945), who was briefly a roommate of Puccini while both were students at the Milan Conservatory. This and other works of a related type were especially in vogue at La Scala in the 1890s, where *Cavalleria rusticana* had twenty-three performances in its first season (1891), more than either Verdi's *Otello* or *Falstaff* in their first seasons.

Cavalleria rusticana is based on a short story and related play by Giovanni Verga (1840–1922). Turiddu returns to his home in Sicily after military service to find his old girlfriend, Lola, married to the working man Alfio. Turiddu takes up with the peasant girl Santuzza, whom he shortly jilts to renew his affair with Lola. He then demands that Alfio fight him to the death, observing a Sicilian custom of biting Alfio's ear as part of the challenge. Word shortly arrives from offstage that Turridu has been killed by his opponent.

Although it is difficult to see much realism in this contrived story, it has an echo in literature of the nineteenth century that focuses objectively on the lives of people from lower social strata. This trend is seen preliminarily in novels such as Charles Dickens's *Oliver Twist* (1837–1838), and later in the century in works of the French writers Gustave Flaubert (1821–1880) and Emile Zola (1840–1902).

In its new formula for opera texts, *verismo* was quickly imitated, as in **Ruggero Leoncavallo**'s *Pagliacci* (*Clowns*, 1892), and it is plain to see in Puccini's later operas, including *Tosca* and *Il tabarro* (*The Cloak*, 1918). Today, *Cavalleria rusticana* and *Pagliacci* are almost always performed back-to-back (opera goers fondly call them "Cav and Pag").

SUMMARY

Italy's most prominent opera house in the late nineteenth century was the Teatro alla Scala in Milan. By the 1880s its repertory had been modernized to consist not only of the newest works of Italian composers but also old favorites and classics, including those of non-Italian origin. A high level of musicianship was achieved by the theater under the leadership of Arturo Toscanini.

The most successful Italian composer of opera in the generation after Verdi was Giacomo Puccini. His *Madama Butterfly* (1904) continues aspects of the older Italian number opera, and Puccini also mixes in modern elements that promote a greater musical continuity and dramatic plausibility. These new features include the use of narrative ensembles to tell the story and to connect the arias, duets, and choruses. Puccini also brings back certain themes outside of the confines of a single number and creates families of related themes to suggest related groups of characters in the libretto.

In the 1890s a new type of opera called *verismo* (realism) emerged in Italy, as a response to competition from such foreign composers as Richard Wagner and Georges Bizet. In *verismo* opera, characters from low social strata are beset by elemental passions that drive them to acts of violence. The first important work of the type was Pietro Mascagni's *Cavalleria rusticana*, and other examples of the idiom were composed by Puccini and Ruggero Leoncavallo.

KEY TERMS

| impresario | Arturo Toscanini | Pietro Mascagni |
| Ricordi | *verismo* | Ruggero Leoncavallo |

Paris in the *Belle Époque:* Debussy, Fauré, and Lili Boulanger

The years straddling the turn of the twentieth century in France are often termed the *Belle époque,* the "beautiful era." The term points to a reigning mood that was at once carefree, high-spirited, and optimistic, all the outcome of a relatively good economy, peace, and satisfaction with a progressive government that had been installed in the 1870s, following France's humiliating defeat by the armies of Prussia. The spirit of the period demanded entertainment and diversion, which were sure to stimulate the arts. Popular culture—cabaret, circus, café-concert, and early cinema—was especially in vogue, and the high arts of literature, painting, and music advanced and prospered.

Music flourished in the Paris of 1900. The Opéra, installed since 1875 in the magnificent Palais Garnier (named for its architect, Charles Garnier), brought the operas of Wagner to an appreciative French audience. Native opera composers largely took their new works to the nearby Opéra-Comique, where Gustave Charpentier's *Louise* premiered in 1900 and Claude Debussy's *Pelléas et Mélisande* in 1902. The operettas of Edmond Audran (1840–1901) and André Messager (1853–1929) increased the great popularity of the genre that had been established in Paris in the 1850s by Jacques Offenbach (1819–1880). There were two major series of orchestral concerts, the Concerts Lamoureux and Concerts Colonne, both named after a founding conductor. New music was supported by the Société Nationale de Musique (National Society of Music), in whose concerts works by Claude Debussy and Maurice Ravel were frequently heard, and wealthy patrons of music, such as the Princesse Edmond de Polignac (an American by birth), sponsored private concerts.

This positive and vibrant atmosphere stimulated the formation of new ideas, which arrived in profusion as younger artists looked for a distinctive tone and method in their work that would be relevant to their own period. Artists in different fields were often closely in touch, egging each other on toward new thinking and new ways in which their disciplines could be brought closer together.

✿ NEW POETRY

The poetry of **Paul Verlaine** (1844–1896) will illustrate this striving for a new tone in French literature of the late nineteenth century and the close affinity that arose between poetry and music. Verlaine's life was disordered and tempestuous, but these qualities are not especially notable in his poetic oeuvre, which is delicate in the extreme. His early style is apparent in the poetic collection *Fêtes galantes* (*Elegant Parties*), which was published in 1869 and later drawn on by Debussy and Gabriel Fauré for song texts. It consists of seventeen short poems that depict fleeting scenes and fragile memories: a momentary conversation between lovers, a comic instant among the clowns at the Comédie-Italienne, a portrait of a silly cleric, an ambiguous dialogue between lovers at the seashore.

The title of the collection gives us a clue to the context in which these fragments arise. A ***fête galante*** was a popular social occasion among the aristocracy of the eighteenth century. In the summer months the courtiers of the day—with precious language, stilted manners, and the finest of dress—met out of doors to converse, flirt, and make music. Such occasions were favorite themes for painters of the eighteenth century, especially for Antoine Watteau (1684–1721), as in his *La gamme d'amour* (*The Scale of Love*; Fig. 63-1). Verlaine's poems resemble the imaginary conversations overheard at such occasions—laden with artifice, but human and emotional beneath a thick layer of masks.

An especially delicate and musical poem from *Fêtes galantes* is "En sourdine" ("Muted"), which was used by Claude Debussy in a song of the same title, to be discussed momentarily. (The

✿ FIGURE 63-1

Antoine Watteau, *The Scale of Love*, 1717. Watteau depicts a scene from a *fête galante* in which the figures, distracted by love, have momentarily forgotten their music.

Bridgeman Art Library

text and its translation are given in full in the Anthology.) The speaker of the poem records a succession of minute and transitory feelings—sensations from the light sifting through the trees and a breeze rustling in the grass, as well as the emotions of love and despair. He is impassive and wishes not to act but to relish the moment, with its network of diverse sensations. Although the structure of the poem is reasonably strict and regular, Verlaine chooses words and creates a syntax that stretch the French language and enrich its sonority.

A comparison with Friedrich Rückert's "Um Mitternacht" (see Chapter 60) points up other distinctive features of Verlaine's poetry. Rückert's narrator speaks from the depths of an anguished soul. He actively searches for calm, and his thoughts have a certain bombast, as when he declares that he has fought the battle of all mankind. Verlaine's poetic imagination is entirely different: his narrator's words are understated, focused on minutiae, and the narrator remains entirely passive, engaged only in the present moment. His inner self is never apparent. These differences between German assertiveness and French refinement are also apparent in the music of these countries at the end of the Romantic period.

✤ IMPRESSIONISM IN PAINTING

Many of the qualities of Verlaine's poetry—its evocation of mood and atmosphere, understatement, passivity, and appeal to the senses—also characterize a new style of painting practiced by a group of French artists of the 1870s and 1880s. The works of these painters—Claude Monet, Auguste Renoir, Camille Pissarro, Edgar Degas, Alfred Sisley among others—were controversial in their day. Their style was dubbed **impressionism** by critics, since it seemed to record mere impressions gained from observing nature rather than advancing the more accepted academic principles and subjects of painting. But, by the turn of the century, impressionism was widely embraced, and in the present such works are among the most celebrated paintings in the entire world of art.

The works of **Claude Monet** are quintessential impressionist paintings. An example is his *Wild Poppies* (1873; Fig. 63-2). The artist depicts a beautiful though unpretentious scene from nature. Like the narrator in Verlaine's "En sourdine," he impassively records what he sees by seeming to float slightly above the landscape. Although the beauty of nature is his main subject, Monet also includes two women with children, who are shown at a distance happily integrated into their natural surroundings. The viewer's eye is drawn to the brilliant red poppies, which are represented with a certain abstraction as flecks of paint that stand out as though electrified by sunlight. A sense of motion is created in the large band of sky, in which clouds seem to sweep toward the viewer. In all, the painting creates a powerful mood of serenity and nostalgia.

✤ NEW REALITIES: CLAUDE DEBUSSY

Claude Debussy (1862–1918), the greatest musician of the *Belle époque*, was flattered to be compared to the leading impressionist

✿ FIGURE 63-2
Claude Monet, *Wild Poppies*, 1873. Monet's landscapes embody the essence of impressionism in their closeness to nature, mood of happy nostalgia, and vision of a world brought alive by sunlight and color.

Bridgeman Art Library

painters. "You do me a great honor by calling me a pupil of Claude Monet," he told his friend Emile Vuillermoz.[1] Despite the obvious differences between painting and music, there is much that connects his works with impressionist painting: understatement, subtlety, a love of the beauty and freedom of nature, a preference for primary orchestral colors, a sense of free motion, and an originality that bypasses academic formulas. But Debussy, like all great composers, did not wish to have his music reduced to an *-ism*. To his publisher Jacques Durand he complained: "I'm trying to write 'something else'—*realities* in a manner of speaking—what imbeciles call 'impressionism,' a term employed with the utmost inaccuracy."[2]

Debussy spent virtually his entire life in Paris. He entered the Paris Conservatory in 1872, at the tender age of ten, and proved brilliantly talented though implacably rebellious in all areas of his study. For a long time he remained obscure as a composer and made his living by giving lessons, writing reviews, and receiving patronage from several wealthy supporters. His existence, rather like that of Schubert earlier in Vienna, was bohemian and fully devoted to art. He achieved general recognition as a composer only in 1902 with the premiere of his opera *Pelléas et Mélisande*, and even after this he was hounded by debt, failing health, and personal crises. He died from cancer in 1918, at the age of only fifty-five.

Debussy's music was written in the leading genres of the late Romantic period, primarily song, character piece for piano, and the symphonic poem for orchestra. He aspired to write dramatic music but was able to complete only one opera (*Pelléas et Mélisande*) and one ballet (*Jeux*). There is also an early string quartet and three late sonatas (for cello and piano; violin and piano; and flute, viola, and harp).

Debussy's song setting of Verlaine's "En sourdine" reveals a tone that he shared with modern French writers and painters, as well as a far-reaching musical originality. Although this is an early work, composed in 1891, Debussy's principal innovations are already apparent. One of the most important of these is a harmonic language that leaves the sense of key in an ambiguous state. Only in the final four measures of the song is a central tonality, B major, firmly established by the appearance of dominant and tonic chords, and even there the tonic triad is decorated by its major sixth, G♯.

We can see Debussy's ambiguity with functional harmony by looking at the chords in the opening phrase of the song in measures 1–10 (these are shown in a condensed form in Ex. 63-1). The chords themselves are certainly familiar, consisting of several different triads, a half-diminished seventh chord (E♯-G♯-B-D♯), and, near the end, a dominant seventh on the root tone C♯. But the progression into which these chords is placed defines no key concretely. There is no strong motion toward an apparent tonic or dominant chord, and the progression is not framed by harmonies that plainly refer to a tonic.

EXAMPLE 63-1

The harmonic freedom in Debussy's songs may have been inspired by the music of Modest Mussorgsky (recall Mussorgsky's song "Within Four Walls" from Chapter 59). Debussy had high praise for Mussorgsky's music: "Nobody has spoken to that which is best in us with such tenderness and depth," he said.[3]

Debussy's harmonic innovations were of great interest to his contemporaries. "His harmonies, without constructive meaning, often served the coloristic purpose

Debussy on Music and Nature

Between 1901 and 1915 Debussy regularly wrote reviews and opinionated essays for leading Paris journals. For the *Revue musicale* in 1913 he contributed a short speculation on the prospects for music. Here he touched upon two of his favorite themes: the relation of music to nature, and the need for music to be free from laborious complication:

> . . . Music is the art that is in fact the closest to Nature, although it is also the one that contains the most subtle pitfalls. Despite their claims to be true representationalists, the painters and sculptors can only present us with the beauty of the universe in their own free, somewhat fragmentary interpretation. They can capture only one of its aspects at a time, preserve only one moment. It is the musicians alone who have the privilege of being able to convey all the poetry of night and day, or earth and sky. Only they can re-create Nature's atmosphere and give rhythm to her heaving breast. . .

> Let us purify music! Let us try to relieve its congestion, to find a less cluttered kind of music. And let us be careful that we do not stifle all feeling beneath a mass of superimposed designs and motives: how can we hope to preserve our finesse, our spirit, if we insist on being preoccupied with so many details of composition? We are attempting the impossible in trying to organize a braying pack of tiny themes, all pushing and jostling each other for the sake of a bite out of the poor old sentiment! If they are not careful the sentiment will depart altogether, in an attempt to save its skin. As a general rule, every time someone tries to complicate an art form or a sentiment, it is simply because they are unsure of what they want to say. . . .[4]

of expressing moods and pictures," wrote Arnold Schoenberg. "In this way, tonality was already dethroned in practice, if not in theory."[5] Schoenberg interpreted the function of Debussy's chords for their capacity, not to define a key, but to create colors. The chords, Schoenberg suggests, make attractive sounds and promote the calm and quiet mood established by the poem.

Debussy's innovative harmonic practice is only one of several ways in which the subtlety and understatement of Verlaine's poetry is communicated. Debussy makes sure that the text is always clearly heard, and the listener is never distracted from it by any elaborate vocal melody. Word paintings are also frequently brought in. The rhythm has a freedom from regular beat and rigid meter, just like the free movements of nature mentioned in the poem.

LISTENING CUE

CLAUDE DEBUSSY
Fêtes galantes I (1891)
"En sourdine"

CD 10/14
Anthology, No. 168

HARMONIC CHEMISTRY IN DEBUSSY'S PIANO MUSIC

Debussy's music for piano consists of some eighty character pieces, which include twelve études, twenty-four preludes, and other works gathered into brief programmatic cycles. His treatment of the instrument continues the line established by Chopin in its exploitation of highly animated motions and bright sonorities, a flamboyant use of arpeggiated arabesques, and the exploration of new harmonies. As a composer of the character piece, Debussy extends the ideas of Schumann by finding ways to create the most diverse and vivid images in the least space.

Debussy's "Reflets dans l'eau" ("Reflections in the Water," 1905) paints an ingenious musical portrait of rippling water, often the subject of the paintings of Monet. To achieve his picturesque objectives, Debussy suppresses the melodic element, which at the beginning is reduced to an isolated three-note figure, A♭-F-E♭ (Ex. 63-2, left hand), and melody per se is replaced by arabesques that splash freely into the bright, high register of the instrument.

EXAMPLE 63-2

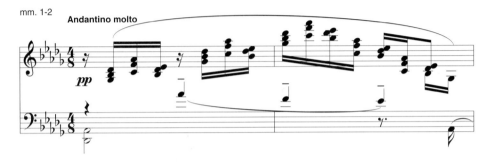

The work is also notable for its harmonic innovations: Debussy told his publisher, Durand, that it contained "the most recent discoveries of harmonic chemistry."[6] One of these "discoveries," which Debussy uses as a means of contrast, is to select tones from a **whole-tone scale** rather than a diatonic scale. This is apparent especially in the middle of the piece, as in the passage shown in Example 63-3. In these measures, all of the tones are drawn from the whole-tone scale B C♯ D♯ F G A, omitting only D♯. The whole tones make the passage stand apart strikingly from its surrounding sections, which are largely diatonic.

EXAMPLE 63-3

Another innovation is the embellishment of triads and seventh chords with a tone a major sixth above the bass or root of the chord. This was a means of harmonic enrichment that in the 1920s was imitated by American popular composers, including Duke Ellington and George Gershwin.

LISTENING CUE

CLAUDE DEBUSSY
Images I (1905)
"Reflets dans l'eau"

CD 10/15
Anthology, No. 169

DEBUSSY'S ORCHESTRAL MUSIC

A culture for orchestral music flourished in Paris during the *Belle époque*, and the medium attracted all of the leading composers of the day. Most of the prominent Parisian musicians—Camille Saint-Saëns, Ernest Chausson, Paul Dukas, and Vincent d'Indy—wrote symphonies of large proportion, but the inflated scope and necessity for development made the genre unattractive to Debussy after his earliest years. He explained his distaste for developmental forms as a constraint upon his artistic freedom:

> Explorations previously made in the realm of pure music had led me toward a hatred of classical development, whose beauty is solely technical and can interest only the mandarins in our profession. I wanted music to have freedom, that is perhaps more inherent in it than in any other art, for music is not limited to a more or less exact representation of nature, but rather to the mysterious affinity between Nature and the Imagination.[7]

Accordingly, Debussy turned not to the symphony but to the more intimate proportions of the symphonic poem and orchestral character piece. His principal works of this type include the Prelude to *The Afternoon of a Faun* (based on a poem by Stéphane Mallarmé), the cycles *Nocturnes* and *Images*, and the powerful *La mer*, which consists of three symphonic portraits of the sea.

Three short and strongly contrasting pieces—"Nuages" ("Clouds"), "Fêtes" ("Festivals"), and "Sirènes" ("Sirens")—make up *Nocturnes*. The first of them, "Nuages," is strongly evocative and pictorial, and it employs harmonic devices that are far in advance of its time. When it was first performed in 1900 at the Concerts Lamoureux, Debussy tried to explain its immense originality by using ordinary visual analogies. The work, he wrote, "renders the immutable aspect of the sky and the slow solemn motion of clouds, fading away in gray tones lightly tinged with white."[8] But this description scarcely does justice to a work of such profound expressivity and novel structure.

Several of the stylistic features encountered in "En sourdine" and "Reflets dans l'eau" are again apparent in "Nuages": like the song, this piece has a symmetrical **A B A'** form in which normal development is replaced by a more static repetition of short phrases. An emphasis here on ostinato and repetition seems intended to dispel any sense of forward motion or, as Debussy explained it, to portray "the immutable aspect of the sky." As in the piano piece, there is a dim reference to a centric triad (here B minor), but otherwise virtually no functional harmonic progressions.

We saw in "Reflets dans l'eau" the alternation of diatonic passages with others whose tones are drawn from a whole-tone scale. In "Nuages" Debussy continues such experiments by using the octatonic scale and pentatonic scale in addition to the more familiar major and minor. The so-called **octatonic scale,** which consists of an alternation of whole and half steps, had been used frequently by Russian composers of the nineteenth century. In this work by Debussy it appears most prominently in the haunting melody given to the English horn (Ex. 63-4). The **pentatonic scale**, a feature of traditional Asian music, duplicates the intervals of the black keys on the piano, and it underlies the tones of the work's subsidiary melody (Ex. 63-5).

EXAMPLE 63-4

It is perhaps the timbre of Debussy's orchestral music that most remains with the listener. Debussy writes for an orchestra of normal constitution, although he omits the brass except for horns. Like French composers throughout the nineteenth century, he tends to segregate the orchestra into distinct choirs, and lines are usually doubled only within a single group. Plainly, the composer did not want the blended or homogeneous sonority of German orchestral music, instead choosing a brighter and more variegated sound. The important thematic elements, which are shortened to appear as mere fragments, are normally given to the contrasting colors of the solo woodwinds, and toward the end Debussy instructs the strings to play with mysterious sonorous effects, including harmonics and tremolos on the fingerboard. Debussy's orchestration was carefully studied by a younger generation of modernist composers—Igor Stravinsky among others—who would shortly put Debussy's orchestrational and harmonic innovations into new and daring contexts.

LISTENING CUE

CLAUDE DEBUSSY
Nocturnes (1900)
"Nuages"

CD 11/1
Anthology, No. 170

GABRIEL FAURÉ

Debussy's innovations went further than most of the progressive French composers of the *Belle époque* were willing to go. One such reluctant contemporary was Gabriel Fauré (1845–1924). "If I like Debussy," he remarked, "I no longer like Fauré. How can I then be Fauré?" Fauré began his career as a church musician and composed religious works for chorus, including his much-admired Requiem (1877). He was later a professor of composition at the Paris Conservatory (his students include Maurice Ravel and Lili Boulanger) and from 1905 was its director. He wrote in all of the major musical genres of his time, of which his songs, piano character pieces, and chamber music with piano are best known.

The song "Dans la forêt de septembre" ("In September's Forest," 1902) reveals Fauré's intensely romantic musical personality. The speaker in the poem by Catulle Mendès (1841–1909) beholds an ancient forest and feels a sympathy with its long and stoic suffering, which he shares. As he enters the forest, a tree sends down a leaf that lights upon his shoulder, which the narrator interprets as a token of their kinship.

Certainly the poem is full of emotion and sentimentality, qualities shared with Fauré's music. Our attention in the song is drawn to its warm melodiousness, which Fauré enhances by the soothing arpeggios in the piano and the enriched harmonies. In form the work is repetitive and symmetrical, cast in a rondo-like design. Fauré's admiration for the music of Wagner is reflected in the harmonic vocabulary, which stretches the key of G♭ major but never disrupts it.

Fauré's music shares with Debussy's its nuance and refinement, but Fauré was more the romantic traditionalist in his love for long and intensely tuneful melodies and a harmonic language that never abandons functional progressions.

LISTENING CUE

GABRIEL FAURÉ
"Dans la forêt de septembre," Opus 85, No. 1 (1902)

CD 11/2
Anthology, No. 171

THE SPREAD OF DEBUSSYISM: LILI BOULANGER

While Debussy's innnovations in harmony and tonality were questioned by the older composer Gabriel Fauré, they were enthusiastically adopted by younger French musicians of the *Belle époque*. One of the most promising of these was Lili Boulanger (1893–1918; Fig. 63-3). She was born in Paris to a family of distinguished musicians. Her older sister, Nadia (1887–1979), became the most renowned French teacher of composition of her day. Lili Boulanger studied composition at the Paris Conservatory, and in 1913 she was the first female composer to be awarded the Prix de Rome, an honor conferred earlier on Hector Berlioz and Claude Debussy, and also on her father, Ernest Boulanger (1815–1900).

Lili Boulanger was plagued throughout her short life by poor health, and she died in 1918 at the age of twenty-four. She left behind primarily choral compositions, including works based on psalm texts such as the imposing *Du fond de l'abîme* (*Out of the Depths*, from Psalm 130). She also composed songs, including the cycle *Clairières dans le ciel* (*Clearings in the Sky*, 1914), and a few piano pieces.

Clairières dans le ciel shows Boulanger's enormous gift as a composer and underscores the tragedy of her untimely death. The work is a cycle of thirteen songs based

FIGURE 63-3

Lili Boulanger was the first female composer to win the coveted Prix de Rome.

on poems in free verse by Francis Jammes (1868–1938). These tell of a blissful love affair, existing close to nature, that is ultimately and inexplicably struck down. Boulanger's songs closely follow the spirit of these words. The thirteen pieces move from major to minor, and in the sixth song Boulanger quotes a motive from the beginning of Wagner's opera *Tristan und Isolde*—a work that tells of another hopeless love affair. In the final poem, the composer brings back motives from earlier in the cycle, just as the poet at the conclusion looks back sadly on what once had been.

"Elle est gravement gaie" ("She Is Solemnly Cheerful") is the second song of the cycle. The music perfectly mirrors the naive and uncomplicated sentiments of the poem. The song has a simple ternary design, and the piano and voice share a warm melodiousness, more like that of Boulanger's teacher Fauré than that of Debussy. But in harmony and tonality, the song speaks clearly in Debussy's language. The tonal context is E major, although there are no functional harmonic progressions, and the tonic triads after the opening are all decorated by nonharmonic tones. The music is painted with colors from Debussy's harmonic palette, which consists mainly of triads, seventh chords, and ninth chords. The music alternates smoothly among pitch fields that are diatonic, pentatonic, and octatonic. Other technical features of the song will be familiar from Debussy's music, including the chain of parallel ninth chords in the middle and the replacement of development by a repetitive mosaic made from small figures.

Boulanger's own musical personality appears most in the treatment of the voice. Written with the French tenor David Devriès in mind, the cycle requires an agile, high voice which can glide effortlessly to sustained high tones. The voice's upper register is repeatedly mined for expressive effects, as on the word *surprendre* ("surprise"), where the voice leaps up a seventh to the tone A, sung *pianissimo*.

LISTENING CUE

LILI BOULANGER

Clairières dans le ciel (1914)

"Elle est gravement gaie"

CD 11/3
Anthology, No. 172

SUMMARY

The *Belle époque* refers to the period in French history before and after 1900 when both popular and serious arts flourished. Poets such as Paul Verlaine introduced a subtle and understated style of poetry that emphasized the creation of mood, and these qualities were often captured in song settings such as in Debussy's "En sourdine." Impressionist painters of the 1870s and 1880s, notably Claude Monet, depicted everyday scenes that reflect the motions and luminosity of the out-of-doors. Monet's fondness for the image of reflecting water has its musical counterpart in Debussy's "Reflets dans l'eau" for piano.

Even in his own lifetime, Debussy was referred to as a "musical impressionist," although he did not accept this term as a good description of his music. Debussy's innovations include the suppression of functional harmonic progressions despite his continued use of triads and seventh and ninth chords. Many of his works alternate diatonic music with passages whose tones are drawn from whole-tone, octatonic, and pentatonic scales. Debussy was a master of orchestral music, as seen in his "Nuages" from *Nocturnes*, in which a motionless sky is depicted by ostinatos and undifferentiated rhythms.

Debussy's older contemporary Gabriel Fauré composed music in a more conventional romantic style, notable for its warmth, lyricism, and harmonies that absorbed the expressive implications of those of Wagner. Younger contemporaries, such as Lili Boulanger, more eagerly adopted Debussy's advances in harmony and tonality, although the melodiousness of Fauré's music also remained a model.

KEY TERMS

Belle époque	impressionism	octatonic scale
Paul Verlaine	Claude Monet	pentatonic scale
fête galante	whole-tone scale	

THE EARLY TWENTIETH CENTURY

The history of music in the first half of the twentieth century is divided into two parts, separated by a major stylistic change that occurred around 1920, just after the end of World War I. Before this dividing point, the Romantic period had come to a blazing end. The longstanding romantic traits of passionate expression, complex ideas, and innovative musical resources drove music at this time to extremes. Gustav Mahler's Symphony No. 8 (1906) is typical of the larger-than-life work of the pre-war years. The sprawling composition lasts for an hour and a half, and its gargantuan orchestra and chorus earned it the

1850	1900

ROMANTIC PERIOD (1820–1914)

Richard Strauss (1864–1949), German composer

Erik Satie (1866–1925), French composer

Scott Joplin (1868–1917), American composer

Alexander Scriabin (1872–1915), Russian composer

Charles Ives (1874–1954), American composer

Arnold Schoenberg (1874–1951), Viennese composer of atonal and twelve-tone music

Maurice Ravel (1875–1937), French composer

Béla Bartók (1881–1945), Hungarian composer

Anton Webern (1883–1945), Austrian composer, student of Schoenberg

Alban Berg (1885–1935), Austrian composer, uses Büchner's play as text

Sergei Prokofiev (1891–1953), Russian piano virtuoso and

Darius Milhaud (1892–1974), French composer

Paul Hindemith (1895–1963), leading German

George Gershwin (1898–1937), American pianist

Kurt Weill (1900–1950), German-American

Aaron Copland (1900–1990), American composer

Ruth Crawford Seeger (1901–1953), American

Richard Rodgers (1902–1979), American

Dmitri Shostakovich (1906–1975),

Samuel Barber (1910–1981),

Leonard Bernstein

Igor Stravinsky (1882–1971)
Russian-American composer

CORBIS

Al Jolson, in The Jazz Singer (1927)

CORBIS

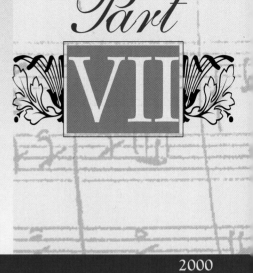

nickname *Symphony of a Thousand*. In its music and text Mahler explored no less a subject than man's destiny and capacity for creativity.

Following World War I, this music of extremes was overturned in favor of a lighter and more life-sized style. The new taste of the 1920s had one unmistakable common feature—to be as unlike late Romantic music as possible. Composers after World War I were far less inclined to take up Mahler's metaphysical contemplations or to call on a thousand performers. Moderation and objectivity became the new order of the day. Composers looked for a new simplicity in their music and cast a sympathetic eye on musical styles and forms of the eighteenth century.

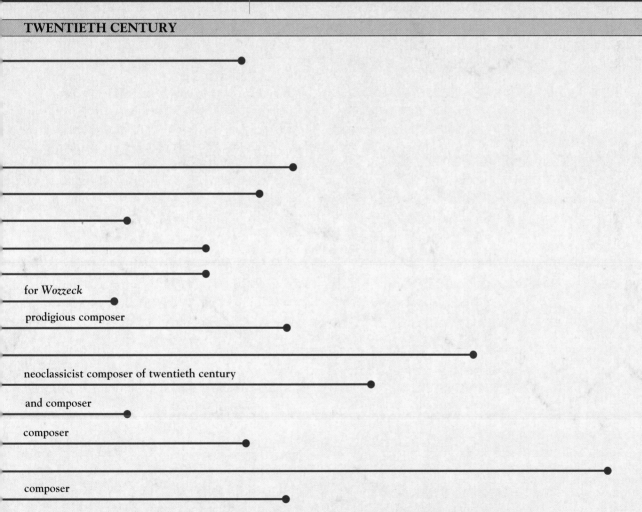

1950   2000

TWENTIETH CENTURY

for *Wozzeck*

prodigious composer

neoclassicist composer of twentieth century

and composer

composer

composer

song writer

Russian composer

American composer

(1918–90), American composer of *West Side Story*

Musical Interlude

7

Music After 1900

Of all the style periods of Western music history, only the one beginning around 1900 has no generally accepted name. There is no counterpart to a critical term like romanticism, classicism, Enlightenment, or baroque that points to common and distinctive features in music composed since the turn of the twentieth century.

Why this is so takes us to the very core of musical culture of this time. Many of its enduring musical works in fact show certain common traits. A freer-than-ever occurrence of dissonant harmony, the removal or reinterpretation of traditional tonality, a new emphasis on the expressive power of sound in itself, an openness to change and experimentation in musical resources, and a dissolution of traditional genres and media are all common features that bind together works that began to appear after 1900. At the same time, overlapping and sharply opposing styles have counteracted any idea that the century forms one single period, by whatever name.

This ambiguity reaches even into the works of individual composers. In earlier eras, the mature works of a major figure sound reasonably alike. The music of Wagner sounds like Wagner, whether from *The Flying Dutchman*, his first major opera, or *Parsifal*, his final composition. But there is often no such consistency in the music of leading composers of the early twentieth century. Samuel Barber is an example. In his romantic *Adagio for Strings*, his homespun songs *Knoxville: Summer of 1915*, or his angular and dissonant Piano Sonata we encounter such diversity of expression that it is scarcely imaginable that these compositions are products of a single mind. This mixing of styles continues to appear in works by major composers later in the century. George Rochberg's Variations on an Original Theme differs little in style from piano music written a hundred years before, in the early Romantic period. His piano "Blues" from *Carnival Music* differs little in style from an improvisation by the jazz pianist Art Tatum from the 1940s. The Variations movement from Rochberg's String Quartet No. 3 is almost indistinguishable in style from a late quartet by Beethoven. So what is the name of Rochberg's style?

Rochberg's eclecticism cannot mask the fact that there has existed a succession of prevailing tastes in music of the early twentieth century. In its first decade, a continuation of romanticism is apparent. As in the nineteenth century, heightened expressivity was paramount at this time, when composers searched for new themes and for new musical materials by which these could be conveyed.

In the 1920s and 1930s these romantic features were questioned, then rejected, by most composers. Many of the leading musicians of these decades, including Igor Stravinsky, Paul Hindemith, and Kurt Weill, swept aside the sort of music that they had grown up with—works with complex expressivity and larger-than-life emotions. Objectivity and coolness of expression became the order of the day in a new type of music that critics labeled "neoclassicism." Romantic emotionalism in music seemed clearly outdated. Also at this time, thanks to advances in sound-recording technology, popular music claimed the attention of audiences throughout the world. Classical composers of these years, such as Kurt Weill, began to question whether a distinction between popular and art music could be maintained.

But, at the same time that Stravinsky and Hindemith were writing music in the new objective style of the 1920s, other major composers of the day headed in opposite directions. Arnold Schoenberg found in neoclassicism only a movement that had removed "all that was good in the preceding period." His own music of the 1920s maintained the complexity, dissonance, and chromaticism that was being shunned by the neoclassicists. The French composer Charles Koechlin (1867–1950) continued to write evocative and impressionistic music inspired by Fauré and Debussy, and he had no sympathy with the neoclassicists' call for a "return to Bach" as an antidote for romanticism.

The very existence of these overlapping and conflicting attitudes and musical styles became one of the distinctive features of musical culture in the early twentieth century. A multiplicity of styles is unique to this period, just as the century itself is unique in its sharp juxtapositions of peace and war, poverty and wealth. The years from 1900 to 1950 witnessed two world wars, a worldwide economic depression, a Holocaust, and unprecedented wealth and technological advance, and the impact of these titanic events upon musical culture will be traced in the following chapters.

Richard Strauss in Berlin

The modern nation of Germany came into existence only in 1871. In January of that year, shortly after German armies had defeated the French in the Franco-Prussian War, leaders representing most of the German-speaking states met in the Palace of Versailles near Paris and proclaimed their allegiance to Wilhelm I, King of Prussia. By doing this they created a unified German *Reich* (Empire), which they proudly called the "Second Reich," the first being the medieval Germanic empire founded by Charlemagne. Recall from Chapter 54 that German lands after the fall of Napoleon were loosely allied in the German Confederation, although the rivalry between Prussia and Austria—the two most powerful members—remained keen. In 1866 Prussia defeated Austria in the Austro-Prussian War, and shortly thereafter Austria was excluded from a new "North German Confederation," which replaced the older alliance. The evolving boundaries that led to the emergence of a unified German nation are illustrated in Map 64-1.

The German Empire that was created in 1871 was much larger than the Germany we know today. It extended westward beyond the Rhine River into what is now France. To the east it stretched along the Baltic Sea to modern-day Lithuania and Estonia, and to the southeast its borders reached well into what is now Poland.

BERLIN

The capital of the new empire was Berlin, which earlier had been the capital of the powerful north European state of Prussia. In the early nineteenth century the city was small and isolated, but by 1900 it had become a great metropolis with a population of over 2.7 million. The center of the city (after World War II, part of Communist East Berlin) was bounded on the west by the Brandenburg Gate, an imposing triumphal arch completed in 1791 (Fig. 64-1). By walking eastward from this point

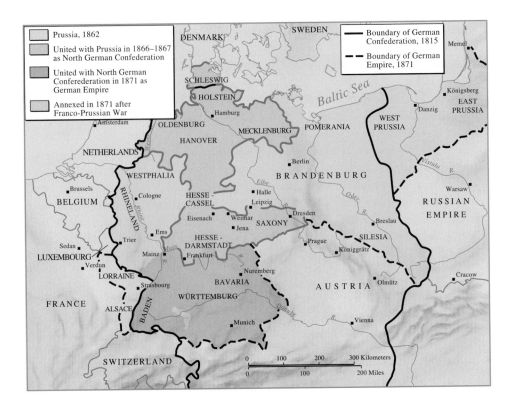

✺ MAP 64-1

The Unification of Germany, 1866–1871.

along the tree-lined avenue called Unter den Linden, one shortly passed the Royal Library, which was home to the greatest collection of composer's manuscripts anywhere in the world. Next to it was the university, where Hegel had earlier lectured on philosophy and where, at the end of the century, Philipp Spitta—then the world's greatest authority on the music of J.S. Bach—taught musicology. Across the street was the Royal Opera, built by King Frederick the Great in 1742. After passing over the Spree Canal, the walker could view the grandiose Imperial Palace before arriving in residential suburbs to the east.

In 1900 the Royal Opera was the city's most prestigious musical institution. The emperor himself, then Wilhelm II, was directly involved with choosing the repertory and overseeing productions. Two years before, Richard Strauss (1864–1949; Fig. 64-2) was brought in as principal conductor and later made music director, a position that he held until 1918. From 1908 he was also music director of the Berlin Philharmonic Orchestra, which was founded in 1882 and grew to prominence under the leadership of Hans von Bülow and Arthur Nikisch. Its later conductors have included Wilhelm Furtwängler (1886–1954) and Herbert von Karajan (1908–1989).

✺ FIGURE 64-1

The Brandenburg Gate is a neo-Grecian portal completed in the center of Berlin in 1791; it remains one of the most imposing monuments in the city.

❂ RICHARD STRAUSS

When Strauss came to the Royal Opera in 1898, he was already recognized as one of the world's leading composers, primarily because of a series of brilliant orchestral pieces. These compositions revived the genre of the one-movement programmatic work for orchestra that had been advanced by Franz Liszt at mid-century. Liszt called a composition of this type a "symphonic poem" (see Chapter 57), while Strauss preferred the equivalent term *Tondichtung*, or **tone poem.** By 1889 Strauss had completed three such works—*Don Juan, Macbeth,* and *Tod und Verklärung* (*Death and Transfiguration*)—whereupon he turned to the genre of opera and wrote *Guntram,* a work in the Wagnerian vein. The opera was a failure in the eyes of the public, who dealt Strauss his first major setback as a composer.

He then returned to his strong suit, composing for orchestra, and wrote one brilliant tone poem after another: *Till Eulenspiegels lustige Streiche* (*Till Eulenspiegel's Merry Pranks,* 1895), *Also sprach Zarathustra* (*Thus Spoke Zarathustra,* 1896), *Don Quixote* (1897), and *Ein Heldenleben* (*A Hero's Life,* 1898). Strauss had also attracted attention with his songs, which began to appear in print in 1887 and increased in number in the 1890s, near the time of his marriage to Pauline de Ahna, a singer and interpreter of his vocal music. His production of songs dwindled after her retirement in 1906.

By this time, Strauss had again taken up the challenge of writing opera, although after *Guntram* he looked for a more original operatic style. Following the comic opera *Feuersnot* (*Need for Fire,* 1901), he made a great success with *Salome* (1905), a work in a modern idiom. *Elektra,* an opera in a similar style, followed in 1909, after which Strauss entered into a collaboration with the Viennese writer **Hugo von Hofmannsthal** (1874–1929) on a series of new operas. These include the ever-popular *Der Rosenkavalier* (*The Cavalier of the Rose,* 1910), *Ariadne auf Naxos* (*Ariadne on Naxos*), *Die Frau ohne Schatten* (*The Woman Without Shadow*), and *Arabella.* In these works Strauss abandons the experimental language of *Salome* and *Elektra* and returns to a fully romantic style, conveyed in classical operatic forms.

After his final opera, *Capriccio* (1941), Strauss contemplated retirement, but a great resurgence of creative spirit toward the end of his life led to several memorable late compositions, including the tone poem *Metamorphosen* (*Metamorphoses,* 1945) and orchestral songs published posthumously under the title *Four Last Songs* (1948). For a discussion of Strauss's late works, see Chapter 78.

Bettmann/CORBIS

FIGURE 64-2
Richard Strauss in mid-career.

Salome

Strauss always hoped for success in the genre of opera. More than most other composers of his generation, he accepted Wagner's idea that opera would be at the center of "music of the future," and the genre seemed to be the perfect outlet for his interest in modern theater and his passionate belief in the expressive power of the orchestra and the human voice. But for a composer around 1900, finding the right subject and musical style for a new opera posed a complex challenge. Strauss had failed in his effort to continue the Wagnerian idiom in his first opera, *Guntram,* and the reception of his second opera, the comedy *Feuersnot,* was limited by its bawdy subject. When he saw **Oscar Wilde**'s highly controversial play *Salome* staged in Berlin in 1902, he recognized material that he could transform into an opera having both musical and dramatic originality.

Even in Berlin—a city known for free thinking in theater—*Salome* was strong stuff. Wilde wrote the play in 1891 in French, with the celebrated French actress Sarah Bernhardt in mind for the title role. Using the biblical story of the beheading of John the Baptist by Herod, Wilde creates a fantasy of forbidden love. At its center

Synopsis of *Salome*

King Herod and his queen Herodias are entertaining in their palace on a moonlit night. Soldiers and attendants wait outside, where they can hear the holy man Jochanaan (John the Baptist) issue prophecies from a nearby cistern, in which he is held prisoner. They are joined by Salome, the daughter of Herodias, who commands that Jochanaan be brought before her. Salome finds him disgusting as he spews forth condemnations of her mother. But suddenly she declares herself enamored of him—especially his body, his hair, and, most of all, his red mouth. "I will kiss your mouth, Jochanaan," she swears, whereupon he asks to return to the cistern.

Herod now leads the party outside, seeking Salome, at whom he stares lasciviously. The voice of Jochanaan is again heard, quoting prophecies from the Apocrypha: The hour is at hand, he says, when the earth will turn black, stars will fall

like ripe figs, and the kings of the earth will grow afraid. The strumpet, he says, will die beneath soldiers' shields.

Herod wants to see Salome dance, for which he promises to grant her any wish. After her seductive "Dance of the Seven Veils," she demands that the head of Jochanaan be brought to her on a silver platter. Paralyzed by fear and drink, Herod allows her wish to be carried out. An arm rises from the cistern bearing the decapitated head, which Salome takes and fondles. Filled with disgust and apprehension, Herod commands that all torches be extinguished, and the stage falls totally dark as clouds temporarily screen the moon and stars. From the darkness, Salome luridly declares that she has kissed Jochanaan's lips, which, she says, had a bitter taste. A moonbeam betrays her at this climactic moment, and Herod screams, "Kill that woman!" Soldiers rush forward and crush her beneath their shields.

---

he places Salome, the daughter of Herodias. Compared to tragic heroines of the nineteenth century, she is plainly a new type—lustful, perverse, a bizarre femme fatale to whom nothing in the realm of sensuality is forbidden. The play went into rehearsal in London in 1892, but the censor forced it to be withdrawn, and it was first brought to the stage only in 1896, in Paris. The work has subsequently been known primarily through Strauss's opera.

The apparent sordidness of the play is attenuated by the absurdity of the dialogue and Wilde's unrelenting parody. His reputation as a writer of satiric social comedies, such as the contemporary *Lady Windermere's Fan*, is never entirely forgotten in *Salome*. The characters themselves, beneath their distorted exteriors, are comic types. Herodias is the shrew, Herod the foolish old lecher, Jochanaan a pompous buffoon. Salome herself reminds us of the mad heroine of romantic tragedy, the maiden who has lost her wits on account of love. Even the circumstances of her madness—her sexual arousal by John the Baptist and her ghoulish delight in his decapitation—are so exaggerated as to make her at home with the other clownish figures.

Strauss immediately recognized in Wilde's play the element of parody, which he considered one of his strengths as a composer. In *Till Eulenspiegel* he had used a choir of bassoons in the low register to draw a devastating portrait of a band of stuffy professors; in *Ein Heldenleben* he called on the solo violin to impersonate his wife—alternately happy or moody, and always talkative. Strauss continues this line of parody in parts of *Salome*, as in the music for Herod, whose whining tenor voice lacks any regal character and whose melodic material has a cloying banality. But Wilde's dark humor is largely missing from the opera, lost in part to the German translation and to the riveting power of Strauss's music, which grips the listener in a way that agrees with Wilde's perhaps ironic designation of the play as tragedy.

Strauss's creation of a libretto from Wilde's play was also atypical. He composed directly from its prose text, with no adaptation other than omitting lines from the original. The more typical way of adapting a literary work for an opera (recall Puccini's *Madama Butterfly*, discussed in Chapter 62) was to remove the complexity of the literary model and flatten the characters into simple types. Typically, the librettist segregated narrative text from other moments that suggested musical arias, ensembles, and choruses. By working directly with a spoken play, Strauss avoids all such artificialities and retains a sophisticated literary content for his opera; he was also freed to compose in short, asymmetrical phrases with few apparent divisions into musical numbers.

MUSIC OF THE OPERA

The overall structure of the opera resembles the structure of the play. Both are based on a large-scale symmetry in which passages of text and music near the beginning—notably Salome's love song to Jochanaan's body, hair, and mouth—return in a varied form in Salome's final monologue (discussed below). The music otherwise is continuously developmental, based on recurrent motives and tonalities that symbolize characters and dramatic situations. These resemble the leitmotives of Wagnerian opera, which was plainly a model for Strauss despite the highly un-Wagnerian text. As in Wagner's operas, traditional musical numbers—arias, recitatives, ensembles, and choruses—are rarely evident.

The large orchestra, enriched by such unusual instruments as **xylophone** and **heckelphone** (a member of the clarinet family), is the primary expressive element, as it also is in Wagner. It states most of the principal motives and takes over entirely from the voices at certain crucial moments, such as Salome's seductive **"Dance of the Seven Veils."**

The climax of the whole work is reached in Salome's concluding monologue, during which she fondles, and finally kisses, Jochanaan's decapitated head. The passage contains a complex network of motives that differ from Wagner's leitmotives in their greater number and complexity of presentation. Some are heard prominently on the surface of the music, and occasionally in the voices, but they are given out more typically deep within the orchestra's dense counterpoint, often fleetingly and subject to extensive transformations.

We can appreciate Strauss's intricate use of motives by tracing the evolution of the principal one that identifies the character Salome. This figure makes its first appearance in the clarinet in the very first measure of the opera (Ex. 64-1a). Salome appears on stage for the first time in scene 2, at which point her motive returns in the violin (Ex. 64-1b). The central measures of its earlier form (bracketed in the example) are now embedded into a new and more lyrical melody. In scene 3, where Salome asks about the prisoner who is spouting prophecies, her motive returns in yet another transformation (Ex. 64-1c). It has the same head motive as in (b), but a new continuation that reiterates an ascending and descending minor third. Later, where Salome sees Jochanaan and declares him disgusting, her motive (Ex. 64-1d) sheds its opening from (c) and adds a descending fourth to the minor thirds. In this form it dominates the music of her final monologue.

EXAMPLE 64-1

a
Ziemlich fliessendes Zeitmass
Clarinet
p

(continued on next page)

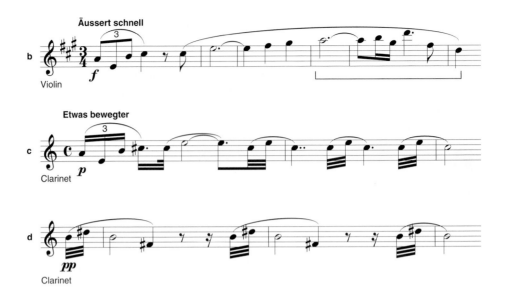

The central tonality of the monologue is C♯ minor and major, but this key appears only sporadically, mainly in moments where Salome gathers her thoughts. Where she drifts off into confusion, Strauss eliminates any unified sense of key. These wavering principles of tonal organization come directly into conflict near the end, after Salome sings her final exultant, "I have kissed your mouth, Jochanaan." As the music approaches a mammoth cadence in C♯ major, the upper instruments outline notes from a dominant chord in the key, but the lower ones go off by a semitone and play an A7 chord (Ex. 64-2). The stridently confused harmony that results is met by Herod's command, "Kill that woman!" This triggers a ten-measure coda in which the key is wrenched down to C minor, and the opera ends with convulsive reiterations of Salome's motive while she is crushed beneath the soldiers' shields.

EXAMPLE 64-2

LISTENING CUE

RICHARD STRAUSS
Salome, concluding scene (1905)

CD 11/4
Anthology, No. 173

✿ STRAUSS AND "PROGRESS"

The success of *Salome* in 1905 brought an unexpected complexity into prospects for the future of music. Before this time most composers and audiences—at least in the German-speaking world—had settled comfortably into the assumption that there were only two available styles for new compositions. The more conservative one was associated with Brahms, the more progressive with Wagner. The Brahmsian model, as discussed in Chapter 58, balanced modern and traditional elements. It was modern in its extended harmonic language, intensive motivic development, and certain liberties in form, but it was traditional in genre, medium, and absolute rather than programmatic expressivity. The Wagnerian model made fewer overt references to the Classical past. It pushed harmony and tonality into new areas of ambiguity, expanded the orchestra to unprecedented size, and expressed a broad spectrum of extra-musical ideas.

Although we can now see that the differences between the styles of Brahms and Wagner are not so extreme, around 1900 there was very little middle ground separating the partisans of the two. You were either a Brahmsian or a Wagnerian. Gustav Mahler—a stalwart Wagnerian—wrote to his wife in 1904: "I have gone all through Brahms pretty well by now. All I can say of him is that he's a puny little dwarf with a rather narrow chest. Good Lord, if a breath from the lungs of *Richard Wagner* whistled around his ears he would scarcely be able to keep his feet."[1] On the other side was a musician like **Hugo Riemann,** the great German music theorist, who saw Wagner's influence as leading only to decadence. Brahms, said Riemann, was like a great tree that could withstand the winds of change:

> [Brahms is the] lone rugged oak that has endured on the paths swept by destructive tempests, its mighty roots having sunk deep into the earth. Its canopy is intact and spreads forth ever more proudly. It commands the present day, where the salvation of the future lies; it restores new powers to the healthy soil.[2]

Strauss's *Salome* changed this dichotomy by introducing a musical style whose novelties seemed to outweigh any indebtedness to Brahms, Wagner, or other late-Romantic models. For many of the progressive musicians of the day, this amounted to a betrayal. A year after the opera's premiere, **Felix Draeseke**—a composer and staunch advocate of Wagner—published a widely read polemic called "Confusion in Music."[3] In it he dismisses contemporary works that seemed to him intentionally ugly and muddled. Although Draeseke does not mention Strauss by name, he drops enough hints to make it clear that he considered Strauss to be the leader of this "Cult of the Ugly," as he called it.

Draeseke's attack provoked Strauss—who normally was not inclined to write about music—to respond. In his essay "Is There an Avant-Garde in Music?" Strauss professes his belief in the necessity in music of "progress." Music, he says, can never stop evolving, even at such an elevated stage as the one reached by a Brahms or a Wagner. He writes:

> Even a perfect work of art should be considered only as a stage in a great organic development. It should be planted as a seed in the souls of our descendants, to inspire and assist in the birth of even higher and more perfect creations.[4]

At the same time, Strauss placed a heavy restriction upon progress. Great works of any period, he said, must be acclaimed by the public in general. "A great artist is instinctively recognized as a natural genius by the public at large, even if its judgment of details is not at all clear headed."[5] This demand for public acceptance ultimately made Strauss appear to be a reactionary, not a progressive. In the eyes of younger modernist musicians such as Arnold Schoenberg, a truly important work could never be fully understood by a contemporary audience, only by one at some future time.

Strauss's *Salome* transcended the arguments between the Brahmsians and Wagnerians, conservatives and progressives. Although the work contains romantic features—intense expression, exploration of the human psyche, harmony and tonality employed as expressive as well as syntactic tools—it also broaches new ideas, including its hitherto untouchable subject, free use of dissonant harmonies, and a higher level of musical complexity than ever before. These constituted a whole new concept of "progress" that onlookers like Draeseke could only interpret as leading to ugliness. In the years just after 1905, younger composers throughout the world fixed their gaze on these novel features in *Salome* and left behind the romantic ones, ultimately ushering in a new period in the history of music.

SUMMARY

Berlin was the German capital city from the founding of the country in 1871. At the turn of the twentieth century, its central musical institution was the Royal Opera, which was led by Richard Strauss from 1898 to 1918. In addition to conducting, Strauss during this period wrote tone poems and operas, among which *Salome* (1905) was his first major operatic success.

The work introduces a new subject matter for opera, filled with grotesquerie and parody that mix explosively with a biblical story. Based on a play by Oscar Wilde, the opera brings the literary content of the genre to a higher level. Strauss's music is equally innovative. Building upon Wagner's technique of the leitmotive, Strauss introduces motives with a withering complexity that make them sometimes virtually impossible to follow. Their complications are only heightened by the raucous dissonance of much of the score and passages in which key is scarcely evident. Strauss later justified these novelties as the result of a necessary progress in music.

KEY TERMS

tone poem	xylophone	Hugo Riemann
Hugo von Hofmannsthal	heckelphone	Felix Draeseke
Oscar Wilde	"Dance of the Seven Veils"	

Chapter

Music in Russia During the Silver Age: Igor Stravinsky

The arts and letters in Russia during the reign of Tsar Nicholas II (1894–1917) entered a prosperous time that is now commonly called the **Silver Age.** Like the Silver Age of literature in ancient Rome of the first century C.E., it was a period of changing tastes. The romantic and melodious style of Tchaikovsky still enjoyed immense prestige in Russia, but to many observers it was a monument to an earlier era rather than a guide for the future. The experimental and nationalistic approach of the *kuchka* (see Chapter 59) held more promise, although the realism of a composer such as Modest Mussorgsky also seemed increasingly dated, as did the anti-Westernism implicit in the aesthetics of these Russian nationalists. For many younger Russian musicians of the Silver Age, the new ideas flowing, especially from France, could not be ignored.

REALISM IN RUSSIAN ART AND LITERATURE

The element of **realism** in Russian literature is well known from the penetrating psychological and social novels of Fyodor Dostoyevsky (1821–1881) and Leo Tolstoy (1828–1910), and it can also be readily seen in the paintings of an artist such as Ilya Repin (1844–1930). His *They Did Not Expect Him* (1884–1888; Fig. 65-1) captures a moment in life. A man unexpectedly returns to his family, whereupon each member registers a different emotion. The painting suggests a moment in a larger story whose full narrative could easily be imagined by any observer.

Compare this painting to Mikhail Vrubel's *The Six-Winged Seraph* (1905; Fig. 65-2). It relies for its effect not on social issues or a readily told story, but on color and form, as the artist reaches back in his theme to some primitive, mystic, and distinctively Russian essence. The artistic visions of Vrubel (1856–1910) point to the new post-realistic tendency in Russian arts of the Silver Age, which emphasizes experimental materials, abstraction more than realism, and an affinity with primitive and ancient Russian themes.

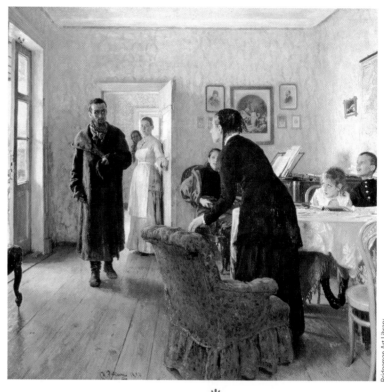

Bridgeman Art Library

FIGURE 65-1
Ilya Repin, *They Did Not Expect Him* (1884–1888). Ilya Repin was a leading Russian realist painter whose direct depictions of everyday life also guided the music of Mussorgsky.

Bridgeman Art Library

FIGURE 65-2
Mikhail Vrubel, *The Six-Winged Seraph* (1905). The paintings of Mikhail Vrubel often depart from the dominant realist style of Repin and use symbolist techniques associated with modern French art and metaphysical or religious themes.

❀ MUSIC DURING THE SILVER AGE

Russian music of the period underwent a similar evolution. Many of the great works of nineteenth-century Russian music have an analogy with the realism of a Tolstoy or a Repin. Realism is especially apparent in the music of Mussorgsky, as in his opera *Boris Godunov* and songs such as "Within Four Walls" (see Chapter 59). Recall how the melody of "Within Four Walls" realistically imitates the depressed muttering of the poem's speaker. Mussorgsky avails himself of unusual musical elements, including aimless chord progressions, changing meters, and the suppression of normal melody, to mimic the spoken word and the poem's underlying emotion.

Although Mussorgsky's experimental musical resources were of interest to the next generation of Russian composers, these younger musicians generally bypassed his realistic attachment to his own world. At the turn of the twentieth century the nationalism that characterized the *kuchka* remained prominent, although this outlook was then expressed by an interest in the mystic or primitive element of the Russian consciousness more than by any anti-Westernism. This orientation led younger Russian musicians of the time to a musical language that relied upon the most contemporary thinking of European musicians.

The Silver Age also witnessed a continued modernization and diversification of Russian musical culture. The amateurism that had characterized native composers in the mid-nineteenth century was diminished, as Russian artists were more readily supported by the aristocracy and also by a rising, wealthy merchant class. The foreign domination of Russian music had also largely ended, and Russian figures, like their Western contemporaries, were all the more ready to export their own ideas abroad.

St. Petersburg continued to be the leading center for music. In addition to the celebrated opera and ballet of the Mariinsky Theater, the city's culture for orchestral and chamber music continued to expand. There were several important new opportunities for modern music to be heard: in 1903 the conductor and piano virtuoso **Alexander Siloti** (1863–1945) founded orchestra concerts that served a mixed fare of new music from both Russian and European figures. The modernist Viennese composer Arnold Schoenberg conducted his tone poem *Pelleas und Melisande* in 1912 with Siloti's orchestra, which he found musically outstanding. In 1901 a group of art-loving amateurs formed a society called the **Evenings of Contemporary Music** specifically to perform new works. Igor Stravinsky and Sergei Prokofiev—the leading young modernists on the Russian musical scene at the time—were both active as players and composers in this organization.

❀ SERGEI DIAGHILEV AND *THE WORLD OF ART*

The new vistas in Russian art associated with the Silver Age come into focus in the work of the remarkable impresario **Sergei Diaghilev** (1872–1929). Diaghilev was born in Gruzino, southeast of St. Petersburg, where he arrived in 1890 to study law. His interests quickly turned to the arts. He took classes in music at the Conservatory, although after publishing several articles on modern Russian painting he seemed headed for the career of an art critic. In 1898 he founded an art journal called **Mir iskusstva (World of Art)** in which he and his fellow writers expressed sympathy with modern European developments. Under the aegis of his journal, Diaghilev also presented a series of art exhibitions in St. Petersburg, and the Evenings of Contemporary Music were organized by several who collaborated on his journal.

Diaghilev's first taste of the professional world of ballet came near the turn of the century when he was asked to coordinate the design of a new production of Léo Delibes's ballet *Sylvia* for the Mariinsky Theater. Diaghilev's imagination was awakened to the creative possibilities available to an impresario, and he was especially keen on producing an opera or ballet as an integral collaboration among artists representing different fields. On a more practical level, his future as an impresario was brightened by his remarkable skill in raising money for artistic purposes from Russia's aristocracy and wealthy middle classes.

Beginning about 1906, Diaghilev looked to Western Europe—especially to Paris—for an outlet for his artistic initiatives. The Parisian social climate was then optimal for the appearance of Russian art, as France was just then reaching out to Russia on the diplomatic front. In 1907 the Russians, French, and British entered into a **Triple Entente,** by which they hoped collectively to balance the power of an opposing alliance among Germany, Austria, and Italy. Russian music—especially the works of Nicolai Rimsky-Korsakov and Mussorgsky—had long appealed to the French taste for the exotic and colorful.

Diaghilev soon turned his attention to music and dance, intending, as he had with Russian painting, to display the riches of modern Russian culture more fully to the French and other European capitals. In 1907 he organized a season of concerts at the Paris Opéra, featuring Russian composers and performers; the next year he brought a production of Mussorgsky's *Boris Godunov* for the Opéra; and in 1909 he presented ballets, using dancers from the Mariinsky Theater.

❀ THE BALLETS RUSSES

Ballet would be Diaghilev's focus from that time forward. In 1909 he established his own company, later named the **Ballets Russes (Russian Ballet)**, which toured Europe and the Americas, with major seasons in Paris, Berlin, Milan, London, and Monte Carlo. The ballets that Diaghilev produced were very different from a typical nineteenth-century ballet such as Tchaikovsky's *The Nutcracker* (see Chapter 59). Those works filled an entire evening, and they told a story by mime, with danced numbers—solos, ensembles, and dances for the full company—periodically inserted. The music had only a loose connection to the story, mainly providing a backdrop to the dancing rather than an expressive enhancement to the drama.

Diaghilev's ballets were entirely different. They were short, and several were needed to fill an evening's entertainment. Their music could come from different sources. Concert works for orchestra (such as Debussy's Prelude to *The Afternoon of a Faun*) were sometimes provided with choreographies, and pastiches of music were specially arranged and orchestrated (as in the ballet *Les sylphides,* based on piano music by Chopin). Diaghilev also commissioned original scores to be joined to original choreographies.

This last type is the most interesting musically and the area in which Diaghilev and his associates exerted their most lasting influence on the history of ballet. Before Diaghilev, ballet music had a mixed reputation. With the exception of Tchaikovsky, music for the genre tended to be written by secondary figures, who provided at most a tuneful and repetitive score that had a limited range of expression and no attempt at originality. By the end of the nineteenth century, these utilitarian features made the entire genre of ballet pale in the eyes of musicians when compared to opera, in which a truer dramatic expression was the norm.

Diaghilev followed up on the achievements of Tchaikovsky by bringing musical respectability back to the genre. He was guided aesthetically by a choreographer from the Mariinsky Theater, **Mikhail Fokine** (1880–1942). Fokine was dismayed by the traditional ballet of his time. It seemed to lack drama, unity, or high artistic intentions, all of which he found being sacrificed to the stock jumps, spins, and poses from classical dance. Ballet, he said in his memoirs, "lacked its most essential element: presentation to the spectator of an artistically created image."[1]

He experienced the same displeasure with his genre that, fifty years earlier, Richard Wagner did with traditional opera, and both had similar ideas for improvement. Fokine insisted that all aspects of a ballet—its scenario, mime, dancing, lighting, costume, stage design, and music—should be integrated into a unified dramatic image. Fokine's prescription was that ballet should become a "total work of art," for which the Wagnerian music drama was plainly a model.

IGOR STRAVINSKY

Igor Stravinsky (1882–1971; see Part VII timeline) rose to fame as a composer by realizing Fokine's conception of the integrated ballet. Fokine was the choreographer of Stravinsky's first two ballets, *The Firebird* (1910) and *Petrushka* (1911), and his ideas concerning the artistic integrity of ballet served Stravinsky well from this time forward.

Stravinsky was born near St. Petersburg to a musical family (his father was a leading singer at the Mariinsky Theater). Typical of the amateuristic tradition of Russian music, he at first did not choose the life of a professional musician. Instead he studied law at the university in St. Petersburg and only at the age of twenty-three began to study music seriously, taking lessons then with Rimsky-Korsakov. Following the death in 1908 of his conservative teacher, Stravinsky deepened his contacts with the modernists of the *World of Art* group, and he was eventually introduced to Diaghilev.

Stravinsky's breakthrough to international celebrity as a composer came in 1910, when Diaghilev presented his new ballet, *The Firebird*, to Parisian audiences. This work was followed by other brilliantly original ballet scores for Diaghilev's company: *Petrushka* (1911), *The Rite of Spring* (1913), *Les noces* (*The Wedding*, 1917, premiere 1923), and *Pulcinella* (1920). During this early period, Stravinsky also composed songs (typically for voice accompanied by small and diverse ensembles of instruments), an opera called *The Nightingale*, and a choral work with large orchestra called *Zvezdoliki* (*King of the Stars*).

During World War I, Stravinsky settled in Switzerland, then later in France, where in the 1920s he became a leader of new thinking in modern music. (His ideas from this time are discussed in Chapter 68.) Between the world wars Stravinsky often toured as pianist, conductor, and composer, and he made several trips to the United States. With the beginning of World War II in 1939, Stravinsky emigrated permanently to America, and in 1940 he settled in California in what is now the city of West Hollywood. He remained there until shortly before his death in 1971, and he is buried in Venice, Italy, near the tomb of his great patron, Sergei Diaghilev.

The Rite of Spring

The basic idea for Stravinsky's *The Rite of Spring (Le sacre du printemps)*—his third ballet for Diaghilev—was a re-enactment of spring rituals in prehistoric Russia. A theme drawn from Russian folklore was squarely in the aesthetic spirit of the *World of Art* group, where delving into national roots and the Slavic subconsciousness was considered a way for the Russian artist to reach a higher reality. Russian folklorism also appealed to European audiences for its color and exoticism, and Stravinsky's two earlier ballets—*Firebird* and *Petrushka*—had successfully used folkloric scenarios.

To work this idea into a ballet, Stravinsky collaborated with Fokine (who later dropped out of the project, replaced as choreographer by the dancer **Vaslav Nijinsky**) and with the painter Nicholas Roerich, who specialized in ancient Russian subjects and was considered an authority on Russian ethnography. The ballet that they foresaw was consistent with the dramatic theories of Fokine. They would produce not simply an artistic or stylized evocation of a subject from Russian folklore, but, to the extent possible, an authentic re-creation of one. To this end Roerich designed historically plausible costumes and decor, the dancing imitating realistic movements more than those of classical ballet, and Stravinsky brought authentic and relevant folk melodies into his score.

The scenario for the ballet consists of a series of scenes disposed in two large parts. Unlike Tchaikovsky's *The Nutcracker*, there is no attempt to tell a connected story. The general idea contained within each section is outlined by headings that Stravinsky placed in the score:

Part 1: Adoration of the Earth	Part 2: The Sacrifice
Introduction	Introduction
The Augurs of Spring	Mystic Circles of the Young Girls
Dances of the Young Girls	Glorification of the Chosen One
Ritual of Abduction	Evocation of the Ancestors
Spring Rounds	Ritual Action of the Ancestors
Ritual of the Rival Tribes	Sacrificial Dance (The Chosen One)
Procession of the Sage	
The Sage	
Dance of the Earth	

This outline was considerably fleshed out in an article (excerpted in Box) that appeared in the Parisian journal *Montjoie!* on 29 May 1913, the day of the work's premiere. The first performance was much anticipated by French audiences. Stravinsky's two previous ballets had been warmly received in the French capital, but by 1913 audiences throughout Europe were more inclined than ever to rise up in protest against music that was unfamiliar in style. Only two months before, a concert at the Musikverein in Vienna, with orchestral pieces by Arnold Schoenberg, Anton Webern, and Alban Berg, was brought to an early end by a tumult in the audience.

Apparently not wanting to be outdone, the Parisians had a similar uprising at the first night of *The Rite of Spring*. The American ballet critic Carl Van Vechten was present on that evening, and he reported:

> This first audience would not permit the composer to be heard. Cat-calls and hisses succeeded the playing of the first few bars, and then ensued a battery of screams, countered by a foil of applause. We warred over art (some of us thought it was and some thought it wasn't). . . . Some forty of the protestants were forced out of the theatre but that did not quell the disturbance. The lights in the auditorium were fully turned on but the noise continued and I remember Mlle. Piltz executing her strange dance of religious hysteria on a stage dimmed by the blazing light in the auditorium, seemingly to the accompaniment of the disjointed ravings of a mob of angry men and women.[2]

"What I Wanted to Express in *The Rite of Spring*" by Igor Stravinsky (excerpts)

"The Parisian public has for some years accorded a good reception to my *Firebird* and *Petrushka*. My friends have observed an evolution in their underlying ideas, from a fantastic fable in the one to a generalization concerning all of humanity in the other. I am afraid that *The Rite of Spring*—in which I project an abstraction of a somewhat broader sort, rather than a fairy tale or the sadness and joy of the human condition—may disconcert those who have extended to me to this point a heartfelt sympathy.

"With *The Rite of Spring* I wanted to express the sublime ascent of nature eternally reborn—the total, panic rising of the universal sap.

"In the Prelude, before the curtain, I express in my orchestra that great fear which weighs upon all sentient beings in the face of things that exert power—a 'thing in itself' that has the *capacity* to grow and infinitely develop. A delicate sound, even on the flute, can contain this element of power and spread above the whole orchestra. It is the obscure and immense sensation that everything experiences at the moment when nature renews its forms; it is the vague and deep anxiety of universal puberty. Even in my orchestration and in the play of melodies, I demand that it be evoked. . . . In sum, I wanted to express in the Prelude the panic fear of nature in the face of a rising beauty, a sacred terror in the glare of the midday sun, a sort of cry of Pan. The musical material itself inflates, expands, grows. Each instrument is like a bud that pushes against the husk in an old tree, each becoming part of an imposing whole. . . .

"Now we hear a procession coming near. The Holy Man arrives, the Sage, the High Priest, the oldest of the clan. A great terror sweeps through all gathered. The Sage then gives a blessing to the earth, stretching on his stomach with arms and legs spread, becoming himself as though one with the earth. His blessing is like a signal for a rhythmic outburst. All cover their heads and run in circles, pouring forth in great numbers, as though representing the new energy of nature. This is the Dance of the Earth.

"The Second Tableau begins darkly with the games of the adolescent girls. At the outset, a musical Prelude is based on a mysterious chant that accompanies their dancing. . . . The Chosen One is the one to be consecrated by spring, the one who must yield to spring that force which her youth had hold over. The young girls dance around the Chosen One, who remains motionless in a sort of apotheosis. Then it is the purification of the earth and the evocation of the ancestors. And the ancestors also circle the Chosen One, who begins her Sacrificial Dance. . . ."[3]

Stravinsky himself seemed none too upset by the stormy reaction, and *The Rite of Spring*—both in its original form as ballet music and as an independent orchestral tone poem—was soon recognized as one of the great masterpieces of the early twentieth century.

The music—which reveals both emotionality and extraordinary new materials—is certainly the core of the work's greatness. The orchestra is very large, expanded to over ninety instruments. Woodwinds are in fives, and there are eight horns and a large battery of percussion. Stravinsky calls for instruments not normally heard in the orchestra—the breathy alto flute, strident small trumpet and small clarinet, bass trumpet (played by a trombonist), Wagner tubas, antique cymbals, and gourd—and all of the instruments are driven to the limits of their ranges and instructed to play in many irregular ways. Plainly, the composer wanted to increase the number of sounds that the orchestra could produce and the diversity of ideas and emotions that such sounds could evoke.

The melodic element does not at first attract our attention because it seems reduced to a mosaic of fragments (many drawn from Eastern European folk songs) that are spun out by repetition and ostinato. The harmonic and tonal organization of the work makes no consistent reference to key and, instead, constantly shifts among passages that are diatonic (for example, in the folk song that Stravinsky quotes in the bassoon at the beginning of the ballet), octatonic (as in the flourish in the trumpets that announces the appearance of the Sage), and whole tone in the frenzied "Dance of the Earth." These passages are shown in Example 65-1.

Authenticity in the Writings of Stravinsky

Stravinsky's first important essay on music is the analysis of *The Rite of Spring* that is excerpted in the box on the facing page. It appears to be a highly valuable and authoritative explanation of one of the great works of music of the twentieth century. But the essay is clouded by controversy over its authenticity. Although published solely with Stravinsky's name as author, the composer received some measure of assistance from the editor of *Montjoie!*, Ricciotto Canudo. Its authenticity was further confused when Stravinsky complained in his *Chronicles of My Life* (1935) that it contained "a distortion of my language and even of my ideas."

Should this complaint be taken seriously? We now know that Stravinsky's *Chronicles* were themselves largely ghost written by Walter Nuvel, an old acquaintance of Stravinsky from Diaghilev's *World of Art* group. The composer's deceptions in claiming authorship for other people's words continued for the rest of his life. His *Poetics of Music*—lectures for the 1939 Charles Eliot Norton Lectures at Harvard University—were written by the French critic Roland-Manuel and the Russian émigré Pierre Suvchintsky. They contain an interesting statement *about* Stravinsky's aesthetic of the

1930s, but they are not what they purport to be—a far more important declaration *by* Stravinsky himself. Stravinsky's unwillingness to speak his own mind has cast doubt upon and created misinformation about his life and musical oeuvre. It has clouded the entire historical record concerning the composer and brought confusion upon the general understanding of his work. Like most plagiarists, Stravinsky was clumsy in his deceptions, sometimes stumbling into ludicrous situations. He was evidently proud of the work done by Roland-Manuel on *Poetics of Music*, and he read one of the lectures to a Parisian gathering of friends that included the poet Paul Valéry. Apparently unknown to the composer, Roland-Manuel had taken ideas from Valéry's own recent college lectures on poetics to put into Stravinsky's mouth, and the composer unwittingly read these to their real author. After the gathering Valéry wrote in his diary: "Stravinsky . . . gets out the text of the lectures he has just written to give at Harvard. He calls them 'poetics' and his main ideas are more than analogous to mine from the course at the Collège."

EXAMPLE 65-1

Diatonic
Solo bassoon, mm. 1-3

Octatonic
Tpts., 2 before reh. 66

(Source octatonic scale)

Whole tone
Bass clar., reh. 75

By 1913 such free harmonic thinking was familiar to the world of new music from the innovations of composers like Richard Strauss and Arnold Schoenberg. It is in rhythmic organization that *The Rite of Spring* breaks new ground. The work contains an unprecedented rhythmic energy, achieved by exploiting a virtual catalog of alternatives to normal rhythmic organization.

In the Introduction to Part 1, for example, there is little sense of beat at all, instead a free intertwining of lines with differing motions. Then in the first scene, "The Augurs of Spring," the rhythm changes to a steady, hypnotic pounding of eighth-note values (Ex. 65-2). These are cut through by irregularly placed accents that dispel any normal or symmetrical meter. Onstage, at this point, a dancer impersonates an old woman who, Stravinsky writes, "runs, bent over the earth, half-woman, half-beast. The adolescents at her side are Augurs of Spring, who mark in their steps the rhythm of spring, the pulse beat of spring."

EXAMPLE 65-2

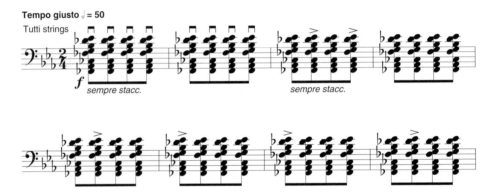

The chord played by the strings in this passage shows Stravinsky's keen ear for dissonant harmonies, which even by themselves can be exciting and rousing. The lower strings play a E-major triad (spelled as F♭) while the upper strings at the same time sound an inversion of an E♭7 chord. The combination arising by a juxtaposition of familiar but unrelated harmonies is often called a **polychord.** Stravinsky's use of key signature (three flats) in this scene may relate to the presence of the E♭ harmonic component, although the scene is not organized by this or any other key. Yet another type of rhythmic organization is found in the concluding "Sacrificial Dance." The meter of this passage changes virtually from one bar to the next, with only a small submetric value (here a sixteenth note) acting as a common element that runs through (Ex. 65-3).

EXAMPLE 65-3

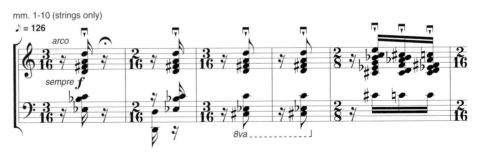

In passages of the "Dance of the Earth," Stravinsky constructs a complex rhythmic canon. At Rehearsal 70 (Ex. 65-4) the part for D-clarinet and D-trumpet contains a repeated rhythm consisting of a quarter-note followed by a dotted half-note, suggesting a meter with four beats; the same figure is heard in the trombones and C-trumpet III but is offset by two beats. Stravinsky notates the passage in $\frac{6}{4}$, which does not conform to the meter expressed in either stratum.

EXAMPLE 65-4

Stravinsky's often brutal rhythms, mesmerizing ostinatos and moments of wrenching tension in *The Rite of Spring* showed once and for all that the new resources and outlook of musical modernism were capable of holding the attention of an audience. They were destined to be the central elements in musical expression of the twentieth century.

LISTENING CUE

IGOR STRAVINSKY
The Rite of Spring (1913)
Procession of the Sage
The Sage
Dance of the Earth

CD 11/5–7
Anthology, No. 174

THE RUSSIAN REVOLUTION

On 15 March 1917, Tsar Nicholas II abdicated his throne amid uncontrollable strikes, rioting, and military insurgency throughout Russia's largest cities. The crisis was most directly provoked by the disastrous economic and social effects of Russia's participation in World War I, during which the country relentlessly descended into chaos and anarchy. After the tsar's departure, a provisional government was established, but the real power was in hands of councils of workers and soldiers (called "soviets"). Those in St. Petersburg (which in 1914 had been renamed Petrograd) gradually threw their support to the **Bolshevik** faction led by **Vladimir Lenin,** who promised to end Russia's involvement in the war, to distribute land to peasants, and to cede power to the soviets. On the night of 6 November 1917, the Bolsheviks seized control from the provisional government, and thus began a long and violent process of consolidation and centralization of power. In 1922 the older Russian empire was reassembled as the Union of Soviet Socialist Republics (USSR), which endured until its ultimate collapse in 1991.

The effect of the **Russian Revolution** on musical culture was profound. Many artists greeted the change of government with a positive idealism. "I and those associated with me," wrote Sergei Prokofiev, "welcomed it with open arms. I was in the streets of Petrograd while the fighting was going on, hiding behind house corners when the shooting came too close."[4] Lenin immediately placed Anatoli Lunacharsky—a respected writer—in charge of culture and education, and Lunacharsky brought such leading younger artists as Marc Chagall, Vasili Kandinsky, and Alexander Blok into his arts ministry. The writer Blok saw the revolution—despite its excesses and violence—as a necessary step in the progress of Russian society and art.

But the desperate economic conditions into which the country was cast caused many of its leading composers and performers to emigrate to Europe. Even earlier, with the outbreak of World War I, Stravinsky had settled in Switzerland and had become increasingly estranged from his homeland. He would not return to Russia until 1962. Diaghilev and his Ballets Russes were likewise permanently established in Europe. Sergei Prokofiev left in 1918 to try his luck in America; the great pianist and composer Sergei Rachmaninoff quickly departed for Scandinavia, never to return.

 # SUMMARY

The arts in Russia near the turn of the twentieth century (commonly called the "Silver Age") are characterized by an absorption of modern developments from western Europe and a reduction in the importance accorded to realism or traditional thinking. The nationalistic element of earlier Russian composers remained in force, but this was often redirected into artistic studies of archaic or primitive aspects of Russian society.

The transformation in taste in Russian music and art was furthered by the impresario Sergei Diaghilev, who in 1909 formed a ballet company later called the Ballets Russes (Russian Ballet) that brought new works to audiences in Paris and other Western capitals.

The leading composer in Diaghilev's troupe was Igor Stravinsky, whose five ballet scores for the Ballets Russes, composed between 1910 and 1920, include *The Rite of Spring*, a work notable for original thinking in rhythm, the use of Russian folk melodies, colorful orchestration, and powerful expression of primitive humanity close to nature. The rhythmic innovations in the work include shifting meters, suppression of regular meter by irregular accents, and rhythmic canons. In passages such as "The Augurs of Spring," Stravinsky's harmonies include polychords—dissonant chords made from juxtaposing two familiar though unrelated harmonies.

The Revolution of 1917 marked a break with the past as the leading Russian composers and performers left the country, their place soon to taken by younger figures.

KEY TERMS

Silver Age
realism
Alexander Siloti
Evenings of Contemporary
   Music
Sergei Diaghilev

Mir iskusstva (*World of
   Art*)
Triple Entente
Ballets Russes
   (Russian Ballet)
Mikhail Fokine

Vaslav Nijinsky
polychord
Bolshevik
Vladimir Lenin
Russian Revolution

Atonality: Schoenberg and Scriabin

Russian-born artist **Vasili Kandinsky** created the painting in Figure 66-1 shortly after hearing a 1911 concert devoted to the works of the Viennese composer Arnold Schoenberg (1874–1951). Kandinsky, who was accompanied by several fellow artists from the Munich area, heard two of Schoenberg's string quartets and a selection of his songs, as well as his Three Piano Pieces, Op. 11. Although Kandinsky was himself an experienced musician, he was apparently startled by the unusual music. Schoenberg's String Quartet No. 2 (1908) brought in a soprano voice in its last two movements to sing poetry by Stefan George—one of Kandinsky's favorite writers—that speaks of an individual's hope for release from a world containing only misery. The music expresses these sentiments in new ways. For long passages its rhythm and texture are turbulent and unsettled, having little sense of regular pulse or metric symmetry. The harmonies are almost entirely dissonances, and a sense of key is evident only sporadically. The brief Piano Pieces go even further in removing normal tonality and banishing triads—long the building blocks of harmony—which are replaced by a large number of unfamiliar dissonances. Despite these novelties, the works are in certain ways traditional, especially in their familiar genres and intense, almost romantic expressivity.

NEW MUSIC AND ABSTRACT ART

Kandinsky's friends began to speculate on the meaning of Schoenberg's innovations and their relevance to modern painting. Franz Marc, who was with Kandinsky at the concert, thought that Schoenberg wanted each note or chord to stand on its own and that the composer intended to remove all traditional musical laws, composing entirely through instinct like a primitive artist.[1]

Kandinsky's own reaction was to paint the "impression." In this powerful work, certain

FIGURE 66-1

Vasili Kandinsky, *Impression 3 (Concert)*, 1911. Kandinsky's partly abstract painting was created shortly after first hearing Schoenberg's atonal music.

realistic images—human forms and the black piano lid—are evident, but these are outweighed by abstract shapes and fields of color (such as the strident yellow area on the right side) and by a freely emotional expression that communicates the artist's feelings about the music. Kandinsky was one of the first important abstract artists, a painter who used largely nonrepresentational shapes in his works.

In an article that he wrote in 1912, Kandinsky tried to explain the artistic effect of an abstract shape by using the example of a simple line.[2] In the "real" world, a written line exists mainly to fulfill certain functions or uses. In an essay, for example, it can be called on to underscore, or stress, an important thing or concept. But when the line is placed on the canvas of an abstract painting, all such uses are abandoned and the shape can only represent what Kandinsky—echoing the ideas of philosophers going back to Plato—called the "thing in itself." By this he meant that the line took on a pure value and meaning rather than a meaning defined by its use. But what meaning? Kandinsky could only indicate this by a musical analogy. The line, he said, had a "pure inner sound."

This "thing in itself" is what Kandinsky and his artist friends found revealed in Schoenberg's music. The compositions that they heard seemed to lack other symbols of the real world—a normal or euphonious blending of elements or utilitarian purposes—all of which seemed to have been replaced by direct references to more elemental or inner states. Kandinsky was sufficiently provoked to write to the composer himself. In a letter of 18 January 1911 he told Schoenberg: "What we are striving for and our whole manner of thought and feeling have so much in common that I feel completely justified in expressing my empathy."[3]

Schoenberg responded enthusiastically. To explain his music to Kandinsky he was not so philosophical as the artist had been; instead, he chose to emphasize the ways that his music had come into being—by instinctive and spontaneous choices rather than by applying rules. Relying on instinct, he said, could tap into his unconscious mind and produce the truest image of the self, which he thought to be the goal of all art. "Art belongs to the *unconscious*!" Schoenberg exclaimed. "One must express *oneself*! Express oneself *directly*! Not one's taste, or one's upbringing, or one's intelligence, knowledge or skill. Not all these *acquired* characteristics, but that which is *inborn, instinctive*."[4]

✿ ARNOLD SCHOENBERG

Schoenberg's music had not always been so unusual as were the works heard by Kandinsky in 1911. His earlier compositions—songs, chamber pieces, a tone poem based on Maurice Maeterlinck's play *Pelléas et Mélisande*, and a massive oratorio called *Gurrelieder*—were typical products of the late Romantic period. They were intensely melodious, highly expressive, serious to the point of overstatement, and they used harmony and tonality in the enriched manner of such late nineteenth-century figures as Richard Strauss, Hugo Wolf, and Gustav Mahler.

These were among the musicians who inspired Schoenberg during his youth in Vienna. He was largely self-taught as a composer, and he made his mark as an independent thinker. Until 1933 (see Fig. 66-2) he resided alternately in Vienna and Berlin and earned his living primarily as a teacher of composition, at which he was especially gifted. All the while his music attracted attention for its originality and audacity. Among his private students in composition were such leading composers as Alban Berg and Anton Webern, performers including Rudolf Kolisch and

Edward Steuermann, and the conductors Heinrich Jalowetz and Karl Rankl.

His final sojourn in Berlin began in 1926 as professor of composition at the Berlin Academy of Arts. When Hitler rose to power in Germany in 1933, Schoenberg—born a Jew but long since a convert to Lutheranism—was dismissed from his position. With his family he fled first to Paris where, in an act of defiance, he reconverted to Judaism. He then traveled to America and settled finally in California, where he was later appointed to the music faculty of the University of California, Los Angeles.

Although Schoenberg at first embraced the romantic language of Wagner, Brahms, and their followers, he felt compelled to move beyond it and to find a style that was original—recognizable as his alone. Between 1905 and 1908 he gradually developed this alternative, the main characteristics of which were the absence of tonal center and the pervasive presence of dissonant rather than triadic harmony. He never settled on a term to designate this style, but in describing it he repeatedly pointed to one of its most salient characteristics—that he used dissonance as though it was "emancipated." By the **emancipation of dissonance** he meant that dissonant chords could appear freely, and be just as readily understood and enjoyed as triads had been in earlier music.

 FIGURE 66-2
Arnold Schoenberg, *Self-Portrait* (1910). Schoenberg was a skillful painter in addition to being a musician, and he created many self-portraits.

THE ATONAL STYLE

Others called Schoenberg's music of this new type **atonal.** The composer himself could never accept this term, which he found inherently negative—something that no composer would want to be known for. The phenomenon of atonality in early twentieth-century music gradually took on a more concrete and positive meaning. Such music has no key, that is, no functional harmonic progressions that extend over and unify large spans of a musical work. Its pitch basis is the entire chromatic scale, each tone of which has, at least theoretically, equal importance. Because of this equality of notes, atonal music normally lacks a key signature (the presence of which suggests that seven notes are natural and the other five only "accidental"). The harmonic basis of atonal music consists primarily of dissonant chords, theoretically of any size and intervallic makeup (although triads and other tertian harmonies occur in passing). Other musical features, such as the choice of forms, melodic styles, and rhythmic motions, are more flexible, depending on the taste of the individual composer.

Schoenberg wrote atonal music until the early 1920s, at which time he abandoned the intuitive and spontaneous processes that were originally at its root and which he had emphasized in his correspondence with Kandinsky. Believing that larger forms were incompatible with the spontaneity of atonality, Schoenberg during this period wrote primarily brief character pieces—for orchestra, piano, and voice. He also composed two short operas, *Erwartung* (*Waiting*) and *Die glückliche Hand* (*The Magic Touch*), and an incomplete symphony with voices.

Despite its great originality in harmony, Schoenberg's atonal style still contains features brought forward from late nineteenth-century music. These include expressive melody, traditional musical textures, irregular phrase lengths, and an intense

Schoenberg on Atonal Music

Schoenberg was reluctant to describe his music as "atonal," since he believed that the tones in any composition had some degree of relatedness. In place of this word, he used the term "emancipation of dissonance" to characterize his works written between 1908 and 1923. Here Schoenberg describes this concept:

> The term *emancipation of dissonance* refers to its comprehensibility, which is considered equivalent to the consonance's comprehensibility. A style based on this premise treats dissonances like consonances and renounces a tonal centre. By avoiding the establishment of a key, modulation is excluded, since modulation means leaving an established tonality and establishing *another* tonality.
>
> The first compositions in this new style were written by me around 1908 and, soon afterward, by my pupils,

Anton von Webern and Alban Berg. From the very beginning such compositions differed from all preceding music, not only harmonically but also melodically, thematically, and motivally. But the foremost characteristics of these pieces *in statu nascendi* were their extreme expressiveness and their extraordinary brevity. At that time, neither I nor my pupils were conscious of the reasons for these features. Later I discovered that our sense of form was right when it forced us to counterbalance extreme emotionality with extraordinary shortness. Thus, subconsciously, consequences were drawn from an innovation which, like every innovation, destroys while it produces. New colourful harmony was offered; but much was lost. . . . [5]

development of motives. Still, Schoenberg's innovations most capture our attention. One of the most controversial of these is his banishing of triads from his atonal music. He explained why these were no longer admissible: "I believe they would sound too cold, too dry, expressionless. Or, perhaps, what I mentioned on an earlier occasion applies here. Namely, that these simple chords, which are imperfect imitations of nature, seem to us too primitive."[6]

Schoenberg also believed that a richness of tone color was appropriate to atonal music. He mentions it in his correspondence with Kandinsky in the context of painting: "Color is so important to me (not 'beautiful' color, but color which is expressive in its relationships)." In his *Theory of Harmony* (1911) Schoenberg proposed a new resource for modern music that he called **tone-color melody** (***Klangfarbenmelodie***) in which a succession of differing timbres could take on a structural role in a composition akin to that of normal melody. In a "melody" of this type, each tone or chord could have its own particular timbre.

Piano Piece, Op. 11, No. 1

Schoenberg's Three Piano Pieces, Op. 11 (1909), are among his earliest compositions in the atonal style. Each is a brief character piece having a definite mood. Piece No. 1 is generally somber, and it frequently erupts into momentary outbursts. One of the difficulties that the piece poses for the listener and performer is that these conflicting moods—and the musical figures that embody them—are so abbreviated. They change quickly from one moment to the next, and the melodic ideas themselves tend to dissolve into minute fragments. The quick moving, abbreviated shapes, lack of keynote, and absence of triadic harmonies make Schoenberg's music difficult for most of us to understand. Schoenberg was well aware of this difficulty and thought that it could be overcome only by many years of familiarity. In a letter of 1937 he remarked about his music: "I am content if they do not dislike it when they hear it the fifteenth time," he confessed.

The tonal organization of Piece No. 1 conforms to the general characteristics of atonality. The notes of the full chromatic scale are drawn on equally, the harmonies are almost entirely dissonant, and there are no functional harmonic progressions. Typical also of the atonal composer, Schoenberg subtly coaxes new colors from the piano. One way that he does this is by using **piano harmonics.** In measures 14–17, Schoenberg instructs the player silently to depress the tones F-A-C♯-E, thus releasing the dampers on those strings. The left hand then plays the same notes in a lower register, which makes the partials of these open strings shimmer with a glassy tone.

The form of the work is closest to the ternary model. The music opens with a theme (measures 1–11), itself having a small ternary design. The middle section follows with a succession of contrasting subsections, each of which plainly develops motives from the theme. At measure 53 the theme is brought back in a recognizable though transformed state. The perpetual development of motives in the piece is something shared with nineteenth-century composers (recall from Chapter 58 Brahms's pervasive use of the motto F - A♭ - F in the first movement of his Third Symphony). Schoenberg, like such forebears, at first aimed in his atonal music for a unified and homogeneous substratum that could support a diverse and changeable surface.

LISTENING CUE

ARNOLD SCHOENBERG
Piano Piece, Opus 11, No. 1 (1909)

CD 11/8
Anthology, No. 175

THE EVOLUTION OF SCHOENBERG'S ATONAL STYLE

Shortly after he completed the Piano Piece No. 1 in February 1909, Schoenberg began to experiment with a far more radical type of atonal music having fewer points of contact with traditional styles and structures. He began at this time to compose in a stream of consciousness, without the development of motives that is apparent in the Piano Piece. "I strive for complete liberation from all forms, from all symbols of cohesion and logic," he wrote to Ferruccio Busoni. "Thus, away with 'motivic working out.'"[7] His opera *Erwartung* (1909) was one of several pieces written in this new way.

Schoenberg's experiment soon led him into a compositional crisis in which he lost his confidence and inspiration. In 1911 he wrote to his student Alban Berg: "I've lost all interest in my works. I'm not satisfied with anything any more. I see mistakes and inadequacies in everything. Enough of this; I can't begin to tell you how I feel at such times."[8] Gradually, Schoenberg pulled himself out of his creative doldrums, which he did by rethinking how atonal music could be created. He dispensed with the procedure that he had described to Busoni and Kandinsky—composing as an "unconscious" act—and moved toward an opposite viewpoint by which composing would once again be methodical, leading to familiar musical forms while retaining the more general features of atonality.

He looked back in time to the great works of Bach, Beethoven, and Brahms, and he found all of these composers working consciously with themes and motives to create unified structures. Their motivic craftsmanship was lacking in his stream-of-consciousness pieces, so he decided to return to an earlier formal outlook and use motives even more pervasively and systematically than ever.

Pierrot lunaire

Pierrot lunaire (*Moonstruck Pierrot*, 1912) was the crucial piece that set Schoenberg on this future direction; it is one of his most original creations in the atonal style. *Pierrot lunaire* is a cycle of twenty-one narrations for a female speaker accompanied by a small ensemble of piano, strings, and woodwinds. Its genre is that of the **melodrama**, a composition that combines spoken recitation with instrumental music (in Chapter 55 we encountered an example of the style in the Wolf's Glen Scene in Weber's opera *Der Freischütz*).

The words of *Pierrot lunaire* are drawn from a collection of French poetry of the same title by **Albert Giraud** (1860–1929), translated into German by Otto Erich Hartleben. They deal with the sad-sack, moonstruck clown Pierrot, whose antics range from the comic to the grotesque. Each of the poems, or "rondels," has thirteen lines of which lines 1–2 are repeated as 7–8, and line 1 returns as line 13.

The delivery of the speaking part was not left entirely to the reciter. Schoenberg instead wrote out a recitation, using musical notation that dictates the rhythms precisely and shows approximate pitches. Schoenberg emphasized that he wanted the reciter to speak, not to sing, although the exact interpretation of the reciter's part occupies an indefinite place between speech and song. Schoenberg called this type of recitation **Sprechgesang** (speech song), and he notated it by placing an X through the stems of notes. An example from the eighth recitation is shown in Example 66-1.

EXAMPLE 66-1

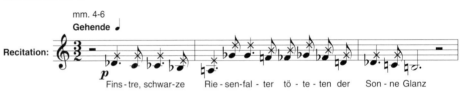

Dark, black, giant butterflies killed the sunshine.

Schoenberg's new way of composing systematically with themes and motives is especially evident in the eighth recitation, titled "Nacht (Passacaglia)." The poem contains a grotesque vision of gigantic butterflies sinking to earth and blotting out the sun, which Schoenberg depicts by growling sounds from the bass instruments and by a contrapuntal texture that ranges from strict canon to free imitation.

The music is saturated by a three-note motive—first heard in the piano in the form E-G-E♭—whose many recurrences suggest the term **passacaglia,** which Schoenberg chose for the title of this movement. Recall from Chapter 31 that a passacaglia in the seventeenth century was a work based on continuous repetitions of a short thematic figure.

While the baroque composer usually confined the recurring thematic figure to the bass line, creating a so-called **basso ostinato,** Schoenberg uses the E-G-E♭ figure in all of the lines, and he also spreads it vertically into several interlocking and adjacent parts. We can see how he does this by observing the instrumental introduction in measures 1–3. As seen in Example 66-2, there are six brief lines present in these measures (four in the piano part alone), and each of them descends by semitone except for the single note in the bass clarinet. The basic motive is presented not linearly but vertically, by joining adjacent tones from several lines. For example, in measure 1 the motive E-G-E♭ arises in the two lowest lines of the piano part.

In this way, the composer extends the unifying power of a motive beyond a single linear dimension into the two-dimensional space that music occupies. Schoenberg believed that this verticalized presence of motives represented a "discovery" that was so logical and so closely connected to trends in great music of the past that it would eventually become standard practice among composers. It led him directly to his **twelve-tone method** of composing, which he devised in 1923 (see Chapter 69).

EXAMPLE 66-2

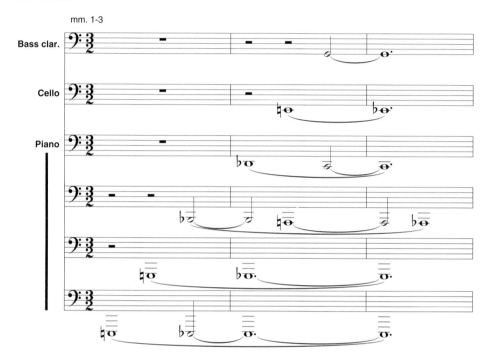

Following the introduction, the basic motive is spread into the two-dimensional texture by means of strict imitation. In measures 4–10, for example, the instruments play a canon on a theme that begins with the three-note motive. In measure 8 the clarinet states the basic motive simultaneously over different spans of time (Ex. 66-3). Here the motive is heard in groups of eighth-notes in three different transpositions; also, the three first notes, three second notes, and three third notes of each eighth-note group state the motive.

EXAMPLE 66-3

LISTENING CUE

ARNOLD SCHOENBERG
Pierrot lunaire (1912)
No. 8, "Nacht (Passacaglia)"

CD 11/9
Anthology, No. 176

❋ OTHER ATONALISTS: ALEXANDER SCRIABIN

The atonal style emerged in the first decade of the twentieth century, not only with Schoenberg in Vienna but also among progressive composers in many other locations worldwide. Its characteristics are seen in works composed between 1905 and 1910 by Béla Bartók in Hungary, Igor Stravinsky in St. Petersburg, and Charles Ives in New York. One of its most important converts was the Russian composer Alexander Scriabin (1872–1915). He was born in Moscow and educated at the Moscow Conservatory, where he developed skills as a pianist. Typical of the nineteenth-century virtuoso, he composed for his own instrument, mainly sonatas, character pieces, and a piano concerto (1896), which he performed on tours in Europe and America. These compositions were at first romantic in style, with a melodiousness and harmonic vocabulary reminiscent of works by Chopin. He began to compose symphonic music in 1900, and his later symphonies and tone poems are programmatic. His Fifth Symphony ("Prometheus—Poem of Fire," 1910) calls for the projection of colored lights that he associated with certain keys (C major, for example, was red). But Scriabin never devised a practical notation for this idea.

Around 1908 Scriabin began to compose atonal music. The distinctive trademarks of his atonal style—and its differences from Schoenberg's brand of atonality—are apparent in his Five Preludes for Piano, Op. 74. These short pieces were completed in 1914, only months before Scriabin's untimely death. Prelude No. 5 is marked *fier, belliqueux* (proud, warlike) and filled with flamboyant and expressive rhetoric, quite unlike Schoenberg's understated Piano Piece, Op. 11, No. 1. Scriabin repeats themes and motives in this Prelude according to a simple plan (**ABAB**), unlike Schoenberg, who avoids repetition in favor of a constant development of motives.

While Schoenberg avails himself of a large number of dissonant chords drawn from the chromatic scale, Scriabin limits himself, in making up his lines and chords, to only two collections of notes. These systematically underlie the tonal organization of his entire atonal oeuvre. The first of these is the **octatonic scale,** the presence of which is not surprising in Scriabin since it had long been used by Russian composers (it is sometimes called the "Rimsky-Korsakov scale," given that composer's fondness for it). The other is called the **mystic chord,** or alternately "'Prometheus' chord" since it is prominent in Scriabin's "Prometheus" Symphony. The mystic chord appears as the first harmony of "Prometheus," taking the form G-D♯-A-C♯-F♯-B (Ex. 66-4). Scriabin uses it not only as a chord per se, but also as the source for notes in lines and themes.

EXAMPLE 66-4

If we place its tones into a compact scalewise order, such as F♯-G-A-B-C♯-D♯, we see that the mystic collection of pitches is closely related to a whole-tone scale, since only one note (F♯ in the preceding example) deviates from a fully whole-tone pattern. The mystic collection is also closely related to a segment of an octatonic scale. By moving the single tone B to become B♭, it forms six of the eight notes of the octatonic scale F♯-G-A-B♭-(C)-C♯-D♯-(E).

Scriabin has several ways of varying the octatonic and mystic collections of tones when he uses them in a piece of music. He presents them equally as lines and chords, he sometimes omits tones from them, and he freely reorders their notes. He also transposes and symmetrically inverts their pitches. A symmetric **inversion** of a collection of notes results if the intervals formed by those notes *above* the first tone are duplicated *below* it. Consider the mystic collection illustrated above: F♯-G-A-B-C♯-D♯. It can be symmetrically inverted by duplicating its *ascending* intervals instead in a *descending* direction, that is F♯-F♮-E♭-D♭-C♭-A.

We can see how Scriabin uses these relationships in the very first measure of his Prelude No. 5 (Ex. 66-5). The notes that make up the second half-note beat of this measure, placed in a compact scalewise form, are B♭-A-G-F-E♭-D♭. On beat three the tones are D-E♭-F-G-A-B. Apparently, the two collections (both versions of the mystic chord) are related by symmetric inversion followed by transposition. On beat one there are seven notes, C-D♭-E♭-F-G-A-B♭, which merge, in a sense, a mystic collection with its inversion, since the first six notes, as shown in the scalewise order, are inversionally related to the last six.

EXAMPLE 66-5

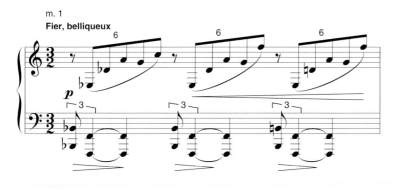

The form of Prelude No. 5 is clarified by shifts between the mystic and octatonic collections. Music A (mm. 1–4 and 9–12) is generally based on mystic collections; music B (mm. 5–8 and 13–17) is almost entirely octatonic. To see how Scriabin uses the octatonic scale, look at measure 5 (Ex. 66-6). The six tones appearing in this measure are drawn from the octatonic scale A-B♭-(C)-C♯-D♯-(E)-F♯-G. The two missing tones (C and E) are supplied in the measures that immediately follow.

EXAMPLE 66-6

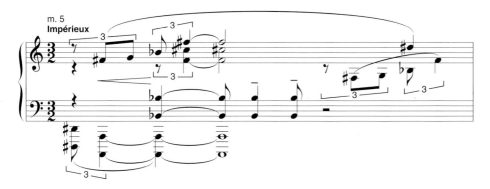

LISTENING CUE

ALEXANDER SCRIABIN
Piano Prelude, Opus 74, No. 5 (1914)

CD 11/10
Anthology, No. 177

SUMMARY

Around 1908, Arnold Schoenberg began to compose "atonal" music, a style characterized by the lack of traditional key and functional harmonic progressions, a free and theoretically equal use of all tones of the chromatic scale, and a free application of dissonant harmonies, which are treated as though equivalent to consonant (triadic) chords. Modern artists of the same time, such as the Russian-born Vasili Kandinsky, recognized similarities between atonal music and their own abstract, nonrepresentational paintings. In his atonal pieces from 1910 and 1911, Schoenberg experimented with composing in a stream of consciousness—very quickly and with a minimum of planning. Beginning with his recitations of *Pierrot lunaire* (1912), he began to compose atonal music more systematically, returning to strict polyphony and reinforcing traditional linear motivic unity by deploying motives throughout a texture.

Schoenberg's Russian contemporary, Alexander Scriabin, also began to compose atonal music around 1908, evolving, as did Schoenberg, from his earlier romantic language. The pitch organization of Scriabin's atonal music is based upon the octatonic scale and the so-called mystic chord, the latter a six-note collection of tones that is close to the whole-tone scale.

KEY TERMS

Vasili Kandinsky
emancipation of
    dissonance
atonal music
tone-color melody
    (*Klangfarbenmelodie*)

piano harmonics
melodrama
Albert Giraud
Sprechgesang
passacaglia
basso ostinato

twelve-tone method of
    composition
octatonic scale
mystic chord
(symmetric) inversion

Chapter 67

French Music at the Time of World War I: Ravel and Satie

The esteem accorded the music of Claude Debussy following the premiere in 1902 of his opera *Pelléas et Mélisande* showed that modernism had reached a considerable degree of acceptance by French audiences. This new work was given no fewer than fourteen performances in its first season at Paris's Opéra-Comique—an extraordinary number for a composition of such complex originality. Its innovations caused a great stir throughout French intellectual and artistic circles; Olivier Messiaen recalled playing the music of *Pelléas* as a child and finding it "a revelation, a thunderbolt." Erik Satie heard the work at the Opéra-Comique shortly after its premiere and described it to his brother as something "absolutely astounding."

Debussy's modernism resided in a great originality of both form and material, and it extended to new ways of presenting melody, a new harmonic and tonal language, and new ideas about rhythmic organization (see Chapter 63). He allied his music with the most recent trends in French painting and literature, and in all of these ways it suggested a certain elitism. It was difficult for his contemporaries to understand and plainly not intended for everyone.

At the same time that Debussy's music appeared triumphant, new or alternative ideas arose among his contemporary composers. Some figures of an older generation—Camille Saint-Saëns (1835–1921) and Vincent d'Indy (1851–1931) are examples—could not accept Debussy's innovations at all, and several younger French composers had their own ideas of how music should progress. Erik Satie (1866–1925) composed in a radically simplified and almost naivist manner. Maurice Ravel (1875–1937), although sharing many of Debussy's romantic inclinations, moved his music into a new relationship with works from the past.

MAURICE RAVEL

Maurice Ravel was the leading younger French contemporary of Debussy. He lived for virtually his entire life in and around Paris. At the age of fourteen he entered the Paris Conservatory, first as a piano student, and later in the composition class of Gabriel Fauré. As a budding composer he at first enjoyed the support of Debussy, who described him as "extraordinarily gifted," although their relations at a later time became strained.

Ravel lived as a freelance musician, primarily from income derived from the sale of his music and from concerts in which he conducted and played piano. He occasionally taught—one of his students was Ralph Vaughan Williams (see Chapter 61), with whom he formed a close friendship—although Ravel never held an institutional teaching appointment. Following World War I, he was recognized internationally as one of the greatest living composers, and he traveled the world giving concerts of his own music. He undertook a triumphant but grueling tour of the United States and Canada in 1928. His last compositions date from 1933, after which he suffered from a degenerative condition that may have been a form of Alzheimer's disease.

Ravel wrote music in all of the important genres of his day—opera, ballet, orchestral tone poems and piano character pieces, songs, chamber music, and concertos. In his early works—those composed before World War I—he concentrated on the piano. After the war he turned decisively to orchestral composition, at which he was especially skilled. Among the orchestral genres he bypassed only the symphony, as did other progressive French composers, including Debussy and Fauré. Among his larger works are the ballets *Daphnis et Chloé* and *Boléro*, the tone poem *La valse* (which was intended as a ballet score), the Piano Concerto, and the monumental piano collections *Miroirs* (*Mirrors*) and *Gaspard de la nuit* (*Gaspard of the Night*).

While the works of Debussy are fairly homogeneous in style, those of Ravel are highly diverse. His early compositions are plainly indebted to Debussy's influence. Ravel generously described Debussy as "the most phenomenal genius in the history of French music," but he added, "I believe that I myself have always followed a direction opposite to that of Debussy's symbolism."[1] Ravel gradually freed himself from Debussy and experimented in a variety of new techniques including jazz adaptations and atonality. Some of these were associated with younger composers, and especially with the music of his friend Igor Stravinsky.

Ravel set off in this "opposite direction" from Debussy primarily by adopting a new outlook on music of the past. This was different from the conservative attitude that was held earlier by a Mendelssohn or Brahms. These composers were concerned mainly with preserving in their music the outlines of Viennese classicism, which they updated and extended in an orderly manner. Ravel was not interested in preserving a particular heritage so much as he was drawing from anywhere and everywhere in the past to create an entirely contemporary musical language. His sources were diverse, some coming from as far back as the Baroque period, others more recent, and others still drawn from such popular musical idioms as American jazz and Spanish flamenco. Ravel revived the forms that he found in his sources and parodied their styles, which he updated with modern harmony.

At the turn of the twentieth century, musicologists in France were hard at work promoting the country's musical past, especially the compositions of Baroque masters such as Jean-Philippe Rameau (1683–1764) and François Couperin (1668–1733). In 1895 the Parisian publisher Durand began to produce an edition of the complete works of Rameau, beginning with his harpsichord music, and in 1903 Durand came out with an edition of Couperin's 1722 *Concerts royaux* (*Royal Concerts*). Ravel apparently studied these sources and drew upon them for ideas for new works.

Le tombeau de Couperin

In the piano suite *Le tombeau de Couperin* (*Couperin's Monument*, 1914–1917), Ravel revives the forms and certain of the styles of harpsichord music from the Baroque period in France, especially as they occur in the works of François Couperin. The word *tombeau* (French for "tomb" or "monument") had been long used by French composers to designate a musical tribute to a great predecessor, especially a deceased teacher.

Recall from Chapter 36 that François Couperin was a harpsichordist and composer employed by King Louis XIV of France. Among his greatest works are twenty-seven dance suites for harpsichord (Couperin called them *ordres*, or "orderings"), and other suites called *Concerts royaux* (*Royal Concerts*) that were playable either by harpsichord alone or with the addition of a few instruments.

Ravel appears to have studied Couperin's fourth *Royal Concert* (c1722) prior to composing his *Tombeau*, and he made it the model for a brilliant and thoroughly modern suite of piano pieces. Ravel's *Tombeau* consists of six movements—Prelude, Fugue, Forlane, Rigaudon, Menuet, and Toccata. These allude to dance types that (with the exception of the Toccata) appear in Couperin's 1722 Royal Concerts. Like Couperin, Ravel writes each of his dances (except for the C-major Rigaudon) in a single key, E minor. Couperin's Fourth Royal Concert is also in E, alternating between minor and major. With some exceptions, Ravel also preserves the binary or rondo forms in which Couperin casts his dance movements. So serious was Ravel's study of Couperin's Fourth Royal Concert at this time that he made an incomplete arrangement for piano of its Forlane movement, probably as a way to absorb Couperin's idiom.

The Rigaudon from Ravel's *Le tombeau de Couperin* is an especially brilliant and festive work. In the seventeenth and eighteenth centuries, a **rigaudon** was a lively social dance in $\frac{2}{4}$ time. It was often imitated in the music of French baroque operas and instrumental suites. The opening of the Rigaudon that appears in Couperin's Fourth Royal Concert is shown in Example 67-1; below it is the beginning of Ravel's Rigaudon. Couperin uses a familiar binary form in his Rigaudon, which is expanded by Ravel into a ternary alternative. Ravel also captures the motoric rhythms of Couperin's baroque style. In harmony, however, Ravel's piece is thoroughly modern. It alludes to the key of C major, although in the interior of the piece chromatic tones are liberally added as the music dashes through a series of conflicting tonal centers.

EXAMPLE 67-1

Couperin's Rigaudon, mm. 1-8

Légérement, et marqué

Ravel's Rigaudon, mm. 1-7

Assez vif

Ravel's way of referring to music of the past was influential on composers living in France after World War I. Especially significant was his tendency in *Le tombeau de Couperin* to treat the past as though it were his musical *subject*—to write music, that is, about music. This outlook would shortly become central to the 1920s style called **neoclassicism,** to which we turn in the next chapter.

LISTENING CUE

MAURICE RAVEL
Le tombeau de Couperin (1914–1917)
Rigaudon

CD 11/11
Anthology, No. 178

ERIK SATIE

Prior to the end of World War I, the works of Erik Satie were unrelated to any general development in French serious music. Satie played piano as a child and, beginning in 1879, attended the preparatory division of the Paris Conservatory. His advancement there was found unpromising, and he dropped out in 1886. He then worked as cabaret pianist—first at the famous **Chat Noir** in the Montmartre district of Paris—composing and arranging popular songs for the establishment and writing whimsical essays for its publications. Through his appearances in this and other

Cabaret Then and Now

Today **cabaret** is a relaxed form of popular musical entertainment in which a singer croons above the soulful tones of a piano for audiences in a nightclub setting. In Satie's day, in Paris, it was something different. In 1888 Satie was hired as a piano accompanist at the Chat Noir (Black Cat) in Montmartre, the first important modern cabaret. The word "cabaret" comes probably from a small tray on which drinks are served. A show at the Chat Noir usually included dramatic skits, shadow plays (forerunners of cinema), and the singing of poet-songsters. The mood was anything but relaxed, being instead satiric and provocative. The style was intentionally rough and always relevant (at least in the eyes of the performers). For artists of all disciplines in the 1880s, cabaret was a way of bringing average citizens face to face with art.

The singer Yvette Guilbert (1865–1944) introduced a new type of cabaret art, that of the *diseuse*. With piano or small-band accompaniment, she partly sang, partly spoke a poem that ridiculed and poked fun at the society of her day. Her performances may well have been a model for Schoenberg's *Pierrot lunaire*.

The old art of cabaret was exported from Paris around the world. It found a thriving home in Germany—especially in Berlin—where the artistic trappings of the Chat Noir were reconstructed. This is the risqué world of entertainment that was recreated in 1966 in the show *Cabaret,* with music by John Kander. The musical was the basis for a highly successful 1972 film starring Liza Minnelli, which captures the spirit of anything-goes that made German cabaret unique. With the rise of the Nazis in the 1930s, the freethinking cabaret was ruthlessly eliminated.

❀ FIGURE 67-1

Satie frequently drew whimsical portraits, often of himself, as in *Projet pour un buste de M. Erik Satie (Project for a Bust of Mr. Erik Satie)*. Their humor and understatement are reflected in his music.

cabarets, he became acquainted with numerous classical musicians, including Debussy and Ravel, who found him to be an eccentric and irrepressible personality (Fig. 67-1). Finding the life of a cabaret pianist increasingly burdensome, Satie aspired to write classical music, and he returned to school in 1905, at the age of almost forty, to study counterpoint.

Satie's first significant exposure as serious composer came in 1911 when Ravel performed three of his piano pieces at a concert of the Société Musicale Indépendante (of which Ravel was a founder). The performance led to the publication of several collections of piano music, and gradually other Parisian pianists, including the virtuoso Ricardo Viñes, took them up.

Satie's reputation grew steadily, and in 1917 Sergei Diaghilev commissioned him to compose the music for a new ballet, **Parade,** on which he collaborated with the painter Pablo Picasso and writer Jean Cocteau. *Parade* attracted attention for its novelty, unpretentious tunefulness, and absorption of popular musical styles, and these features seemed to forecast a new spirit in the arts, which Satie and Cocteau continued to encourage in the years to come.

Satie wrote mainly short piano pieces, to which he gave eccentric and witty titles such as "Three Pieces in the Shape of a Pear" and "Three Truly Limp Preludes (For a Dog)." The humorous tone was probably a carryover from Satie's work in cabaret, where parody was the order of the day.

There are also a few songs and pieces using small orchestra or instrumental ensembles, including the scores for the ballets *Parade, Mercure* (1924), and *Relâche* ("Closed," 1924).

One of Satie's piano pieces played by Ravel in 1911 was the Sarabande No. 2, one of three works with this title that Satie had composed in 1887. The piece must have baffled the listeners of 1911 because its complete artlessness was so opposite the highly elaborate new music of the day. The Sarabande resembles a mere improvised succession of chords, presented in a monotonously repetitive form, with very little melody and rhythm and absolutely no counterpoint or development of ideas.

The chords themselves alternate among triads, major sevenths, and major ninths, only occasionally presented with functional harmonic implications. The central sonority is the major ninth chord (for example, E-G♯-B-D-F♯ in m. 18). These harmonies are presented mainly in streams in which the dissonant tones are neither prepared nor resolved, and the chords rarely fulfill tonal harmonic functions. Throughout the piece we can almost hear Satie—wearing his famous wry smile—ask his listeners why harmonies must progress and why dissonances must resolve!

Following World War I, with the onset of a broad reaction against the late Romantic style, Satie's music of simplicity, humor, and naiveté emerged as a precursor of important events and trends. Satie himself relished this newfound significance, and musicians worldwide praised his music for its refreshingly anti-Romantic profile. The American composer and critic **Virgil Thomson,** who while a student in Paris in the 1920s met Satie, became a lifelong admirer. For him Satie's music is "as simple, as straightforward, as devastating as the remarks of a child."

LISTENING CUE

ERIK SATIE
Sarabande No. 2 for Piano (1887)

Thomson-Schirmer Website
Anthology, No. 179

WORLD WAR I

During the summer of 1914, Ravel vacationed on the French coast, working on a new string trio "with an insane certainty and lucidity," as he told his friend Maurice Delage. On 1 August news arrived that Germany had declared war on Russia; two days later Germany declared war on France, and all of Europe then descended into general warfare. The issues that precipitated war—militarism, economic rivalry, and nationalistic hostility, among others—had before 1914 exerted little effect on musical culture. The major concert halls and opera houses of Europe presented a cosmopolitan repertory, and on a personal level European composers of different nationalities got along reasonably well.

Internationalism seemed to be the order of the day throughout the musical world. The Englishman Edward Elgar was an outspoken admirer of German culture, and the German Richard Strauss praised Elgar's progressivism. "I raise my glass to the welfare and success of the first English progressivist, Meister Edward Elgar, and of the young progressivist school of English composers," he said in a 1902 speech. The Austrian Arnold Schoenberg respected Claude Debussy's avant-gardism, and the Russian Igor Stravinsky considered France a second home.

Given these cordial international contacts among leading musicians, the declaration of war took virtually everyone by surprise. Many musicians were on vacation in August, when the announcement of war was made, and most thought that the conflict would be quickly settled. Still, there was great uncertainty. Schoenberg hurriedly returned to Berlin from his vacation, spent with the Russian painter Vasili Kandinsky in the Bavarian resort of Murnau. Ravel returned to Paris from his vacation retreat on the French coast, Elgar from Scotland to London.

Composers had different reactions to the onset of war. Many felt helpless and bewildered by world events, with a dark apprehension about their future as musicians. Debussy wrote to his publisher shortly after war was declared: "I'm nothing more than a wretched atom hurled around by this terrible cataclysm, and what I'm doing seems to me so miserably petty!"[2] Others rethought old allegiances. Ferruccio Busoni—an Italian composer and pianist living in Berlin—cynically reassessed his adopted German identity:

> I used to say: there exist in the world, all in all, either *incipient* or *moribund* cultures. Only the diminutive area between London and Rome, between Paris and Moscow [i.e., Germany], can credit itself with a culture which is florescent and vigorous, mature yet still youthful (I used to say). I declare this opinion to be one of the greatest mistakes I ever made.[3]

Most musicians became rabid patriots, willing to exchange their instruments for rifles. Schoenberg at the age of forty enlisted in the Austrian army; Ravel, despite poor health, joined the French forces. "Vive la France!" he wrote to Cipa Godebski. "But, above all, down with Germany and Austria! Or at least what those two nations represent at the present time. And with all my heart: long live the Internationale and Peace!"[4] Paul Hindemith, whose father would shortly be killed in battle, wrote from Frankfurt: "Many French pretend to be wounded or dead, then shoot our troops in the back. It is entirely the fault of the French if German troops become outraged and act thoughtlessly."[5]

For the duration of the war, 1914 to 1918, musical culture throughout Europe was much reduced. Travel was restricted, and many composers were deprived of an income from foreign royalties. Although efforts existed in most countries to spare artists from combat, many composers, painters, and writers were killed, including the German painters Franz Marc and August Macke, the French composer Albéric Magnard and his countryman, the writer Charles Péguy.

What would be the outcome of this war for music? The question was pondered by musicians everywhere, and most foresaw profound and lasting changes looming on the horizon. In 1914 the English music critic Ernest Newman wrote:

> The war, if it be prolonged, will mean the drawing of a line across the ledger and the commencement of a new account. It is impossible for the Continent to pass through so great a strain as this without a setting free of great funds of dormant emotion, and a turning of old emotions into new channels. These tremendous crises always have a far-reaching nervous effect.[6]

The "new channels" so accurately predicted by Newman will be outlined in chapters to follow.

 SUMMARY

Although Debussy's approach to modernism was the most important direction in French music in the decade before World War I (see Chapter 63), alternative styles are seen at the same time in the works of Maurice Ravel and Erik Satie. Ravel began his career as a composer by writing piano music that could not escape Debussy's powerfully evocative Impressionism, but Ravel later tried to distance himself from Debussy by finding his own style. He did so in part by adopting a new approach to music of the past, which he drew upon in the manner of parody. In his piano suite *Le tombeau de Couperin* he derives forms and stylistic ideas—motoric rhythms, ornamented melodic lines, and a percussive treatment of the keyboard—from François Couperin's *Royal Concerts* (1722), which he updates with modern harmonies and tonal organization.

The piano pieces of Erik Satie, such as his Sarabande No. 2 (1887), are highly simplified and primitivized in technique. With a puckish humor, they seem to question hallowed rules of traditional music, such as the necessity for goal-directed harmonic progressions and the preparation and resolution of dissonances.

World War I (1914–1918) marked the end of an era in musical history.

KEY TERMS

rigaudon	Chat Noir	*Parade*
Neoclassicism	cabaret	Virgil Thomson

Chapter

68

New Music in Paris After World War I: Stravinsky and The Six

On 11 November 1918, three German diplomats arrived in the village of Compiègne near Paris to meet Marshal Ferdinand Foch, the commander of the Allied armies during the final stages of World War I. The visitors accepted Foch's terms for German surrender, and all signed an armistice that ended the war. As news of this event swept through France, there was an outpouring of exhilaration and also utter exhaustion. On the positive side for France, their armies had spearheaded the successful Allied war effort, conquering the mighty German Empire and regaining the lands lost to Germany after the humiliating defeat in the Franco-Prussian War of 1870–1871. The war had forged a close alliance between the French and the people of the United States—by 1918 the world's greatest economic power—and cultural interchange soon increased between the two countries. But the French people had suffered greatly. Four years of horrific warfare had been fought largely on French lands, at the staggering cost of 1.4 million of its citizens killed.

✸ MUSICAL LIFE IN PARIS

Although the northern and eastern provinces of France had experienced a drastic level of destruction during the war, Paris was spared, and after the Armistice its musical culture quickly rebounded. Opportunities to hear new music multiplied. The Russian émigré conductor **Serge Koussevitsky** (1874–1951) founded an orchestra in Paris in 1920 that performed new works by French and Russian composers. Stravinsky's Octet (discussed momentarily) and Maurice Ravel's brilliant orchestration of Modest Mussorgsky's *Pictures at an Exhibition* were among the compositions first heard in Koussevitsky's concerts. In 1924 Koussevitsky was appointed director of the Boston Symphony Orchestra, with which he diligently supported new symphonic compositions by American composers.

Ballet companies specializing in new repertory also proliferated following the war. The Ballets Russes, led by Sergei Diaghilev (see Chapter 65), continued to present a season in Paris every year, and after the war they gave the premier performances there of new works by Igor Stravinsky, Sergei Prokofiev, Erik Satie, and younger French-born musicians. In the 1920s Diaghilev had to compete with several new rivals, including the modernistic **Ballets Suédois** (Swedish Ballet) and the **Ballets Ida Rubinstein,** which first presented Maurice Ravel's ballet *Boléro* in 1928.

An important musical discovery in postwar Paris was **jazz.** Immediately after the end of the war, American and English dance bands arrived in Paris to play at casinos and fashionable bars such as Le Boeuf sur le Toit (The Ox on the Roof, named after a trendy 1919 ballet by Darius Milhaud). Their music ignited a craze for dancing and helped to dispel the bitter memories of war. They called their playing "jazz," although it had little in common with what we now call jazz. The typical dance band that came to Paris after 1918 was a large ensemble that mixed strings, woodwinds, brass, piano, plucked instruments, and drums, and it played written arrangements in which improvisation had little if any role. The music was filled with lively syncopations, crisp and polished playing, and the musicians were adept at creating special sound effects by glissandos, mutes, exaggerated vibrato, and the resources of the percussionist's **drum set.**

The high-spirited dance music had a powerful attraction for classical composers. In jazz they discovered a style that was down to earth, something distinctly appealing after a period when grandiosity and complexity in music had left many listeners bewildered. It was also the source of many new musical ideas, especially in its rhythm, whose originality was underscored by the young Parisian composer Darius Milhaud:

> The power of jazz comes from a novelty of technique that extends to all of its elements. In rhythm there is an exploration of resources resulting from the constant use of syncopation, opening up in this music a realm of expression with the simplest means that does not need a rich or varied orchestration.[1]

Jazz rhythms were quickly imported into many new works by the leading French classical composers—including Igor Stravinsky, Maurice Ravel, Erik Satie, Georges Auric, and Milhaud himself—as a mingling of the high and popular arts became the order of the day. The pianist **Jean Wiéner** (1896–1982) launched a concert series in Paris in 1920 in which new experimental pieces were performed side-by-side with jazz band music.

REGAINING CONTROL

Jazz dancing was a welcome antidote to the dismal aftermath of war, whose appalling chaos made all Europeans look to regain control. This became an underlying theme in the arts in the decades after 1918, and in music it helped to produce one of the clearest and most definitive stylistic changes in its history.

Like many other shifts in artistic temperament, the change of taste after the war can be most readily assessed in the visual arts. We find examples in the works of the Dutch artist **Piet Mondrian** (1872–1944), who lived in Paris both before and after World War I. His paintings before the war extend the language of the French impressionists (see Chapter 63). An example from 1908 is his *The Winkel Mill in Sunlight* (Fig. 68-1). Here Mondrian, like the impressionists before him, depicts a familiar object found in the countryside. But, unlike the im-

FIGURE 68-1
Piet Mondrian, *The Winkel Mill in Sunlight,* 1908.

pressionists, he interprets it through a hotly expressive composition, in which the realistic appearance of the windmill largely dissolves beneath large brush strokes, strident colors, and abstract shapes. All of these convey the painter's apparently volatile feelings about the object. A degree of anxiety reigns within the painting, as serenity and order are sacrificed to the painter's emotions.

Compare this painting to Mondrian's *Vertical Composition with Blue and White* (Fig. 68-2), executed after World War I. In this work the depiction of natural objects is replaced by fields of color ordered by a strict and abstract geometry. The viewer finds a certain coolness in the painting as the hot patch of blue is forced almost entirely off the canvas by the large and immoveable rectangles. Everything is under control, as construction has replaced free emotion and subjective expression.

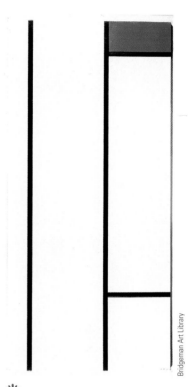

❀ FIGURE 68-2

Piet Mondrian, *Vertical Composition with Blue and White*, 1936.

IGOR STRAVINSKY AND THE NEOCLASSICAL STYLE

The redirection of expressivity seen in Mondrian's postwar painting is also encountered in the music of Igor Stravinsky composed after World War I. In 1914 Stravinsky permanently left Russia and settled in Switzerland, where he lived until 1920. From then until his emigration to America in 1939, he resided primarily in France, although he led a footloose existence in which he was often on tour or shuttling between various French locations. In 1934 he settled with his family in Paris and obtained French citizenship.

Stravinsky composed music between the world wars that continued, as before World War I, to emphasize ballet and other theatric types of composition. These works include the ballets *Pulcinella* (1920), *Apollo Musagetes* (1928), *The Fairy's Kiss* (1928), and *Jeu de cartes* (*Card Game*, 1936), the opera *Mavra* (1922) and an "opera-oratorio" *Oedipus Rex* (1927). Far more than before World War I, he composed in Classical instrumental genres, including symphonies, concertos for piano (1924) and violin (1931), and chamber music.

In these compositions, Stravinsky established himself as the leader of a new style of modern music that corresponds to the general postwar spirit in the arts (Fig. 68-3). Its principal distinguishing feature is its rejection of the aesthetic of late Romantic music, as Stravinsky consciously broke with the dominant style of the immediate past. Certainly, an erasing of memories of a culture that had led to a devastating war contributed to his new outlook. Romantic music was supremely emotive and expressive, so in the 1920s Stravinsky made his new works cool, objective, sometimes witty and full of parody, and often abstract or absolute in asserting a purely musical content. The composer—certainly with a bit of overstatement—declared in his *Autobiography* that music had no expressive power at all. He wrote:

> I consider that music is, by its very nature, essentially powerless to *express* anything at all, whether a feeling, an attitude of mind, a psychological mood, a phenomenon of nature, etc. . . . *Expression* has never been an inherent property of music. That is by no means the purpose of its existence. If, as is nearly always the case, music seems to express something, this is only an illusion and not a reality.[2]

Stravinsky also spoke out in the 1920s against what he termed "modernism" in music of the recent past. "I despise all modern music, outside of jazz," he told an interviewer in 1925. "I myself don't compose modern music at all." This statement seems confusing because Stravinsky's music of the 1920s is thoroughly modern in its novelty of means. It is likely that he was referring to the modern music of the turn of the century, such as that of a

❀ FIGURE 68-3

Stravinsky drawing, *This is my music*. Stravinsky's famous drawing of his music suggests works with a spare linearity, irregularly placed meters, and the complexity of a maze.

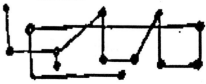

Richard Strauss or Arnold Schoenberg, music whose larger-than-life rhetoric and complexity had built upon the works of their German Romantic forebears.

Stravinsky's new music would instead be aimed to please a broad audience in its directness and relative simplicity, and it would be written expressly to appeal to listeners of his own time. He was less inclined to delve—as he himself had done in a work such as *The Rite of Spring*—into timeless matters and to use experimental or unfamiliar means of expression whose acceptance could be hoped for only in the future. "It would be a great mistake," said the composer at the end of his *Autobiography*, "to regard me as an adherent of *Zukunftsmusik*—the music of the future. Nothing could be more ridiculous. I live neither in the past nor in the future. I am in the present."

Stravinsky's desire to live in the present rather than in the past or future is especially evident in his banishing of regionalism and folklorism from his new music. These features were at the very core of his own early ballets, as we have already seen in *The Rite of Spring* (see Chapter 65), in which the composer addresses a subject from Slavic folklore and lavishly quotes folk melodies. Such things were now ruled out. Folklorism, among artists, Stravinsky wrote, "is a naive and dangerous tendency which prompts artists to remake an art that has already been created instinctively by the genius of the people. It is a sterile tendency and an evil from which many talented artists suffer."[3] In the place of a regional outlook, Stravinsky asserted an international—indeed universal—perspective in compositions that contain nothing that can positively identify them as Russian or French.

Stravinsky's break with romanticism suggested to many of the critics of the 1920s that the composer was trying to turn the clock back, by imitating elements of music more characteristic of the Classic and Baroque periods than those of the nineteenth and twentieth centuries. This was something that had recently been seen in Ravel's *Le tombeau de Couperin* (see Chapter 67) or Sergei Prokofiev's *Classical* Symphony (1917). It led the critics to give the name "**neoclassicism**" to Stravinsky's new style. "In impulse and incentive there is quite a remarkable affinity between Bach and Stravinsky," wrote the English critic Edward Evans in 1921, "and I feel that it will become more apparent as time goes on."[4]

Stravinsky himself was at first leery of the notion that he was primarily attempting to revive Classical styles, although he later warmed to the idea. In a 1924 article in which he described his newly completed Octet (excerpted in Box), Stravinsky does not mention the term "neoclassicism" or the idea of a revival of earlier styles. But when he wrote about the same piece in 1963, he was quick to give credit to Bach:

> Bach's two-part Inventions were somewhere in the back of my mind while composing this [third] movement, as they were during the composition of the last movement of the Piano Sonata. The terseness and lucidity of the inventions were an ideal of mine at the time, in any case, and I sought to keep those qualities uppermost in my own composition.[5]

The Octet (*Octuor*)

The octet was a familiar medium for chamber music of the Classical period. Beethoven's Octet, Op. 103, calls for wind instruments and it resembles Mozart's Serenades, especially the wind octets of K. 375 and K. 388. Stravinsky's Octet (1923) is also for winds: flute, clarinet, and pairs of trumpets, bassoons, and trombones. In his essay "Some Ideas About My Octuor" (see Box), the composer explained his choice of this heterogeneous ensemble by praising its potential for a cold, rigid, and distinct sound. The subgroups, he continued, could produce strong contrasts in volume and serve to clarify the music's form, which was synonymous with its content.

"Some Ideas About My Octuor" by Igor Stravinsky (excerpts)

"My Octuor is a musical object. This object has a form and that form is influenced by the musical matter with which it is composed. The differences of matter determine the differences of form. One does not do the same with marble that one does with wood. My Octuor is made for an ensemble of wind instruments. Wind instruments seem to me to be more apt to render a certain rigidity of the form I had in mind than other instruments—the string instruments, for example, which are less cold and more vague. . . . My Octuor is not an 'emotive' work but a musical composition based on objective elements which are sufficient in themselves. . . . The aim I sought in this Octuor, which is also the aim I sought with the greatest energy in all my recent works, is to realize a musical composition through means which are emotive in themselves. These emotive means are manifested in the rendition by the heterogeneous play of movements and volumes. This play of movements and volumes that puts into action the musical text constitutes the impelling force of the composition and determines its form. . . .

"Form, in my music, derives from counterpoint. I consider counterpoint as the only means through which the attention of the composer is concentrated on purely musical questions. Its elements also lend themselves perfectly to an architectural construction.

"This sort of music has no other aim than to be sufficient in itself. In general, I consider that music is only able to solve musical problems; and nothing else, neither the literary nor the picturesque, can be in music of any real interest. The play of musical elements is the thing. . . ."[6]

The Octet's diminutive medium—hard and clear in sound—is only one of several means by which Stravinsky dispels the mists of romanticism. The work is concise. Its three movements—titled "Sinfonia," "Theme with Variations," and "Finale"—last scarcely thirteen minutes. Its spirit is light, melodious, and witty—there is no angst, no hyper-emotionality, nothing that would make those in the audience listen with their heads in their hands.

Especially in the fast tempos, the controlled rhythmic chaos of Stravinsky's earlier *Rite of Spring* is replaced by an almost motoric sense of beat, which is occasionally draped over changes of meter. The music has a cosmopolitan tone, devoid of regionalisms or folk song quotations and cleansed of anything that could identify the nationality of its creator. The design of the first movement suggests a concise sonata form with slow introduction.

These and other features remind the listener of aspects of the music of the Classical period, although the work has a thoroughly modern harmonic and tonal language. Stravinsky's high spirits suggest that the work's classicism is—as it was for Ravel in *Le tombeau de Couperin*—more of a witty parody than any naive revivalism. The American composer Aaron Copland—who was present at the Paris premier performance of the work in October 1923—aptly described Stravinsky's parody as "art grafted on art."

LISTENING CUE

IGOR STRAVINSKY
Octet (1923)
First movement, "Sinfonia"

CD 11/12
Anthology, No. 180

DARIUS MILHAUD AND "THE SIX"

The lighthearted spirit of Stravinsky's Octet also appeared in the new music of younger native-born French composers during the decades following World War I. An article published in 1920 in a Paris journal identified a group of these figures as **"The French Six,"** and those named—Darius Milhaud, Georges Auric, Francis

Poulenc, Germaine Tailleferre, Louis Durey, and Arthur Honegger—found the term to be good publicity and gave a series of joint concerts. They were encouraged in their efforts by Erik Satie and by the influential French writer **Jean Cocteau** (1889–1963), whose works trumpeted many of the anti-romantic ideals for postwar music also espoused by Stravinsky. In his widely read pamphlet *Le coq et l'arlequin* (*The Cock and Harlequin*, 1918), Cocteau demanded a music of tuneful and entertaining simplicity. It would be the opposite of late Romantic German music, which "grimaces" and "wears a mask."

Darius Milhaud (1892–1974) readily complied with Cocteau's demand. Milhaud (pronounced MEE-OH) was born in the south of France and educated at the Paris Conservatory. He lived in the United States after 1940, and following the end of World War II held teaching positions both at Mills College in Oakland, California, and the Paris Conservatory. He was an immensely prolific composer whose early works, those from about 1915 through the 1920s, are best known. These include ballets and operas, chamber works, and piano pieces.

Milhaud was fascinated by popular music, whose styles he frequently brought into his own compositions. He had a special affinity with American jazz, which he heard on a trip to Harlem in 1922 and then re-created in his ballet *La création du monde* (*Creation of the World*, 1923). During a two-year sojourn with the French diplomatic corps in Rio de Janeiro, he became familiar with Brazilian popular dance music. He remarked on its special rhythmic character:

> I was intrigued and fascinated by the rhythms of this popular music. There was an imperceptible pause in the syncopation, a careless catch in the breath, a slight hiatus which I found very difficult to grasp. So I bought a lot of maxixes and tangoes and tried to play them with their syncopated rhythms that run from one hand to the other. At last my efforts were rewarded and I could both play and analyze this typically Brazilian subtlety.[7]

Milhaud made use of Brazilian dance rhythms in his collection of piano character pieces titled *Saudades do Brazil* (*Longing for Brazil*, 1920). In addition to the presence of syncopated rhythms, these pieces are all studies in **polytonality.** This is a simultaneous presentation of two or more keys or diatonic collections of tones in different strata of a composition, and it was long a Milhaud specialty. He described its attraction for him as a resource for emphasis and expression in new music: "I think that it gives to music a sort of particular brilliancy. It can mean much more powerful fortissimi, much more tender pianissimi. It increases the field of expression that we have at our disposal," he wrote.[8]

"Botafogo" (the name of a beach in Rio), from *Saudades do Brazil*, illustrates Milhaud's imaginative use of his diverse resources. The piece imitates the Brazilian samba, with its comfortable syncopations and simple repetitive form. In the first section (mm. 1–26) the two hands quickly pull apart into a polytonal texture (Ex. 68-1). The right plays in F♯ minor, the left in F minor, and the two come together at cadences. In the middle part (mm. 27–42), the right hand plays mainly white keys, suggesting C major against the left hand's black keys.

EXAMPLE 68-1

LISTENING CUE

DARIUS MILHAUD
Saudades do Brazil (1920)
"Botafogo"

CD 11/13
Anthology, No. 181

SUMMARY

Parisian musical culture quickly returned to life following the end of World War I in 1918, at which time a new spirit emerged throughout the artistic world. An emphasis on simplicity, directness, construction, and objectivity tended to replace the older romantic notions of a warm string sound, a large colorful orchestra, a programmatic agenda, and overt displays of emotion. Many French music critics found the new spirit in music embodied in a return to the styles and forms of the Classical and Baroque periods, and they termed the new musical taste "Neoclassicism." The leading figure of the movement was the Russian émigré Igor Stravinsky, whose Octet (1923) is an example of the leaner, clearer style of Neoclassicism.

A group of younger native-born French composers called "The Six" shared in Stravinsky's Neoclassical style. One of their most adventuresome members was Darius Milhaud, who brought popular music into his original compositions and experimented with new harmonic ideas including polytonality. In this style, differing keys exist simultaneously in different strata of a composition.

KEY TERMS

Serge Koussevitsky
Ballets Suédois
Ballets Ida Rubinstein
jazz

drum set
Jean Wiéner
Piet Mondrian
neoclassicism

The Six (The French Six)
Jean Cocteau
polytonality

Chapter

69

Vienna in the Aftermath of War: Twelve-Tone Methods

> I shall never forget what an opera performance meant in those days of direst need. For lack of coal the streets were only dimly lit and people had to grope their way through; gallery seats were paid for with a bundle of notes in such denominations as would once have been sufficient for a season's subscription to the best box. The theater was not heated, thus the audience kept their overcoats on and huddled together and how melancholy and gray this house was that used to glitter with uniforms and costly gowns![1]

The writer Stefan Zweig made these observations when he returned to Vienna following World War I and found his native city in a state of chaos, its economy shattered, its people in the grip of a famine so severe that many of them literally starved to death.

Zweig discovered that in this time of "direst need" the Viennese turned as never before to music. "The conductor lifted his baton, the curtain parted and it was as glorious as ever," he wrote, "and we strained and listened, receptive as never before, because perhaps it was really the last time. That was the spirit in which we lived, thousands of us, multitudes, giving forth to the limit of our capacity in those weeks and months and years, on the brink of destruction. Never have I experienced in a people and in myself so powerful a surge of life as at that period when our very existence and survival were at stake."[2]

AUSTRIA AFTER 1918

Austria and its empire had been totally transformed by the war. In 1916, after sixty-eight years on the throne, Emperor Franz Joseph died, and with him passed a symbol of Austria's political stability and cultural identity. Shortly after his death, under the burden of war, the Hapsburg Empire itself broke apart. The eastern regions declared their independence and reconstituted themselves as the new nations of Czechoslovakia, Yugoslavia, Hungary, and Poland. On the day of armistice, the Hapsburg monarch, King Charles I, abdicated his throne and fled to Switzerland, leaving behind only a small German-speaking country. Austria on that day was declared a republic.

These political and social changes had important implications for music. The Opera in Vienna was no longer the "Court Opera" but the "State Opera," and it had to rely for its very existence on a subsidy from a faceless city government. Still, music flourished. The management of the Opera scored a coup by bringing in Richard Strauss as co-director. The Vienna Philharmonic Orchestra, then under the leadership of Felix Weingartner, continued to present highly acclaimed concerts in the splendid Musikverein (see Chapter 58). A strict diet of modern music could be had at the concerts of the Society for Private Musical Performances, founded by Arnold Schoenberg in 1918.

ORGANIZING THE TWELVE TONES

Just as in Paris following World War I, in Vienna too composers felt the demand for control and organization in new music. In Paris the call for order had been answered by Igor Stravinsky's turning away from both radical modernism and from the entire musical language of late Romanticism. Stravinsky replaced the older outlook on music with an objective and plainly structured modern music that seemed attuned to the day.

Musicians in Vienna similarly looked for laws and systems that could justify the advances in music that had arisen largely from instinct. Several of the leading Viennese composers of the postwar period looked to the tones of the chromatic scale—which in earlier atonal music had been drawn upon freely and interchangeably—as a resource especially in need of organizational principles. One such musician in Vienna was **Josef Matthias Hauer** (1883–1959). Self-taught as a composer, Hauer wrote songs and brief piano pieces prior to World War I. "I worked by instinct," he recalled, "without any external theory, following only my inspiration with no conscious thought."[3] By 1920 his attitude had changed, and he then announced the discovery of a simple "twelve-tone law" that provided him with the conscious guidance he then desired. "Within a given succession of tones," Hauer proclaimed, "no note may be repeated and none may be omitted."[4]

The way that Hauer applied his twelve-tone law can be gathered from the opening of his Etude for Piano, Op. 22, No. 1 (1922; Ex. 69-1). The melodic line in the work consists of a succession of statements of the twelve tones (Hauer called each one a "building block"), and within each block no tone is repeated and none omitted. Hauer did not extend his law to the chords of the piece, which consist of simple triads and their extensions. Here are the tones in the first four melodic building blocks:

1. E♭ B♭ G G♭ D D♭   G♯ E B F A C   (mm. 1–2)
2. E G B♭ D F♯ C♯   B D♯ G♯ C A F   (m. 3)
3. C♯ G E D B♭ C   G♯ A G♭ E♭ B F   (m. 4)
4. E C C♯ B♭ D A♭   D♯ A G F F♯ B   (mm. 5–6)

EXAMPLE 69-1

mm. 1-11

Since Hauer does not repeat or omit any tones within a block, he has observed his own twelve-tone law. Writers today often use the term **aggregate** to designate one of Hauer's twelve-tone building blocks. This term—which will be useful for the discussion that follows—refers to a contiguous presentation of all twelve notes, with none repeated except in an immediate context. Reformulated using this more modern terminology, Hauer's twelve-tone law states that the melodic stratum of a composition should consist entirely of a succession of aggregates.

Hauer also had a method for promoting continuity from one aggregate to the next and for allowing twelve-tone organization to govern the form of the work as a whole. Throughout the Etude, the first and second halves (or **hexachords**) of each aggregate share five of the six tones with the corresponding hexachord in the next block. Compare blocks 1 and 2. The first hexachords of both differ in total pitch content only by one tone (E♭ and E are exchanged). Blocks 2 and 3 exchange F♯ and C; blocks 3 and 4, G and A♭. After all twelve tones have been exchanged in this way (which occurs at the end of the seventh block in m. 11), a section of the work ends and music with a new surface design follows.

Hauer's twelve-tone pieces—which enjoyed a measure of prominence in modern music circles during the 1920s—are intentionally primitive in style, as they lack indication of tempo, dynamics, or expressive character, and they have only a limited rhythmic and textural variety. Their austere style comes from Hauer's wish to eliminate traditional expressivity from his music: "The purely physical, sensual, also the trivial and sentimental are, so far as possible, ruled out," he wrote. Plainly, his music embodies a reaction against romanticism and represents the same wish to erase the immediate past that composers such as Stravinsky experienced at the same time.

❁ SCHOENBERG'S TWELVE-TONE METHOD

A more artistic method for organizing the twelve-tones emerged in the works of Arnold Schoenberg following World War I. As we saw in Chapter 66, Schoenberg's earlier atonal compositions drew freely on the full resources of the chromatic scale. In his 1911 *Theory of Harmony*, Schoenberg declared that the chromatic scale was the "conceptual basis" for his new harmonic practices. In a few passages in compositions written before and during World War I, he experimented in forming aggregates, which represents a far more systematic use of tones than before. An instance of this from 1913 is seen in Example 69-2, from an isolated passage in the orchestral song "Seraphita," Op. 22, No. 1. The violins in these two measures play a six-note chord having the tones C♯ F A C E G♯. Against this harmony the clarinets play lines made from these notes transposed down a tone. Since these two hexachords are **complementary** (that is, they share no tones in common) an aggregate is formed. The passage resembles one of Hauer's building blocks, except that Schoenberg has made his twelve-tone structure extend throughout the two-dimensional musical space made from melody plus chord. This desire to integrate musical space is plainly akin to Schoenberg's objective in using the motif E-G-E♭ in "Nacht (Passacaglia)" from *Pierrot lunaire*, discussed in Chapter 66.

EXAMPLE 69-2

For a ten-year period following the composition of "Seraphita," Schoenberg continued to experiment with new methods for bringing order into his hitherto intuitive and freely spontaneous way of composing. In 1923 he consolidated the results of his research into a **twelve-tone method,** which he used in most of his later major compositions.

Schoenberg's twelve-tone method, as it existed in the 1920s and 1930s, contains two entirely different procedures: aggregate formation is one, and the other is a new principle by which melodic phrases are varied. The latter process concerns melodic "shapes," which was Schoenberg's term for what we call phrases—that is, melodic units that can usually be sung in one breath. An example of Schoenberg's innovative way of deriving one shape from another is found within the phrases that make up the main theme of the first movement of his String Quartet No. 4 (the entire movement is given in Anthology, No. 182). This theme, shown in Example 69-3, has three shapes (phrases), which are played in succession by Violin I, Violin II, and Violin I.

EXAMPLE 69-3[†]

Each of the three phrases embodies an aggregate, since each contains a statement of the twelve tones with none repeated except in an immediate or repetitive context. But this twelve-tone feature is not our main concern at this point. Instead, see how Schoenberg varies the first, or "basic" shape, to create the second and third ones. The variational relation among the three occurs, first of all, in a traditional way by the recurrence of small and plastic motives. Notice, for example, that the motive in measure 2 made from three successive eighth notes on the tone A returns in freely varied forms in measures 3, 4, 6, 8, 11, and 12. It is heard finally in measure 13, where the rhythm has broadened to three successive quarter notes on the tone A.

At the same time, a stricter and more systematic variational process is at work, one that is at the core of Schoenberg's twelve-tone method. This involves only tones and the intervals that separate them—not rhythms, contours, or gestures, as in motivic variation—and it concerns the entire succession of notes as they are presented in a given order in the various shapes. Here are the three ordered successions, or **rows,** of tones as they occur in the three phrases:

Phrase 1 (mm. 1–6)
D C♯ A B♭ F E♭ E C A♭ G F♯ B

Phrase 2 (mm. 6–9)
G A♭ C B E F♯ F A C♯ D E♭ B♭

Phrase 3 (mm. 9–14)
B F♯ G A♭ C E E♭ F B♭ A C♯ D

The notes in phrase 3 have the same order as in phrase 1, only reversed (presented, that is, in **retrograde**). The order of tones in phrase 2 also derives from phrase 1, but in a more complex fashion. The notes of phrase 1 are first **transposed** up five semitones, to render the row G F♯ D E♭ B♭ A♭ A F D♭ C B E. Next, this transposed row is symmetrically **inverted.** Recall from Chapter 66 that a symmetric inversion of a group of notes occurs if the intervals formed by those notes are duplicated in the opposite direction. For example, the first interval of the transposed row (G - F♯) is a descending minor second. To begin the formation of an inversion, the second note must form an *ascending* minor second, so the F♯ is replaced by A♭. When this process of replacement is carried out on each tone of the transposed row, the notes of phrase 2 result.

To summarize: Schoenberg in his twelve-tone method treats the entire succession of notes in an original shape as an integral, ordered unit, and he reproduces that unit in the notes of later shapes, albeit changing the tones by transposition, inversion, retrogression, or a combination of these. It is also apparent from the opening of the Fourth Quartet that Schoenberg freely repositions tones in different registers when they return. Schoenberg's process of variation is an example of what has come to be known as **serialism** in music, which means that the order of occurrence of some element in a composition (pitches, in this case) is governed by a predetermined plan or arrangement.

There is one additional aspect of this serialized method of variation that Schoenberg himself considered to be of the utmost importance. This is the capacity of variations upon a shape to unify a two-dimensional musical texture. We have already observed Schoenberg moving in this direction in his *Pierrot lunaire* and song "Seraphita." In the twelve-tone method he extended the idea so as to achieve a homogeneous intervallic unity throughout an entire composition—from beginning to end, and in both the linear and harmonic or textural dimensions. We can see his thinking at work in a passage from the first movement of the Fourth Quartet (Ex. 69-4). In these measures, Schoenberg applies a tone row derived from the basic row (the one encountered in the main theme in mm. 1–6) by inversion and transposition to begin on the note C:

C D♭ F E A B B♭ D F♯ G A♭ E♭

EXAMPLE 69-4

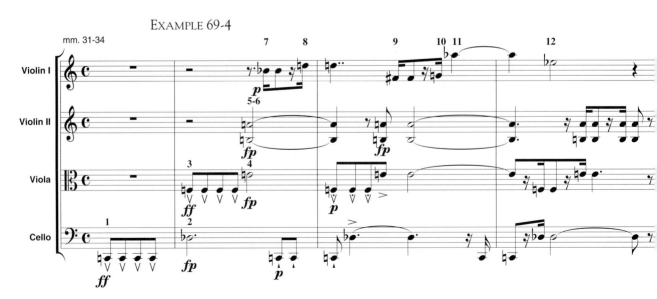

In the measures shown in Example 69-4, Schoenberg does not place this row into any single line or melody but distributes its notes throughout the texture (a process now called **partitioning** the row). The row's distinctive order is still maintained. The first two tones are given to the cello, the next two to the viola. The next two are deployed as a chord in Violin II, and the remaining six are given to the line in Violin I (the notes of the row are numbered in Ex. 69-4). By partitioning the row, the entire four-part texture embodies a variation of the basic shape.

Schoenberg's String Quartet No. 4

Schoenberg's compositional career entered a new phase in 1923, when he established his twelve-tone method. During his earlier period of free atonal composition (1908–1923), he had written primarily short character pieces. But with the twelve-tone method at his disposal, he returned to large instrumental genres, since he then had a structural scaffold on which to build extended compositions. In these works he often uses or approximates Classical forms.

Among Schoenberg's major twelve-tone compositions are his String Quartets No. 3 and 4 (1927 and 1936), String Trio (1946), Woodwind Quintet (1924), Suite for chamber ensemble (1926), concertos for violin (1936) and piano (1942), and Variations for Orchestra (1928). He continued to write melodramas for reciter and instruments, as in the *Ode to Napoleon Buonaparte* and *A Survivor from Warsaw* (this powerful composition is discussed in Chapter 78). Schoenberg also composed numerous twelve-tone works for chorus, and there are two twelve-tone operas—*Von heute auf morgen* (*From One Day to the Next*) and *Moses und Aron* (*Moses and Aaron*). Schoenberg almost entirely abandoned the composing of songs during his twelve-tone period.

Schoenberg's String Quartet No. 4, Op. 37 (1936), is one of his greatest compositions, one that shows that the twelve-tone method is adaptable to music that is inventive and emotionally—as well as intellectually—engaging. The work has four movements, each of which reveals analogies in form and style to quartets from the Classical period.

This Classical tone is especially apparent in the clarity of rhythm and texture in the first movement. The design of the movement is also loosely reminiscent of sonata form, which Schoenberg had not used at all in the diminutive works of his atonal period. Notice the traditional relationship between the bold main theme (see Ex. 69-3) and the lyrical second theme, the beginning of which is shown in Example 69-5. The contrast in character between these themes is often found in Classical movements in sonata form. Also observe in the second theme the underlying tone row, which Schoenberg partitions between the cello and viola. This is the original row transposed up a fifth, just as the second theme in a Classical first movement is normally in a key a fifth above the original one. When Schoenberg brings back the main theme at the recapitulation in measure 239, he returns to the "tonic" by using the original, un-transposed form of the row.

EXAMPLE 69-5

mm. 66-68

In studying the work, we are tempted to focus on the ingenious ways that the composer applies his twelve-tone method. But Schoenberg adamantly rejected this practice. He considered the intricacies of the method itself to be purely a guideline for the composer and virtually irrelevant to the listener. To the violinist Rudolf Kolisch—whose quartet gave the premier performance of the Fourth Quartet— Schoenberg in 1932 commented on twelve-tone analysis:

> This isn't where the aesthetic qualities reveal themselves, or, if so, only incidentally. I can't utter too many warnings against overrating these analyses, since after all they only lead to what I have always been dead against: seeing how it is *done*; whereas I have always helped people to see: what it *is*! . . . My works are twelve-note *compositions*, not *twelve-note* compositions. In this respect people go on confusing me with Hauer, to whom composition is only of secondary importance.[5]

A discovery of what the music "is," in Schoenberg's view, results primarily from listening carefully to the unfolding of themes and motives. Aspects of form, color, pacing, harmony, and contrast all contribute to an understanding of this central thematic element.

LISTENING CUE

ARNOLD SCHOENBERG
String Quartet No. 4 (1936)
First movement, *Allegro molto, energico*

CD 11/14
Anthology, No. 182

ANTON WEBERN

In the 1920s and 1930s, Schoenberg's twelve-tone method was adopted by several of his students, including Alban Berg and Anton Webern, and a few other Viennese composers such as Theodor Adorno and Ernst Krenek. These musicians all developed their own distinctive ways of applying the general idea of the method, and they all created music in different and highly individualized styles. This diversity makes it impossible to speak of any single twelve-tone style in music, or even of any single twelve-tone method.

One of the most distinctive followers of Schoenberg along the twelve-tone road was his student Anton Webern (1883–1945). A lifelong resident of Vienna, Webern received a Ph.D. degree in musicology from the University of Vienna, where he wrote a dissertation on the Renaissance composer Heinrich Isaac (see Chapter 24). In 1904, while at the university, he began to take lessons privately with Schoenberg, with whom he formed a close personal and professional relationship. After a few attempts at tonal composition, Webern began to write atonal music, and in 1924 he adopted a version of Schoenberg's twelve-tone method for his own compositional purposes.

Webern's music received little attention during his lifetime, and he was better known as a conductor than as a composer. He also taught and worked as a consultant for the Austrian radio and for music publishers. He died as the result of a tragic mishap at the very end of World War II. He and his wife had fled from Vienna, which was under bombardment, to live with his daughter and son-in-law in the mountainous western regions of Austria, an area that had recently come under American occupation. On 15 September 1945 he was accidentally shot to death by an Occupation soldier.

Schoenberg Writes to Webern's Widow

18 January 1946
Dear Minna,

For several weeks now I and my friends here have been terribly upset over Anton's death, and we have not been able to understand what took place and how it could have happened to him. And this just now—when at last there are again brilliant prospects for the international recognition of his works. We have all found this tragic in highest measure, and try as I may I cannot convince myself that it is really true that I shall never see him again. We were also shaken by the death of Peter [Webern's son], whom I knew only as a small child and whom I cannot at all imagine as a soldier. This dreadful war has been a frightful disaster for the whole world, and it has brought even greater misery to your family. . . . [Library of Congress]

Arnold Schönberg Center, Vienna

🌸 FIGURE 69-1
Anton Webern.

Webern conferred an opus number on works that he considered complete and important to his oeuvre, although many of these were not published in his lifetime. There are thirty-one works with opus numbers, which include songs, choral music (including two cantatas), a variety of chamber pieces, and short orchestral works (including a brief symphony, which will be discussed momentarily). When he fled Vienna in 1945, he left behind an even larger number of compositions in varying states of completion. These were recovered only in 1965 by Webern's biographer Hans Moldenhauer, and many of these additional works have now been published and recorded.

Webern's music bemused everyone—even his teacher Schoenberg—by its extreme brevity, radical understatement, and textures so disjunct that melodic lines sometimes dissolve into a succession of minute splotches of color. These kaleidoscopic surfaces in his works have been compared to the painting technique called **pointillism,** in which dots of pure and contrasting color merge into recognizable images. An example of the pointillistic technique in painting is seen in Camille Pissarro's *Woman in the Meadow at Eragny* (Fig. 69-2).

Webern's musical pointillism, as in the work of painters like Pissarro, represents an art of the greatest concentration and the most subtle refinement. Performers and listeners

🌸 FIGURE 69-2
Camille Pissarro, *Woman in the Meadow at Eragny, Spring,* 1887. Using a technique termed "pointillism," Pissarro applied dots of pure color that merge at a distance to create realistic images.

Bridgeman Art Library

must diligently attempt to recreate the element of image and continuity that Webern always intended his music to have but which is almost always hidden beneath its fragmented surfaces.

This quality of concentrated and fragmented image is encountered in his Symphony, Op. 21 (1928). The work is for chamber orchestra, consisting of pairs of clarinets and horns, harp, and a string quartet, in which the composer allowed for either one player on a part or for more normal orchestral doublings. There are two movements, and the whole composition lasts about nine minutes.

In the second movement, "Variations," Webern fits a lively range of expression into a duration of less than three minutes and a variety of moods into a rigid form. The music—which Webern originally wanted as the first movement of the Symphony—consists of a theme, seven variations, and coda, each spanning eleven measures. The theme is played in measures 1–11 by the clarinet (Ex. 69-6), and it states the following twelve-tone row (whose notes are numbered from 1 to 12 in the example):

F A♭ G F♯ B♭ A   E♭ E C C♯ D B

EXAMPLE 69-6

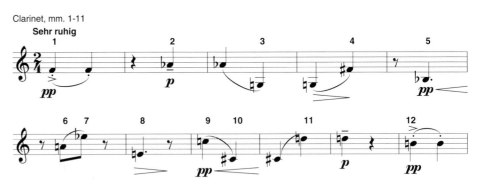

This row has many distinctive features. Its two halves, for example, are symmetrical in that the tones of the second half, transposed to the tritone, are the retrograde of the first half. This symmetrical feature of the row strongly influences the form of the whole movement. An example of this is found in Webern's choice of rhythms and dynamics. The sequence of rhythmic values, dynamic levels, and attack types in the second half of the theme returns in a nearly exact retrograde of that in the first half, just as the notes of the row return in retrograde. This linking of row structure to the order of occurrence of rhythms, dynamics, and attack amounts to a serialization of these non-pitch elements and an integration of them into the twelve-tone structure. The idea of extending the principle of pitch serialism explicitly to other musical elements would become a powerful inspiration to composers following World War II (see Chapter 79).

A comparison of the Variations movement with the first movement of Schoenberg's String Quartet No. 4 will show that the two composers had little in common as to style, form, or even their interpretation of the twelve-tone principle. After the initial presentation of the main theme, Webern tends to avoid conventional themes altogether, allowing his music to explode into a montage of small motives. In comparison, Schoenberg's textures, based on lines and chords, seem entirely traditional.

Webern's way of using tone rows is also very different from Schoenberg's. Recall from Schoenberg's Fourth Quartet that the notes of a row are easily traced in lines and chords, since Schoenberg uses one row (or at most two) at any one time. But Webern tends to interweave numerous forms of the basic row, both within a single line and within the texture. This interlacing often makes it difficult to find the rows and it also usually dispels any straightforward creation of aggregates.

We can see how this happens by studying the second variation (mm. 23–33). The horn part (its beginning is shown in Ex. 69-7) is the easiest to decipher. In this line, Webern alternates tones as they occur in two forms of the row— an inversion beginning on F and a transposition beginning on E:

F D E♭ E C C♯ G F♯ B♭ A A♭ B
(inversion beginning on F)

E G G♭ F A G♯ D D♯ B C C♯ B♭
(transposition beginning on E).

EXAMPLE 69-7

Horn (nontransposing), mm. 23-28

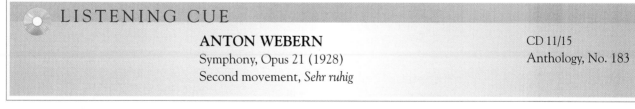

The other instruments in this variation play notes drawn from two additional forms of the basic row (an inversion beginning on E♭ and a transposition beginning on G):

E♭ C C♯ D B♭ B F E G♯ G F♯ A
(inversion beginning on E♭)

G B♭ A G♯ C B F F♯ D D♯ E C♯
(transposition beginning on G).

Webern partitions these two rows into the texture so that segments of no more than two notes of any row are heard one after the other in any line. Plainly, Webern didn't want us to follow the rows, whose role in the music is to provide an abstract unity in the background.

In the Variations movement from the Symphony, Webern generally bypasses Schoenberg's principles of serialized variation and aggregate formation, and he essentially follows his own method of composing.

 LISTENING CUE

ANTON WEBERN
Symphony, Opus 21 (1928)
Second movement, *Sehr ruhig*

CD 11/15
Anthology, No. 183

 SUMMARY

Although Austria was greatly reduced in size following World War I, it continued to be the source of new musical ideas. Several of its progressive composers, including Josef Matthias Hauer, Arnold Schoenberg, and Anton Webern, devised new ways of bringing order into the presentation of tones from the chromatic scale.

Schoenberg's way of doing this was by devising a "twelve-tone method of composition." A work coming from his method has a succession of "aggregates," which are contiguous presentations of the twelve tones with none omitted and none repeated except in an immediate context. The initial melodic phrase in a twelve-tone work is also subject to a new variational process called "serialism," by which its entire succession of notes is reproduced in later phrases and passages, albeit changed by transposition, symmetric inversion, retrogression, or a combination of these. Schoenberg used his twelve-tone method in most of his major new works written after 1923.

Twelve-tone composition was adopted shortly thereafter by Anton Webern, Schoenberg's student. Webern's works are unusually brief and deliberately fragmented in texture, inviting a comparison with the technique of modern French painters called "pointillism." Webern's application of the twelve-tone method is very different from Schoenberg's, with less emphasis on forming aggregates or consistently relying upon serialized variations. Multiple tone rows are often presented simultaneously, tightly interlaced throughout the texture.

KEY TERMS

Josef Matthias Hauer	twelve-tone method	inversion
aggregate	row	serialism
hexachord	retrograde	partitioning
complementary hexachords	transposition	pointillism

Chapter

70

Musical Theater in Germany in the 1920s: Berg and Weill

Theater in Germany in the 1920s enjoyed a popularity surpassing that in any other country in the world. Attending plays, operas, and revues was a passion for the Germans, and in the capital city of Berlin alone the demand for staged entertainment supported some forty professional playhouses, three major opera theaters, and countless "specialty" stages for cabaret, variety, and vaudeville. Berlin's theatergoers could choose from a seemingly infinite variety of plays. The classics—great works of the past from Sophocles to Schiller—were amply available, although these were frequently staged using updated interpretations and technologies.

More recent plays often embodied modern literary styles that also appeared in operas of the day. One such was **naturalism.** Here the playwright looked realistically at the lives of people from the lower social classes, usually underscoring their struggle with the society in which they live. Recall that naturalism (or "realism") is the literary movement that in the 1890s underlay *verismo* opera, such as Pietro Mascagni's *Cavalleria rusticana* (see Chapter 62). In the politicized atmosphere of German theater of the 1920s, these plays often tended toward a proletarian outlook that meshed with Communist ideology by showing class conflicts and laborers struggling to improve their lot in life.

Another modern literary movement with resonance in the world of opera was **expressionism.** Plays of this sort began to appear just before World War I. Typically, they contain a symbolic treatment of characters' irrational impulses, which often lead to grotesque or violent conclusions. An example is August Stramm's *Sancta Susanna* (1914), which deals with the repressed sexual desires of a nun. Aroused by the beauty of a spring night, the nun Susanna tears off her habit and rushes naked to embrace the crucifix. Her performance is interrupted by a huge spider that falls into her hair and leaves her shrieking. As other nuns arrive for prayer, Susanna stands defiant before their cries of "Satan!" The play was made into an opera in 1921 by Paul Hindemith.

❂ GEORG BÜCHNER

Among the major discoveries of Berlin theater culture of the 1920s were the plays of **Georg Büchner** (1813–1837). He was a scientist by profession and an amateur writer who lived in Germany and Switzerland before his death at the age of only twenty-three. Büchner's writings—which include the plays *Woyzeck, Danton's Death* and *Leonce and Lena,* and the novella *Lenz*—were virtually unknown until the end of the nineteenth century, and they first attracted widespread attention even later, in the explosively polarized social climate in Germany and Austria that followed World War I.

Woyzeck was performed repeatedly in Berlin in the 1920s, both as a spoken drama and as the basis for an opera by Alban Berg first given at Berlin's State Opera in 1925. The play itself has a curious history. When Büchner died in 1837 he left it incomplete, consisting of a tangle of disconnected scenes with no title, no clear order of events, and no conclusion. These were all provided by an editor, Karl Emil Franzos, when the play appeared in print in 1879. Franzos titled the drama *Wozzeck*—his reading of the name of its leading character—and he also made up an ending and tried to provide the fragments with a logical order despite the absence of continuity from one to the next.

A later editor, Georg Witkowski, had learned that Büchner's play was based on a historical event: an 1822 trial in Leipzig of a soldier, **Johann Christian Woyzeck,** for the murder of his commonlaw wife. The trial was highly sensational in its day, and reports of it were drawn on extensively by Büchner. During the trial, Woyzeck was examined by Dr. Johann Clarus, who found symptoms of mental disorder, although these did not prevent Woyzeck from being put to death for his crime by a public beheading. The title of Büchner's play in Witkowski's 1920 edition was appropriately changed from *Wozzeck* to *Woyzeck* (in older German handwriting the letter *z* is almost indistinguishable from *y*), and this is the spelling that is now used for the spoken play.

Although a product of the early nineteenth century, Büchner's *Woyzeck* has much about it that is similar to modern German drama of the period following World War I. There is a strong element of naturalism, with a leading character drawn from the lowest levels of a society that brutalizes and ultimately destroys him. It can also be read as a proletarian drama that shows a certain dignity in the laborer Woyzeck, a man with nothing in the world except for Marie, whom he is ultimately driven to murder.

The text also has an uncanny similarity to expressionist plays. Just as in later expressionist writing, some characters have no names (they are called simply "the captain" or "the doctor"), and these figures represent whole social and professional

Synopsis of *Woyzeck* by Georg Büchner

(This synopsis is based on the order of scenes in a 1909 edition by Paul Landau of the Büchner-Franzos text.)

The story of the play unfolds in series of disconnected scenes. The impoverished soldier Wozzeck (Woyzeck in later editions) lives with his commonlaw wife Marie and their child. Marie watches a parade led by the dashing Drum Major, who embraces her. "You're some woman," he says. "We'll have a whole litter of little drum majors!" "If you want," Marie responds. "What's the difference."

At a local tavern, Wozzeck sees Marie dancing with the Drum Major, and his jealousy is aroused. Back in the regimental barracks, Wozzeck hears the Drum Major brag about his pleasures with Marie, and, for good measure, he throttles Wozzeck, who then mutters menacingly "One after the other!"

Village women listen to a folk tale told by an old woman: A poor boy had nothing in the world so he goes into the heavens only to find that the moon is a lump of wood, the sun a withered sunflower, and the stars only gnats. He returns to earth to find that it is an overturned chamber pot, whereupon he sits and cries.

On a walk with Marie by a lake, Wozzeck shrieks out "If not I, then no one else!" whereupon he stabs her to death. Now in a demented state, he returns to the tavern and dances wildly, then returns to the lake and drowns while trying to wash off the blood. The next morning Marie's child is playing in front of his house and other children tell him that his mother is dead, whereupon they leave to see the corpse. Following an autopsy a judge declares that this was the most beautiful murder in a long time.

🌿 FIGURE 70-1

Stage painting by Ludwig Sievert (1887–1966) for the murder scene in *Wozzeck*. Sievert was one of the most famous German operatic set designers of his day. He brought ideas of expressionistic painting to the stage.

Theater Museum of the University of Cologne

classes. The grotesque ending, with its murder and suicide, became stock features of expressionist plays (Fig. 70-1). *Woyzeck*, like many plays in Germany following World War I, also has an anti-military theme through its unflattering portrait of a captain and his insensitive dealings with the common soldier Woyzeck.

❋ ALBAN BERG'S WOZZECK

Büchner's play was used as the text of one of the great operas of the twentieth century, *Wozzeck* by Alban Berg (1885–1935). The composer was Viennese, a student of Arnold Schoenberg, and he saw Büchner's drama when it was given in Vienna in 1914. Feeling an empathy with its leading character, Berg was determined to transform the material into an opera text. But his work on it was delayed by service in the Austrian army, and he completed the opera only in 1922. He left the spelling of the title as *Wozzeck*, the same as in pre-1920 editions of the source play.

At the time when he wrote the opera, Berg was still relatively unknown as a composer, having written only songs and a few short chamber and orchestral pieces. Following the premiere of *Wozzeck* in 1925 at Berlin's State Opera, he vaulted to international recognition and gained confidence as a composer, although he continued to work in a painstakingly methodical manner. He subsequently composed a Chamber Concerto for Piano, Violin, and Winds; a passionate string quartet called the *Lyric Suite*, a Violin Concerto, and a second opera, *Lulu*, based on plays by Frank Wedekind.

For *Wozzeck*, Berg himself made up the libretto—much as Richard Strauss had done for *Salome*—by using material directly from the spoken play. Using Paul Landau's 1909 edition (see Box), Berg selected fifteen of Büchner's scenes and distributed these equally into three acts. His choice of which scenes to include and which to omit shows that he wanted the opera text to be interpreted primarily as a social drama that could elicit sympathy for the world's downtrodden, symbolized by the figure of Wozzeck. He eliminated scenes, such as the old woman's bleakly existentialist tale, that suggest alternative readings, and he ended his opera—as did the editor Franzos—with the grotesque and expressionistic image of Marie's child mindlessly following the other children to see his mother's corpse.

The libretto of *Wozzeck* is markedly different from the opera texts used by the great romantic composers. Wagner's texts for *Der Ring des Nibelungen* (see Chapter 55), for example, contain a pointed critique of contemporary European society—so distracted, in his view, by materialism that the higher values of brotherly love have vanished. But in Wagner's works there is always a hero who can lead mankind toward a better future. His operas are filled with clouds that have silver linings; all end optimistically with a world in which love can again flourish, and all glorify compassionate and fearless heroes who will ride to mankind's rescue.

Berg's *Wozzeck* is entirely different. Its central figure, Wozzeck, is the opposite of a hero, instead a crazed murderer who is snuffed out by his world rather than having any capacity to reshape it. At the end of the play and opera, the audience has no sense that the conditions that produced Wozzeck and brought him down have changed. The cynicism and hopelessness that pervade the work will be encountered often in twentieth-century art and music.

When Berg began to compose the music for the opera, he faced a quandary in choosing the form that the work should take. Büchner's scenes were mostly short and unconnected in time and place with their neighboring scenes. Any attempt at the seamless through-composed operatic form used by Wagner would have been impossible given these disjunctions in the narrative. Also, just as Berg was composing the work between 1914 and 1922, the Wagnerian model was itself being set aside by several important German opera composers in favor of a return to the more traditional scheme of "number opera," in which subdivisions into arias, duets, ensembles, recitatives, and choruses are unmistakable.

The leading figure in this retrospectivist movement was Richard Strauss, the composer who in his earlier opera *Salome* (see Chapter 64) had shown himself to be a stalwart adherent to the Wagnerian conception of operatic form. But beginning in the opera *Der Rosenkavalier* (*The Cavalier of the Rose*, 1910) and even more emphatically in his *Ariadne auf Naxos* (*Ariadne on Naxos*, 1912), Strauss returned to the form of number opera, more reminiscent of the age of Mozart than of Wagner.

Although Berg realized that it was futile to try to apply the Wagnerian form to *Wozzeck*, he was no advocate of Strauss's glance toward the operatic past. So his solution to the question of form in *Wozzeck* was to adopt a highly original compromise. In each of the fifteen scenes, Berg employs some unifying element that gives the scene closure and distinguishability from its surroundings. In some scenes Berg uses a genre, form, or style associated with traditional instrumental music; in others he deploys an ever-present musical figure to lend unity.

Each of the five scenes of Act 3, for example, brings in a musical element as a "principle of cohesion," to quote Berg himself. The first scene dwells upon a theme to produce a theme and variations form; the second uses a single note, B♮, as its point of focus. The third introduces a particular rhythmic figure, the fourth a persistent six-note chord, and the last scene is presented over a steady eighth-note rhythm.

At the end of a scene within an act the curtain falls and the orchestra continues to play transitional music until the curtain again rises. The overall impression of Berg's formal compromise is one of musical continuity with an underlying level of architecture characteristic of instrumental music.

The distinguishability of the scenes is bridged over by thematic recurrences that span and help to unify the music of the entire work. These are similar to Wagner's leitmotives in that they often symbolize elements in the drama. Berg's music also mirrors the drama by a flexibility in style. Depending on the text, for example, the voices in the opera speak or sing in ways that range from the "speech melody" that Schoenberg had used in *Pierrot lunaire* (see Chapter 66) to a pronounced lyricism.

The work's harmonic language is equally varied. The general idiom of the opera is atonal, although moments in the key of D minor are heard in the work's final interlude (which Berg said was a musical representation of his own voice commenting on the fate of Wozzeck). In Act 1, scene 4, there is a passacaglia upon a twelve-tone theme.

A climax of intensity in the opera is reached in Act 3, scene 2, in which Wozzeck murders Marie. The form of the scene is among the freest of the opera since it has almost none of the architectural symmetry that is found in other scenes. Instead, Berg in this scene writes through-composed music that meticulously follows the text, and he brings in an ever-present tone, B♮, as a unifying element and musical symbol.

This note had appeared ominously at the end of Act 2, just after Wozzeck had been thrashed by the Drum Major. After watching the fight, the soldiers in the barracks return to their bunks "one after the other," "einer nach dem Andern," according to Berg's staging instruction. Wozzeck mutters these same words to himself (Example 70-1), but the final note—a hushed low B♮—tells us that by this he means murder, Marie first of all. The note is then heard in every measure of Act 3, scene 2, as a sustained pedal point, representing Wozzeck's murderous obsession.

EXAMPLE 70-1

In his 1929 "Lecture on *Wozzeck*," Berg describes some of the extraordinarily complex methods by which his music represents Marie's murder.[1] He singles out the tangle of her leitmotives—symbols of herself and her world—which race through her mind at the moment of her death (mm. 103–105). He also points to the imaginative way in which the scene-change music (mm. 109–21) at the end of the passage mixes together the unifying tone B♮ with the rhythm that will dominate the next scene. The winds and brass play a great crescendo on the unison tone B (Ex. 70-2), and their entrance points create the rhythm shown on the lower line of the example. This rhythm then becomes the unifying element of Act 3, scene 3, set among dancers in a noisy bar.

EXAMPLE 70-2

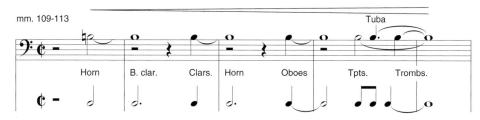

By these and other ingenious ways of linking the music to the drama, Berg in *Wozzeck* showed that the atonal style could be successfully adapted to the genre of opera. His music grippingly expresses even the most human emotions conveyed in Büchner's text.

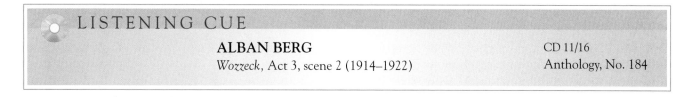

LISTENING CUE

ALBAN BERG
Wozzeck, Act 3, scene 2 (1914–1922)

CD 11/16
Anthology, No. 184

✿ KURT WEILL

Shortly after Alban Berg had taken a small step away from the Wagnerian form of opera in *Wozzeck*, Kurt Weill (1900–1950) made a giant leap away from it in his *Die Dreigroschenoper* (*The Threepenny Opera*). Earlier in the 1920s, while still a student of Ferruccio Busoni at Berlin's Academy of Arts, Weill had attracted attention in Berlin as a composer of modernistic instrumental pieces. Shortly following his apprenticeship with Busoni, he turned to opera and wrote a series of successful works collaborating with the playwright Georg Kaiser. For his *The Threepenny Opera* (1928) he worked with the writer Bertolt Brecht to create one of the most successful and influential works in the entire history of musical theater.

With the rise of the Nazis, Weill was forced to flee from Germany. He moved first to Paris and then permanently to New York City. There he established himself as a Broadway composer, creating a series of hits that include *Lady in the Dark* (1940), *One Touch of Venus* (1943), *Street Scene* (1946), and *Lost in the Stars* (1949).

Weill's music represents an extreme stage in the rebellion against romanticism that in the 1920s came to characterize modern music worldwide. In France critics called the new style neoclassicism, and they pointed to Igor Stravinsky as its leading figure. Weill described his own anti-romantic music as **Gebrauchsmusik,** or "music for use." (This word was also mentioned by the German composer Paul Hindemith for practical pieces aimed at young players and singers.) Weill applied the word differently, for pieces that were useful in their capacity to satisfy the need of a mass audience for music of high quality. In both cases, utilitarianism had replaced the ideal of "art for the sake of art," which was characteristic of music from the late Romantic period.

After his youthful essays in instrumental music, Weill turned decisively to the theater as an outlet for his notion of useful music. He was especially attracted to the writings of the Berlin poet and playwright **Bertolt Brecht** (1898–1956). In such early plays as *Drums in the Night* (1923) and *A Man Is a Man* (1926), Brecht assessed German society of the postwar period with a biting cynicism. In 1928, Brecht and

Synopsis of *The Threepenny Opera*

The opera is set in London in the 1700s. Following an overture, a balladeer appears and sings about the legendary highwayman Macheath, known for his evil deeds as "Mac the Knife." Jonathan Peachum runs a supply shop for beggars, whom he organizes and trains. Those that disobey him are impeached (turned in to the law), hence his name (from "Impeach them!"). Mrs. Peachum brings news that Polly, their daughter, has a new boyfriend, and Peachum suspects that he must be the notorious Macheath. As they speak, Macheath is preparing the stable where he has taken shelter for his wedding to Polly. His gang of thieves is on hand, the sheriff Tiger Brown (an old friend, bought off by Macheath) drops by, and Rev. Kimball arrives to perform the ceremony.

In Act 2 Polly confesses to her parents about her intention to marry Macheath, and the news is not well received. He already has several wives, says Mrs. Peachum. Macheath will receive the usual treatment—the Peachums will have him arrested, impeached, and hanged. But Polly tips Macheath off and he flees. Mrs. Peachum pays one of his whores, Jenny—whose part was originally sung by Weill's wife Lotte Lenya—to lead the police to him, and he is arrested and taken to jail. The plot thickens as the sheriff's daughter, Lucy, reveals that she too is married to Macheath and claims to be pregnant. She helps him to escape from jail.

Outraged by sloppy police work, Peachum threatens Sheriff Brown with a disruption of the forthcoming coronation of a new Queen. Brown arrests him for this, but Peachum threatens blackmail and is released. Macheath is again arrested and a hanging now seems sure. But suddenly there arrives a royal messenger: the new Queen has commanded that Macheath be freed and knighted! At Peachum's command, the moral of the story is given out as everyone sings a hymn: "Don't punish every wrong so harshly," they sing. Concentrate instead on making our own world a better place to live.

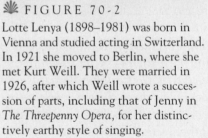

🌸 FIGURE 70-2

Lotte Lenya (1898–1981) was born in Vienna and studied acting in Switzerland. In 1921 she moved to Berlin, where she met Kurt Weill. They were married in 1926, after which Weill wrote a succession of parts, including that of Jenny in *The Threepenny Opera,* for her distinctively earthy style of singing.

his assistant Elisabeth Hauptmann were planning a revival of John Gay's famous English ballad opera **The Beggar's Opera** (1728). This older work (discussed in Chapter 41) is set among London's thieves and beggars, who act out a devastating satire on the culture and politics of the time, one in which Brecht saw parallels with his own day. Spoken dialogue in *The Beggar's Opera* alternates with songs and other musical numbers that Gay's musical collaborator, Johann Christoph Pepusch, arranged from traditional or well-known tunes.

Brecht and Hauptmann translated the text of *The Beggar's Opera* into German, made certain revisions, and added a few song texts from poetry by François Villon and Rudyard Kipling. Weill was brought in to provide musical tunes that would conform to the light and satiric style of the work as a whole, and the team renamed their work: *The Beggar's Opera* was reborn as *Die Dreigroschenoper, The Threepenny Opera.*

The differences separating *The Threepenny Opera* from late Romantic opera reach to the very bedrock of the genre, and they mirror the essential differences separating classical from popular musical theater. The operas of Wagner, for example, were products of the composer's individual imagination, and these arrived at a fixed state that is usually represented by an early performance or edition. The composer could revise this conception at a later time—Wagner did so extensively for several of his operas—but then another fixed and unchanging conception is established. *The Threepenny Opera* is different. It is the product of a collaboration among numerous artists—Weill, Brecht, and Hauptmann, to name only three—and it has no definitive or fixed form. The versions heard in the original performances in Berlin in 1928 were in a constant state of change dictated by circumstances—changes in cast, ad libitum playing and singing, extemporaneous adjustments in length, adding and deleting dialogue and music. The creative team never agreed on a definitive version of the work. Like the score of a later Broadway show, the original editions of Weill's music resemble anthologies of songs rather than a comprehensive record of the thing itself, and Brecht had no hesitation in rewriting the work's dialogue—even changing its meaning—in later published versions of the libretto.

Despite these idiosyncrasies, a general portrait of the work can be drawn. The 1928 staging of *The Threepenny Opera* was especially distinctive and original. There was no attempt to portray the London of 1728 realistically or to transport the audience back in time. The stage was instead plainly a stage and the objects on it were products of the 1920s. A small jazz band sat in plain view in front of the pipes of a barrel organ, and still images and texts were projected on screens to provide the audience with an explanation of the events that they witnessed. The simple vocal parts were performed by actors and operetta stars rather than opera singers, and their pieces tended to interrupt the narrative rather than to advance it. The songs resemble reports on the events and characters in the play more than personalized expressions of individuals in roles.

By these means, Weill and Brecht wanted to avoid normal theatric illusion and to prevent the audience member from being drawn emotionally into an imaginary narrative. Instead, they hoped to detach or "alienate" the listener from the fictitious action so that its relevance to the real world of 1928 could become more apparent. This highly mixed and loose form for a theatric work is now termed **epic theater,** and it is an idea with which Brecht is most closely associated.

Weill's music for the play consists of some twenty numbers, mainly solo songs, duets, and choruses. Larger ensembles ("finales") are situated at the ends of each act, and instrumental music is added here and there. The style of the music evokes jazz—not so much the American variety as the bouncy dance music of tangos, fox-trots, and shimmies that was part of Berlin night life in the 1920s. The accompaniment is for a small jazz band consisting of saxophones and other reeds, brass, plucked instruments, drums, and keyboard instruments played by the conductor. The musical style is highly simplified: the songs are mainly repetitive in form, homophonic in texture, and they use simple triadic harmonic progressions. There is a degree of stridency and linearity in the music that distinguishes it from popular music per se.

The best known of Weill's songs for *The Threepenny Opera* is the very first one, "The Ballad of Mac the Knife." In the 1928 performances it followed the overture, which was played by the band on stage with this message projected on two screens: "Tonight you'll see an opera for beggars. Since this opera is as splendidly conceived as only beggars can do and since it has to be cheap enough for them to pay for it, it'll be called *The Threepenny Opera*."

The curtain was then briefly lowered and, when raised, the actors had taken their places on a darkened stage. The title of the first song, "The Ballad of Mac the Knife," was then projected on the screens, and an actor cast as a balladeer stood to sing the tale of the murderous Mac, accompanied by barrel organ with other instruments gradually added. Weill indicates the character of the strophic song by the words "blues tempo," which suggests something slow and lazy, but the music has no relation to the distinctive form of the American blues song. "Mac the Knife" quickly became a hit song and jazz standard, performed by pop singers including Louis Armstrong, Ella Fitzgerald, and Bobby Darin.

> ### LISTENING CUE
>
> **KURT WEILL**   CD 11/17
> *The Threepenny Opera* (1928)   Anthology, No. 185
> "Ballad of Mac the Knife"

SUMMARY

Opera and spoken theater flourished in Germany in the 1920s and early 1930s. New literary styles in dramas from this time—including naturalism, expressionism, and epic theater—were shared with new operas. *Wozzeck*, by Alban Berg, is based on a play by Georg Büchner and is a literary precursor of both naturalism and expressionism. Its atonal music takes on a novel form by which scenes imitate forms or styles drawn from instrumental music or, in its third act, an ever-present musical element. In this opera, Berg demonstrates that the atonal style could be successful in opera and could express a wide range of emotions.

The Threepenny Opera by Kurt Weill and Bertolt Brecht revives an eighteenth-century English ballad opera in its use of spoken dialogue alternating with musical numbers. It exemplifies Brecht's notion of "epic theater," in which ordinary dramatic illusion is dispelled as the audience is coaxed to focus on the meaning of events for contemporary society. Weill's music consists primarily of songs having a popular flavor, one of which, "The Ballad of Mac the Knife," became a hit song.

KEY TERMS

naturalism	Johann Christian Woyzeck	Bertolt Brecht
expressionism	*Gebrauchsmusik* ("music	*The Beggar's Opera*
Georg Büchner	for use")	epic theater

Chapter 71

Béla Bartók and Hungarian Folk Music

World War I had a disastrous outcome for the nation of Hungary. Prior to the war it enjoyed a position of preeminence within the Austro-Hungarian Monarchy. While recognizing the German-speaking Hapsburg emperor as their king, the Hungarians

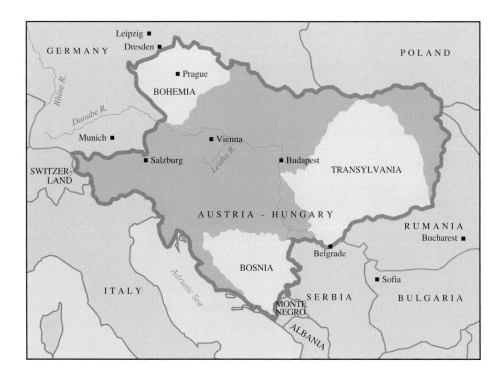

MAP 71-1
Austro-Hungarian Empire
before World War I.

formed their own government that ruled over the internal affairs of a large region
east of the Leitha River. The borders of Hungary at this time reached south to the
Adriatic Sea, east into what is now Romania, and north into present-day Russia,
Czech Republic, and Poland (see Map 71-1).

Hungary was a restless kingdom, cobbled together from a hodge-podge of competing enclaves of language and culture. Hungarians—those who spoke the Magyar
language—lived beside Slovenians, Serbians, Croatians, Bulgarians, Armenians,
Ruthenians, Poles, and Germans. After World War I, during which the Austro-
Hungarian Empire dissolved, the country was greatly reduced in size and left as a
small, landlocked nation stripped of its regions of mixed ethnicity. Until World War II
it was ruled by the authoritarian government of Admiral Nicholas Horthy.

The Hungarian capital is Budapest, a city of great beauty that lies
astride the Danube River some one hundred fifty miles east of Vienna.
Since the late nineteenth century, its musical culture has centered on the
Opera House, built in 1884, where conductors including Gustav Mahler
have worked. Nearby is the Academy of Music, with its excellent concert
hall. Since its opening in 1875, the academy has trained many of Europe's
leading performers and composers.

BÉLA BARTÓK

Perhaps the greatest of these musicians is Béla Bartók (1881–1945; Fig.
71-1). He was born in a farming village in what is now Romania, and his
childhood was unsettled. His father died when he was only seven years
old, and he then lived in several different cities with his mother, a piano
teacher, and his sister. He attended the Budapest Academy of Music,
where he concentrated mainly on piano playing, and in 1907 he was
appointed to its piano faculty.

FIGURE 71-1
Béla Bartók's imagination as a
composer was stimulated by simple
Hungarian peasant songs, whose
spirit and materials he brought to
his own original works.

Like many Budapest artists and intellectuals, he was an avid Hungarian nationalist. "For my own part," he wrote to his mother in 1903, "all my life, in every sphere, always and in every way, I shall have one objective: the good of Hungary and the Hungarian nation."[1] While pursuing the career of a touring piano virtuoso and pedagogue he also composed, although he was periodically discouraged by the lack of understanding his works received.

Bartók's nationalistic pride led him to examine the folk music of his country, and from 1905 he traveled repeatedly, often accompanied by his friend **Zoltán Kodály** (1882–1967), to farming regions to record folk songs. He explored the possibilities by which peasant music could be integrated into his own original compositions.

In the 1920s and 1930s, Bartók's music was at last recognized for its originality, and he toured throughout the world, giving concerts that brought him ever greater acclamation. His life in Budapest was unsettled by the rise of the Nazis—"a band of thieves and murderers" he called them—who to his alarm found increasing support in the Hungarian government. In October 1940, well after the outbreak of World War II, Bartók and his wife made an audacious dash across Europe to Lisbon, where they boarded a ship that took them to safety in New York City. The composer spent his last five years there, created some of his greatest works, and continued with his folk music research.

Bartók composed in all of the genres of his day. His music for solo piano includes a Sonata (1926) and various collections of character works, and also a cycle of pedagogical pieces called *Mikrokosmos,* many of which are based on folk songs. Bartók is one of the greatest composers of modern chamber music, and his six string quartets are monuments in the literature. He wrote one opera (*Duke Bluebeard's Castle,* 1911), two ballets (*The Wooden Prince,* 1916, and *The Miraculous Mandarin,* 1919), and his orchestral music includes the dazzling *Music for Strings, Percussion and Celesta* and Concerto for Orchestra. He also wrote two concertos for violin, three for piano, and one (incomplete) for viola.

❀ HUNGARIAN PEASANT MUSIC

Bartók's career as a musician is closely tied to his study of the folk music of peasants of Hungary, Romania, and Slovakia. His interest in this repertory was both musical and scholarly, and it developed into a passion for field research that he described as "the one thing that is as necessary to me as fresh air is to other people."[2] He collected thousands of folk songs and meticulously classified them according to certain stylistic features. His central contribution to the knowledge of this music was to clarify the distinction between an ancient repertory of Hungarian peasant songs and a more modern repertory. He also advanced criteria by which to distinguish the Hungarian songs from those of neighboring regions.

The old Hungarian songs especially attracted his attention. These had been preserved in isolated Hungarian farming villages, and they were relatively untouched by modern European musical styles. Their unaffected artistry, stripped bare of everything superfluous, appealed to the musician in Bartók. Having learned of this ancient type of Hungarian music, Bartók dismissed the importance of other, better-known types, such as the flashy instrumental playing of Gypsies that had been celebrated in Franz Liszt's *Hungarian Rhapsody* No. 15 (see Chapter 57). All of this Bartók disdainfully termed "**popular art music**"; true folk music, he believed, was the product of the peasant uncorrupted by city life and modern culture.

An example of the old Hungarian peasant song is "Fekete főd" ("Black Is the Earth"), which Bartók recorded on a research trip to Transylvania in 1906 or 1907 (Ex. 71-1). The region of Transylvania occupies roughly the northwest quarter of modern Romania, and Bartók found it to be the richest location of all for finding ancient Hungarian songs. They were preserved there in isolated farming communities populated by a Hungarian ethnic group called the Székely.

EXAMPLE 71-1

Fe-ke- te főd, ___ fehérazén zsebken - dőm, Elhagyott a legked-vesebb sze-re - tőm.

Black is the earth, snow white is my kerchief. He abandoned me; love's curse falls heavily on me.

The song "Fekete főd" has most of the features that Bartók found characteristic of its type. It is unaccompanied in medium and strophic in form. One stanza (see Ex. 71-1) has two lines of text (four is more typical). Each has the same number of syllables (in this case, eleven), and the musical setting is entirely syllabic. The rhythm of the melody is flexible and free from regular beat—Bartók described it as **parlando-rubato**—although other old Hungarian songs often have a strict beat, a type of rhythm that Bartók called "tempo giusto," which was appropriate for dancing. The short-long rhythm at the beginning is a characteristic rhythmic figure, and the leap of a descending fourth to the final note E is also a common cadential marker. The melody is entirely pentatonic, using only the notes E G A B D.

The terseness and stark simplicity of such music represented for Bartók a pinnacle of artistry. He wrote:

> According to the way I feel, a genuine peasant melody of our land is a musical example of a perfected art. I consider it quite as much a masterpiece, for instance, in miniature, as a Bach fugue or a Mozart sonata movement is a masterpiece in larger form. A melody of this kind is a classic example of the expression of a musical thought in its most conceivably concise form, with the avoidance of all that is superfluous.[3]

BARTÓK'S USE OF FOLK MUSIC

Given his exuberant praise for the artistry of peasant tunes, Bartók naturally wanted to bring such melodies into his own compositions. He was encouraged in this when he found quotations of peasant songs made in passing by Haydn and Beethoven in their symphonies. For the modern composer, the use of folkish materials, Bartók said, could bring an element of nature into new music, promoting ease of understanding.

Bartók also found in the old folk tunes models for progressive thinking about musical materials. The tune "Fekete főd" (see Ex. 71-1), for example, does not outline functional harmonic progressions, so it is not illogical, Bartók said, to harmonize it in a way that bypasses functional harmony. But the peasant melodies are otherwise totally different from new music. They are never chromatic in their pitch content and they always exhibit a tonality based on motion toward a final focal tone. Still, Bartók insisted that there was no inconsistency in absorbing such melodies into a fully atonal style. In an essay of 1931, he defined three ways in which a peasant tune could enrich an original composition:

We may, for instance, take over a peasant melody unchanged or only slightly varied, write an accompaniment to it and possibly some opening and concluding phrases. This kind of work would show a certain analogy with Bach's treatment of chorales. . . . [Second:] The composer does not make use of a real peasant melody but invents his own imitation of such melodies. There is no true difference between this method and the one described above. . . . [Third:] Neither peasant melodies nor imitations of peasant melodies can be found in his music, but it is pervaded by the atmosphere of peasant music. In this case we may say, he has completely absorbed the idiom of peasant music which has become his musical mother tongue.[4]

Bartók's compositions contain examples of all three ways of using folk music. His arrangements of folk tunes—made for voice, chorus, and piano—are especially imaginative. One such is his treatment of "Fekete főd," for voice and piano, which he prepared around 1907 and published in 1922 in his *Eight Hungarian Folksongs*. The voice sings two stanzas of the unadorned tune while the piano adds a subtle accompaniment that preserves the character of the song. The piece opens with billowing arpeggios in the piano, whose tones are limited to those of the pentatonic scale used in the tune. Here Bartók—like Liszt before him in *Hungarian Rhapsody* No. 15—evokes the sound of the **cimbalom,** a Hungarian dulcimer. Gradually the accompaniment adds additional notes to create familiar chords and harmonic progressions, although Bartók entirely avoids the dominant chord in the home key of E minor, presumably since the strong dominant-to-tonic motion is not suggested within the tune itself.

LISTENING CUE

BÉLA BARTÓK
Eight Hungarian Folksongs
"Fekete főd" (c1907)

CD 11/18
Anthology, No. 186

Concerto for Orchestra

Bartók's Concerto for Orchestra (1943) exemplifies his third way of using folk materials. There are no quotations of peasant songs per se, although their influence is often apparent, having been thoroughly absorbed into the composer's "musical mother tongue." The Concerto for Orchestra comes from Bartók's final years, composed while he was living in the United States. This was the most difficult period in his life. He was unable to make a living in any way acceptable to him, and he was plagued by failing health.

A commission for a new orchestral work from Serge Koussevitsky, conductor of the Boston Symphony Orchestra, was a godsend that brought the creative winds back into his sails. Many émigré composers of this time—Paul Hindemith, Arnold Schoenberg, and Igor Stravinsky are other examples—turned to orchestral composition when they arrived in America during World War II. Orchestras were the strong suit of American musical culture, and conductors such as Koussevitsky were ready to reach out to composers for new works.

Bartók's Concerto for Orchestra is a five-movement composition whose form has more in common with the symphony than with the concerto. In his notes for the premier performance in Boston in December 1944, the composer explained the term "concerto" as a reference to a virtuosic treatment of instruments in the orches-

Bartók and the Golden Section

In the visual arts, an aesthetically pleasing point at which to divide a line is one that creates the so-called **Golden Section.** Imagine that the original line has the length a and that it is divided into two segments of lengths b (the longer of the two) and c:

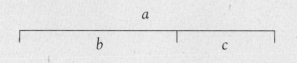

The division point forms the pleasing Golden Section if the lengths $b/a = c/b$. In terms of absolute measurements, these ratios form a constant value of about 0.618.

This simple relationship has for centuries fascinated both mathematicians and artists. It is also found in a number series named for the medieval mathematician Leonardo Fibonacci. The Fibonacci series consists of a string of numbers beginning with 0 and 1 and continuing with numbers that equal the sum of the preceding two. The Fibonacci series thus begins 0, 1, 1, 2, 3, 5, 8. . . . Higher up in the series, the ratio formed by any two adjacent terms is roughly 0.618, the same ratio as in the Golden Section.

If artists have found this proportion to be pleasing, so too have musicians. From the Renaissance to the twentieth century, composers have sometimes shaped the proportions of a musical work to equal or approximate those of the Golden Section and the related Fibonacci series. In his *Klavierstück XI* (*Piano Piece XI*, 1956), for example, the German composer Karlheinz Stockhausen explicitly used numbers from the Fibonacci series to govern the lengths of sections.

Did Bartók do the same? Bartók himself was entirely silent on this. Still, the Hungarian scholar Ernő Lendvai has found in his music a pervasive use of Golden Section proportions, both in the divisions of a work into parts and in Bartók's harmonic language. The first movement of Bartók's Sontata for Two Pianos and Percussion (1937), for example, has 443 measures. The Golden Section occurs approximately in measure 274, which is just where Bartók begins the recapitulation of the movement's sonata form. Other scholars find this a provocative accident, not the product of any systematic thinking on Bartók's part.

tra, most of which step forward periodically to display their skills. But the principal formal model for the work is the symphony. The first movement is fast with a slow introduction, and it uses Bartók's reinterpretation of sonata form. This is followed by a lighthearted *scherzo* movement, then a slow movement, another *scherzo,* and the work ends with a brilliant finale.

Bartók provided the movements with titles—the third, for example, is called "Elegia" ("Elegy")—that hint at some programmatic meaning. He also alluded to this dimension in his program notes for Boston: "The general mood of the work represents—apart from the jesting second movement—a gradual transition from the sternness of the first movement and the lugubrious death-song of the third, to the life-assertion of the last one."[5]

When he composed the concerto, Bartók was almost certainly aware that he suffered from a fatal disease, the blood disorder polycythemia, and it seems likely that the concerto is a highly personalized reflection upon his fate. The personal voice speaks plainly in the fourth movement, titled "Interrupted Intermezzo," in which Bartók quotes part of a theme from the first movement of the recent Symphony No. 7 by Dmitri Shostakovich—a composer whom Bartók considered kitschy, but who was a great favorite of Koussevitsky's. In Bartók's version, the theme is immediately hooted down by various instruments of the orchestra.

Such high spirits are little in evidence in the somber first movement. It begins with a slow introduction that presents motivic and tonal material that is later reshaped into main themes. An economical interconnection of motives is a distinctive characteristic of the movement, in which development is ever-present and variety among themes is achieved on a relatively superficial level of tempo, character, and instrumentation. Notice how the mysterious opening motive in the cellos and basses—moving by fourths and major seconds to outline a **pentatonic** collection of tones—is linked to these same features in the themes at measures 76 and 134. In Example 71-2, a few of the most obvious such connections among these themes are shown in brackets. Bartók's thematic economy and insistence on a multidimensional process of development is also revealed by his use of fugue, as in the virtuosic passage in the brass in measures 316–396.

EXAMPLE 71-2

Celli, basses, mm. 1-6

Violins, mm. 76-81

Trombone, mm. 134-141

Pentatonic collections of tones are the principal means by which Bartók relates the music to its Hungarian folk roots. Other folklike materials are also in evidence. The rhythms of the slow introduction remind us of the flexible freedom from beat of a "parlando-rubato" song such as "Fekete főd," and Bartók also resorts—as in the phrase in Violin I in measures 95–101 (Ex. 71-3)—to the short-long rhythmic figure that characterizes Hungarian music.

EXAMPLE 71-3

Violin I, mm. 95-101

The style of the piece has certain features in common with the dominant anti-romantic trend of the 1920s, 1930s, and 1940s (see Chapter 68). Bartók's music, even before World War I, anticipated this rejection of romanticism in its spareness and avoidance of romantic extravagance. But after the war he generally held himself aloof from the neoclassic movement led by Stravinsky. Still, a clarity of form in the Concerto for Orchestra, its general melodiousness and ease of understanding, and its use of classic forms and genre suggest a connection between the work and the prevailing artistic spirit of its time.

LISTENING CUE

BÉLA BARTÓK

Concerto for Orchestra (1943)

First movement, *Andante non troppo; Allegro vivace*

CD 11/19

Anthology, No. 187

The Kodály Method

Bartók's research companion on many of his folk song forays into the Hungarian countryside was Zoltán Kodály (1882–1967). His career in music shadowed that of Bartók. Both attended the Academy of Music in Budapest and both were later on its faculty. Both had a passion for folk song research, and their discoveries were largely made together. Both were leading composers, and Bartók was always unstinting in his praise for the new music of his friend.

But Kodály's greatest contribution to the history of music lay in his effort to improve the musical education of children and youth. As early as the 1920s he wrote singing exer-

cises using solfège syllables to promote musicianship and musical literacy. By 1950 these initiatives had coalesced into the "Kodály Method," which is based on the premise that choral and vocal training is basic to the musical awareness and skill of younger students.

His outlook has continued to flourish. Kodály societies now exist in cities around the world and continue to be praised not only for their effectiveness in training pre-professional musicians but also in bringing musical sensitivity to the public at large.

SUMMARY

The nation of Hungary was greatly reduced in size following World War I. At this time its rural people still preserved a rich culture of folk songs, some of which were ancient in origin. The Hungarian composer Béla Bartók collected and studied this musical repertory, and he was able to distinguish between older and newer styles. He especially valued the old Hungarian songs, which tended to be simple in expression, pentatonic in pitch content, and flexible in their freedom from a strict beat.

Bartók often made artistic arrangements of these songs, and his original compositions, such as his Concerto for Orchestra, more subtly reveal elements of the folk style combined with modern harmonic practices. Bartók's Concerto for Orchestra is close to the symphony in form, although the virtuosic treatment of various instruments from the orchestra ties in with the idea of a concerto. The themes and motives of the work are closely unified, and the Concerto also has a classical tone in form and genre that hints at Stravinsky's neoclassicism.

KEY TERMS

Zoltán Kodály
"popular art music"

parlando-rubato rhythmic style
cimbalom

Golden Section
pentatonic

Early Jazz

What is **jazz**? Even so basic a question defies any simple answer. The word began to appear in print around 1915, and at first it was attached to many different types of popular music that existed then in America. The early writers on jazz seemed themselves baffled about what it was and where it came from, and they gradually tried to give the word a more specific meaning. Aaron Copland, in 1927, defined jazz purely as a musical style. Jazz occurred in popular music, he said, when a rhythmically regular accompaniment is joined to a syncopated or metrically asymmetrical melodic line.[1] In an interview in 1938, Jelly Roll Morton claimed to have used the word "jazz" as early as 1902 to refer to a style of performance that was freer in rhythm than in the strict style of ragtime. In 1958 the pioneering jazz historian Rudi Blesh limited jazz to the playing of African American musicians in New Orleans bands. "To this day," he wrote, "with rare exceptions, only New Orleans Negroes can play real jazz."[2] The jazz authority Gunther Schuller found improvisation to be the central factor in true jazz. This was its "heart and soul," he wrote in 1968.[3]

Today there is still no general agreement on the origin of the term or exactly what music it should designate, and it is now apparent that any but the most general definition is arbitrary. One reason for this impreciseness is the nature of the phenomenon itself. The styles and genres of jazz have constantly intermixed and hybridized, never remaining stable for long. A definition of jazz cannot be limiting because it is a musical phenomenon always in progress. With this reality in mind, our search for the general outlines of jazz can begin by studying the types of music from which it came.

✿ THE SOURCES OF EARLY JAZZ: RAGTIME

Jazz, in its early stages, resulted from an interaction of four principal genres of American popular music that existed around 1900: ragtime, blues, popular songs, and dance music. In the 1890s the term **ragtime** was applied to popular music having a "ragged," or syncopated, rhythm. Gradually the term became associated more exclusively with music for the piano, whereupon it indicated a character piece (each one called a **rag**) that was carefree in spirit, syncopated in melody, and similar to a march in form. Rags were primarily used to accompany march-like dances such as the "two-step" and "cakewalk," the latter being a revival of a dance that had been performed by plantation slaves. The heyday for the composing of piano rags was from about 1895 until 1920, although in more recent times the genre has experienced a revival among both composers and pianists.

We can gather the principal characteristics of a piano rag by studying the most famous composition of its type, "Maple Leaf Rag" by **Scott Joplin** (1868–1917). Joplin was born in Texas and lived primarily in Missouri—a center of ragtime culture at the turn of the twentieth century—and he spent his last decade in New York City. Although known primarily as a composer of rags, he also adapted the ragtime style to classical genres, as in his opera *Treemonisha* (1911).

Joplin's "Maple Leaf Rag" (1899) was named after the Maple Leaf Club, a dance hall where Joplin worked as a pianist in Sedalia, Missouri. Except for the syncopated melody and the medium of piano, the music is similar in almost all ways to a contemporaneous American band march. It has a duple meter and moderate tempo—"Never play ragtime fast," he warned—and it consists of a succession of phrases, or "strains," each of sixteen measures and most immediately repeated. In the middle of the work, at the point marked "trio," the key shifts to the subdominant. The strains in a rag are sometimes brought back to form a repetitive pattern: in "Maple Leaf Rag" the first strain returns just before the trio.

The most distinctive feature of the style is the syncopated melody in the right hand, which is accompanied in the left hand by a rhythm of absolute regularity.

A **syncopation** is a temporary metric irregularity, and several types are encountered in the tunes of ragtime. The one in "Maple Leaf Rag" comes from a metric displacement (Ex. 72-1). At the top of the example the rhythm in the right hand (mm. 1–2) is barred as a regular figure in $\frac{2}{4}$ time. The very same rhythm appears below, but here the bar line is shifted to the left by a sixteenth-note value, which produces the syncopated rhythm as given by the composer.

EXAMPLE 72-1

Such rhythmic figures were strictly interpreted when Joplin played his own rags. He apparently stayed close to the printed music and avoided any extensive embellishment or improvisation. "Each note will be played as it is written," he said in his *School of Ragtime*.[4]

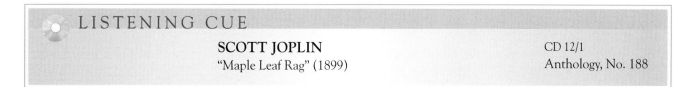

LISTENING CUE

SCOTT JOPLIN
"Maple Leaf Rag" (1899)

CD 12/1
Anthology, No. 188

James P. Johnson's "Carolina Shout" (c1921) shows a later stage in the evolution of ragtime, one in which the process of hybridization among several types of popular music is well underway. Johnson (1894–1955) lived in the New York area amid a highly competitive group of ragtime pianists that also included Willie "The Lion" Smith, Luckey Roberts, and the young Duke Ellington. Like Joplin, he aspired to bring jazz styles into the composition of classical genres, as in his "blues opera" *De Organizer* (1940), on which he collaborated with the Harlem poet Langston Hughes.

The overall form of "Carolina Shout" embodies the ragtime archetype seen in Joplin's "Maple Leaf Rag." Following a four-measure introduction, there is a succession of sixteen-measure strains, of which the fourth begins a trio in the subdominant key (in which the work ends). But differences between the two compositions abound. Johnson's rag is in $\frac{4}{4}$ with a driving tempo, not the moderate march-like $\frac{2}{4}$ of Joplin. Johnson's virtuosic playing imitates styles that are less pianistic than they are vocal, especially those found in the blues songs to be discussed presently. His rhythms are not made from the motoric eighths and sixteenths of Joplin's piece but from a swinging triplet subdivision of the beat that always leans forward and resembles the way that words are normally spoken or sung. On the repeats of phrases, Johnson introduces improvisatory variations upon the harmony and melody of the strain just played.

Listen especially for the bass line and left hand in Johnson's piece (the first four measures of the first strain are shown in Ex. 72-2). Johnson's left hand moves regularly from a tone in the bass to a chord in the middle register, creating a striding motion. This distinctive pattern was common, not only in Johnson's music but also in that of a group of post-ragtime pianists in Harlem in the 1920s. Their style is now called **stride.** Notice also that Johnson overcomes the disruption of the striding motion to create a predominantly stepwise bass line, which takes on a melodic identity that is not heard in Joplin's piece. In this way Johnson forecasts the **walking bass** of jazz combos of the 1930s, 1940s, and 1950s. In these later ensembles (see Chapter 81), the walking bass was adopted by string bass players, who create a stepwise line in quick, even rhythmic values. Finally, listen for Johnson's remarkable rhythmic inventiveness as he departs effortlessly from the regularity of duple meter to insert bass patterns temporarily suggesting triple time.

EXAMPLE 72-2

mm. 5-8

Ragtime influenced jazz in its syncopated rhythms and in the tension existing between a rhythmically regular accompaniment and irregular melody. The essential form of ragtime—multi-thematic and multi-sectional—also provided jazz with a basic archetype to which it has periodically returned.

LISTENING CUE

JAMES P. JOHNSON
"Carolina Shout" (c1921)

CD 12/2

✿ BLUES

The early history of **blues** is more shadowy than that of ragtime. Originally, a blues was a type of improvised song that by the early twentieth century had emerged among African Americans of the South. It probably borrowed on styles of folk singing that reach back considerably earlier, although it attained its mature form only after the turn of the twentieth century.

The words of blues are worldly—often sad and dejected, sometimes coarse or vulgar—and the early blues singers made them up on the spot. In their classic form, the words of an entire blues song consist of an open-ended succession of three-line stanzas. In each, the first two lines are identical and the third comments on the first two. Here is a typical blues stanza by the singer Bessie Smith from her 1926 recording of "Lost Your Head Blues":

> I was with you, baby, when you didn't have a dime;
> I was with you, baby, when you didn't have a dime;
> Now that you got plenty money, you done throw'd your good gal down.

Blues singing is highly expressive, and the vocalist often bends and slides between tones to underscore the bittersweet sentiments contained in the words. The expressive lowering of a note by a half-step—especially the third or seventh degree of the major scale—creates so-called **blue notes,** which are distinctive features of the blues style.

The accompaniment of a blues song is sometimes provided by a single instrument such as piano or guitar—played often by the singer—or it might come from a small band. The role of the instruments goes well beyond simple accompaniment. The players often improvise in a way that enriches the harmony and reinforces the emotions and vocal delivery of the singer. Typically, the singer engages in an outright dialogue with at least one of the instruments, which imitates and shadows the singer's melody. Their interchange is reminiscent of the improvised **call-and-response** singing between an individual and a group that is known to have existed among slaves. This closeness between singer and accompaniment made it inevitable that bands quickly took up the playing of blues, dispensing with the singer.

Like all improvised music, blues relies upon a widely understood form to guide and organize the performers' extemporaneous creativity. In the first stanza, the singer **improvises** a melody or uses a preexisting blues tune. In either case, the melody accommodates a simple and standardized harmonic progression that spans twelve measures in $\frac{4}{4}$ time. It has three four-measure phrases, with a line of words situated in each. The first four-measure phrase rests steadily on the tonic chord; the second moves from subdominant to tonic harmonies, and the third begins on the dominant, usually moves then to the subdominant, and arrives for its final two measures back on the tonic chord. Other stanzas (usually called **choruses**) consist of further variations upon these harmonies and, generally, upon the melodic ideas from the main tune in the first stanza.

A handsome example of the early blues song is Bessie Smith's "Lost Your Head Blues" (1926). Bessie Smith (1894–1937) was the most successful professional blues singer of her time; she achieved an unprecedented polish and expressive force in a string of successful recordings that began to appear in 1923. For "Lost Your Head Blues"—recorded in New York in 1926—she is accompanied by the pianist Fletcher Henderson and cornetist Joe Smith. The song has the classic blues form, although its length is limited by the three-minute duration of phonograph discs of this period. There is an introduction, in which the cornetist prefigures the basic melody, then five choruses (stanzas). The emotional power of Smith's singing is enhanced by her bending and sliding between tones and her imaginative variations upon the basic melodic ideas. The cornetist completes the space at the end of each four-measure phrase with a chattering solo (called a **fill**) that imitates the voice and engages sympathetically with the singer's tale of woe.

The blues influenced jazz through its improvisatory and expressive element. Blue notes became the stock in trade of later jazz musicians, and the form of blues—monothematic with variations upon an unchanging harmonic progression—was a basic design to which jazz musicians often returned.

LISTENING CUE

BESSIE SMITH   CD 12/3
"Lost Your Head Blues" (1926)

POPULAR SONGS

Songs played an important role in the musical life of Americans throughout the nineteenth century. Some were written for music-making in middle-class homes, and these were geared to the rudimentary performing skills of amateurs and used homespun and sentimental words. Religious songs, or **spirituals,** were performed in churches and religious meetings, and these were richly developed in African American congregations. Other songs were written for use in traveling **minstrel shows,** a popular form of theatric entertainment that rested on a comic caricature of black dialect and culture and included songs, dances, and skits.

By the later nineteenth century, most popular songs used a common strophic form with refrain. Following an introduction, each stanza was divided into a verse and a chorus. The words of the verse changed from stanza to stanza, the chorus (refrain) remained unchanged in both words and music. In the days of the minstrel shows, the refrain was a true chorus, typically having four voice parts that were sung by the whole minstrel troupe. If multiple singers were not available, then the "chorus" melody could be sung soloistically.

In Chapter 77 we will return to the popular song, with classic examples from the 1920s through the 1950s. In them the traditional **verse-and-refrain form** is still in effect, and it remains in evidence in songs by the Beatles, Elton John, Michael Jackson, and other songsters to the present day.

Popular songs contributed to the history of early jazz by providing its material, its tunes. The familiar song melodies and their harmonies became **jazz standards**—works that jazz musicians could be expected to know from memory and use to accompany dancing, have as a basis for improvisation, or write out in arrangements. They exerted an ever-greater importance on jazz during the Big Band era beginning in the late 1920s (see Chapter 81).

❀ DANCE MUSIC

Like the singing of songs, dancing was an important traditional form of entertainment throughout American history. In the early twentieth century its popularity grew steadily, and in the 1920s social dancing—in clubs, hotels, and restaurants—became a national passion. But, prior to the appearance of the swing bands of the late 1920s, dance pieces had no distinctive musical identity—no particular medium, form, or style beyond a meter and tempo that could accommodate the popular dance steps of the day. At the turn of the century, triple-time dances such as waltzes and "Bostons" were still popular, and music for them could be played by piano or bands of any size, using original compositions or song arrangements. Rags, played by piano or ensembles of varying size, were at the height of their popularity, and these were danced to syncopated march-like steps.

After 1910 the older triple-time dances lost favor at the hands of newer and more vigorous duple-meter dances such as the **foxtrot** and the syncopated **Charleston.** As dancing became more popular, the larger dance halls required larger musical ensembles. The demand was answered primarily by dance orchestras, in which fifty members were not unusual. These groups typically mixed strings, brass, woodwinds, drums, and plucked instruments, and their music relied upon new compositions and arrangements. These works adhered generally to the ragtime prototype, with a succession of melodies freely repeated. Improvisation had little role, although a controlled embellishment of a melody and addition of special playing effects—flutter tongue, glissandos, growls, mute effects—were typical of the style. The "Society Orchestra" led by **James Reese Europe** (1881–1919) was one of the most successful of the New York dance orchestras of this day, and Europe saw a need to keep improvisation out of his band's playing:

> I have to call a daily rehearsal of my band to prevent the musicians from adding to their music more than I wish them to. Whenever possible they all embroider their parts in order to produce new, peculiar sounds. Some of these effects are excellent and some are not, and I have to be continually on the lookout to cut out the results of my musicians' originality.[5]

Music at Congo Square

The American architect Benjamin Latrobe visited New Orleans in 1819 and recorded this account of music-making on Sundays at Congo Square:

> In going up St. Peters Street & approaching the common I heard a most extraordinary noise. . . . It proceeded from a crowd of 5 or 600 persons assembled in an open space or public square. I went to the spot & crowded near enough to see the performance. All those who were engaged in the business seemed to be *blacks*. I did not observe a dozen yellow [i.e., Creole] faces. They were formed into circular groupes in the midst of four of which, which I examined (but there were more of them), was a ring, the largest not 10 feet in diameter. In the first were two women dancing. . . .
>
> The music consisted of two drums and a stringed instrument. An old man sat astride of a cylindrical drum about a foot in diameter, & beat it with incredible quickness with the edge of his hand & fingers. . . . The most curious instrument, however, was a stringed instrument which no doubt was imported from Africa. On the top of the finger board was the rude figure of a man in a sitting posture, & two pegs behind him

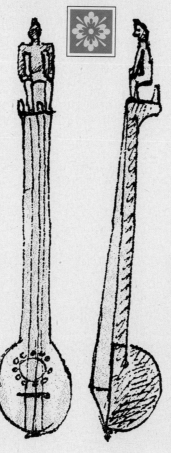

to which the strings were fastened. [Latrobe made the accompanying drawings of the two instruments.]

> The women squalled out a burthen [refrain] to the playing at intervals, consisting of two notes, as the negroes, working in our cities, respond to the song of their leader. . . .[6]

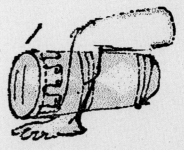

FIGURE 72-1

Benjamin Latrobe, drawings of instruments used by slaves in New Orleans. These instruments were handmade from common materials. The art of drumming is especially sophisticated among African musicians.

NEW ORLEANS AND THE EMERGENCE OF JAZZ

New Orleans musicians near the turn of the twentieth century played a special role in the creation of the new idiom called jazz. It was here that the intermixture of existing popular musical genres—especially band marches, ragtime, and blues—produced, not a simple development of these individual types of music but an amalgamation with its own spirit and character. The term "jazz" was most often used to designate this phenomenon.

Why did jazz first flourish in New Orleans? The presence of riverboats, bordellos in the red-light district of Storyville, festivals such as Mardi Gras, and parades for any and all occasions ensured a demand for music. Much about the city's musical culture was special. Throughout the nineteenth century, slaves living in and around New Orleans were allowed to express themselves musically; in other cities their music-making was generally forbidden. On Sundays, their day of rest, slaves gathered in central New Orleans at Congo Square to dance, sing, and play native African instruments. An eyewitness account of their music can be found in the Box.

New Orleans also had a well-developed tradition of serious music, which promoted musical literacy and supported music teaching. Musical instruments were readily available. Opera was especially advanced in New Orleans by the later nineteenth century, thanks to the existence of the French Opera House, which from 1859 until 1919 produced numerous American premieres of operas by modern French composers.

A distinctive feature of musical culture in New Orleans was the brass band. Bands were popular throughout America around 1900, and especially so in New Orleans. They played for every imaginable social occasion—funerals, weddings, parties—and they had their own informally joyous style. Jelly Roll Morton recalled their spirited playing:

> Those parades were really tremendous things. The drums would start off, the trumpets and trombones rolling into something like *Stars and Stripes* or *The National Anthem* and everybody would strut off down the street, the bass-drum player twirling his beater in the air, the snare drummer throwing his sticks up and bouncing them off the ground, the kids jumping and hollering, the grand marshall and his aides in their expensive uniforms moving along dignified.[7]

To accompany dancing, these bands were pared down and adjusted in their instrumentation, but they kept the spirited freedom of playing that Morton recalled. The typical New Orleans dance band early in the century was small, generally five to seven players. These were divided into two groups: the cornet, clarinet, and trombone were typically entrusted with the melody and the piano, drums, and bass—called the **rhythm section**—played an accompaniment. Many of the bandsmen could only play by ear, others apparently read music, and their tunes included rags, marches, popular songs, and blues-like pieces.

An example of the **New Orleans style** of jazz is "Dippermouth Blues," recorded in 1923 by **Joe "King" Oliver**'s Creole Jazz Band (Fig. 72-2). Oliver (1885–1938) was a leading New Orleans cornetist who, like many musicians following World War I, left the city for greater opportunities in Chicago and New York. The band on the recording is typical of the New Orleans medium. It has seven players consisting of a melody group of two cornets (Oliver and his protégé, Louis Armstrong), clarinet, and trombone, and a rhythm section of piano, bass (doubling on banjo), and drums.

The music has the character of ragtime and the form of blues. After a four-measure introduction, there are nine blues choruses, each with the classic twelve-measure harmonic structure. The playing most characteristic of the New Orleans style occurs in choruses 1, 2, 5, and 9, when all four of the melody instruments improvise in group fashion over the blues harmonies. In these passages there is no distinguishable melody, which is replaced by a comfortably blended polyphony. The group playing alternates with solo choruses. In numbers 3 and 4 the clarinetist Johnny Dodds leads while the band accompanies in **stop time**—playing only on the first three beats of each measure. Oliver's cornet solo in chorus numbers 6 through 8 is especially distinctive in its closeness to the sound of the human voice, which Oliver imitates with blue notes, playing with the valves pushed halfway, and using the mute. At the end of

✿ FIGURE 72-2
King Oliver's Creole Jazz Band, 1923, was formed in Chicago in 1922 and had the makeup of New Orleans bands. Oliver is seated; standing from the left are Baby Dodds, Honoré Dutrey, Bill Johnson, Louis Armstrong, Johnny Dodds, and Lillian Hardin, soon to be Armstrong's wife.

CORBIS

his solo, the band suddenly falls silent (observing a characteristic **break**), and a player shouts out "O shake that thing!"

LISTENING CUE

JOE "KING" OLIVER
"Dippermouth Blues" (1923)

CD 12/4

By the mid-1920s, the New Orleans style was losing focus. Most of the city's leading musicians had moved elsewhere, and the ensemble concept was undergoing a far-reaching transformation (see Chapter 81). Echoes of New Orleans' jazz can still be heard in recordings from the late 1920s by one of New Orlean's greatest musical expatriates, **Louis Armstrong** (1901–1971). Born in dire poverty in New Orleans, Armstrong grew up in the city's Home for Colored Waifs, where he learned to play cornet. His skills advanced under King Oliver, his mentor, and he followed Oliver to Chicago in 1922. In 1925 Armstrong founded his own band, the Hot Five, which conformed in general to the New Orleans concept but which increasingly focused on his own individualized virtuosity rather than the group playing of Oliver's band. By this time Armstrong had dispensed with the cornet—an instrument suited to ensemble playing—in favor of the more brilliant and soloistic trumpet.

His recording of "West End Blues," made by Louis Armstrong and His Hot Five in 1928, shows the new directions in which Armstrong pointed the New Orleans style. Armstrong's band was made up according to New Orleans standards, with a melody group consisting of trumpet, trombone, and clarinet, and a rhythm section of piano, banjo, and drums. The form of the work is the standard instrumental blues, the same as in Oliver's "Dippermouth Blues."

A version of the melody "West End Blues" had shortly before been composed and recorded by the Dixie Syncopators, a New Orleans–type band that Oliver then led. In Armstrong's version, the tune is not basic to the structure of the work, which depends more on true improvisation than on the restrained melodic embellishment that was Oliver's specialty. Armstrong's "West End Blues" is both a tribute to Oliver and the New Orleans style and also a brash declaration of independence from it. The new spirit is heard straightaway in the introduction, played by Armstrong alone as a flamboyant improvisation over a few blues chords. Here Armstrong breaks free from the temporal and harmonic restrictions of the idiom. His playing exploits the high register of his instrument—so different from Oliver's exclusively middle-register playing—and it has an expressive impetuosity, as though Armstrong is demanding that he be listened to as an individual.

The five blues choruses that follow the introduction cover a range of emotions from Armstrong's comfortable **scat singing** in number 3 to the happy ragtime virtuosity of the pianist Earl Hines in number 4. "Scat" is an improvised singing on nonsense syllables that usually imitates the playing of an instrument. It was often used by early New Orleans jazz musicians, and Louis Armstrong was its first important practitioner.

LISTENING CUE

LOUIS ARMSTRONG
"West End Blues" (1928)

CD 12/5

SUMMARY

Jazz refers to several styles of American popular music that emerged in the early twentieth century. The term has always been used imprecisely, although in general it is a type of music that at first mixed together elements from ragtime, blues, popular songs, and dance music. Its roots reach back to earlier types of improvised music of African Americans.

A "rag" is a march-like piano character piece in which a syncopated melody is joined to a rhythmically regular accompaniment. A "blues" was originally an improvised strophic song whose stanzas (or "choruses") span twelve-measure phrases and rest upon a fixed and simple harmonic progression. Popular songs around 1900 were strophic compositions in which each stanza (or "verse") was ended by a refrain (called a chorus because at an earlier time it was sung in group fashion). Dance music prior to the late Big Band phenomenon of the late 1920s had no single identity in medium or form.

The most likely birthplace of jazz is New Orleans, where, following the turn of the twentieth century, the term "jazz" was applied to music played in a free manner by small dance bands. These were subdivided into a group of instruments playing melody (often cornet, clarinet, and trombone) and other instruments playing accompaniment (a "rhythm section" often made up by piano, drums, and bass). A distinctive feature of their music-making was group improvisation, in which all of the melody instruments created a closely knit polyphony.

KEY TERMS

jazz	call-and-response	Charleston
ragtime	improvise	James Reese Europe
rag	chorus	rhythm section
Scott Joplin	fill	New Orleans style
syncopation	spiritual	Joe "King" Oliver
stride	minstrel show	stop time
walking bass	verse-and-refrain form	break
blues	jazz standard	Louis Armstrong
blue notes	foxtrot	scat singing

Chapter

73

Paul Hindemith and Music in Nazi Germany

On 30 January 1933, Paul von Hindenburg, Germany's aging president, made a desperate move to stabilize his country and stave off its political and social collapse: he appointed **Adolf Hitler** (1889–1945) to be Germany's chancellor, its head of state. Hitler was the leader of the country's strongest and most radical political party, the National Socialist German Workers' Party, derisively nicknamed the **Nazis.** During his rise to prominence, Hitler had made no secret of his plans for Germany. He wished to rid the country of Communists and Jews, revive the army after its defeat in World War I, expand the country's borders, and replace its recent attempt at democratic government with a centralized authoritarian rule. Germans, he believed, were a "master race" who were destined to rule over the people of the world that he considered less advanced.

MUSICAL LIFE UNDER THE NAZIS

Immediately after they came to power, the Nazis began to make their ideas a reality, and the lives of Jewish musicians in Germany were among the first to be disrupted. In April 1933 a new law banned Jews from civil-service positions, which in Germany at the time included virtually all teaching appointments. The effects were immediately felt by composers who were teachers, and Bernhard Sekles, Franz Schreker, and Arnold Schoenberg were only a few of those who lost their jobs.

Schoenberg, for one, had anticipated the dismal outlook for Jews in Germany. In 1924 he had written to the painter Vasili Kandinsky:

> But what is anti-Semitism to lead to if not to acts of violence? Is it so difficult to imagine that? You are perhaps satisfied with depriving Jews of their civil rights. Then certainly Einstein, Mahler, I, and many others will have been got rid of. But one thing is certain: they will not be able to exterminate those much tougher elements thanks to whose endurance Jewry has maintained itself unaided against the whole of mankind for 20 centuries. For these are evidently so constituted that they can accomplish the task that their God has imposed on them: To survive in exile, uncorrupted and unbroken, until the hour of salvation comes![1]

With such thoughts no doubt in mind, Schoenberg in May 1933 fled from Berlin to Paris and then to the United States, where he continued his career as a teacher and composer.

For non-Jewish musicians in Germany, prospects temporarily brightened. The Nazis wanted the arts to flourish in their new empire, which they called the **Third Reich,** and Hitler was himself a devotee of classical music. He once bragged that he had carried a score to Wagner's *Tristan und Isolde* in his backpack during his army service in World War I. **Joseph Goebbels,** the minister of the new Department of Education and Propaganda, which oversaw the arts, held a Ph.D. degree in literature and aspired to be a writer. At first, the cooperation of leading German musicians—including the composers Richard Strauss and Hans Pfitzner and the conductor Wilhelm Furtwängler—was solicited, but later any disagreement with Nazi control or ideology by these or other figures was ruthlessly crushed.

Music by Jewish composers, including romantic pieces by Felix Mendelssohn and Gustav Mahler, was soon effectively banned from performance, and ultramodern directions in new music—such as free dissonance, atonality, and twelve-tone composition—were also ruled out. American jazz was dismissed as decadent.

Goebbels wanted German composers to write music that had traditional materials but that could still be recognized as original and innovative. He was uncertain about the new music of the 1920s and 1930s that mixed elements of old and new and was hard to categorize as tonal or atonal, consonant or dissonant. Such music, which critics alternately termed "neoclassical" or "objective," had much about it that could appeal to the Nazis. Its chords, rhythms, forms, and textures were basically familiar, and it seemed to honor the traditions of past masters—especially the German J.S. Bach. But other features of neoclassical music, such as its tendency to incorporate elements from jazz or an eclecticism that mixed traditional with modern thinking, were less acceptable. Also, composers like Stravinsky had only a few years earlier written compositions—*The Rite of Spring* is an example—that made use of blatant dissonance and atonality, styles that were now dismissed as degenerate or an example of **cultural bolshevism.**

The Nazis' shallowness in understanding the music of their time manifested in their dealings with Paul Hindemith (1895–1963), the leading German neoclassicist composer of the twentieth century. Hindemith's career placed him at the crisis points of music of his day. As much as any major figure in the century, he grappled head on with the essential questions that faced the classical composer of the early twentieth century: Could the basic materials of music—including triadic harmony, consonant intervals, and fluent melody—be set aside in favor of new alternatives? Could composers of the future develop a distinctive style using alternative materials? Could such new musical vocabularies contribute positively to society?

❀ HINDEMITH'S LIFE AND WORKS

Hindemith (pronounced HIN-duh-mit) first made his living as a professional violinist (he was appointed concertmaster of the Frankfurt Opera orchestra at the age of nineteen). Following World War I he gained attention as a composer in a modernistic vein, although he gradually became an adherent of the more conservative anti-romantic artistic movement of the 1920s, one that asserted objectivity, traditionalism, and craft. Like Stravinsky at the same time, he expressed disdain for unrestrained experimentation in music.

In 1927 Hindemith was appointed to the faculty of the Hochschule für Musik (Technical College for Music) in Berlin, and he began an intense study of musical pedagogy, history, and theory. He also searched for ways by which music could establish a stronger presence throughout contemporary society. With this social objective in mind, he composed a series of educational works intended for young players and singers. Given their utilitarian purpose, he called them *Gebrauchsmusik* (music for use)—a term also used by Kurt Weill for a different phenomenon (see Chapter 70).

In 1938 Hindemith emigrated from Germany, first to Switzerland, then to the United States, where in 1941 he was appointed to the faculty of the School of Music at Yale University. He returned to Europe in 1953, where he lived primarily in Switzerland, not Germany, and he increasingly occupied himself as an orchestral conductor.

Hindemith's large musical oeuvre emphasizes the instrumental genres. He wrote concertos, symphonies, pieces for chamber orchestra and band, six string quartets, piano music, and sonatas for virtually every instrument. He was also attracted to opera, and his principal works of this type are *Mathis der Maler* (*Mathis the Painter,* 1935), *Cardillac* (1926, revised 1952), and *Die Harmonie der Welt* (*The Harmony of the World,* 1957). His other major vocal compositions include the monumental song cycle *Das Marienleben* (*The Life of Mary,* 1923, revised 1948), which is based on poetry by Rainer Maria Rilke, and a Mass (1963).

❀ HINDEMITH'S THEORY OF THE TWELVE TONES

Like many composers of the 1920s, Hindemith searched for laws and principles by which the expanded musical resources of the early twentieth century could be organized and put to productive use in new compositions. Stravinsky, for example, said that his Octet was a work concerned primarily with form, counterpoint, and architecture. Schoenberg in the 1920s turned to twelve-tone rows as means of organization, an answer to his wish "to know *consciously* the laws and rules which govern the forms which he has conceived 'as in a dream.'"

Hindemith's exploration for laws led him, first, to study the history of music theory (he taught himself Latin to be able to do this), and then to write his own theory capable of extending traditional thinking on the subject to the new chromatic tonal resources of the modern period.

In 1937 he published his findings in a treatise called *Unterweisung im Tonsatz* (Hindemith's English equivalent was **The Craft of Musical Composition**). Here he presents a theory concerning the twelve tones of the chromatic scale, and his conclusions are all based on the fundamental premise that these tones and the intervals that they form have a hierarchy of differing strengths. A fifth, for example, must always be structurally different from a second. Such differences derive, he asserted, from acoustical laws that could not be denied or ignored by any composer or any musical style.

Plainly, Hindemith's ideas are rooted in musical traditions, not in the liberated thinking about musical structure characteristic of the years before World War I. They differ sharply from notions of earlier atonal composers, for whom all twelve tones and all intervals were available as though essentially equivalent. For Arnold Schoenberg, a consonant interval such as a fifth occurring in new music was not different structurally from a dissonant interval such as a second. One was no more a product of nature than the other, he wrote. They both occurred between adjacent tones in the overtone series, the fifth lower down in the series, the second higher up—differences that for Schoenberg were insignificant and arbitrary. "They are no more opposites than two and ten are opposites," he wrote.

Hindemith was totally opposed to this outlook. For him, all intervals and chords had differing weights and strengths that had to be respected if a musical structure was to stand on its own. He compared composing to designing and building a house:

> Harmonic progressions—governed by [interval] relationships—are laid out in a sort of ground plan that shows, first of all, the structure's main support points, between which the connecting building elements are subsequently added. Devising this ground plan depends on an assessment of the harmonic weight of chords. . . . The outcome of this working procedure, when elaborated with elementary rhythmic effects and ornamental building elements, is the completed composition.[2]

Mathis der Maler

Hindemith began to apply his theory of tones in his masterpiece—the opera *Mathis der Maler*—which he conceived of just when Hitler took power in 1933. This composition ultimately incorporated not only his ideas about musical materials but also his consciousness of the role of the artist in a society that was evidently in crisis. Hindemith wrote the libretto himself, and he chose as his topic a fictionalized account of the life of the Renaissance German painter **Matthias Grünewald** (c1470–1528). Grünewald's greatest works—studied by Hindemith as he wrote the libretto—are the paintings made for a large altarpiece installed in the chapel of a hospital monastery in Isenheim, a village near Colmar, France. These spectacular paintings are now displayed at the Musée d'Unterlinden in Colmar.

When the altarpiece is closed (Fig. 73-1a), the viewer sees a disturbingly realistic view of the crucifixion. Grünewald's conception is both symbolic and passionately

Synopsis of *Mathis der Maler*

The opera is divided into seven scenes, or "tableaux." The painter Mathis is at work at the monastery of the Order of St. Anthony, where he is completing a year's leave from the service of his patron, Albrecht, who is the ruler of the region around Mainz and an archbishop of the Catholic Church. Both Mathis and Albrecht are facing personal dilemmas. The peasants of the region are in revolt against the ruling classes, and Mathis sympathizes with their cause and wonders what value his art can have in a time of social and political turmoil. Albrecht's court is in an uproar between adherents to the Catholic Church and its pope and others who are followers of the reform movement led by Martin Luther. The latter group wants Albrecht to join their cause, and he is tempted to do so. Still, he obeys an order from the pope to burn Lutheran books.

Hans Schwalb, the leader of the peasants' revolt, is brought wounded to the monastery by his daughter, Regina, and Mathis sympathetically gives them his horse with which to escape. Mathis decides to put aside his art and to take up the cause of the rebels, but he is appalled by their brutality. Albrecht meanwhile has resigned his position as ruler and archbishop but remains with the Church, taking on the life of a hermit.

In the climactic sixth tableau, Mathis and Regina have fled for safety into the forest. Here Mathis has a complex dream in which he imagines that he is St. Anthony. In the desert he is tempted by a series of worldly distractions, each embodied by an earlier acquaintance. Now utterly confused, he visits with a holy man, St. Paul of the Desert (represented in the dream by his patron, Albrecht), who advises him to return to his art, by which he can best serve God and his fellow man. "Go forth and create!" commands Paul.

The last scene depicts Mathis at the end of his life as he retires his painting gear and prepares for death, having obeyed the command of Paul.

🌿 FIGURE 73-1a

Matthias Grünewald, Isenheim altarpiece. Grünewald's masterpiece is the collection of altar paintings created for a hospital monastery in the French-German village of Isenheim near Colmar. Its scenes are duplicated in the sets used in Hindemith's opera *Mathis der Maler.*

Bridgeman Art Library

dramatic. In the central panel to the left of the crucifix, the Virgin Mary (in white) faints while the anguished figure of Mary Magdalene kneels beside in prayer; to the right, John the Baptist points to Jesus and utters Latin words meaning, "It is fitting that He increase and I diminish." Flanking panels show St. Anthony and St. Sebastian; the entombment of Christ is depicted below the central panel.

The ingeniously constructed altarpiece can be opened, first, to display three scenes from the life of Christ: the annunciation, the birth of Jesus serenaded by an angelic concert (Fig. 73-1b), and the brilliant resurrection. The central panels can be opened yet again to show a depiction of St. Anthony's legendary temptation in the desert and his consultation with St. Paul of the Desert (Fig. 73-1c).

To a considerable extent Hindemith's text is a symbolic representation of contemporary events. The composer wrote much of himself into the character of Mathis—the man who is torn between serving society and serving art. The portrait of an explosively polarized nation that has been driven to the breaking point depicts the Germany of 1933 as much as that of the 1500s. In creating the libretto, Hindemith was also plainly attempting to meet the Nazis halfway, to appeal to their artistic interests, as he understood them, while at the same time exposing false directions. His choice of a great German artist as his central character conformed to the Nazis' worship of nationalism, and Mathis's decision to renounce revolution for art was in line with their ideas of a centralized political authority. But Hindemith's scene in which Lutheran books are burned was an obvious criticism of a recent book burning in Berlin orchestrated by Goebbels, and the open-mindedness of the political leader Albrecht was not at all part of the Nazis' thinking.

Ultimately, the struggle dramatized in *Mathis der Maler* comes not from external forces or characters who represent good and evil, instead an internal conflict within Mathis himself—between art as moral obligation and art as willful indulgence. For Hindemith, as for Mathis, art had to represent a moral dimension if it was to continue to be relevant to modern society.

The music that Hindemith wrote for *Mathis der Maler* (1935) reflects the international neoclassical style of the 1920s and 1930s, as well as Hindemith's attempt to accommodate the Nazis' conservatism in artistic taste. The opera's form continues the departure—already seen in Alban Berg's *Wozzeck*—from the Wagnerian model of through composition. Neither Hindemith or Berg went so far as to return outright to number opera, although Hindemith's music has unmistakable subdivisions into traditional musical forms and operatic media such as choruses, ensembles, arias, and melodious narrations. The composer makes these numbers all the more distinguishable from one another by giving them a symmetrical musical form akin to that in instrumental music as well as a distinct tonality.

An example of his approach to operatic structure is found in the climactic third *Auftritt* ("entrance") of scene 6, in which Mathis, dreaming that he is St. Anthony, seeks advice from Albrecht, whom he imagines to be St. Paul of the Desert. Hindemith directs that the scenery should duplicate the appearance of Grünewald's painting of this meeting (see Fig. 73-1c). The music of the entrance is divided into three connected subsections: a dialogue between Anthony and Paul in rondo form, an aria for Paul in varied strophic form, and a through-composed duet for both characters that is worked out as a two-part contrapuntal invention. The principal themes of the three sections are shown in Example 73-1.

FIGURE 73-1b

The concert of angels from Grünewald's Isenheim altarpiece.

FIGURE 73-1c

St. Anthony (left) is advised by St. Paul of the Desert in Grünewald's Isenheim altarpiece.

EXAMPLE 73-1

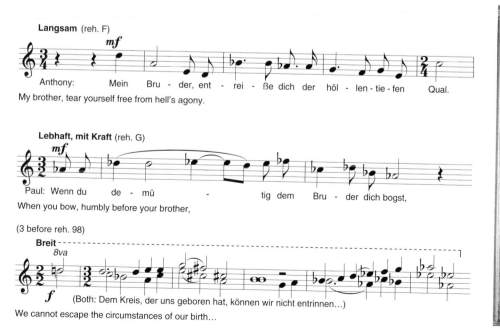

Anthony: Mein Bru-der, ent-rei-ße dich der höl-len-tie-fen Qual.
My brother, tear yourself free from hell's agony.

Paul: Wenn du de-mü-tig dem Bru-der dich bogst,
When you bow, humbly before your brother,

(Both: Dem Kreis, der uns geboren hat, können wir nicht entrinnen...)
We cannot escape the circumstances of our birth...

Although the three subsections flow into one another without pause, they are made noticeably distinct by their contrasting tonal centers. The rondo touches repeatedly on a D-minor pitch collection and triad, the aria on D♭ minor, and the duet on D major. These subsections are not "in" these keys in any traditional sense, since the music has no significant functional harmonic progressions.

Another distinctive feature of the opera's music is Hindemith's borrowing preexistent melodies from folk songs, Lutheran hymns, and Gregorian chants. These well-known tunes give a work populated by peasants, Lutherans, and Catholics all the more dramatic plausibility, and their presence also allows Hindemith to tie the work more closely to the spirit and substance of Grünewald's altar paintings. For example, Hindemith quotes repeatedly from the chants used at Mass in the Catholic Feast of Corpus Christi. This is the day when the Church celebrates Holy Communion, a Christian sacrament that reenacts the crucifixion, which is the principal subject of Grünewald's altarpiece.

Hindemith apparently felt the need to spread thematic elements beyond the boundary of a single scene or musical number, but he did not adopt Wagner's device of the leitmotive. Instead, he isolates a few motivic fragments within the chants and folksongs that he quotes and then reuses them among the work's melodies. These recurrent motives give the opera a purely musical unity and provide a counterbalance to its subdivision into distinct musical parts. An example comes from the melody that ends scene 6, entrance 3, sung by Anthony and Paul on the word "Alleluia." The tune is taken from Gregorian chant, from the Alleluia used at Mass on the Feast of Corpus Christi. The opening of the two melodies is shown in Example 73-2.

EXAMPLE 73-2

The rising scalar motive C-D-E at the beginning of Hindemith's alleluia melody is embedded in numerous other important melodies in different parts of the opera. Example 72-3, for example, shows the main themes of the opera's Prelude, where the alleluia motive (shown in brackets) figures prominently.

EXAMPLE 73-3

"The Hindemith Case" by Wilhelm Furtwängler (excerpts)

This article by **Wilhelm Furtwängler**—conductor of the Berlin Philharmonic Orchestra and the leading German conductor of his day—appeared in a Berlin newspaper on 25 November 1934. The previous March, Furtwängler had conducted the premiere of the Symphony *Mathis der Maler*, and he now wished to bring out the entire opera, permission for which was still pending from the Nazi authorities. Although reasonable in tone, Furtwängler's article outraged the Nazis for its presumptuousness, and *Mathis* was essentially banished from the stage in Germany. The opera was first given in Zurich, Switzerland, in 1938.

> A campaign has been launched in certain circles against Paul Hindemith on the grounds that he is "not acceptable" to the new Germany. Why? What is he accused of? . . .
>
> His reputation has spread abroad not only because of his skill as a performer but also due to [the] progressive and pioneering quality of his music. He deliberately broke with the emotionalism of the Whilhelmine era, the false romanticism that still lingered after the time of Wagner and Richard Strauss. He has avoided music that serves philosophical ideas or wallows in an indulgent neo-romantic sentimentality, as does the music of many of his contemporaries, and he has instead cultivated the values of straightforwardness, objectivity, and simplicity.
>
> His most recent work, the Symphony *Mathis der Maler,* has served to confirm these qualities. Since its first performance in March 1934 it has made a deep impression wherever it has been played, notably on those not otherwise particularly well-disposed toward him. This does not signify, I repeat, any ideological change of direction on his part, but instead a return to his beginnings, to his real self.
>
> Eight months ago, when the *Mathis* Symphony was first heard, the authorities made no move against Hindemith, perhaps because of an unconscious reluctance to interfere in the course of the nation's culture. Now, although he has published nothing in the meantime, they have decided to mount a campaign of public vilification against him with the object of forcing him to leave the country. No tactic seems too petty. They have even sunk to the depths of quoting the occasional parody of Wagner and Puccini in his works, completely missing the point of such badinage. Obviously, with a composer who has written so much and whose works are there in published form for everyone to inspect, it is not difficult, years after the event, to find youthful indiscretions. Moreover Hindemith has never engaged in political activity. Where will it lead if we begin to apply the methods of political denunciation to art? . . .[3]

LISTENING CUE

PAUL HINDEMITH
Mathis der Maler (1935)
Scene 6, entrance 3

CD 12/6
Anthology, No. 189

Symphony *Mathis der Maler*

The first music to be completed for the opera was a set of three orchestral passages, each depicting one of Grünewald's altar paintings. Well before he finished the remainder of the opera or even its libretto, Hindemith assembled these into a separate orchestral showpiece in symphonic form that he called Symphony *Mathis der Maler* (1934). The first of the symphonic movements is titled *Engelkonzert* (*Concert of Angels*), and it refers musically to the painting in Figure 73.1b. The second movement, *Grablegung* (*Entombment*), depicts another part of Grünewald's altarpiece, and the third movement, *Versuchung des heiligen Antonius* (*Temptation of St. Anthony*), has its equivalent in the Grünewald's depiction of this legendary event.

The music of the three movements also reappears in the completed opera. The *Engelkonzert* is synonymous with the work's Prelude (overture), the *Grablegung* is situated at the conclusion in scene 7, and the *Versuchung des heiligen Antonius* is distributed into passages at the beginning of scene 6.

Hindemith's music for *Mathis der Maler* shows a new and important development in the spirit of music between the world wars. Hindemith not only embraces the musical language of neoclassicism but also interprets this choice on a moralistic basis. After his time, a composer's adoption of a musical style could convey not merely taste but an embodiment of right versus wrong.

SUMMARY

When the Nazis took over the German government in 1933, they immediately dismissed Jews from employment and banished music by Jewish composers. Atonal and twelve-tone music was also ruled out as an example of "cultural bolshevism," and American jazz was dismissed as decadent. Nazi leaders supported the music of other leading figures such as Richard Strauss and Hans Pfitzner, although they seemed confused over trends in the music of their day. Their attitude toward the music of Paul Hindemith was especially ambivalent, despite Hindemith's efforts to accommodate their wishes.

In addition to his musical compositions, Hindemith was a music theorist who attempted to establish laws based on timeless natural principles for the use of chromatic tones. He applied his ideas in his opera *Mathis der Maler* and in the Symphony *Mathis der Maler,* the latter an orchestral work that pre-dates the opera. Both compositions are based on paintings by the Renaissance German artist Matthias Grünewald.

In the opera, Hindemith continues the general departure from Wagnerian principles that had been begun earlier by Richard Strauss, Alban Berg, and Kurt Weill. Hindemith partly returns to a division of the work into number-like passages suggesting arias, duets, choruses, and ensembles. He abandons Wagner's use of leitmotives, although he reinforces a broad melodic unity throughout the work by shared motives, and he quotes many preexisting chants and folksongs. In his writings, Hindemith justified his stylistic preferences in music on a moral basis.

KEY TERMS

Adolf Hitler   cultural bolshevism   Matthias Grünewald
Nazis   *Gebrauchsmusik*   Wilhelm Furtwängler
Third Reich   *The Craft of Musical*
Joseph Goebbels   *Composition*

Chapter 74

Music in Soviet Russia: Prokofiev and Shostakovich

Prospects for music in Russia following the October Revolution of 1917 were uncertain at best. The country was economically devastated by its participation in World War I and by the upheaval of revolution. The future role for classical music—an art

long associated with privileged social classes and a product of the individual imagination—was still undefined for a state that professed proletarian and collectivist values. Over the next few years, most of Russia's leading musicians—including Jascha
Heifetz, Serge Koussevitsky, Alexander Glazunov, Vladimir Horowitz, Sergei Rachmaninoff, and Sergei Prokofiev—left their homeland for more certain terrain abroad.

SERGEI PROKOFIEV

Many relocated in France, but Sergei Prokofiev (1891–1953) emigrated instead to
the United States. When he arrived in New York in 1918, he attracted attention as
a piano virtuoso and prodigious composer, one with a whole portfolio of works in a
modernist vein. But he found audiences here unprepared for his innovative outlook, although he had praise for America's high performance standards. In his *Autobiography* he recalled these years:

> Discussion of new music, new trends and composers had become an integral part of
> our musical life. America, on the contrary, had no original composers, apart from those
> who came from Europe with ready-made reputations, and the whole accent of musical
> life was concentrated on execution. In this field the standard was rather high.[1]

Between the time of his arrival in America in 1918 and 1932, Prokofiev lived
what he later called a "nomadic concert-tour existence." He concertized all over
the world, including the Soviet Union, composed all the while in a highly disciplined way, and when not traveling lived alternately in the United States, Germany, and France. Between 1932 and 1936 he shuttled between Moscow and Paris,
and finally returned with his family permanently to Russia.

His return came as a surprise to other Russian émigrés such as Stravinsky and
Rachmaninoff, who had expressed only disdain for the political developments in
their native land and refused at first even to visit Soviet Russia. Prokofiev was of a
different mind. He never gave up the idea that he was a Russian musician at heart,
and his return was provoked by a homesickness for his mother country, a search for
more time to compose, and the presence of a sympathetic Russian audience.

Prokofiev was an immensely prolific composer. Operas and ballets—including the
comic opera *Love for Three Oranges* (1919), the epic *War and Peace* (1943), and the
ballets *Romeo and Juliet* (1936) and *Cinderella* (1944)—are central to his oeuvre.
Orchestral works include his five concertos for piano, two concertos for violin,
seven symphonies, and numerous suites. He wrote nine piano sonatas, character
piano pieces, sonatas for solo instruments (violin, cello, and flute), two string quartets, songs, and choral works. Prokofiev was especially drawn to composing for cinema, and his scores for the films *Alexander Nevsky* and *Lieutenant Kijé* were also
reworked in concert forms. His charming musical narration *Peter and the Wolf*
(1936) is known by children worldwide (see Box on pages 681–682).

MUSICAL CULTURE IN THE SOVIET UNION

The year 1932—when Prokofiev began the renewal of his ties to Russia—was a turning point for the country and for its musicians. Before this time there had existed in
the Soviet Union a heated debate on the role of music. One faction was open to
Western ideas and modernistic styles; another was more ideological in its opposition
to Western music and to art music in general. Still, there was considerable openness
in the practice of the arts. Traditionalists and experimentalists lived side by side, and

new music by major European figures was often heard, especially in Leningrad (the name given in 1924 to the old capital city of St. Petersburg). Lenin's minister for the arts was the respected writer and critic **Anatoli Lunacharsky** (1875–1933), who tried to balance opposing factions while supporting artistic freedom from the threat of political and proletarian ideology.

The atmosphere of tolerance created by Lunacharsky gradually eroded under the rule of Joseph Stalin (1879–1953). Stalin distrusted the West and wanted to centralize control over the arts, which he accomplished partly through organizational means, partly through repression and terror. A resolution issued by the central Communist Party in April 1932 abolished the various proletarian organizations among artists and led to the founding of a "Union of Soviet Composers." For most musicians in the country, this was a positive step, since it seemed to give the musicians themselves— rather than proletarian amateurs—a larger voice in the control of their art. Dmitri Shostakovich spoke out immediately praising the decree: "I personally see the Resolution as a sign of faith in the composer."[2] But the musicians could not have been happy about Stalin's delegation of ultimate control over these organizations to political or military figures, such as his trusted ally **Andrei Zhdanov,** rather than to artists and intellectuals like Lunacharsky. All the same, the decree was apparently a principal reason why Prokofiev felt confident in reestablishing ties with Russia in 1932.

More crucial questions concerned artistic freedom and individual versus collective expression. What type of music would be approved of and supported by the Party? The answer first came in connection with literature. At a meeting in 1934 of the Soviet Writers' Congress, Zhdanov enunciated a policy of **socialist realism** as the single overriding objective in the future. This was not unexpected, since realism had long been a distinguishing feature of Russian literature and music. Recall the song "Within Four Walls" by Modest Mussorgsky (see Chapter 59), in which a text expressing everyday sentiments seems to override the music of the song, which is stripped bare of any elaborate melody or harmonic enrichment.

But realism for Zhdanov was not to be "objective," not a disinterested portrait of life or of working people. Instead it would of necessity be colored by optimism and idealistic thinking. In his 1934 speech he gave these guidelines for the new concept of realism:

> In the first place, it means knowing life so as to be able to depict it truthfully, in works of art, not to depict it in a dead, scholastic way, not simply as "objective reality," but to depict reality in its revolutionary development. In addition to this, the truthfulness and historical concreteness of the artistic portrayal should be combined with the ideological remolding and education of the toiling people in the spirit of socialism. This method in *belles lettres* and literary criticism is what we call the method of socialist realism.[3]

He cautioned writers to avoid subjects that deal with "non-existent life and non-existent heroes" or "a world of utopian dreams." Artists should instead "actively help to remold the mentality of people in the spirit of socialism."

The implications of these statements for music were clear enough. Composers would be urged to concentrate on programmatic or texted works glorifying the Revolution and the worker. Their music would have to be geared to the understanding and enjoyment of the masses. The admonition against utopianism and "non-existent life" could only refer to music that was advanced beyond the understanding of the present day—music, in other words, that deviated from the norm in harmony, rhythm, tonality, and form.

Music of this latter sort was dismissed as **formalism.** The term itself is nebulous, although it suggests a work in which abstract musical elements outweigh programmatic content. But, practically speaking, it was used as a catchall condemnation for any-thing in music—atonality, emancipated dissonance, rhythmic dislocation, disturbing or erotic subject matter—that was difficult for or unsettling to the average listener.

Although Prokofiev was ready to compose "great works" that glorified the Soviet Union and the ideals of the Revolution, he saw the dangers inherent in bureaucrats trying to distinguish between realism and formalism. Shortly after Zhdanov's speech, an interview with Prokofiev was published in the Moscow newspaper *Izvestia*, and here the composer warned against banality in the guise of realism:

> The danger of becoming provincial is unfortunately a very real one for modern Soviet composers. It is not so easy to find the right idiom for this music. To begin with it must be melodious; moreover the melody must be simple and comprehensible, without being repetitive or trivial. . . . The same applies to the technique and the idiom: it must be clear and simple, but not banal. We must seek a new simplicity.[4]

Prokofiev's call for a "new simplicity" touched on an issue not limited to Soviet Russia. It echoed throughout the entire world of music during the 1920s and 1930s. The Soviets' demand for realism, in other words, was a symptom of a broad move-ment in the arts of the time, not a cause of that movement. Given his years of travel, Prokofiev was uniquely placed to understand the direction that music had taken following World War I, especially among the younger composers in France and in the works of Igor Stravinsky. Prokofiev's own music generally followed the same course as these contemporaries, moving toward a relative simplicity and melodious-ness mixed with certain modernistic thinking in harmony and tonality. By person-ality, Prokofiev was not inclined to be a follower of trends, and he was very unmoved by much of the neoclassical music that he had heard in Paris in the 1920s. His rela-tionship to neoclassicism would always be ambiguous.

In an *Autobiography* written in 1941, Prokofiev assessed his own musical style and found in it four principal characteristics: a classical trait represented by the use of classical forms, a modern element seen mainly in an enriched harmonic language, motoric rhythms, and a pronounced lyricism. While his list of characteristics pro-vides an excellent general definition of neoclassicism, Prokofiev was not in favor of any "back to . . ." return to eighteenth-century composers or styles. He regretted his own youthful foray into music of this type—the "Classical" Symphony (Symphony No. 1, 1917)—and he found the retrospectivist outlook to be especially dismaying in recent works by Stravinsky. In a letter to Boris Asafiev in 1925, Prokofiev de-scribed Stravinsky's Concerto for Piano and Wind Instruments as "monkey see, monkey do":

> Stravinsky's concerto is a continuation of the line he adopted in the finale of his Octet—that is, a stylization in imitation of Bach—which I don't approve of, because even though I love Bach and think it's not a bad idea to compose according to his principles, it's not a good idea to produce a stylized version of his style. . . . Unfortu-nately, Stravinsky thinks otherwise; he doesn't see this as a case of "monkey see, mon-key do," and now he's written a piano sonata in the same style. He even thinks this will create a new era.[5]

Piano Sonata No. 7

Prokofiev's attempt to juggle realism, formalism, and the pitfalls of neoclassicism is especially evident in his Seventh Piano Sonata (1939–1942). All four of the traits that the composer described as characteristic of his oeuvre are plainly discernible in it. Classicism is found in the choice of genre and the work's overall form; lyricism is evident in the slow movement, and motoric rhythms and modernistic harmonies are plain to hear in its first and third movements.

The sonata is dominated by its third movement, an impetuous finale. The musical idiom owes much to Stravinsky's brand of neoclassicism, although it avoids the outright "back to Bach" allusions that Prokofiev found objectionable in Stravinsky's contemporaneous music. Still, it is Stravinskian in its driving ostinatos and motoric eighth-note pulse, which is draped over an asymmetrical $\frac{7}{8}$ meter (Ex. 74-1). As in Stravinsky's works of the 1920s and 1930s, Prokofiev mixes together octatonic, diatonic, and freely chromatic pitch fields, and the movement has a cool, witty tone, not unlike Stravinsky's Octet. Also typical of neoclassicism is a parody of jazz, represented at the beginning by the blue note C♯ in the left hand (equivalent to the lowered-third scale degree in the implied B♭ major tonality). Prokofiev, like Stravinsky, was a self-declared fan of American jazz, which he had many opportunities to hear on his American tours.

EXAMPLE 74-1

The Seventh Sonata is the product of a great composer at work in the musical culture and taste of his day, oblivious to bureaucrats' attempts to limit his imagination with labels such as realism and formalism. Certainly the finale of the Sonata is formalistic by the Soviets' definition, but the work was still greeted with great enthusiasm on its first hearing in Moscow in January 1943 at the height of World War II—as functionaries like Zhdanov were apparently too involved with the war to notice.

Still, some explanation for its modern resources had to be given. After Prokofiev's death, its first interpreter—the virtuoso pianist **Sviatoslav Richter** (1915–1997)—offered up an interpretation of the Seventh Sonata that was geared to please the authorities. Despite appearances, Richter claimed, the work is actually a realist composition whose modernism is only an expression of wartime anxiety. Richter writes:

> The sonata immediately throws one into the anxious situation of the world losing its equilibrium. Anxiety and uncertainty reign. Man is witnessing the riot of the violent forces of death and destruction. However what he had lived by before did not cease to exist for him. He feels, loves. Now the full range of his emotions bursts forth. Together with everyone and everything he protests and poignantly shares the common grief. The impetuous, advancing race, full of the will for victory, sweeps away everything in its path. It gains its strength in struggle and develops into a gigantic life-affirming force.[6]

The duplicity apparent in Richter's description became ever more widespread among Russian artists in their effort to cope with a meddlesome government.

LISTENING CUE

SERGEI PROKOFIEV
Piano Sonata No. 7 (1939–1942)
Third movement, *Precipitato*

CD 12/7
Anthology, No. 190

Peter and the Wolf

One of Prokofiev's most beloved and ingenious works is **Peter and the Wolf,** a "symphonic tale" for narrator and orchestra, which the composer wrote in 1936 for the Children's Musical Theater in Moscow. The story, written by Prokofiev himself, is narrated against a musical background. Peter, our youthful hero, ventures out into the meadow and greets the bird and duck, ignoring Grandfather's warnings about the wolf. A prowling cat is outsmarted by a clever bird. Just after Peter returns home at the insistence of Grandfather, the wolf comes out of the forest and swallows up the duck in one gulp. Peter sees this and intrepidly snares the wolf's tail in a noose and hoists him up. Hunters arrive and triumphantly carry the wolf off to the zoo.

Prokofiev's music has a memorable simplicity and warmth, and it demonstrates for children and adults alike the capacity of music to illustrate specific ideas. Each of the characters in the story has its own identifying motive, and these are played on instruments that precisely fit the character's qualities. Peter's motive is played primarily by the strings, in a happy and self-confident manner.

🌿 FIGURE 74-1

Reg Cartwright's painting shows Peter, the intrepid hero, with the other characters in Prokofiev's timeless musical fable.

EXAMPLE A

The bird is represented by the flute, whose music is filled with a rhythmic effervescence.

EXAMPLE B

The duck's instrument is the oboe, played with a waddling rhythm in the low register where its tone can be more than a bit duck-like.

EXAMPLE C

The cat's motive is taken by the clarinet in an even rhythm that suggests menace beneath a nonchalant exterior.

EXAMPLE D

(continued on next page)

Peter and the Wolf (continued)

Grandfather's chastisements are captured perfectly by the bassoon in the gruff low register:

EXAMPLE E

And, finally, the fox appears, embodied by horns whose music, in the minor mode, is spaced closely together to produce a sound of shrill penetration.

EXAMPLE F

The story is told most obviously by the narrator, but far more vividly by the instruments and their music.

DMITRI SHOSTAKOVICH

The fifteen years in age that separate Dmitri Shostakovich (1906–1975; Fig. 74-2) from Prokofiev ensured that their musical careers would develop differently. Shostakovich was only eleven years old at the time of the Revolution. When he graduated in 1925 from the Conservatory in his home city of Leningrad, he had become a loyal citizen and apparently an idealistic believer in the official objectives of the Soviet state. Like many younger musicians who had remained in Russia, he was optimistic about prospects for its future musical culture. The Soviet economy had been stabilized by Lenin's New Economic Policy, and the arts were flourishing despite ideological debates.

The German conductor Bruno Walter came to Leningrad in 1926, and he too sensed an optimism about the future: "The Leningrad Philharmonic Orchestra, the members of the Opera, and the audiences," he wrote, "made me joyfully aware of that spirit of enthusiasm which imparts to Russia's musical life its pulsating force."[7]

EARLY WORKS AND SUCCESSES

During his 1926 visit, Walter met Shostakovich and heard his Symphony No. 1, written at the age of nineteen while the composer was still a student. Walter performed the work with the Berlin Philharmonic Orchestra, and it was then taken up by orchestras elsewhere in the West and

🌸 FIGURE 74-2

The brilliant Soviet composer Dmitri Shostakovich was born in St. Petersburg in 1906, and died in Moscow in 1975.

CORBIS

Shostakovich on Music and Ideology

In this article-interview in *The New York Times* in 1931, Dmitri Shostakovich contends that all music contains a political and social message:

There can be no music without an ideology. The old composers, whether they knew it or not, were upholding a political theory. Most of them, of course, were bolstering the rule of the upper classes. Only Beethoven was a forerunner of the revolutionary movement. If you read his letters, you will see how often he wrote to his friends that he wished to give new ideas to the public and rouse it to revolt against its masters.

On the other hand, Wagner's biographies show that he began his career as a radical and ended as a reactionary. His monarchistic patriotism had a bad effect upon his mind. Perhaps it is a personal prejudice, but I do not consider Wagner a great composer. It is true he is played rather frequently in Russia today; but we hear him in the same spirit as we go to a museum to study the forms of the old régime. We can learn certain technical lessons from him, but we do not accept him.

We, as revolutionists, have a different conception of music. Lenin himself said that "music is a means of unifying broad masses of people." Not a leader of masses, per-

haps, but certainly an organizing force! For music has the power of stirring specific emotions in those who listen to it. No one can deny that Tchaikovsky's Sixth Symphony produces a feeling of despair, while Beethoven's Third awakens one to the joy of struggle. Even the symphonic form, which appears more than any other to be divorced from literary elements, can be said to have a bearing on politics. Thus we regard Scriabine as our bitterest musical enemy.

Why? Because Scriabine's music tends to an unhealthy eroticism. Also to mysticism and passivity and escape from the realities of life.

Not that the Soviets are always joyous, or supposed to be. But good music lifts and heartens and lightens people for work and effort. It may be tragic but it must be strong. It is no longer an end in itself, but a vital weapon in the struggle. Because of this, Soviet music will probably develop along different lines from any the world has known. There must be a change! After all, we have entered a new epoch and history has proved that every age creates its own language. Precisely what form this development in music will take I cannot say, any more than I can say what the idioms of speech will be fifty years from now. The notes will be same![8]

held up as evidence that music of originality could still come from Russia. Shostakovich was soon recognized as Russia's leading young composer and, like Prokofiev somewhat later, he became a spokesperson for socialist realism in music. "There can be no music without an ideology," he said in an article in *The New York Times* in 1931 (see Box). "Even the symphonic form, which appears more than any other to be divorced from literary elements, can be said to have a bearing on politics."[9]

Symphonic forms were much on Shostakovich's mind in their relation to Soviet artistic policy. Like many Russian composers in the early twentieth century, Shostakovich concentrated on the genre of the symphony. He wrote fifteen symphonies in all, and in them he continues the conception of the genre as it was inherited from the late romantic works of Gustav Mahler. Progressive composers elsewhere in the world had generally abandoned the symphony after the turn of the century, although they returned to it in the 1920s under the aegis of neoclassicism. Like Mahler, Shostakovich frequently uses chorus and solo voices in his symphonies, and most have strongly implied programs.

His most often performed symphony is No. 5 (1937), which uses the traditional classical form and has no explicit program despite the presence of many musical figures—marches, fanfares, bombastic orchestration, surging rhythms—that could plausibly support a programmatic interpretation. Shostakovich encouraged such thinking. Concerning the Fifth Symphony, he wrote: "The central idea of the work is man, with all his sufferings. The finale of the symphony resolves the tragic, tense elements of the first movements on a joyful, optimistic level."[10]

In addition to his fifteen symphonies, Shostakovich's huge oeuvre includes fifteen string quartets, sonatas, concertos, songs, choral music, and over thirty film scores. In his earlier years he had shown an affinity for theatric composition. Between 1928 and 1935 he wrote a series of operas and ballets of which the opera *Lady Macbeth of the Mtsensk District* (1932) proved to be hugely successful both in Russia and abroad. Its text has the realism characteristic of nineteenth-century Russian literature, but little of the revolutionary optimism that Zhdanov had demanded. Katerina, the wife of a merchant, is involved in an affair with a worker. She murders her husband and subsequently her lover, whereupon she commits suicide. Despite the grimness of the libretto, Shostakovich's music is full of parody, especially in the sex scenes, which were daringly explicit for Soviet Russia of the time.

LATER WORKS AND CONTROVERSIES

Following the great success of *Lady Macbeth*, Shostakovich was emboldened to speak out on more sensitive issues, such as the possibility that socialist realism could have a negative effect on artistic creativity. In an article in the newspaper *Izvestia* in 1935, he joined with Prokofiev to warn that realism could easily lapse into banality:

> To brand any work as formalistic on the grounds that its language is complex and perhaps not immediately comprehensible is unacceptably frivolous. Now my main goal is to find my own simple and expressive musical language. Sometimes the aspiration for a simple language is understood rather superficially. Often "simplicity" merges into epigonism [i.e., sterile imitation]. But to speak simply does not mean to speak as people did 50 or 100 years ago. This is a trap into which many modern composers fall, afraid of being accused of formalism. Both formalism and epigonism are harmful to Soviet music.[11]

It may have been such outspoken and independent pronouncements as this that contributed only a few months later to Shostakovich's being taken down a peg. In January 1936 his opera *Lady Macbeth* was the subject of an article, "Chaos Instead of Music," in the Communist Party newspaper *Pravda*. The essay was anonymous, which suggested that it came from the highest Soviet authorities, perhaps even from Stalin, who was reportedly indignant when he had seen the opera in Moscow only days before. In the article, Shostakovich's opera is denounced as "a confused stream of sound," a "distortion" that was filled with "fidgety, screaming, neurotic music." The writer continues:

> The composer has clearly not made it his business to heed what the Soviet public looks for in music and expects of it. As if by design, he has encoded his music and jumbled up all the sounds in such a way that it can only appeal to aesthetes and formalists who have lost all touch with good taste. He has ignored the determination of Soviet culture to banish crassness and crudeness from every corner of Soviet daily life.[12]

"This is a meaningless game," the writer says menacingly, "that may well come to a very bad end." The effect of this attack was immediate and profound, for Shostakovich and for all Russian composers. The year 1936 was the beginning of Stalin's murderous purge of citizens from all walks of life, many of whom were artists and several of whom were personal acquaintances of the composer. Shostakovich would have to watch his step and move even more decisively toward a "simple and expressive musical language." His next major work, the Symphony No. 5, seemed to satisfy his critics and his career was again on track, although the specter of threats from bureaucrats and rivals periodically resurfaced.

Following Stalin's death in 1953, a greater measure of artistic freedom was granted to Soviet composers, and Shostakovich again became an artistic ambassador for the Soviet system. In 1979, some four years after the composer's death, a book called *Testimony*, purporting to contain Shostakovich's memoirs, was published in the United States.[13] Here Shostakovich presents himself as an embittered dissident with no sympathy for Soviet ideology, a composer who communicated his disdain for the Soviet regime through subtle and ironic hints in his music. His complicity with the Soviets, he says, was only a pretense, "a survival tactic that permits you to maintain a minimal decency." The Russian authorities and many Shostakovich specialists dispute the authenticity of these memoirs.

Piano Concerto No. 1

Shostakovich's emphasis on the orchestral medium produced not only fifteen symphonies but also pairs of concertos for piano, violin, and cello. The earliest of these is his Piano Concerto No. 1 (1933), which he wrote "to fill a gap in Soviet instrumental music, which lacks full-scale concerto-type works." The genre of the concerto, like the symphony, was generally shunned by progressive composers following the turn of the century, although it returned to favor in the 1920s, the period of neoclassicism.

The First Concerto plainly shows the influence of this movement. It was composed on the heels of Ravel's Piano Concerto and Prokofiev's Fifth Piano Concerto—both squarely in the vein of Stravinskian neoclassicism. Like Ravel's Concerto, Shostakovich's is high-spirited and full of parody, as much "music about music" as are Stravinsky's neoclassical works from the 1920s (see Chapter 68).

Shostakovich was very enthusiastic about Stravinsky's music and his new aesthetics of the 1920s: "I certainly do not believe that he should be imitated in every respect," Shostakovich wrote, "but he is very interesting and original in that he has opened up new paths in modern music. This is why I single him out among contemporary West European composers." In his 1931 interview for *The New York Times* (see Box) he parrots Stravinsky's well-known dismissal of the music of Wagner and Scriabin, and also Stravinsky's contention that music had in the 1920s entered a new epoch. But Shostakovich, as always, attributed the playful quality of his Concerto not to Stravinsky's "new paths" but to the special role of the Soviet composer. "Our age, as I perceive it, is heroic, spirited and joyful. This is what I wanted to convey in my concerto."[14]

The work has a classical three-movement form, although a prelude to the finale is shown in the score as a separate movement, bringing the total to four. Typical of the Classical style, the work is brief and the orchestra small, calling only for strings and a solo trumpet that banters off and on with the piano.

The first movement is cast into a free sonata form whose main and second themes (both introduced by the piano) are shown in Example 74-2. The movement has many comic touches. References to keys are spoofed, as tonalities careen and collide. In several passages the cellist enters with his own themes, as though mistakenly thinking that it is his concerto. By the end all are exhausted by the madcap antics, and the music seems to deflate into the low register, where it dies.

EXAMPLE 74-2

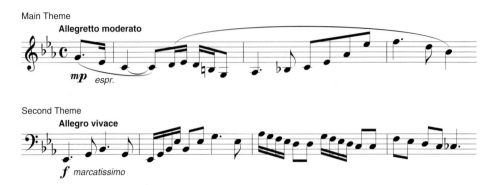

Main Theme

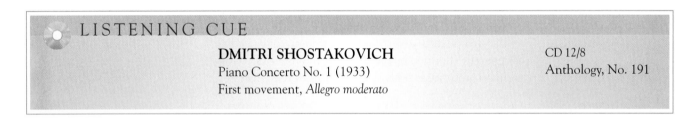

Second Theme

In the music of Shostakovich we see the neoclassical element of parody carried over into outright satire and humor. "I want to fight for the right of laughter to be accepted in so-called serious music," Shostakovich demanded.

LISTENING CUE

DMITRI SHOSTAKOVICH
Piano Concerto No. 1 (1933)
First movement, *Allegro moderato*

CD 12/8
Anthology, No. 191

SUMMARY

In the early post-revolutionary period (1917–1920), many of Russia's leading musicians emigrated to the West. These include Sergei Prokofiev, who lived in the United States, France, and Germany from 1918 to 1932, during which time he worked as both a concert pianist and composer. Between 1932 and 1936 he gradually strengthened his ties with Soviet Russia and embraced Soviet ideology concerning the role of music, which demanded "socialist realism" rather than "formalism." The former quality is found in works that are understandable by the average listener and positive in outlook; the latter in abstract or difficult works.

The objective of realism in music conforms in general to the musical style of neoclassicism, which was most closely associated with works by Stravinsky from the 1920s and 1930s and influential on Russia's leading composers. Prokofiev did not accept the "back to Bach" element of Stravinsky's music of the time, although he agreed with Stravinsky concerning the need for a return to clarity and simplicity in music, an eclectic harmonic style that mixed diatonicism with alternative pitch resources, and an emphasis on lyrical melody.

Dmitri Shostakovich was the leading younger composer in Soviet Russia in the 1920s and 1930s, although his music was harshly criticized by Soviet authorities for its formalism. Shostakovich, like Prokofiev, attempted to conform to bureaucratic wishes by finding a simple and expressive style rooted in neoclassicism. Shostakovich emphasized parody and satire in his music.

KEY TERMS

Anatoli Lunacharsky	socialist realism	Sviatoslav Richter
Andrei Zhdanov	formalism	*Peter and the Wolf*

Self-Reliance in American Music: Ives, Seeger, Nancarrow

In his landmark 1841 essay "Self-Reliance," **Ralph Waldo Emerson** appeals to his American readers for individualism and independent thinking. "Imitation is suicide," he declares. "Whoso would be a man, must be a nonconformist." Emerson then elaborates: "Insist on yourself; never imitate. Your own gift you can present every moment with the cumulative force of a whole life's cultivation; but of the adopted talent of another you have only an extemporaneous half possession."[1]

Emerson's words have an uncanny relevance to the history of American music, which has been driven by opposing instincts, on the one hand for self-reliance and on the other for an "adopted talent," an imitation of European styles.

MUSIC IN COLONIAL AMERICA

America's first important composer, **William Billings** (1746–1800), was a nonconformist. "I don't think myself confin'd to any Rules for Composition laid down by any that went before me," he proclaimed. "Neither should I think (were I to pretend to lay down Rules) that any who came after me were any ways obligated to adhere to them."[2]

Billings lived in Boston, taught himself music, and worked as a tanner. His compositions consist primarily of unaccompanied choral pieces used in church services and singing schools. Some are **fuguing tunes,** which contain a simple point of imitation usually inserted toward the end, and Billings also composed longer, multisectional pieces that he called "anthems." In addition to his rough-and-ready originality, Billings had a gift for creating a memorable tune. An example is in the rousing "Chester" (c1770; Ex. 75-1). Its words, written by Billings himself, capture the patriotic mood in the colonies just before the American Revolution. The tune appears in the tenor voice, surrounded by simple and direct harmonies.

EXAMPLE 75-1

mm. 1-8

(continued on next page)

and   slav - 'ry   clank____   her   gall - ing   chains;

✿ NINETEENTH-CENTURY DEVELOPMENTS

In the nineteenth century, a modern musical culture was gradually created in the United States. Its centerpiece was (and continues to be) the symphony orchestra. In New York a permanent orchestra—forerunner of the New York Philharmonic—was founded in 1842. The Boston Symphony Orchestra followed in 1881, and in 1900 occupied its acoustically splendid Symphony Hall (Fig. 75-1). The Chicago Orchestra was formed in 1891, and the Philadelphia Orchestra in 1900. The Philadelphians were brought to great prominence by the English-born conductor **Leopold Stokowski** (1882–1977), who daringly programmed the works of modern composers.

Other types of music also flourished in nineteenth-century America. Pianos appeared in ever-greater numbers in the homes of middle-class families, with excellent instruments provided by American makers including Jonas Chickering, William Knabe, and Henry Steinway. Opera was slower to develop, but flourished in New Orleans and later in New York. The **Metropolitan Opera** was founded in New York in 1883. Alongside the culture for artistic music in nineteenth-century America was an unusually vigorous and diverse popular music, which led early in the twentieth century to the birth of jazz (see Chapter 72). Domestic music-making created a demand for both popular and serious piano music and songs, which was met by a thriving sheet music trade.

Just as William Billings exemplifies the beginnings of self-reliance in American music, **Edward MacDowell** (1860–1908) typifies the adopted talent, the composer who aspired primarily to elevate American musical culture to the level of contemporary European music. MacDowell was born in New York and spent the years from 1876 to 1888 living in Europe, primarily in Germany. There he gave piano concerts, taught, and composed in the style of modern German musicians. He then returned to America and resumed his career. In 1896 he was appointed the first professor of music at Columbia University. His home in Peterborough, New Hampshire, was left as an artists' retreat, the "MacDowell Colony," that still exists today. MacDowell's music includes two piano concertos, orchestral tone poems, songs and choruses, and a large number of compositions for piano, including four sonatas and collections of character pieces.

The "Song" from *Sea Pieces*, Op. 55 (1898), for piano, shows MacDowell's skillful adoption of an existing style. *Sea Pieces* is a collection of eight character piano pieces squarely in the idiom of similar works by Romantic-era composers such as Mendelssohn and Liszt. Each piece depicts an aspect of the sea as seen through the eyes of an imaginary traveler. MacDowell adds poetic lines to

✿ FIGURE 75-1

Boston's Symphony Hall—home of the Boston Symphony Orchestra—was completed in 1900. The building is a symbol of the great importance of orchestras to American musical culture.

CORBIS

the beginning of the pieces to reinforce the image that the music is intended to convey. The "Song" is introduced by these verses:

> A merry song, a chorus brave,
> And yet a sigh regret
> For roses sweet, in woodland lanes—
> Ah, love can ne'er forget!

Each of these thoughts is represented by a theme. The first one—"a merry song, a chorus brave"—imitates a sea **shanty,** a rousing type of work song that MacDowell no doubt encountered among sailors during his own ocean travels. Its beginning is shown in Example 75-2. Although repetitive and more than a bit sentimental, the *Sea Pieces* have a great charm and melodic imagination.

EXAMPLE 75-2

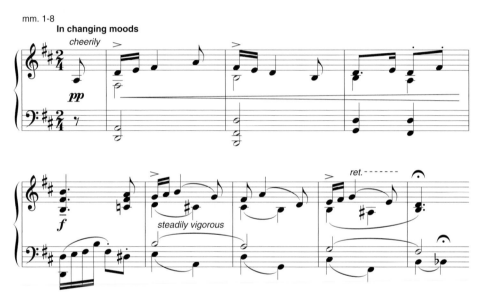

CHARLES IVES

The Emersonian ideal of self-reliance bloomed in American music in the works of Charles E. Ives (1874–1954). He was born in Danbury, Connecticut, the son of a musician. In his youth Ives learned piano and organ and received a good knowledge of European music and its rules from his father, a free-thinking musician who was entirely open to musical experiments. "Father was not against a reasonable amount of 'boy's fooling,'" Ives wrote, "if it were done with some sense behind it (maybe not very much or too good a sense, but something more than just thoughtless fooling)—as playing left-hand accompaniment in one key and tune in right hand in another. . . . He made us stick to the end, and not stop when it got hard."[3]

As a youngster Ives began to compose in a vein that was alternately homespun, humorous, and experimental. He wrote more polished and conventional works during his undergraduate days at Yale University, where he studied composition with **Horatio Parker** (1863–1919), a German-trained composer and teacher who had little sympathy for Ives's experiments.

An especially skillful work that Ives wrote for Parker is the song "Feldeinsamkeit" ("Alone in the Fields," 1897). Parker often asked his students to compose songs to texts that had already been used by the great nineteenth-century musicians, and here Ives takes up a German poem by Hermann Allmers that had been famously set to music by Johannes Brahms (see Chapter 58.)

Ives's treatment of the poem shows a thorough knowledge of the contemporary progressive style of German music, associated more with a Richard Strauss or Hugo Wolf than with Brahms. In the middle section of the song's **ABA** form, where the poetic voice speaks of sailing disembodied through space, Ives's harmony detaches itself from the principal key and moves tonally far afield, finally returning to earth with the reprise of the opening stanza. In his autobiographical *Memos*, Ives recalled Parker playing "Feldeinsamkeit" in the presence of the composer George Chadwick:

> When Chadwick came in Parker was objecting to the too many keys in the middle. . . .
> C. said, "The melodic line has a natural continuity—it flows . . . as only good songs
> do. And it's different from Brahms, as in the piano part and the harmony it takes a
> more difficult and almost opposite aspect to Brahms, for the active tranquility of the
> outdoor beauty of nature is harder to express than just quietude. In its way it's almost
> as good as Brahms."[4]

LISTENING CUE

CHARLES IVES
"Feldeinsamkeit" (1897)

CD 12/9
Anthology, No. 192

Following graduation, Ives moved to New York and entered the insurance business, first as an actuary, then as the head of his own agency. He and his partner, Julian Myrick, proved immensely successful, in large part due to Ives's systematic ideas for insurance marketing. Ives is now recognized as a leading figure in the creation of the modern American insurance industry, and he brought the same passion to his business life as he did to his music, seeing many connections between the two worlds. He composed in his spare time and dispensed with the European romantic style demanded by Parker to return to the experimental ideas of his youth, which he enriched with new and original aesthetic intentions. His works had virtually no public performances.

Ives composed little after suffering a heart attack in 1918, following which he turned his attention to making his music known. In 1920, at his own expense, he published his Piano Sonata No. 2 (subtitled *Concord, Mass., 1840–60*) and an explanatory pamphlet titled *Essays Before a Sonata*. Two years later he published a collection of *114 Songs*. Gradually, performances of his music increased, and its scope and originality became better known. In 1939 the "Concord" Piano Sonata was hailed in the *New York Herald-Tribune* as a "masterpiece," and in 1947 Ives won a Pulitzer Prize for his Symphony No. 3.

❋ AESTHETICS

Much about Ives's music resembles traditional European compositions of the late nineteenth and early twentieth century. He composed in traditional genres, and, like the musician of the Romantic era, he made his instrumental music expressive through familiar programmatic strategies such as melodic quotations and free forms. His penchant for novel materials—dissonant chords, polyrhythms, microtones, among others—is not so unusual for this period. But Ives's musical aesthetic was largely his own. Inspired by reading Emerson and recalling his father's free-thinking about music, he developed his own philosophy, which guided him in the creation of a body of compositions that was essentially unlike anything that had come before.

In the Epilogue to *Essays Before a Sonata,* Ives describes what he was aiming for in his music. He proposes that any musical work has two sides: one is its "manner" (its outer aspect, the form in which it is presented), and the other its "substance" (its spiritual or poetic content). "Substance has something to do with character," he writes. "Manner has nothing to do with it. The 'substance' of a tune comes from somewhere near the soul, and the 'manner' comes from— God knows where."[5] Manner is the lesser quality since it relies only on ephemera; substance is higher since it expresses the real world—filled with everyday concerns in addition to higher moral and spiritual insights. Ives insisted that the substance of art was as much the property of the common man as it was the specialist. He foresaw a future "when every man while digging his potatoes will breathe his own Epics, his own Symphonies."[6]

Although other composers have written about this two-sidedness of music— Schoenberg called the distinction "style" versus "idea"—Ives is unusual in that he sees the two as opposites. The more apparent the manner in a composition, Ives says, the less its substance. This reciprocity, he thought, had caused a crisis in late Romantic music. Composers such as Tchaikovsky and Richard Strauss, Ives says, overly emphasize manner in their striving for beauty and perfection of form. For this reason their compositions lose touch with the real world and are diminished in substance. A composer like Debussy, Ives writes, could have improved his music "if he had hoed corn or sold newspapers for a living, for in this way he might have gained a deeper vitality and truer theme to sing at night and of a Sunday."[7] This imbalance in manner and substance was the reason that Ives could not continue to write such sonorous music as "Feldeinsamkeit." In purely musical terms, he saw the truth in Emerson's warning about imitation.

IVES'S MUSIC: VOCAL WORKS

Ives's music exhibits no single style. Some compositions use traditional musical materials, others are dissonant, atonal, microtonal, or otherwise experimental. Some appear to be written in an improvisatory stream of consciousness, while others are carefully planned out to produce unified structures. A recurrent feature of his music is the quotation of tunes that he recalled from his Connecticut childhood.

Ives's vocal works consist of more than one hundred fifty songs plus music for chorus, including psalm settings, *Three Harvest Home Chorales,* and *The Celestial Country* for chorus, orchestra, and organ. In these pieces Ives uses several strategies for bringing his music into contact with the real world and giving it substance. One was to make it depict the musical memories of his own past—thus the quotations of tunes and other evocations of the musical world of his boyhood. At the same time he saw the need for his music to rise above the everyday, to achieve a more timeless level that was worthy of art, while still being rooted in the mundanities of the real world. Just as Emerson believed that universal truth came to the individual through a flash of intuition, Ives wanted to find in the everyday experience some momentary insight that revealed a higher meaning. He then searched for an appropriate musical language to depict the special within the commonplace.

The dichotomy that underlay Ives's outlook on art is apparent in one of his most charming songs, "Charlie Rutlage" (c1920). This is a setting of a ballad by the Montana cowboy and writer, D.J. O'Malley. It tells the supposedly true story of a fellow cowboy, Charlie Rutlage, who was killed in an accident while herding cattle. The image of a common man about his daily work suddenly coming face to face with his destiny was just what Ives was looking for in a musical text, and his setting of the scene finds a musical equivalent of its juxtaposition of opposites.

The work begins with a portrait of Charlie's everyday world, expressed in a quirky folk-like music with a pentatonic melody and an accompaniment that constantly changes key. In the middle part, where Charlie's number is up, Ives looks for a non-conventional style. The vocalist speaks rather than sings, while the pianist impersonates Charlie, crying out "Whoopee ti yi yo, git along little doggies." The music rises to a frenzy, and at the point where Charlie is killed, the pianist uses the fists to pound out **tone clusters** (dissonant groups of adjacent notes; Ex. 75-3). Following this spiritual flash, Charlie goes to heaven to be reunited with his kinfolk and the music returns to the everyday world of the opening.

EXAMPLE 75-3

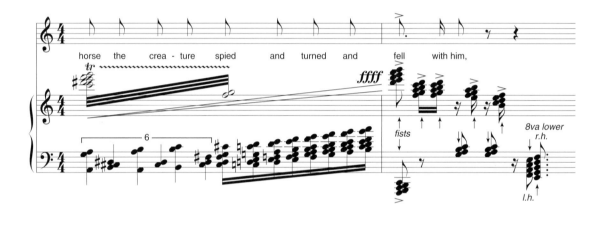

LISTENING CUE

CHARLES IVES
"Charlie Rutlage" (c1920)

CD 12/10
Anthology, No. 193

IVES'S INSTRUMENTAL MUSIC: THE UNANSWERED QUESTION

Ives composed four symphonies and numerous tone poems, four violin sonatas and two string quartets, two piano sonatas and a variety of character pieces for piano. Virtually all of his mature instrumental music is programmatic. It deals with topics that include recollections of his boyhood, portraits of people he admired, locations in New England, Americana, and metaphysical speculations. His tone poem *The Unanswered Question* (1906, later revised) is an example of the last. According to a Foreword in the score, the music portrays the universe. We repeatedly hear a question raised concerning the meaning of existence, and mankind's attempts to answer the question are futile, leading only to frustration.

To express this idea Ives uses a spatial device also exploited by late Romantic composers. He instructs the strings to sit offstage, or at least separated from the other instruments. Ives also finds another ingeniously effective way to communicate the idea of the work, one that had not been used by any of his contemporaries. Each of the three elements in the program—the silent universe, the question of existence, and mankind's futile answers—is represented by a distinguishable stratum of music, and these are put together without strict coordination in time. The universe—or as Ives calls it "The Silences of the Druids, Who Know, See, and Hear Nothing"—is represented by soothing and featureless music in the strings. They play diatonically, form consonant chords, and dispense with any strong sense of beat or meter. The "Perennial Question of Existence" is raised repeatedly by a short figure in the solo trumpet (Ex. 75-4). Its motive is chromatic in content and its notes do not duplicate tones of the string chords. Human beings are represented by four flutes (Ives allows for them to be replaced by other woodwinds). After every question they bicker furiously, each time with great animation and stridency. They can never answer the trumpet's question of existence.

EXAMPLE 75-4

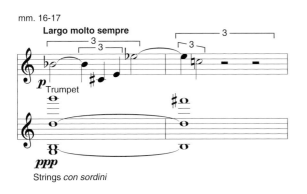

LISTENING CUE

CHARLES IVES
The Unanswered Question (1906)

CD 12/11
Anthology, No. 194

The works of Charles Ives created a new way of thinking about music for composers in the United States. The American composer, Ives seemed to say, need not join in the mainstream of music established by European classical composers. American musicians were instead free to move in new directions, to mix styles, and even to rethink the very laws that composers on the other side of the Atlantic had long accepted.

LATER FIGURES: RUTH CRAWFORD SEEGER AND CONLON NANCARROW

Ives's spirit of self-reliance resurfaced in American music later in the twentieth century. It is plain to hear in the works of **Harry Partch** (1901–1974). Partch had little use for traditional classical music, which he condemned as "abstract," something of interest only to a handful of snobs. What he wanted instead was "corporeal" music:

> The approved Abstraction is a full musical fare for only a small percentage of our people, and the resulting hunger is satisfied by anything that breaks the formal barriers in the direction of Corporeality—hillbilly, cowboy, and popular music, which, whatever its deficiencies, owes nothing to scholastic and academic Europeanisms.[8]

Photo Courtesy of Peggy Seeger

❧ FIGURE 75-2
Ruth Crawford, c1926. Ruth Crawford (later Ruth Crawford Seeger) was one of the most original voices in American music in the 1920s and 1930s.

Partch's disdain for "Europeanisms" led him to compose music for home-made instruments, to which he added earthy recitations.

A more sophisticated expression of the Ivesian spirit is found in the music of **Ruth Crawford Seeger** (1901–1953; Fig. 75-2). She was born in Ohio, grew up in Florida, and studied piano in Chicago. There she began to compose modernistic songs, piano pieces, and chamber music, and her independence of mind attracted the attention of other free-thinking musicians. In 1929 she moved to New York and began to study with **Charles Seeger** (1886–1979), whom she married in 1932. Seeger, a man of broad interests in music, taught composition by a method that he called **dissonant counterpoint.** His idea was to liberate a student's thinking about music while maintaining its craft. He asked his students to write exercises in species counterpoint, but he reversed the roles of consonance and dissonance. In his exercises, dissonances became the basic, stable intervals and consonances were restricted in rhythm and meter. They appeared only in passing until "resolved" to a dissonance.

In a self-reliant fashion, the Seegers looked for a musical style that was different from the more established American musical idioms of their day, such as folklorism and neoclassicism, for which they had no affinity. They were attracted to the serial music of Arnold Schoenberg, although as always they insisted on finding their own way, independent of the Europeans.

Ruth Crawford Seeger's String Quartet (1931) illustrates their objectives. The work has four short movements of contrasting character. The third movement, *Andante,* is the most original of the four. The part for each instrument consists of long-held tones, which create slowly changing and densely chromatic chords. These sound masses come to life through constantly shifting and subtly overlapping crescendos and decrescendos, which gather with a wave-like force until reaching a climax in measure 75, whereupon the music quickly collapses and evaporates.

The movement has only a single melodic line, created as the instruments enter or change their tones, one by one. The line is highly chromatic. For example, in measures 1–17 it has the tones C♯-D-C-D♯-F-F♯-A-B♭-G♯-B, covering ten of the twelve notes before the tone C is repeated on the downbeat of measure 18. The line weaves its way upward through generally small intervals that avoid the outlining of familiar chords. The Seegers called a melody of this type "dissonant," not only because it moved through primarily dissonant intervals but also because its diverse and heterogeneous materials suggested a freedom from familiar patterns. The work's concentration into a single, free melodic line represented for the Seegers a progressive step toward the future. Charles Seeger wrote:

> The proposition is here advanced that by decreasing the number of lines and increasing their freedom, two ends are served: first, the correction of the abuses of polyphony; second, the reinstatement of the single melodic line, whose return to preference in the not too distant future is at least a probability.[9]

An element of counterpoint enters the work, not by any multiple melodies but by simultaneous strata, each formed from the instruments' distinctive patterns of dynamics. "This movement," said Ruth Crawford Seeger, "is built on a counterpoint of dynamics. The crescendi and diminuendi should be exactly timed."[10] We can see what she means by examining a passage near the opening of the movement (mm. 16–20 in Ex. 75-5). Each instrument repeatedly plays small crescendos and decrescendos, and within every section of the movement the crescendo in each instrument reaches its high point at a fixed location within the measure. In the section shown in Example 75-5, for example, the viola reaches its loudest moment on the downbeat of each measure; Violin II on the second beat of every measure, Violin I on the last beat of the measure, and the cello on the next to last beat. At measure 28 the pattern changes, as though the "counterpoint" has shifted to a new key.

EXAMPLE 75-5

(The dotted tie indicates that the first tone of each new bow is not to be attacked.)

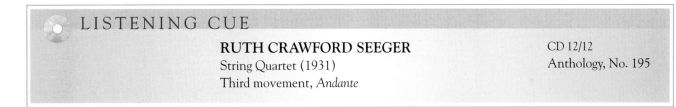

LISTENING CUE

RUTH CRAWFORD SEEGER
String Quartet (1931)
Third movement, *Andante*

CD 12/12
Anthology, No. 195

The Seegers' independent outlook is also found in the music of **Conlon Nancarrow** (1912–1997). He was born in Arkansas to a family that was, by his description, tone deaf. Growing up, he played jazz while he received a good musical education. In the 1930s he began to compose, mainly jazzy instrumental pieces.

In 1940 he emigrated permanently to Mexico City, although he found himself isolated there from a culture for new music. Out of necessity he began to compose for the medium of player piano (see Chapter 77), first sketching out a work and then painstakingly punching a paper roll to encode it in a performable medium. His player-piano pieces—all of them are called simply "studies"—are often jazz inspired, and they exploit the precision of his medium by using complex **polyrhythms,** often far more complex than could be realized by any human performer. His music was long unknown, except to a few musicians such as Elliott Carter who were sensitive to his rhythmic originality, and he went through long periods when he did not compose at all.

His breakthrough to international recognition came only in the 1970s, when recordings of his player-piano studies finally captured the attention of modern music enthusiasts. Except for a small number of pieces for piano and instrumental ensembles, his entire oeuvre is devoted to about fifty player-piano studies, which are remarkable for their imaginative use of the instrument and for their stunning rhythmic complication.

Study 3a for player piano (c1948) has the form of a boogie-woogie piano blues. **Boogie woogie** (or "honky tonk") is a style of blues piano playing developed in the 1920s by Meade "Lux" Lewis and other blues pianists. The most distinctive feature is a fast, driving tempo and a bass line that outlines the blues harmonies through a percussive ostinato. The idiom of boogie woogie lived on into the 1950s and 1960s in the music of **rhythm-and-blues,** which was the direct forerunner of rock 'n' roll.

Nancarrow's Study 3a consists of twenty-two blues choruses. The boogie-woogie bass line (Ex. 75-6) runs unchanged from beginning to end. Above it we hear variations upon several short riff-like motives, the first of which is shown in Example 75-7. As the series of variations continues, new lines are added, each with its own rhythmic and metric organization. The last seven choruses undergo a steady increase in contrapuntal complexity until finally eight separate streams of sound are present. Three of these lines create a mensuration canon. Recall from Chapter 18 that this type of canon is made from simultaneous lines that contain the same music performed at different rates of speed. In the lowest line of Nancarrow's canon (Ex. 75-8), each note of the blues bass has a duration equivalent to two sixteenths. Above it, the blues bass is stated more slowly, with three sixteenths per tone, and higher still it reappears with five sixteenths per note. Other contrapuntal lines add asymmetrical rhythmic ostinatos until the limits of complication are reached, whereupon the piece suddenly ends.

EXAMPLE 75-6

EXAMPLE 75-7

EXAMPLE 75-8

SUMMARY

Throughout its history, classical music in America has alternately imitated European models and broken free from them. The colonial hymn composer William Billings declared himself unrestrained by conventional rules, although nineteenth-century figures such as Edward MacDowell wrote music squarely in the manner of German romantic contemporaries.

Charles E. Ives began in the same imitative mold, but soon broke with the musical traditions of his time and professed a self-reliance in composing that he found in the writings of Ralph Waldo Emerson. He sometimes strove for substance in his music by making it reflect everyday life, into which a glimpse of a higher spirituality is usually granted. Many of his pieces quote tunes that he heard as a child. Other pieces express metaphysical ideas by a variety of innovative means, and Ives music alternates in style between conventional forms and experiments with dissonance, spatiality, and noncoordination among strata.

The music of Ruth Crawford Seeger continues the self-reliant spirit of Ives. In the *Andante* movement of her String Quartet she experiments with a new concept of counterpoint, made not from simultaneous melodies but from distinct patterns of crescendos and decrescendos in the four lines.

Virtually all of the music of Conlon Nancarrow is written for the medium of player piano. His player-piano studies are often jazzy, and they combine layers of sounds having differing metric organization. These create complex polyrhythmic and polymetric textures.

KEY TERMS

Ralph Waldo Emerson	shanty	dissonant counterpoint
William Billings	Horatio Parker	Conlon Nancarrow
fuguing tune	tone cluster	polyrhythm
Leopold Stokowski	Harry Partch	boogie woogie
Metropolitan Opera	Ruth Crawford Seeger	rhythm-and-blues
Edward MacDowell	Charles Seeger	

American Composers Return from Europe: Copland and Barber

In June 1921, Aaron Copland (1900–1990) set off for Europe to continue his musical education. In doing so he was following the pattern of the leading American composers of the later nineteenth century, including George Chadwick and Horatio Parker, mentioned in Chapter 75. But there was an important difference, since Copland was headed for Paris, whereas the earlier musicians had studied composition primarily in Germany. During World War I, Germany had been the enemy and France an ally, and, following the armistice, America's longstanding musical connection with Germany was largely transferred to France.

In the 1920s, Paris became a home away from home for an entire generation of American musicians, writers, and painters. The shift from Germany to Paris was not simply a matter of geography. For the musician it indicated a change of orientation from the German world of complex emotionality to France's up-to-date modernism.

✤ COPLAND'S LIFE AND MUSIC

Copland studied during his first summer at a music school for American students in Fontainebleau, near Paris. Here he met the remarkable teacher **Nadia Boulanger** (1887–1979), who was the older sister of Lili Boulanger (see Chapter 63). Copland immediately recognized Nadia Boulanger's gift as a teacher. "Her sense of involvement in the whole subject of harmony made it more lively than I ever thought it could be," he wrote. "She created a kind of excitement about the subject, emphasizing how it was, after all, the fundamental basis of our music, when one really thought about it. I suspected that first day that I had found my composition teacher."[1] Copland followed "Mademoiselle," as Boulanger was known to her students, to Paris, where for the next three years he studied with her privately, forming a warm friendship.

In 1924 Copland returned to New York and took up the life of a professional composer. Predictably, his early works favored the orchestra, which was the strong suit of American musical culture of the day. He remained for his whole career an independent composer, although he periodically taught (for example, during the summers from 1940 to 1965 at the Berkshire Music Center in Tanglewood, Massachusetts) and wrote books and essays on music. In the 1940s he came repeatedly to Hollywood to write film scores, and in 1949 he received an Oscar for his score for the movie *The Heiress*. He was much involved in arts organizations that supported new American music, and in the 1950s he began the career of an orchestral conductor, specializing in his own music.

Copland's best known works include his three symphonies, ballet scores, orchestral character pieces including *Fanfare for the Common Man* (1942), *El Salón México* (1936), *An Outdoor Overture* (1938), and the patriotic narration *Lincoln Portrait* (1942). His smaller works include a Violin Sonata (1943), Nonet for strings (1960), Piano Sonata (1941), Piano Variations (1930), and the songs *Twelve Poems of Emily Dickinson* (1950). His folksong arrangements, *Old American Songs*, are often performed today.

✤ THE FORMATION OF A STYLE

When Copland arrived in Paris in 1921, his own future language as a composer was still largely unformed. Different from many European musicians of the day, he came from an environment in the United States that did not by itself set him on any particular path. The Brooklyn of his childhood, he wrote, "had little or no connection with serious music. My discovery of music was rather like coming upon an unsuspected city—like discovering Paris or Rome if you had never before heard of their existence."[2] Understandably, Parisian musical culture of the 1920s exerted a powerful and lasting influence, especially through the modern works of Fauré, Debussy, Ravel, and, most of all, the new music of Igor Stravinsky, who then lived in France and was greatly admired by Nadia Boulanger.

But this European connection posed a danger in Copland's mind. He did not want to be a mere follower of his European contemporaries. He found this a failing in nineteenth-century American composers such as Chadwick and Parker: "They were essentially practitioners in the conventional idiom of their own day, and therefore had little to offer us of a younger generation."[3]

Copland instead wanted his music to bring together apparent opposites—Americanism at the same time as universality, and accessibility with the trappings of high art. "We wanted to find a music that would speak of universal things in a vernacular of American speech rhythms," Copland wrote. "We wanted to write music on a level that left popular music far behind—music with a largeness of utterance wholly representative of the country that Whitman had envisaged."[4]

Copland's mention of the poet **Walt Whitman** (1819–1892) was no accident. He was one of Copland's favorite writers, one whose legacy combined the same opposites that Copland wanted to bring to music. Whitman's poetry dealt with American themes but had an international appeal, and his principal subject is America's common men and women, whom he extolled as though the material of high art.

In the preface to his 1855 *Leaves of Grass*, Whitman elaborated on his artistic outlook: "The genius of the United States is not best or most in its executives or legislatures, nor in its ambassadors or authors or colleges or churches or parlors, nor even in its newspapers or inventors . . . but always most in the common people."[5] The role of the artist, Whitman continued, was to be the voice of the common man ("his spirit responds to his country's spirit"), and this could only succeed by adopting a plain and simple style: "The art of art, the glory of expression, and the sunshine of the light of letters," Whitman concluded, "is simplicity. Nothing is better than simplicity . . . nothing can make up for excess or for the lack of definiteness."[6]

These ideas had a powerful influence on Copland, and they reflect the distinctively American emphasis on individuality and self-reliance that we have already encountered in the writings of Ralph Waldo Emerson and the music of Charles Ives (see Chapter 75). Ives had grappled with the same fundamental question that concerned Copland: How can classical music have relevance to American society? Ives's answer was to create a naivist music celebrating everyday experience, but Copland could not accept this outlook. Despite his appreciation for Ives's imagination, Copland found Ives's music lacking in structure, polish, and craft—all things that Ives had dismissed as worthless "manner." Copland would not accept the idea that manner was something insignificant in music, and it was exactly what he found missing in Ives. "At its worst his music is amorphous, disheveled, haphazard—like the music of a man who is incapable of organizing his many different thoughts," wrote Copland about Ives.[7]

Organization—what Copland found so lacking in Ives's music—was the quality that Boulanger most prized in a work. She called this formal element *"la grande ligne"* ("the long line"), and Copland interpreted it to mean continuity and "flow:"

> Every good piece of music must give us a sense of flow—a sense of continuity from first note to last. Every elementary music student knows the principle, but to put it into practice has challenged the greatest minds in music! A great symphony is a man-made Mississippi down which we irresistibly flow from the instant of our leave-taking to a long foreseen destination. Music must always flow, for that is part of its very essence, but the creation of that continuity and flow—that long line—constitutes the be-all and end-all of every composer's existence.[8]

His rejection of Ives's self-reliance in music only increased the dilemma that Copland faced in finding his own style. At first he tried to write compositions that combined modern harmonies with jazz rhythms, an alternative that was encouraged by Mlle. Boulanger and squarely in the French manner of the 1920s. But by 1930 he had abandoned this practice because he believed that jazz was limited in its emotional range. He finally decided to compose alternately in two styles. Some pieces would be modernistic and close to the contemporary neoclassical model; others were made simple, folkloric and American in theme, and musically accessible to almost everyone.

Piano Variations

The Piano Variations (1930) is the first masterpiece of the former type—music taking its departure from Stravinskian neoclassicism but transformed in Copland's own way. The work consists of an eleven-measure theme, twenty connected variations, and a coda. Copland gives his variations distinguishable and contrasting moods: "expressive," "naive," "clangorous," "blurred," "scherzando," and "threatening" are some of the playing instructions. Despite these contrasts, the entire composition is tightly unified by a continuous development of ideas.

Like Stravinsky's neoclassical music of the 1920s, the Piano Variations is relatively brief, contrapuntal in texture, and classical in form and genre. The fast passages display a motoric rhythm set against changing and asymmetrical meters, and the sound of the work is transparent, lean, and hard. The harmonies are modernistically dissonant, as they mix together diatonic, octatonic, and freely chromatic pitch structures. Traditional tonality plays no role, although—as in the music of Stravinsky—triads remain important sonorities and certain pitches are temporarily given priority. There is nothing overtly regional or American about the work.

All of these are features of Stravinsky's music from the 1920s, but Copland departs from his model in several ways. He avoids Stravinsky's witty parody of earlier musical styles, and he writes for the piano with a more rawboned texture and rhythm. Perhaps bearing in mind Boulanger's admonition about the need in music for "the long line," Copland also introduces a principle of unity in the Piano Variations that derives more from Arnold Schoenberg than from Stravinsky.

Copland freely admitted Schoenberg's influence in the work: "I *did* make use to some extent, but in my own way, of the method invented by Arnold Schoenberg that came to be known as 'twelve-tone' and from which developed 'serialism.' The *Variations* incorporates a four-note motive on which the entire piece is based. Almost every note and chord in the piece relate back to these four notes."[9]

Copland's principal tone row consists of the opening four notes: E-C-D♯-C♯ (Ex. 76-1, top). The figure is then expanded into an eleven-measure theme by free development and by the addition of new motivic ideas. The tone row, as well as the other motivic features of the theme, are then continually developed in the variations that follow. Copland brings back the basic four-note row in transpositions, inversions, and retrogrades (see Ex. 76-1), and he promotes variety by placing the notes of a row in different registers. As with Schoenberg's early serial music, Copland at times freely reorders the tones within a row, and row-based passages alternate with others made from free motivic development.

EXAMPLE 76-1

mm. 1-3

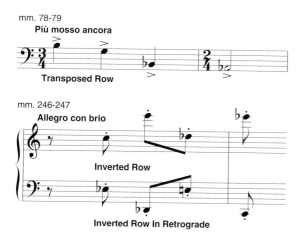

mm. 78-79
Più mosso ancora
Transposed Row

mm. 246-247
Allegro con brio
Inverted Row
Inverted Row In Retrograde

LISTENING CUE

AARON COPLAND
Piano Variations (1930)

CD 12/14
Anthology, No. 196

Appalachian Spring

Copland's ballet scores—*Billy the Kid* (1938), *Rodeo* (1942), and *Appalachian Spring* (1944)—were written in the composer's second style, in which he appealed to the understanding of a large audience through familiar materials, Whitmanesque simplicity, and American themes. The music of *Appalachian Spring* is an especially distinguished example of this style. The work was commissioned by the dancer and choreographer **Martha Graham** (1893–1991) for a performance in the Coolidge Auditorium in the Library of Congress in Washington, D.C. Since this auditorium is small, Copland was limited to a thirteen-piece chamber orchestra of strings, woodwinds, and piano.

Graham's idea for the scenario of the ballet underwent several changes—some made even after Copland had composed the music—and by the time of the 1944 premiere she had settled on this story:

> The action of the ballet concerns "a pioneer celebration in spring around a newly-built farm house in the Pennsylvania hills in the early part of the last century. The bride-to-be [Fig. 76-1] and the young farmer-husband enact the emotions, joyful and apprehensive, their new domestic partnership invites. An older neighbour suggests now and then the rocky confidence of experience. A revivalist and his followers remind the new householders of the strange and terrible aspects of human fate. At the end the couple are left quiet and strong in their new house."[10]

🌿 FIGURE 76-1

Martha Graham ecstatically dances the role of the Bride in the premier performance of Copland's *Appalachian Spring* (1944), while the followers of a revivalist minister sit by stoically.

In 1945 Copland reworked the music of *Appalachian Spring* into a suite for full orchestra, and it is in this form that the work is now best known. (Later, Copland also created additional suites, both for full and chamber orchestras, some containing the music of the entire ballet.) The climax of the 1945 Suite comes near the end, in music for a scene that depicts events of everyday farm life. For this passage, Copland took Graham's suggestion to write variations on a song melody, which he chose from an anthology of Shaker hymns. Copland frequently used traditional melodies in his works of the populist type. The Shaker hymn that he chose for *Appalachian Spring*—called "**Simple Gifts**"—provides an appropriate local color in a ballet about pioneering life in America, and its simple tunefulness helps the audience to understand the work. Its opening is shown in Example 76-2.

EXAMPLE 76-2

'Tis the gift to be sim - ple, 'tis the gift to be free, 'tis the

gift to come down where we ought to be,

Copland insisted that the use of such a preexisting melodic source had to be more than decoration, its musical and expressive essence somehow worked out through the entire composition. He explained: "A hymn tune represents a certain order of feeling: simplicity, plainness, sincerity, directness. It is the reflection of those qualities in a stylistically appropriate setting, imaginative and unconventional and not mere quotation, that gives the use of folk tunes reality and importance."[11] The "order of feeling" of the hymn is abundant in Copland's score, with its uncluttered texture, largely triadic harmony, and clear-cut rhythms. The composer also integrates the tune into the work's musical substance by anticipating its triadic head motive in earlier themes.

LISTENING CUE

AARON COPLAND   CD 12/15
Appalachian Spring (Suite, 1945)   Anthology, No. 197
Variations on a Shaker Hymn

Copland pointed to the last section of the 1945 Suite—just following the variations—as containing his favorite music of the entire work. Certainly, it has the touching, Whitmanesque simplicity that he wanted: "I had become convinced that simplicity was the way out of isolation for the contemporary composer," he later wrote.[12] The melody (Ex. 76-3) is harmonized to evoke an African American gospel hymn—blue notes E♭ and B♭ are brought in, there are parallel fifths and octaves, and the V-IV harmonic motion at the cadence recalls the ninth and tenth measures of a typical blues harmonic progression.

Copland on Art and the Affirmative Spirit

In the early 1950s, Copland, together with many other American artists, was attacked in the press and in Congress for alleged Communist sympathies. Copland strenuously denied such accusations, but the climate of fear created by McCarthyism took a toll on his creative spirit. At the end of his book *Music and Imagination* (1952), Copland commented obliquely on this dilemma:

> One of the primary problems for the composer in an industrial society like that of America is to achieve integration, to find justification for the life of art in the life about him. I must believe in the ultimate good of the world and of life as I live it in order to create a work of art. Negative emotions cannot produce art; positive emotions bespeak an emotion about something. I cannot imagine an art work without implied convictions; and that is true also for music, the most abstract of the arts.

It is this need for a positive philosophy which is a little frightening in the world as we know it. You cannot make art out of fear and suspicion; you can make it only out of affirmative beliefs. This sense of affirmation can be had only in part from one's inner being; for the rest it must be continually reactivated by a creative and yea-saying atmosphere in the life about one. The artist should feel himself affirmed and buoyed up by his community. In other words, art and the life of art must mean something, in the deepest sense, to the everyday citizen. When that happens, America will have achieved a maturity to which every sincere artist will have contributed.[3]

EXAMPLE 76-3

Reh. 67

The music of the ballet ends delicately with a special five-note chord that was a favorite Copland harmony. Here it consists of notes of the tonic C-major triad together with those of the dominant G-major triad (Ex. 76-4). This chord, which is heard sporadically throughout the work in differing transpositions, again subtly alludes to the Shaker hymn since, in its simplicity, the melody outlines solely tonic and dominant harmonies.

EXAMPLE 76-4

The music of Aaron Copland shows two sides of the American artistic consciousness during the period between the world wars. One is modern, biting in its dissonant harmony and angularity of line, and abstract in meaning; the other is warm, filled with Americana, and traditional in musical materials. In the latter type, Copland succeeded in creating a musical idiom that seemed to many to be the very embodiment of the American spirit.

SAMUEL BARBER

Samuel Barber (1910–1981) repeatedly visited Europe and acquired a lifelong fascination for its culture and society. His European experiences had a very different effect on his music from those of Copland or most of the other American students of Nadia Boulanger. Barber had no special affinity with French modern music, and he was one of the few major composers of his day who professed to be uninterested in the works of Stravinsky. "With all Stravinsky's talent and imagination," Barber wrote, "his lack of lyricism and utter inability to work in more than small periods weigh heavily against him."[14] Barber's music rarely delves into Americana, and he had no sympathy for the self-made aesthetic of Ives. "He [Ives] was an amateur, a hack, who didn't put pieces together well," Barber wrote.

Barber's sympathies were mostly with German romantic musicians of the nineteenth century. He did not participate in the general rebellion against romanticism that spread throughout the musical world in the 1920s, and he rose to fame as a composer by extending the language of romantic composers, always in his own distinctive way, far into the twentieth century.

BARBER'S LIFE AND WORKS

Barber attended the Curtis Institute of Music in Philadelphia, where he studied composition with Rosario Scalero (1870–1954) and became an accomplished singer. He soon attracted attention with orchestral works such as his Overture to *The School for Scandal* (1933). Following service in the army during World War II, he received numerous prestigious commissions, one of which led to the opera *Antony and Cleopatra,* written for the opening in 1966 of the new Metropolitan Opera house at New York's Lincoln Center.

Like all of the major American composers of his period, Barber wrote for orchestra—symphonies, shorter character pieces, and concertos—and he was also a leading composer of songs. Among his chamber works are a String Quartet (1936), a Piano Sonata (1949), and a Sonata for Cello and Piano (1932). In addition to *Antony and Cleopatra,* he also composed the opera *Vanessa* (1957) and several ballets.

Barber's music has an astonishing diversity of styles. He was most at home in a traditional but still distinctive type of music characterized by lyric and affective melody and by traditional harmony. These features suggest a continuation of values of the Romantic period.

Beginning in the 1940s, Barber apparently became self-conscious about the character of his music and the direction it had taken. He was willing then to experiment in styles associated with other composers, as if to show that he could outdo his contemporaries at their own game. His "Capricorn" Concerto (1944) is an outright adaptation of Stravinsky's neoclassical style; his *Excursions* for piano (1944) use jazz idioms, and his songs *Knoxville: Summer of 1915* suggest the folkloric regionalism of Copland. Gradually, Barber slid into a bleak self-criticism. Fully twenty years after he composed his Symphony No. 2 (1944), he attempted to withdraw and destroy the work (which he was not able to do), and in his later years he fell nearly silent as a composer.

Adagio for Strings

Barber's orchestral music includes three *Essays,* two symphonies, and the ever-popular **Adagio for Strings** (1938). He also wrote concertos for violin (1939), cello (1945), and piano (1962), and a concerto grosso called "Capricorn" Concerto (1944). His essentially romantic spirit is apparent in his most often performed work, the *Adagio for Strings*. The piece had its origin as the slow movement of his String Quartet, which Barber composed in 1936 while living in Austria near Salzburg. At the time, he was studying music by Wagner, especially Wagner's *Siegfried Idyll*, an orchestral character piece whose warm melodiousness, free form, and extended harmonic language are all reflected in the *Adagio*. In 1938 the quartet movement was arranged for string orchestra and performed by Arturo Toscanini with the NBC Symphony Orchestra, an event that helped to establish Barber's standing among the leading American composers. The popularity of the work has never waned, and Barber arranged it again in 1967 for chorus, giving it the traditional *Agnus dei* text from the Catholic Mass.

The *Adagio* contains a skillful adaptation of the Wagnerian style. The piece has a passionate melodiousness, rich texture, and an intensity of expression that is pushed almost to the point of becoming maudlin. The form involves a free development of lines heard in the first eight measures (Ex. 76-5). These gather into ever-increasing waves until the motions reach a climax, whereupon they fall back into an exhausted recapitulation of the opening.

EXAMPLE 76-5

The lasting popularity of the *Adagio* is evidence that importance in music of the twentieth (or any other) century cannot be judged solely by its relation to a dominant style or a musical "mainstream." Certainly, the *Adagio for Strings* stands far apart from the major competing trends in music of the 1930s—Schoenbergian serialism, Stravinskian neoclassicism, and Copland's regionalism, among others. It looks to the past, but not by way of any parody. Copland (Fig. 76-2) found its value to reside in its authenticity: "It's really well felt, it's believable you see, it's not phoney. He's not just making it up because he thinks that would sound well. It comes straight from the heart, to use old-fashioned terms."[15]

❀ FIGURE 76-2
Samuel Barber and Aaron Copland, photographed together in 1950, were the two leading European-trained American composers of the early twentieth century.

Barber's *Hermit Songs*

Barber's songs also come straight from the heart. He wrote some fifty of these, including *Knoxville: Summer of 1915* (1947) on words by James Agee, a setting of Matthew Arnold's *Dover Beach* for voice and string quartet (1931), and the cycle *Hermit Songs* (1953), which consists of ten settings of medieval Irish poetry translated into modern English.

The texts of the *Hermit Songs* are predominantly religious, although spoken in an entirely worldly and personalized tone. "Sea-Snatch," the sixth of the ten songs, paints a miniature portrait of a boat caught in a violent storm, its planks consumed as though by a great fire, its sailors left to cry out to the all-powerful King of Heaven. The title "Sea-Snatch" was apparently given to the poem by Barber, a "snatch" referring to a succinct song or poetic fragment. The brevity of such poems came from their being entered hurriedly by medieval scribes into the narrow margin of a manuscript.

Barber's music for the song brings the storm alive through a relentless and surging rhythm. There is no regular meter, as the lines toss violently up and down. The voice has no respite from the storm as it moves breathlessly, accompanied by a twisting ostinato in the piano. By repeating the opening lines, Barber makes a concise ternary form out of his diminutive text. The expressive harmonic language of the *Adagio for Strings* is replaced in the *Hermit Songs* by more dissonant sounds, especially chords made from intervals of the fourth. "Sea-Snatch" is strictly limited to the notes of a C-minor scale, which Barber limits further by dwelling on pentatonic collections of tones.

LISTENING CUE

SAMUEL BARBER
Hermit Songs (1953)
"Sea-Snatch"

CD 12/16
Anthology, No. 198

In Barber's works we see a cross-section of the stylistic diversity of mid twentieth-century music. The romanticism evident in the early *Adagio for Strings* gives way in later pieces such as "Sea-Snatch" to a more modernistic harmonic organization.

SUMMARY

Following World War I, American musicians established a stronger contact with French musical culture. Aaron Copland was only one of the leading younger composers of the 1920s who studied in France with Nadia Boulanger. Copland, like many of his fellow American musicians, made his music express distinctively American themes and values, which he accomplished (as in the ballet *Appalachian Spring*) by a simple and traditional style and, as with Ives, by the quotation of folk melodies. Copland also wanted his music to have the universality and sophistication of contemporary European music, and this was his goal in his Piano Variations.

Samuel Barber came to prominence by composing music in a traditional romantic style, although he often tried his hand at other, more contemporary trends in music. His *Adagio for Strings* is an example of his extension of the Wagnerian idiom in its intense expressivity and enriched harmonic language. His *Hermit Songs* (1953), which are settings of medieval Irish poetry, depart from the romanticism of the earlier pieces, although they maintain the traditional values associated with song composition.

KEY TERMS

Nadia Boulanger   Martha Graham   *Adagio for Strings*
Walt Whitman   "Simple Gifts"

Chapter

77

Tin Pan Alley and the Broadway Musical

Around 1900, popular songs were the type of music most frequently heard by the average American. A piano was installed in many middle-class homes, and one of its main functions was to accompany the singing of parlor songs, providing an enjoyable form of family entertainment before the days of TV and DVDs. A thriving sheet music industry evolved in America to make songs available to amateur players and singers, and a successful new song could produce astonishing sales and instant wealth for its publisher—sometimes also for its composer. Harry Von Tilzer's "A Bird in a Gilded Cage" (1900) sold 2 million copies of sheet music in its first year alone; Charles Harris's "After the Ball" (1892) brought in $25,000 per week—a virtual fortune at this time. George Gershwin's song "Swanee" (1919) earned its still unknown composer $10,000 in royalties during its first year and made his name familiar around the world.

An easy way to perform songs in the home was to purchase a **player piano.** These began to appear in the 1890s, and at first consisted of a cabinet-like apparatus that was placed in front of a normal piano keyboard. A perforated paper roll that encoded the song's piano accompaniment was inserted into the device, and a pneumatic action driven by a pair of pedals activated mechanical fingers that "played" the instrument. After 1900 the player mechanism was most often mounted into the piano itself. Although sometimes used to distribute classical music (rolls were made by Debussy, Ravel, Mahler, Richard Strauss and many other composers and performers of the day), the player piano had its greatest success in bringing popular songs into American homes, allowing families to sing along with the tunes.

THE POPULAR SONG BUSINESS

The explosion in demand for songs near the turn of the century went hand in hand with the rise of new forms of theatric entertainment—especially the **vaudeville show** and **musical play.** Unlike classical or "art" songs, which are independent and free-standing musical works, popular songs at this time were normally functional music that first achieved popularity in a theatric show. Professional singers in shows introduced audiences firsthand to new songs, and sheet music was normally available for purchase on the spot. The vaudeville show and musical play had by 1900 largely replaced the old minstrel shows, whose racial humor had at last been recognized by American audiences as crude and bigoted.

Vaudeville was more attuned to the times. This was a type of variety show consisting of a succession of independent "acts"—comedy routines, short skits, juggling, animal tricks—and songs were essential. Musical plays, which were forerunners of the Broadway musical, consisted of a succession of songs and dances strung together by a simple story line.

The center of the lucrative song-publishing business at the turn of the twentieth century was New York City, in downtown Manhattan. Vaudeville theaters had sprung up there, especially on Broadway, which angled across the center of town. Crossing Broadway near Madison Square Park were 27th and 28th Streets, where so many music publishers were located that their pianos made the neighborhood sound like a jangle of tin pans. **Tin Pan Alley** became the nickname for the whole popular-song industry.

The marketing of songs was done by **song pluggers**—musicians who worked for a publisher and demonstrated its new offerings for the customers. At the age of fifteen, George Gershwin dropped out of high school to became a song plugger for the firm of Jerome H. Remick & Co. He earned only $15 per week, but he thoroughly learned the art and craft of song writing and the business that supported it.

In the 1920s the distribution of popular songs was revolutionized by the new technologies of radio, sound film, and sound recording, which quickly cut into the sale of sheet music. The first commercial radio station in America, KDKA, was founded in 1920 in Pittsburgh, and by the end of the decade radio receivers were in most homes. For the first time, songs could be heard in the home with no active participation on the part of the listener—certainly a mixed blessing for the history of music. The development of radio soon led to a transformation in sound recordings from a primitive acoustical technology to a modern electronic one. The earliest "electronic discs"—superior in sound quality to the older mechanical phonograph recordings—began to appear around 1925, although these were for a long time limited to about three minutes in duration. The first sound film, *The Jazz Singer* starring Al Jolson, appeared in 1927, and many of the movies that followed were of Broadway musicals, bringing the tunes of George Gershwin, Jerome Kern, Irving Berlin, and other leading New York songsmiths to a larger audience than ever before.

❀ FIGURE 77-1

George Gershwin, c1932. In his short life, George Gershwin brought the art and craft of popular song writing to a new level of sophistication.

CORBIS

❀ GEORGE GERSHWIN

The art of the popular song rose to new heights in the works of George Gershwin (1898–1937; Fig. 77-1). Born in Brooklyn, he acquired a solid training in music, became an accomplished pianist, and had a good knowledge of classical works. He began writing songs as a teenaged song plugger, and he composed his first musical (*La-La-Lucille!*) in 1919. In his short career he wrote more than three hundred fifty songs, which were placed into some forty musicals and films. Gershwin also wrote classical works with a popular or jazzy flavor, including three Piano Preludes, *Rhapsody in Blue* for piano and jazz band (1924), a Piano Concerto (1925), the orchestral character pieces *An American in Paris* (1928) and *Cuban Overture* (1932), and the opera *Porgy and Bess* (1935).

The reasons for his success as a songwriter are easy to hear in "The Man I Love" (1924; Fig. 77-2). This was written for the musical *Lady, Be Good* (1924), but withdrawn before its opening and later re-situated in *Strike Up the Band* (1927). The story of *Lady, Be Good*, written by Guy Bolton, tells of a struggling brother-and-sister dance team (roles created for Fred and Adele Astaire), whose cleverness leads ultimately to their success. The lyrics of the song are by Gershwin's brother, Ira, and they are general enough—expressing wistful sentiments of love—to fit into almost any musical of the day.

Gershwin's music for the song is an example of a **ballad,** which in the context of Tin Pan Alley refers to a love song in a slow tempo. Its form agrees with the norm for popular songs of the 1920s. It begins with a four-measure introduction in $\frac{4}{4}$ time, in which a motive from the following section is introduced. Next comes the **verse,** which spans sixteen measures that are divided into two symmetrical eight-measure phrases, both ending on a dominant-seventh chord in the home key of E♭ major. The **chorus** (also called the **refrain**) follows the verse. Both terms are vestiges of earlier songwriting practices. Recall from Chapter 72 that the late nineteenth-century American popular song had a strophic form in which each stanza ended with a true refrain taken by a four-part chorus. By the 1920s the terms remained for this section of the song, but it was then sung by a solo voice rather than a chorus. Since songs by this time had usually been whittled down to a single stanza, there could be no literal refrain.

The weight of Gershwin's song falls in the chorus, which has the most memorable tune and words that state the idea of the song most directly. The verse is left with an introductory function, and this section could be (and often was) omitted. The chorus of "The Man I Love," as in most other songs of the 1920s, covers thirty-two measures that are divided into four eight-measure phrases, each with a line of text. Within the four phrases there are only two different eight-measure musical components (call them **A** and **B**), and these are repeated according to some simple scheme, here **AABA,** the most common plan.

Phrase **A** remains close to the home key of E♭ major, but phrase **B** (sometimes called the **release** of the song) creates tonal contrast by shifting briefly to the key of C minor. Typical of many Gershwin songs, the chorus of "The Man I Love" is performed twice in succession. The words of the song are entirely typical of the genre, with their sentiment of reaching out beyond the drab everyday world for a happiness that is just beyond grasp.

In addition to being an inexhaustible font of memorable tunes, Gershwin left his mark on popular music by bringing to it an enriched harmonic and tonal language—one borrowed from classical music of the late nineteenth century—and also using elements from African American jazz. The main melody in the refrain of "The Man I Love" immediately lights on a blue note, here D♭, the flatted seventh in E♭ major. The points of harmonic arrival and departure throughout the song are all simple tonics and dominants, but Gershwin connects these basic chords with a variety of harmonies that arise through an advanced compositional thinking. Notice the augmented chords in the verse in measures 10 and 11

FIGURE 77-2

Gershwin's manuscript for the verse of "The Man I Love" suggests that he composed at the piano and first wrote down the music for the piano accompaniment. The vocal line per se, as well as the chorus of the song, was entered only later.

(Ex. 77-1), and listen for the diminished chords and secondary dominants that Gershwin brings in here and there. Such harmonic inventiveness was an important element of expansion in the tradition of song writing. Gershwin's originality brought a new depth to the genre that also found its way into jazz at about the same time.

EXAMPLE 77-1

LISTENING CUE

GEORGE GERSHWIN
"The Man I Love" (1924)

CD 12/17
Anthology, No. 199

THE BROADWAY MUSICAL

Almost all of Gershwin's songs first became known through their placement in a **musical.** This is a genre of popular musical theater (also called "Broadway musical" or "musical comedy") that emerged in America shortly after 1900. One of its antecedents was **operetta,** a type of opera that had garnered success in Paris and Vienna after 1850. Operettas were made from songs, choruses, and dances—all with a certain operatic pretense—interspersed into a lighthearted spoken play. The American musical did not at first have the artistic aspirations of operetta, since it consisted only of a string of songs and dances hung together on the thinnest of story lines.

The central figure in establishing the identity of the Broadway musical was the songwriter **Jerome Kern** (1885–1945). Like most American composers of classical music of his generation, he received his musical education in Germany, and he returned to New York to work as a song plugger and composer of songs to be inserted in shows given by visiting English troupes. During World War I he began to compose the music for his own new productions, which were instantly successful. Kern's songs include such timeless favorites as "Smoke Gets in Your Eyes," "All the Things You Are," and "Ol' Man River," and these have a solid musical substance that was an inspiration to later songsters like Gershwin and Richard Rodgers.

Kern's *Show Boat* (1927)—his most important work—created a prototype for the classic American musical. Its story is based on a contemporaneous novel by Edna Ferber and makes for more sophisticated drama than is found in earlier musicals. Kern's music is not simply a succession of unrelated songs and dances but an integrated whole that included large choral and ensemble numbers reminiscent of opera.

Synopsis of *Oklahoma!*

Singing as usual, the cowboy Curly McClain pays a visit to the Williams farm on the Oklahoma frontier. Laurey Williams—a headstrong orphan of eighteen—lives there with her Aunt Eller Murphy. Curly has come to invite Laurey to the social that evening at Skidmore's, but he learns that she has already been asked by the new hired man, Jud Fry. Other neighbors arrive: Will Parker has just returned from Kansas City having won $50, and now he wants to marry his girlfriend, Ado Annie, although—unable to say no to a man—she arrives in the company of the slick-talking peddler, Ali Hakim. Curly goes to confront Jud over Laurey.

In a dream ballet, Laurey imagines that she has married Curly, but Jud enters, strangles him, and carries her off. At the party that evening, Curly is in a tense stand-off with Jud while the cowboys are arguing, as always, with the farmers. Jud quarrels with Laurey, who angrily tells him not to come on her farm any more. She runs to Curly, who blurts out a marriage proposal that she accepts.

At Laurey's place after the wedding the neighbors celebrate, and the future looks bright for living in Oklahoma. The menfolk haze the newlyweds by a "shivaree" (a noisy celebration), which is interrupted when Jud arrives. He fights with Curly and is killed as he falls on his knife. A judge and marshall are at the party, and they convene an informal court that finds Curly "not guilty!"

RODGERS AND HAMMERSTEIN: *OKLAHOMA!*

Kern's classic type of musical was brought to its highest level in the shows of Richard Rodgers (1902–1979). Between 1919 and 1942 he collaborated with the writer Lorenz Hart on more than thirty musicals, including *On Your Toes* (1936), *Babes in Arms* (1937), and *Pal Joey* (1940). Rodgers subsequently teamed with the writer **Oscar Hammerstein II** (1895–1960) on a series of hugely successful musicals including *Oklahoma!* (1943), *Carousel* (1945), *South Pacific* (1949), *The King and I* (1951), *Flower Drum Song* (1958), and *The Sound of Music* (1959). Rodgers also wrote the stirring incidental music for *Victory at Sea* (1952), a televised documentary on naval warfare during World War II.

Oklahoma! was the first show by Rodgers and Hammerstein, and their most successful collaboration of all. Going well beyond the norm for Broadway composers and writers, they worked together like an opera composer and librettist. Earlier, as in the musicals of Gershwin, the story line of a show—the "libretto" that would ultimately be given in spoken dialogue—was made by a writer using some tried-and-true formula. The words for the songs were written by a second writer, the **lyricist,** who was adept in clever rhymes and turns of phrase. Hammerstein wrote both the libretto and the song lyrics for Rodgers, a consolidation of effort that helped to produce a more unified and integrated dramatic effect.

Just as an opera librettist, Hammerstein started with a literary work—the play *Green Grow the Lilacs* (1931) by the Oklahoma playwright Lynn Riggs (1899–1954). The play has certain themes that were promising for a musical in the mold of *Show Boat*—a folkish American subject set among common people, a love story with a happy ending, and plenty of action, local color, and clearly drawn characters. But the play also has many sharp edges. Oklahoma for Riggs was not an idyllic place, but a region on the very edge of civilization. Some of his characters are vulgar and violent beneath their folksy surface, and the play leaves the bleak message that we are all trapped by an existence in which the only certainty is death. Needless to say, Hammerstein removed all of these unsettling features, reinforced the comic situations, and flattened the characters into mainly good-natured types.

Rodgers's music begins with an overture that is a medley of the song melodies to come. The principal music in each act consists of songs, most based on the verse-and-refrain model seen in Gershwin's "The Man I Love." Rodgers cautiously expands this prototype by making the songs strophic and by adding extraneous musical sections. The melody of a song is often elaborated upon in a dance that follows, and song tunes are frequently repeated as fragmentary "reprises" that serve to integrate the music more closely into the spoken play. To accompany Laurey's dream ballet, Rodgers breaks free from the simple confines of the song to write a longer multi-sectional instrumental number, although this music, like the overture, is still a medley of song tunes already heard. The ballet—which is the dramatic high point of the work—was choreographed by **Agnes De Mille,** who was trained in classical dance. A version of her gripping choreography can be seen in the award-winning 1955 film version of *Oklahoma!*

"I Cain't Say No!" shows Rodgers' irrepressible wit and his expansion of the typical verse-and-refrain song. The number is sung by the neighborhood girl Ado Annie, who has taken up with the peddler Hakim while her boyfriend, Will, is in Kansas City. She confesses to Laurey that attention from any man makes her "all shaky from horn to hoof." Except for adding a contrasting section to the song, Rodgers formal plan for "I Cain't Say No!" is virtually the same one used by Gershwin in "The Man I Love." Rodgers begins with an eighteen-measure verse followed by a refrain with the standard **AABA** form, and the refrain is sung twice over.

Between the refrain and its repetition, Rodgers inserts a contrasting section that he calls a "trio," probably because it is in a contrasting key, like the trio of a band march or piano rag. Rodgers takes more liberties than Gershwin with the phrase structure of the song, bringing the music closer to the words and giving it more flexibility and naturalness. The eight-measure phrases are sometimes extended to make the music underscore an important point in the text. For example, the final statement of the A melody is extended to twenty-four measures to allow the voice part chromatically to ascend to a mock-dramatic climax, showing that Ado Annie positively cain't say no.

LISTENING CUE

RICHARD RODGERS AND OSCAR HAMMERSTEIN II
Oklahoma! (1943)
"I Cain't Say No!"

CD 12/18
Anthology, No. 200

❋ LEONARD BERNSTEIN: *WEST SIDE STORY*

The differences that separated opera from musicals in the 1940s dwindled on Broadway following World War II. The growing affinity between opera and musical is especially apparent in one of the great works in the entire genre of the Broadway musical, *West Side Story* by Leonard Bernstein (1918–1990).

Bernstein was a phenomenon in the history of American music, someone equally gifted as a composer, pianist, and conductor, and at home in both classical and popular music. He was a New Englander, educated at Harvard and the Curtis Institute of Music, and he followed the dual careers of orchestral conductor and composer.

Synopsis of *West Side Story*

On a summer evening on the Upper West Side of New York, members of a local gang, the Jets, begin to appear. Their leader is Riff, and they all act tough and cool. Members of the rival Puerto Rican gang, the Sharks, led by Bernardo, appear menacingly, taunting and picking fights. Riff asks his old friend Tony to come to the evening's gym dance, where both gangs will be present and where a challenge will be made for a rumble (a gang fight). Tony agrees, although he has lately shown little interest in his old gang and seeks something new and better in life.

In a Puerto Rican bridal shop, Anita makes a white party dress for her friend Maria, sister of her boyfriend, Bernardo. Bernardo brought Maria to America to marry Chino, but she is not attracted to him. The gangs arrive for the gym dance, and as a tumultuous mambo is played, they dance passionately. Suddenly, Tony and Maria see each other and stand as though transfixed. After only a few words they kiss, whereupon Bernardo pushes Tony away. After the dance Tony rushes to the alley behind Maria's apartment, climbs the fire escape, and they embrace. The gangs meet for a "war council" at Doc's drug store, and despite admonitions to keep cool, they erupt into wild dancing. Finally, Riff and Bernardo agree that the rumble will happen the next evening—using fists only.

Maria tells Tony to stop the fight, but he cannot do so and knives are soon drawn despite the agreement. Tony tries to hold back Riff, only to see him stabbed to death by Bernardo. In a fury, Tony grabs the knife and kills Bernardo. Tony rushes back to Maria and they both sense that they are helplessly trapped by their fate. Tony then goes into hiding, but he overhears Anita say wrongly that Maria has been killed by Chino. With no more reason to hide, he wanders the dark streets, only to be shot dead by Chino. At last stunned and silent, the gangs carry his body away.

Bernstein was the musical director of the New York Philharmonic Orchestra from 1958 to 1969, and later a regular visiting conductor of the Vienna Philharmonic Orchestra. His principal compositions were for Broadway, including the musicals *On the Town* (1944), *Wonderful Town* (1952), *Candide* (1956), and *West Side Story* (1957). He also composed the ballet *Fancy Free* (1944), three symphonies, orchestral suites derived from his musicals, and the choral work *Chichester Psalms* (1965).

West Side Story continued the collaborative creative process that was normal for the genre of the Broadway musical, although ultimately the work is so overwhelmed by its music that it is usually thought of as Bernstein's alone. The initial idea was hatched in 1949 by the choreographer **Jerome Robbins** (1918–1998), who enlisted Bernstein for a musical having a large element of dance, based on Shakespeare's *Romeo and Juliet*. His idea did not progress until 1955, a time of widely publicized gang violence in New York that pitted Puerto Rican youths against others. The playwright Arthur Laurents then rewrote Shakespeare's feuding Montague and Capulet families as New York gangs called the Jets and Sharks. Romeo becomes Tony, a former member of the Jets; Juliet is Maria, sister of the leader of the Sharks. **Stephen Sondheim** (b. 1930)—who later became famous as both a Broadway composer and writer—was brought in to create the lyrics. The idea of basing a musical on Shakespeare's bleakly tragic story was only the first of many innovations in the work, which had its premiere in 1957.

From the very opening curtain, the differences in musical conception between *West Side Story* and *Oklahoma!* are unmistakable. Instead of Rodgers's easy-going overture medley, Bernstein begins with a grippingly dramatic instrumental "Prologue" that accompanies Robbins's choreography, in which the gangs taunt each other with a mixture of ballet and street dancing. The music has a degree of difficulty and complexity exceeding anything seen before on Broadway. Bernstein himself oversaw the orchestration of the work (something unusual for a show composer), and he enlarged the normal Broadway pit orchestra to allow it to evoke different jazz styles—big band swing, combos playing bebop or cool jazz, and the jazz of high-voltage Latin bands.

The musical numbers that follow the Prologue are in a variety of styles and forms. Riff's "Jet Song" or Tony's ballad "Maria" are based on the verse-and-refrain model of the traditional popular song. Other numbers—the extended ballet music for the "Dance at the Gym" or the pseudo-operatic finale in "Tonight"—are essentially new types for a musical, given their complexity.

The song and dance "Cool" illustrates many of these innovative features. In the drugstore where the Jets hang out, their gang members await the arrival of the Sharks to have their war council. Riff tells his men to be cool, but their tension flares up in a frenzied dance, after which calm returns. Structurally, the number has four contrasting sections, all held together by shared motives. The first section is a verse-and-refrain song for Riff. In the verse, Riff and the others speak rather than sing while a jazzy ostinato riff is introduced. The ostinato continues in the refrain, which is conventional in phrase structure, with thirty-two measures arranged in an **ABAB** pattern.

The second section begins when the restless gang members start to dance to the music of a strict fugue. The opening of the fugue subject, a countersubject, and the first fugal answer are shown in Example 77-2. The third section—an orchestral development—follows the fugue, as the dance grows ever more frenzied. This section concentrates on the fugal countersubject, which is stated as an intricate canon between the basses and muted trumpet (Ex. 77-3). Calm returns in the final section, in which the song refrain is brought back and sung in unison by the whole gang. The breathless number is rounded off by a short coda.

EXAMPLE 77-2

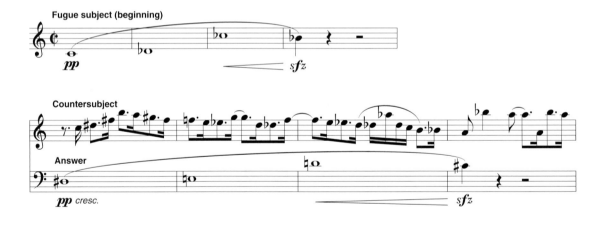

EXAMPLE 77-3

The music for "Cool" defies any distinction between popular and serious art. Bernstein uses advanced harmonic, rhythmic, and structural materials—shared at the time by jazz musicians and by some classical composers, notably Igor Stravinsky—and he brings these into an intimate fusion. "Cool" is ostensibly in the key of

C major, but the harmonies that support this key are altered to produce chords whose common feature is that their tones are all available in an octatonic scale. For example, the first chord in the number has the tones C E♭ E G (Ex. 77-4), which is also the first chord of the Prologue. Certainly, this harmony represents the tonic in C major, but the added E♭ (in addition to evoking a blue note in the key) also suggests an octatonic origin, which is reinforced by the tones added just after the downbeat—F♯ and A. These notes flesh out an almost complete octatonic scale: C (D♭) E♭ E F♯ G A (B♭).

EXAMPLE 77-4

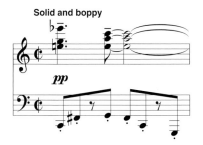

West Side Story is also remarkable for the extent to which a few central motives recur throughout the entire work. These create a unity that is more at home in the genre of opera (think of the recurring motives in a music drama by Wagner) than in a musical, which generally consists of a sequence of largely unrelated numbers.

The ostinato figure C-F♯-G in the left hand of Example 77-4 is an example of one of these central recurring motives. A few of the subtle ways in which Bernstein uses the small figure are shown in Example 77-5. At the top is Tony's outcry "Maria!" from his song of this title (No. 5). Here the motive has the same shape as in "Cool"—an ascending tritone followed by an ascending semitone—although in "Maria" it is transposed and used in a different musical context. Tony's last call to Maria at the end of the song (shown in the middle of the example) finds the notes of the motive transposed and shuffled in order. A still more subtle transformation occurs in the whistle-like figure heard in the Prologue (No. 1), at the point when Bernardo enters (shown at the bottom of the example). Its tones are yet another transposition and reshuffling of the basic figure.

EXAMPLE 77-5

 LISTENING CUE

LEONARD BERNSTEIN   CD 12/19
West Side Story, "Cool" (1957)   Anthology, No. 201

Leonard Bernstein's *West Side Story* revealed the capacity of the musical to rise above comedy and simple entertainment. Many dimensions of the work have such richness and depth that they can only be grasped by repeated listening and study. But *West Side Story* also has songs and dances of immediate appeal, thus honoring the traditions of musical theater established by Kern, Gershwin, and Rodgers.

MUSICALS OF THE 1960s AND BEYOND

Both the classical musical as seen in *Oklahoma!* and Bernstein's sophisticated *West Side Story* have continued to provide models for musicals to the present day. But many innovations have also appeared on Broadway since the 1960s. Musicals nowadays are often sung straight through, without the spoken dialogue of *Oklahoma!* or *West Side Story.* There has also been a diversification of musical styles beyond that of the Tin Pan Alley song. For example, rock began to be imported into Broadway shows beginning in the 1960s. An early example of the rock musical is *Hair* (1967), an anti–Viet Nam War piece in which the music is provided largely by an amplified rock band playing on stage, with Galt MacDermot's songs interspersed.

An even more fundamental innovation was the birth in the 1980s of the so-called **megamusical,** which is a show in which grandiose staging, stunning visual effects, and massive danced or choral numbers are characteristic. Early examples include *Les Misérables* (1980) and *Miss Saigon* (1989), both with music by Claude-Michel Schoenberg and lyrics by Alain Boublil.

The megamusical reached unprecedented acclamation in the shows of **Andrew Lloyd Webber** (b. 1948). Lloyd Webber was born in London and educated at the Royal College of Music. As a composer he is at home in classical and virtually any style of pop music, and the musical types present in his shows range from rock (*Jesus Christ Superstar,* 1971) to opera (*Phantom of the Opera,* 1986). The latter of these and his immensely successful *Cats* (1981) are classic examples of the megamusical.

SUMMARY

The popular song was the type of music most often heard by the average American around 1900. Songs were distributed mainly through sheet music and player-piano rolls, whose sale created a thriving business. The art and industry of the popular song of the early twentieth century is now commonly called "Tin Pan Alley." One of the greatest song composers of the 1920s and 1930s was George Gershwin, whose songs became known in musical comedies and early sound films. Gershwin generally adhered in his songs to a simple verse-and-chorus prototype. To this conventional framework, he added harmonic enrichment and also elements from jazz.

The Broadway musical flourished in America in the early twentieth century in the hands of Jerome Kern, and it reached a classic stage in the 1940s in works such as *Oklahoma!* by Richard Rodgers and the librettist Oscar Hammerstein II. *Oklahoma!* consists of a spoken folk comedy in which Rodgers inserted songs as well as longer instrumental numbers to accompany dancing.

Leonard Bernstein's musical *West Side Story* goes far beyond Rodgers in musical and dramatic complexity. It mingles diatonic and octatonic fields of pitches, and its numbers are unified by small recurring motives. *West Side Story* is based on Shakespeare's *Romeo and Juliet,* which is updated to a contemporary New York setting among West Side gangs. The music mingles elements of jazz with Tin Pan Alley songs.

Musicals since the 1960s regularly bring in rock styles of music and playing, and they often dispense with the spoken dialogue present in earlier shows. Since the 1980s they often use grandiose visual and scenic effects, creating a genre called the "megamusical."

KEY TERMS

player piano
vaudeville show
musical play
Tin Pan Alley
song plugger
ballad
chorus (refrain)

song "release"
musical (Broadway musical)
operetta
Jerome Kern
Oscar Hammerstein II
lyricist

Agnes De Mille
Jerome Robbins
Stephen Sondheim
megamusical
Andrew Lloyd Webber

CONTEMPORARY MUSIC

*M*usic flourishes today as never before. Both live and recorded music seem to be everywhere, and virtually all of music—in every style, from any period—is at our fingertips. The landscape for music also has a different appearance from any time in the past. It has been reshaped by the spectacular rise of popular music and by advances in musical technology that bring the art to more people than ever.

New classical music (art music) shares in this prosperity. In its report on a recent season, the American Symphony Orchestra League noted increases in both concert attendance and endowments for its member orchestras. Composers of classical music are free as never before to follow their imaginations in any and all directions. Like a John Zorn, they can defy the traditional dis-

---

1900	1950

Fletcher Henderson (1897–1952), central figure in big band phenomenon and swing style

Edward "Duke" Ellington (1899–1974), American composer and big band leader

Elliott Carter (b. 1908), American composer

Benny Goodman (1909–1986), clarinetist and bandleader

Pierre Schaeffer (1910–1995), French radio engineer, inventor of *musique concrète*

John Cage (1912–1992), American composer

Milton Babbitt (b. 1916), American composer

John "Dizzy" Gillespie (1917–1993), trumpeter

Charlie Parker (1920–1955), alto saxophonist, one of founders of bebop

György Ligeti (b. 1923), Hungarian composer

Luciano Berio (1925–2003), Italian composer

Miles Davis (1926–1991), jazz trumpeter

George Crumb (b. 1929), American composer

Terry Riley (b. 1935), American minimalist

Arvo Pärt (b. 1935), Estonian composer

Steve Reich (b. 1936), American

Philip Glass (b. 1937), American

Joan Tower (b. 1938), American

World War II (1939–1945)

Olivier Messiaen (1908–1992), French composer

CORBIS

Bill Haley and Elvis Presley, Germany, 1958

CORBIS

Beatles take America by storm, 1964

CORBIS

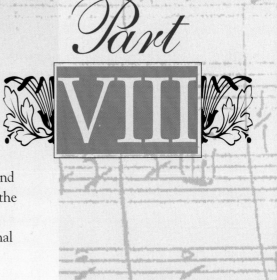

tinctions between popular, experimental, and artistic music. Like a Morten Lauridsen, they can re-create the serene harmonies of Renaissance polyphony. Or, like a Brian Ferneyhough, they can write music of withering complexity and abstraction. In classical music of today, anything goes.

This tolerant atmosphere is completely unlike the mood that dominated music following World War II. During the postwar decades, a demand for conformity and abstraction ruled the world of classical music. But, by the mid-1970s, this largely depersonalized context for music had evaporated, to be superseded by the present spirit of openness and eclecticism. The final chapters of this book trace this remarkable transformation.

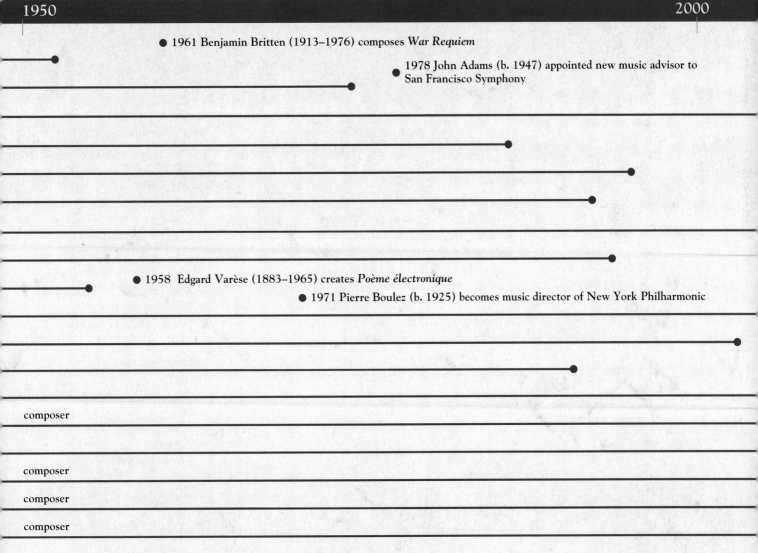

1950   2000

● 1961 Benjamin Britten (1913–1976) composes *War Requiem*

● 1978 John Adams (b. 1947) appointed new music advisor to San Francisco Symphony

composer

composer

composer

composer

● 1958 Edgard Varèse (1883–1965) creates *Poème électronique*

● 1971 Pierre Boulez (b. 1925) becomes music director of New York Philharmonic

● 1955 Bill Haley's "Rock Around the Clock" vaults to top of charts

● 1960 Krzysztof Penderecki (b. 1933) composes *Threnody for the Victims of Hiroshima*

After World War II

In the preceding chapters, we encountered music composed after World War I that represented a clean break with the past. These works were created in a world recovering from war, whose horrors made a new order in music seem imperative. If World War I led to an upheaval in the world of music, what could the greater tragedy of World War II have in store? By the early 1950s the answer was evident. At this time the culture for modern music worldwide underwent yet another shift of taste every bit as decisive as the one in 1918.

This new style had three principal characteristics: depersonalization, control, and innovation. Its most typical works were depersonalized by composers' willing removal of their own taste from their music and their own capacity to exercise free choice. These were sacrificed to procedures of composing by system or by chance. Emotionality was hidden behind abstraction and complexity. In the place of a familiar emotional content in music, form became its be-all and end-all. "To write poetry after Auschwitz is barbaric," said Theodor Adorno, and his dictum echoed in the musical world throughout the 1950s and 1960s.

The desire for control was felt in several ways. The first was in a demand for conformity in how to write music. There was little tolerance in the musical world of the 1950s and 1960s. Virtually all ambitious younger composers at this time fell into line with the accepted formalism and abstraction of the day. Control was also exerted by systems of composition—total serialism and phase processes are examples—that reduced free choice.

Finally, the postwar period was one of unprecedented innovation, produced in large part by the desire to efface the past. If musical styles such as neoclassicism were to be rejected, then a whole new order in music would have to be discovered, and composers after World War II were tireless in finding new materials and outlooks, reaching even to elements that earlier had defined music as an art. Younger composers of the 1950s and 1960s tried their hand at creating an entirely new idea of music, sometimes not even involving sound, much less traditional organization, communication, or meaning.

Predictably, a musical style so rigid as that of the postwar period was not destined to last very long. It collapsed as soon as the anxieties that beset society following World War II had eased. In its place yet another taste in music emerged, one that in virtually every way was the opposite of the one immediately before. Beginning in the 1970s, composers replaced the striving for control with tolerance and musical diversity. Individuality and personalized outlooks on music returned to center stage. The constant search for innovation ended as composers returned to known values and materials. The taste of the 1970s and beyond was for a simpler style that embodied and enshrined any and all values from the past, so long as they were familiar and relatively untroubling.

The twentieth century came to its end with a music that embodied the inner spirit of the time and reflected, however indirectly, the society in which it originated. When listening to music of earlier eras, we often find a haven, a respite from our occupations. But when we go to music of the twentieth century, we rarely find a sanctuary from the world. Instead we are brought face to face with all of its realities.

Reflections on War:
Britten, Penderecki, and Others

On 1 September 1939, German armies swept into Poland in an attack that marks the beginning of **World War II.** Two days later, Britain and France responded by declaring war on Germany, but, using the new technique of "lightning" warfare, Germany's conquest of Europe continued. In 1940 its armies overran Scandinavia, the Lowlands, and, finally, France. By this time Germany had formed an alliance, called the "Axis," with other nations, most importantly Japan, which had used military force to extend its dominion into China and Southeast Asia. In Europe, Great Britain was left virtually alone in opposing Germany's onslaught, as the United States tried to remain neutral. In the fall of 1940, the cities and strategic centers of England came under a withering bombardment, or "blitz," by the German air force, and the English feared an invasion was imminent.

America was finally drawn into the war on 7 December 1941, when Japan attacked the American navy at Pearl Harbor in Hawaii. Germany then declared war on the United States. In both Europe and the Far East, the "Allies," led by America and Great Britain, gradually gained the upper hand against the Axis nations. On 7 May 1945, following massive destruction of its cities, Germany unconditionally surrendered, and on 14 August 1945—after the United States unleashed nuclear weapons on the cities of Hiroshima and Nagasaki—the Japanese likewise capitulated.

The world was profoundly and permanently changed by this devastating conflict. The degree of destruction, loss of life, and general degradation of society was unprecedented. The Nazis had attempted to wipe out the entire Jewish population of Europe through a methodical genocide, now called the **Holocaust.** The world had witnessed the appalling human consequences of nuclear weapons in Hiroshima and Nagasaki, and "the bomb" seemed a permanent and menacing threat to all of civilization. World War II triggered the Cold War, which for nearly fifty years pitted the Communist countries of Eastern Europe and Asia against the West in a bitter and often deadly struggle.

Music—whose direction and character have always been sensitive to the society around it—shared in the upheaval brought by the war. Tragic consequences were plain to see. Talented musicians—Viktor Ullmann, Erwin Schulhoff, Hans Walter David, to name only a few—were sent to their death in Hitler's concentration camps. Others, such as Schoenberg, Bartók, and Stravinsky, left Europe and permanently resettled in America. In Germany and Austria, virtually every major opera house and concert hall was destroyed by war's end. The Prussian State Library in Berlin, which housed the musical manuscripts of Bach, Beethoven, Mozart, and Mendelssohn, was bombed, although its priceless musical documents were saved, in part by the foresight of its music librarian, Georg Schünemann, who hurriedly shipped them out of Berlin. After seeing his library destroyed, Schünemann committed suicide.

The war also changed the inner spirit of music. Neoclassicism—the dominant trend in music between the world wars—appeared to many to be naive and outdated. For most of the younger postwar composers, Stravinsky's witty parody of earlier musical styles could no longer serve in a world that had experienced the Holocaust, and reviving the past only reawakened bleak and unspeakable memories. A new order in music would have to be found, and the search for it is the subject of the following two chapters of this book. In this chapter we explore music that reflects upon war in a direct way, in works that embody the theme of warfare by composers who attempted in them to give artistic expression to its horror.

✿ RICHARD STRAUSS, *METAMORPHOSEN*

Richard Strauss remained in Germany and Austria throughout the war. Strauss was then Germany's most famous living composer, and he tried to continue his career by accommodating the Nazis, who manipulated him and his reputation to serve their own purposes. The fact that his daughter-in-law and grandchildren were Jewish created for him a special level of anxiety and reluctance to speak out against the Nazis.

Strauss was deeply distressed by the destruction of the great musical institutions that had been the centers of his life's work. He was especially affected by the ruin of the National Theater in Munich, his home town. It was the place where his father had served for nearly fifty years as principal hornist, and after the theater was bombed in October 1943, Strauss wrote, "This is the greatest catastrophe that has ever been brought into my life, for which there can be no consolation and in my old age no hope." Most of his operas had received their premiere in the beautiful Semper opera house in Dresden, and on 12 February 1945 this structure, along with the rest of the city, was destroyed in a devastating firestorm following a bombing raid. Hearing the news, Strauss could only exclaim "My beautiful Dresden— Weimar—Munich, all gone!"

In this depressive frame of mind, the 80-year-old composer was forced out of retirement to write songs and one major instrumental work, an orchestral elegy for a destroyed German culture. He titled it *Metamorphosen* (*Metamorphoses*, 1945), with the subtitle "a study for twenty-three solo strings." The half-hour composition calls for ten violins, five violas, five cellos, and three basses, each having its own line of music. This unique orchestration makes for a rich texture and dark sound, which conform to Strauss's romantic musical language, one filled with a poignant melancholy mixed with resignation.

In the *Metamorphosen*, Strauss returns to the orchestra and to the genre of the tone poem, which had brought him international recognition some sixty years earlier but was long since put aside in favor of operatic composition. The title word "**metamorphoses**" refers to changes of form. Although Strauss gave no definitive explanation of what the term meant in the context of this work, he copied into its manuscript a poem by Goethe that speaks of the metamorphoses of history. We cannot hope to understand why things change, Goethe says in this poem, but only to persist.

Another aspect of the idea of metamorphosis is captured by the work's continual development and transformation of its themes. The main theme, heard near the opening, is shown in Example 78-1. It reappears in different guises, becoming ever more insistent toward the end, as though pointing to something positive. Its final metamorphosis occurs in the work's last ten measures, marked in the score "IN MEMORIAM!" Here the theme (Ex. 78-2) evolves to take the shape of the main theme of the Funeral March of Beethoven's "Eroica" Symphony. Recall from Chapter 50 that Beethoven's "Eroica" was itself a work that memorialized what had once existed—it was "composed to celebrate the memory of a great man," as Beethoven wrote on it. By quoting Beethoven, Strauss appears to be saying that civilization— even at its most highly evolved stages—contains the seeds of its own destruction and renewal. Strauss leaves us with an epitaph written by Beethoven, whose tribute to the past is as relevant to the world of 1945 as the one of 1804.

EXAMPLE 78-1

mm. 9-17

Adagio ma non troppo

EXAMPLE 78-2

Reh. 500-end

Molto lento

In memoriam!

dim.   *pp*

✿ ARNOLD SCHOENBERG: A SURVIVOR FROM WARSAW

Schoenberg was dismissed from his professorship at Berlin's Academy of the Arts immediately after Hitler came to power in 1933 (see Chapter 66). More clearly than many others at the time, he foresaw the threat of extermination that Hitler represented for Jews, and the composer fled with his family to America. In 1934 he settled in Southern California, where he continued to compose and teach, surrounded by a group of friends and émigré artists that included Edward Steuermann, Theodor Adorno, Hanns Eisler, and Alma Mahler.

In August 1947, shortly after the end of the war, Schoenberg composed a short orchestral work, *A Survivor from Warsaw*, that is his tribute to the spirit of European Jews who faced annihilation at the hands of the Nazis. In addition to the orchestra, *A Survivor from Warsaw* calls for narrator and male chorus. The narrator's words were written in English by Schoenberg himself, and they outline a brief drama told by a Jewish survivor of Nazi persecution. Schoenberg reportedly based the story on the recollections of a Jewish refugee who had hidden from the Nazis in Warsaw, only to be sent to a concentration camp. Beaten senseless by a camp guard, the narrator recalled a group of Jewish men who, about to be sent to the gas chamber, spontaneously and defiantly sang the *She'ma*, a central text of Judaism from the Old Testament book of Deuteronomy: "Hear, O Israel, the Lord our God, the Lord is one. And you shall love the Lord your God with all your heart and soul and mind. . . ." Pious Jews often recite these words when facing death.

A Survivor from Warsaw is in two distinct parts. The first is recitational, as the speaker tells the story of his persecution and brutal imprisonment (the opening of the recitation is shown in Ex. 78-3). In this part, the orchestra shadows and underscores the words by adding distorted bugle signals, nervous string tremolos played on the bridge, frantic rhythms, and a fragmented, strident texture. Schoenberg uses his twelve-tone method with great freedom, occasionally creating twelve-tone aggregates (see Chapter 69), but making no strict use of tone rows. The music is dissonant and atonal, and it shares with Strauss's *Metamorphosen* its direct emotional impact.

EXAMPLE 78-3

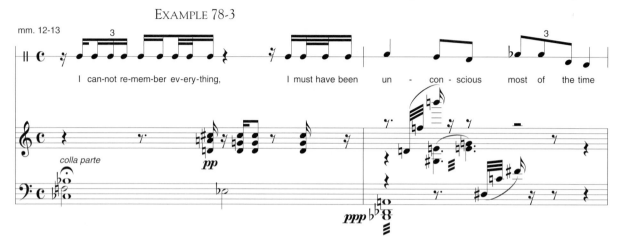

The music becomes more connected and determined in the second part, where the male chorus sings the *She'ma* prayer in a resolute unison to a strict twelve-tone melody. Its beginning is shown in Example 78-4.

EXAMPLE 78-4

BENJAMIN BRITTEN AND THE *WAR REQUIEM*

The career of Benjamin Britten (1913–1976) was much affected by World War II. He received his musical education at London's Royal College of Music, where he studied composition and piano playing, becoming proficient on this instrument. He attracted attention in the later 1930s primarily for his orchestral music. His first international success came with his *Variations on a Theme of Frank Bridge* for string orchestra, which was heard in Salzburg in 1937 and then played around the world. By 1939 Britten was widely regarded as England's leading younger composer.

As war clouds gathered over Europe, Britten—an avowed pacifist—emigrated to America. During his absence, the war began and the blitz inflicted its ghastly toll on his homeland. His absence was noted by England's musical community. The editor of London's influential *Musical Times* snapped: "Mr. Britten is only one of many thousands of young men who 'wished to continue their work undisturbed'; and if they had all followed him to America, Hitler would have had a walk-over."[1]

Britten returned to England in 1942, making no apologies for his unconditional rejection of warfare, and he soon reestablished his public reputation. Just after the war he began to specialize in composing operas. The seventeen that he ultimately wrote include *Peter Grimes* (1945), *Billy Budd* (1951), *The Turn of the Screw* (1954), and *Death in Venice* (1973). In addition to his operas, he wrote a large number of choral compositions including *A Ceremony of Carols* (1942), *Spring Symphony* (1949), and *War Requiem* (1961). His music for solo voice includes five Canticles, a Serenade for tenor, horn, and strings (1943), and several volumes of folk song arrangements. His music for orchestra includes symphonies, concertos, and his always popular *The Young Person's Guide to the Orchestra* (1946).

Britten's *War Requiem* is one of his very greatest works and the one that most directly embodies his conscientious rejection of warfare. It was commissioned for the consecration of a new St. Michael's Cathedral in Coventry, a city in central England. Prior to the war, Coventry was home to one of the most magnificent gothic churches in the world. Its nave and altar are shown in Figure 78-1a as they once were. On the night of 14 November 1940 the city was attacked by the German air force and the cathedral entirely destroyed (Fig. 78-1b). By 1962 a new cathedral (Fig. 78-1c) was built beside the ruins of the old one, and for its commemoration Britten was commissioned to write a work that became the *War Requiem*.

It is music on a monumental scale, powerful in its emotionality. And, although Britten wrote for a world that had been victimized by warfare, he speaks with a voice that unflinchingly refuses to take sides—instead condemning all war.

Recall from Chapters 48 and 58 the traditional features of the musical Requiem Mass. Since the fifteenth century, composers had written works that drew their Latin texts

(a)

Photograph courtesy of Robert Orland

(b)

🌿 **FIGURE 78-1**

The splendid gothic nave and altar of the Cathedral of St. Michael are shown in (a); (b) shows the same cathedral after bombardment in 1940; in (c) is the new church, completed in 1962 and the site of the premiere of Britten's *War Requiem*.

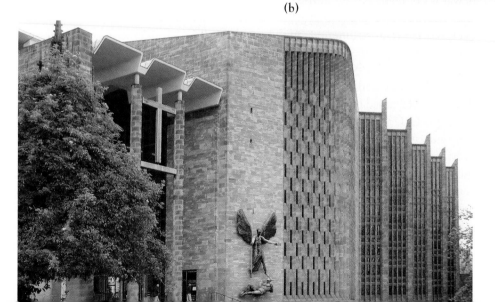

(c)

CORBIS

❈ FIGURE 78-2
Wilfred Owen is one of the greatest English poets at the time of World War I, during which he was killed in battle. His poetry was used by Britten in the *War Requiem*.

from, and could be subsequently used for, the Catholic Mass for the Dead, prescribed for funerals and commemorations of the deceased. In the nineteenth century, the musical requiems of Hector Berlioz, Giuseppe Verdi, and others had taken on the dramatic trappings and huge proportions of opera, making them more appropriate to the concert hall than the church. Composers beginning in the Baroque period also wrote "requiems" that do not use words from the Catholic liturgy, but other texts on the subject of death. Brahms's *German Requiem*—a concert work with texts chosen freely from the German Bible (see Chapter 58)—is an example of this non-liturgical type of requiem.

Britten's *War Requiem* refers to these earlier conceptions, but creates an essentially new composite genre. Like the requiems of Berlioz and Verdi, the *War Requiem* is huge in length and medium, and boldly expressive, sharing styles with the composer's own operas. Like Brahms, Britten dispenses with the notion of a requiem as a composition that is limited to certain traditional and preordained texts. He intertwines the war poetry of **Wilfred Owen** (1893–1918; Fig. 78-2) with the Latin texts from the traditional Catholic requiem.

The two textual strands are carefully knit together. Owen's poetry is sometimes situated to expand upon the Latin words, giving their universal sentiments a more personal resonance. At other times, Owen's English poetry is placed so as to question and even contradict the ideas expressed in the Latin words.

Wilfred Owen was a schoolteacher and amateur poet. He enlisted in the English army during World War I and was wounded near Somme. While convalescing in a hospital in Edinburgh, he discovered a great talent for poetry and also a central theme for his writing—warfare—which he condemned unconditionally. His poetry expresses a deep compassion for the individual soldier—enemy as well as ally—and an indignation at social conditions that lead to war. In 1918 Owen returned to combat in France, where he was killed one week before the armistice.

Owen's antiwar sentiments were shared by many people in England during World War I, when the issues underlying the conflict often seemed unclear and not commensurate with its horrible human toll. Britten's decision to bring them forward into a commission dealing with the aftermath of German aggression during World War II proved highly controversial, especially since Owen's poetry allows for no distinction between right and wrong in war—it is all wrong, he says—and attributes the cause of warfare to the warmongering press, misguided national allegiances, and even to the church.

The interweaving of the traditional Latin texts and Owen's personalized visions of war is especially skillful in the fifth movement, Agnus Dei. Here, as elsewhere in the work, the distinctions that separate the English from the Latin words are made even sharper by instrumentation. Throughout Britten's *War Requiem*, the Latin words are sung by mixed chorus, boys' choir, or soprano soloist, accompanied by a large orchestra (the boys are accompanied only by organ). The English poetry is sung by baritone and tenor soloists—who represent the individual voices of soldiers—accompanied by a separate chamber orchestra.

In this fifth movement, the chorus, accompanied by full orchestra, sings the Agnus dei. This text has a special form in the Requiem Mass that is slightly different from its reading in the regular Mass. The sentence "Lamb of God, who takes away the sins of the world, grant them rest" is sung three times, the final repetition ending ". . . grant them eternal rest." These three statements alternate with the tenor voice, accompanied by chamber orchestra, singing Owen's poem "At a Calvary Near the Ancre." In it, the poet compares Jesus at the time of the crucifixion to a soldier in

war, separated from his comrades and in the hands of a ruthless enemy. He is cruci-
fied with the complicity of smug priests and writers who fan the flames of nationalism. In a short coda the tenor intones "Dona nobis pacem" ("Give us peace"), these
words taken from the Agnus dei in the regular Catholic Mass.

The music is haunting, with a disarming simplicity. An ostinato runs throughout,
made at first from a figure (Ex. 78-5) with notes of a descending B-minor scale segment followed by a C-major scale. The music itself is a study in opposites—ascending motions placed next to those descending, major triads and scale segments beside
those in minor, the tone C placed opposite F♯. The tenor's music constantly changes
and evolves, while the music of the chorus is ever the same, and the voice of protest
in Owen's words stands in stark contrast to that of unquestioning acceptance in the
Latin ones.

EXAMPLE 78-5

In the coda, the unaccompanied tenor, singing the words "give us peace," struggles
to overcome the opposites but cannot do so. In one of the most memorable conclusions in all of modern music, the voice dies away on the tone F♯, with peace but no
resolution (Ex. 78-6).

EXAMPLE 78-6

Do - na no - bis pa - cem.

LISTENING CUE

BENJAMIN BRITTEN
War Requiem (1961)
Agnus dei

CD 13/1
Anthology, No. 202

KRZYSZTOF PENDERECKI, *THRENODY FOR THE VICTIMS OF HIROSHIMA*

The aftermath of World War II drove Strauss, Schoenberg, and Britten toward a renewed emotionalism and led them to avoid, each in his own way, the cool emotional detachment that characterized much of the modern music between the world
wars. This new element of *espressivo* is also found in postwar music by the Polish
composer Krzysztof Penderecki (b. 1933), although his musical materials are experimental, very different from those of his older contemporaries.

Penderecki (pronounced pen-der-RET-skee) was born in Dębica (south of the
Polish capital city of Warsaw), and after World War II he resumed his education at

the conservatory in Kraków. His music began to attract attention in the late 1950s, just as Poland was leading the way among Communist Bloc countries in allowing its artists greater freedom of expression. Penderecki's works were heard at the modern musical festival called **Warsaw Autumn,** where younger Polish composers boldly separated themselves from an old-fashioned socialist realism (see Chapter 74) and made contact with new ideas in music among European contemporaries. From 1966 Penderecki lived abroad, mainly in Germany and the United States, although he returned to Poland in 1972.

His music includes the operas *The Devils of Loudon* (1968) and *The Black Mask* (1986), five symphonies and numerous concertos, two string quartets and two violin sonatas, and a large amount of Latin sacred music for chorus. This includes *St. Luke Passion* (1966), *Psalms of David* (1958), *Te Deum* (1980), *Magnificat* (1974), and *Stabat mater* (1962). His *Polish Requiem* (1984) was inspired by the Solidarity uprising in Poland that led to the country's liberation from Soviet domination. Several of his pieces were used by Stanley Kubrick in the 1980 movie *The Shining*.

Threnody for the Victims of Hiroshima (1960) was one of Penderecki's earliest compositions to attract international attention. It calls for fifty-two string instruments, and it was at first given the most neutral of titles, 8'37". The extent to which the music is a **threnody** (a song of lamentation) is not clear, but the shrieking sounds of the violins at the opening, the crackling whip-like noises in the middle, and the sense of disintegration at the end could easily suggest to the listener images of the terrible suffering of Hiroshima's victims. In all likelihood the title—which suggests a protest against the West—was primarily chosen to make the boldly experimental composition more appealing to conservative Polish authorities.

The style of the *Threnody* is based upon ideas drawn from electronic music of the 1950s (see Chapter 80). Penderecki worked in an electronic music studio at the Polish Radio in Warsaw just at the time that he was composing *Threnody*, and he was probably familiar with the 1950s electronic compositions by the Europeans Karlheinz Stockhausen and Iannis Xenakis. The tape works of Xenakis are especially relevant. In his *Concret PH*, written for the Brussels Exposition in 1958 and much publicized at the time (see Chapter 80), Xenakis made up a piece of music by recording the sound of burning charcoal. Its crackling noises were then amplified, edited, and returned to tape as a work of music that was devoid of regular rhythm, line, chord, interval, and all such traditional building blocks.

These older materials were replaced by **sound masses,** which become the basic elements of the composition. The composer casts the sonorous textures into an artistic shape by molding their density and volume. Xenakis referred to such works as **stochastic** (that is, involving chance and probability) since he could not control individual sounds—these behaved randomly—but only their totality, which he could accurately predict and manipulate.

This is essentially Penderecki's approach in the *Threnody*, although he achieves comparable effects by sounds from the string instruments playing in real time. The basic elements of the piece are not notes, intervals, and rhythms per se, only masses of sounds achieved by giving the orchestra a variety of unusual playing instructions. For example, the instrumentalists are told that at a certain time they should play and sustain the highest note on their instrument. At another point they are instructed to tap on its sound board, or scrape on the wood of the bridge, or noodle on tones and microtones chosen randomly within some fixed interval. Much of what they do is left for them to decide, allowing the players to make sounds that are random incidents—not determined by the composer—much as Xenakis had no control over the individual sounds of his burning charcoal.

Penderecki devises special notational symbols, or **graphic notations,** to guide the players, and he controls their coordination by laying out the score in a succession of blocks, each of a specific duration. See how this works by studying the very beginning of the score (Ex. 78-7). The first graphic figure is a black wedge, which tells the strings to play and sustain their highest possible note, which will be different for every player. During the first block of time, fifteen seconds long, other groups of strings enter, also on their highest tones. The second block lasts for eleven seconds, and here some of the string groups are instructed by the wavy line to play their high tone with a slow, wide vibrato, others with a smaller, faster vibrato.

EXAMPLE 78-7†

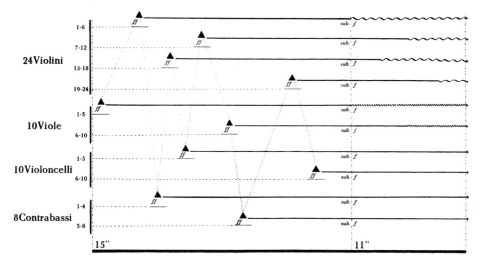

The piece has no form in the traditional sense—no thematic exposition, development, and return—although it has a definite shape as it moves through passages of tension and relaxation. At the opening, the shriek of each instrument's highest tone gradually erodes into a softer dynamic level. This first sound mass soon gives way to one characterized by popping and crackling noises, then by more tranquil tone clusters.

Penderecki's ideas were widely influential on modern music in the 1960s. His insistence on music as an expressive art formed a bridge between the postwar tendency toward abstraction and a return in the 1970s to more traditional values. This transition will be the subject of later chapters.

LISTENING CUE

KRZYSZTOF PENDERECKI

Threnody for the Victims of Hiroshima (1960)

CD 13/2
Anthology, No. 203

---

†Krzysztof Penderecki, *Threnody for the Victims of Hiroshima.* Copyright © 1961 P.W.P. Przedstawicielstwo Wydawnictwo Polskich, Warsaw, Poland. Copyright assigned to SESAC, Inc., New York.

SUMMARY

World War II (1939–1945) was unprecedented in the loss of life, destruction, and upheaval that it brought upon civilization. It produced not only a change of style in modern music but also a group of compositions that deal with the theme of warfare. *Metamorphosen* (1945), by Richard Strauss, is a work of mourning, written in an elegiac romantic style in which the composer at the end quotes the Funeral March theme from Beethoven's "Eroica" Symphony. Arnold Schoenberg's *A Survivor from Warsaw* (1947) calls for orchestra, male chorus, and narrator to present the drama of a survivor of Nazi persecution. The narrator recalls a group of Jewish prisoners, about to be sent to the gas chamber, who break defiantly into the singing of a Hebrew prayer. The work uses a free version of the twelve-tone method and achieves a powerful effect.

Benjamin Britten was a pacifist who refused service in the British military during World War II, and his *War Requiem* (1961) makes a monumental statement in opposition to all warfare. The work is for two orchestras, two choruses, and solo voices, and it uses poetry by Wilfred Owen in addition to Latin texts from the traditional Roman Catholic Requiem Mass. Krzysztof Penderecki's *Threnody for the Victims of Hiroshima* (1960), for large string orchestra, deploys sound masses to communicate the anguished images of the victims of war.

KEY TERMS

World War II	Wilfred Owen	sound mass
Holocaust	Warsaw Autumn Festival	stochastic music
metamorphoses	threnody	graphic notation

Chapter 79

Twelve-Tone Music and Serialism after World War II

As World War II came to an end, most observers of the arts expected that neoclassicism would return to center stage in modern music, just where it was before the war. Stravinsky—the leading figure in this style—was then living on the American West Coast and at the height of his powers. During the war he had composed the magnificent Symphony in C and the Symphony in Three Movements, and he was about to begin one of his most important works of the neoclassical type: the opera *The Rake's Progress* (completed in 1951). This was "an opera of arias and recitatives, choruses and ensembles," as he called it, which would fit into the number opera mold of Mozart's comic Italian operas.

The German neoclassicist Paul Hindemith, living during the war on the East Coast, had been equally productive. Following war's end his music was briskly in demand in Germany. His publisher, Willy Strecker, wrote to him in 1946 to report that the music of other composers could not be obtained: "In consequence Krenek, Schönberg, Bartók, Weill, Berg etc. have been consigned to virtual oblivion. You and Stravinsky are the only ones of the whole former group still left." Stravinsky and Hindemith had ever fewer rivals among established composers. Berg, Webern, and Bartók were dead; Weill died in 1950, and Schoenberg in 1951.

But shortly after the war concluded, the whole style and aesthetic of neoclassicism came under attack in both Europe and America, especially from younger composers. Elliott Carter (b. 1908) found the idiom out of touch with a world that had experienced total warfare. "The whole conception of human nature underlying the neoclassical aesthetic," he said, "amounted to a sweeping under the rug of things that, it seemed to me, we had to deal with in a less oblique and resigned way."[1]

Pierre Boulez (b. 1925) was even more emphatic. In 1951 he asked:

Can a "universal" language be established now? By means of "neoclassicism"? One scarcely needs to deny it, given the total gratuity of the game thus played, its historical necessity not being at all evident. The distracting sudden movements—as distracted as distracting—from Bach to Tchaikovsky, from Pergolesi to Mendelssohn, from Beethoven to the Renaissance polyphonists, mark off the steps toward an eclectic, miserable insolvency without the smallest embryo of a language being forced into birth.[2]

❋ THE TWELVE-TONE REVIVAL

It was Carter, Boulez, and other younger composers—far more than the older, established figures—who set the agenda for modern music after World War II. They rejected neoclassicism in favor of a dizzying variety of experimental approaches to music. One of the earliest and most striking aspects of their revisionist thinking was the emphasis on and extension of twelve-tone composition and serialism. Recall from Chapter 69 that these terms refer to interrelated compositional procedures put forward in the early 1920s by Arnold Schoenberg and used in different ways by him and his students Alban Berg and Anton Webern.

Recall that a twelve-tone composition by Schoenberg presents a succession of twelve-tone aggregates, which are lines and harmonies that contain all twelve notes of the chromatic scale with none omitted and none repeated out of context. These arise methodically in Schoenberg's music by "serialism" applied to the choice of tones. In general, serialism is a compositional procedure in which choices are influenced or dictated by a pre-compositional ordering of elements. In a twelve-tone piece by Schoenberg, serialism is evident in the use of a basic ordering of the twelve tones—a "tone row," that is—which then governs the choice of pitches throughout the composition.

Prior to the end of World War II, Schoenberg's method had exerted only a minor impact on the musical world outside of his own circle. Twelve-tone music was usually thorny and difficult, full of dissonance and chromaticism, which made it jarring to audiences attuned to the greater simplicity and diatonicism of neoclassical works. During World War II itself, performances of twelve-tone music virtually disappeared in Europe and scores became unavailable. A few composers in the 1930s experimented with aspects of Schoenberg's method—Copland in the *Piano Variations* (see Chapter 76), the Viennese composer **Ernst Krenek,** the Swiss-French composer Frank Martin, and the Italian Luigi Dallapiccola—but Schoenberg's bold prediction that the method would "insure the supremacy of German music for the next hundred years" seemed by 1945 to be an idle boast.

✸ MILTON BABBITT AND "TOTAL SERIALISM"

The impulse to revive twelve-tone and serial composition was strongly felt in the United States after the war. In this country, scores by Schoenberg, Berg, and Webern were readily available for study, and Schoenberg himself occasionally lectured on the workings of the method. An important factor in the dispersal across the United States of information on twelve-tone music was the writing of the émigré composer and scholar Ernst Krenek (1900–1991). Krenek was Viennese, and made his reputation in the 1920s as a composer in a neoclassical vein. In the 1930s he changed his outlook and adopted a version of the twelve-tone method, first in his opera *Karl V* (1933). In 1938 he immigrated to America, where, unlike Schoenberg, he frequently wrote on the subject of twelve-tone composition, even producing a textbook, *Studies in Counterpoint Based on the Twelve-Tone Technique* (1940). His ideas were especially important for the twelve-tone music of his student George Perle (b. 1915) and for the twelve-tone compositions of Igor Stravinsky.

Twelve-tone and serial procedures were taken in an important new direction following World War II by the American composer **Milton Babbitt** (b. 1916). Beginning in the 1930s, Babbitt taught at Princeton University—both in mathematics and music—and his influence was exerted through his teaching and theoretical writings on the twelve-tone idea as well as through his musical compositions. His point of departure as a composer was the twelve-tone music of Schoenberg, which he found uniquely revolutionary "in its nature and implications, the degree to which it imposes new demands of perception and conception upon the composer and listener, and—therefore—the degree to which it admits of further and extensive exploration and discovery."[3]

Babbitt studied the systematic aspects of Schoenberg's method (something never emphasized by Schoenberg himself), with the intention of broadening its applicability and reinforcing its capacity for organization in his own new works. He began to apply this expanded notion of serialism in 1947, in his Three Compositions for Piano (published in 1957). Stylistically, Composition No. 1 reflects several influences: it has the strictly linear texture of a two-part invention, exemplifying the counterpoint that Krenek considered a necessary outcome of the twelve-tone technique. Its syncopated and jazzy flavor may recall Babbitt's own background as a jazz performer, and aspects of the work's twelve-tone method come from Schoenberg.

Composition No. 1 is based on the tone row: Bb-Eb-F -D-C-Db-G-B-F#-A-Ab-E. Babbitt lays out forms of the basic row (transpositions, inversions, and retrogrades) in each of the work's two lines. Except for a few measures in which only one hand plays, the two hands simultaneously state different row forms, and these are always chosen to exhibit a special relationship—also found in Schoenberg's twelve-tone music—that Babbitt called **combinatoriality** (it is sometimes also called "complementarity").

Combinatoriality refers to the capacity of two or more forms of a row to create aggregates when stacked vertically. A simple example of the phenomenon can be observed in the first two measures of Composition No. 1. The left hand states the basic row while the right hand states this row transposed to the tritone:

	measure 1		**measure 2**	

right hand:

	E	A	B	Ab	F#	G		Db	F	C	Eb	D	Bb

left hand:

	Bb	Eb	F	D	C	Db		G	B	F#	A	Ab	E

Not only does each line contain the twelve tones, but twelve-tone aggregates are also formed in each measure, and thus the twelve tones more completely penetrate the entire two-dimensional texture.

Babbitt also extends the principle underlying the inversion and retrogression of tone rows to the work's rhythms. Recall from Chapter 69 that Anton Webern in his Symphony, Op. 21, had presented a series of rhythmic durations in retrograde when he used a retrograded tone row. Babbitt goes considerably beyond Webern in his own system for serializing such compositional decisions. In Composition No. 1, he begins with a basic rhythmic figure made by grouping together first five, then one, then four, and finally two sixteenth-notes. Look at Example 79-1 (showing the rhythm in the left hand in mm. 1–2) to see how this works. There are four groups of sixteenth-notes, each ended by a rest or by having its last note lengthened, and these groups contain 5, 1, 4, and 2 values, respectively. The rhythmic numbers 5 1 4 2 create a row that can be retrograded, just like a tone row. Whenever a retrograded row of pitches occurs, Babbitt applies the retrograded rhythmic row (2 4 1 5). An example arises in the right hand in measures 3–4, as shown in Example 79-2.

EXAMPLE 79-1

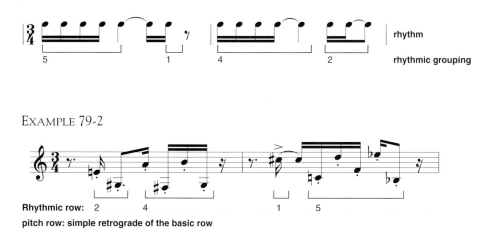

EXAMPLE 79-2

Rhythmic row: 2   4   1   5

pitch row: simple retrograde of the basic row

But how can such a rhythmic row be inverted? Babbitt answers the question by resorting to a simple numerical operation by which a pitch row can be inverted, and he then uses the same operation on the rhythmic numbers. He first represents the notes of the basic series by integers from 0 to 11. He defines 0 as the first note in the row and replaces the other tones by their number of semitones above the first note. In this way the basic row of Composition No. 1 can be represented as this number set:

0   5   7   4   2   3   9   1   8   11   10   6

(B♭ E♭ F D C D♭ G B F♯ A A♭ E)

An inversion of the tone row can be obtained simply by subtracting each number from 12 (the number 12 in the result is replaced by 0):

Inversion:

0   7   5   8   10   9   3   11   4   1   2   6

(B♭ F E♭ G♭ A♭ G D♭ A D B C E)

"Who Cares If You Listen?" by Milton Babbitt (excerpts)

Babbitt's 1958 article "Who Cares If You Listen?" (originally titled "The Composer as Specialist") unequivocally states the composer's reaction to public indifference toward his music. Such works have evolved beyond the understanding of most people, Babbitt writes, so it follows that there is no longer a reason for a composer to present this music to the public at large.

. . . . The unprecedented divergence between contemporary serious music and its listeners, on the one hand, and traditional music and its following, on the other, is not accidental and—most probably—not transitory. Rather, it is a result of a half-century of revolution in musical thought, a revolution whose nature and consequences can be compared only with, and in many respects are closely analogous to, those of the mid-nineteenth-century revolution in mathematics and the twentieth-century revolution in theoretical physics. . . .

Why should the layman be other than bored and puzzled by what he is unable to understand, music or anything else? It is only the translation of this boredom and puzzlement into resentment and denunciation that seems to me indefensible. After all, the public does have its own music, its ubiquitous music: music to eat by, to read by, to dance by, and to be impressed by. Why refuse to recognize the possibility that contemporary music has reached a stage long since attained by other forms of activity?

The time has passed when the normally well-educated man without special preparation could understand the most advanced work in, for example, mathematics, philosophy, and physics. Advanced music, to the extent that it reflects the knowledge and originality of the informed composer, scarcely can be expected to appear more intelligible than these arts and sciences to the person whose musical education usually has been even less extensive than his background in other fields. . . .

I say all this not to present a picture of a virtuous music in a sinful world, but to point up the problems of a special music in an alien and inapposite world. And so, I dare suggest that the composer would do himself and his music an immediate and eventual service by total, resolute, and voluntary withdrawal from this public world to one of private performance and electronic media, with its very real possibility of complete elimination of the public and social aspects of musical composition. By so doing the separation between the domains would be defined beyond any possibility of confusion of categories, and the composer would be free to pursue a private life of professional achievement, as opposed to a public life of unprofessional compromise and exhibitionism. . . .[4]

This same operation is then applied to the rhythmic row 5 1 4 2. It is "inverted" by subtracting each number from 6, which produces the row 1 5 2 4. Babbitt brings this rhythmic row into play whenever an inverted pitch row is present, as in the right hand in measures 7–8 (Ex. 79-3).

EXAMPLE 79-3

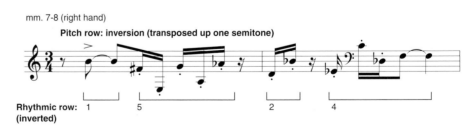

mm. 7-8 (right hand)

Pitch row: inversion (transposed up one semitone)

Rhythmic row: (inverted)   1   5   2   4

LISTENING CUE

MILTON BABBITT
Composition for Piano No. 1 (1947)

CD 13/3
Anthology, No. 204

In these and related ways, Babbitt in Composition No. 1 takes a step toward what he later termed "total structuralization" (others call it **total serialism),** since a single serial principle has been extended beyond pitch to organize multiple elements of the work. Plainly, total serialism represents a reduction in the free choices available to a composer and a step toward a degree of automatism in the compositional process. These were very much in the spirit of the postwar period, when artists wished to reestablish control in the arts, after a time when all of society seemed out of control. At virtually the same moment—apparently independently from Babbitt—the European composer Olivier Messiaen was experimenting with a similarly automated approach to composing. This will be addressed in the next chapter.

IGOR STRAVINSKY, AGON

The rumblings of serialism among younger composers in both Europe and America in the late 1940s broke into a loud roar in 1952, with the premiere of Stravinsky's *Cantata.* The fourth movement of this work begins with a tenor soloist singing the melody shown in Example 79-4. The brackets (which were placed into the score by Stravinsky himself, as though marking something not to be missed) show tone rows: the first is a basic series, the second its retrograde, the third its inversion, and the fourth the inversion in retrograde. The strictly linear presentation of these units and their overlap—the final one or two tones of one row become the first such in the next row—had been a distinctive features of row usage in the music of Anton Webern, which Stravinsky is said to have studied while composing the work.

EXAMPLE 79-4

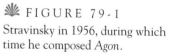

FIGURE 79-1
Stravinsky in 1956, during which time he composed *Agon*.

In his new music, composed between 1952 and 1958, Stravinsky (Fig. 79-1) gradually reinforced the use of serialism and, later, the formation of twelve-tone aggregates. These changes of technique mark one of the most important moments in the history of twentieth-century music. Stravinsky's new procedures signaled a partial abandonment of the neoclassical style by its leading figure and an indication that serialism and twelve-tone composition were poised to become the new common practices of the postwar period.

Why did Stravinsky change his way of composing? He never wrote in detail about this matter, although he insisted that he did not calculate a style: "I can follow only where my musical appetites lead me," he wrote. He held also that the ideas in his serial music were not so different from those of his neoclassical works, only expressed in a more evolved language: "A step in this evolution does not cancel the one before."

Certainly, the critical writings of authors such as Boulez—already cited for his attack upon neolassicism—must have influenced the older composer, who understandably did not wish to be left behind in the new postwar order. Boulez grew ever more strident on the issue: "I, in turn, assert that any musician who has not experienced—I do not say understood, but, in all exactness, experienced—the necessity for the dodecaphonic language is USELESS. For his whole work is irrelevant to the needs of his epoch," Boulez wrote in 1952.[5]

Other writers of the day were relentless in asserting the priority of Schoenberg over Stravinsky. Theodor Adorno in his influential *Philosophie der neuen Musik* (*Philosophy of New Music*, 1949) dismissed Stravinsky as the composer of "fashionable commercial music," something for "listeners who wish their music to be familiar, but at the same time to be labeled modern."[6] The twelve-tone method, Adorno continued, grew from the bedrock of music itself: "Among the rules of twelve-tone technique, there is not one which does not proceed necessarily out of compositional experience—out of the progressive illumination of the natural material of music."[7]

Stravinsky may have read such polemics as harbingers of a new taste, to which he decided to conform. The stages in his conversion from neoclassicist to twelve-tone composer are apparent in the sections of his ballet *Agon* (1953–1957). In creating this twenty-minute work, Stravinsky collaborated with the Russian-American choreographer **George Balanchine** (1904–1983). The ballet calls for twelve dancers—four men and eight women—who dance twelve short numbers that suggest an abstract competition (*agon* is the Greek word for a contest). There is no plot. Some of the dance types, like the *pas de deux* (see Chapter 59), are customary in modern ballet; others—a sarabande, galliard, and three branles—are in the style of old French court dances. The score is tied together by recurrent instrumental passages, and some of the dances share musical materials with their neighboring ones.

This continuity from dance to dance is especially evident in the center of the work, in the series of three branles. These were among the last parts of the ballet to be composed, and they contain a fairly strict serialism and, in the last of the three, also twelve-tone organization. This is unlike the sections of the ballet composed earlier, which have a diatonicism reminiscent of the neoclassical style.

The name of the old French dance called the **branle** (or bransle) comes from the verb *branler*, to shake or swing. The seventeenth-century lexicographer Randle Cotgrave—apparently searching for just the right word—described it as "a totter, swing, or swindge; a shake, shog, or shocke." It was a dance, Cotgrave continued, "wherein many (men and women) holding by the hands sometimes in a ring, and otherwise at length, move all together."[8] There were several different types of branles, distinguished by character, meter, and phrasing, and Stravinsky chose ones called "simple," "gay," and "double" for his group of three. Although he consulted a seventeenth-century dance treatise, he seems to have been concerned with historical authenticity only in general features of tempo and meter.

There is much about the Bransle Double—the last of the group—that still reminds us of Stravinsky's earlier neoclassical music. It has a rigidity of beat that suggests the motoric rhythms of his earlier works and a hard, clear sound made from an orchestra that juxtaposes small groups of brass, woodwinds, and strings. But the movement has many new features. It is chromatic rather than diatonic, dissonant rather than triadic, and it has none of the witty parody and leisurely tunefulness of neoclassicism. All such features are replaced by a tone of concise abstraction.

The pitch structure of the movement is entirely serialized, based on this twelve-tone row:

C D E♭ F E A G A♭ B♭ C♭ D♭ G♭

As in the *Cantata*, the row forms are laid out linearly—not partitioned into the accompanimental texture, as was Schoenberg's preference. Again, Stravinsky links rows together so that they overlap by one or two notes. This can be observed in the main theme, shown in Example 79-5, which is made from the basic series followed by its retrograde inversion, the two elided on the note G♭. Also like Webern's technique is Stravinsky's placement of tones of the row into widely distant registers, which weakens the sense of line. The accompaniment of the main theme—in the brass and, later, in the string instruments—does not use full twelve-tone rows, instead, only half-rows.

EXAMPLE 79-5

LISTENING CUE

IGOR STRAVINSKY
Agon (1953–1957)
Branle Double

CD 13/4
Anthology, No. 205

Several important conclusions concerning the history of twentieth-century music can be drawn from Stravinsky's conversion to serial and twelve-tone composition. It confirmed, first of all, that a new style period had dawned on the musical world in the 1950s and that serial composition would be one of its principal features. It underscored the primary relevance of the Viennese School of composers—especially Schoenberg and Webern—for the larger direction of music in this century. Since it represented the third major style embraced by Stravinsky—unquestionably one of the leading composers of the century—it showed that the evolution of musical taste and idiom had taken on a quicker pace in the twentieth century than ever before. In the past, a few major composers stood astride two eras in music history. Claudio Monteverdi, for example, bridged both the Renaissance and Baroque periods; Beethoven, the Classic and Romantic periods. Now, in the twentieth century, Stravinsky's career and music spanned fully three major periods, and a sorting out of overlapping styles would be more difficult than ever in the past.

❋ PIERRE BOULEZ, *LE MARTEAU SANS MAÎTRE*

While Stravinsky and Babbitt turned in the 1950s to twelve-tone music in a form that was reasonably close to the ways that Schoenberg and Webern had used this technique, many European composers of the 1950s hatched their own highly idiosyncratic interpretations of serialism that had little to do with their Viennese forebears. Many of Europe's younger composers learned about twelve-tone composition and shared ideas for its reinterpretation at the International Summer Courses for New Music, founded in 1946 in the German town of **Darmstadt** (near Frankfurt). With established composers including René Leibowitz and Olivier Messiaen looking on approvingly, the younger musicians Luigi Nono (1924–1990), Karlheinz Stockhausen (b. 1928), and Pierre Boulez (b. 1925) led discussions, study sessions, and concerts that soon linked the name Darmstadt with a doctrinaire outlook on the need for serialism in new music.

Pierre Boulez was closely associated with Darmstadt beginning in the mid-1950s. He had come to Paris as a student in 1942 and entered the conservatory, where he studied with Olivier Messiaen, among others. He learned about twelve-tone music in private study with René Leibowitz, and began to compose serial pieces from 1945 onward. In the early 1950s, in works such as his *Structures* for two pianos, Boulez arrived at a highly automated system of total serialism. Shortly thereafter he became active as a conductor, and in 1971 rose to the position of music director of the New York Philharmonic Orchestra (Fig. 79-2). Since 1974 he has directed the Institut de Recherche et Coordination Acoustique/Musique (Institute for Musical Research and Collaboration, called **IRCAM**) in Paris, which is devoted to explorations into and performance of new music.

Boulez has always been outspoken in his demand that modern music must wipe the slate clean of styles from the past—and not only those inherited from the neoclassicists. Only months after Schoenberg's death in 1951, Boulez published an inflammatory article titled "Schoenberg Is Dead." This did not contain the heartfelt eulogy that everyone expected. Instead, Boulez lashed out at Schoenberg's traditionalism—especially his familiar textures made from melody and accompaniment—and also against his limited use of the serial principle. Schoenberg's twelve-tone music, Boulez asserted, was a "catastrophe," heading in "a direction as wrong as any in the history of music." "So let us not hesitate to say," he concluded, "without any silly desire for scandal, but equally without shamefaced hypocrisy or pointless melancholy: SCHOENBERG IS DEAD."[9]

But by the mid-1950s Boulez had backed away from his dogmatism concerning the necessity for strict serial composition, and he looked for freer ways of composing. He stopped writing totally serialized music and created his own private method for tonal organization. He began to admit chance procedures into his music (see Chapter 80), and he looked for ways to balance "freedom of invention and the need for discipline in invention," as he wrote.

The interchange between freedom and discipline is apparent in Boulez's most often performed work, *Le marteau sans maître* (*The Hammer Without a Master*, 1955). This half-hour composition calls for alto voice and six instrumentalists: viola,

❋ FIGURE 79-2

The outspoken Pierre Boulez served as music director of the New York Philharmonic Orchestra from 1971 to 1977. He continues to compose and conduct today.

CORBIS

alto flute, guitar, vibraphone, xylorimba (a xylophone with an extended low register), and one percussionist playing multiple instruments. The voice sings in four of the work's nine movements, using poetry by **René Char** (1907–1988), and (like Schoenberg's *Pierrot lunaire*) each movement has a different instrumentation.

The overall structure of the work is complex. The nine movements are intertwined into three cycles, each containing a setting of one of Char's surrealistic poems and also instrumental commentaries upon these poems. The three cycles are summarized in this diagram:

↓*Cycle 1* (based on the text "The raging proletariat")

　　↓*Cycle 2* (based on "Hangmen of loneliness")

　　　　↓*Cycle 3* (based on "Beautiful edifice and forebodings")

1. Before "The raging proletariat" (instruments)

　　2. Commentary I to "Hangmen of loneliness" (instruments)

3. "The raging proletariat" (voice and instruments)

　　4. Commentary II to "Hangmen of loneliness" (instruments)

　　　　5. "Beautiful edifice and forebodings" (voice and instruments)

6. "Hangmen of loneliness" (voice and instruments)

7. After "The raging proletariat" (instruments)

　　8. Commentary III to "Hangmen of loneliness" (instruments)

　　　　9. Counterpart to "Beautiful edifice and forebodings"
　　　　　 (voice and instruments)

The third movement, "L'artisanat furieux" ("The raging proletariat"), for voice and alto flute, is by far the simplest and most conventional part of this immensely complicated work. The poem is drawn from a 1934 collection of Char's poetry, also titled *Le marteau sans maître*, that stemmed from the literary movement called **surrealism.** Here a poet gives out images, feelings, and memories, often disconnected and incongruous, that seem to spill from the unconscious mind. "L'artisanat furieux" is a poem in prose that uncovers a grotesque and fantastic dream:

> La roulotte rouge au bord du clou
> Et cadavre dans le panier
> Et chevaux de labours dans le fer à cheval
> Je rêve la tête sur la pointe de mon couteau le Pérou
>
> The red caravan beside the prison
> And a body in the basket
> And work horses in the horseshoe
> I dream with my head on the point of my Peruvian knife.

Boulez does not set the poem to music in a traditional way, in which its ideas are underscored by music. Instead, the words create sounds as though detached from meaning, and these are floated into a freely ornamental dialogue with the alto flute. One of the composer's stated premises in the work is to synthesize word sounds with instrumental tones and to find a common sound shared by both instruments and voice, all leading to a unity on the basis of sound alone. (In Chapter 82 we will see Italian composer Luciano Berio continue with this experiment.)

Boulez removes all feeling of beat or regular rhythm, allowing the music to float without a sense of moving from beginning to end. There are no musical themes or motives in the normal sense. These are dispelled through the avoidance of a connected line and the absence of any thematic development or return.

The work's tonal organization is the product of Boulez's own private system. It takes its departure from serial and twelve-tone procedures, but these lead to music that has virtually nothing in common with traditional twelve-tone or serialized structures. In composing *Le marteau sans maître* Boulez began with a twelve-tone row that he divided into segments of different sizes. These were then "multiplied" with one another. In simple terms, multiplication reproduces the intervals of one segment of the row on each note of some other segment, and the products are treated as pitch collections without any inherent ordering. They are deployed in the composition in a way that is partly predetermined, partly free. There is no possibility in Boulez's system for a tone row being identified with a theme—something that he found objectionable in earlier twelve-tone music.

LISTENING CUE

PIERRE BOULEZ   CD 13/5
Le marteau sans maître (1955)   Anthology, No. 206
"L'artisanat furieux"

 ## THE WANING OF THE TWELVE-TONE METHOD

Stravinsky's adoption of twelve-tone and serial procedures in his music was soon matched by other established figures. Aaron Copland, William Walton, Benjamin Britten, and Roger Sessions all wrote twelve-tone music of some type shortly thereafter. But Boulez's rejection of doctrinaire twelve-tone and serial procedures in *Le marteau sans maître* was the harbinger of a general turning away from these methods.

Stravinsky persisted in writing strictly twelve-tone music to the end of his composing career in 1966, but by then the method had been dropped by most other musicians, both young and old. Increasingly, serialism represented a mentality about composition that came under attack. Krzysztof Penderecki wrote: "Anyone can learn to write twelve-tone music—you don't even have to be a composer. There were no standards. Anyone who had been in Darmstadt for one or two weeks thought that he could compose."[10] For Luciano Berio, serialism was close to fascism, something that could only produce music that was "dull on the outside and empty inside." By 1960 it was clear that other alternatives would have to be found for music in a postwar society.

 ## SUMMARY

Following World War II, younger composers in Europe and America rejected neoclassicism, which before the war had been the dominant style of modern music worldwide. It its place they at first proposed a revival of twelve-tone and serial composition, extending the thinking that underlay these methods to encompass not only the selection of pitch but also rhythm and other variables in a composition, thus producing "total serialism." In America, Milton Babbitt used a mathematical model to create a common procedure by which both rhythms and pitches could be inverted.

Babbitt's interest in serial procedures received a boost when they were adopted in the 1950s by Igor Stravinsky, who took the twelve-tone music of Webern as his principal model. Stravinsky's use of the twelve-tone method confirmed the existence of a new style period in the 1950s, with serial composition as one of its principal features.

Pierre Boulez began his career as a composer of strictly serialized music, but in *Le marteau sans maître* (1955) he reinterpreted its methods for tonal organization in a far freer manner. This was the harbinger of a general rejection of the twelve-tone method and other strict serial procedures.

KEY TERMS

Ernst Krenek
Milton Babbitt
combinatoriality
total serialism
George Balanchine

branle (bransle)
Darmstadt
IRCAM (Institut de
    Recherche et Coordination
    Acoustique/Musique)

René Char
surrealism

Chapter

80

Alternatives to Serialism: Chance, Electronics, Textures

During the quarter-century that followed the end of World War II in 1945, serialism was one of many approaches to music that seemed appropriate to a time of international readjustment. Total serialism—with its tendency to automate the compositional process—had the effect of imposing a strict control on music, something that seemed fitting after a wartime period when society lacked control. The postwar years were also filled with a great anxiety that found expression, often indirectly, in music. Warfare continued sporadically in Southeast Asia—first in Korea, then in Viet Nam—and the threat of nuclear destruction now hung over mankind. The spread of Communism and the prospect of a renewed worldwide conflict between America and the Soviet Union were also in people's minds. What type of classical music could have meaning in such a world?

Composers during the quarter-century after 1945 found no unanimous answer to this question. Pierre Boulez was one of numerous musicians who had loudly insisted on the necessity of twelve-tone and serial music, but by 1955 he had backed away from a strict serialism and opted instead for greater freedom (see Chapter 79). Others could not accept serialism at all. Elliott Carter commented in 1960 on twelve-tone music: "I have found that it is apparently inapplicable to what I am trying to do, and is more of a hindrance than a help."[1] These composers experimented with drastically different types of music, in which the only apparent common feature is a rejection of the past and a search for novelty.

In this chapter we turn to three such innovative outlooks that were prominent in the 1950s and 1960s: chance music, electronic music, and experiments with new musical textures. For each of these we will focus on one of its most representative composers.

✿ CHANCE MUSIC: JOHN CAGE

The most radical of all the postwar experiments was the composing of music by **chance,** that is, making compositional choices at random rather than basing them on taste, musical laws, or traditions. Its most vigorous proponent was the American composer John Cage (1912–1992).

Cage was born in Los Angeles, and in the 1930s he began to compose in an independently modern fashion. He was briefly a student of Arnold Schoenberg, who advised him to give up music since he showed no feeling for harmony. Not discouraged by this advice, Cage went on to write music without harmony. In the 1940s he attracted attention with pieces for percussion ensemble—a medium explored earlier in music by the French-American composer Edgard Varèse (discussed later in this chapter).

At first, Cage composed in a highly systematic way—just the opposite of his later reliance on chance. To organize the durations and sectional divisions in his music, he devised a numerical system that would have made a serialist proud. See how it works in his Sonata No. 5, from *Sonatas and Interludes* (1948; Ex. 80-1). A series of numbers, 4 4 5 5, controls the formal durations and phrasing in both the large and small dimensions of the piece. On the large scale, the work has an **AABB** form, and the length of each section measured in numbers of half-notes is 36, 36, 45, and 45, which reduces to 4 4 5 5. The same number sequence also influences the division into smaller units. Look, for example, at the first phrase of the **B** section (mm. 19–27, marked off by double bars). Within this smaller segment, the four notes in the right hand have durations equivalent to 4, 4, 5, and 5 half-notes.

EXAMPLE 80-1[†]

[†]John Cage, Sonata No. 5, from *Sonatas and Interludes*. Copyright © C. F. Peters Corp. Reprinted by permission of Hemar Press, Inc.

The piece is stunningly original in its diversity of sound. Cage composed here for what he called **prepared piano,** which is a piano that has been transformed into a one-person percussion ensemble by inserting screws, bolts, and rubber erasers between the instrument's strings. Except in rhythm and an occasional unprepared string, the appearance of the notation is very unlike the sound of the work. In other ways, Sonata No 5 is a reasonably traditional composition. Cage chose its sounds intuitively, and he worked out the piece by improvising at the keyboard. The sonata has a regular rhythm, a normal repetitive form, and in it the composer intended to communicate emotions to the listener.

Around 1950, inspired by his readings in Zen, Cage began to replace these familiar features with various applications of the principle of chance. His *Music of Changes* (1951) takes a first step toward this new orientation, by which a composer willingly relinquishes control over the details or even the entire substance of a new work.

Music of Changes is a lengthy composition for piano, in four large parts. A sequence of numbers, comparable to that in Sonata No. 5, is still operative in *Music of Changes*, but let us turn our attention instead to the way that Cage creates the musical material itself—its tones, rhythms, dynamics, and textures. In Sonata No. 5, Cage had chosen these elements based on taste. He picked the notes, rhythms, and sounds, he said, because he liked them. In *Music of Changes* this element of composer's taste is largely removed because the materials are selected by processes involving chance.

Cage began by constructing charts showing a variety of sounds, durations, and dynamics. Each of the sound charts, for example, contained sixty-four figures with one or a few tones in each. Fully half of the sixty-four figures in each sound chart are left void, containing only silence. Cage then tossed coins to choose a figure, which was given a rhythm selected from another chart by a similarly random process. The tempo, dynamics, and polyphonic density of a passage were chosen by comparable routines.

The result is music having **indeterminacy of composition,** as Cage called it, because the choice of musical materials is not directly controlled by the composer. "Value judgments are not in the nature of this work as regards either composition, performance, or listening," Cage concluded. "A 'mistake' is beside the point, for once anything happens it authentically is."[2]

LISTENING CUE

JOHN CAGE	CD 13/6
Music of Changes (1951)	Anthology, No. 207
Part 1	

Soon after *Music of Changes,* Cage went even further in the removal of compositional order and personal taste from his music. In these later compositions, "silence"—the absence of a musical sound—grows in importance and, ironically, becomes the context in which a different kind of sound—unpredictable ambient noise—occurs. In Cage's music, these "silences" are occasions during which the listener can meditate upon unintended sounds of nature and environment, by which we are always surrounded. He was exuberant about them—about their inevitability and closeness to life and nature—and for him they held out the possibility for the "sudden enlightenment" of Zen. Silence, he contended, is "urgent, unique, uninformed about history and theory, beyond the imagination, central to a sphere without surface, its becoming is unimpeded, energetically broadcast. There is no escape from its actions."[3]

Cage's most emphatic silent work is the famous *4′ 33″* (1952), in which a pianist sits before the instrument and audience for four minutes, thirty-three seconds without playing at all. (Cage insists that the piece is in three movements.) *4′ 33″* is not a musical "work" in the normal sense, only an occasion for a Zen-like meditation. Its existence led the writer Paul Griffiths to the witty conclusion that if you're not listening to anything else, you're listening to Cage.

In other compositions following *Music of Changes,* Cage creates pieces that are **indeterminate of performance,** meaning that the performers share with the composer in making decisions about what and how to play. Cage writes most pieces of this type in graphic notation, using visual symbols other than conventional musical notations. Recall from Chapter 78 that Krzysztof Penderecki used graphic notation in his *Threnody for the Victims of Hiroshima,* although Cage's visual materials are far more imprecise in their musical implications than are Penderecki's.

An example is found in the score for Cage's *Concert for Piano and Orchestra* (1958) shown in Example 80-2. To the graphic design, Cage adds only this minimal instruction:

> Any pitch area having at least 20 chromatic tones. Space
> vertically = frequency. Horizontally = time. Horizontal lines =
> duration of single tones. Vertical lines = clusters or legati.
> Points = short tones.

John Cage on Chance Music

In 1958, John Cage was invited to lecture at the Darmstadt Summer School, a center for the rationalized music of serialism. His subject was "experimental" music in the United States, but it soon became evident to his audience that by this term he referred primarily to his own chance music. Experimental music, Cage said, was the outcome of an action whose result is not foreseen, thus quite the opposite of the works that the Darmstadters thought experimental. Cage's witty language and juggling of ideas is seen in this excerpt from his talk:

. . . . Actually America has an intellectual climate suitable for radical experimentation. We are, as Gertrude Stein said, the oldest country of the twentieth century. And I like to add: in our air way of knowing nowness. Buckminster Fuller, the dymaxion architect, in his three-

hour lecture on the history of civilization, explains that men leaving Asia to go to Europe went against the wind and developed machines, ideas, and Occidental philosophies in accord with a struggle against nature; that, on the other hand, men leaving Asia to go to America went with the wind, put up a sail, and developed ideas and Oriental philosophies in accord with the acceptance of nature. These two tendencies met in America, producing a movement into the air, not bound to the past, traditions, or whatever. Once in Amsterdam, a Dutch musician said to me, "It must be very difficult for you in America to write music, for you are so far away from the centers of tradition." I had to say, "It must be very difficult for you in Europe to write music, for you are so close to the centers of tradition."[4]

EXAMPLE 80-2[†]

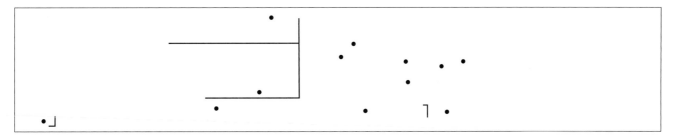

In other works, Cage communicates with the performers by way of a **verbal score**—a short narration of what the performer is intended to do. Here is the score for *4' 33" No. 2* (1962): "In a situation provided with maximum amplification (no feedback), perform a disciplined action."

The music of John Cage moved to an extreme point in the postwar rethinking about what music could become. Although to many his innovations are pure absurdity, he dramatically represents the spirit of the 1950s and 1960s, when experimentation in music seemed to be both relevant and limitless.

ELECTRONIC MUSIC: EDGARD VARÈSE

Postwar developments in audio technology led in the 1950s to the creation of a whole new genre—**electronic music.** This term refers to works whose sounds are directly realized by a composer using electronic equipment. Music of this type was

[†]John Cage, Concert for Piano and Orchestra, pp. 30–31. Copyright © 1960 Henmar Press (a division of C. F. Peters Corp.).

nourished by the liberated thinking of the 1950s concerning musical materials, but it became practical only with the development and distribution of the tape recorder.

The technology for the tape recorder was created primarily in Germany before and during World War II, and the first commercial versions were marketed to the public in the late 1940s. The ease of editing sounds on tape lured musicians of the day to experiment with a type of music that could admit any and all sounds, produce wholly new forms and textures, and give the composer total control over the musical outcome.

The first important type of electronic music was **musique concrète** (concrete music), which is electronic music made from recordings of natural or man-made sounds. This was the brainchild of **Pierre Schaeffer** (1910–1995), a French radio engineer. Beginning in 1948, Schaeffer used sound-effects discs available at his radio station to create a series of musical "studies." He called his genre "concrete" music because he worked directly with sounds, rather than abstractly through musical notation. He began with recordings of everyday sounds—pots and pans, musical instruments, a locomotive—and then edited and manipulated them so that they would take on musical features including regular rhythm and motivic recurrences.

Trained musicians soon took notice of his experiments, and Pierre Boulez, Olivier Messiaen, and Edgard Varèse were among those who composed in his Paris studio in the 1950s. They approached the idiom with far more freedom than had Schaeffer, typically disguising the source of the sounds and bypassing the elements from traditional music that Schaeffer had thought necessary.

Around 1952, the New York composers Vladimir Ussachevsky (1911–1990) and Otto Luening (1900–1996) created what they called **tape music,** which was a variant of Schaeffer's musique concrète. They composed and recorded their own instrumental pieces on tape and then modified the sound—especially by adding reverberation, or "feedback," which was easily provided by the tape recorder itself.

A different type of electronic music was created at about the same time by German musicians including Herbert Eimert (1897–1972) and Karlheinz Stockhausen (b. 1928) at West German Radio in Cologne. Their point of departure was not acoustical sound but tones and noises generated by electronic equipment, and they called their idiom "electronic music," although this term was soon used to refer to a more general phenomenon. The source sounds of purely electronic music were manipulated and reassembled as musical works on tape, often organized with the structural trappings of serialism.

In 1958 Edgard (or Edgar) Varèse (1883–1965) brought together several of these directions into one of the earliest important pieces of electronic music, *Poème électronique* (*Electronic Poem*). Varèse was born in Paris and lived alternately in France and Germany, working as a composer and conductor. In 1915 he emigrated to the United States and settled in New York, where he continued to compose and teach. He helped to found the **International Composers' Guild,** an organization devoted to performing new music. His compositions written before coming to America are almost entirely lost, and Varèse is now known for a small number of orchestral and chamber works that he composed after about 1920. These include *Ionisation* (1931) for percussion ensemble, *Déserts* (1954) for instruments alternating with sounds on tape, and the purely electronic *Poème électronique*.

Varèse pursued a career in music that was always outside of the establishment. His dissonant and atonal music of the 1920s and 1930s made no concessions to the neoclassical taste that reigned in Europe and America at the time. "In neoclassicism, tradition is reduced to the level of a bad habit," he quipped.[5] He argued in favor of a music in which sound per se—more than intervals, lines, or accompaniments—became the central element. In a lecture in 1936 he said:

> When new instruments will allow me to write music as I conceive it, taking the place of the linear counterpoint, the movement of sound-masses, of shifting planes, will be clearly perceived. When these sound-masses collide the phenomena of penetration or repulsion will seem to occur. Certain transmutations taking place on certain planes will seem to be projected onto other planes, moving at different speeds and at different angles. There will no longer be the old conception of melody or interplay of melodies.[6]

The "new instruments" that he foresaw finally became available to him in the context of electronic music. Varèse considered the elimination of live performance, implicit in the electronic medium, to be a progressive step. "The interpreter will disappear like the storyteller after the invention of printing," he predicted.[7]

A music of colliding sound masses became a reality in Varèse's *Poème électronique*. It was written for use in the Philips Pavilion at the 1958 World's Fair in Brussels, where it was part of a visionary multimedia display, also called "Poème Électronique," that was conceived of by the Swiss-French architect **Le Corbusier** (1887–1965). Le Corbusier intended it to "show the new resources that electronic technology has placed at the disposition of the arts, sound, color, image, and rhythm." To realize his vision of an electronic poem, Le Corbusier brought together a team of artists and technicians. **Iannis Xenakis** (1922–2001) designed the pavilion itself, which was a spectacular structure (Fig. 80-1) that was destroyed after the fair. In addition to being an architect and engineer, Xenakis was also a prominent composer.

Visitors to the pavilion experienced an eight-minute multimedia event in which Varèse's electronic composition swept through the space on hundreds of loudspeakers. At the same time, a film by Philippe Agostini was projected on the structure's inner walls, showing images that represented the advance of civilization. Colored lights and additional projections added to the sensory barrage, and Xenakis composed a short electronic work, *Concret PH* (discussed in Chapter 78) that was played while the audiences departed.

In *Poème électronique* (Fig. 80-2), Varèse adopted several of the styles of electronic music in existence in the early 1950s. Some of his raw materials—as in the musique concrète studies of Schaeffer—are drawn from easily identified acoustic sources. The bells at the opening, the human voice at 3:40, and the organ at 7:15, provide familiar milestones for the listener. Also like Schaeffer, Varèse adds formal elements from traditional music, most obviously a recurrent motive made from three tones ascending by half-steps (heard at 0:56, 1:34, and 7:31). Following the example of Ussachevsky and Luening, Varèse quotes from music that he had earlier composed and recorded—specifically, percussion music from his Study for *Espace* (1947),

Bibliothèque de la Ville, La Chaux-de-Fonds

❀ FIGURE 80-1

Le Corbusier and Iannis Xenakis, Philips Pavilion, Brussels World's Fair, 1958. The visionary pavilion was the site of Le Corbusier's "Poème électronique," an eight-minute multimedia display for visitors to the fair. Edgard Varèse composed an electronic piece, also called *Poème électronique*, for use in this display.

❀ FIGURE 80-2

Sketch for *Poème électronique* by Edgard Varèse.

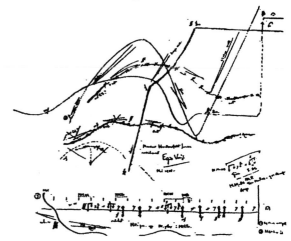

which appears at 2:10 and later. Like Eimert and Stockhausen, Varèse also adds a variety of purely electronic sounds, and these seem to merge seamlessly into the percussion sounds.

Varèse initially thought that the music would illustrate the film, but this plan was abandoned, and there was ultimately no coordination between Varèse's sound and visual images. Still, the music is expressive and dramatic—quite different in this respect from the 1950s tendency toward abstraction and depersonalization in much new music. Sound images suggesting the church (the bells, the organ, a chorus at 7:02) run throughout the piece, and the purely electronic sounds conjure up many human images. The interplay at 1:39 may well remind us of the antics of R2-D2 and C-3PO from *Star Wars.* The dramatic high point occurs at 3:40, when the human voice enters with its unearthly cry, "Hu-gah!" Varèse himself was never explicit about the meaning of the work, although he remarked that it was intended "to express tragedy and inquisition."

LISTENING CUE

EDGARD VARÈSE   CD 13/7
Poème électronique (1958)

Electronic music continued to hold a place in modern music circles after the time of Varèse. Composers were stimulated by the appearance of new equipment—synthesizers, computer programs, and sampling devices—that widened the avenues toward new sounds and textures. But by the 1970s the phenomenon began to wane among classical composers. Electronic music in the 1950s and 1960s was sustained by widespread support for experimentation in the arts and by a sense that exploration was necessary. By the 1970s these sentiments began to evaporate as composers reawakened to traditional musical values. Electronics suggested novelty and academicism—features that gradually became remote to the evolving culture for new music.

From the 1970s onward, electronic music was also increasingly swallowed up by commercial music and popular culture. The Beatles were the first to bring advanced electronic music into their recordings. Songs like "Tomorrow Never Knows" and "Revolution 9" include sounds developed in electronic music studios of the 1950s. Since the Beatles, bands such as Velvet Underground, Talking Heads, and Tangerine Dream have been on the leading edge of electronic music. Today, in addition to experimental rock, the technology for electronic music has found a greater outlet in computer games, MTV, and heavy-metal bands than in the world of classical music.

NEW MUSICAL TEXTURES: OLIVIER MESSIAEN

The experience with electronic music in the 1950s and 1960s opened two principal avenues for further developments—a greater range of sounds admissible to music, and textures based on sound masses rather than on lines and chords. The second of these, new textures, was especially important for the postwar period and was worked out by composers in virtually every medium.

The revolutionary expansion in musical materials earlier in the century had almost entirely bypassed textures. Polyphonic and homophonic patterns created by lines and chords continued to exist in music that otherwise had audaciously overthrown traditional resources. In some of the music of Anton Webern (see Chapter 69) the texture is so spare, the notes so disjunct in register, and the musical fabric so permeated with silences that the distinguishability of lines and chords is blurred. But these are relatively superficial appearances, and Webern himself claimed that familiar textures would emerge in his music provided it received a sensitive performance. In the experimental atmosphere in music following World War II, texture at last became a focal point for new ideas and experiments. The music of Webern was studied and imitated precisely for its originality in this area, as well as for its sense of abstraction and strict use of serial and twelve-tone thinking.

Olivier Messiaen (1908–1992) was one of the first major postwar composers to seek alternatives to the familiar patterns of lines and chords. He was born in Avignon in the south of France and educated at the Paris Conservatory. From 1931 he was organist at the Church of the Trinity in Paris, and he became one of the major composers of twentieth-century organ music. His influence was exerted also through his teaching, which he did both privately and at the Paris Conservatory. Pierre Boulez and Karlheinz Stockhausen are among his students.

Messiaen, like Varèse, was relatively little involved with the neoclassical movement that dominated French modern music in the 1930s and 1940s. Messiaen's music was generally chromatic, colorfully dissonant, and always expressive—features that did not conform to the dominant prewar taste for musical objectivity. In the 1950s Messiaen attracted attention with works that incorporated melodic ideas inspired by **bird song.** He had become an avid ornithologist, and he attempted to capture bird songs in musical notation, even though this could only be done by an often-remote approximation. The bird songs stimulated his musical imagination and gave him "the right to be a musician," he said. "Nature is always beautiful, always grand, always new, inexhaustible in colors and sounds, forms and rhythms—an unequalled model for total development and perpetual change. Nature is the supreme resource!"[8]

Just before turning to nature for guidance, Messiaen in 1949 and 1950 explored an opposite sort of music—abstract in tone, partly automated in composition, and utterly original in texture. In these years he composed four "rhythmic studies" for piano, which proved highly influential upon the younger composers of the day. The second of these is called "Mode de valeurs et d'intensités" ("Mode of Durations and Dynamics," 1949)—the very title suggesting a spirit of abstraction and formalism. For Messiaen a "mode" is a fixed collection of musical elements to which the composer limits himself in a composition. The mode in this piece contains exactly thirty-six different pitches, twenty-four durations, twelve attack types, and seven dynamic levels.

In composing the study, Messiaen chose the pitches freely and intuitively, and he laid them out in three simultaneous strata—high, middle, and low—each given its own staff in the score. There are certain motivic recurrences in the music, but no sense of thematic exposition, development, or return. All twelve chromatic tones were available to him in each stratum. To this extent, the work is a fairly traditional atonal character piece for piano. But Messiaen worked out the composition in a highly original fashion. Virtually all compositional decisions outside of the choice of pitch were automated, as Messiaen assigned a predetermined and unchanging register, duration, attack type, and dynamic level to each of the twelve notes in each stratum.

This system integrates the compositional process and exerts the control that composers of the time apparently desired. The integration of elements is somewhat akin to the system used by Milton Babbitt in his Composition for Piano, No. 1 (see Chapter 79), although Babbitt structures his piece in units corresponding to full twelve-tone rows, while Messiaen thinks in terms of the individual tone.

To see how Messiaen's system works, look at the middle stratum of "Modes de valeurs et d'intensités." The register, duration, attack type, and dynamic level of each of the twelve tones is established in advance, as shown in Example 80-3. Whenever the note G is used in this part, for example, it will be placed an octave and a fifth above middle C, have a duration of one sixteenth-note, be attacked *sforzando* with an accent and staccato dot, and played *fortissimo*.

EXAMPLE 80-3

Messiaen's system exerts its effect mainly on the resulting musical texture. Although the score suggests three polyphonic lines, these are not apparent when the piece is played because any sense of line is dispelled by the maximal diversity in register, dynamics, attack quality, and duration from one note to the next. The texture becomes almost entirely pointillistic—made from an array of individualized tones rather than from lines and chords. Recall from Chapter 69 that the term "pointillism" is also used to describe the music of Webern.

LISTENING CUE

OLIVIER MESSIAEN
"Mode de valeurs et d'intensités" (1949)

CD 13/8
Anthology, No. 208

SUMMARY

Following World War II, modern music took on a variety of styles and compositional methods in addition to serialism. One of the most novel was the making of compositional choices by chance, an approach associated with the music of the American composer John Cage around 1950. A work such as *Music of Changes* for piano is notated in detail, but the compositional choices are made from a number of options by chance routines. Earlier, Cage had written more traditional types of music, often for "prepared piano"—an instrument converted into a virtual percussion ensemble. In works composed later in the 1950s, Cage used a style that he termed "indeterminacy of performance," with which he turned decisions about what to play almost entirely over to performers. His involvement with a "composition" dwindled to brief graphic notations and verbal scores.

Another postwar alternative to serialism was the composition of electronic music. An early version was "musique concrète," which is electronic music made from recordings of natural or man-made sounds that are manipulated electronically and reassembled on disc or tape in a musical form. Other composers opted for pure electronic music, in which the source sounds were produced by electronic devices. Edgard Varèse's *Poème électronique* (1958) uses both approaches.

Composers following World War II also experimented with new musical textures, alternatives to the traditional homophony and polyphony. Varèse praised the value of "sound masses"—conglomerations of sound in which no single tones or intervals are apparent. Olivier Messiaen, in his piano study "Mode de valeurs et d'intensités" (1949), linked together the choice of register, duration, dynamic level, and attack type to produce a "pointillistic" texture in which individual tones seem to leap out without association into lines or chords.

KEY TERMS

chance music	verbal score	International
prepared piano	electronic music	Composers' Guild
indeterminacy of	musique concrète	Le Corbusier
composition	Pierre Schaeffer	Iannis Xenakis
indeterminacy of	tape music	bird song
performance		

Harlem in the 1930s, 1940s, and 1950s: Big Bands, Bebop, and Cool Jazz

By 1930 New York City had become the world's capital for jazz. During the teens and twenties this constantly changing type of music had spread from points of origin such as New Orleans, Kansas City, and Chicago (see Chapter 72) to cities in the West, North, and East. It found its most vibrant home in Harlem, which was then the center of African American culture in the United States.

 ## JAZZ IN HARLEM

Around the time of World War I, African Americans from the South and East migrated in large numbers to **Harlem**—a district in north-central Manhattan—where they hoped to find greater economic prosperity and a more sympathetic environment. In the 1920s Harlem became a center for the arts, and writers including Langston Hughes, James Weldon Johnson, and W. E. B. Du Bois fostered the **Harlem Renaissance** in literature that focused on the black experience in America. At the same time Harlem became a mecca for the lighter entertainments of dancing, theater, and nightclub, for which popular music was needed. Some of the most famous venues in the history of jazz were opened in Harlem during this period. The Apollo Theatre on 125th Street at first presented shows and reviews and later brought the leading names of jazz on stage to perform. At the Cotton Club on Lenox

Darius Milhaud Recalls a Visit to Harlem in 1922

The French composer Darius Milhaud came to New York in 1922 to give concerts, and he eagerly visited Harlem to hear jazz. He recalled the experience:

... Harlem had not yet been discovered by the snobs and aesthetes: we were the only white folk there. The music I heard was absolutely different from anything I had ever heard before, and it was a revelation to me. Against the beat of the drums, the melodic lines criss-crossed in a breathless pattern of broken and twisted rhythms. A Negress whose grating voice seemed to come from the depths of the centuries, sang in front of the various tables.

With despairing pathos and dramatic feeling, she sang over and over again, to the point of exhaustion, the same refrain to which the constantly changing melodic pattern of the orchestra wove a kaleidoscopic background.

This authentic music had its roots in the darkest corners of the Negro soul, the vestigial traces of Africa no doubt. Its effect on me was so overwhelming that I could not tear myself away. From then on, I frequented other Negro theatres and dance-halls. In some of their shows, the singers were accompanied by a flute, a clarinet, two trumpets, a trombone, a complicated percussion section played by one man, a piano, and a string quintet. ...[1]

Avenue, Duke Ellington's band was in residence from 1927 until 1931, after which the bands of Cab Calloway and Jimmie Lunceford could be heard. The Savoy Ballroom, the largest dance hall in Harlem, was only a block away. With two jazz bands alternating, the dancing never stopped. The Harlem Stompers, led by the drummer Chick Webb, was one of the most popular bands at the Savoy, and Webb brought in the still-unknown Ella Fitzgerald as a vocalist, to launch her career as the "First Lady" of jazz.

The diversity of popular music available in Harlem by 1930 seemed endless. A group of virtuoso pianists—James P. Johnson, Luckey Roberts, Fats Waller, Willie "The Lion" Smith, among others—were active in Harlem developing a post-ragtime style called **stride.** The name comes from the striding motions of the pianist's left hand, from chord roots in the low register of the instrument on strong beats of the measure to inner voices on weak beats. An example of the style is heard in James P. Johnson's "Carolina Shout" (see Chapter 72).

Dance music played by bands and orchestras was increasingly in demand as social dancing in the 1920s became a virtual craze. Small bands playing in the New Orleans style (see Chapter 72) seemed old fashioned in comparison to larger dance orchestras made from strings, winds, and brass, playing arrangements in an eclectic style sometimes called "symphonic jazz." In the late 1920s and early 1930s, several dance bands in New York took on a clearer identity. These new groups were soon dubbed **big bands,** and they led to a new style, marked by impulsive energy, called **swing,** which dominated jazz into the 1940s.

✺ THE BIG BANDS: FLETCHER HENDERSON AND DUKE ELLINGTON

Although no one musician can be credited with the emergence of the big band phenomenon and the swing style, a central figure in their development was **Fletcher Henderson** (1897–1952; Fig. 81-1). Born in Georgia, Henderson arrived in New York in 1920, whereupon he worked as a song-plugger and later as a band leader. In 1924 his band was hired to play at the Roseland Ballroom on 51st Street, the most prestigious dance hall in the city, and his distinctive style was soon widely imitated. His band often went uptown to play at the Savoy Ballroom in Harlem.

Frank Driggs Collection

🌿 FIGURE 81-1

Henderson in the 1930s led a typical big band, made from saxophones, trumpets, and trombones, with a rhythm section of guitar, drums, bass, and piano (Henderson's own instrument).

Shortly after arriving at Roseland, Henderson's band was invigorated by the addition to the trumpet section of Louis Armstrong, who brought to the group an improvised solo playing that was more forceful than usual in the sedate style of symphonic jazz. Don Redman (1900–1964), who played reed instruments in Henderson's band, wrote arrangements in a style that would later be widely imitated.

Henderson's initiatives laid the groundwork for the emergence of one of jazz's greatest musicians, **Edward "Duke" Ellington** (1899–1974; Fig. 81-2). Ellington grew up in Washington, D.C., where he was largely self-taught in music and where he learned to play piano in the stride style. Like Henderson (also a pianist), he moved to New York and formed his own band. His group entered the spotlight in 1927 when it became the resident band at Harlem's Cotton Club, where Ellington played for dancing and as back-up to production numbers and floor shows. To accompany imitation African dances, Ellington players evoked the menacing sounds of the jungle: the brass players growled and the drummer played tom-toms, all creating a **jungle style** which became an Ellington specialty.

Duke Ellington devoted his entire career to this ensemble. He composed, arranged, and played piano for the group, toured the world over, and made a series of celebrated recordings and films. In addition to such big band hits as "Take the A Train," "Mood Indigo," and "Satin Doll," Ellington also composed film scores, musicals, and longer concert works—including concertos, suites, and programmatic music—for his jazz orchestra.

Ellington rose to prominence in the 1920s on the tide of big band music, a functional genre which he advanced, transformed, and ultimately surpassed. By the 1930s his orchestra had reached a size of fourteen or fifteen instrumentalists (sometimes adding a vocalist), which was a number typical of other big bands. The players were divided into four basic groups—saxophones (doubling on clarinets), trumpets, trombones, and "rhythm" (an accompanying group consisting of piano, drums, bass, and guitar). The Ellington orchestra's music, like that of other bands, used a form based on the variations model inherited distantly from the blues. Melodic material was taken from (or imitated) the popular songs of the day, and these were molded into shape by arrangers such as Redman and Ellington's assistant, **Billy Strayhorn** (1915–1967).

The musical styles and forms of big bands can be studied in their classic state in "Take the A Train" (1941). Named after a familiar subway line in New York, "Take the A Train" became Ellington's signature work and his orchestra's greatest hit. After a four-measure introduction in $\frac{4}{4}$ time, the

🌿 FIGURE 81-2

Duke Ellington brought a composer's outlook to jazz, and with it helped to enrich the big band style.

CORBIS

band plays the first chorus (i.e., section), which contains the main theme. It is entirely written out, involving no improvisation. The melody is given to the saxophones, accompanied by crisp and syncopated chords in the trumpets and trombones, while the rhythm group plays unobtrusive chords in the background. The melody spans thirty-two measures, laid out in the form **AABA**—a pattern that will be recognized as the standard form for the chorus of a popular song of the day (see Chapter 77). Phrase A is shown in Example 81-1.

EXAMPLE 81-1

In the big band era, the main themes of dance pieces were usually borrowed from preexisting popular song choruses, which were considered **jazz standards** and the common property of all dance bands and their arrangers. These songs could be played instrumentally (as in "Take the A Train") or sung by a vocalist—in either case functioning primarily as an accompaniment to dancing. In "Take the A Train," the melody was not preexistent, nor was it literally a song, having been composed by Billy Strayhorn expressly for use in this instrumental piece.

The remainder of "Take the A Train" consists of two variations (choruses) on the song melody, this number limited by the roughly three-minute duration of sound recordings at the time. The first variation features a relaxed improvised solo for muted trumpet, its accompaniment entirely written out (probably by Strayhorn). In a four-measure interlude before the second variation, the key changes from C major to E♭ major, in which key the remainder of the piece is played. The second variation has a more intricate and forceful character than the first, as the solo trumpet alternates with the saxophone section. The arrangement builds to a climactic chord at 2:15, just before the final statement of the A phrase. The end of this variation is extended by two additional statements of phrase A during which the band fades out, just beating the three-minute limit.

Additional elements of the big band style are also evident. Improvisation is strictly limited to a few solo variations, as the music is essentially a written arrangement of a song-like melody. The arranger pits the saxophones against the brass in a crisp and lively dialogue, and the beat is a steady and regular $\frac{4}{4}$. The entire work has a polished surface with an energy geared to dancing.

The swing band pieces of Ellington and Strayhorn, such as "Take the A Train," go beyond other works of their type in their wholeness and symmetry. There is no arbitrariness as to the number or character of variations and no ideas that are left undeveloped. Listen, for example, for how Ellington on piano brings back the descending whole-tone motive from the introduction (Ex. 81-2) in the very last statement of the A phrase (at 2:45), and notice the relation of this whole-tone figure to the augmented chord in measures 3–4 of the main melody (see Ex. 81-1).

EXAMPLE 81-2

Maurice Ravel Visits America, 1928

Maurice Ravel, like most French composers of the 1920s, was a fan of American jazz. In Paris he was a regular at Le Boeuf sur le Toit, a nightclub where jazz was played. On his 1928 tour of the United States Ravel gladly accepted George Gershwin's invitation to join him on a trip to Harlem to hear authentic American jazz. He gave his opinion about it in this interview:

> . . . You Americans take jazz too lightly. You seem to feel that it is cheap, vulgar, momentary. In my opinion it is bound to lead to the national music of the United States.

Aside from it you have no veritable idiom as yet. Most of your compositions show European influences, either Spanish, Russian, French, or German—rather than American individuality. Nor do I believe those who claim that this is due to the admixture of foreign peoples who comprise the American people. *Pas du tout. C'est ridicule, ça!* [Not at all—that's ridiculous!]. . . . I am also happy to have come to America at last and although I have hardly been out of doors I can testify that Broadway After Dark is *ravissant* [delightful].[2]

The form of the piece is not an open-ended series of variations; instead, it is a concentric design that creates a unified whole. The theme in the first chorus constitutes an exposition of materials, which are then developed in the variations following. In this development the melody itself does not explicitly reappear, only its harmonies, and these coherently support a massing of ever-new melodic ideas that grow in intensity. After the climactic chord at 2:15, a reprise occurs, as the melodic phrase A reemerges plainly in the saxophones, its energy quickly dispelled as the band fades out in a short coda.

It is often said that jazz is essentially improvisatory—a performer's art—but the long-range formal unity and integration of materials of Ellington and Strayhorn in a piece like "Take the A Train" plainly come from the thinking of a composer.

LISTENING CUE

EDWARD "DUKE" ELLINGTON
"Take the A Train" (1941)

CD 13/9

In the 1930s and early 1940s, the big band phenomenon became virtually synonymous with the word jazz. By virtue of radio and sound recordings it achieved the status of a national style, associated with no single city or regional audience. By the late 1930s the country's most successful big band was the one led by clarinetist **Benny Goodman** (1909–1986). His organization was based in New York, and his band occasionally played in Harlem, although it was known nationwide through its radio broadcasts. Goodman recorded both with his big band and with smaller ensembles, and he favored the intense and driving style that was the essence of swing. The character of his music was shaped in part by Fletcher Henderson, who provided Goodman's bands with many of their most celebrated arrangements. Goodman was one of the first major band leaders to promote racial integration in his musical organizations, and his popularity led to his receiving the nickname "King of Swing."

🌿 FIGURE 81-3
Charlie Parker was one of
the founders of bebop.

🌸 BEBOP

As World War II neared its end in the 1940s, many jazz musicians began to tire of the big band style, which, except in a few orchestras such as Ellington's and Goodman's, had become mired in predictable musical formulas. A rebellion against its clichés was fomented not so much by the famous band leaders themselves, but by their players, or **sidemen.** They met after hours at Harlem jazz clubs, such as Minton's Playhouse on 118th Street, to play informally for their own enjoyment, in **jam sessions** involving smaller groups in which new ideas could be tried out. By about 1945 a new style, called **bebop** (or simply **bop**) had emerged that would move to a central position in the history of jazz as the swing bands lost popularity after World War II.

The two musicians most closely identified with the origins of bop are the trumpeter John "Dizzy" Gillespie (1917–1993) and alto saxophonist Charlie Parker (1920–1955; Fig. 81-3). Both musicians established their reputations in big bands. In the 1930s and early 1940s Gillespie played in the bands of Teddy Hill and Cab Calloway, among others. Parker, who hailed from Kansas City, played in the bands of Earl Hines and Billy Eckstine at the same time as did Gillespie. In the mid-1940s the two collaborated on recordings that helped to establish the identity of bebop and, with it, change the direction of jazz.

The bebop style carried over many elements from the big bands; at the same time it rebelled against the big band style. The typical bebop ensemble was not the large dance orchestra of fourteen or fifteen players, instead a much smaller ensemble, or **jazz combo,** made from one or a few melody instruments and a rhythm section usually having piano, drums, and bass. The music played by bop combos used the same form as the big band arrangement—introduction, theme (usually a blues in twelve measures or a song chorus in thirty-two), and a succession of variations on the theme's harmonies.

Improvisation, strictly limited in the big band arrangement, returned to central importance in bebop, and the texture of such works was thin, focused on solo improvisations with rhythm section accompaniment. The improvisations, especially when done by a Gillespie or Parker, were virtuosic, often exploding torrents of sound that were scarcely held in check by a heavy beat, strict harmonic progression, or familiar melody.

The most distinctive feature of bebop—the element most unlike the big band arrangement—is its rhythm. Recall the role of the bass and drum set in Ellington's "Take the A Train." They play almost entirely in the background, and unvaryingly on the beat in a moderate $\frac{4}{4}$. In bebop, by contrast, the typical tempo is headlong fast, and the beat is kept mainly by the "walking" bass, which plays a stepwise line with even rhythmic values. The drum set is freed from marking the beat and instead creates impulsive sound textures on the cymbals and other percussion instruments. The piano typically **comps,** that is, plays irregularly spaced chords. Bebop numbers were often used for dancing, but they invited a deeper level of attention to themselves as pure music than did the more rhythmically regular big band arrangements.

Many of these characteristics of bebop may be heard in "Koko," a celebrated 1945 recording featuring Parker and Gillespie (who plays trumpet and is also credited with playing piano). They are joined by the bassist Curly Russell and drummer Max Roach. The piece is based on the jazz standard "Cherokee," written by Ray Noble and often arranged for use by big bands. The main theme of "Cherokee" spans sixty-four measures laid out in the standard **AABA** form. Phrase **A** is shown in Example 81-3. The familiar pentatonic melody of the song plays no role in "Koko." Only its harmonies are retained, which are played quietly by the pianist. The tempo is amazingly fast, with the half note at the rate of about 150.

EXAMPLE 81-3

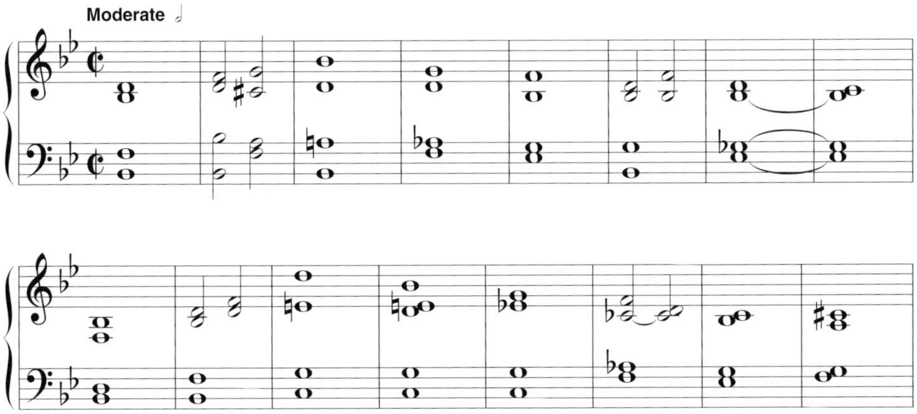

The introduction spans thirty-two measures in the fast tempo, creating music that was apparently worked out in rehearsals as a **head arrangement,** that is, an entirely composed but unwritten musical conception. Gillespie and Parker first play eight measures in a precise unison (a typical gambit in bebop), they then improvise eight measures each, and the final eight measures is another unison. Parker then takes charge, playing two successive sixty-four-measure choruses in a breathlessly virtuosic improvisation, free from any preexistent melody and imaginatively extending the harmonies of "Cherokee." A high-voltage drum interlude follows with little apparent sense of strict beat, and the work ends with a return to the music of the introduction, concluding on the dominant harmony in the key of B♭ major.

LISTENING CUE

CHARLIE PARKER   CD 13/10
"Koko" (1945)

❋ COOL AND FREE JAZZ

The modernism and rebellion embodied in bebop led in the 1950s and 1960s to a splintering of jazz styles. An important new direction that emerged in the 1950s is a style called **cool jazz.** In many ways cool jazz is close to bebop, but without the breakneck tempos or aggressive virtuosity heard in "Koko." The mood of cool jazz is instead relaxed and homogeneous, the tempos moderate, and the dynamics calm. An early example of the style is heard in "Boplicity," recorded in 1949 by Miles Davis and His Orchestra. Miles Davis (1926–1991) grew up in St. Louis, learned trumpet, and in 1944 moved to New York, where he played in the big bands of Benny Carter and Billy Eckstine. He was closely associated with Charlie Parker in the early development of bebop, and he began to make recordings with his own groups in the late 1940s. Always of an experimental temperament, Davis was an originator of the cool style and, in the late 1960s, of jazz-rock fusions.

"Boplicity" looks backward to the music of the big bands and bebop combos as well as forward to the future of jazz. Davis's orchestra has nine members, larger than the typical bop combo. The brass include French horn and tuba, unusual instruments in a jazz ensemble, and there are two saxophones plus a standard bop rhythm section of piano, drums, and bass. The instruments are used by Davis's arranger, Gil Evans (1912–1988), to produce a mellow sound, not the thin or linear texture of bebop. The playing of the rhythm section is totally unlike bebop, as the drummer, Kenny Clarke, restricts himself to the hi-hat cymbal with a regularity that would be at home in a big band arrangement. Some aspects of the piece still recall bebop, especially the opening melody, which is played in a near unison by the trumpet and saxophone.

Other features have the relaxation of cool jazz. Davis plays his trumpet in the middle register with an airy tone that has none of the drive or sharpness of a Gillespie or a big band section player. Note also the differences separating Gerry Mulligan's baritone saxophone solo at 0:58, played with a relaxed confidence, from the aggressive virtuosity of Charlie Parker in "Koko."

The form of "Boplicity" mixes the regular and irregular. The piece begins with a thirty-two measure theme (composed apparently by Davis) in the predictable **AABA** form. The opening is shown in Example 81-4. The second chorus (from 0:57), begins with Mulligan's improvisation, but the clear eight-measure phrases of jazz and its simple variational form soon dissolve into a freer development, leading to a recapitulation of the theme's phrase **A** at 2:40.

EXAMPLE 81-4

 LISTENING CUE

MILES DAVIS   CD 13/11
"Boplicity" (1949)

Gradually, the preeminence of Harlem as a source of new ideas in jazz began to diminish. Cool jazz was as much a product of the West Coast as it was the East, and, from the 1960s, jazz musicians traveled on different paths with no evidence of a dominant style. Many jazz performers began to look backward to revive earlier types of jazz, including ragtime and New Orleans ("Dixieland") band styles. Some performers, such as Ornette Coleman and Cecil Taylor, have experimented with styles drawn from contemporary artistic music, including atonality, in an idiom called **free jazz.** The composer Gunther Schuller wrote what he called **third stream music,** in which the two mainstreams of jazz and classical music flowed together. New alliances were built between jazz and rock, opening up a style called **fusion.**

 SUMMARY

In the 1920s and 1930s Harlem, an African American district in New York City, became the world's capital of jazz. Musicians from all other centers of jazz—New Orleans, Chicago, Kansas City—migrated there, and a native group of pianists explored a type of playing called "stride," which was loosely based on the model of ragtime.

In the late 1920s Harlem witnessed the development of "big bands"—dance bands numbering some fourteen or fifteen players, divided into choirs of trumpets, trombones, and saxophones, with a rhythm section typically consisting of piano, drums, bass, and guitar. Under the leadership of musicians including Fletcher Henderson, Duke Ellington, and Benny Goodman, dance music took on a standard form based on a theme (usually a blues melody or the chorus section of a popular song) followed by soloistic variations. The music of Duke Ellington's orchestra regularly went beyond this formula to create unified and integrated jazz compositions.

The big bands lost popularity shortly after World War II, and their place was taken by a more experimental style called bebop. This type of music was played by a small combo of instruments, it was often extremely fast in tempo, and it was based on virtuosic improvisations that were largely freed from a strict adherence to a pre-existing melody and its harmonies. A branch of bebop popular in the 1950s was "cool jazz," in which the aggressive virtuosity of bebop was replaced by a relaxed and homogeneous type of playing.

KEY TERMS

Harlem	jungle style	jazz combo
Harlem Renaissance	Billy Strayhorn	comp
stride	jazz standards	head arrangement
big bands	Benny Goodman	cool jazz
swing	sidemen	free jazz
Fletcher Henderson	jam sessions	third stream music
Edward "Duke" Ellington	bebop (bop)	fusion

Musical Interlude

The Birth of Rock

9

For a decade following World War II, the popular song industry in America rolled in the same traces that had been formed in the 1920s. The most successful songs were still composed in the style of Tin Pan Alley, and many of the most popular recordings were still made from jazz standards that had been around for decades. Sheet-music editions of new songs remained a profitable source of income. The most popular song in America for the year 1953 was the sentimental and quasi-religious "I Believe," sung by Frankie Laine to music by Ervin Drake. Among the older standards, "Tea for Two," composed in 1923 by Vincent Youmans for the show *No, No, Nanette*, was still a substantial money-maker.[1] The leading singers of the day—Bing Crosby, Perry Como, and Frank Sinatra, among others—had risen to fame during the Big Band era.

All of this changed in 1955 when the song "Rock Around the Clock" vaulted to the top of the charts in a recording made by Bill Haley and The Comets. Music for this song had been composed several years earlier by Jimmy deKnight and it had already been recorded, but it was Haley's "cover" (a new recording of a previously known song) that garnered attention. Haley's rendition had a drive and intensity that is completely unlike the sedate crooning of a Bing Crosby or Perry Como. The accompaniment was provided not by satin strings but by a lean combo that featured a walking bass, amplified guitars, and drum set playing relentlessly on beats 2 and 4 in a fast $\frac{4}{4}$ time. The form of "Rock Around the Clock" is a straightforward blues filled with the driving ostinatos of boogie-woogie and the saucy twang of blue notes. The words ("We're gonna rock around the clock tonight; we're gonna rock rock rock till the broad day light") refer obliquely to sex, something kept politely out of sight in songs such as "Tea for Two." Plainly, Haley's recording was music for a rebellious youth for whom cute and sentimental songs were merely emblems of a stodgy older generation.

The style of music heard in "Rock Around the Clock" was certainly known by 1955, but before this year it was marketed mainly to African American audiences, not to the white middle-class listeners who bought recordings of Crosby and Como. The trade journal *Billboard* categorized recordings targeted to African Americans as "rhythm and blues" (or "R&B"); those for the white working-class listener as "country and western" ("C&W"). Music of the former type—including recordings by Big Joe Turner, Fats Domino, and Little Willie Littlefield—was closest to "Rock Around the Clock," with its astringent medium, driving tempo, and blues-based form. Country and western recordings made by Hank Williams, Eddie Arnold, and Jimmy Dean (later of sausage fame) were more relaxed and mellifluous, and their lyrics usually told a story that resonated with the working class.

The revolution begun by "Rock Around the Clock" was not so much the appearance of a new style as it was the crossing over of existing styles to new audiences. The music that earlier had appealed mainly to blacks and working-class whites was now ecstatically embraced by the burgeoning young and privileged white audience.

❀ FIGURE 1

Chuck Berry was one of the founders of rock 'n' roll.

© Neal Preston/CORBIS

Disk jockeys, such as Cleveland's Alan Freed, began to use the term "rock 'n' roll" to designate this music of mixed tastes, and with it a new era in the history of popular music was born. Bill Haley's success with "Rock Around the Clock" was soon matched by other performers from the worlds of R&B and C&W. The early rock 'n' roll recordings of African American performers like Chuck Berry (Fig. 1) and Little Richard reached not only the R&B charts but also those earlier dominated by white performers. Elvis Presley's recordings, which ranged in style over R&B, gospel, country, and older-type ballads, achieved their unprecedented level of success by transcending racial and social divisions.

The birth of rock 'n' roll was in large measure a product of the social and economic upheaval of the postwar period in America. It coincided with the decision of the U.S. Supreme Court that racial segregation in public schools is unconstitutional, and also with the civil rights movement that would ultimately transform all of American society. It came at the same time as older social patterns in this country were being disrupted by massive suburbanization and relocation between rural and urban areas. It was a harbinger of the ascendancy of youth, dramatically symbolized by the election in 1960 of John F. Kennedy, then only forty-three years old, as President of the United States.

Although rock was a product of its time, it proved very controversial in musical terms. Many performers in the jazz world admired Elvis's revival of blues singing with a country twang and his success in bridging racial divisions, but they uniformly condemned the commercialism of rock that drove Elvis to try to be all things to all people. This was the assessment made in 1958 by Rudi Blesh, who praised Elvis's musical origins but lamented his forays into styles of pure entertainment. "He is [now] singing mainly Tin Pan Alley trash," snorted Blesh, "and his preeminence is being threatened by sophisticated 'folk' singers, the breed that infests the cities today with their guitars and their crooning. Exactly thus, in 1926, was New Orleans jazz replaced."[2]

Classical musicians had equally mixed feelings about early rock 'n' roll. The American composer John Harbison found rock recordings to be musically empty when compared to the older compositions of Tin Pan Alley:

> It isn't *Heartbreak Hotel* or *Hound Dog* that survives as a cultural artifact, it is *Elvis Presley* or his posthumous doubles singing them. Sheet music disappeared or became hopelessly primitive. The *song* became the *record*: few tunes circulated among performers; they were instead identified definitely with a single recorded performance, which that performer tried to duplicate exactly in live performance or "lip-synched" to the record. The beat, the harmonies, and the forms emphasized clear reiterated shapes ("hooks"), root position chords, and hypnotic, crushing pulsations, physicality and presence above all.[3]

Other classical musicians, especially those who had tired of the abstractions of postwar modernism, found much to praise in the energy and inventiveness of rock 'n' roll. The composer and critic Ned Rorem valued the Beatles' songs for their sense of fun, something he thought had been driven from classical music by the abstractions of Boulez and Babbitt. "They have removed sterile martyrdom from art, revived the sensual," Rorem wrote. "Their sweetness lies in that they doubtless couldn't care less about these pedantic explications."[4]

The infancy of rock 'n' roll came to an end in the 1960s, when the Beatles took America by storm. Although their early songs sprang from the same roots as the recordings of Bill Haley and Elvis Presley, their music soon diversified and began to suggest a new and broadly unpredictable future for popular songs. So different was their eclecticism from early rock 'n' roll that many journalists began to call their idiom simply "rock." By whatever name, the pioneers of rock 'n' roll—Haley, Presley, Berry, Jerry Lee Lewis among others—began a movement that ultimately changed the entire landscape of American musical culture.

Chapter

Music in the 1960s and 1970s: Live Processes, Minimalism, Metric Modulations

By 1960 modern music seemed to be trapped in an identity crisis. After World War II the impulse to forget the past had driven it in so many opposing directions that agreement among musicians was hard to find and the audience for new music ever more scarce. Total serialism, chance, electronic music, sound masses, stochastic textures, and pointillism (see Chapters 79 and 80) were musical responses to the spirit of the time, but they seemed to have little in common except for an audacious novelty.

Almost no one was happy. Leonard Bernstein declared the year 1966 to be "a low point in the musical course of our century":

> Pop music seems to be the only area where there is to be found unabashed vitality, the fun of invention, the feeling of fresh air. Everything else suddenly seems old-fashioned: electronic music, serialism, chance music—they have already acquired the musty odor of academicism. Even jazz seems to have ground to a painful halt. And tonal music lies in abeyance, dormant.[1]

Composers of this time bickered furiously among themselves. Elliott Carter proclaimed that total serialism "produces disastrous results, from any artistic standpoint." John Cage found that Carter's ideas only build "a new wing on the academy." Cage's use of chance in composing was dismissed by the composer Luigi Nono as "a method for those who fear decisions and the freedom that they entail." Nono's countryman Luciano Berio judged serialism—Nono's compositional method—to be close to fascism.

Such opposing viewpoints suggest that music of the 1960s and early 1970s was in a state of transition. Composers during this period tried to find their place within an unstable musical culture, often repeatedly changing their allegiances to achieve affirmation for their work. Although they continued to experiment with new ideas, they gradually dispensed with the doctrinaire attitudes of the 1950s and looked instead for consensus and new avenues toward acceptance.

We turn in this chapter to musical styles of the 1960s and early 1970s that embody this transitional outlook. In works by Luciano Berio and George Crumb we find new ways of using the voice and of joining words to tones. Both composers intended their music to speak to a larger audience than had existed hitherto for new compositions. Steve Reich was one of several American musicians of the 1960s who developed an influential style called "minimalism," which held a special appeal for younger listeners attuned to pop music. In his music of the early 1970s, Elliott Carter simplified the complex principles of rhythmic organization of his earlier works. In all of the compositions studied in this chapter we will see a continuation of the search for novelty, but at the same time an effort to find a basis for communication and broader appeal.

✿ NEW USES OF THE VOICE: LUCIANO BERIO AND GEORGE CRUMB

The music of Luciano Berio (1925–2003) typifies the conflicting viewpoints of the 1960s. Berio was devoted to **modernism**—he wanted to expand his inherited musical language, to find new materials and novel principles of organization. But he was dissatisfied with the musical culture that had been created by modernism, especially by serialism, which produced a music that seemed to him sterile and lifeless. Music could expand its language, he thought, so long as it remained a "live process"—a product, that is, of people making musical sounds that could communicate to listeners.

Berio was born in the town of Oneglia, on the Italian Riviera near San Remo, to a family of musicians. Following the end of World War II, he enrolled at the conservatory in Milan, and in the 1950s he regularly attended the courses for modern music in Darmstadt. He rose to prominence as a composer of serial music, and he was also one of the first Italians to write electronic works. But by the late 1950s Berio had become disenchanted with much of the thinking associated with Darmstadt. "Serial procedures in themselves guarantee absolutely nothing," he wrote. "No idea is so wretched that it cannot be *serialized,* just as ideas and images that have no interest can always be versified."[2] What was needed in the place of sterile serialism was "a living and permanent contact with sound material."

In the 1960s Berio composed music that rejected rigid formalisms in favor of the live processes he had come to favor. One group of pieces, each called a *Sequenza,* explored the capacity of a single instrumentalist or singer to sustain an entire composition. Another group consists of "songs" in which Berio addresses the apparent incompatibility between ultramodern poetry—works by writers such as James Joyce, e. e. cummings, Samuel Beckett, and Edoardo Sanguineti—and traditional musical forms and principles of expression. In these latter works, Berio creates a new type of song involving **extended techniques** of singing, such as singing with the mouth closed, on the breath, with phonetic symbols instead of words, or using imprecise pitch. In these ways Berio's songs become soundscapes like those of electronic music, and they invoke a new aesthetic concerning the relation between words and tones. His use of the voice was influenced by the virtuosic skills of the American soprano Cathy Berberian (1928–1983), to whom Berio was married in the 1950s. He also owed a debt to Pierre Boulez's *Le marteau sans maître* (see Chapter 79), in which the voice and text are treated in novel ways.

One of the most influential of Berio's song-like compositions from this period is *Circles* (1960) for soprano, harp, and two percussionists. The work uses poetry by e. e. cummings (1894–1962), which is laid out in five song-like sections connected by instrumental interludes. The overall form of the composition is made from a variety of symmetric or circular gestures, as suggested by the title word. For example, the text in the fourth song is the same as the second (but with new music); the text of the fifth is the same as the first. The two percussionists are instructed to place their instruments in circles, around which they move. The singer takes differing positions as the cycle progresses, again partly outlining a circle. The cycle rises to a climax in the third song, where words are entirely replaced by resonant nonsense syllables that are accompanied by an explosion of sounds in the percussion instruments.

Berio's point of departure in this highly imaginative work is cummings' poetry. The writer experiments playfully with the sounds of words, their odd juxtapositions, and new rhythms suggested by how the words are placed on the page. In cummings' poetry the reader often encounters a succession of unrelated images and musical effects that override any narrative or logical meaning.

An example is the poem "stinging" (from cummings' collection *Tulips and Chimneys,* 1923), which Berio uses in the first and fifth sections of *Circles:*

> stinging
> gold swarms
> upon the spires
> silver
>
>   chants the litanies the
> great bells are ringing with rose
> the lewd fat bells
>   and a tall

(continued on next page)

wind

is dragging

the

sea

with

dream

-S

A poem like this is not a good choice for a traditional song. The music of song, by its very nature, projects ideas and emotions. Music expands upon the poem and reinforces its atmosphere and elements of continuity. None of these characteristics have analogies in this poem. There is no continuity of thought, no apparent emotion, no unifying ideas upon which the music might expand.

Like a true modernist, Berio brushes such problems aside. He focuses on two aspects of the poem—its sounds (especially the recurrent hissing s's and the nasal -ing's), and its formal disposition on the page, which suggests a certain rhythm, pacing, and two-dimensional form. Berio shapes these word sounds as though composing *musique concrète*. Recall from Chapter 80 that musique concrète is a type of electronic music in which the composer begins with recorded natural or man-made sounds. These raw materials are then manipulated into soundscapes. The harp in Berio's song creates sounds and noises that echo and punctuate those of the voice. Berio's medium also retains some elements from the traditional song. The voice is often lyrical and melismatic, and certain words are subtly painted in music. Note the "stinging" of tones at the opening and the bell-like sound tolled by the harp on the words "great bells are ringing." Cummings's spatial arrangement of words on the page also has an analogy in Berio's composition, in which the movements of the players and their position on stage are part of the expressive content of the work.

LISTENING CUE

LUCIANO BERIO
Circles (1960)
"stinging"

CD 13/12
Anthology, No. 209

Berio's new approach to the genre of song was continued later in the 1960s by the American composer George Crumb (b. 1929). Crumb was born in West Virginia and followed an academic path in music. He received graduate degrees from the University of Illinois and University of Michigan, and for more than thirty years was a professor of music at the University of Pennsylvania.

As a composer, Crumb attracted attention beginning in 1963 with a series of settings of Spanish poetry by Federico García Lorca (1898–1936) for voice and various chamber ensembles. He collaborated in these works with the American soprano Jan DeGaetani (1933–1989), whose virtuosity and extended singing techniques inspired Crumb in much the same way that Berberian did Berio.

Crumb's *Ancient Voices of Children* (1970) is one of the most celebrated of his García Lorca settings. It calls for soprano, boy soprano, oboe, mandolin, harp, amplified piano, toy piano, and a grand assortment of percussion instruments that include Japanese temple bells, Tibetan prayer stones, and a musical saw. *Ancient Voices* has five vocal movements, each using an excerpt from García Lorca's poetry, and there are also two instrumental interludes that may optionally be danced.

The five García Lorca poems outline a cycle of life and death in which the central symbolic image is that of the child. The first two poems use vivid metaphors to situate the spirit of the child in a fantasy world, presumably before birth. In the central third poem, "¿De dónde vienes?" ("Where Are You From?"), the child becomes a personification of love who converses with the woman who will give it birth. The child of love comes to her from afar, delights in nature, and demands sensuality. "What do you ask for, child, from afar?" demands the woman. "The white mountains of your breast," responds the child. Finally the child inflicts the pain of birth upon the woman. The cyclic view of life continues in the final two poems. In the fourth, the child dies, and in the fifth its spirit goes beyond the stars to regain its child-like soul, ready then to begin the cycle anew.

Crumb represents the symbolic and ritualistic poetry through a great mixture of means in which no sonorous or expressive device is ruled out. Motives from the first song, for example, are brought back at the end of the work to reinforce the connection between the beginning and end of the poetic cycle. Crumb also quotes from earlier music, in different historical styles, suggesting that the cycle of creation lies outside of any definite or historic time. In the fourth piece, where the child dies and returns to the spirit world, Crumb quotes from J.S. Bach's harmonization of the song "Bist du bei mir," BWV 508, whose unspoken words read "If you remain with me I will go gladly to death and to my rest." The quotation is played by a toy piano, the instrument of the child (Ex. 82-1). In the fifth movement, in which the speaker departs the earth for heaven, Crumb quotes the oboe solo in "The Farewell" movement of Gustav Mahler's *Das Lied von der Erde* (Ex. 82-2), music that deals with the departure of the soul at the time death.

EXAMPLE 82-1

EXAMPLE 82-2

The third piece, "¿De dónde vienes?"—subtitled "Dance of the Sacred Life-Cycle"—lies at the center of *Ancient Voices*, the point in the cycle representing creation itself. Crumb's notation of the music is laid out partly as a circle, symbolizing the content of García Lorca's poetry. The music begins with the soprano singing inarticulate syllables into an amplified piano, whereupon the percussionists begin an ostinato **bolero rhythm** (Ex. 82-3). The bolero is a sensual and erotic Spanish dance (one by Maurice Ravel was used with this effect in the film *10*, starring Bo Derek and Dudley Moore), so it is appropriate to this text.

EXAMPLE 82-3

The soprano, impersonating the woman, then begins her dialogue with the child, represented by a boy soprano situated offstage. The performers move three times around the notational circle, finally reaching the coda in the lower right corner of the score. In this piece, as in Berio's, our attention is drawn most directly to its sounds, as the composer devises an endless variety of ways in which the performers can create new and engaging colors. Note the shimmering effect of the soprano singing into the amplified piano, and the exuberance of her vocalization as well as the startling shouts from the percussionists as they play their bolero.

LISTENING CUE

GEORGE CRUMB   CD 13/13
Ancient Voices of Children (1970)   Anthology, No. 210
"¿De dónde vienes?"

❋ ELLIOTT CARTER

The movement from an abstract modernism toward a more accessible style is also seen in the career of Elliott Carter (b. 1908). Carter was born in New York City, educated at Harvard University and the École Normale de Musique in Paris, where he studied for three years with Nadia Boulanger (recall that she was also the teacher of Aaron Copland and numerous other American composers). Carter returned to New York in 1935 and taught, wrote essays on music, and made his way as a composer in a neoclassical vein.

Around 1950 Carter sharply changed the style of his music, bringing it closer to the modernist spirit of the period and greatly increasing its complexity. Carter's new musical rhetoric and method were self-made—typically American in their independence from trends. "I feel that my music is really something developed by myself," he wrote, "and whatever value and character it has is a result of the way I've thought about it. . . . That may be an American way of thinking in itself."[3]

But, at the same time that he joined the modernist movement, Carter expressed only disdain for most of the -isms of the 1950s. He wrote:

The neo-avant-garde has a very great preoccupation with the physical materials of music. . . . There seems to be very little concern with the perception of these sounds, their possibilities of intellectual interrelation by the listener, and, therefore, their possibilities of communication on a high level. Most of the time the possibility of communication is denied, or, if admitted, kept on the primitive level of any music that has only a sensuous effect.[4]

This "communication on a high level" is what Carter aimed for beginning in the 1950s in his new music. This consisted almost entirely of instrumental compositions in traditional genres—string quartets, concertos, symphonies, character pieces. Despite the composer's praise for communication in new music, these works are uncompromisingly complex in texture and material.

A celebrated example of Carter's music from this time is his String Quartet No. 2 (1959). This is a twenty-minute work having four movements in a traditional sequence, fast/*scherzo*/slow/fast, the whole framed by a brief introduction and conclusion. The movements are played without pause, and each movement is connected to the one following by a cadenza (for viola, cello, and violin, respectively).

The Introduction and first movement (*Allegro fantastico*) illustrates Carter's attempt to communicate on a high level. We are first confronted by the work's difficulties and complexities. The texture is densely contrapuntal and the harmonic language entirely dissonant and atonal. There are no themes, developments, or recapitulations in the normal sense. Our attention turns instead to a high-speed interaction among the four instruments, each of which has its own character. Notice in Example 82-4 the independence of the four lines. In addition to its own "behavior," to use Carter's term, each line has its own distinct musical materials. The first violin is "fantastic, ornate, and mercurial," to quote the composer, and it tends to dominate the other lines. Violin II has a "laconic, orderly character which is sometimes humorous." The viola is expressive, the cello impetuous. Together, the four instruments act out a wordless drama. At one moment, a musical character struts pompously on stage and ignores the others; the next moment there is an exchange of ideas and an attempt to get along, only to dissolve into furious confrontations. This fast-moving drama creates the form of the composition, which lacks traditional recurrences and symmetries.

EXAMPLE 82-4

(*continued on next page*)

The distinctions in character among the four musical actors are reinforced by their different intervals and rhythms. Look, for example, at the passage near the beginning of the first movement, shown in Example 82-4. Violin I in these measures moves entirely by step, minor third, and perfect fifth. Violin II has different intervals. The notes of its chords are separated by major thirds, major sixths, and major sevenths—fewer intervals than in the flashy first violin and more appropriate to its stodgy persona.

The contrasts and interrelationships in rhythmic structure among the four parts are especially complex and inventive. In general, the lines in a work by Carter each have quickly changing tempos and unstable (or sometimes negligible) metric organization. The rhythmic structure of one line is normally not shared with the other lines.

To understand this element of Carter's language, we must first recognize an additional player in the drama—the notation of the score itself—which is clearly seen by the string-playing actors on stage as they struggle through their parts, but entirely unseen by the audience. We can observe notation playing the role of devil's advocate in the first few measures of Example 82-4. Here, it seems that a beat is marked by the first violin—showing off as always—with its sixteenth-note quintuplets at a tempo of 112. The other parts seem left behind, perplexed as to beat and meter.

But the notation has laid down a smoke screen, beneath which the rhythm is simpler and more regular than it appears. Its basic simplicity is shown by the re-notation in Example 82-5, where the two violins are seen to proceed hand-in-hand at a tempo of the quarter-note at 140, not 112. The impetuous cello and emotive viola at first cannot conform, as they press ahead irregularly. Finally, the cello gets the rhythmic upper hand in measure 60, where it establishes a regular pulse for itself at the rate of 186.7 for each note, and at this tempo it shortly joins hands with the viola. Carter's notation—the appearance of which often does not conform to the music's rhythmic organization—keeps all of the musical actors in a state of motion.

EXAMPLE 82-5

The rapid-fire changes in tempo—112 to 140 to 186.7 in only a few measures—are not arbitrarily selected, but based on simple numerical proportions. The rate of 140, taken by Violin II in measure 58, is exactly ¼ of the first violin's 112; the cello's 186.7 is ⅓ of the second violin's 140. Carter referred to a proportional change of tempo such as this as a **metric modulation,** which is a change of tempo produced when a small division of a beat is regrouped as part of a new beat. An example is found in measures 59–60. The sixteenth-note in measure 59 (which spans one-fifth of a beat in the tempo of 112), is regrouped in measure 60 as one-third of a new beat, producing a new tempo of 186.7 (that is, ⅗ of 112).

LISTENING CUE

ELLIOTT CARTER   CD 13/14
String Quartet No. 2 (1959)   Anthology, No. 211
Introduction and first movement (*Allegro fantastico*)

By the mid-1970s, Carter may have sensed that he had set the level of communication too high in a work such as the String Quartet No. 2. Just then a broadly based reaction against postwar modernism, with its complication and abstraction, was becoming apparent. Carter turned away from the complexities of the String Quartet No. 2 and began to write music for solo voice that communicates on a far more immediate plane. In works including *A Mirror on Which to Dwell* (1975, for soprano and nine instruments), *Syringa* (1978, for mezzo-soprano, baritone, and eleven instruments), and *In Sleep, in Thunder* (1981, for tenor and fourteen instruments) only a shadow of the audacious rhythmic complications of the Second String Quartet remains.

MINIMALISM: STEVE REICH

Carter's retreat from the no-holds-barred modernism of the Second String Quartet followed the path taken by a group of younger American composers of the 1960s and 1970s who mixed innovation with a return to recognizable melody, counterpoint, and harmony. These musicians—Steve Reich (b. 1936), Terry Riley (b. 1935), La Monte Young (b. 1935), and Philip Glass (b. 1937)—experimented in the mid-to-late 1960s with a style having a minimum of materials (a simple beat, a few tones) that are spun out—often to great lengths—by repetition varied by gradual change. Although some precedents for their type of music can be found—in John Cage's static and slowly evolving *String Quartet in Four Parts* (1950), for example—the group worked in a distinctly American, self-reliant manner, bolstered by direct personal contact and mutual collaboration.

An early example of their type of music is Terry Riley's *In C* (1964). The score consists of fifty-three short melodic fragments, each made from a few notes of a C-major scale (some F♯'s crop up in the middle, a few B♭'s at the end). The first four of the figures are shown in Example 82-6. A piano sets a pulse by repeatedly playing octave C's, and an ensemble of any makeup begins by repeating figure 1 in unison. Gradually everyone moves to figure 2, which is similarly repeated. The piece ends when everyone has played all fifty-three motives and decides to stop. *In C* is obviously novel and experimental—it resonates with the spirit of the 1960s—but, different from most other modernist developments of the time, it also has the familiar elements of simple pulse, normal rhythm, and tones from a major scale.

EXAMPLE 82-6

In the 1970s, the style of pieces like Riley's was dubbed **minimalism,** a term borrowed from art criticism. Another type of minimalism arose in the mid-1960s in the music of Steve Reich. He was born in New York and educated in music at Cornell University, the Juilliard School, and Mills College in Oakland, California, where he studied with Luciano Berio. Typical of the times, he began as a composer of twelve-tone and serial works, but he could sustain no affinity for such music.

In the mid-1960s, while experimenting with taped musique concrète, Reich discovered an acoustic phenomenon that led him in a new direction. By putting a phrase of speech on a tape loop (by which it is sounded over and over as an ostinato) and by playing the loop on two tape recorders, Reich noticed that a succession of new rhythms would emerge if the two tape players turned at slightly different speeds, as the coordination of the looped ostinatos came further and further apart. He termed the phenomenon **phasing** and used it in his *concrète* pieces *It's Gonna Rain* (1965) and *Come Out* (1966).

These works were audaciously modernistic, squarely in the spirit of the 1960s. They were as completely depersonalized as the chance pieces by John Cage and as strictly controlled as an automated composition by Milton Babbitt. Reich considered them not so much compositions as processes, which, when set in motion, generate an entire musical substance on their own. The objective of the phasing process was the creation of an evolving series of secondary rhythmic patterns, arising and then evaporating as the ostinatos came ever further out of phase.

The phenomenon had similarities with a movement in the graphic arts of the 1960s called "conceptual art" (or sometimes "minimal art"). An example, *Arcs from Corners and Sides* by the New York artist Sol LeWitt (b. 1928), is shown in Figure 82-1. The design, like Reich's phase music, is made from a minimum of materials—semicircular arcs—and a simple plan by which the arcs radiate from the four sides of a square. The design that results is enriched by other symmetrical patterns created by areas of varying densities of lines. These additional patterns—like the secondary rhythmic figures in Reich's music—are a by-product of the artist's concept and process.

🌿 FIGURE 82-1

Sol LeWitt, *Arcs from Corners and Sides* (in various venues, 1968–1993). LeWitt's graphic works—like a phase composition by Steve Reich—are the product of a relatively simple process. The radiating arcs also produce interlocking rose-like designs, just as Reich's phase works produce secondary rhythmic patterns.

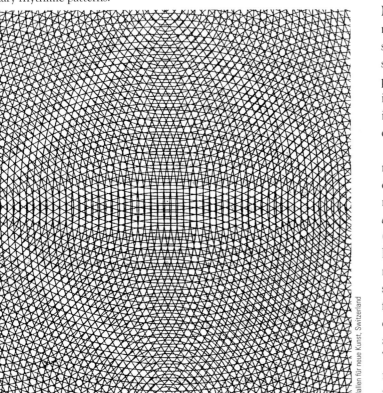

Hallen für neue Kunst, Switzerland

Reich later transferred his idea of phasing to a live medium, replacing the tape loop and concrète sound with a performed ostinato. This led him to pieces such as *Clapping Music* (1972), which is for two performers using only their hands to clap out rhythms. The two clappers start in unison with the figure shown in Example 82-7, which is repeated numerous times. The first clapper continues this pattern from beginning to end, but the second player at the beginning of each measure leaps ahead by an eighth-note. The figure has twelve eighth-note values, so in the thirteenth measure the two come back into unison, whereupon the piece ends. The phase process creates many unexpected rhythmic patterns. For example, rests in both parts occur only on the fourth, seventh, ninth, and twelve eighth-notes within any measure. Although the metric pattern arising in most measures is asymmetric and irregular, in the seventh measure the clouds suddenly part to reveal a perfectly regular $\frac{3}{8}$ meter (Example 82-8).

EXAMPLE 82-7

EXAMPLE 82-8

m. 7 (composite)

 LISTENING CUE

STEVE REICH

Clapping Music (1972)

CD 13/15
Anthology, No. 212

Minimalism proved to be the most enduring new musical style of the postwar decades. It was born from the audacious spirit of innovation that was dominant during this time, and it spread to composers in Europe, influencing experimental rock as well as classical music. Minimalism outlived the waning of this experimental phase in the history of postwar music, a phenomenon that will be taken up again in the next chapter.

SUMMARY

The 1960s and early 1970s were a transitional period in the history of music, during which composers continued to explore and search for new styles but dropped doctrinaire attitudes to look for ways that modern music could communicate and regain the interest of audiences. The song-like compositions of Luciano Berio and George Crumb are examples of this thinking. Both composers rely on sound per se to enhance the poetry that they set to music, and Crumb adds additional expressive techniques such as quotations from preexisting music.

Elliott Carter's music of the 1950s and 1960s was unrelentingly complex, especially in its multiple and changeable tempos and the complex counterpoint of lines. The composer intended these features to create a wordless drama in his instrumental music. In the 1970s, in works such as the songs *A Mirror on Which to Dwell,* he simplified his music's texture and returned to a more traditional model of song composition.

The mixture of audacious novelty and traditional materials is also seen in minimalist music, composed from the mid-1960s by a group of American composers including La Monte Young, Terry Riley, Philip Glass, and Steve Reich. Minimalism is a style that uses a minimum of materials that are spun out by repetition with gradual change. It is seen in the music of the 1960s and early 1970s by Steve Reich as the result of a "phasing" process by which an ostinato begun in unison by two or more sources of sound (performers or taped sounds) gradually moves out of synchrony, thus producing a changing series of secondary rhythmic patterns.

KEY TERMS

modernism	metric modulation	phasing
extended techniques	minimalism	conceptual art
bolero rhythm		

Chapter 83

Returning to the Known: Music of the Recent Past

By 1975 a rejection of postwar modernism in music and a return to more familiar musical values were in full swing. This change of taste was accompanied and provoked by changes in the society that supported music. The unspeakable memories of World War II had lost some of their jagged edge and the anxieties that attended the Cold War had eased. People were wealthier than ever before. Popular culture had grown exponentially in importance all over the world, and with it came the expectation for simple and immediate entertainment—things that were scarce in the classical music that had dominated the 1950s and 1960s. The factors that nourished postwar musical modernism—a desire among artists to forget the past and to hide the personality behind complexity, abstraction, and intricate form—had by 1975 largely evaporated.

As often in the twentieth century when styles have changed, new thinking was accompanied by a forceful rejection of the immediate past. Pierre Boulez in the 1950s had demanded conformity to the principle of serialism, so composers after 1975 tended to go in the very opposite direction by preaching tolerance for any and all styles and procedures. While Elliott Carter wrote music of daunting complexity in the 1960s, composers of the 1970s and later brought simplicity to their music. In a lecture in 1984, the American composer John Harbison assured his students that it was then acceptable to write simple diatonic music:

In the early seventies it took more nerve, it was more out of step to explore a nonchromatic language than now. The chromatic revolution had been certified by the universities, was socially and academically acceptable. . . . Younger composers [today] are fortunate that they confront in their early years an unpressured multiplicity of options; the rewards will be clear.[1]

The modernists' demand that composers wipe out the musical past seemed especially undesirable. In the 1950s, Pierre Boulez had insisted that new music should have historical amnesia: "Strong expanding civilizations have no memory," he said. "They reject and forget the past. They feel strong enough to be destructive because they know they can replace what has been destroyed."[2] By the later 1970s this outlook was discredited by almost everyone. Embracing all of music—old and new, popular and classical, Western and non-Western—had become the order of the day. In 1972 the American composer George Rochberg spoke for this new outlook: "Unlike Boulez, I will not praise amnesia," he wrote.

> The desperate search in the second half of the twentieth century for a way out of cultural replication, i.e., being influenced by others, borrowing, leapfrogging, etc., has let loose a veritable Pandora's box of aberrations which have little or nothing to do with art.[3]

Composers, wrote Rochberg, must once again frankly express their personalities and emotions: "There can be no justification for music, ultimately, if it does not convey eloquently and elegantly the passions of the human heart," he wrote.[4]

In this chapter we turn to representative compositions from the last quarter of the twentieth century, in which the new taste of these years is apparent. In all of them we will see a greater simplicity and accessibility than before, a free use of styles from the past, and non-doctrinaire thinking on how to write music. György Ligeti's *Hungarian Rock* joins disparate musical styles into a happy amalgam. John Adams's opera *Nixon in China* reveals the evolution of minimalism from a thorny experimental music to a friendly and agreeable one. Joan Tower's *Fanfare for the Uncommon Woman*, No. 1, calls to mind Aaron Copland's *Fanfare for the Common Man*—one of the best-known pieces of classical music in the entire twentieth century. Arvo Pärt's *Berlin Mass* revives the outwardly serene features of Renaissance vocal music, although it also preserves aspects of minimalist and serial methods of composition.

✳ MIXING STYLES: GYÖRGY LIGETI

The career of the composer György Ligeti (pronounced JERGE LI-geti, b. 1923) illustrates the changes of direction in modern music during the 1970s. Ligeti was born to Hungarian parents in a village in Romania and, as a Jew, only miraculously survived World War II while living in Budapest. Following the war he enrolled at the Budapest Academy of Music—the institution where Béla Bartók had earlier studied and taught—and Ligeti too served on its faculty from 1950 to 1956.

During the Hungarian Revolution against the Soviet Union in 1956, Ligeti fled to Vienna and then settled in Cologne, Germany, where he composed electronic works and met important figures in the world of contemporary European music. From 1959 he was active at the Darmstadt Summer Courses for New Music, and he established a reputation as an essayist on technical aspects of avant-garde composition.

Ligeti burst into view as a composer in 1960 and 1961 with his orchestral works *Apparitions* and *Atmosphères*. These pieces—somewhat similar to the orchestral works of Krzysztof Penderecki from the same time (see Chapter 78)—use sound masses made from what Ligeti calls **micropolyphony.** This is a texture created by large numbers of lines, so many that the individual lines, intervals, and rhythms are not distinguishable and are absorbed instead into a web-like mass. An example of micropolyphony can be seen in a few measures from *Atmosphères*, shown in Example 83-1. Here, twenty-eight violins, ten violas, ten celli, and eight basses have their own distinct lines, each playing chromatically in uncoordinated and complex rhythms. The individual lines cannot be heard, only a texture made from a sound mass that has a certain color and dynamic level.

EXAMPLE 83-1[†]

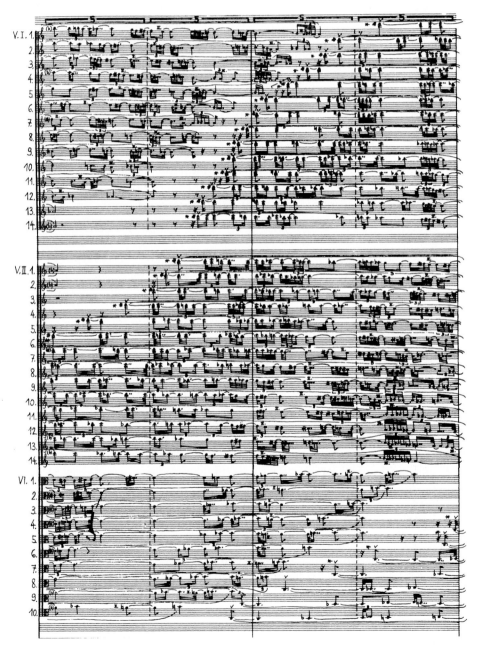

†György Ligeti, *Atmosphères*, study score, p. 9. Copyright © 1963 Universal Edition (no. 13590), Vienna.

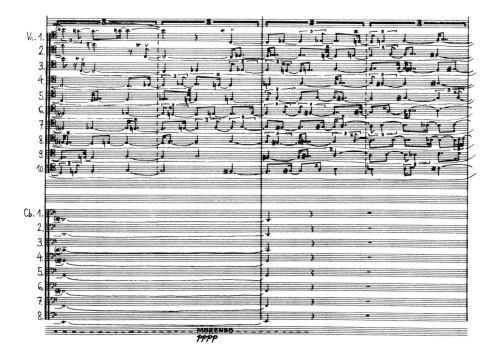

By the 1970s Ligeti had moved beyond textural composition into an eclectic style that was more clearly connected to familiar earlier models. He explained this change of outlook:

> If 30 or even 20 years ago I may have belonged to some group of composers that considered itself "avant-garde," today I adhere to no group ideology. The avant-garde protest action was a political gesture of an elite. With the collapse of the socialistic utopia and with the change in civilization's technology, brought by the spread of microelectronics, the time for an artistic avant-garde is past. Since for me "beautiful" postmodernism is only an illusion, I am looking for some "other" modernism, neither a "back to" nor a modish protest or "criticism." [5]

One of Ligeti's "other modernisms" in the 1970s was to combine disparate styles, which is evident in his *Hungarian Rock* (1978) for harpsichord. The work cleverly intertwines aspects of jazz, baroque keyboard music, and modern harmony. The baroque element comes from the use of harpsichord and from the form of the chaconne. Recall from Chapter 31 that the form of the chaconne, which appeared in both instrumental and vocal music of the Baroque period and is virtually synonymous with the form of the passacaglia, is characterized by continuous variations on a short ostinato figure in the bass, a short harmonic progression, or both simultaneously. Often the tones of the bass of a chaconne leap by intervals of the fourth and fifth, as in Claudio Monteverdi's celebrated chaconne "Zefiro torna" of 1632 (Example 83-2). Ligeti's bass figure shares the fourths and fifths of the baroque model, although the composer compresses the motive into a single measure with an asymmetrical rhythm (Example 83-3).

EXAMPLE 83-2

EXAMPLE 83-3

Ligeti's next step is to use the ostinato figure like a jazz musician constructing a blues. A four-measure harmonic progression is made by repeating the bass figure four times in succession, each time with different chords (Ex. 83-4), and this phrase is played in the left hand forty-four times, with no alterations. Above it, the right hand—like a bebop saxophonist—adds an ever more complex series of melodic variations. These begin with only a few tones and adhere to the 2 + 2 + 3 + 2 rhythm of the bass, but gradually the right hand becomes more complex and chromatic, and it imposes changing rhythms, meters, and irregular phrase patterns above the bass. Eight measures before the end, the breathless motion grinds to a halt and an improvisatory coda completes the piece.

EXAMPLE 83-4

One whole bar = mm. 50

sempre simile

LISTENING CUE

GYÖRGY LIGETI
Hungarian Rock (1978)

CD 13/16
Anthology, No. 213

THE TRANSFORMATION OF MINIMALISM: JOHN ADAMS

The change of taste in music in the late 1970s is apparent also in the evolution of minimalism. Recall from Chapter 82 that minimalism is a musical style that arose in America in the 1960s. In it, a minimum of musical material—often contained in a short ostinato figure—is expanded, often to great lengths, by repetition with gradual change. At its time of origin the style reflected the spirit of the avant-garde—minimalistic pieces tended to be automated, depersonalized, and unprecedented in their materials (recall the hand clapping in Reich's *Clapping Music*). But, in the 1970s and 1980s, minimalism was defanged, losing its modernistic bite and gaining footholds in the world of rock. The minimalistic ostinatos were then often shunted into an accompaniment, to which normal melodies and rock lyrics were readily added.

The transformation of minimalism is apparent in the music of John Adams (b. 1947). Adams was educated at Harvard, and in 1978 appointed **new music advisor** to the San Francisco Symphony Orchestra. Many American orchestras of the 1970s created a position of this type, which has proved to be an important alternative to academic employment for the modern American composer. In addition to longer orchestral works such as *Harmonielehre* (1985), Adams also revitalized the genre of the short orchestral character piece in compositions such as *Short Ride in a Fast Machine* (1986) and *The Chairman Dances* (1985). Works of this type, typically bright and lively, are often programmed by orchestras nowadays at the beginning of a concert, to give the audience a relatively painless dose of modern music.

Adams's early music is minimalistic in concept, but with important differences from the minimalism of ten years before. This distinction can be observed in his *China Gates* for piano (1977), the opening measures of which are seen in Example 83-5. The work is plainly minimalistic, as it uses relatively few materials that are spun into ostinatos that undergo—in the middle voice—gradual change.

EXAMPLE 83-5

Several distinctive features of Adams's style can also be observed in this piece. The first is the presence of what the composer calls **gates,** which are points at which pitch collections change, akin to modulations in earlier music. The first gate occurs

Synopsis of *Nixon in China*

Richard M. Nixon, President of the United States, arrives with his wife, Pat, and national security advisor Henry Kissinger, in the Chinese capital of Peking, to make direct diplomatic contact with the Chinese government. They meet the Chinese premier, Chou En-lai, and the elderly Chairman Mao Tse-Tung, whose conversation Nixon finds mysterious. At the evening's banquet, spirits are high and many toasts are proposed. In the second act, Pat Nixon visits monuments of the city and in the evening attends a performance of the ballet "The Red Detachment of Women," which has been devised by Mao's wife, Chiang Ch'ing. Many misunderstandings occur during the performance. Although a staging or context is not specified for the third act, the principals reminisce nostalgically about their earlier years and differing aspirations while a band plays old-fashioned dance music.

🌸 FIGURE 83-1
The Finnish graphic artist Pekka Loiri created this poster for a performance of Adams's *Nixon in China*.

Photograph courtesy of Pekka Loiri

in measure 16, where the previous collection of tones, all drawn from a D♭-major scale, shifts to tones from a B-major scale. (The term "gate" comes from a device used by electronic composers to create sudden shifts in the amplitude of an electronic signal.)

Another distinctive feature of the piece is in its layering of textures. There are three strata, each containing an ostinato, but each distinguishable by rhythmic motion and register. The top level moves in eighth notes, the middle in longer values, and the lowest is a simple drone. Note especially the differences separating *China Gates* from an earlier minimalistic piece like Steve Reich's *Clapping Music* (see Chapter 82). Adams's minimalism has become beautiful—relaxing, sonorous, comfortable—not difficult or unsettling, as was often true of 1960s minimalism.

Gates and layers are still present in the music of Adams's opera *Nixon in China* (1987), but the shadows of minimalism have receded even further, relegated to the musical accompaniment. The opera is distinctly unusual in its subject matter, which is drawn from current events. The libretto, by the poet Alice Goodman, deals with the visit of President Richard Nixon to Mainland China in February 1972. This occasion was of immense historical importance, as it helped to defuse the hostile relations that had long existed between China and the West and proved a milestone in the waning of the Cold War.

Goodman's focus is not so much on historical fact as on the personalities involved. The librettist intended to make these realistic and "heroic," but since contemporary political figures are known almost entirely by one-dimensional portrayals in the media, any true realism in such an opera is largely an illusion. Nixon is drawn, predictably, as paranoid, someone who slips easily off the track into trivial nostalgia. Pat Nixon is the long-suffering wife, Mao is inscrutable, Henry Kissinger is bu-reaucratic. Given these one-sided character types and certain ludicrous situations into which they are placed, the work most resembles the archetype of traditional comic opera. Also like comic opera is the form, which is made from a succession of distinct arias, narrations, choruses, and ensembles. Finally, there is a comic parody of traditional operatic forms.

Nixon's aria "News" is the first major musical number of the opera. Just after arriving in Peking and greeting Premier Chou, the President becomes transfixed by the importance of the moment. Historic news is being made at this very time, he thinks, and he compares the event to the Apollo astronauts walking on the moon. He imagines that his arrival is just then being broadcast on the evening news, its importance consecrated by this uniquely American ritual. But his thoughts then dart toward his enemies, those ungrateful for his achievements. But he will ignore them: "My hand is as steady as a rock," he declares. His reverie is finally interrupted by Henry Kissinger—his part sung in this scene by a male chorus—who brings word that a meeting with Chairman Mao has been arranged.

The overall form of the aria is free, following the shifting ideas of the text, although an element of da capo form (see Chapter 32) is present as the opening music returns at measure 582. Nixon sings in a partly repetitive, partly lyrical style to a minimalistic accompaniment.

⊙ LISTENING CUE

JOHN ADAMS
Nixon in China (1987)
Act 1, scene 1, "News"

Nonesuch CD 79177 or
Nonesuch CD 79193
Anthology, No. 214

✤ REVIVING THE RECENT PAST: JOAN TOWER

The music of Joan Tower (b. 1938; Fig. 83-2) reflects the change of taste by which musical modernism in the 1970s was swept aside. Her earlier works were serialized and abstract, but from the mid-1970s they became simpler, more eclectic, and more familiar in material. She describes this change:

> When I first got out of school, I hung around a lot of serial composers and was into the twelve-tone stuff, heavily, I was playing it, so my music was fairly twelve-tone based at that time. But after about ten years I found my own voice. . . . This was at a time [earlier on] when you didn't do anything simple. [Later] it was a real door-opener for me, because after that my own voice started to take shape.[6]

Tower was born in New York State and attended Bennington College and Columbia University. A pianist, she specialized in performing modern music with her own ensemble, the Da Capo Chamber Players, for which she has written numerous works. She composes primarily instrumental music, including orchestral character pieces, concertos, and chamber compositions.

Her *Fanfare for the Uncommon Woman*, No. 1 (1986), is an example of the short orchestral character piece that has increasingly become the stock-in-trade of the serious American composer. It is made not only from familiar pitch materials and expressive gestures, but in its title and in musical content refers explicitly to Aaron Copland's ever-popular *Fanfare for*

✲ FIGURE 83-2
Joan Tower is a leading voice in contemporary American music.

Photograph © Steve J. Sherman

the Common Man (1942). Written during World War II, Copland's *Fanfare* is a patriotic work that evokes the sound of cannons and bugles, all leading to a triumphant conclusion.

Tower's *Fanfare* has a different context. Although written for the same medium as Copland's *Fanfare*—orchestral brass and percussion—Copland's war-like allusions are replaced by a more lilting and festive spirit. "It is dedicated," Tower writes about the *Fanfare*, "to women who take risks and who are adventurous."

Tower's fanfare, like Copland's, begins with a trumpet figure based on a pentatonic scale and chords made from fourths and fifths (Ex. 83-6). Copland's opening figure (top) imitates the intervals available on a valveless bugle, while Tower's opening material (bottom) is more pervasively quartal. In the middle of Tower's fanfare, the lines become complex in makeup, based alternately on diatonic, whole-tone, and chromatic scales, and the opening music and its pentatonicism return near the end.

EXAMPLE 83-6

LISTENING CUE

JOAN TOWER
Fanfare for the Uncommon Woman, No. 1 (1986)

CD 13/17
Anthology, No. 215

THE RENAISSANCE REBORN: ARVO PÄRT

As composers of the 1970s searched the past for new alliances with the present, they found an especially fruitful source of inspiration in Renaissance choral music. Recall from Chapters 21 and 25 the features of this body of music, which achieves a balance and serenity that seemed appropriate to the relaxed spirit of the 1970s and also an antidote to the complex dissonances of the immediate musical past. Renaissance choral music became the stylistic framework for the works of Arvo Pärt (pronounced PAIRT). Pärt was born in Estonia in 1935, when this small country, lying on the Baltic Sea just below Finland, was an independent republic. Following World War II, Estonia was absorbed into the Soviet Union, although its independence was recovered in 1991. Pärt attended the conservatory in Tallinn, the capital city, and established a reputation in the Soviet Union as a rebellious composer writing complex serialized music. Even in 1980 he was little known in the West; in that year he emigrated from Russia, first to Vienna, and settled finally in Berlin.

Pärt's compositional evolution neatly shows a cross section of the broad changes in modern music following World War II. In the 1960s he was a serialist, although he found this idiom unsatisfying. Composers at Darmstadt, he said later, were like children playing in a sandbox. He then turned to an eclectic style that mixed modern elements with quotations from the past (recall a similar feature in George Crumb's *Ancient Voices of Children,* see Chapter 82). Finally, in the later 1970s, Pärt developed a personalized idiom that outwardly imitates Renaissance choral music. Since 1980 he has composed primarily for voices, using Latin texts from the Roman Catholic liturgy. These pieces include Masses, motets, passions, and a Magnificat.

Pärt calls the style of his works after 1976 **tintinnabuli** (Latin for "bells"), which refers to his method for constructing a polyphonic texture. A work in the tintinnabuli style has one or more pairs of polyphonic lines. In each pair one line is melodic, the other harmonic (or bell-like) in nature. The melodic line resembles a Gregorian chant, progressing largely stepwise in a diatonic motion that tends to focus on a keynote. The harmonic line is restricted to the notes of the tonic triad.

An example of a tintinnabuli pair of lines is shown in Example 83-7, music that is drawn from the *Credo* of Pärt's *Berlin Mass* (1990). The lower line is the melodic voice. It is entirely diatonic, in the key of E major, and it moves predominantly by step. The upper voice is the bell line. Its notes are limited to those of an E-major triad, and these tones are chosen to meet the melodic line only at the intervals of the fourth, fifth, sixth, and octave.

EXAMPLE 83-7

mm. 1-11 (Bass and tenor, text omitted)

Pärt's *Berlin Mass* shows other aspects of his revival of Renaissance music. Like the Mass in the fifteenth and sixteenth centuries, Pärt's *Berlin Mass* is functional music, intended to be performed in a Catholic service of worship. With its primarily consonant harmony and clear declamation of the text, the work has a serenity reminiscent of a Mass by Palestrina or a motet by Josquin. The second tintinnabuli pair (made by the altos and sopranos) relates to the first (bass-tenor) by a strict canon.

Pärt deviates from his ancient model by adding an instrumental accompaniment to the chorus; also, his music is more static than a Renaissance work because it contains an unchanging triad in the harmonic lines. The work has many subtly modernistic touches—a repetitiveness suggesting minimalism and even a few holdovers from the days of serialism—but with Pärt these all contribute to a personalized and expressive objective.

LISTENING CUE

ARVO PÄRT
Berlin Mass (1990)
Credo

CD 13/18
Anthology, No. 216

🌸 MUSIC IN THE TWENTY-FIRST CENTURY

Arvo Pärt's tying the past together with the present is an appropriate theme with which to end this study of music in Western civilization. Pärt's outlook on the past would be impossible if music throughout our history did not possess so many recurrences and symmetries, so many similar patterns of change provoked by recurring conditions. The liberation of dissonance that characterizes Monteverdi's "second practice" in 1600 has an uncanny similarity to the emancipation of dissonance proclaimed by Arnold Schoenberg around 1908. Both were declared to sharpen the expressive resources available to the musician, and both initiated a new period in musical history that followed on a time when musical expression had become limited and predictable. Stravinsky's attacks of the 1920s on music of the recent past reminds us strikingly of Johannes Tinctoris' complaint, made in 1477, that no music composed more than forty years earlier "is thought by the learned as worthy of performance."

Given these cycles and symmetries of music history, can we look with any confidence at what music will be in the future? The near future appears clear enough. Now, at the beginning of the twenty-first century, classical music retains its allegiance to known values, its tolerant embracing of all music of the past, and its basic simplicity. We can be fairly sure that classical composers will continue in the near future to seek as large an audience as possible and continue to find alliances with popular music, non-Western music, film, and all earlier styles of classical works.

But beyond this, the crystal ball for music grows dim. Although we cannot reliably predict what music will be in the future, we can with reasonable certainty say *why* it will become what it will. The first factor is contained within music itself. Music changes in part because of its own life cycles. In the nineteenth century, for example, the trend toward ever-greater expressivity led to greater and greater lengths and grandiosity. Finally, these had reached their own limit. How could music be longer than Wagner's operas or more grandiose than Mahler's symphonies? The late romantic style collapsed under its own weight and a new style grew from it.

Music also changes because of non-musical factors, especially the character and course of the society in which it exists. The muscular impulsiveness of Beethoven's music was shaped, in part, by the era in which he lived, a time of continuous warfare, when the exploits of heroic individuals were praised. In the twentieth century, the two world wars produced sharp changes in musical styles as artists struggled to regain control by rejecting a past filled with unsustainable memories.

What will music be in the future? Almost certainly it will be an outgrowth of its own evolution, expansion, and ultimate exhaustion. With equal certainty it will be a product of the society around it and, as such, a reflection of our own experiences, brought back to those of us who listen and study with a greater clarity and meaning.

SUMMARY

Around 1975 a major change of style occurred in the world of classical music. The complexity, desire for control, and experimentation of the preceding decades were replaced by a simpler and more familiar style. Composers no longer rejected the past but embraced it, in all its dimensions. György Ligeti's *Hungarian Rock* combines disparate styles from the past—jazz and baroque chaconnes—into an eclectic mixture. John Adams's music, as in his opera *Nixon in China,* transforms minimalism from an experimental type of music to one with familiar features and comforting sonorities. Joan Tower's *Fanfare for the Uncommon Woman,* No. 1, alludes to a specific earlier composition by Aaron Copland. Arvo Pärt's music after 1976, which uses what this composer calls the "tintinnabuli" (bells) style, imitates Renaissance vocal counterpoint.

KEY TERMS

micropolyphony   gate
new music advisor   *tintinnabuli* style

NOTES

Abbreviations

History in Documents   *Music in the Western World: A History in Documents,* ed. Piero Weiss and Richard Taruskin (New York, 1984).

JAMS   *Journal of the American Musicological Society*

Letters of Mozart   Emily Anderson, *The Letters of Mozart and His Family,* ed. and trans. Emily Anderson, 3 vols. (London, 1966).

NG   *The New Grove Dictionary of Music and Musicians,* ed. S. Sadie and J. Tyrrell (London, 2001).

PART VI

Musical Interlude 6   1. E.T.A. Hoffmann, "Beethoven's Instrumental Music," ed. Oliver Strunk, in *Source Readings in Music History: The Romantic Era* (New York, 1965), 37. 2. Letter of 26 September 1781 in the *Letters of Mozart and his Family,* ed. Emily Anderson, 3 vols. (London, 1938), III, 1144.

Chapter 52   1. Anselm Hüttenbrenner, "Fragments from the Life of the Song Composer Franz Schubert" (1854), in Otto Erich Deutsch, *Schubert: Memoirs by his Friends,* trans. Rosamond Ley and John Nowell (New York, 1958), 182–83. 2. Deutsch, *Schubert,* 178–79, 185–86. 3. Deutsch, *Schubert,* 337.

Chapter 53   1. *Selected Correspondence of Fryderyk Chopin,* trans. Arthur Hedley (New York, 1963), 100–101. 2. Hector Berlioz, *Memoirs,* trans. Rachel Holmes and Eleanor Holmes, rev. Ernest Newman (New York, 1932), 19. 3. Berlioz, "On Conducting" (1856), in Hector Berlioz and Richard Strauss, *Treatise on Instrumentation,* trans. Theodore Front (New York, 1991), 410. 4. Hector Berlioz, *A Selection from his Letters,* ed. and trans. Humphrey Searle (New York, 1973), 27. 5. *Selected Correspondence of Fryderyk Chopin,* 97–98. 6. George Sand, *My Life,* trans. Dan Hofstadter (New York, 1979), 236–37. 7. *Selected Correspondence of Fryderyk Chopin,* 220. 8. *Selected Correspondence of Fryderyk Chopin,* 329–30. 9. Quoted and discussed by Arthur Hedley in *Selected Correspondence of Fryderyk Chopin,* 377–87.

Chapter 54   1. *Neue Zeitschrift für Musik,* 13 (19 December 1840): 198. 2. Robert Schumann, "A Symphony by Berlioz," in *Berlioz Fantastic Symphony,* Norton Critical Score, ed. Edward T. Cone (New York, 1971), 248. 3. *Letters of Clara Schumann and Johannes Brahms, 1853–1896,* ed. Berthold Litzmann, 2 vols. (New York, 1973), II, 300.

Chapter 55   1. Richard Wagner, "Pasticcio" (1834), in *Richard Wagner's Prose Works,* vol. 8, trans. William Ashton Ellis (London, 1899), 60. 2. From Weber's *Tonkünstlerleben,* quoted in John Warrack, *Carl Maria von Weber,* 2nd ed. (Cambridge, 1976), 97. 3. *The Complete Correspondence of Clara and Robert Schumann,* ed. Eva Weissweiler, trans. Hildegard Fritsch and Ronald L. Crawford, 2 vols. (New York, 1994), I, 3.

Chapter 56   1. Stendhal, *Life of Rossini* (1824), trans. Richard N. Coe (New York, 1970), 3. 2. Hans von Bülow, *Briefe und Schriften,* 8 vols.(Leipzig, 1896), III, 357. 3. Alexis-Jacob Azevedo, *G. Rossini: Sa vie et ses oeuvres* (Paris, 1864), 114. 4. Quoted in Mary Jane Phillips-Matz, *Verdi: A Biography* (Oxford, 1993), 612. 5. Phillips-Matz, *Verdi,* 669.

Chapter 57   1. Letter of 7 May, 1873 to Antal Augusz, in Franz Liszt, *Briefe aus ungarischen Sammlungen, 1835–1886,* ed. Margit Prahács (Kassel, 1966), 160. 2. From memoirs of Ilka Horowitz-Barnay, cited by Alan Walker, *Franz Liszt,* 3 vols. (New York, 1983), I, 83. 3. Vladimir Stasov, *Selected Essays on Music,* trans. Florence Jonas (New York, 1968), 121. 4. Letter of 1837 to Adolphe Pictet, in Franz Liszt, *Gesammelte Schriften,* ed. Lina Ramann, 6 vols. (Leipzig, 1888), II, 151. 5. Franz Liszt, *The Gipsy in Music* (1859), trans. Edwin Evans, 2 vols. (London, n.d.), II, 337. 6. *Franz Liszts Briefe,* ed. La Mara, 8 vols. (Leipzig, 1902), VII, 57–58. 7. Felix Mendelssohn-Bartholdy, *Briefe aus Leipziger Archiven,* ed. Hans-Joachim Rothe and Reinhard Szeskus

(Leipzig, 1972), 174. 8. The text of the manifesto is given in full in Peter Latham, *Brahms* (London, 1975), 31.

Chapter 58   1. *Selected Correspondence of Fryderyk Chopin,* trans. Arthur Hedley (New York, 1963), 72. 2. Robert Schumann, "Neue Bahnen," *Neue Zeitschrift für Musik,* 39 (28 October 1853): 185–86. 3. Letter to Hans von Wolzogen, in Bruckner, *Gesammelte Briefe,* ed. Max Auer (Regensburg, 1924), 168.

Chapter 59   1. Nikolay Rimsky-Korsakov, *My Musical Life,* trans. Judah A. Joffe (London, 1974), 28. 2. Quoted in Francis Maes, *A History of Russian Music: From "Kamarinskaya" to "Babi Yar,"* trans. Arnold J. Pomerans and Erica Pomerans (Berkeley, 2002), 43. 3. *The Musorgsky Reader,* ed. Jay Leyda and Sergei Bertensson (New York, 1947), 215. 4. *The Musorgsky Reader,* 112. 5. From Roland John Wiley, *Tchaikovsky's Ballets* (Oxford, 1985), 373–74. 6. Wiley, *Tchaikovsky's Ballets,* 229.

Chapter 60   1. Natalie Bauer-Lechner, *Recollections of Gustav Mahler,* trans. Dika Newlin (Cambridge, 1980), 130. 2. Bauer-Lechner, *Recollections of Gustav Mahler,* 130. 3. Alma Mahler, *Gustav Mahler: Memories and Letters,* ed. Donald Mitchell, trans. Basil Creighton, 3d ed. (Seattle, 1975), 217–18. 4. *Selected Letters of Gustav Mahler,* eds. Alma Mahler and Knud Martner, trans. Eithne Wilkins, Ernst Kaiser, and Bill Hopkins (New York, 1979), 179. 5. Alma Mahler, *Gustav Mahler,* 297. 6. Letter of 19 December 1901. The text is given in full in Henry-Louis de La Grange, *Gustav Mahler,* 3 vols. (Oxford and New York, 1995), II, 448–52.

Chapter 61   1. Quoted in Alan Walker, *Franz Liszt,* 3 vols. (Ithaca, 1996), III, 486. 2. *Leeds Mercury,* 6 October 1898, cited in Jerrold Northrop Moore, *Edward Elgar: A Creative Life* (Oxford, 1984), 244. 3. Rosa Burley and Frank C. Carruthers, *Edward Elgar: The Record of a Friendship* (London, 1972), 68–69. 4. Cited in Moore, *Edward Elgar,* 260. 5. From program notes for the premier performance, 19 June 1899, quoted in Moore, *Edward Elgar,* 270.

Chapter 62   none

Chapter 63   1. Letter of 25 January 1916, in *Debussy Letters,* ed. François Lesure and Roger Nichols, trans. Roger Nichols (Cambridge, MA, 1987), 313. 2. *Debussy Letters,* 188. 3. Claude Debussy, "The Nursery, Poem and Music by M. Moussorgsky" (1901), in *Debussy on Music,* trans. and ed. Richard Langham Smith (Ithaca, 1988), 20. 4. *Debussy on Music,* 295–97. 5. Arnold Schoenberg, "Composition with Twelve Tones" (1941), in *Style and Idea,* ed. Leonard Stein, trans. Leo Black (Berkeley, 1984), 216. 6. *Debussy Letters,* 155. 7. *Debussy on Music,* 74. 8. Quoted in Léon Vallas, *Claude Debussy: His Life and Works,* trans. Maire and Grace O'Brien (London, 1933), 112.

PART VII

Chapter 64   1. Alma Mahler, *Gustav Mahler: Memories and Letters,* ed. Donald Mitchell, trans. Basil Creighton, 3d ed. (Seattle, 1975), 239. 2. Hugo Riemann, "Degeneration und Regeneration in der Musik" (1908), in *Die Konfusion in der Musik: Felix Draesekes Kampfschrift von 1906 und ihre Folgen,* ed. Susanne Shigihara (Bonn, 1990), 248. 3. *Die Konfusion in der Musik,* 41–62. 4. Richard Strauss, *Recollections and Reflections,* ed. Willi Schuh, trans. L. J. Lawrence (Westport, CT, 1974), 16. 5. Strauss, *Recollections and Reflections,* 13.

Chapter 65   1. Michel Fokine, *Fokine: Memoirs of a Ballet Master,* trans. Vitale Fokine (Boston and Toronto, 1961), 49. 2. Carl Van Vechten, "Music and Bad Manners," in *Music and Bad Manners* (New York, 1916), 34. 3. Igor Stravinsky, "Ce que j'ai voulu exprimer dans *Le Sacre du Printemps*" (1913), in *Le Sacre du Printemps: Dossier de Presse,* ed. François Lesure (Geneva, 1980), 13–15. 4. Sergei Prokofiev, "Autobiography," in *Soviet Diary 1927 and Other Writings,* trans. Oleg Prokofiev (Boston, 1992), 258.

Chapter 66   1. August Macke and Franz Marc, *Briefwechsel* (Cologne, 1964), 40. 2. Vasili Kandinsky, "Über die Formfrage," in *Der blaue Reiter* (Munich, 1912), 74–100. 3. Arnold Schoenberg, *Wass-*

ily Kandinsky: Letters, Pictures and Documents, ed. Jelena Hahl-Koch, trans. John C. Crawford (London and Boston, 1984), 21. 4. *Arnold Schoenberg, Wassily Kandinsky*, 23. 5. Arnold Schoenberg, "Composition with Twelve Tones" (1941), in *Style and Idea*, ed. Leonard Stein, trans. Leo Black (Berkeley, 1984), 217. 6. Arnold Schoenberg, *Theory of Harmony*, trans. Roy E. Carter (Berkeley and Los Angeles, 1978), 420. 7. Letter to Ferruccio Busoni, ca. August 1909, in *Busoni, Selected Letters*, ed. and trans. Antony Beaumont (New York, 1987), 389. 8. *The Berg-Schoenberg Correspondence: Selected Letters*, ed. Juliane Brand, Christopher Hailey, and Donald Harris (New York and London, 1987), 60.

Chapter 67 1. Maurice Ravel, "Contemporary Music" (1928), in *Composers on Modern Musical Culture*, ed. Bryan R. Simms (New York, 1999), 92. 2. *Debussy Letters*, ed. François Lesure and Roger Nichols, trans. Roger Nichols (Cambridge, MA, 1987), 291. 3. Ferruccio Busoni, *Selected Letters*, trans. and ed. Antony Beaumont (New York, 1987), 186. 4. 20 August 1914, in *A Ravel Reader: Correspondence, Articles, Interviews*, ed. Arbie Orenstein (New York, 1990), 152. 5. Letter to Familie Weber, 23 September 1914, in *Paul Hindemith Briefe*, ed. Dieter Rexroth (Frankfurt, 1982), 35. 6. Ernest Newman, "The War and the Future of Music," *Musical Times*, 55 (1 September 1914): 571.

Chapter 68 1. Darius Milhaud, "The Evolution of the Jazz Band and Music of the Negroes of North America" (1923), in *Composers on Modern Musical Culture*, ed. and trans. Bryan R. Simms (New York, 1999), 239. 2. Igor Stravinsky, *An Autobiography* (New York, 1962), 53. 3. Stravinsky, *An Autobiography*, 97. 4. Edward Evans, "Igor Stravinsky: Contrapuntal Titan," *Musical America* (February 12, 1921). 5. Igor Stravinsky and Robert Craft, *Dialogues* (Berkeley and Los Angeles, 1982), 40. 6. Igor Stravinsky, "Some Ideas About my Octuor," *The Arts* 5/1 (January 1924): 5–6. 7. Darius Milhaud, *My Happy Life*, trans. Donald Evans, George Hall, and Christopher Palmer (London and New York, 1995), 70–71. 8. Darius Milhaud, "The Composer on His Work: 'I am always interested in what is coming,'" *Christian Science Monitor*, May 20, 1968.

Chapter 69 1. Stefan Zweig, *The World of Yesterday* (Lincoln, NE, 1964), 295–96. 2. Zweig, *The World of Yesterday*, 296. 3. Josef Matthias Hauer, "Die Tropen," *Musikblätter des Anbruch* 6/1 (1924): 18. 4. Josef Hauer, *Vom Wesen des Musikalischen* (Vienna, 1920), 53. 5. Arnold Schoenberg, *Letters*, ed. Erwin Stein, trans. Eithne Wilkins and Ernst Kaiser (New York, 1965), 164–65.

Chapter 70 1. "Berg's Lecture on 'Wozzeck'" (1929), in H. F. Redlich, *Alban Berg: The Man and his Music* (London, 1957), 261–85.

Chapter 71 1. Béla Bartók, *Letters*, ed. János Demény, trans. Péter Balabán, István Farkas (New York, 1971), 29. 2. Bartók, *Letters*, 153. 3. Béla Bartók, "The Folk Songs of Hungary" (1928), in *Béla Bartók Essays*, ed. Benjamin Suchoff (Lincoln and London, 1976), 333. 4. Béla Bartók, "The Influence of Peasant Music on Modern Music" (1931), in *Béla Bartók Essays*, 341–44. 5. Béla Bartók, "Explanation to Concerto for Orchestra," in *Béla Bartók Essays*, 431.

Chapter 72 1. Aaron Copland, "Jazz Structure and Influence," *Modern Music* 4/2 (1927): 9–14. 2. Rudi Blesh, *Shining Trumpets: A History of Jazz* (New York, 1958), 176. 3. Gunther Schuller, *Early Jazz: Its Roots and Musical Development* (New York and Oxford, 1968), 58. 4. Scott Joplin, *School of Ragtime: Exercises for Piano* (New York, 1908), 3. 5. James Reese Europe, "A Negro Explains 'Jazz'" (1919), in *Readings in Black American Music*, ed. Eileen Southern (New York, 1971), 225. 6. Benjamin Latrobe, *Impressions Respecting New Orleans*, ed. Samuel Wilson, Jr. (New York, 1951), 49–50. 7. Alan Lomax, *Mister Jelly Roll: The Fortunes of Jelly Roll Morton, New Orleans Creole and "Inventor of Jazz,"* 2nd ed. (Berkeley, 1973), 12.

Chapter 73 1. Arnold Schoenberg, *Letters*, ed. Erwin Stein, trans. Eithne Wilkins and Ernst Kaiser (New York, 1965), 92–93. 2. Paul Hindemith, "Sterbende Gewässer" (1963), in *Aufsätze, Vorträge, Reden*, ed. Giselher Schubert (Zurich and Mainz, 1994), 326–27. 3. Wilhelm Furtwängler, "The Hindemith Case," in *Furtwängler on*

Music: Essays and Addresses, ed. and trans. Ronald Taylor (Brookfield, VT, 1991), 117–20.

Chapter 74 1. Sergei Prokofiev, "Autobiography" (1941) in *Soviet Diary 1927 and Other Writings*, trans. Oleg Prokofiev (Boston, 1991), 264. 2. *Dmitri Shostakovich About Himself and his Times*, trans. Angus and Neilian Roxburgh (Moscow, 1981), 33. 3. Andrei Zhdanov, "Soviet Literature: The Richest in Ideas, the Most Advanced Literature," in *Problems of Soviet Literature: Reports and Speeches at the First Soviet Writers' Congress*, ed. H. G. Scott (New York, 1935), 21. 4. Sergei Prokofiev, "Autobiography," 297. 5. *Selected Letters of Sergei Prokofiev*, ed. and trans. Harlow Robinson (Boston, 1998), 94–95. 6. Sviatoslav Richter, "On Prokofiev," in *Sergei Prokofiev: Materials, Articles, Interviews* (Moscow, 1978), 193. 7. Bruno Walter, *Theme and Variations: An Autobiography*, trans. James A. Galston (New York, 1946), 277–78. 8. Rose Lee, "Dimitri Szostakovich: Young Russian Composer Tells of Linking Politics with Creative Work," *New York Times*, 20 December 1931. 9. Lee, "Dimitri Szostakovich." 10. From an article in *Vechernaya Moskva*, 11 December 1940, in *Dmitri Shostakovich About Himself and His Times*, 83. 11. From an article in *Izvestia*, 3 April 1935, in *Dmitri Shostakovich About Himself and His Times*, 58. 12. The entire essay is found in Francis Maes, *A History of Russian Music from "Kamarinskaya" to "Babi Yar,"* trans. Arnold J. Pomerans, Erica Pomerans (Berkeley, 2002), 299–300. 13. *Testimony: The Memoirs of Dmitri Shostakovich*, ed. Solomon Volkov, trans. Antonina W. Bouis (New York, 1979), 14. From an article in *Sovetskoye Iskusstvo*, 14 December 1933, in *Dmitri Shostakovich About Himself and His Times*, 43.

Chapter 75 1. Ralph Waldo Emerson, "Self-Reliance," in *Selected Essays, Lectures, and Poems*, ed. Robert D. Richardson, Jr. (New York, 1990), 168. 2. William Billings, *The New-England Psalm-Singer: or American Chorister* (Boston, 1770). 3. Charles E. Ives, *Memos*, ed. John Kirkpatrick (New York, 1972), 46. 4. Ives, *Memos*, 183–84. 5. Charles E. Ives, *Essays Before a Sonata*, in *Three Classics in the Aesthetic of Music* (New York, 1962), 162. 6. Charles E. Ives, "Notes to *114 Songs*," in *Composers on Modern Musical Culture*, ed. Bryan R. Simms (New York, 1999), 213. 7. Ives, *Essays Before a Sonata*, 166. 8. Harry Partch, *Genesis of a Music: An Account of a Creative Work, Its Roots and Its Fulfillment*, 2nd ed. (New York, 1974), 52. 9. Charles Seeger, "Tradition and Experiment in (the New) Music," in *Studies in Musicology II: 1929–1979*, ed. Ann M. Pescatello (Berkeley, 1994), 211. 10. Cited in Matilda Gaume, *Ruth Crawford Seeger: Memoirs, Memories, Music* (Metuchen, NJ, and London, 1986), 204.

Chapter 76 1. Aaron Copland and Vivian Perlis, *Copland: 1900 Through 1942* (New York, 1984), 50. 2. Aaron Copland, *Music and Imagination* (New York, 1959), 104. 3. Copland, *Music and Imagination*, 108. 4. Copland, *Music and Imagination*, 111. 5. *Walt Whitman's Leaves of Grass: The First (1855) Edition*, ed. Malcolm Cowley (New York, 1959), 5–6. 6. *Walt Whitman's Leaves of Grass*, 12. 7. Copland, *Music and Imagination*, 112. 8. Aaron Copland, *What to Listen For in Music*, rev. ed. (New York, 1957), 30. 9. *Copland 1900 Through 1942*, 182. 10. Aaron Copland, *Appalachian Spring—Ballet for Martha*, full score (New York and London, 1945), Preface. 11. Copland, *Music and Imagination*, 110–11. 12. *Copland 1900 Through 1942*, 279. 13. Copland, *Music and Imagination*, 117–18. 14. Quoted in Barbara B. Heyman, *Samuel Barber: The Composer and His Music* (New York and Oxford, 1992), 244. 15. Cited in Heyman, *Samuel Barber*, 174.

Chapter 77 none

PART VIII

Chapter 78 1. Editor's note, *Musical Times* (London), 82 (no. 1182: August 1941), 308.

Chapter 79 1. Allen Edwards, *Flawed Words and Stubborn Sounds: A Conservation with Elliott Carter* (New York, 1971), 61. 2. Pierre Boulez, "A Time for Johann Sebastian Bach" (1951), in *Notes of an Apprenticeship*, trans. Herbert Weinstock (New York, 1968), 14. 3. Milton Babbitt, "Twelve-Tone Invariants as Compositional Determinants,"

Musical Quarterly 46 (1960): 246. 4. Milton Babbitt, "Who Cares If You Listen (The Composer as Specialist)" (1958), in *Composers on Modern Musical Culture*, ed. Bryan R. Simms (New York, 1999), 153–59. 5. Pierre Boulez, "Eventually . . ." (1952), in *Notes of an Apprenticeship*, 148. 6. Theodor W. Adorno, *Philosophy of Modern Music*, trans. Anne G. Mitchell and Wesley V. Blomster (New York, 1973), 203. 7. Adorno, *Philosophy of Modern Music*, 68. 8. Randle Cotgrave, *A Dictionarie of the French and English Tongues* (London, 1611), s.v. *Bransle*. 9. Pierre Boulez, "Schönberg Is Dead, *Score* (May 1952): 22. 10. Thomas Meyer, "'Man kann nur einmal Avantgardist sein': Gespräche mit Krzysztof Penderecki," *Neue Zeitschrift für Musik* 150 (December 1989): 19.

Chapter 80   1. Elliott Carter, "Shop Talk by an American Composer" (1960), in *The Writings of Elliott Carter*, eds. Else Stone and Kurt Stone (Bloomington and London, 1977), 206. 2. John Cage, "Composition" (1952), in *Silence* (Middletown, CT, 1961), 59 3. John Cage, "Experimental Music: Doctrine" (1955), in *Silence*, 14. 4. John Cage, "History of Experimental Music in the United States" (1959), in *Silence*, 73. 5. Louise Varèse, *Varèse: A Looking-Glass Diary* (New York, 1972), 257. 6. Edgard Varèse, "New Instruments and New Music" (1936), in "The Liberation of Sound," *Perspectives of New Music* 5 (1966–67): 11. 7. Louise Varèse, *Varèse*, 276. 8. Olivier Messiaen, "Musikalisches Glaubensbekenntnis," *Melos* 25 (1958): 385.

Chapter 81   1. Darius Milhaud, *My Happy Life: An Autobiography*, trans. Donald Evans, George Hall, and Christopher Palmer (New York and London, 1995), 110. 2. Maurice Ravel, "Take Jazz Seriously!," *Musical Digest* 13/3 (March 1928): 49–50.

Musical Interlude 9
1. Based on "Peatman's Annual Survey of Song Hits on Radio and TV," *Variety* (13 January 1954): 50. 2. Rudi Blesh, *Shining Trumpets: A History of Jazz* (New York, 1958), 352. 3. John Harbison, "Uses of Popular Music" (1984), reprinted in *Composers on Modern Musical Culture*, ed. Bryan R. Simms (New York, 1999), 200. 4. Ned Rorem, "The Beatles," in *Music and People* (New York, 1968), 18.

Chapter 82   1. Leonard Bernstein, *The Unanswered Question: Six Talks at Harvard* (Cambridge, MA, and London 1976), 420–21. 2. Luciano Berio, "Poesia e musica: Un' esperienza," from the German version in *Darmstädter Beiträge zur neuen Musik* 2 (1959); 44–45. 3. Jonathan Bernard, "An Interview with Elliott Carter," *Perspectives of New Music* 28/2 (1990): 190. 4. Elliott Carter, "Letter from Europe" (1963), in *The Writings of Elliott Carter*, ed. Else Stone and Kurt Stone (Bloomington and London, 1977), 220.

Chapter 83   1. John Harbison, "Two Tanglewood Talks" (1984), in *Composers on Modern Musical Culture*, ed. Bryan R. Simms (New York, 1999), 204. 2. Pierre Boulez, *Conversation with Célestin Deliège* (London, 1976), 33. 3. George Rochberg, "Reflections on the Renewal of Music" (1972), *Composers on Modern Musical Culture*, 193–94. 4. Rochberg, "Reflections on the Renewal of Music," 195. 5. György Ligeti, "Rhapsodische, unausgewogene Gedanken über Musik, besonders über meine eigenen Kompositionen" (1991), *Neue Zeitschrift für Musik* 154 (January 1993): 28. 6. Quoted in Ann McCutchan, *The Music That Sings: Composers Speak About the Creative Process* (New York and Oxford, 1999), 58–59.

BIBLIOGRAPHY

What follows is a brief, preliminary bibliography. Far more comprehensive bibliographies are included in the Student Workbook and Instructor's Manual for *Music in Western Civilization*, and are also available on the Thomson-Schirmer website (where they are updated). These bibliographies cite only works in the English language. Each of the books and articles contains either its own bibliography or copious footnotes that suggest still more useful sources for research. For help in the challenging task of writing about the ephemeral art of music, see the essay "Writing a Research Paper on a Musical Topic" by Sterling Murray that is included in the Workbook.

DICTIONARIES AND ENCYCLOPEDIAS

By far the most useful tool for research in music—both for scholars and students—is **The New Grove Dictionary of Music and Musicians,** 2nd edition (London: Macmillan, 2001). It is available both in a 29-volume printed edition and online (www.grovemusic.com). Many colleges and universities subscribe to the online version, making it accessible to students at many locations on campus and at home. The online version is continually updated, as contemporary scholarship requires. In addition, the online version includes articles from the more specialized *The New Grove Dictionary of Opera* and *The New Grove Dictionary of Jazz.* Almost every subject dealing with classical and popular, Western and non-Western music, can be found in *The New Grove Dictionary.* Each entry is written by a world-renowned scholar and is followed by its own detailed bibliography. For major composers, a complete list of compositions is given, along with the date of publication or first performance, as well as references to scholarly editions in which a specific piece may be found. Other, much smaller but nonetheless useful, reference tools include:

Baker's Biographical Dictionary of Musicians. New York: Schirmer Books, 2001.

The Harvard Biographical Dictionary of Music. Cambridge, MA: Harvard University Press, 1996.

The Harvard Dictionary of Music, 4th ed., ed. Don Randel. Cambridge, MA: Harvard University Press, 2003.

The Norton/Grove Concise Encyclopedia of Music, ed. Stanley Sadie and Alison Lathan. New York and London: Norton, 1988.

The Norton/Grove Dictionary of Women Composers, ed. Julie Anne Sadie and Rhian Samuel. London and New York: MacMillan and Norton, 1994.

The Oxford Companion to Music, ed. Alison Lathan. Oxford: Oxford University Press, 2002.

PRIMARY-SOURCE DOCUMENTS FOR WESTERN MUSIC

Music in the Western World: A History in Documents, ed. Piero Weiss and Richard Taruskin. New York: Schirmer Books, 1984.

Opera: A History in Documents, ed. Piero Weiss. Oxford: Oxford University Press, 2002.

Readings in the History of Musical Performance, ed. Carol MacClintock. Bloomington, IN: Indiana University Press, 1979.

Source Readings in Music History, ed. Oliver Strunk; rev. edition ed. Leo Treitler. New York and London: Norton, 1998.

HISTORICAL SURVEYS OF WESTERN MUSIC

Part VI: The Romantic Period

Dahlhaus, Carl. *Nineteenth-Century Music,* trans. J. Bradford Robinson. Berkeley and Los Angeles: University of California Press, 1989.

Palantinga, Leon. *Romantic Music.* New York: Norton, 1984.

Whittall, Arnold. *Romantic Music: A Concise History from Schubert to Sibelius.* London: Thames and Hudson, 1987.

Part VII: The Early Twentieth Century

Cook, Nicholas and Anthony Pople, eds. *The Cambridge History of Twentieth-Century Music.* Cambridge: Cambridge University Press, 2004.

Morgan, Robert P. *Twentieth-Century Music: A History of Musical Style in Modern Europe and America.* New York: Norton, 1992.

Salzman, Eric. *Twentieth-Century Music: An Introduction.* Upper Saddle River, NJ: Prentice Hall, 2002.

Simms, Bryan R. *Music of the Twentieth Century: Style and Structure.* New York and London: Schirmer Books, 1996.

Part VIII: Contemporary Music

Griffiths, Paul. *Modern Music and After.* New York: Oxford University Press, 1995.

Nyman, Michael. *Experimental Music: Cage and Beyond.* Cambridge: Cambridge University Press, 1999.

Schwartz, Elliott and Daniel Godfrey. *Music Since 1945: Issues, Materials, and Literature.* New York: Schirmer Books, 1993.

MUSIC JOURNALS

There are hundreds of journals (periodicals containing scholarly articles) dealing with various aspects of the history and performance of Western classical music. Some of these journals regularly publish an index to the articles found in previous issues, but most do not. There are, however, three useful indexes to journals that encompass English as well as foreign-language journals: *Music Index, International Index to Music Periodicals,* and *RILM* (acronym for *Répertoire international de littérature musicale*). All three are available online, usually through a university or college computer network, for a quick search of specific topics.

Thus, to find out more about Mozart's *Don Giovanni* or Copland's *Appalachian Spring*, for example, simply go to one of these sites and type in the title in the appropriate search box. *RILM*, perhaps the most useful of the three, often provides helpful abstracts that allow the reader to determine if the article in question will be of use. For dissertations about musical topics, *Dissertations and Theses—Full Text* has not merely abstracts but, as the title states, entire dissertations and theses online (those written after 1997). Finally, more than forty of the most important music journals now also have back issues online through a link called JSTOR (*Journal Storage: The Scholarly Journal Archive*). Most university and college libraries subscribe to this online service.

❀ ONLINE SEARCH ENGINES FOR ARTICLES, DISSERTATIONS, AND THESES ABOUT MUSIC

Music Index (Warren, MI: Harmony Park Press) http://www.hppmusicindex.com

International Index to Music Periodicals (Alexandria, VA: Chadwyck-Healey Inc.) http://iimpft.chadwyck.com/home

RILM (*Répertoire international de littérature musicale*; New York: International Musicological Society) http://www.rilm.org

Dissertations and Theses—Full Texts (Cambridge: ProQuest Company) *http://proquest.umi.com*

JSTOR (*Journal Storage: The Scholarly Journal Archive*; New York: JSTOR) http://www.jstor.org

❀ IMPORTANT ENGLISH LANGUAGE MUSIC JOURNALS

Journal (earlier *Proceedings*) *of the Royal Musical Association* (British, 1874–)

Musical Quarterly (American, 1915–)

Music and Letters (British, 1920–)

Journal (earlier *Bulletin*) *of the American Musicological Society* (American, 1948–)

Ethnomusicology (American, 1953–)

Journal of Music Theory (American, 1957–)

Perspectives of New Music (American, 1963–)

Early Music (British, 1973–)

19-Century Music (American, 1977–)

Music Theory Spectrum (American, 1979–)

Early Music History (British, 1981–)

Journal of Musicology (American, 1981–)

Popular Music (British, 1981–)

American Music (American, 1983–)

CREDITS

472 (above) CORBIS; 472 (below) CORBIS; 473 CORBIS; 477 COR-BIS; 481 An Evening at Baron von Spaun's: Schubert at the piano among his friends, including the operatic baritone Heinrich Vogl (1845–1900) (drawing), Schwind, Moritz Ludwig von (1804–71) Historisches Museum der Stadt, Vienna, Austria. Bridgeman Art Library, London, UK/www.bridgeman.co.uk; 486 Liberty Leading the People, 28 July 1830 (oil on canvas) Delacroix, (Ferdinand Victor) Eugene (1798–1863) Louvre, Paris, France. Bridgeman Art Library, London, UK/www.bridgeman.co.uk; 501 (above) The Leipzig Gewandhaus with a piece of music by Felix Mendelssohn (1809–47) (w/c on paper), German School, (19th century) Private Collection. Bridgeman Art Library, London, UK/www.bridgeman.co.uk; 501 (below) Bildarchiv Preussischer Kulturbesitz/Art Resource, NY; 509 CORBIS; 515 Portrait of Richard Wagner (1813–83) (oil on canvas), Lenbach, Franz Seraph von (1836–1904) Wagner Museum, Bayreuth, Germany. Bridgeman Art Library, London, UK/www.bridgeman.co.uk; 516 © Vanni/Art Resource, NY; 522 Portrait of Gioacchino Rossini (1792–1868) (oil on canvas), Italian School, (19th century) Museo Civico, Bologna, Italy, Alinari. Bridgeman Art Library, London, UK/www.bridgeman.co.uk; 527 Guiseppe Verdi (1813–1901) 1877 (b/w photo) (see also 124001), Carjat, Etienne (1828–1906) Museo di Storia della Fotografia Fratelli Alinari, Florence. Bridgeman Art Library, London, UK/www.bridgeman.co.uk; 531 Portrait of Franz Liszt (1811–86) August 1832 (litho) (b/w photo), Deveria, Achille (1800–57) Bibliotheque de L'Opera, Paris, France, Giraudon. Bridgeman Art Library, London, UK/www.bridgeman.co.uk; 532 Portrait of the Countess Marie d'Agoult (1805–76) 1843 (oil on canvas), Lehmann, Henri (Karl Ernest Rudolf Heinrich Salem) (1814–82) Musee de la Vie Romantique, Paris, France, Archives Charmet. Bridgeman Art Library, London, UK/www.bridgeman.co.uk; 534 Caricature depicting Franz Liszt (1811–1886) playing the piano, 1845 (litho) (b/w photo), French School, (19th century) Musee de la Ville de Paris, Musee Carnavalet, Paris, France, Archives Charmet. Bridgeman Art Library, London, UK/www.bridgeman.co.uk; 540 (above) © Snark/Art Resource, NY; 540 (below) CORBIS; 541 Court Ball at the Hofburg, 1900 (w/c), Gause, Wilhelm (1853–1916) Historisches Museum der Stadt, Vienna, Austria. Bridgeman Art Library, London, UK/www.bridgeman.co.uk; 551 Portrait of Modest Petrovich Moussorgsky (1839–81) 1881 (oil on canvas), Repin, Ilya Efimovich (1844–1930) Tretyakov Gallery, Moscow, Russia. Bridgeman Art Library, London, UK/www.bridgeman.co.uk; 553 Marie Taglioni (1804–84) in 'Flore et Zephire' by Cesare Bossi, c.1830 (litho), Chalon, Alfred-Edward (1780–1860) (after) Victoria & Albert Museum, London, UK. Bridgeman Art Library, London, UK/www.bridgeman.co.uk; 558 Portrait photograph of Gustav Mahler/Private Collection. Bridgeman Art Library, London, UK/www.bridgeman.co.uk; 564 CORBIS; 567 Sir Edward Elgar (1857–1934) (photo) Private Collection. Bridgeman Art Library, London, UK/www.bridgeman.co.uk; 571 CORBIS; 575 Photo courtesy of Opera News; 580 The Scale of Love, 1715–18 (oil on canvas), Watteau, Jean Antoine (1684–1721) National Gallery, London, UK, Giraudon. Bridgeman Art Library, London, UK/www.bridgeman.co.uk; 581 Wild Poppies, near Argenteuil (Les Coquelicots: environs d'Argenteuil), 1873, Monet, Claude (1840–1926) Musee d'Orsay, Paris, France, Giraudon. Bridgeman Art Library, London, UK/www.bridgeman.co.uk; 587 Bibliothèque Nationale, Paris; 590 (above) CORBIS; 590 (below) © Underwood & Underwood/CORBIS;

594 © Hugh Rooney; Eye Ubiquitous/CORBIS; 595 Bettmann/CORBIS; 601 (above) Unexpected, 1884–88 (oil on canvas), Repin, Ilya Efimovich (1844–1930) Tretyakov Gallery, Moscow, Russia. Bridgeman Art Library, London, UK/www.bridgeman.co.uk; 601 (below) The Six Winged Seraph, from 'The Prophet', by Alexander Pushkin (1799–1837), 1905 (charcoal and gouache on paper), Vrubel, Mikhail Aleksandrovich (1856-1910) Pushkin Museum, Moscow, Russia. Bridgeman Art Library, London, UK/www.bridgeman.co.uk; 611 Impression no. 3 (Concert) 1911 (oil on canvas), Kandinsky, Wassily (1866–1944) Stadtische Galerie im Lenbachhaus, Munich, Germany, Peter Willi. Bridgeman Art Library, London, UK/www.bridgeman.co.uk; 613 Self portrait (oil on canvas), Schoenberg, Arnold (1874–1951) Private Collection. Bridgeman Art Library, London, UK/www.bridgeman.co.uk; 624 Self Portrait, early 20th century (pen and ink on paper) (b/w photo), Satie, Erik (1866–1925) Bibliotheque Litteraire Jacques Doucet, Paris, France, Archives Charmet. Bridgeman Art Library, London, UK/www.bridgeman.co.uk; 628 Molen (Mill) The Winkel Mill in Sunlight, 1908 (oil on canvas), Mondrian, Piet (1872–1944) Haags Gemeentemuseum, The Hague, Netherlands. Bridgeman Art Library, London, UK/www.bridgeman.co.uk; 629 (above) Vertical Composition with Blue and White, 1936 (oil on canvas), Mondrian, Piet (1872–1944) Private Collection. Bridgeman Art Library, London, UK/www.bridgeman.co.uk; 629 (below) From Igor Stravinsky and Robert Craft, Conversations with Igor Stravinsky (Berkeley: Univ. of Calif. Press, 1980): p.108; 641 (above) Arnold Schönberg Center, Vienna; 641 (below) Woman in the Meadow at Eragny, Spring, 1887 (oil on canvas), Pissarro, Camille (1831–1903) Musee d'Orsay, Paris, France, Giraudon. Bridgeman Art Library, London, UK/www.bridgeman.co.uk; 646 Cologne, Theater Museum of the University of Cologne; 650 CORBIS; 653 CORBIS; 666 CORBIS; 672 The Isenheim Altarpiece, c.1512–15 (oil on panel) (for details see 81214, 622, 71772), Grunewald, Matthias (Mathis Nithart Gothart) (c.1480–1528) Musee d'Unterlinden, Colmar, France, Giraudon. Bridgeman Art Library, London, UK/www.bridgeman.co.uk; 673 (above) Nativity and concert of angels from the Isenheim Altarpiece, central panel (oil on panel), Grunewald, Matthias (Mathis Nithart Gothart) (c.1480–1528) Musee d'Unterlinden, Colmar, France, Giraudon. Bridgeman Art Library, London, UK/www.bridgeman.co.uk; 673 (below) St. Anthony and St. Paul, detail from the Isenheim Altarpiece, c.1512–16 (oil on panel), Grunewald, Matthias (Mathis Nithart Gothart) (c.1480–1528) Musee d'Unterlinden, Colmar, France. Bridgeman Art Library, London, UK/www.bridgeman.co.uk; 681 Peter and the Wolf (oil on board), Cartwright, Reg (b.1938) Private Collection. Bridgeman Art Library, London, UK/www.bridgeman.co.uk; 682 CORBIS; 688 CORBIS; 694 Photograph courtesy of Peggy Seeger, www.pegseeger.com; 701 CORBIS; 705 CORBIS; 708 CORBIS; 709 Gershwin Trust; 718 (center) CORBIS; 718 (left) CORBIS; 718 (right) CORBIS; 725 Photographs courtesy of Robert Orland, http://historiccoventry.co.uk; 726 CORBIS; 735 CORBIS; 738 CORBIS; 747 Bibliothèque de la Ville, La Chaux-de-Fonds; 747 (below) Marc Treib, Space Calculated in Seconds: The Philips Pavilion, Le Corbusier, Edgard Varèse (Princeton: Princeton Univ. Press, 1996); 753 (above) Courtesy of the Frank Driggs Collection; 753 (below) CORBIS; 756 CORBIS; 760 © Neal Preston/CORBIS; 770 Hallen für neue Kunst, Switzerland; 778 Photograph courtesy of Pekka Loiri, Original Loiri, Inc., www.originalloiri.fi; 779 Photograph © Steve J. Sherman.

GLOSSARY

a cappella: singing without instrumental accompaniment

Abendmusik: an hour-long concert of sacred music with arias and recitatives—something akin to a sacred opera or oratorio; a single religious theme unfolded in music over the course of five late-afternoon performances on the Sundays immediately before and during Advent in the city of Lübeck, Germany

Académie royale de musique: in effect, a French national opera company directly licensed and indirectly financed by the king; it performed in the center of Paris at the Palais Royal

academy: a learned society, sometimes devoted to presenting concerts; in Germany in the eighteenth century the term often referred to a public concert

acciaccatura: a technique of crunching dissonant chords used by Domenico Scarlatti

accompanied recitative: a recitative that features a full orchestral accompaniment; it appears occasionally in the sacred vocal music of Bach, but was used more extensively in the operas of Gluck and later composers.

Aeolian: the first of the four new modes added to the canon of eight medieval church modes by Heinrich Glarean in 1547; first official recognition of the minor mode

aggregate: in twelve-tone composition, a contiguous statement of the twelve notes with none repeated except in an immediate or repetitive context

agréments: French word for ornaments, or embellishments

air de cour: the French term for a simple, strophic song for a single voice or a small group of soloists

Alberti bass: an animation of simple triads brought about by playing the notes successively and in a pattern; a distinctive component of the style of keyboard composer Domenico Alberti (c1710–1746)

allemande: French for the "German" dance and usually the first dance in a Baroque suite; a stately dance in $\frac{4}{4}$ meter at a moderate tempo with upbeat and gracefully interweaving lines that create an improvisatory-like style

alternatim technique: a technique in which the verses of a chant are assigned to alternating performing forces, such as an organ and a choir

Ambrosian chant: a body of chant created by Ambrose (340?–397 C.E.) for the church of Milan in northern Italy

Amen cadence: a final phrase setting the word "Amen"; more specifically, a plagal cadence that English composers in particular employed to set "Amen" giving a piece an emphatic conclusion

antecedent phrase: the opening, incomplete-sounding phrase of a melody; often followed by a consequent phrase that brings closure to the melody

anthem: a sacred vocal composition, much like a motet but sung in English, in honor of the Lord or invoking the Lord to preserve and protect the English king or queen

antiphon: in antiphonal singing the short chant sung before and after a psalm and its doxology

antiphonal singing: a method of musical performance in which a divided choir alternately sings back and forth

Aquitanian polyphony: a repertory of about sixty-five pieces of two-voice organum surviving today from various monasteries in Aquitaine in southwestern France

arcicembalo: a sixteenth-century harpsichord constructed in Ferrara, Italy, that had two keyboards, each with three rows of keys

aria: an elaborate, lyrical song for solo voice more florid, more expansive, and more melodious than a recitative or arioso; an aria invariably sets a short poem made up of one or more stanzas

arioso style: an expressive manner of singing somewhere between a recitative and a full-blown aria

Ars antiqua: the music of the thirteenth century characterized by a uniform pace and clear ternary units (as contrasted with the *Ars nova* of the early fourteenth century)

Ars nova: musical *avant garde* of the early fourteenth century characterized by duple as well as triple relationships and a wide variety of note values (as contrasted with the *Ars antiqua* of the thirteenth century)

Ars subtilior: (more subtle art) a style of music exhibited by composers working in Avignon and other parts of southern France and northern Italy during the late fourteenth century; marked by the most subtle, sometimes extreme, rhythmic relationships

Artusi-Monteverdi Controversy: the conflict between Claudio Monteverdi, who composed in a new style inspired by a text-driven approach to musical composition, and Giovanni Maria Artusi, a churchman and conservative music theorist who advocated the older style of music that followed traditional rules of harmony and counterpoint, and who characterized Monteverdi's music as harsh and offensive to the ear

atonal music: twentieth-century harmony lacking consistent tonal center; atonal music normally has no large-scale functional harmonic progressions, uses tones of the full chromatic scale as though structurally equivalent, and emphasizes dissonant chords of any size and intervallic make-up

atonality: see atonal music

aulos: an ancient Greek wind instrument played in pairs that produced a high, clear, penetrating sound

authentic mode: in the eight church modes the authentic is the first of each of the four pairs of modes; each authentic mode has a corresponding lower mode (plagal), but both modes of the pair end on the same final pitch

BACH motive: a motive consisting of the tones B♭ A C B♮ (the musical letters in Bach's name, according to German usage); found in compositions by J.S. Bach himself and many later composers

Bach Revival: a movement originating in Germany in the early nineteenth century by which Bach's entire compositional oeuvre was published and performed

Bach-Abel concerts: a series of public concerts begun in London in 1764 by J.C. Bach (son of J.S.) and another German musician, Carl Abel; the concerts featured the most recent works of Bach and Abel as well as other fashionable composers; continuing for nearly twenty years, they became a model for the public concert series in London and on the Continent

bagatelle: a short instrumental composition

ballad: (1) a narrative poem or its musical setting; (2) a traditional, usually strophic, song that tells a lengthy story; in popular music, a love song in a slow tempo

ballad opera: a type of popular eighteenth-century English musical theater using re-texted ballads (or other popular songs) and spoken dialogue rather than recitative

ballade: one of the three French *formes fixes* that originated in the Middle Ages; a song always with the form AAB setting a poem with from one to three stanzas, or strophes; employs a lyrical melody accompanied by one or two voices or instruments

ballata: a dance song with a choral refrain; one of the three *formes fixes* of secular music in trecento Italy

ballet: a theatrical genre made from regulated dancing and mime, accompanied by orchestra

ballet de cour: (court ballet) a type of elaborate ballet with songs and choruses danced at the French royal court from the late sixteenth to the late seventeenth century in which members of the court appeared alongside professional dancers

ballet variations: passages in a ballet featuring soloistic dancing

Baroque: the term used generally to describe the art, architecture, and music of the period 1600–1750

baryton: a *viola da gamba*-like instrument with six strings

bas instruments: (soft instruments) one of the two classifications of instruments in the fifteenth century; constituted no set group but could include recorder, vielle, lute, harp, psaltery, portative organ, and harpsichord, individually or in combination

basse danse: the principal aristocratic dance of court and city during the early Renaissance; a slow and stately dance in which the dancers' feet glided close to the ground

basso continuo: a bass line that provided a never-ending foundation, or "continuous bass," for the melody above; also a small ensemble of usually two instruments that played this support

basso ostinato: a bass line that insistently repeats, note for note

bebop: a style of jazz originating in the 1940s for small improvising ensembles, often in fast tempos

Bebung: German term for the vibrating sound produced by the clavichord technique of holding and "wiggling" a key up and down

Belle époque: (beautiful era) name often given to the years straddling the turn of the twentieth century in France

big band: the dominant medium of jazz during the 1930s and 1940s; big bands typically numbered about fifteen players, divided into a rhythm section (usually piano, bass, guitar, and drums) and choirs of saxophones (doubling on clarinets), trumpets, and trombones

binary form: a structure consisting of two complementary parts, the first moving to a closely related key and the second beginning in that new key but soon returning to the tonic

blue note: a lowered scale degree (usually the third and seventh) in the major mode in blues and other jazz styles

blues: originally an improvised strophic folk song containing a succession of three-line stanzas, each sung to a twelve-measure phrase and using a standard recurrent harmonic progression; the blues form is also applicable to instrumental jazz

blues chorus: a principal subsection of a jazz work in blues form, usually twelve-measures in duration

bolero: Spanish dance in triple meter

boogie woogie: a style of piano blues with a driving ostinato accompaniment

bop: see **bebop**

branle (bransle): a fifteenth- and sixteenth-century group dance

break: in jazz, a sudden and momentary pause during which a player introduces an improvised solo

breve: one of the three basic note values and shapes recognized by Franco of Cologne around 1280 in his classification of musical durations

bridge: see **transition**

brindisi: a drinking song, often found in nineteenth-century Italian opera

Broadway musical: see **musical**

broken consort: a mixed ensemble of different types of instruments

burden: the refrain with which an English carol begins and which is repeated after each stanza

Burgundian cadence: (octave-leap cadence) when three voices are present, the contratenor often jumps an octave at a cadence to avoid parallel fifths and dissonances and to fill in the texture of the final chord

Buxheim Organ Book: one of the largest sources of Renaissance organ music; written about 1470, it contains 256 mostly anonymous compositions notated in tablature for organ, almost all of which are arrangements of sacred and secular vocal music

BWV (Bach Werke Verzeichnis): Bach Work List; an identifying system for the works of Johann Sebastian Bach, which functions much like the "K" numbers used for Mozart's works

Byzantine chant: the special dialect of chant developed by the Byzantine Church; it was eventually notated and a body of music theory emerged to explain it

cabaletta: the fast, virtuosic concluding part of an aria or duet, often found in nineteenth-century Italian opera

cabaret: a popular entertainment including songs, skits, and dancing

caccia: a piece involving a musical canon in the upper two voices supported by a slower moving tenor; one of the three *formes fixes* of secular music in trecento Italy

cadenza: a technically demanding, rhapsodic, improvisatory passage for a soloist near the end of a movement

call and response: a style of African-American song alternating phrases

between two individuals, or between an individual leader and a group

canon: imitation of a complete subject at a fixed interval and time delay; in a canon (round) the following voice(s) must duplicate exactly the pitches and rhythms of the first, as for example in "Row, row, row your boat"

canonical hours (liturgical offices): a set of eight periods of worship occurring throughout the day and observed in monasteries and convents; first prescribed in the Rule of St. Benedict (c530 C.E.)

canso: the name for a song in southern medieval France, in langue d'oc (occitan)

cantata: the primary genre of vocal chamber music in the Baroque era; it was "something sung" as opposed to a sonata, which was "sounded" on an instrument; in its mature state it consisted of several movements, including one or more arias and recitatives; cantatas can be on secular subjects, but those of J.S. Bach are primarily sacred in content

cantate française: virtually identical to the late seventeenth-century Italian chamber cantata except that it set a French rather than an Italian text

canticle: a particularly lyrical and memorable passage of scripture usually drawn from the New Testament of the Bible

cantiga: a medieval Spanish or Portuguese monophonic song; hundreds were created on subjects of love, epic heroism, and everyday life

cantor: the practitioner who performs music, as distinguished from the *musicus*; in a medieval monastery or nunnery the person specially trained to lead the music of the community who sat with one of the two groups and led the singing

cantrix in a convent, the main female singer and, in effect, the director of the choir

cantus: the highest vocal part in an early polyphonic composition, what would later come to be called the superius and finally the soprano

cantus firmus: a well-established, previously existing melody, be it a sacred chant or a secular song, that usually sounds in long notes and provides a structural framework for a polyphonic composition

cantus firmus Mass: a cyclic Mass in which the five movements of the Ordinary are unified by means of a single cantus firmus

canzona: a freely composed instrumental piece, usually for organ or instrumental ensemble, which imitated the lively rhythms and lightly imitative style of the Parisian chanson

cappella: (1) a building consecrated for religious worship; (2) an organized group of highly trained musicians who sang at the services in such a chapel

cappella pontificia sistina: the pope's private vocal ensemble as it came to be called in the early seventeenth century and that sang in the Sistine Chapel

carnival song: a short, homophonic piece associated with carnival season, the text of which usually deals with everyday life on the streets

carol: a strophic song for one to three voices setting a religious text, usually associated with Christmas

carole: one of two main types of dances of the Middle Ages; a song and dance that often made use of the musical form called strophe plus refrain, in which a series of stanzas would each end with the same refrain; singers and dancers grouped in a circle and a soloist sang each successive strophe of text, while everyone else joined in for the refrain

castrato: an adult male singer who had been castrated as a boy to keep his voice from changing so that it would remain in the soprano or alto register

cauda (pl., caudae): in the vocabulary of the medieval musical theorist, a long melisma on a single syllable; used in a conductus to set off key words

cavatina: in eighteenth- and nineteenth-century Italian opera, an entrance aria; in German opera a simple aria in a slow or moderate tempo

Cecilianism: movement in Catholic Church music in Germany in the nineteenth century that favored the reintroduction of a pure style based on sixteenth-century principles

celesta: a small keyboard instrument on which tones are sounded by hammers striking metal bars

chamber cantata: a cantata performed before a select audience in a private residence; intimate vocal chamber music, principally of the Baroque era

chance music: twentieth-century music in which compositional decisions are made by chance procedures

chanson: the French word for song, monophonic or polyphonic

chansonnier: a book of songs, as created by musicians in the Middle Ages and Renaissance; a collected anthology of chansons

chant: monophonic religious music that is sung in a house of worship

character piece: a short instrumental work (especially for piano or orchestra) that establishes a particular mood

Charleston: a popular dance of the 1920s, fast in tempo with a distinctive asymmetrical rhythm

chekker: original name for the clavichord in England

choir: the eastern end of a cathedral or large church; contained the high altar and was the area in which most music was made; an ensemble of singers

choir festival: special occasion for the performance of choral and orchestral music; especially prominent in Germany and England during the nineteenth and twentieth centuries

choir school: a school that took boys at about the age of six, gave them an education with a strong emphasis on music, especially singing, and prepared them for a lifetime of service within the church

choirbook format: a layout common for writing religious music from the late Middle Ages onward in which the soprano voice was on the upper left, the alto or tenor on bottom left, alto or tenor in upper right, and the bass on the bottom right; contrasted with written music today where all the parts are superimposed on one another

chorale: a monophonic spiritual melody or religious folksong of the Lutheran church, what today is called by many Christian denominations a "hymn"

chorale cantata: a genre of sacred vocal music that employs the text and tune of a pre-existing Lutheran chorale in all or several of its movements

chorale fantasia: a lengthy composition for organ that takes a chorale tune as a point of departure but increasingly gives free rein to the composer's imagination

chorale prelude: an ornamental setting of a pre-existing chorale tune intended to be played on the organ before the singing of the chorale by the full congregation

Choralis Constantinus: a collection of nearly three hundred fifty motet-like compositions of Heinrich Isaac (c1450–1518) setting polyphonically all the Proper chants of the Catholic Mass; the first systematic attempt to provide polyphony for the entire church year since the twelfth century

chord inversion: a revolutionary principal codified by Jean-Philippe Rameau in his *Treatise on Harmony* holding that a triad may have different pitches other than the root in the bass but without changing the identity of the triad

choreographer: in ballet, the creator of the dance steps

chorus: a group of singers performing together; in jazz, a basic phrase in blues

(usually spanning twelve measures), or a refrain in a popular song

chromatic genus: a tetrachord employed by the ancient Greeks consisting of two semi-tones and a minor third

chronos: in ancient Greek musical notation the basic unit of time—a short value

church modes: the eight melodic patterns into which medieval theorists categorized the chants of the church; the four principal ones are Dorian, Phrygian, Lydian, and Mixolydian

ciaconna (chaconne): originally a separate and distinct bass melody, but during the seventeenth century the term came to mean almost any repeating bass pattern of short duration

cimbalom: a Hungarian dulcimer

circle of fifths: an arrangement of the tonic pitches of the twelve major and minor keys by ascending or descending perfect fifths, C-G-D-A etc., for example, which, because of the enharmonic equivalency of F♯ and G♭, ultimately come full circle back to C

clarino register: the very high register of the trumpet; playing in this register was a special technique of Baroque trumpeters that was exploited by Baroque composers

clausula (pl., clausulae): section, phrase, or "musical clause" in a medieval composition

clavecin: French word for harpsichord; the favorite chamber keyboard instrument in the late seventeenth and early eighteenth centuries

clavichord: a keyboard instrument that makes sound when a player depresses a key and thereby pushes a small metal tangent in the shape of a "T" upward to strike a string; the sound produced is very quiet, the softest of any musical instrument

closed ending: the term used in the Middle Ages for what we today call a second ending

coda: the musical section appended to a piece to add extra weight to the end to give it a feeling of conclusion

Codex Calixtinus: manuscript that survives today at the cathedral at Santiago de Compostela, Spain, written around 1150 and once believed to be the work of Pope Calixtus II; contains a service for St. James, which includes twenty polyphonic pieces; important in the history of Western music because it is the first manuscript to ascribe composers' names to particular pieces

colla parte: a technique in which all the instrumental parts double the vocal lines

collegium musicum: an association of musicians in eighteenth-century Germany, consisting usually of university students, who came together voluntarily to play the latest music in a public setting such as a large café or beer hall

color: the melodic unit that serves as a structural backbone in an isorhythmic composition

coloratura: florid figuration assigned to the soprano voice in an opera; also the high female voice capable of singing such a florid part

colossal Baroque: name for the style of large-scale sacred music employing multiple choirs of voices and instruments and sung in largest churches in Rome, Venice, Vienna, and Salzburg

combinatoriality: the capacity of two forms of a twelve-tone row to create multidimensional aggregates

combo: a small jazz ensemble

comic opera: a simple, direct type of musical theater that made use of comic characters, dealt with everyday social issues, and emphasized values more in step with those of the middle class

comping: the playing of accompanimental chords by a pianist or other instrumentalist in jazz

complementary hexachords: two collections of notes, each having six tones, which together contain all tones of the chromatic scale

complete works edition: a musical edition containing the complete oeuvre of a composer

compound melody: a melody made from two or more simultaneous stepwise strands whose tones are touched alternately

conceptual art: a loosely defined movement in art of the 1960s and 1970s in which the artist calls attention to ideas by which the art work is created rather than to traditional artistic objects

concert overture: an orchestral piece in one movement, usually programmatic in content, and intended for concert purposes

Concert spirituel: one of the first and foremost public concert series founded in Paris in 1725; originally formed to give a public hearing to religious music sung in Latin, its repertory soon came to emphasize instrumental symphonies and concertos as well

concert symphony: a three- or four-movement instrumental work projecting the unified sounds of an orchestra; has its origins in the Enlightenment

concertante: a special orchestral style; a concerto-like approach to the use of the orchestra in which individual instruments regularly emerge from the orchestral texture to function as soloists

concerted madrigal: a madrigal in the concertato style with strong contrasts in textures and timbres involving voices and instruments

concerted motet: a motet in the concertato style with strong contrasts in textures and timbres involving voices and instruments

concertino: the small group of solo performers in a concerto grosso

concerto: a purely instrumental piece for ensemble in which one or more soloists both complement and compete with a full orchestra

concerto delle donne: (ensemble of ladies) a group of female singers employed by the duke of Ferrara at the end of the sixteenth century; they constituted the first professional ensemble of women employed by a court

concerto grosso: a concerto in which a larger body of performers, namely the full orchestra (the ripieno, or tutti), contrasts with a smaller group of soloists (the concertino)

concerto-sonata form: a form, originating in the concerto of the Classical period, in which first the orchestra and then the soloist present the primary thematic material; much like sonata form but with two expositions

concrete music: see musique concrète

conductus: an extra-liturgical piece written for one, two, three, or occasionally four voices with texts that are metrical Latin poems arranged in successive stanzas; although not part of the canonical liturgy, most were serious and moralistic in tone; often used to accompany the movement of the clergy from one place to another in and around the church

confraternity: a Christian society of laymen emphasizing religious devotion and charity; in Florence performing laude was an essential part of their fraternal life

Congress of Vienna the meeting called by Emperor Francis I, King of Austria—after Napoleon Bonaparte abdicated his throne and fled France—inviting all the leaders of Europe to meet to redraw the boundaries of their continent and reestablish principles of legitimate rule

consequent phrase: the second phrase of a two-part melodic unit that brings a melody to a point of repose and closure

consort: an ensemble of instruments all of one family

consort song: one of two forms of the solo art song that flourished in England around 1600; the voice is accompanied by a group of independent instruments, usually a consort of viols

contenance angloise: the "English manner" of composition that fifteenth-century Continental musicians admired and adopted, though the exact nature of this style is not known

contrafactum (pl., contrafacta): the transformation of a piece of music from a secular piece to a sacred one, or (less often) from a sacred to a secular one

contralto: a low alto (a low female voice)

contratenor altus the upper of the two contratenor voices (the other being the bass); the medieval equivalent of our alto voice

contratenor bassus: the lower of the two contratenor voices (the other being the alto); the medieval equivalent of our bass voice

conversation books: notebooks used (by Beethoven and others with a hearing impairment) to communicate; one hundred forty of Beethoven's conversation books survive today

cool jazz: a style of jazz of the 1950s characterized by subdued playing and moderate tempos

Coptic chant: the music of the Christian Church of Egypt, which still exists today, passed along for nearly 2000 years entirely by oral tradition

cori spezzati: music for two, three, or four choirs placed in different parts of a building

cornett: a wooden instrument with fingerholes that is played with a mouthpiece and sounds in the soprano range with a tone something like a soft trumpet

Council of Trent: (1545–1563) a congress of bishops and cardinals held at the small town of Trento in the Italian Alps; the institutionalization of the spirit of the Counter-Reformation; its decision regarding music insisted that music must never interfere with the comprehension of the sacred word

counterpoint: from the Latin punctus contra punctum (one note moving against another note); the harmonious opposition of two or more independent musical lines

counterpoint, dissonant: see dissonant counterpoint

Counter-Reformation: the movement that fostered reform in the Roman Church in response to the challenge of the Protestant Reformation

countersubject: in a fugue, a unit of thematically distinctive material that serves as a counterpoint to the subject

countertenor: a male performer who sings in the alto or soprano range in falsetto voice

couplet: a term used in the rondo form of the seventeenth and eighteenth centuries to indicate an intermediate section (episode) distinctly different from the refrain

courante: a lively dance in triple meter characterized by intentional metrical ambiguity created by means of hemiola; one of the four dances typically making up a Baroque dance suite

Credo: a profession of faith formulated as the result of the Council of Nicaea in 325; one of the five parts of the Ordinary of the Mass

crook: a small piece of pipe that could be inserted in a horn if the player needed to change key; it altered the length of tubing within the instrument and consequently its pitch

crumhorn: a capped double-reed wooden instrument with a curving shape; has the range of a tenth and makes a sound like a kazoo

cultural bolshevism: a catch phrase used by Nazi ideologues to condemn art that was considered decadent on account of its association with foreign, Jewish, or Communist influences

cyclic Mass: a Mass in which all of the movements are linked together by a common musical theme; the first was Machaut's *Mass of Our Lady* composed in the mid fourteenth century

cyclicism: the recurrence of melodic ideas (often transformed) throughout a multimovement or multisectional composition

da camera: (of the chamber) a seventeenth-century designation for music that was not intended primarily for the church

da capo aria: an aria in two sections with an obligatory return to and repeat of the first (hence ABA); the reprise was not written out but signaled by the inscription "da capo" meaning "take it from the top"

da chiesa: (of the church) a seventeenth-century designation for music that was intended primarily for the church

dance suite: an ordered set of dances for solo instrument or ensemble, all written in the same key and intended to be performed in a single sitting

development: in sonata form, the middlemost section in which the themes of the exposition are varied or developed in some fashion; it is often the most confrontational and unstable portion of the movement

diabolus in musica: (devil in music) the dissonant, or disagreeable tritone such as F-B

diatonic genus: the basic genus within the ancient Greek musical system; reflects the primary tetrachord spanning the intervals S-T-T

Dies irae: (*Day of Wrath*) an anonymous thirteenth-century sequence; today the most famous of all medieval sequences, one which serves as the sequence of the requiem Mass

discant: a style of music in which the voices move at roughly the same rate and are written in clearly defined modal rhythms (as compared to organum purum)

diseme: in ancient Greek musical notation a long value of time—formed by two chronoi

dissonant counterpoint: term coined by Charles Seeger to refer to counterpoint in which the traditional roles of consonance and dissonance are reversed

dithyramb: in ancient Greece, a wild choral song, mingled with shouts, that honored Dionysus; a term applied today to any poem with these characteristics

divertimento: originally simply a musical diversion, it came to imply a lighter style of music and a five-movement format: fast/minuet and trio/slow/ minuet and trio/fast; the term was used interchangeably with serenade

divertissement: (1) a lavishly choreographed diversionary interlude with occasional singing set within French *ballet de cour;* (2) an "entertainment" in an opera or ballet, only loosely connected to its surrounding scenes

Doctrine of Affections: a theory of the Baroque era that held that different musical moods could and should be used to influence the emotions, or affections, of the listeners

dot: following a note, a dot adds fifty percent to the value of the note; this concept entered music history in the early fourteenth century

double escapement action: a piano action in which a hammer falls back only halfway after striking a string, allowing the hammer to restrike more quickly

double leading-tone cadence a cadence with two leading tones in the penultimate chord, one pulling upward to the primary tone of the final chord and the other upward to the fifth degree

double verse structure: a distinctive feature of the sequence; each musical phrase is sung twice to accommodate a pair of verses

doxology: a standard formula of praise to the Holy Trinity

drum set: a collection of percussion instruments in a jazz ensemble that can be wielded by a single player

duplum: second voice in two- three- or four-voice organa

electronic music: works whose sounds are directly realized by a composer using electronic equipment

emancipation of dissonance: term used by Arnold Schoenberg to refer to a phenomenon in modern music by which dissonant chords and intervals are used as though equivalent to consonant ones

empfindsamer Stil: term applied to the hyper-expressivity that affected northern European, and particularly German, arts generally in the second half of the eighteenth century

emulation technique: see parody technique

English cross (false) relation: the simultaneous or adjacent appearance in different voices of two conflicting notes with the same letter name

English discant: a general term for the technique in fifteenth-century English music, both written and improvised, of using parallel 6/3 chords and root position triads in a homorhythmic style

English Madrigal School, The: the name given to the composers who fashioned the great outpouring of English secular music vocal music, mostly madrigals, in London between 1588 and 1627

enharmonic genus: a tetrachord found in ancient Greek music consisting of a major third and two quarter-tones; used for music demanding more subtle variations of pitch than that of the diatonic or chromatic genera

Enlightenment: a philosophical, scientific, and political movement that dominated eighteenth-century thought

ensemble finale: an energetic finish to an operatic act that is sung by a vocal ensemble rather than a soloist

envoi: one or more lines of verse added to the end of a chanson to suggest a leave taking

epic theater: a theatric style, associated with the plays of Bertolt Brecht, that dispels normal theatric illusion and "alienates" the audience from the narrative

episode: a passage in a musical work occurring between other passages that have more central thematic importance (as in a rondo form); in a fugue, a section full of modulation and free counterpoint that is based on motives derived from the subject

equal temperament: a division of the octave into twelve equal half-steps, each with the ratio of approximately 18:17; first advocated by some musicians in the early sixteenth century

estampie: one of two main dance types of the Middle Ages; originally a dance-song in which the dancers also sang a text, usually a poem about love; however, during the thirteenth and fourteenth centuries it evolved into a purely instrumental piece

étude: a study; a work intended to build a player's technique and often also having artistic value

Evensong: the final service of the day in the Anglican religion, an amalgam of Vespers and Compline

exposition: in sonata form the first main section in which the primary thematic material of the movement is presented or exposed; of a fugue, an opening section in which each voice presents the subject in turn

expressionism: a movement in twentieth-century literature and art in which symbolic means are used to explore irrational states of mind and grotesque actions

extended techniques: playing and singing in unusual ways in order to expand the sounds available in a musical work

faburden: a style of English medieval choral music that arose when singers improvised around a given chant placed in the middle voice; it is important because English composers began to incorporate this improvisatory style into their more formal written work

falsobordone: an improvisatory technique used by church singers that originated in Spain and Italy around 1480; at first three voices chanted along with the psalm tone making simple chant sound more splendid; by the seventeenth century, psalm tone and improvisation were abandoned and it became a newly composed piece for four or five voices but with the same simple, chordal style

fantasia: an imaginative composition the exact nature of which depends on the period of origin; in earlier eras these were usually contrapuntal works; later, the term suggested an improvisatory piece in free form, or sometimes pieces incorporating preexisting themes

fauxbourdon: the Continental style related to the English faburden; in fauxbourdon singers of sacred music improvised at pitches a fourth and a sixth below a given plainsong

fête galante: a popular social occasion among the French aristocracy of the eighteenth century

figured bass: a numerical shorthand placed with the bass line that tells the player which unwritten notes to fill in above the written bass note

fill: in jazz, a brief figure added between phrases performed by the principal soloist or singer

fin'amors: the theme of ideal love, an important value in chivalric society, as expressed in the poetry of the troubadours

flat trumpet: a slide trumpet, but one for which the sliding tube extended backward over the player's left shoulder, rather than extending forward from the right; had the capacity to play in minor keys more easily

formalism: in general, emphasis on strict formal principles or patterns in music; more specifically, a pejorative term used in the Soviet Union for music that seemed abstract or difficult, not in tune with the taste of the masses or with Soviet artistic ideology

formes fixes: the three fixed forms—ballade, rondeau, virelai—in which nearly all French secular art songs of the fourteenth and early fifteenth centuries were written

foxtrot: a social dance in $\frac{4}{4}$ time, popular in America in the 1920s

free jazz: a type of jazz of the 1950s and 1960s characterized by the removal or reinterpretation of key, normal harmonic progressions, and familiar jazz forms

French horn: the English term for the instrument that in other languages is simply called a horn; introduced into English ensembles only after 1700

French overture: a distinctive type of instrumental prelude created by the composer Jean-Baptiste Lully; came to be understood as an overture in two sections, the first slow in duple meter with dotted note values, the second fast in triple meter and with light imitation

frottola (pl., frottole): a catch-all word used to describe a polyphonic setting of a wide variety of strophic Italian poetry; the frottola flourished between 1470 and 1530 but had its origins in the improvisatory, solo singing that arose in Italy during the 1400s

fugue: a contrapuntal composition for two, three, four, or five voices, which begins with a presentation of a subject in imitation in each voice (exposition), continues with modulating passages of free counterpoint (episodes) and further appearances of the subject, and ends with a strong affirmation of the tonic key

fuguing tune: a hymn, often composed by American musicians of the eighteenth century, having fugal passages

functional harmony: a theory of harmonic syntax that defines the role of a chord as a point of departure or arrival (a tonic), a secondary point of arrival or moment of harmonic tension (a dominant), or a prefix to a dominant

fusion: a style of popular music that mixes elements of jazz and rock

galant style: French term used by music historians (rather than "Enlightenment style") to describe eighteenth-century music that is graceful, light in texture, and generally symmetrical in melodic structure

galliard: a fast leaping dance in triple meter especially popular during the Renaissance

Gallican chant: the Christian music of early-medieval Gaul; it later mixed with chant coming from Rome and that fusion formed the basis of what we call Gregorian chant

gate: in electronic music, a device allowing for shifts in amplitude in an electronic signal; in the music of John Adams a point of modulation from one collection of tones to another

Gebrauchsmusik: (music for use) a term used in the 1920s by Paul Hindemith to designate his compositions for amateurs or for everyday settings; also used by Kurt Weill for music of artistic value that was accessible to a general audience

German flute: what is today called the flute (the transverse flute)

gigue: a fast dance in $\frac{6}{8}$ or $\frac{12}{8}$ with a constant eighth-note pulse that produces a galloping sound; the gigue is sometimes lightly imitative and in the Baroque era was often used to conclude a suite

Gloria: a hymn of praise originating in early Christian times; one of the five parts of the Ordinary of the Mass

Golden Section: the division of a line into two parts such that the ratio of lengths of the smaller to the larger division equals the larger to the whole

Gothic architecture: the style of architecture that emerged in Paris and surrounding territories in the twelfth century; a lighter style than its Romanesque predecessor, it was characterized by greater height, greater light, and an almost obsessive application of repeating geometrical patterns

Gradual: the first of the two melismatic, responsorial chants of the Proper of the Mass that are sung between the Gloria and the Credo; consists of two parts: a respond and a psalm verse

grand opera: a style of opera originating around 1830 in France characterized by lavish use of chorus and ballet and elaborate spectacle

grand piano: a term that first appeared in England toward the end of the eighteenth century that denoted a large piano with sturdy legs and strings running roughly in the same direction as the keys

graphic notation: in twentieth-century compositions, musical notation that includes unusual graphic designs

Greater Perfect System: the framework of the Greek two-octave scale formed by four tetrachords and the proslambanomenos

Gregorian chant (plainsong): a vast body of monophonic religious music setting Latin texts and intended for use in the Roman Catholic Church; the music sung daily at the eight canonical hours of prayer and at Mass

ground bass: the English term for *basso ostinato*

Guidonian hand: ascribed to Guido of Arezzo that involves a system of using the left hand to inscribe mentally all the notes of the Guidonian scale and thus provide a portable mnemonic aid for the musical staff and the notes set upon it

Gypsy scale: a scale used by Gypsy musicians of the nineteenth and twentieth centuries containing two augmented seconds (such as C D E♭ F♯ G A♭ B C)

hand-crossing: a technique in keyboard playing in which the left hand must cross over the right to create an exciting three-level texture (left hand, right hand, and left over)

hard hexachord: in the Guidonian system, the hexachord—six-note pattern of TTSTT—set on G

Harlem Renaissance: a literary and artistic movement of the 1920s in Harlem (an African-American district in New York City)

harmonics: overtones, or frequencies, that are components of a fundamental tone

Harmonie: German name for an eighteenth-century independent wind band; called thus because winds played mostly harmony and not melody in the symphony of the day

Harmoniemusik: music written for an eighteenth-century *Harmonie*, or independent wind band

harpsichord: a string keyboard instrument that first appeared in the West in the fifteenth century; it utilized a key-jack mechanism to pluck the taut wire strings; during the Baroque era it was the principal keyboard instrument for realizing the basso continuo, but it lost favor as the piano grew in popularity during the second half of the eighteenth century

hautboys: another name for the shawm; the term was in use in England and France in the sixteenth century, and in England was eventually transformed into "oboe"

hauts instruments: (loud instruments) one of the two classifications of instruments in the fifteenth century; included trumpets, sackbuts, shawms, bagpipes, drums, and tambourine

head arrangement: a jazz arrangement rehearsed and memorized by musicians, but not written down

heckelphone: a double-reed woodwind instrument in the bass range sounding as notated

Heiligenstadt Testament: Beethoven's will that he prepared while staying in Heiligenstadt, Austria, in 1802; ostensibly addressed to his two brothers, it is actually an expression of his innermost feelings for all posterity

hexachord: a collection of six pitches

Hoboken (Hob.) number: number by which Josef Haydn's individual works may be identified following the catalogue prepared by the Dutch musicologist Anthony Hoboken

hocket: a contrapuntal technique and a musical genre; it occurs when the sounds of two voices are staggered by the careful placement of rests, thereby creating a highly syncopated piece

Hofkapelle: the group of singers responsible for the religious music at the Hapsburg court of Emperor Maximilian I; they were the center of religious and musical life at the court

horn fifths: a characteristic musical figure assigned to the French horns in which the instruments slide back and forth through sixths, fifths, and thirds, sometimes ornamenting along the way

hot jazz: an intense and exciting style of jazz

hymn: a relatively short chant with a small number of phrases, often four, and a rather narrow vocal range; hymns are invariably strophic, the usual hymn having three or four stanzas

idée fixe: (obsession): term used by Hector Berlioz to describe a recurrent melody in his *Symphonie fantastique*; the *idée fixe* melody symbolizes the beloved in the work's program

imitation: duplication of the notes and rhythms in one voice by a following voice; from the mid fifteenth century onward it became an oft used technique to enliven polyphonic music and sacred polyphonic music in particular

impresario: a manager, as of a ballet or opera company

impressionism: a realistic style of French painting of the late nineteenth century using everyday subjects (especially sea- and landscapes) and emphasizing the effects of sunlight upon colors; used in music to designate the style of Claude Debussy and others composing evocative music partially freed from strict beat and normative harmonic progressions

improvisation: playing or singing without reference to an existing musical composition

indeterminacy: see chance music

indeterminacy of composition: term associated with the composer John Cage by which compositional decisions are largely determined by chance routines; see also chance music and indeterminacy of performance

indeterminacy of performance: term associated with the composer John Cage by which music results from spontaneous decisions made by players, not strictly dictated by a composer; see also chance music

intabulation: a piece of music notated in tablature and specifically for certain solo instruments such as lute or keyboard; an intabulation implies that a preexisting polyphonic vocal piece has been arranged for a single instrument

intermezzo: a musical diversion between the acts of an opera or a play

introduction: a passage at the beginning of a composition or movement that prepares for and is often slower in tempo than the music to come; in nineteenth-century opera, a musical number (usually called an *introduzione*) at the beginning of the first act that is multisectional and composite in medium

Introit: an introductory chant for the entrance of the celebrating clergy; the first item of the Proper of the Mass

inversion: (1) in traditional harmony, the placement of a bass tone into an upper voice; a melody is inverted if its contour is replaced by its mirror image; (2) a tone row in a twelve-tone composition (or set of pitches in freely atonal music) is inverted if each interval separating the notes is replaced by the octave complement—sometimes said to be a "symmetric" inversion

invertible counterpoint: counterpoint carefully written so that the vertical position of two or more voices can be switched without violating the rules of counterpoint or creating undue dissonance

Ionian: added to the canon of eight medieval church modes by Glarean in

1547; first official recognition of the major mode

isorhythm: in isorhythm (same rhythm) a rhythmic pattern is repeated again and again in a line, usually in the tenor voice; a technique introduced by composers in the early fourteenth century

jam session: in jazz, an informal making of music by improvisation

jazz: a collective term for various types of twentieth-century popular music originating among African-American musicians and often involving improvisation; see also swing, hot jazz, free jazz, cool jazz

jazz break: see break

jazz combo: a small jazz ensemble

jazz dance bands: bands of moderate to large size and flexible makeup, freely incorporating jazz idioms, that played for dancing in the period from about 1915 to 1925

jazz standard: see standard

jubilus: the melisma on the final syllable of the word Alleluia; called this because at that moment the full choir and community celebrates with jubilation the redemptive life of Christ

jungle style: a big band style, associated especially with Duke Ellington in the 1920s and 30s, evoking African or primitive musical effects

just tuning: a system in which, in addition to the ratios required by Pythagorean tuning, the major and minor thirds were also tuned according to strict ratios (5:4 and 6:5)

Kapellmeister: chief of music at court; the German equivalent of *maestro di cappella* (chapel master) in Italy

keyboard tablature: a combination of note symbols (for the fast-moving upper part) and pitch-letter names (for the lower parts)

kithara: the largest of all ancient Greek string instruments (an especially large lyre) usually fitted with seven strings and a resonator of wood

Köchel (K) number: an identifying number assigned to each of the works of Mozart, in roughly chronological order, by German botanist and mineralogist Ludwig von Köchel (1800–1877)

kuchka: (handful) the sobriquet given in 1867 to a group of Russian composers living in St. Petersburg: Mily Balakirev (the mentor of the group), Nicolai Rimsky-Korsakov, César Cui, Alexander Borodin, and Modest Mussorgsky; the group is sometimes called "The Five"

Kyrie: an ancient Greek text and the only portion of the traditional Mass not sung in Latin; in this the first section of the Ordinary of the Mass the congregation petitions the Lord for mercy in threefold exclamations

La Guerre des Bouffons: (The War of the Buffoons) a paper war over the relative merits of Italian and French musical style; it raged, on and off, for several years in Paris during the 1750s and centered on the question of what sort of opera was appropriate for the French stage

lament bass: a descending tetrachordal *basso ostinato* employed during the Baroque era as a musical signifier of grief

Landini cadence: the name for a cadential gesture used frequently by Francesco Landini in which he ornamented a cadence by adding a lower neighbor-tone to the upper voice as it moves up to the octave

langue d'oc (occitan): the vernacular language of southern France in the high Middle Ages; the language of the troubadours and trobairitz

langue d'oïl: the vernacular language of northern France in the high Middle Ages; the language of the trouvères

lauda (pl., laude): Italian for a song of praise; a simple, popular sacred song written, not in church Latin but in the local dialect of Italian; from its beginning in the thirteenth century, the lauda had been sung by members of a confraternity

Le nuove musiche: (*The New Music*, 1602) published by Giulio Caccini; an anthology of solo madrigals and strophic solo songs gathered over time, rather than all new music as was implied; the preface contains invaluable information on vocal performance practices of the early Baroque era

leitmotive: a musical motive, normally occurring in the orchestral part of an opera, which symbolizes a character or dramatic entity; associated primarily with the operas of Richard Wagner, and also used by later composers

libretto: the text of an opera or an oratorio written in poetic verse

Lied (pl., Lieder): (song) a German art song or popular song

ligature: in early notation a group of two, three, or four individual notes

lira da braccio: a Renaissance fiddle; a bowed five-string instrument tuned in fifths and played on the shoulder

Lisztomania: Heinrich Heine's term for the emotional effect that Liszt had on his audiences

liturgical drama: a religious play with music intended to be performed as an adjunct to the liturgy, sometimes before Mass

liturgical offices: see canonical hours

liturgy: the collection of prayers, chants, readings, and ritual acts by which the theology of the church, or any organized religion, is practiced

long: one of the three basic note values and shapes recognized by Franco of Cologne around 1280 in his classification of musical durations

lute: a pear-shaped instrument with six sets of strings called courses, as well as frets created with thin strips of leather wrapped around the fingerboard at measured intervals, and a distinctive peg box that turns back at a right angle to the fingerboard; during the sixteenth century the most popular of all musical instruments

lute ayre: one of two forms of the solo art song that flourished in England around 1600; the soloist is accompanied by a lute and possibly a bass instrument such as the *viola da gamba*; a strophic piece that depended on the solo singer to employ the expressive nuances of the voice to make each stanza sound distinctive

lute tablature: a special type of notation for lute music that directs the fingers to stop strings at specific frets so as to produce sounds

lyre: in ancient Greece a medium-sized instrument usually fitted with seven strings of sheep gut and a resonator of turtle shell; plucked with a metal or bone plectrum and used most often to accompany a solo singer

lyricist: the writer of the words of a popular song, especially the songs in a musical

madrigal: (fourteenth century) originally a poem in the vernacular to which music was added for greater emotional effect; having the form AAB, it was one of the three *formes fixes* of secular music in trecento Italy; (sixteenth century) like the frottola, a catch-all term used to describe settings of Italian verse; sixteenth-century madrigals were through composed rather than strophic and employed a variety of textures and compositional techniques

madrigalism: the term for a musical cliché in which the music tries to sound out the meaning of the text, such as a drooping melody that signals a sigh or a dissonance to intensify a "harsh" word

magister cappellae: musician who is leader of the chapel

Mannheim crescendo: a gradual increase from very soft to very loud with a repeating figure over a pedal point; a specialty of the highly disciplined orchestra at the court of Mannheim

Mannheim rocket: a triadic theme that bursts forth as a rising arpeggio; another specialty of the highly disciplined orchestra at the court of Mannheim

masque: an elaborate courtly entertainment using music, dance, and drama to portray an allegorical story that shed a favorable light on the royal family

Mass: the central and most important religious service each day in the traditional liturgy of the Roman Catholic Church

Matins: the night office of the canonical hours, required much singing, and on high feasts such as Christmas or Easter, might go on for four hours

mazurka: a triple-time Polish dance

megamusical: a type of musical appearing in the 1980s with large cast and lavish spectacle

melisma: a lengthy vocal phrase setting a single syllable of text

melismatic chant: chants in which there are many notes per syllable of text; Matins, Vespers, and the Mass have the most melismatic chants

mélodie: (melody or song) a French art song of the nineteenth century

melodrama: a musical genre in which spoken text is accompanied by, or alternates with, instrumental music

mensural notation: symbol specific notation developed in the late thirteenth century; the direct ancestor of the system of notation used today (in contrast to modal notation, a contextual notation system used prior to the late thirteenth century)

mensuration canon: a canon in which two voices perform the same music at different rates of speed, the corresponding notes of which grow progressively distant from one another

metamorphoses: changes in form; used by Richard Strauss as the title of his final orchestral tone poem (1945)

metric modulation: a term associated with the composer Elliott Carter designating a proportional change of tempo by which a small division of a beat is regrouped into a new beat so that a new tempo results

Micrologus: (Little Essay) music theory treatise written c1030 by Guido of Arezzo setting forth all that a practicing church musician needed to know to sing the liturgy

micropolyphony: a term associated with the composer György Ligeti designating a texture in which a large number of lines merge into a sound mass

mime: the art of portraying a character or narrative solely by bodily movements and facial gestures

minim: a new short note value recognized by the fourteenth-century theorists of the *Ars nova*; a subdivision of the semibreve

minimalism: a musical style originating in the United States in the 1960s in which works are created by repetition and gradual change enacted upon a minimum of basic materials

Minnesang: (a song of love in old high German) a song created by a Minnesinger

Minnesinger: in the high Middle Ages the name for a German poet-musician writing love songs

minstrel show: a theatric entertainment originating in the United States in the middle of the nineteenth century, containing skits, songs, and dancing, which parodies the language and manners of African Americans

minuet: originally a triple-meter dance that was often added toward the end of the Baroque dance suite; in the Classical period it was invariably written in rounded binary form and coupled with a matching rounded binary movement called a trio

minuet and trio: a pair of movements with each usually constructed in rounded binary form; the trio was often scored for fewer instruments, sometimes only three (thus the name); often served as the third movement of a symphony or piece of chamber music

modal notation: a new type of notation that came into music gradually around 1150–1170 and that allowed composers to specify rhythmic duration as well as pitch; in modal notation the context determines the rhythm as opposed to the modern system of mensural notation in which each sign (note) indicates a specific duration

mode: (*modus*) the division of the long into two or three breves

modernism: in general, a style that departs from traditional norms of musical materials and aesthetic principles in the name of contemporaneity and progress; the term is often encountered in musical criticism of the twentieth century, especially for music arising in its early years and in the decades following World War II

monochord: a ancient device with a single string stretched over a wooden block and anchored at each end; distances were carefully measured on the string to correspond to specific pitches

monody: the overarching term for solo madrigals, solo arias, and solo recitatives written during the early Baroque era

Morning Prayer: the first service of the day in the Anglican religion, an amalgam of Matins and Lauds

motet: (thirteenth century) originally a discant clausula to which sacred words were added; in a motet each of the upper voices declaims its own poetic text that comments on the significance of the single Latin word being sung by the tenor; (later) the term generally used to connote a sacred choral composition, either accompanied by instruments or sung *a cappella*

motet-chanson: (fifteenth century) a hybrid of a motet and a chanson; a genre in which a vernacular text in an upper voice is sung simultaneously with a Latin chant in the tenor

motetus: the second voice (immediately above the tenor) in the thirteenth-century motet

movable type: individual small pieces of metal type cut with the letters of the alphabet or musical symbols that can be arranged to form words or music; once a sheet using the type has been printed the pieces of type can then be "moved"—rearranged to create a completely different page

Mozarabic chant: the old Christian church music as sung by Christians living in Spain under Moslem rule; survives today in more than twenty manuscripts but is nearly impossible to transcribe and perform

multiple cantus firmus Mass: when two or more cantus firmi sound simultaneously or successively in a Mass

multiple stops: on a violin (or other bowed string instruments) playing two or more notes simultaneously as chords

multiple-impression printing: a process for printing musical notation in which the lines of the staff are first printed horizontally across the sheet, then the sheet is pressed a second time to place the notes on the staff, finally a third pressing adds the text, title, composer's name, and any written instructions

murky bass: German name for a rumbling octave bass, created by repeating a bass note in alternating octaves, that became a favorite technique of both Italian and German keyboard composers of the eighteenth century

muses: in ancient Greek mythology, the nine goddesses who attended Apollo and presided over the arts and sciences; root of our word "music"

music drama: a term associated with the operas of Richard Wagner, who rejected the genre term "opera" for his mature works; Wagner preferred the word "drama"—sometimes "music drama"—for his operas to stress their heightened literary value; but in his essay "On the Name 'Music Drama'" (1872) Wagner also rejected this term as misleading

music of the future: a slogan derived from the writings of Richard Wagner that points to a utopian state in which the various arts coalesce into an integrated or "total" work of art

music of the spheres: part of the ancient Greek world-view of music, which held that when the stars and planets rotated in balanced proportions they made heavenly music

Musica enchiriadis (Music Handbook): a music theory treatise that dates from the 890s and is ascribed to Abbot Hoger; it describes a type of polyphonic singing called organum and aimed to teach church singers how to improvise polyphonic music

musica ficta: accidentals not found on the Guidonian scale but that had to be added by medieval performers because, being theoretically "off the scale," they had to be imagined

musica humana: music of the human body—one of the three harmonies Boethius posited as part of his cosmology of music

musica instrumentalis: earthly vocal and instrumental music—one of the three harmonies Boethius posited as part of his cosmology of music

musica mundana: music of the spheres—one of the three harmonies Boethius posited as part of his cosmology of music; the belief that all the universe resonates with music as sounding number

musica reservata: text-sensitive music reserved for a small circle of connoisseurs

musica secreta: (*musica reservata*) progressive chamber music reserved for a small, elite audience; used to describe the performances by the *concerto delle donne* before the ducal family in Ferrara

musical: a form of popular musical theater of the twentieth century, normally with spoken dialogue alternating with songs, dances, ensembles, and choruses; synonymous with musical comedy, musical play, and Broadway musical

musical play: see musical

musicologist: a scholar of music

musicus: as defined by Boethius, the musicologist who studies and understands music; as distinguished from the *cantor*, who is a practitioner

musique concrète: (concrete music) electronic music (q.v.) made from recordings of natural or man-made sounds

mystic chord: a collection of six tones used in the later music of Alexander Scriabin; an example of the mystic

chord, placed into a compact scalewise order, is B C D E F♯ G♯

nationalism: in general, the love for or allegiance to a region of birth and its people, culture, and language; in music, nationalism is often expressed by the quotation of folk songs and dances or the use of folk stories

natural hexachord: in the Guidonian system, the hexachord—six-note pattern of TTSTT —set on C

naturalism: a movement in literature of the late nineteenth century that depicts society in an objective and truthful manner

nave: the western end of a cathedral or large church; the public part of the church, which functioned as town hall and civic auditorium as well as a space for religious processions and votive prayers

neoclassical architecture: term for the architecture of the eighteenth century that copied classical Roman qualities of balance, harmonious proportions, and an absence of ornate decoration

neoclassicism: a critic's term designating a dominant musical style of the 1920s through 1940s, especially associated with the music of Igor Stravinsky of that time; characteristics of neoclassical music include parody-like references to earlier music (especially works of Baroque and Classical periods), motoric rhythms, changing meters, a cool and detached tone, modernistic harmony, and an international tone rather than regional allegiances

neumatic chant: chants in which there are three, four, or five notes for each syllable of text

neume: in medieval musical notation, a sign used to delineate single pitches or groups of pitches; originally, around 900 C.E., neumes were just laid out on the parchment above text as a reminder of how it should be sung

New German School: a group of musicians gathering around Franz Liszt in Weimar and supporting the artistic outlook of Liszt and Richard Wagner

new music advisor: a position existing since the 1970s with many American symphony orchestras; the new music advisor typically composes new works for the orchestra and recommends other contemporary compositions

New Orleans style of jazz: a jazz style emerging in New Orleans in the early twentieth century characterized by small bands, an energetic ("hot") style of playing, and group improvisation

Nimrod variation: ninth variation in Edward Elgar's *Enigma* Variations for

orchestra; a musical portrait of Elgar's publisher, August Jaeger

nocturne: a type of piano character piece appearing in the nineteenth century distinguished by a dreamy mood, a lyric melody in the right hand, and widely-spaced, arpeggiated chords in the left hand

nota: (Latin for note) a symbol on a line or space representing a single, precise pitch

notes inégales: in which a succession of equal notes moving rapidly up or down the scale are played somewhat unequally, such as "long-short, long-short"

Notre Dame School: the name given by historians to the composers Leoninus, Perotinus, and their colleagues who created a huge musical repertory of more than a thousand pieces during the period 1160–1260 at and around Notre Dame of Paris

number symbolism: a system prevalent during the Middle Ages and Renaissance in which meaning in music was conveyed by the use of numbers representing religious themes and concepts; a composition might have certain structural proportions such as 6:4:2:3 in Dufay's motet that mirror the proportions of the cathedral of Florence

obbligato: indication that a composer has written a specific part for an instrument and intends it to be played as written

obbligato recitative: recitative in which the full orchestra is necessary to the desired effect (also known as accompanied recitative)

oblique motion: motion occurring when one voice repeats or sustains a pitch while another moves away or toward it; used in medieval organum as a way to avoid dissonant tritones

oboe d'amore: an oboe-like instrument in A, slightly lower in range than the oboe; used by J.S. Bach and revived in works by Gustav Mahler and Richard Strauss

occitan: see langue d'oc

occursus: a running together, Guido of Arezzo's term for cadence

octatonic scale: a symmetric scale alternating half and whole steps

ode: a multi-movement hymn of praise to a person or ideal usually lasting about twenty minutes and containing an instrumental introduction, choruses, duets, and solo arias, but no recitative because there is no story

Odhecaton: the first book of polyphonic music printed from movable type; although published in Venice, most of the nearly one-hundred compositions in it were the works of the great northern masters of counterpoint

open ending: the term used in the Middle Ages for what we today call a first ending

opera: a dramatic work, or play, set to music; in opera the lines of the actors and actresses are sung, not spoken, and music, poetry, drama, scenic design, and dance combine to produce a powerful art form

opera buffa: the name for Italian comic opera but which, unlike most other forms of comic opera, uses rapid-fire recitative rather than spoken dialogue

opéra comique: similar to Italian *opera buffa*, has characters from the everyday world, singing in a fresh, natural style, and the dialogue is generally spoken or sometimes delivered in recitative; the principals sing either simple airs or popular melodies

opera seria: serious, not comic, opera; the term is used to designate the heroic, fully sung Italian opera that dominated the stage at the courts of Europe during the eighteenth century

operetta: a genre of light or comic opera with spoken dialogue and traditional operatic numbers originating in the mid nineteenth century

ophicleide: an early nineteenth-century bass brass instrument, forerunner of the tuba

opus dei: "work of the lord"; the services of the canonical hours as referred to in the Rule of St. Benedict

oratorio: a genre of religious music developed in the seventeenth century to satisfy the desire for dramatic music during Lent; a musical setting of a dramatic text in Latin or Italian or, later, other languages that usually elaborates upon an event in the Old Testament; uses the essential processes of opera but without the lavish sets, costumes, or acting

oratory: a prayer hall set aside just for praying, preaching, and devotional singing

Orchésographie: lengthy treatise on dance published by Thoinot Arbeau in 1589; it details all the popular dances of the day with their steps, tells what is in fashion and what is not, and provides unexpected information about performance practices of the day

Ordinary of the Mass: chants of the Mass with unvarying texts that can be sung almost every day of the year; *Kyrie, Gloria, Credo, Sanctus,* and *Agnus dei*

ordre: the term used by François Couperin to designate a group of pieces loosely associated by feeling and key; similar to what other composers of the Baroque era would call a dance suite

organ Mass: a Mass in which an organ alternates with, or entirely replaces, the choir

organ verset: an independent organ section in an *alternatim* organ Mass; a short piece that replaces a liturgical item otherwise sung by the choir

organum (pl., organa): a type of polyphonic religious music of the Middle Ages; the term came to be used generally to connote all early polyphony of the church

organum purum: florid two-voice organum of medieval Paris continuing the tradition of earlier Aquitanian polyphony in sustained-tone style

ostinato: see *basso ostinato*

overdotting: practice in which a dotted note is made longer than written, while its complementary short note(s) is made shorter

paean: in ancient Greece, a hymn that celebrated the deeds of primary gods such as Zeus or Apollo; today any poetic hymn of praise

pan-consonance: music in which almost every note is a member of a triad or a triadic inversion and not a dissonance

pan-isorhythm: a technique whereby isorhythm is applied to all voices, not just the tenor in an isorhythmic piece

parallel organum: organum in which all voices move in lockstep, up or down, with the intervals between voices remaining the same

paraphrase Mass: a Mass in which the movements are united by a single paraphrased chant

paraphrase motet: a motet that contains a paraphrased chant throughout

paraphrase technique: when a composer takes a preexisting plainsong and embellishes it somewhat, imparting to it a rhythmic profile; the elaborated chant then serves as the basic melodic material for a polyphonic composition

Parisian chanson: a newer (after 1500) style of French chanson in which the rhythm of the text begins to animate the rhythm of the music; almost every note has its own syllable and the duration of that note is often determined by the length or stress of the syllable; subject matter was also more "down to earth" and might include lusty lovers or drinking scenes

parlando-rubato rhythm: term used by Béla Bartók to describe the flexible rhythm of most ancient Hungarian peasant songs

parody technique (emulation technique): when one composer emulates another by borrowing entire polyphonic sections of an earlier work

part book: a volume that contains the music of one voice part and only one voice part

partita: term used by J.S. Bach as a synonym for suite

partitioning: in twelve-tone music, the distribution of the notes of a tone row into several strands in a texture

partsong: a strophic song with English text intended to be sung by three or four voices in a predominantly homophonic musical style

passacaglia: (1) a musical form involving continuous variations upon a *basso ostinato*, originating in the Baroque period and virtually synonymous with the term chaconne; (2) originally a separate and distinct bass melody but during the seventeenth century it came to mean almost any repeating bass pattern of short duration

passion: a large-scale musical depiction of Christ's crucifixion as recorded in the Gospels; an oratorio on the subject of the passion

pastoral aria: a slow aria with several distinctive characteristics: parallel thirds that glide mainly in step-wise motion, a lilting rhythm in compound meter, and a harmony that changes slowly and employs many subdominant chords

patter-song: the rapid delivery of text on repeated notes

pavane: a slow gliding dance in duple meter performed by couples holding hands; replaced the fifteenth-century *basse danse* as the primary slow dance of the court

pedal point: on the organ, a sustained or continually repeated pitch, usually placed in the bass and sounding while the harmonies change around it

Penitential Psalms: the seven of the one hundred fifty psalms of the Psalter that are especially remorseful in tone and sung in the rites of the Catholic Church surrounding death and burial

pentatonic scale: a scale with five tones per octave; specifically, a scale having the form C D E G A (or a transposition or reordering of these tones); "pentatonic music" makes use of pentatonic scales

pes: (Latin for foot) the English name for a bottom voice that continually repeats throughout a polyphonic composition

phasing: a term associated with composer Steve Reich; a phase piece is one that begins with two sources of sound giving forth an identical ostinato; one sound source gradually pulls ahead, creating a constantly-changing rhythmic interaction with the other source

pianoforte: original name for the piano because, unlike the harpsichord, its mechanism allowed the player to control the force of a blow to the string and thus could play piano or forte

Picardy third: a shift from minor to major in the final chord of a piece

plagal cadence: a IV-I chordal movement with the bass in root position falling down by the interval of a fourth or rising up by a fifth

plagal mode in the eight church modes the plagal is the second of each of the four pairs of modes; plagal means "derived from" and each plagal mode is a fourth below its authentic counterpart; the Dorian mode, for example, has its plagal counterpart in the Hypodorian mode

plainsong: see Gregorian chant

player piano: a piano provided with a mechanical device that "plays" the instrument according to musical instructions entered on a perforated paper roll

point of imitation: a distinctive motive that is sung or played in turn by each voice or instrumental line

pointillism: an artistic style of the late nineteenth century in which dots of color merge into recognizable images in the eye of the viewer; a similar phenomenon occurs in music by modern composers including Anton Webern and Olivier Messiaen in which notes seem isolated and detached from larger context

polychord: a chord made by juxtaposing two familiar harmonies

polymeter: two or more meters sounding simultaneously

polyrhythm: the simultaneous appearance in a musical work of two or more rhythmic patterns or principles of rhythmic organization

polytonality: the simultaneous appearance in a musical work of two or more keys

popular art music: a term coined by Béla Bartók to describe songs composed by nineteenth-century composers, of low artistic value, that had been accepted by the populace as folk songs

portative organ: a small movable instrument that sounded at courtly entertainments, usually to accompany singers rather than dancers

positive organ: a large stationary instrument that began to appear in large numbers in churches in the West shortly after 1300; considered one of the technological wonders of its day, it was usually attached high on the wall in the nave of the church and was the only instrument sanctioned for use in the church

preghiera: a prayer scene, often found in nineteenth-century Italian opera

prelude: a preliminary piece, one that comes immediately before and introduces the main musical event

prepared piano: a piano whose sound is modified by the introduction of mutes and other objects between strings

prima donna: leading lady

prima pratica: a traditional style for church music that is in contrast to the freer writing found in some madrigals of the late sixteenth century; the musical embodiment of the restrained spirit of the Counter-Reformation

program music: instrumental music that explicitly embodies extra-musical content

programmatic symphony: a multimovement symphony that is explicitly programmatic

prolation: (*prolatio*) the division of the semibreve into two or three minims

Proper of the Mass: chants of the Mass whose texts change each day to suit the religious theme, or to honor a particular saint on just that one day

proportions: time signatures often written as fractions that modify the normal value of notes

proslambanomenos: term used by the ancient Greeks to indicate the lowest sounding pitch in their Greater Perfect System

psalm tone: eight simple recitation formulas (simple repeating patterns) to which psalms were chanted

psalmody: act or process of singing the psalms (of the Psalter); done each week during the services of the canonical hours

Psalter: the book of one hundred fifty psalms found in the Old Testament

punctum (pl., puncta): a pair of musical phrases (couplet) usually associated with medieval instrumental music

Pythagorean tuning: a process in which the octaves, fifths, and fourths are tuned in perfect 2:1, 3:2, and 4:3 ratios

quadrivium: the four scientific disciplines of the seven liberal arts—arithmetic, geometry, astronomy, and music— that used number and quantitative reasoning to arrive at the truth

quadruplum: fourth voice in four-voice organa

quattrocento: Italian for what we refer to as "the 1400s"

quodlibet: a genre of music created when several secular tunes are brought together and sound together or in immediate succession

rag see ragtime

ragtime: a style of American popular music, especially found in piano character pieces (called "rags"), in which a syncopated melody is joined to a rhythmically-regular accompaniment

rank: each group of similar sounding pipes in an organ

realism: in Russian music of the nineteenth century a style portraying people objectively and truthfully, often using a melodic style that is close to speech

recapitulation: in sonata form, the return of the first theme and the tonic key following the development; although essentially a revisiting of previous material it is usually by no means an exact repeat

recital: a concert given by a single performer or a small number of musicians

récitatif ordinaire: a style of recitative, developed by French composer Jean-Baptiste Lully, noteworthy for its length, vocal range, and generally dramatic quality

recitation tone: a constantly repeating pitch followed by a mediation or a termination; the recitation tone is the heart of the psalm tone

recitative: a musically heightened speech, often used in an opera, oratorio, or cantata to report dramatic action and advance the plot

reform opera: first created in the 1760s by Christoph Willibald Gluck and Ranieri Calzabigi in an attempt to combine the best features of the Italian and French operatic traditions, to yoke Italian lyricism to the French concern for intense dramatic expression

Reformation: the religious revolution that began as a movement to reform Catholicism and ended with the establishment of Protestantism

release: a contrasting phrase in a popular song refrain

requiem Mass: the burial Mass of the Roman Catholic Church

respond: the opening chant in responsorial singing; usually sung by the full choir, it is followed by a verse sung by a soloist, and is repeated by the full choir

responsorial singing: when the full choir prefaces and responds to the psalm verse, which is sung by a soloist (choral respond, solo verse, choral respond)

retransition: in sonata form, the point near the end of the development where tonal stability returns, often in the form of a dominant pedal point, in preparation for the return of the first theme (in the tonic key) and the beginning of the recapitulation

retrograde: backward in motion, as in twelve-tone music where a tone row is deployed with its tones in reverse order

reverberation time: the time it takes a sound to die out

rhapsody: a type of character piece of the nineteenth century, usually for piano, having no established form or mood

rhythm and blues: a style of American popular songs appearing in the 1940s that use the traditional blues form; forerunner of rock

rhythm section: in jazz, an accompanimental group of instruments

rhythmic imitation: process in which each voice in turn sings the same rhythmic motive, but to melodic motives that differ slightly in pitch

rhythmic modes: simple patterns of repeating rhythms employed in the polyphony created in Paris during the twelfth and thirteenth centuries; modal notation evolved into a system of six rhythmic modes

ricercar: (sixteenth century) an instrumental piece, usually for lute or keyboard, similar in style to the imitative motet; (seventeenth century) Frescobaldi perfected a tightly organized, monothematic ricercar that influenced the later fugal writing of J.S. Bach

rigaudon: a Baroque dance in duple meter

ripieno: the larger ensemble (full orchestra) in a concerto grosso

ripresa: a refrain

Risorgimento: (resurgence) the movement toward Italian political and social unification that began in 1814 and culminated in 1861 when much of Italy was brought together as a single nation under King Victor Emmanuel II

ritornello: a return or refrain

ritornello form: a carefully worked out structure for a concerto grosso, which employs regular reappearances of the ritornello

Robertsbridge Codex: the earliest surviving collection of keyboard music; preserves various pieces typically heard at the French royal court in the mid fourteenth century

rock 'n' roll (or rock): a type of popular song, gaining prominence in America in the 1950s, accompanied typically by amplified guitars, drums, and a few other instruments; early rock songs often had the form of a blues, elements of country music, and sexually-suggestive lyrics

rococo: term used to describe the decorative arts and the music of mid eighteenth-century France, with all their lightness, grace and highly ornate surfaces

Roman chant: the dialect of chant sung in the early churches of Rome; the principal repertory from which Gregorian chant would later emerge

romance: in nineteenth-century French music, a simple strophic song

romantic opera: a genre term used by Carl Maria von Weber for certain of his operas and by Richard Wagner for his early operas; the term suggests that the texts stressed mysterious or supernatural elements, as in the contemporary literary genre of the "romance"

Romantic period: a basic period in the history of Western music extending from the early nineteenth to the early twentieth century; although the music of this time is too diverse to admit meaningful generalizations about its style, there is a recurring impulse toward intense expressivity, which often drives the music to free forms expressed through innovative materials

romanticism: the general style of music of the Romantic period

rondeau: (fourteenth and fifteenth centuries) one of the three French *formes fixes* that originated as a dance-song with the troubadours and trouvères; its musical and textual form is ABaAabAB; (seventeenth and eighteenth centuries) a composition based on the alternation of a main theme (refrain) with subsidiary sections called *couplets* to allow musical diversity

rondellus: a distinctly English musical technique in which two or three voices engage in voice exchange, or more correctly, phrase exchange

rondo: one of the main musical forms of the Classical period; a Classical rondo sets a refrain (A) against contrasting material (B, C, or D) to create a pattern such as ABACA, ABACABA, or even ABACADA; it usually projects a playful, exuberant mood, and is often used as the last movement of a sonata or symphony, to bid a happy farewell to the audience

Rossini crescendo: a characteristic feature in operas by Gioachino Rossini in which a long crescendo is accompanied by ever shorter phrases, a thickening of orchestration, and quicker harmonic motions

rota: the English name for a canon that endlessly circles back to the beginning

rotulus: an oblong sheet of paper or parchment on which chansons were inscribed; the sheet music of the late Middle Ages and the Renaissance

Royal Academy of Music: George Frideric Handel's London opera company started in 1719; a publicly held stock company, its principal investor being the king

Russian Revolution: an uprising in the major cities of Russia in 1917 during which Tsar Nicholas II abdicated and power was seized by the Bolshevik political faction

sackbut: a slide trumpet common in the fifteenth and sixteenth centuries; precursor of the modern trombone

sarabande: a slow, stately dance in $\frac{3}{4}$ with a strong accent on the second beat; one of four dances typically found within a Baroque dance suite

Sarum chant: England's special dialect of Gregorian chant; called that from the old Latin name of the cathedral town of Salisbury; melodies and texts were somewhat different from the chant sung on the Continent

scat singing: in jazz, singing on nonsense syllables

scena: a passage of a nineteenth-century opera given largely in recitative and often leading to an aria or duet

scenario: the story outline of a ballet

scene: a passage in an opera or ballet calling to the stage a particular selection of characters

scherzo: (Italian for joke) an exuberant triple-meter dance that frequently replaced the more stately minute as the third movement in symphonies and chamber works of the Classical period; was favored first by Haydn (in his Opus 33 quartets) and then especially by Beethoven in his symphonies

scholasticism: the mode of thinking that rose to prominence at the University of Paris in the thirteenth century; it managed information by constructing chains of hierarchical categories and relationships

Schubertiad: a social gathering organized within the circle of Franz Schubert at which his music was performed

scordatura: tuning a string instrument to something other than standard tuning

seconda pratica: Claudio Monteverdi's term for the new text-driven approach to musical composition that he practiced; it allowed for "deviations" from conventional counterpoint if these moments were inspired by an especially expressive text

semibreve: one of the three basic note shapes recognized by Franco of Cologne around 1280 in his classification of musical durations

semi-opera: a spoken play in which the more exotic, amorous, or even supernatural moments in the story were sung or danced

sequence: a Gregorian chant, sung on high feasts during the Proper of the Mass immediately after the Alleluia, in which successive verses were paired into double verses; the most famous sequence today is the *Dies irae*

serenade: a piece of outdoor music for a small ensemble usually in at least five movements; the term was used interchangeably with divertimento

serialism: a compositional method in which the choice and ordering of elements is governed by a precompositional arrangement or system; see also total serialism

seven liberal arts: a framework of seven intellectual disciplines set forth by Martianus Capella (c435 C.E.) composed of the trivium and the quadrivium

shanty: a sailor's work song

shawm: a double-reed instrument with a loud penetrating tone, used to provide dance music during the Middle Ages and Renaissance; the ancestor of the modern oboe

sideman: in jazz, a section player

Silver Age: (in Russian art) common designation for an artistic period in Russia during the reign of Tsar Nicholas II (1894–1917); a time of changing tastes

simple recitative: a basic form of recitative in operas of the eighteenth and nineteenth centuries: narrative in text, speech-like in melody, and accompanied solely by keyboard or a minimal number of instruments; a recitative accompanied only by a basso continuo

sincopa: the medieval term for syncopation, a temporary shift of the downbeat

sinfonia: (Italian for symphony) a three-section or three-movement instrumental work that might preface an opera or stand alone as an independent concert symphony

single-impression printing: utilizes individual pieces of movable type that are both the note and a small vertical section of the staff; required only one pressing and was thus much more economical than multiple-impression printing

Singspiel: (sung play) a genre of German opera appearing in the eighteenth and nineteenth centuries using a folkish or comic spoken play with musical numbers inserted

Six, The: a critic's sobriquet given in 1920 to a group of six French neoclassical composers: Darius Milhaud, Arthur Honegger, Germaine Tailleferre, Georges Auric, Francis Poulenc, and Louis Durey

skolion: a song setting an aphoristic poem; the primary musical entertainment at an ancient Greek symposium

socialist realism: an officially-approved doctrine guiding the arts in Soviet Russia that promoted a style geared to the understanding of the masses

soft hexachord: in the Guidonian system, the hexachord—six-note pattern of TTSTT—set on F

soggetto cavato: *soggetto cavato dale vocali*—a cantus firmus extracted from the vowels of a name

solfege: the system of singing different pitches to the syllables "do (ut), re, mi, fa, sol, la, ti (si), do (ut)"

solo concerto: a concerto composed for only one solo instrument

solo sonata: a sonata played by a single melody instrument such as a violin, flute or oboe usually accompanied, in the Baroque era, by a basso continuo

sonata: originally "something sounded" on an instrument as opposed to something sung (a "cantata"); later a multi-movement work for solo instrument or ensemble

sonata form: the most important formal innovation of the Classical period, used by composers most often when writing a fast first movement of a sonata, quartet, or symphony; an expansion of rounded binary form, it consists of an exposition, development, and recapitulation, with optional introduction and coda

sonata-rondo form: a design often found in the finales of symphonies and concertos of the eighteenth and nineteenth centuries that merges elements of sonata and rondo forms

sonatina: a name sometimes used for the easiest and shortest sonatas

song "release": see release

song collection: a group of art songs having a loose connection, such as that coming from a single poet or literary theme

song cycle: a group of songs intended by the composer to be performed as a unit, having definite musical and textual interconnections

Song of Songs: (also called the Song of King Solomon) a particularly lyrical book in the Old Testament of the Bible portions of which have often been set to music over the centuries

song plugger: in the American popular song industry of the early twentieth century, a musician who demonstrated new works for a publisher

sound mass: a basic element in a modern composition made from a conglomerate of tones, lines, and rhythms

Spanish guitar: see *vihuela*

spiccato: designation requiring performers to play in a detached fashion, but not quite as short as *staccato*

spiritual: an American religious song

Sprechgesang: (speech song) a term coined by Arnold Schoenberg to describe the recitational part of his melodrama *Pierrot lunaire* (1912); in *Sprechgesang*, rhythms are notated exactly and pitches are only approximated; a synonym is *Sprechmelodie* (speech melody); the reciter herself is called the *Sprechstimme* (speaking voice); the style was later used in the operas of Alban Berg

square piano: a small box-shape piano with strings running at right angles to the keys, which could be set upon a table or simple stand

standard: in jazz, a popular song that is frequently arranged or used as the basis for improvisation; also called a "jazz standard"

stile antico: the name given to the conservative music emanating from the papal chapel in the seventeenth century

stile concertato: Italian for concerted style; a term broadly used to identify Baroque music marked by grand scale and strong contrast, either between voices and instruments, between separate instrumental ensembles, between separate choral groups, or even between soloist and choir

stile concitato: an agitated style particularly suited to warlike music; Claudio Monteverdi used this term for a new style of music he created that was more direct and insistent than previous martial music

stile rappresentativo: (dramatic or theater style) a type of vocal expression somewhere between song and declaimed speech

stochastic music: a term brought to music from probability theory by the composer Iannis Xenakis to designate works in which individual sonic events are not controlled by the composer, who focuses instead on shaping only their aggregate appearance and behavior

stop: a small wooden knob on an organ that activates a rank of pipes when pulled out

stop time: in jazz, a temporarily simplified rhythm in the accompaniment, which allows for a soloist briefly to improvise

stretta: the climactic section of a number in a nineteenth-century opera, often in a fast tempo; the masculine form *stretto* usually alludes to a passage in a fugue in which a subject is imitated at a shorter than normal time span

stride: a style of ragtime piano playing and composing in which the pianist's left hand moves regularly from chord tones in a low register to harmonies in the middle register

strophe plus refrain: a common musical form in which the strophe, or stanza, is sung by a soloist while all the singers join in with the burden, or refrain

strophic form: a song form in which the music composed for the initial stanza of text is repeated for each additional stanza

strophic variation aria: an aria in which the same melodic and harmonic plan appears, with slight variation, in each successive strophe

Sturm und Drang: (German for "Storm and Stress") as a musical term it refers to a small but significant group of works written around 1770 that are marked by agitated, impassioned writing, such as Mozart's Symphony No. 25 (K. 183) of 1773

style brisé: a modern term for a type of discontinuous texture in which chords are broken apart and notes enter one by one; such a style is inherent in lute music because the sounds of the lute are delicate and quickly evaporate

subject: in a fugue, the theme

substitute clausula: one clausula written in discant style intended to replace another

suite: a musical work that consists of a succession of short pieces, especially dances; also used for a concert work made from excerpts from an opera, ballet, or film score

surrealism: twentieth-century literary and artistic movement that confounds superficial reality or logic in order to evoke unconscious states of mind

sustained-tone organum: organum in which the bottom voice holds a note while the faster-moving top voice embellishes it in a florid fashion

swing: in jazz, a rhythm that drives forward in a triplet pattern; also a style of jazz of the 1930s and 1940s often involving big bands that play in an impulsive and dynamic mood

syllabic chant: chants in which there is usually only one note and only one note for each syllable of text

symmetric inversion: see inversion

symphonic poem: a one-movement programmatic orchestral work; roughly synonymous with tone poem

symphonie concertante: a concerto-like composition of the Classical period with two or more soloists

symposium: in ancient Greece, a tightly organized social gathering of adult male citizens for conversation and entertainment

syncopation: a temporary metric irregularity or dislocation by which beats or divisions of beats do not conform to their normal placement within the meter

syncope: the Renaissance term for a suspension

tablature: directs a performer's fingers to a specific spot on an instrument

tactus: the term used to indicate the beat by music theorists of the Renaissance

Tafelmusik: German name for chamber music, both vocal and instrumental, for the dinner table

talea: a rhythmic pattern, or unit appearing in an isorhythmic composition

tape music: a style of electronic music associated with Vladimir Ussachevsky and Otto Luening in which compositions are recorded and subsequently distorted (especially by reverberating feedback)

temperament: the tuning of intervals in something slightly more or less than strict mathematical ratios

tenor: one of the standard four voice parts; in early medieval polyphony the bottom most voice, often a preexisting chant, upon which the composition is built; called that because in these early works it holds or draws out the notes

Tenorlied: a polyphonic German song in which a preexisting tune is placed in the tenor and two or three other voices enhance it with lightly imitative polyphony

tetrachord: a succession of four pitches

text painting (word painting): the use of striking chord shifts, musical repetition, controlled dissonance, and abrupt textural changes to highlight the meaning of the text; a very popular technique with sixteenth-century madrigal composers

theorbo: a large lute-like instrument with a full octave of additional bass strings descending in a diatonic pattern

third stream: a term coined by the composer Gunther Schuller to describe a musical style merging jazz and classical elements

threnody: a musical lament

through composed: containing new music for every stanza of text, as opposed to strophic form in which the music is repeated for each successive stanza

tibia: Roman name for the aulos

time: (*tempus*) the division of the breve into two or three semibreves

Tin Pan Alley: the art and business of the American popular song of the early twentieth century

tintinnabuli **style:** (bells style) a term coined by the composer Arvo Pärt for a polyphony in which a melodic line is joined to a "bells" line limited to the three tones of the tonic triad

toccata: an instrumental piece, for keyboard or other instruments, requiring the performer to touch the instrument with great technical dexterity; designed to show off the creative spirit of the composer as well as the technical skill of the performer

tombeau: an instrumental piece commemorating someone's death

tonal answer: a following voice that imitates the subject at the interval of a fifth above or fourth below and changes the subject so as to keep the music in the home tonality

tone cluster: a dissonant chord made from sounding all of the tones within a boundary interval

tone poem: a one-movement programmatic work, usually for orchestra, and roughly synonymous with symphonic poem

tone-color melody (*Klangfarbenmelodie***):** a term coined by Arnold Schoenberg to designate a melody-like line made from changing tone colors

tonos (pl., tonoi): ancient Greek term for a scale

total serialism: a compositional method in which the choice of most of the principal elements of a composition (including pitches, rhythms, and dynamics) is governed precompositionally by an integrated system or arrangement

total work of art (*Gesamtkunstwerk***):** a term used by Richard Wagner to designate a goal for art in which its various branches are merged into a integrated and dramatic whole

tragédie lyrique: the term used to designate French opera in the late seventeenth and eighteenth centuries, which was a fusion of classical French tragedy with traditional French ballet (*ballet de cour*)

transformation of themes: a technique of thematic unity throughout a multisectional work by which one or a few initial themes recur, albeit changed in character

transition (bridge): in sonata form the passage of modulation between the tonic and the new key

treble: the highest of the three voices for which much late-medieval English polyphony was written; evolved in general musical terminology to mean the top part as well as the top clef (G clef), the highest clef in music

trecento: short for *mille trecento*, or the century of the 1300s, in Italian

trio: a composition for three solo instruments; also, a contrasting section of a work originally played by a trio of instruments; in minuets, band marches, and rags, the term refers to a contrasting section or episode, with no implications for medium

trio sonata: comprised a line for two treble instruments (usually two violins) and basso continuo

triplum: third voice in a piece of three- or four-voice organum of the Middle Ages

triseme: a triple unit long value of time in ancient Greek musical notation—formed by three chronoi

trivium: the three verbal disciplines of the seven liberal arts—grammar, logic, and rhetoric—which deal with language, logic, and oratory

trobairitz: a female troubadour (poet-musician)

trope: an addition of music or text, or both, to a preexisting chant; they more fully explain the theology inherent in the chants to which they are added

troubadour: a poet-musician of the courtly art of vernacular sung poetry that developed in the Middle Ages in southern France

trouser role: an opera role designed to be sung by a woman dressed as a man

trouvère: a poet-musician of the courtly art of vernacular sung poetry that developed in northern France during the late twelfth and thirteenth centuries

tuba: Roman name for the trumpet; a long, straight instrument with a cylindrical bore and a bell at the end, which originated with the Etruscans

Turkish music: the noise of Turkish military percussion instruments, which were introduced into Western European music in the eighteenth century during the Turkish Wars; some pianos of the day were equipped with special devices to effect the sounds of "Turkish" music, such as bass drum, cymbals, and the like

twelve-tone composition: a composition in which the twelve tones of the chromatic scale are systematically recirculated; the term usually refers to works using Arnold Schoenberg's "twelve-tone method," formulated in 1923, in which the recirculation of tones is joined to a serialized principle of order

unmeasured prelude: an opening piece without specific indications for rhythmic duration or metrical organization

variation technique: a procedure in which successive statements of a theme are changed or presented in altered musical surroundings

variations: a work, movement of a work, or a form in which an initial theme is subject to a series of modifications or paraphrases; see also ballet variations

vaudeville show: a popular theatric entertainment in America made from acts including dances, songs, and skits

verbal score: a musical composition represented not by conventional musical notation but by verbal instructions to the performers

verismo: (realism) a style of Italian opera appearing in the 1890s in short works in which characters from lower social strata are driven by the passions to violent acts

verse and refrain: a form for popular songs in which each stanza (sometimes only a single stanza) is divided into an introductory passage (the verse) followed by a more tuneful refrain

Vespers: the late-afternoon service, and most important of the eight canonical hours for the history of music; not only were psalms and a hymn sung but also the Magnificat

vida: a brief biographical sketch of a troubadour or trouvère; appears along with a small portrait of the artist in some French chansonniers

vielle: a large five-string fiddle capable of playing the entire Guidonian scale; often provided dance music during the thirteenth and fourteenth centuries

Viennese School: historians' term for composers Haydn, Mozart, Beethoven, and Schubert who capped their careers in Vienna and knew one another personally, however indirectly

vihuela **(Spanish guitar):** a plucked string instrument with a waisted body, and a long pole-neck that serves as a fingerboard; the direct ancestor of the modern classical guitar

Vingt-quatre violons du roi: twenty-four instruments of the violin family that formed the string core of the French court orchestra under Louis XIV (six violins, twelve violas, and six *basse de violons*)

viol: a six-string instrument fretted and tuned like the lute and *vihuela*, but bowed and not plucked; it came in three sizes—treble, tenor, and bass—and was played with the instrument resting on the lap or legs

viola da gamba: Italian name for the bass viol, so called because it was held between each leg (*gamba* in Italian)

violino: (little viol) original name for the violin

violino piccolo: a small violin usually tuned a minor third higher than the normal violin

virelai: one of the three French *formes fixes* of the Middle Ages yet more playful than a serious ballade; originated with the troubadours and trouvères as a monophonic dance that involved choral singing; the form is AbbaA

virginal: a diminutive harpsichord possessing a single keyboard with the strings placed at right angles to the keys

vox organalis: (organal voice) one of the two voice parts in an early organum; it is a newly created line added to the preexisting chant

vox principalis: (principal voice) one of the two voice parts in an early organum; it is a preexisting chant that served as a foundation for another newly created line

Wagner tuba: nickname for a tenor-range tuba used by Richard Wagner in his *Der Ring des Nibelungen*

walking bass: a bass line, especially in jazz, with a predominantly stepwise motion and steady rhythm (for example, entirely quarter or eighth notes)

waltz: a triple-time dance for couples that rose to great popularity in the nineteenth century

whole-tone scale: a scale with six notes per octave separated entirely by whole tones

Winchester Troper: a troper—chant manuscript mainly preserving additions to the liturgy called tropes—dating from c1000 C.E. from a Benedictine Monastery at Winchester, England; shows that the singers had a repertory of about 150 two-voice organa, but the troper was a memory aid and is not a prescriptive document that allows singers today to perform the music with confidence

Wolf's Glen Scene: the finale to Act 2 of Carl Maria von Weber's *Der Freischütz*, its most striking and most popular scene

WoO numbers: (*Werk ohne Opuszahl,* or work without opus number) a number given in a catalog of a composer's works designating those pieces lacking a traditional opus number; first used in the 1955 catalog of Beethoven's works compiled by Georg Kinsky and Hans Halm

word painting: see text painting

xylophone: a percussion instrument in which wooden bars are sounded with a mallet

INDEX